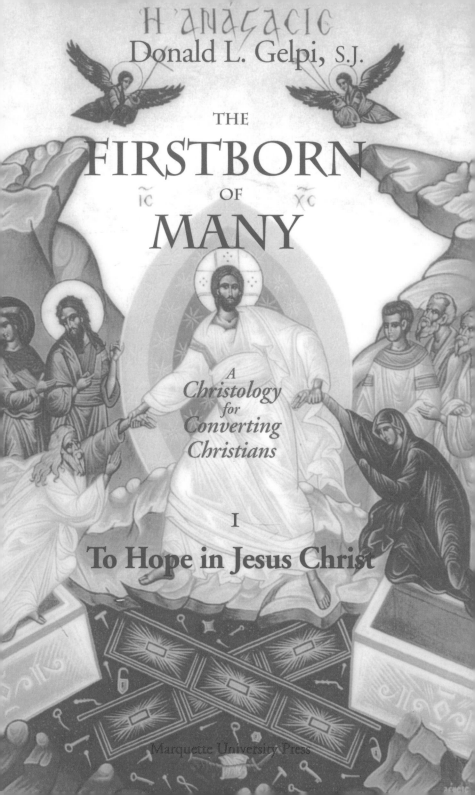

H ἈΝΆϹΑϹΙϹ

Donald L. Gelpi, S.J.

THE
FIRSTBORN
OF
MANY

ĪC͞   Χ͞C͞

A Christology for Converting Christians

I

To Hope in Jesus Christ

Marquette University Press

Donald L. Gelpi, S.J.

THE
FIRSTBORN
OF
MANY

A CHRISTOLOGY FOR
CONVERTING CHRISTIANS

VOLUME 1
TO HOPE IN JESUS CHRIST

MARQUETTE
UNIVERSITY

PRESS

MARQUETTE STUDIES IN THEOLOGY
No. 20

ANDREW TALLON, SERIES EDITOR

Library of Congress Cataloging-in-Publication Data

Gelpi, Donald L., 1934-
  The firstborn of many : a christology for converting Christians / Donald
  L. Gelpi.
    p. cm. — (Marquette studies in theology ; no. 20, 21, 22) Includes
bibliographical references and index.
    ISBN 0-87462-644-7 (pbk. : alk. paper), Volume 1: To hope in Jesus
Christ; ISBN 0-87462-645-5 (pbk. : alk. paper), Volume 2: Synoptic
narrative Christology; ISBN 0-87462-646-3 (pbk. : alk. paper). Volume
3: Doctrinal and practical Christology.
    1. Jesus Christ—Person and offices. 2. Conversion—Christianity.
    3. Catholic Church—Doctrines. I. Title. II. Marquette studies in the-
ology ; #20, #21, #22.
    BT205 .G37 2001
    232—dc21   00-012328

Cover image compliments of St. Isaac of Syria Skete.

We gratefully acknowledge the generous support of The New Orleans
Province of the Society of Jesus, also known as The Southern Province,
in making possible the publication of these three volumes.

MARQUETTE UNIVERSITY PRESS
MILWAUKEE

The Association of Jesuit University Presses

For My Mother, Alice,
Who Died As She Lived
with Great Hope, Faith, Love, Courage,
and Dignity

Volume 1
Table of Contents

Author's Preface

Not long ago a friend and colleague described me as a theologian who writes a lot of books on a variety of subjects but without any apparent intention of constructing a theological system. Shortly thereafter Gregory Zuschlag, a graduate student at Notre Dame University who was trying to write something on my theology, contacted John Markey, one of the most gifted doctoral candidates whom I have had the grace and pleasure of directing at the Graduate Theological Union in Berkeley. Greg wanted to know whether or not I was in fact constructing a system. John replied with an emphatic "Yes."

The close temporal juxtaposition of these two events convinced me that the time has arrived for me to come out of the closet. I confess. I am trying to construct a theological system. I realize that in this era of post-modern skepticism,[1] systematic theological thinking has lost much of its allure. This disfavor seems to stem largely from an intellectual fail-

1. Post-modernism designates a vague and diverse impulse in *fin du siècle*, twentieth-century culture characterized by dissatisfaction with "modernity." Post-modernist thinking questions the omnipotence of modern technology, doubts the claims of universalizing thought, and deplores individualism. I find myself sympathetic to all three critiques of the presuppositions of modern culture. Cf. Albert Borgmann, *Crossing the Postmodern Divide* (Chicago, IL: The University of Chicago Press, 1992) Indeed, by some standards, the philosophical position developed in these three volumes builds on "constructive post-modern philosophy." Cf. David Ray Griffin, John B. Cobb, Jr., Marcus P. Ford, Pete A.Y. Gunter, and Peter Ochs, *Founders of Constructive Postmodern Philosophy: Peirce, James, Bergson, Whitehead, and Hartshorne* (Albany, NY: SUNY, 1993); Robert Cummings Neville, *The Highroad Around Modernism* (Albany, NY: SUNY, 1992).

More typically, however, post-modernist philosophical thinking shows an affinity for deconstructionist patterns of thought. Deconstructionism tends to deny the existence of any subject of discourse. It typically refuses to discern any pattern in history. In its more extreme formulations, deconstructionism portrays language as floating signifiers without any extra-linguistic referant. Deconstructionism resists universal generalizations and focuses on the concrete and the particular. In its least acceptable philosophical formulation, deconstructionism depicts a non-subject projecting self-contradictory meanings on an utterly particular and surd reality. Such a philosophy perpetuates some of the least tenable, nominalistic presuppositions of modernity instead of replacing them with a defensible "post-modern" realism. Cf. Madan Sarup, *An Introductory Guide to Post-Structuralism and Post-Modernism* (Athens, GA: The University of Georgia Press, 1993); Philippa Berry and Andrew Wernick, eds., *Shadow of Spirit: Postmodernism and Religion* (New York, NY: Routledge, 1992); Huston Smith, *Beyond the Post-Modern Mind* (Wheaton, IL: Theosophical Publishing House,1989); Joe Holland, *The Birth of Postmodern Culture: Challenge to Catholic and American Identities* and *Conservative and Liberal Explorations of the Postmodern Stage of the Human* (South Orange, NJ: The Warwick Institute, 1989); Alan M. Olson, "Postmodernity and Faith," *Journal of the American Academy of Religion*, 58(1990), pp. 37-50; Fred Lawrence, "The Fragility of Consciousness: Lonergan and the Postmodern Concern for the Other," *Theological Studies*, 54(1993), pp. 55-94; David

ure of nerve; but the reluctance to construct a theological system does not mean that no one can do it.

The fact that some friends and colleagues seem to find it hard to credit that I am at least attempting to construct a theological system could reflect the fact that the pragmatic logic which I employ in thinking theologically requires me to approach system building fallibilistically. Allow me to explain what I mean.

I espouse a contritely fallibilistic, Peircean logic. Fallibilism holds that one has a better chance of arriving at truth if one admits one's capacity for error than if one does not. Fallibilism has, then, nothing to do with a gloomy, deconstructionist assessment of human cognitive capacities. On the contrary, fallibilism promotes a cautiously optimistic assessment of the human mind's ability to grasp reality truthfully. It does so because it functions as a logical principle within a realistic epistemology and metaphysics.

The theory of knowledge defended in these pages asserts that all conscious human evaluative responses exemplify the mind's presence to reality. Descartes, then, erred profoundly when he asked whether the human mind can know reality. He would have done better to ponder how the human mind becomes present to reality. The mind does so truly when it anticipates correctly how reality is going to behave. It grasps reality falsely when it predicts that things will act one way when in fact they act in another. Thus reality schools the mind to truth by the way it behaves.

Peircean epistemological realism implies a metaphysical realism as well. When the mind anticipates truly the behavior of the realities it encounters, it grasps the laws, the general tendencies, which constitute those autonomously functioning realities. Peirce's philosophical vindication of real generals breaks decisively with the nominalistic tradition which has skewed European philosophy from Descartes to Derrida. Indeed, the nominalistic caste of post-modern thinking situates it solidly in the modern European philosophical tradition and raises serious questions about how post-modern "post-modernism" really is.[2]

By endorsing Peicean epistemological and metaphysical realism, this study advances the project of which the great Catholic novelist Walker Percy dreamed before he died. Percy hoped to construct a systematic de-

---

Tracy, "The Uneasy Alliance Reconceived: Catholic Theological Method, Modernity, and Postmodernity," *Theological Studies*, 50(1989), pp. 548-570; Bruce J. Nichols, ed., *Evangelical Review of Theology: Christ, Modernity, and Post-Modernity*, 22(1998).

This study endorses Thomas Guarino's analysis of the theological challenge posed by deconstructionist post-modernism. It also endorses his proposal for a response to that challenge. Cf. Thomas Guarino, "Postmodernity and Five Fundamental Issues," *Theological Studies*, 57(1966), pp. 654-689.

2. Cf. Donald L. Gelpi, S.J. *The Turn to Experience in Contemporary Theology* (Mahwah, NJ: Paulist, 1994).

fence of Christianity on the foundations of Peircean realism.[3] Percy seems not to have realized that Josiah Royce had already begun such a defence in his monumental work *The Problem of Christianity*.[4] *The Firstborn of Many* further advances Percy's dream by building on the solid philosophical and theological foundations laid by both Peirce and Royce.

Anyone who defends fallibilism must eschew the a priori reasoning invoked by more than one theological system builder. Not only does Peircean logic require one to validate theological language in verifiable experiences; but that logic also requires one to confess that the human mind formulates its hypotheses without knowing whether or not it has taken into account all the relevant data. The same logic also requires that one admit that even validated inductions can become problematic should evidence turn up which they cannot explain or which contradicts them.

One who endorses Peirce's insistence on the finitude and fallibility of the human mind need not, however, thereby abjure system building. Peirce himself prized architectonic, and therefore systematic, philosophizing. In constructing a system, however, a consistent fallibilist needs to invoke the principle of alternation. Viewed as a norm for thinking speculatively, the principle of alternation holds that systematic thinking needs to alternate between detailed studies of specific problems and ongoing reflection on one's account of reality in general. Presumably, every detailed study will yield new insights into reality which could force one to revise one's fallible metaphysical hypothesis.

This study in Christology represents one of a series of detailed, systematic studies in theological foundations. Perhaps, then, the reader will find it helpful if I situate it in the total systematic project on which I embarked over twenty years ago.

In 1973 I joined the faculty of the Jesuit School of Theology at Berkeley with the idea of laying systematic foundations for a North American Catholic theology by pursuing foundational theology in Lonergan's sense of that term. By foundational theology Lonergan means the elaboration of a systematic, strictly normative account of conversion.

---

3. Cf. Patrick H. Samway, S.J., ed., *A Thief of Peirce: The Letters of Kenneth Laine Ketner and Walker Percy* (Jackson, MI: University of Mississippi Press, 1995).

4. By the time Royce wrote *The Problem of Christianity*, he had reached what he called his "Peircean insight" and, despite his denigration as a German idealist, correctly regarded himself as a Peircean realist and pragmatist. Moreover, Peirce, who received *The Problem of Christianity* shortly before his death by cancer, endorsed in a general way Royce's position. That suggests that Peirce himself realized the theological implications of his metaphysical and epistemological realism. Cf. Frank M. Oppenheim, S.J., *Royce's Mature Philosophy of Religion* (Notre Dame, IN: University of Notre Dame Press, 1987).

I also hoped to develop an inculturated foundational theology by drawing broadly on the North American philosophical tradition. Over the years I have analyzed dialectically the development of the intellectual tradition in the United States from Jonathan Edwards to Roberto Unger. On the basis of that analysis, I have constructed the metaphysics of experience which contextualizes all the theology which I have written since coming to Berkeley.

In addition, I have sought to inculturate the writing I do by targeting in each major book important issues in contemporary North American culture. The pastoral applicability of what I have written could also have led some to misprize its systematic intent. Much systematic theological thinking distinguishes dualistically between theoretical truth and its practical application. Peircean logic, however, demands that one regard the practical pastoral consequences of theological doctrines as integral to their speculative meaning.

I find myself at the age of sixty-five about mid-point in the project I began over twenty years ago. I made some false starts, as the reader shall soon see; but at this point in my theological odyssey I feel right on course.

In the project's early stages, I sometimes questioned whether it deserved all the time and effort I was spending on it. I now believe, however, that its completion would indeed make a significant contribution to theology in this country. The completed project promises to address theological needs of the wider Church as well.

During my first year at the Jesuit School of Theology, the administration asked me to teach three courses in the school's Master of Divinity program: the theology of the human person, sacramental theology, and a trinitarian theology of the Holy Spirit. I decided that I would approach all three questions from the standpoint of a theology of conversion. I hoped eventually to turn each of these three lecture courses into a book.

I succeeded. The course on sacraments became *Charism and Sacrament*. The course on the human person became *Experiencing God*. The course on the trinity became *The Divine Mother*.

At the time, I tried to write the best theology I could; but I now regard all three books as trial balloons. In all three studies I was wrestling with doctrinal questions; but I was also creating as I went along the rules for pursuing foundational theology in Lonergan's sense of the term.

Lonergan's *Method in Theology* calls for the creation of a theology of conversion which will provide the norms for distinguishing between sound and unsound doctrines. Unfortunately, however, Lonergan grows extremely laconic when it comes to describing the operational procedures which foundational theologians ought to use. He simply says that they must somehow synthesize metaphysical categories, theological categories, and categories from other sciences which study human religious experience. How one derives an integrated account of conversion from three different speculative disciplines whose conclusions flow from different presuppositions and methods remains a mystery in the pages of *Method in Theology*.

Each of my three trial balloons wrestled with a different methodological problem. In *Charism and Sacrament*, I began to formulate the metaphysics of experience which I subsequently developed in later writings. In *Experiencing God*, I wrestled with the question: how does one draw systematically on philosophy, theology, and scientific studies of human experience in order to elaborate a consistent, strictly normative account of conversion? In *The Divine Mother*, I addressed the question of validating theological language in human experience. Since much contemporary theology argues a priori, the question of validating religious language rarely comes up in many theological discussions; but if one espouses a Peircean logic of relations, one has to face the issue of validation. I decided to take trinitarian theology as a test case on the presupposition that if one could ground trinitarian language in validating human experiences, one could probably validate any theological proposition.

As I advanced in the attempt to do foundational theology, I grew in an understanding of how to go about it. I finally pulled these insights together in *Inculturating North American Theology: An Experiment in Foundational Method*. I sharpened some of those methodological insights in *The Turn to Experience in Contemporary Theology*. This last book I did as a preliminary study for the Christology whose first volume you hold in your hands.

I look on the first three books I did as trial balloons for another reason. As I wrote them, the construct of conversion which I was developing evolved considerably. By the time I finished writing *The Divine Mother*. I had convinced myself that one can speak of five different kinds of conversion and of at least seven different dynamics and counter-dynamics within the conversion process.

In my first three books, I was also beginning to move toward the formulation of a metaphysics of experience which corrects the more obvious fallacies in Whitehead's nominalistic, di-polar construct of experience. The first two books made a false start. I had decided to modify the technical philosophical language of process theology by redefining some key Whiteheadian terms. I hoped to make Whiteheadian language more amenable to a triadic, realistic, social construct of experience.

While I enjoyed playing around with Whitehead's terminology, most readers found the language jargon. In writing I had assumed that contemporary American theologians would understand technical Whiteheadean vocabulary; but I had sorely underestimated the Eurocentrism of the North American theological community. In *The Divine*

Mother, Inculturating North American Theology, and *Grace as Transmuted Experience and Social Process*, I shifted from Whiteheadian language to ordinary language. Moreover, in writing those three books I was finally able to convince myself of the tentative viability of the metaphysics of experience on which I was working.

By the time I had published *Inculturating North American Theology*, I had, then, formulated the method, the metaphysical position, and the construct of conversion I needed in order to begin the work of laying systematic theological foundations for an inculturated North American theology. With *The Divine Mother*, I had actually began constructing my system; but, having refined both my method and my metaphysics through a systematic application of the principle of alternation, I realized that I had to go back and revise both my sacramental theology and the theology of the human person I had tried to develop in *Experiencing God*.

Committed Worship: A Sacramental Theology for Converting Christians revised and updated the positions which I had originally put forth in *Charism and Sacrament*. In *Grace as Transmuted Experience and Social Process*, I had partially revised the theology of nature and grace which I had developed in *Experiencing God*. I realized the need for a much more systematic restatement of those issues; but I decided to postpone revising *Experiencing God* until after I had completed this study in Christology, since I anticipated that I would view questions of nature and grace differently after having wrestled with the question of the incarnation. That expectation has proved true.

This Christology advances my project of constructing a systematic foundational theology in significant ways. It develops a Christology coordinate with the sacramental theology in *Committed Worship* and with the trinitarian theology developed in *The Divine Mother*. After revising my theological account of the human person, I would like eventually to undertake a foundational ecclesiology. Such a study would have to deal with the complex question of the conversion of institutions as such.

After completing the ecclesiology, I would anticipate that I would want to reformulate the theology of the Holy Spirit I articulated in *The Divine Mother*. I have also begun work on a theology of education which views Christian humanistic education from the standpoint of the forms and dynamics of conversion. Eventually, I would also like to lay out in a systematic way the metaphysics of experience which I have developed. Whether I shall live long enough to do all this writing, I do not know; but I intend to complete as much of the project as I can in the time remaining to me.

One can ask any theological question foundationally. How ought the fully converted Christian to experience grace and the saving Breath of God? How ought a fully converted Christian to worship sacramentally?

What shape would a Church take whose institutions all fostered initial and ongoing conversion?

This study focuses on Christology. It too approaches the figure of Jesus from the standpoint of integral conversion. This study asks and tries to answer the following question: How does commitment to Jesus Christ in faith transform every aspect of conversion?

One can convert in natural, secular contexts as well as in a graced, religious context. Hence, a foundational Christology studies how integral commitment to Jesus Christ in faith transvalues the secular forms of conversion.

In the first volume of this study, I begin by addressing the related questions of problem and of method. In the first chapter I argue that contemporary Christology has not exhibited so much confusion since the Christological controversies of fourth and fifth centuries. The second chapter examines methods which some modern and contemporary Christologists have employed to reground Christology. I find all of them suggestive but none of them finally adequate. The third chapter elaborates the method which structures the present study.

The second section of volume one deals with Jesusology. It attempts to clarify what one ought to mean in a contemporary context by Jesus' "humanity." In section two I draw a multi-disciplinary portrait of the man Jesus by blending insights from philosophy, from the social and personality sciences, and from the new quests for the historical Jesus. To the best of my knowledge, this multi-disciplinary portrait of Jesus marks the first attempt ever to validate a philosophical construct of His humanity in the results of contemporary personality and social sciences. I conclude that one may legitimately understand Jesus as a thoroughly finite, developing human experience.

Section three of volume one begins Christology proper. It reflects on the way in which commitment to the Christ revealed in the paschal mystery transforms natural human hopes. Section three deals with Pauline Christology and with the apocalyptic Christology of the book of Revelation. A Christology of hope also clarifies the proper object of a foundational Christology. I argue that in pursuing Christological thinking, foundational theology needs to reflect on what I call "Christological knowing." By "Christological knowing," I mean the unique kind of knowledge which results from practical assimilation to Jesus in the power of His Breath. Part three brings the first volume of this study to a close.

Volume two deals with the intuitive dimensions of Christological faith by undertaking a dialectical analysis of synoptic narrative Christology. In the second volume I use a pragmatic logic of consequences in order to clarify the meaning of Christological knowing. In it I argue that the synoptic gospels all tell the story of Jesus with the same generic purpose in mind: namely, to promote practical assimilation to Jesus in faith and in the power of His Breath. Because the synoptics stress the practical dimension of faith more than doctrine, they elucidate well the concrete demands of Christological knowing. Volume two closes with a reflection on ways in which the narrative imagination shapes the Christian conscience.

Volume three reflects on doctrinal and practical Christology. It analyzes the narrative Christology of the gospel of John. That analysis portrays the fourth gospel as marking an historical transition from narrative to doctrinal Christology. I argue that the fourth Gospel makes an important contribution to narrative Christology when it insists, quite correctly, that one must coordinate Christological and trinitarian doctrine.

I also argue that with the gospel of John, New Testament narrative Christology reached the limits of what narrative thinking can contribute to the development of Christological doctrine. In the synoptic gospels Jesus chiefly summons others to submit to the moral demands of life in the kingdom. In John's gospel He constantly harangues unbelieving Jews and challenges them to believe in His divine pre-existence. I find the Johannine depiction of Jesus theologically correct from the standpoint of the paschal mystery but not altogether convincing as an historical portrait. The analysis of Johannine Christology brings to a close my account of the way in which commitment to Jesus Christ in faith transforms intuitive, imaginative beliefs about religious realities.

The second part of volume three deals with the way in which Christological faith transforms inferential perceptions of those same religious realities. The first chapter recalls and summarizes the experiential construct of Jesus' humanity presented in volume one. Chapter two builds upon that construct by developing a thoroughly experiential account of the hypostatic union. The third chapter coordinates an experiential understanding of the hypostatic union with the trinitarian theology developed in The Divine Mother.

Subsequent chapters also approach Christological doctrine inferentially. They examine what it means to confess the risen Christ as savior, as prophet, as priest, as king, and as judge. In these four chapters I argue that the person of Jesus redefines the meaning of all these key Christological concepts and in the process endows them with novel, even subversive, significance.

The account of narrative Christology in volume two together with the first two doctrinal sections of the third volume describe the ways in which commitment to Jesus Christ in faith transforms intellectual conversion. The third part of volume three deals with the ways in which commitment to Jesus Christ in faith transforms personal and public morality.

Part three, then, deals with the gracing both of personal moral conversion and of socio-political conversion.

Throughout the second part of volume three I argue that, like intuitive, imaginative beliefs about Jesus Christ, rational, inferential beliefs also have an inherently practical character because they reflect on the experience of Christological knowing. The practical consequences of a Christological doctrine, moreover, constitute its clarified speculative meaning.

In the matter of personal morality, I defend the position that Christological knowing chiefly demands the healing of disordered human passions. This chapter builds on creative insights into the nature of passion put forward by Roberto Unger.

The final chapter of this study examines how commitment in faith to Christ transforms socio-political conversion. In it I examine some of the reasons why people living in the United States find it hard to convert socio-politically. I propose a theological argument for the necessity of socio-political conversion. Finally, I suggest a concrete pastoral strategy for prolonging Jesus' prophetic ministry by advancing the Christian search for a just social order.

I should, perhaps, alert readers unfamiliar with my other writings to some stylistic conventions which I shall adopt in the pages and volumes which follow. I shall refer to the third person of the trinity as "the Holy Breath." I shall also call her "the Divine Mother" and refer to Her with a feminine personal pronoun. In so speaking, I am not cultivating novelty for its own sake. This shift in language reflects speculative positions which I argue in this study and in others which I have already published. Allow me then to explain the reason for these linguistic shifts.

The metaphysics of experience which I espouse in these pages eschews the philosophical categories "spirit" and "matter." These categories entered the theological tradition through its assimilation of classical Graeco-Roman philosophy. That philosophy rests on a metaphysical essentialism which this study systematically repudiates. Because the terms "spirit" and "matter" connote the philosophical essentialism from which they derive, I have abandoned them as well.

In classical philosophy, the metaphysical reification of essences breeds a variety of dualisms, which I shall discuss in greater detail later. The dualistic mind conceives two interrelated realities in such a way as to render their real relationship to one another unintelligible. Among the troublesome and misleading dualisms which Christian theology has derived from the Greeks, spirit-matter dualism surely ranks as one of the most troublesome, since it spawns many other kinds of dualism: cosmic dualism, substantial dualism, operational dualism, subject-object dualism, just to name a few. The relational metaphysics of experience developed in these pages rejects all forms of dualism. It therefore rejects dualistic categories and especially those which breed other forms of dualism.

Finally, in modern transcendental Thomism, the term "spirit" connotes the virtual infinity of the human mind, its alleged *a priori* orientation to the whole of Being, truth, and goodness. The metaphysics of experience developed below rejects the *a priori*, deductive logic on which this understanding of the human rests. It also rejects the virtual infinity of the human mind as an unverifiable hypothesis. It therefore replaces this false and misleading understanding of the human mind with a radical cognitive finitude which renders all human thinking irreducibly social and dialogic.

Since I cannot consistently invoke the term "spirit" in order to describe the third person of the trinity, I have replaced it with the term "breath." The new term translates fairly adequately, I believe, the Hebrew term "*ruah*," which the term "spirit" has traditionally translated. The term "breath" has none of the objectionable metaphysical and psychological connotations under which the term "spirit" labors; and, like the term "*ruah*," it connotes life-breath, breathing, wind in motion. Be warned, then, that when I speak in the pages which follow of the "Holy Breath" of God I mean what others mean by the "Holy Spirit."

I also refer to the divine Breath as "She" and speak of Her as "the divine Mother." In other volumes, I explain the reason for this linguistic convention in greater detail. Suffice it to say in the present context that both the Bible and Christian tradition give sanction to imagining the third person of the trinity as the feminine wisdom of God. Not every Christian theologian invokes this strain of Christian theology in speaking about the divine Breath; but it stands completely within the realm of orthodoxy. Moreover, the failure to invoke feminine images of the Breath goes hand in hand with a deplorable and dangerous neglect of pneumatology especially in the Roman tradition.

The subtitles of all three volumes in this study echo that of *Committed Worship*. Both foundational studies focus on the restored catechumenate, which bears as its official title The Rite of Christian Initiation of Adults (RCIA). In both works, I am writing for converting Christians. By converting Christians I mean in the first instance adult neophytes entering the Church; but I also mean baptized Christians who are engaged in the life-long process of ongoing conversion. In targeting the RCIA, I therefore am also targeting any adult Christian interested in understanding his or her Christian faith.

I fully intend the pun in the subtitle of both works. I have tried not only to write for people who are experiencing either initial or ongoing conversion but also to write in such a way as to challenge them to deepen their converted commitment to Christ. If this study helps only some people to know Jesus better through assimilation to Him in the power of His Breath, it will have justified the years of work which produced it.

I owe a deep debt of gratitude to the many friends, students, and colleagues who have helped make this a much better study than I could have done left to my own limited resources. I especially thank Scott Sinclair and Barbara Charlesworth Gelpi for their careful, critical reading of this first volume. Their suggestions much improved it. The John Courtney Murray Group also gave me extremely helpful suggestions for recasting significant sections of the following text. I especially thank Joseph Tetlow, S.J., Frank Oppenheim, S.J., William Spohn, John Markey, O.P., Robert Lassalle-Klein, Elizabeth Linehan, R.S.M., Alejandro Garcia-Rivera, and Simon Hendry, S.J. With the assistance of these and other good colleagues, I must myself take responsibility for any defects in the pages which follow. I also thank Herman Waetjen, a friend and colleague, for his suggestions for improving volume two.

Donald L. Gelpi, S.J.
The Jesuit School of Theology at Berkeley

PART I
THE PROBLEM AND THE METHOD

Chapter 1
The Contemporary Christological Crisis

Measured by almost any standard, contemporary Christological think-ing has not wallowed in a comparable state of confusion since the fifth century, when Cyril, the patriarch of Alexandria, (389-444 a.d.) excom-municated Nestorius, the patriarch of Antioch, (386-451 a.d) for dis-seminating Christological heresy. The controversy between the two pa-triarchs came to a head at the council of Ephesus, (431 a.d.) where Cyril, in the absence of Nestorius, persuaded the assembled bishops to endorse his own approach to Christology and to condemn that proposed by the patriarch of Antioch.

History does not repeat itself; but, as Mark Twain once remarked, it does rhyme. When, for example, Barbara Tuchman wrote *A Distant Mir-ror*, she told the story of the "calamitous" fourteenth century because she felt that its disasters had light to throw on the chaos of the twentieth century.[1]

Theologians can make similar profitable use of earlier periods of theo-logical chaos in order to throw light on contemporary doctrinal babble. Understanding how one period of doctrinal muddle resembles another as well as how the two periods differ enables one to begin to name the sources of contemporary theological misunderstanding. Once one has identified the present sources of confusion, one can begin to draw on the stable elements in one's doctrinal situation in order to bring some semblance of order out of chaos.

In this chapter I shall attempt just such a "rhyming" analysis of the contemporary crisis in Christology. In it I shall document the existence of a contemporary crisis in Christological faith. I shall also analyze some of the major cultural impulses which contribute to that crisis by compar-ing and contrasting it with the Christological crisis of the fourth and fifth centuries.

This chapter, then, divides into five parts. In the first I shall recall how the Christological question reached an initial formulation at the council of Ephesus. In part one, I also examine the events which led to the at-

---

1. See: Barbara Tuchman, *A Distant Mirror: The Calamitous Fourteenth Century* (New York, NY: Knopf, 1978).

tempt to formulate an initial response to that question at the council of Chalcedon. In the second part of this chapter I shall analyze the cultural impulses which contributed to major confusions in patristic Christological thought. In the third part of this chapter I shall identify how the contemporary crisis in Christology resembles its patristic counterpart. I then analyze how the two crises differ. In part three and in the two parts which follow it, I shall examine the cultural impulses which have led to the contemporary crisis. Those issues set the speculative agenda for the rest of this study.

In the chapter which follows this one, I shall examine some of the principal theological strategies for "regrounding" Christology. Regrounding Christology means developing a successful method for resolving the current Christological crisis. In my judgment none of the proposed attempts at regrounding Christology have succeeded. We need, therefore, to understand why they have failed.

In chapter three, I shall elaborate the strategy for regrounding Christology which I shall pursue in this and in subsequent volumes. I shall argue that the kind of foundational Christology which I ambition provides norms for distinguishing between sound and unsound Christological doctrine. Foundational Christology examines how Christological faith transforms conversion. Those doctrines which advance the conversion process count as sound. Those which fail to foster conversion or which even subvert it count as unsound.

Approaching Christology in the context of conversion offers a second speculative advantage. It allows one to de-objectify Christology by rethinking it in relational theological categories. Patristic and especially medieval theologians used metaphysics in order to "objectify" Christology. Today Christologists prefer to objectify Christology through the scholarly discipline of history. Foundational Christology asks, by contrast, the following question: *How ought the fully converted Christian to relate to the person of Jesus Christ?* Answering that question requires, as we shall see, rethinking Christology in the context of a relational metaphysics of community. In answering that same question I shall invoke a pragmatic, relational logic of consequences.

Finally, because a foundational Christology reflects directly on the experience of conversion, it also forces one to explore the experiential basis for abstract Christological doctrines, including the doctrine of the hypostatic union. In the third part of this volume I shall begin that exploration by examining the experiences which lie at the basis of a Christology of hope. I shall complete that exploration in volume three when I address some of the major issues in doctrinal and practical Christology.

The Christology developed in this study shares many of the concerns of P.J. Labarriere's *Le Christ avenir* (Paris: Desclée de Brouwer, 1983).

Our thought has developed quite independently and rests on very different philosophical and methodological presuppositions. Still, like Labarriere, I believe that any sound Christology needs to develop in the eschatological context created by Jesus' death, resurrection, and mission of His divine Breath. Like Labarriere, I believe that any sound Christology includes a normative account of the relationship of the believing Christian community to the glorified Jesus as an integral part of Christology itself. With Labarriere, I locate Christopraxis at the heart of Christology. While I might want to qualify particular statements in Labarriere's work, I regard the preceding positions as doctrinally sound; and I develop them in greater methodological, exegetical and doctrinal detail than Labarriere himself.

(I)

What then have the Christological controversies of the fifth century to teach us about the current Christological crisis?

The disagreement between Cyril and Nestorius came to a head at the council of Ephesus; but their doctrinal confrontation brought to a culmination over four centuries of sometimes brilliant, sometimes confused, sometimes heterodox Christological thinking. In that sense Christological speculation preceded Ephesus.

In another sense, however, Ephesus created Christology as a realm of theological thinking distinct from trinitarian theology. Here two points need noting. 1) Until Ephesus conciliar teaching had focused on trinitarian issues. The council of Nicea (325 a.d.) had condemned Arianism and vindicated the divinity of the Son of God and His co-equality with the Father. Nicea taught that within the trinity Father and Son share an identical reality (*homoousios*). (*DS* 125) The first council of Constantinople (381 a.d.) had extended the same divine dignity possessed by Father and Son to the third member of the divine triad, the Holy Breath. (*DS* 134) These two councils, then, advanced official trinitarian doctrine in significant ways. Of the two, the council of Nicea especially enunciated a trinitarian doctrine with Christological implications; but trinity rather than Christology preoccupied the bishops at Nicea.

At Ephesus, however, the Christological question—the question of how to relate the divine and the human within Jesus—crystallized for the first time in official conciliar teaching. In this sense, then, the council of Ephesus created Christology as a distinct realm of theological reflection by focusing the attention of the entire Church on one of the most fundamental issues which any Christology has to face.

2) Having created Christology by formulating a central Christological question with official clarity, the council of Ephesus also made it imperative that subsequent conciliar teaching find a satisfactory answer to the

question it had raised. The action taken against Nestorius at Ephesus created a major rift within the Church and set at loggerheads two major patriarchal sees. As a consequence, theological efforts at finding a formula of reconciliation to restore Church unity bore fruit with historical inevitability in the council of Chalcedon. Chalcedonian Christology not only offered a formula for reconciling the sees of Alexandria and Antioch, but it also sought to bring theological and pastoral order out of over four centuries of positive Christological breakthrough and divisive confusion.

While they precipitated a major Christological crisis, neither Cyril nor Nestorius offered an adequate answer to the Christological question they had raised. I shall examine their Christological positions in greater detail below. Here it suffices to note that Nestorius lacked the conceptual means to think clearly about the unity of the divine and human in Jesus. Cyril, for his part, had a clear insight into the theological need to assert that unity; but his own way of talking about it had heterodox connotations which seem to have eluded him.

The council of Chalcedon attempted to amend the problems in both positions. It formulated and promulgated the doctrine of the "hypostasic union." Chalcedon discovered in the incarnate Word a single subsistent reality, or "*hypostasis*," and two complete natures, or "*physeis*," one divine and one human. Chalcedon also taught that these two natures co-exist within the subsistent reality of the incarnate Word without blending into some third kind of fictive "theandric"[2] reality.[3]

2. The term "theandric" takes on heterodox connotations when it asserts the blending of the divine and human in Jesus into a third reality. One can, however, also use it in a perfectly orthodox manner as did the first major American Catholic theologian, Orestes Brownson. Brownson used the term "theandric" to designate the co-presence of divinity and humanity within the person of Jesus without their blending into a third reality. For Brownson, then, "theandric life" presupposed rather than denied the unity-in-distinction of divinity and of humanity in Jesus, on the one hand, and of supernatural and natural life in the Christian on the other. Cf. Orestes A. Brownson, *Works*, edited by Henry F. Brownson (20 vols.; Detroit, MI: H.F. Brownson, 1898), XII, p. 484.

3. The creed of Chalcedon asserted:

> Following then the holy Fathers, we all with one voice teach that it should be confessed that our Lord Jesus Christ is one and the same Son, the same perfect in Godhead, the same perfect in humanity; one in being (*homoousios*) with the Father as to His Godhead, and one in being (*homoousios*) with us as to His humanity; in all things like us, sin only excepted; begotten of the Father before the ages as to His Godhead, and in the last days, born for us and for our salvation of the mother of God (*tês Theotokou*) as to His humanity: One and the same Christ, Son, Lord, Only Begotten, made known in two natures (*en duo physesin*) without confusion, without change, without division, without separation; the difference of the natures having been in no wise taken away by reason of the union, but rather the properties of each being preserved, and [both] concurring into one person (*eis hen prosôpon*) and subsistent reality (*kai hypostasin*)—not parted or divided into two persons (*eis duo prosôpa*), but one and the same Son and Only Begotten, the divine Word (*Logon*), the Lord

The council of Chalcedon sought to set the linguistic parameters for all subsequent Christological catechesis; and for centuries it succeeded. Today as well, any speculative Christology needs to come to terms with Chalcedon's answer to the Christological question. Indeed, the failure on the part of more than one contemporary Christology to deal adequately with "the Chalcedonian settlement" has created a good deal of the chaos which currently characterizes much Christological thinking.

The Christological question which Ephesus formulated and which Chalcedon tried to answer asks: How ought one to understand the relationship of the divine and the human in Jesus? Clear Christological thinking demands therefore an historically verifiable and adequate way of talking about three things: humanity, divinity, and their mode of union in Jesus. Serious confusion concerning even one of these three intimately interrelated notions cannot help but produce systematic confusion in one's attempt to answer the Christological question.

Some commentators on the development of patristic theology charge the early councils of the Church with "Hellenizing" the Christian creed. Most likely, however, the bishops at the first councils saw themselves as "de-Hellenizing" a creed which Christian theologians had over-Hellenized and in the process falsified.

All the early councils of the Church, from Nicea to Chalcedon, sought to interpret the early Christian witness to God and to Jesus which had taken canonical shape in what we call the New Testament. The bishops at these councils looked therefore to the New Testament rather than to Graeco-Roman philosophy to endow their doctrinal pronouncements with concrete meaning. By the same token, the doctrinal positions which earned their condemnation did so for having replaced the New Testament witness with other notions, often of philosophical origin, which either denied or seriously distorted that witness. A sound interpretation of these early councils demands, therefore, that a New Testament language of faith, rather than the language of philosophy, ultimately validate the conceptual content even of more or less technical conciliar doctrines like "the hypostatic union."[4]

In my judgment, those who argue that contemporary Christology can dispense with the Chalcedonian Christology immediately contradict themselves by wrestling with exactly the same issues as preoccupied the bishops at Chalcedon. That epic council raised and answered the fundamental question: How do divinity and humanity relate in the subsistent reality we call "Jesus of Nazareth."

> Jesus Christ; even as the prophets from of old [taught] concerning Him, and as the Lord Jesus Christ Himself has taught us, and as the creed (to symbolon) of the Fathers has delivered to us. (DS 301-302)

4. Cf. André de Halleux, "La réception du symboloécumenique de Nicée à Chalcedoine," *Ephemerides Theologicae Lovaniensis*, 61(1985), pp. 5-47.

Even so-called "low" Christologies which deny that in Jesus of Nazareth we encounter a divine person nevertheless end by explaining how divinity and humanity relate in Jesus' person. They may reduce the divine presence in Jesus to His graced relationship with God, or explain it as an instance of Whiteheadean reversion, or speak of the symbolic way in which Jesus makes God present. Still, even in repudiating Jesus' co-equality with God, contemporary Christologies, including the lowest of the "low," nevertheless end by wrestling with the very same issues which preoccupied the bishops at Chalcedon.

Articulating the Church's shared faith and handing it on authentically constitutes the fundamental task of all theology, including Christology. No contemporary Christology can, then, ignore the Chalcedonian settlement; for, one must decide whether it or revisionist Christology provides the more adequate formulation of the shared faith of the Christian community.

(II)

The preceding section of this chapter reflected on the emergence of a major Christological crisis during the fifth century. The present section probes some of the speculative and cultural impulses which gave rise to that crisis.

If one compares Christology in the late fourth and fifth centuries with contemporary Christology, these periods of Christological confusion both resemble one another and differ in significant ways. Both periods betray considerable confusion when it comes to explaining the meaning of the three key terms which structure the Chalcedonian doctrine of the hypostatic union: namely, "humanity," "divinity," and "the relationship between the two in the subsistent reality named Jesus." The reasons for the speculative confusion then and now differ, however, in very significant ways.

In a sense, confusions in patristic Christology resulted in no small measure from the over-identification of Christological thinking with Platonic modes of thought. The contemporary crisis, by contrast, does not result from an overdose of any single philosophical system. Instead, it grows out of an overdose of speculative pluralism.

Let us, then, begin to explore in a more systematic manner the ways in which the contemporary Christological crisis resembles the fifth century crisis and the ways in which they differ; for that exploration promises to enable us to name with greater clarity the kinds of issues which a contemporary foundational Christology needs to face and to resolve if it hopes to end the contemporary crisis in doctrinally and pastorally satisfying ways.

While not all of the fathers of the Church looked benignly on the speculative attempt to render Christian faith in philosophical language, many did; and most of those who did so turned to Platonism as a major font of the theological categories they needed in order to think the Christian reality with philosophical sophistication.

Needless to say, the fathers of the Church tended to think rhetorically and eclectically rather that rationally and systematically. As a consequence, no single philosophical system fueled patristic theological thinking. Among the going philosophies, however, Middle and Neo-Platonism exerted notable speculative influence. The Platonic tradition provided more than one Patristic Christologist not only with a conceptual account of the human but also with a set of metaphysical categories for thinking the divinity of Jesus as well. As a consequence, at the heart of the patristic debates over the relationship between divinity and humanity in Jesus lay a number of speculative confusions which Platonic thinking helped popularize: cosmic dualism, substantial dualism, and the lack of a clear notion of person.

In dualistic philosophical systems, one defines the nature of two really interrelated realms of reality in such a way as to make their relationship to one another either speculatively problematic or utterly unintelligible.

1) *Cosmic dualism:* Platonic metaphysics sundered the cosmos into two essentially different realms: the realm of Spirit and the realm of matter. It described the realm of Spirit as essentially eternal, metaphysically unchangeable, and as ultimately real. It described matter as essentially ephemeral, constantly changing, and as ultimately unreal. (*Theatetus*, 208 c 7-e 4; *Republic*, 509 d 6-511 e 5)

Platonizing Christian thinkers naively identified the reality of God with the Platonic realm of Spirit. As a result, many of the ambiguities and confusions which colored a dualistic Platonic account of the relationship between Spirit and matter also colored patristic discourse about the reality and physical incarnation of God. As we shall see below, cosmic dualism helped fuel the controversy between Cyril and Nestorius at Ephesus.

2) *Substantial dualism:* Platonic philosophy sundered human nature into two essentially distinct kinds of substances: one material, mortal, physical; the other, spiritual, immaterial, and eternal. Substantial dualism implied an operational dualism. Physical substances deal with ephemeral, illusory sensible realities, while spiritual substances deal with immaterial, eternal, unchanging truths. (*Phaedo*, 65 c 2 ff., 72 e 3-77 d 5; *Meno*, 84 ff.)

Substantial dualism left Christian theologians with virtually no speculative resources for conceiving humanity in a unified and coherent way. Operational dualism left it hard pressed to explained human knowing as a unified process.

3) *The Lack of a Conception of "Person":* Like the rest of Graeco-Roman speculation, the Platonic philosophical tradition had no clear concept for "person." Indeed, speculative concern with the meaning of "person" grew out of Christian theological concerns. It resulted historically from the attempt of Christian thinkers to wrestle with two thorny, interrelated questions: How, on the one hand, ought an orthodox Christian to think monotheistically about a God who consists of three conscious, subsisting, co-equal divine realities; and how, on the other, should one understand a single divine subsisting reality who became fully human?

Confusions in Patristic Christological Speculation

How did the preceding philosophical influences play themselves out in the development of patristic Christology?

1) *Confusions about the Logos.* In the second century, Justin Martyr (ca. 100-ca.168 a.d) drew creatively on Middle Platonism in order to interpret the *"Logos,"* the eternal Word of God to which the gospel of John alludes in its first verse. (Jn 1:1) Under the influence of the Platonizing Jewish theologian, Philo of Alexandria, (30 b.c.-45 a.d.) Justin identified the *"Logos"* of St. John with the "intelligence (*nous*)" of Middle Platonism.

In classical Platonic philosophy, the realm of spirit coincides with the realm of abstract ideas and ideals which measure the truth or falsity of all human thinking. These ideas include mathematical, philosophical, and ethical concepts. Classical Platonism portrayed these ideas and ideals as subsisting in the unchanging realm of the eternal, for only essential immutability allowed them to function as a permanent measure of truth and falsity.

As the Platonic tradition developed, however, it located these same ideas and ideals in a subsistent, eternal, divine intelligence. Philo of Alexandria, a Jewish theologian and contemporary of Jesus, sought to effect a synthesis between Jewish faith and Platonic speculation. He discovered in the intelligence of Middle Platonism a philosophical way of speaking about the eternal Word and Wisdom of God. Justin Martyr, a second-century Christian apologist, identified that same intelligence with the Word who became flesh.

A number of Alexandrian Christian theologians endorsed Justin's position and began to explore some of its speculative implications. The list includes Clement of Alexandria, Origen, Athanasius, and the heresiarch Arius.[5]

One can make a plausible historical argument that Justin's identification of the Johannine *Logos* with the intelligence of middle Platonism led

---

5. Cf. Donald L. Gelpi, S.J., *The Divine Mother: A Trinitarian Theology of the Holy Spirit* (Lanham, MD: University Press of America, 1984), pp.61-63.

directly to the Arian heresy.[6] It transformed the second person of the trinity into a divine intellect in which reside all the ideas in which the material universe participates. The Platonic doctrine of participation afforded Alexandrian theologians and other Christian thinkers a way of understanding God's creative and saving activity. The participation of the whole of nature in the ideas conceived by the divine *Logos* accounted for creation. Conscious participation in the same *Logos* through supernatural faith explained God's saving action in the world.

Unfortunately, however, the speculative association of the second person of the trinity with the intelligence of Middle and Neo-Platonism also linked Him to the notion of multiplicity. In a Platonic world of degenerating metaphysical perfection, multiplicity connoted ontological inferiority. Multiplicity also linked the second person of the trinity to the illusory realm of matter. Both associations suggested the Son's ontological inferiority to the Father, whose absolute simplicity manifested His undiminished divine perfection.[7]

Arius conceded that God had created the world through the Son; but he also argued that the Son's link to the material realm of multiplicity

6. By the beginning of the fourth century, Christian theology divided into two major streams: diohypostatic theology and miahypostatic theology. Diohypostatic theologians acknowledged one God who is the source (*archê*) of all things. This God they equated with the Father of Jesus; but they also found a second hypostatic reality within the Christian God, namely, the Son, the *Logos*, whom they described as either begotten or created before all ages. The eternal existence of the Son they left obscure. While diohypostatic thinkers recognized the mediatorial character of the Son and acknowledged that as (a Platonized) *Logos*, He confronts humans as the source of all saving truth, the diohypostatic tradition tended to describe the Son in subordinationist terms. Arius brought this tradition to provocative and systematic expression.

The miahypostatic tradition found only one subsistent reality (*hypostasis, ousia, prosôpon*) in the triune God. These theologians tended to associate the notion of plurality with the Word's historical incarnation, which for them began a new stage in the history of the *Logos*. The miahypostatic tradition also suffered, then, from serious theological problems. First, it made any explanation of the trinity, of plurality within unity in God, extremely difficult. Miahypostatic theologians stressed the saving action of God in the history of salvation.

In the course of the Arian controversy, miahypostatic theologians tended to prefer the term "*homoiousios* (similar in being)" to the Nicean term "*homoousios* (one in being)." Since, however, the so-called "*homoians*" saw themselves as fundamentally anti-Arian, they tended to mean by "*homoiousios*" what the Nicene theologians meant by "*homoousios*." Eventually, the *homoians* were absorbed by the orthodox and disappeared from history. Cf. Joseph T. Lienhard, S.J., "The 'Arian' Controversy: Some Categories Reconsidered," *Theological Studies* (1987), 48:415-437.

7. The Christology of Origen of Alexandria, (ca. 185-254 a.d) illustrates this tendency. Platonic mysticism, with its spiritual ascent from the apparent symbol to transcendent reality, motivated his account of Christ. That same mysticism rather than concern with speculative metaphysics caused his fascination with the "titles," or "expressions (*epinoiai*)," of Christ. In contrast to the absolute simplicity of the Father, Origen's Christ confronts the believer as a complex reality and, hence, as nameable by a variety

transformed Him into a kind of Platonic demiurge, a super-creature whom God employed to create the universe, but a creature none the less.

In *The Divine Mother: A Trinitarian Theology of the Holy Spirit* I examined the negative effect which these theological innovations had on the development of Christian pneumatology. There I argued that contemporary trinitarian theology ought to conceive of the *Logos* of St. John the evangelist, not as the conceived, but as the spoken word of God. A second strain in patristic theology lends strong support to such an interpretation of the *Logos*. Moreover, the notion of a spoken word better accords with the dispensational thinking of the New Testament.[8] Dispensational thinking describes the historical self-revelation of God as people have experienced it, instead of organizing it into an abstract creedal or doctrinal system.

I shall argue a similar position in the doctrinal section of volume three, when the need arises to coordinate the Christology developed in these pages with Christian trinitarian faith. Here, however, it suffices to note that the Platonization of Christology led many of the fathers of the Church and virtually all medieval theologians to misconceive the Johannine *Logos* as the conceived rather than as the spoken Word of God.

2) *Confusions About the Humanity of Jesus.* As we have seen, Platonic anthropology divided human nature dualistically into two distinct substances: one spiritual, the other material. While the spiritual substance ruled the material substance, it related to it instrumentally, the way a charioteer relates to the horses he drives. When Christian theologians attempted to implement this dualistic conception of human nature in a Christological context, it led to another heresy called monophysitism.

Platonizing Christian thought drifted gradually into this heresy, just as it drifted gradually into the Arian heresy of subordinationism. "*Logos-sarx*" Christology helped sow the seeds of heterodoxy. "*Logos-sarx*" Christology, like Justin's *Logos* Christology, drew upon the prologue to the gospel of John and portrayed the incarnation as the union of an eternal divine intelligence with human "flesh (*sarx*)."

Some theologians who espoused this way of talking about the incarnation meant the same thing by "flesh" as the fourth evangelist had: namely, the whole of human nature, but viewed as vulnerable and death-bound. The early Athanasius defended such an orthodox form of *Logos-sarx* Christology. Despite the ambiguities of his rhetoric, flesh for Athanasius

---

of titles. The Son's complexity flows from the fact that He is divine wisdom, the pattern of all intelligible reality. In the Father these same titles lack all objective multiplicity. In the Son, each distinct title enjoys substantial reality. (Origen, *Comm. in Jo.*, I. 20; *In Lib. Jesu Nav. Hom.*. VII, 7). This association of the Son with real, created multiplicity re-enforced the subordinationist tendencies in Origen's thought.

8. Cf. Gelpi, *The Divine Mother*, pp. 45-82; 151-182.

seems, in the last analysis to have meant a complete humanity constituted of both soul and body.[9]

Others, however, understood "flesh" Platonically as the lower material
substance which constituted the inferior half of a complete human nature. Since, moreover, they also realized that this lower substance needed
only one spiritual governing principle, in their account of the incarnation they replaced the human spiritual substance, or soul, with the *Logos*.
In the process they deprived the humanity of Jesus of a human soul. In
the heterodox forms of *Logos-sarx* Christology, the *Logos*, understood ordinarily as the divine intellect, attached Himself directly to a soulless,
material body. In this construct of the incarnation, the *Logos* acted like
the equivalent of a human soul: it governed its material body directly.[10]

9. In his Christology, Athanasius sought to portray the eternal *Logos* as the force from
which all life and movement comes. The *Logos* relates to the cosmos as a quasi-animating
principle, as its quasi-soul. The "flesh" of Christ, which constitutes a portion of the
material cosmos enjoys a privileged indwelling. For Athanasius, then, if the *Logos*
dwells in a privileged way in a particular human body, it follows that the *Logos* mediates life in its fullness to that body. The incarnate indwelling of the *Logos* in the body
of Christ does not circumscribe His cosmic indwelling, because in becoming incarnate, the *Logos* in no way forfeits His infinite divine power, which continues to up-
hold the universe. (Athanasius, *De Incar.*, 17, 41, 44; *Ctr. gen.*, 30-4, 41)

   Athanasius, then, saw the death of Christ as the separation of the *Logos* from the
body it had assumed. The *Logos* descends personally into hell. (*De Incar.*, 16-32)
With the departure of the *Logos* the movement (*kinesis*) of the flesh ceases until the
resurrection. (*Ctr. gen.*, 33)

   Athanasius probably knew the philosophical definition of death as the separation
of soul from body. Still, his sense of the *Logos* as a universal animating principle led
him to underplay the role of Christ's soul in the incarnation, although in his mature
thought he probably recognized the importance of positing a human soul in Christ.
Nevertheless, at the heart of Athanasius's understanding of the incarnation lay the
idea that it enabled the second person of the trinity to function as the vicarious representative of the rest of humanity before God. Cf. Charles C. Twombly, "The Nature
of Christ's Humanity: A Study of Athanasius," *Patristic and Byzantine Review*, 8(1989),
pp. 227-241. See also: Christopher R. Smith, "The Life-of-Christ Structure of
Athenasius's De Incarnatione," *Patristic and Byzantine Review*, 10(1991), pp. 7-24.

10. The young Cyril of Alexandria developed his early Christology largely under the
influence of Athanasius. As a consequence, his early Christological thinking advanced
within the parameters of a *Logos-sarx* model. He saw the *Logos*, on one hand, as the
spiritual power dwelling in Jesus and regarded the incarnation, on the other hand, as
the gradual unfolding of the divine Wisdom the *Logos* contained. He found suffering
only in the "flesh" of Christ and regarded the "flesh" as the recipient of gifts, of holiness, and of glory. (Cyril of Alexandria, *Thesaurus*, 22-4) The human soul of Jesus
lacked any significance in his early writings, not from denial, but from absence. As a
consequence, his thought, like Athanasius's, lay open to development in the direction
of a *Logos-anthrôpos* construct of the incarnation.

   We find a similar Christology in the early writings of John Chrisostom (347-407
a.d.). Prior to his consecration as bishop of Constantinople in 399 a.d., he rarely
mentioned the soul of Christ. Like Cyril and Athanasius he saw the incarnation primarily as the gradual disclosure of the *Logos* in His human flesh. In Chrisostom's

Besides denying the divinity of Jesus, Arius and the Arians defended a heterodox *Logos-sarx* interpretation of the humanity of Jesus and of the incarnation of the *Logos*.[11] In the fourth century, Apollinarius transformed this peculiar understanding of the humanity of Jesus into the monophysite heresy. Apollinarius's thought blended Platonic with Aristotelian philosophical motifs.

Aristotle rejected the substantial dualism which characterized Platonic anthropology and replaced it with his own "hylemorphic" theory. In his treatise on the human soul, he described the human soul, not as a complete substance, but as the "form" of the human body. In informing the human body the soul endows the body with intelligibility as well as vital activity. In Aristotelian theory, then, the informing human soul and the matter it informs together create a third reality, the complete human substance.

Apollinarius, following Aristotle, argued that in a *Logos-sarx* construct of the incarnation something analogous happens in the incarnation. The *Logos* functions as one part of the incarnate reality called Jesus, the animating part. It animates the other material part of that same reality, Jesus' "flesh," or matter. Together, then, the divinity and the physical body it informs blend into a third reality, a complete nature which contains both "divine" and "human" elements. In a sense, however, monophysitism portrays the incarnate Word as neither fully divine nor fully human. The idea that divinity and humanity blend into a some sort of third reality went uncondemned until the council of Chalcedon.[12]

theology, a divine actuation (*energeia*) always commands the flesh of the *Logos*. As a consequence, the sub-rational passions function in Christ only insofar as the *Logos* allows them. Only after Chrisostom's episcopal consecration did he recognize the threat of monophysitism and go on the attack against those who denied the need for a human soul in Christ. (Alois Grillmeier, *Christ in Christian Tradition*, translated by John Bowden (Atlanta, GA: John Knox Press, 1975) pp. 418-421.

11. Cf. Grillmeier, *op.cit.*, pp. 238-239.

12. Apollinarius portrayed the *Logos* as blending with Christ's human flesh in order to form a third reality, a compound unity in human form (*synthesis athrôpoeides*), a complete, unified, substantial reality. (Apollinarius, *Ep. ad Dionys.*, A 9; *Anaceph.*, 16) Accordingly, Apollinarius called the incarnate Word a "heavenly man" because the *Logos* combines with His human flesh in order to form a complete substance. The divine origin of the animating principle in Jesus distinguishes Him from all other created humans. (*Apodeix.*, frag. 25) *Logos* and *sarx* therefore relate to one another as parts to the whole:

A nature (*physis*) is made up of two parts, as the *Logos* with His divine perfection contributes a partial energy to the whole. This is also the case with the ordinary man, who is made up of two incomplete parts which produce one nature (*physis*) and display it under one name. (*De Unione*, 5)

The reality which results from the incarnation qualifies as "neither fully man nor God (alone), but a mixture of God and man." (*Syllog. frag.*, 113) Apollinarius, therefore, found in the incarnate Word, not two natures, but one:

3) *Vagueness about "Person"*: Platonic presuppositions about time and eternity also helped fuel the Nestorian controversy. So did the failure of the whole of Graeco-Roman philosophy to develop a speculative account of the person.

Nestorius had no adequate language for talking about the union of the divine and human in the incarnation. He spoke instead of three "*prosôpa*" in the incarnation. By the Greek term "prosôpon" Nestorius seems to have meant the self-disclosure or self-manifestation of a reality. In what concerns the incarnation, therefore, Nestorius found it useful to distinguish three "*prosôpa*": 1) the *prosôpon*, of self-manifestation of the divinity of Jesus, 2) the *prosôpon*, or self-manifestation of His humanity, and 3) the *prosôpon*, or self-manifestation of the union between the two in the incarnation. At the heart of Nestorian Christology lay a concern to separate an impassible divinity from a suffering humanity.[13]

> The created body does not live in separation from the uncreated Godhead, so that one could distinguish a created nature, and the uncreated Logos does not dwell in the world in separation from the body, so that one could distinguish the nature of the uncreated. (Ep. ad Dionys., A 8)

13. Nestorius insisted that all Christology must begin with the one Lord Jesus Christ who is twofold in nature; but he failed to see clearly or to show that the *Logos* is the subject and bearer of both divinity and humanity. He distinguished between the eternal *Logos* and "Christ," that manifestation (*prosôpon*) of the *Logos* which reveals the properties of both divinity and humanity. For Nestorius, then, the term "Christ" meant "the common name of the two natures." What, therefore, we predicate of "Christ" we cannot predicate of the eternal *Logos*. In so speaking, however, Nestorius insisted that he was making a semantic, not an ontological point. (*Nestoriana*, 174-176)

He did not teach, as the orthodox would claim, that two persons exists in Christ. (*Nestoriana*, 269) Nor did he draw a distinction between the *Logos*, on the one hand, and "Son" and "Lord," on the other. He never regarded Christ as a "mere man." (*Nestoriana*, 184, 248-249, 259)

When confronted with Arianism and monophysitism, Nestorius clearly realized the need to distinguish between the divine and the human natures in Christ. Anticipating in some measure, the Chalcedonian settlement, Nestorius recognized one and the same reality in the eternal and in the incarnate Word. (*Nestoriana*, 330-1). He invoked the term "*hypostasis*" to designate the persons of the trinity and contrasted their hypostatic character with the nature they share in common. He did speak of the presence of two "*hypostaseis*" in Christ, but he seems by that to have meant two distinct natures, not two distinct persons.

For Nestorius, the term "*prosôpon*" connoted the term "*morphê*" used in Phil 2:5-8. It meant, not a person, but an external, undivided appearance, a unified manifestation of some reality. In Nestorius's Christ one finds therefore *prosôpa* (manifestations) of two distinct realities: divinity and humanity; but in "Christ" one finds them manifested in a unified way. Moreover, as a concrete, historical reality, the Christ event has a *prosôpon* distinct from that proper to each of the two natures it reveals. (*Nestoriana*, 224) In the incarnation, the *prosôpon* of the *Logos* uses the *prosopon* of His humanity instrumentally. (*Nestoriana*, 196, 299) (Cf. Grillmeier, *op.cit.*, 247-260.) Nestorius had no clear definition of the term "person."

In Greek the term "*prosôpon*" meant the mask worn by actors on the stage. The mask identified the person, or character, whom the actor portrayed. A horrified Cyril of Alexandria misread Nestorius as teaching that only an accidental relationship unites the Word to His humanity. Cyril in opposition to Nestorius insisted on the need to affirm only a single, subsistent reality in the incarnation, both divine and human; but he proved as unfortunate as Nestorius in his choice of terms. Cyril called the principle of unity in the incarnation "*mia physis*" (literally, "one nature"). For him the term seems to have connoted the dynamic character of the union of the divine and human in Jesus; but it sounded too much like monophysitism to Nestorius, despite Cyril's protestations to the contrary.[14] In all of these misunderstandings, the lack of an adequate conceptual language for talking about the notion of "person" plagued both patriarchs.

A second issue divided them, one which implicitly connoted the dualistic Platonic split between the eternal realm of spirit and the physical realm of matter. Platonizing Christian thinkers, as we have seen, naively identified the reality of God and the Platonic realm of Spirit. So did Nestorius. He held that the *prosôpon* of the divinity of the Son subsists from all eternity in the immutable realm of the divine. He denied, therefore, that any woman, including Mary, could function as its mother, since the eternity of the *Logos* understood as a divine *prosôpon* meant that it could never come into being in the way in which created material things do. Nestorius conceded, however, that Mary might function as the mother of the *prosôpon* of "Christ"; but Christ, for Nestorius, involved a different "*prosôpon*" from that of the divinity. In this convoluted sense, Nestorius denied that Mary can function as the "mother of God."

Had the bishops at Ephesus waited until Nestorius arrived, had they also waited until he and Cyril had profited from the chance to understand one another better, the Nestorian controversy might never have divided the Church. Unfortunately, the bishops chose not to wait and proclaimed instead Cyril's doctrine of the "*theotokos*," namely, that Mary is indeed "mother of God."[15]

14. Because he discovered in the incarnate Word a single principle of life and movement, namely, the *Logos*, Cyril spoke of the presence of a single nature (*mia physis*) in the incarnate Word. The term "*mia physis*" connoted for Cyril a single, divine source or life and movement within the incarnate Word. In other words, the phrase designated for him the unity of the subject present in Christ. (Cyril of Alexandria, *Ad dominas*, 3; *Ad Monach.*, PG 76, 33 A).

15. The council of Ephesus issued no new creedal formula. The council did two things: 1) It reaffirmed the teaching of Nicea, and 2) it endorsed the dogmatic idea that it said it found in the second letter of Cyril. The bishops saw the two affirmations as intimately related.

In the course of considering several documents, the bishops read Cyril's second letter to Nestorius. After its reading, Cyril rose and asked the bishops for a vote con-

In the Nestorian controversy, then, the dualisms implicit in the Platonic distinction between time and eternity, between changeless, divine, impassibility, on the one hand, and changing, suffering humanity, on the other, combined with philosophical vagueness about the meaning of "person" in order to turn the exchange between Cyril and Nestorius into a dialogue of the deaf.[16]

In what precedes, I have been arguing the following two theses: *1) Among the cultural impulses which fed the Christological controversies of the fourth and fifth centuries, over-identification with Platonic modes of thinking contributed in significant ways to the confusions which resulted. 2) Specifically, Platonic assumptions and oversights rendered problematic the three key terms which shape the Christological question: namely, "humanity," "divinity," and "the union of the two in the person of Jesus Christ."*

I have then examined the emergence a major Christological crisis during the patristic period; and I have pondered some of the cultural impulses which produced it. How does the contemporary crisis in Christology resemble this earlier crisis? How do they differ? To these two questions I turn in the section which follows.

(III)

Clearly, the Church in the fifth century faced a more serious Christological crisis than we do today. Then doctrinal confusion in Christology had reached such a pitch that it actually divided the Church. We face no such actual divisions today. To date no one has suffered excommunication for propagating Christological error.

As in the fifth century, however, confusions abound in contemporary Christological thinking. Moreover, even the popular press is beginning to take notice. We read in the news about the contradictions which dog the new quest for the historical Jesus. The media reported the censure of Hans Küng in part for what the Holy Office regarded as Christological

cerning the compatibility of what he had said with Nicene orthodoxy. The bishops voted that it did conform to Nicene orthodoxy. Cyril then requested the reading of a letter by Nestorius and requested a similar vote concerning its contents. The bishops voted negatively, even though Nestorius had not yet arrived at Ephesus to explain or defend his position. Ephesus did, however, anticipate Chalcedon in one respect: Cyril's letter did speak of a "union according to *hypostasis*" in the incarnation. (Cf. Grillmeier, *op.cit.*, pp.484-487.)

In his denial of the *Theotokos*, the doctrine that Mary is mother of God, Nestorius had in mind primarily the Arians and monophysites. He believed that only a denial of the *theotokos* could avoid both errors. His own confused doctrine of the multiple *prosôpa* in the *Logos* and in "Christ" also functioned in this denial.

16. John J. O'Keefe correctly insists that the current scholarly attempt to discover a "low Christology" in Antiochene theology and a "high Christology" in Alexandria indulges in serious anachronism. It would appear, rather, that Nestorius objected to the theopaschite language which Cyril espoused. See: John J. O'Keefe, "Impassible Suffering? Divine Passion and Fifth-Century Christology," *Theological Studies*, 58(1997), pp. 39-60.

heterodoxy. The media also reported the possible censure of Edward Schillebeeckx's New Testament Christology.

Some will probably prefer to dismiss the concerns of the Holy Office as symptomatic of the policies of the conservative, restorationist papacy of John Paul II. A sober study of the issues, however, reveals that serious problems trouble contemporary Christology. The collapse of the traditional philosophical foundations of Christological thinking, the inability of many contemporary Christologists to find a method adequate to the challenge of historical thinking, major paradigm shifts in theological thinking, and the impact of secularism have all combined to transform Christological pluralism into confusion and even contradiction. Overreaction to the excesses of medieval Christology has even produced in some areas of the theological academy a gradual drift back toward a kind of neo-Arianism.[17]

At present, the problems remain confined largely to the theological community. The example of the fifth century teaches us, however, that unless theologians find some way of dealing with the confusions and contradictions which currently trouble Christology, those same confusions and contradictions will probably one day bear bitter fruit.

I am not suggesting the self-evidence of the present crisis. On the contrary, I recognize the need to argue for its existence. Having studied contemporary Christology in some detail, however, I have come to believe that anyone who denies the existence of a contemporary crisis in Christology has either failed to do his or her home work or else is contributing to the problem.

Reflection on fifth century Christology has another important lesson to teach us. One finds confusion today over exactly the same Christological issues as in the fifth century. Today vagueness and confusion dog exactly the same key Christological categories: "divinity," "humanity," and "their union in Jesus"; but, while over-identification with a particular philosophy helped fuel the Christological confusions of the fourth and fifth centuries, very different speculative motives fuel the Christological confusions which currently confront us. The current Christological crisis flows more from the erosion of speculative and philosophical consensus rather than from naive acquiescence in the same set of philosophical presuppositions. An overdose of Platonism created the Christological crisis of the fifth century. Today Christological pluralism is beginning to degenerate into contradiction.[18]

17. In point of fact, the Arians, who regarded the Son of God as a species of demiurge, or super-creature, would almost certainly have viewed many contemporary "low" Christologies with horror.

18. For another analysis of the contemporary situation in Christology see: Roger Haight, S.J., "The Situation in Christology Today," *Ephemerides Theologicae Lovaniensis*, 69(1993), pp. 315-334.

Three different kinds of cultural impulses fuel the contemporary Christological crisis. Some of these impulses have a predominantly theoretical component. Others express pervasive cultural attitudes. Let us try to name these cultural impulses.

Three Dead Ends

First of all, in our day and age, Christological thinking has reached three dead ends. 1) The classical conceptions of divinity and humanity have collapsed and nothing has to date replaced them. 2) Theologians have generally rejected the so-called "high" Christologies popular during the middle ages. 3) Overspecialization in the pursuit of academic Christology has led to the dissociation of Christology from trinitarian theology.

Paradigm Shifts

In addition to finding itself trapped in three major *culs de sac*, contemporary Christology is also wrestling with four major paradigm shifts in theological thinking.

1) The shift from metaphysical to historical thinking has forced Christology to assimilate the results of the new quests for the historical Jesus. This paradigm shift also raises the specter of historical relativism.

2) The shift from a normative, classical understanding of culture to the search for inculturated modes of theological thinking has raised the specter of cultural relativism.

3) The feminist demand that theology shift from sexist modes of thought to gender-inclusive thinking has raised serious questions about the "masculinist" presuppositions of Christological faith.

4) At Vatican II, Catholicism shifted from a triumphalist ecclesiology to a vision of a Church committed not only to ecumenical dialogue among Christians but also to dialogue among the world religions. Initial involvement in the dialogue among the world religions has led some to call for muting the Christological focus of Christian faith.

The Challenge of Secularism

Besides finding itself forced to grope its way out of three Christological dead ends and to cope with four major paradigm shifts in theological thinking, contemporary Christology must also face the erosion of faith which has resulted from the impact of secularism on religious beliefs and attitudes.

American secular society took shape under the aegis of the Enlightenment. As a consequence, secularism in the United States frequently promotes what Robert N. Bellah has aptly called "Enlightenment fundamentalism." Enlightenment fundamentalism accepts as self-evident truth some of the demonstrably erroneous and misleading presuppositions of

Enlightenment thinking. In the United States, Enlightenment fundamentalism thrives in both the academy and in popular culture. From the standpoint of this study, Enlightenment fundamentalism takes theological shape in three important ways:

1) In the academy, Enlightenment fundamentalism leads some theologians to confine religion strictly within the bounds of reason.

2) In its more popular cultural manifestations, Enlightenment fundamentalism inculcates an individualistic ideology which erodes shared religious commitment and shared religious faith.

3) A utilitarian individualism renders capitalism in the United States predatory. It also spawns an aggressive consumerism. The combined moral impact of institutionalized capitalistic greed and a materialistic consumerism so contradicts the moral demands of gospel living that among nominal Christians it tends to promote something like practical atheism.

Let us reflect on each of these cultural impulses in turn; for an insight into each of them clarifies the issues with which a contemporary foundational Christology must deal. Let us begin by pondering the three dead ends into which Christology has wandered and from which it is trying to emerge.

The First Dead End

The collapse of classical conceptions of both humanity and divinity has left contemporary Christology floundering in its first theological dead end. Let us try to understand how Christology wandered down this *cul de sac*.

Here we face a variety of interrelated issues. In pondering this first dead end, I shall first reflect on the persistence of Platonic anthropology during the early middle ages and on the rise of Christian Aristotelianism in the work of Thomas Aquinas. I then cite the theology of Karl Rahner as evidence that Thomistic Aristotelianism persists as a major influence on theological perceptions of the human. I next examine some of the speculative issues which Aquinas's domestication of Aristotle raises. I criticize especially the essentialism and operational dualism of Thomistic anthropology. I then examine the impact of Transcendental Thomism on contemporary theological anthropology; and I call into question the virtual infinity which it discovers in the spiritual powers of the soul. Finally, I reflect on the contemporary collapse of Thomistic anthropology and of classical conceptions of God. I begin, then, by examining the Aristotelian critique of Plato and Aquinas's Platonization of Aristotelian anthropology.

As the preceding reflections on patristic Christology suggest, one can read its development as in no small measure a failed attempt to think the reality of the incarnation within a Platonic philosophical frame of reference. That failure, however, did not prevent Christian thinkers from invoking the presuppositions and categories of Platonism in order to reformulate Christian doctrine.

From the beginning of patristic speculation, some theologians, like Irenaeus of Lyons (ca.140-ca.202 a.d.) and Basil of Caesarea (329-379 a.d.), had sniffed suspiciously at the rationalizing tendencies which Justin had introduced into the tradition and which seemed to burgeon in an intellectually vibrant cultural center like Alexandria.

After the Arian controversy, some of the fathers of the Church turned from philosophy to mysticism as the proper context for approaching theology. Even Christian mysticism, however, succumbed to the blandishments of both Middle Platonism and especially of Neo-Platonic philosophy, which together provided Christian mystical theologians with many of their initial assumptions about the nature of mystical prayer.

In the Latin Church, well until the thirteenth century, Platonism in one intellectual form or another continued to provide theology with its chief assumptions and philosophical categories. In the doctrinal section of this study I shall have occasion to reflect on the "essentialist" Christologies of the twelfth century which early medieval Christian Platonism helped inspire.[19]

In other words, during the first six centuries and in the western, medieval Church the fact that Platonism had helped inspire some of the major heresies of the patristic period did not discourage many theologians from continuing to try to develop an orthodox Christian Platonism. In the thirteenth century, however, the rediscovery of Aristotle in the west forced theologians to face the often devastating criticism of Platonic metaphysics which Plato's most brilliant student had formulated.

Arab philosophers and theologians had found the philosophy of Aristotle more intellectually congenial than Christian thinkers. The contact with Arab thought and culture which resulted from the Islamic conquest of Africa and of parts of Spain combined with cultural contacts between Arab and Christian during the crusades in order to alert Christian theologians to both the challenge and the resources which Aristotelian philosophy offered them for doing theology.

In the thirteenth century, a Dominican professor of extraordinary genius at the university of Paris, Thomas Aquinas, (1225-1274 a.d.) faced that challenge squarely and systematically for the first time. His attempt to re-think Christian theology within the context of a somewhat Platonized

---

19. Cf. Walter S. Principe, *William of Auxerre's Theology of the Hypostatic Union* (Toronto: Pontifical Institute of Medieval Studies, 1963); *Alexander of Hale's Theology of the Hypostatic Union* (Toronto: Pontifical Institute of Medieval Studies, 1967); *Hugh of St. Cher's Theology of the Hypostatic Union* (Toronto: Pontifical Institute of Medieval Studies, 1970); *Philip the Chancellor's Theology of the Hypostatic Union* (Toronto: Pontifical Institute of Medieval Studies, 1975).

Aristotelianism defined the philosophical presuppositions which have undergirded much theological speculation well into the twentieth century.

Aquinas's influence continues to make itself felt in our own day in the thought of major theological giants like Karl Rahner and Bernard Lonergan. Both thinkers mediate between the classical world of medieval theology and modern historical modes of thinking. Of the two, however, Rahner constructed what one might legitimately call a creative, last-ditch defense of Thomism against the incursions of modernity. Rahner based his defense on a philosophically questionable synthesis of insights derived from Thomas Aquinas, Immanuel Kant, and Martin Heidegger.[20]

Later in this study, I shall argue that Rahner's defense of Thomism rests on a demonstrably inadequate method and that it propounds an unverifiable understanding of human nature. Here it suffices to note that Rahner's metaphysical anthropology, which blended in problematic ways three different philosophical systems, lies at the basis of virtually everything he wrote. As a consequence, the philosophical fallacies which mar that anthropology also distort his best theological thought. Those distortions require that any contemporary use of Rahner begin by regrounding his insights in a demonstrably sound method and in an empirically verifiable understanding of the human. That process will also entail their reformulation.

I shall reflect on Rahner's Christology in greater detail below. Here I undertake the more modest task of trying in a preliminary way to understand the scope of the current Christological crisis. In that context, I have cited the case of Rahner as clear evidence that classical philosophical patterns of thought continue to shape even contemporary Christology in significant ways.

How, then, did Christian Aristotelianism transform theological perceptions of the human? To this question I turn in the paragraphs which follow. In them I shall focus on two fallacies of Thomistic anthropology: its essentialism and its operational dualism.

The emergence of Christian Aristotelianism and its dominance of much theological thinking in the west has meant that until only very recently Christian attempts to understand both "humanity" and "divinity" have acquiesced in the assumptions of classical Graeco-Roman philosophy.

In his own day, Aristotle mounted some telling criticisms of Platonic philosophy. Specifically, he demolished a central presupposition of Platonism: namely, that concrete, sensible, material things derive their intelligibility from participation in a transcendent world of ideas. Aristotle ar-

---

20. Cf. Karl Rahner, S.J., *Spirit in the World*, translated by William Dych, S.J. (Montreal: Palm Publishers, 1968); *Hearers of the Word*, translated by Michael Richards (New York, NY: Herder and Herder, 1969).

gued, correctly in my estimate, that the intelligibility of things lies within them, not in some transcendent realm of ideas. Indeed, he formulated his "hylemorphic theory" as a way of insisting on the immanent intelligibility of things. The forms (*morphai*) of things in Aristotelian theory function as immanent, metaphysical principles of action and intelligibility which unite with quantified matter (*hylê*). Hence the name "hylemorphic."

Nevertheless, a Platonic and an Aristotelian understanding of reality both agree on one fundamental point. Both philosophies assume the validity of the same root metaphor in elaborating their account of reality. They both assume that in the last analysis reality resembles an idea. They therefore equate the real with the fixed, the immutable, the unchanging. Both assert that reality consists of fixed, unchanging, essential principles of being. In assuming these positions, both philosophies commit what contemporary philosophy correctly identifies as "the essence fallacy." The essence fallacy in one of its legitimate philosophical formulations naively reifies ideas as metaphysical principles of being.

Ideas exist, of course, but they do not exist as metaphysical principles of being. Rather they exist in human perceptions and judgments of reality: in human hearts and minds. Ideas define the way human hearts and minds become present to the realities they confront.

Essences also exist, but not as metaphysical principles of being. Rather the term "essence" refers to the meaning of some human evaluative response abstracted from both the one who responds and the reality to which it responds. When, for example, in strolling through a zoo I identify a horned, long-necked, long-legged, herbivorous, brown and tan spotted animal as a "giraffe," I apply the idea "giraffe" to a concrete, individual animal or group of animals. In itself, however, the idea "giraffe" refers, not to some abstract essence of "giraffeness" residing in the beast I see but to the human conception "giraffe" when I completely abstract that conception from the context in which I use it at the zoo, both from myself and from the beast I see. The essence "giraffe" describes any animal which exhibits the same traits as the one in the zoo. "Giraffe," in other words, becomes an essence precisely when I abstract it from my own mind and from the caged animal it designates.

The philosophical attempt to construct reality from fixed and immutable essences accorded well with the static, hierarchical societies which flourished during antiquity and the middle ages. Essentialist philosophies tend to imagine the world as a "great chain of Being" comprised of entities hierarchically ordered according to their fixed and immutable degree of perfection, i.e., according to their essences. As a consequence, essentialist philosophies function ideologically as a metaphysics of conservatism which demands that one acquiesce in one's fixed and determined place within a hierarchical system.

Moreover, precisely because they freeze reality by portraying it as essentially static and only superficially changing, philosophies built on the essence fallacy find themselves hard pressed to account adequately for the dynamic development of the real. In a contemporary context, essentialist philosophies cannot account adequately, if at all, for the fact of natural evolution and for the dynamics of human historical development.

Among contemporary essentialist philosophies, Alfred North Whitehead's process philosophy comes closest to reconciling the reification of essences with a dynamic, evolutionary view of the word. In the end, however, it too fails as a result of its tacit nominalism which deprives it of the speculative means to account for process as a reality. I shall reflect on this failure in greater detail in a later chapter.

Because essentialism reifies unchanging and sometimes contradictory essences, dualisms tend to mar essentialistic thinking and to make it inherently incredible. As we have seen, in the development of Christian theology, Platonic dualisms have made it difficult, if not impossible, to explain the unity of the human person, the organic relationship between sensory and intellectual knowledge, and the relation of time to eternity. One can also mount a plausible argument that in Platonism too narrow a focus on individual, human interiority obscures the relationship between the individual and society.

To the essentialist principles of being which Aristotle described, Aquinas added the act of being, which accounts, not for the essence, but for the actuality of created things, although in God Being and essence coincide. Nevertheless, in other respects Aquinas endorsed Aristotelian essentialism by reifying essences as principles of being. In its Thomist formulation, Christian Aristotelianism attempts to overcome Platonic substantial dualism; but in the end it too falls victim to an operational dualism which renders the sensory origin of knowledge inexplicable. Let us reflect on the reasons why.

Aristotle in his treatise on the human soul concluded that his hylemorphic theory led logically to the denial of the Platonic doctrine of the immortality of the soul. Aristotle seems to reserve immortality to the active intellect, which exists apart from the soul which informs the human body. (Aristotle, *De Anima*, A, 3, D 3, 5, 430 a 17) Aquinas in adapting Aristotle to the needs of Christian theology realized that he would have to modify Aristotelianism on this point. With Aristotle he regarded the soul as the form of the body; with Plato he argued to its essential spirituality and immortality.

Aquinas built his argument on an analysis of the powers of the soul. In the world of classical philosophy each power of the soul, like the soul itself, embodies a fixed, determined essence. The power's "formal object" determines its essence. The formal object of a human power of operation consists of the reality on which it works and the aspect under which it attains that reality. The sense of sight, for example, grasps material sensible things as colored; the sense of smell, as odoriferous; the sense of touch as extended and resistant; etc. (Thomas Aquinas, *Summa Theologiae*, I, lxxv, 1; lxxvi, 3, 5-8; lxxvii, 3)

Aquinas argued that two powers of the soul, the intellect and will, operate on immaterial objects and therefore have an immaterial formal object. The will follows the intellect; and the intellect abstracts the forms of things from the matter in which they inhere and grasps ultimately the immaterial reality of God. Aquinas concluded therefore to the essentially spiritual character of intellect and will. The essential spiritual independence of intellect and will from organic processes allowed Aquinas to argue to the soul's essential spirituality and immortality. (*Ibid.*, I, lxxix, 1, 8-10; *In I Sent.*, xix, 5)

In a classical conception of the human, however, the powers of the soul must "move" one another to act. Since, however, organic powers deal only with material things, they can have no effect on spiritual realities, which belong to a different and higher order of being; for the realm of the spiritual, in virtue of a different and more perfect essence, transcends the physical, the sensible, the material.

Aquinas, with Aristotle, asserted the sensory origin of all knowing. Having done so, however, he found himself hard pressed to explain how a lower sensory power can "move" a spiritual power like the intellect to act. He resolved this dilemma by postulating the presence of two spiritual, intellectual powers in the human soul, one active and the other passive. He then argued that the active intellect uses the material phantasm in the sensory imagination in order to impress, not a concrete image, but an abstract idea on the passive intellect, just as one uses a pencil to make not just a physical mark but an intelligible one.[21]

As an argument Aquinas's theory of the sensory origin of intellectual knowledge does not conclude. One writes with a material pencil on another material reality, i.e., on a piece of paper. Aquinas's theory equivalently required that one purely spiritual medieval angel use a slide projector in order to project not an image but an idea onto another purely spiritual medieval angel.

I have reflected on the essentialism and operational dualism which mar Thomistic anthropology. Modern Transcendental Thomism highlights yet another questionable aspect of a Thomistic construct of the human: namely, its discovery of a virtual infinity in the spiritual powers of the soul. To this third issue I turn in the following paragraphs.

---

21. Cf. Etienne Gilson, *The Christian Philosophy of St. Thomas Aquinas*, translated by L.K. Shook (New York, NY: Random House, 1956).

Talk of active and passive intellects may sound dated and irrelevant to contemporary ears. I cheerfully concede the point. Close study of the way the human mind develops does not support the idea that cognition results from essentially distinct powers of the soul which "move" one another to act. Instead, one can trace a continuum of cognitive responses from sensation through emotion to imagination, hypothesis, prediction, verification, and deliberation.

That fact does not, however, prevent these arcane, medieval ideas from coloring contemporary theological understandings of the human. In the case of Karl Rahner, for example, these presuppositions subtend his theology of the "supernatural existential" and of "anonymous Christianity." In Rahner's thought the "supernatural existential" results from the expansion of the formal object of the Thomistic "active intellect." His doctrine of anonymous Christianity presupposes the truth of his doctrine of the supernatural existential.[22]

Other developments in contemporary psychology have made a Thomistic construct of the human inherently implausible. In strict Thomism, especially as reformulated in the modern Transcendental Thomism of Karl Rahner and of Bernard Lonergan, the human intellect, in virtue of the fact that it has "Being" as its formal object enjoys a dynamic virtual infinity. That means that it has an insatiable thirst to know all truth. Both Rahner and Lonergan derived their understanding of the human intellect from the metaphysical anthropology of Joseph Maréchal.

I personally find the virtual infinity of the human intellect incredible. I have been teaching all my life and have never encountered such a mind. Moreover, developmental psychology has made it clear that human cognition begins finite and remains finite. Finitude rather than virtual infinity characterizes human knowing.[23] I shall consider these issues in greater detail in a later chapter.

I have considered some of the most questionable aspects of Thomistic anthropology. In the course of that considertion, I have argued that developments in contemporary philosophy have combined with the results of empirical studies of human cognition to make a Thomistic anthropology inherently implausible. Unfortunately for Catholic Christology, however, Thomism until relatively recently provided it with its basic construct of the human. As Catholic theology has abandoned the Thomistic consensus which has shaped its thinking since the middle ages, it has

---

22. Cf. Karl Rahner, S.J., *Schriften zur Theologie* (Cologne: Benziger, 1961 ff.), I, pp. 251-254, 324-363, IV, 124-127, 142-143, 210-234. Cf. Donald L. Gelpi, S.J., *Life and Light: A Guide to the Theology of Karl Rahner* (New York, NY: Sheed and Ward, 1966), pp. 45-57.

23. Cf. Donald L. Gelpi, S.J., *Grace as Transmuted Experience and Social Process: and Other Essays in North American Theology* (Lanham, MD: University Press of America, 1988), pp. 68-80.

found itself unable to replace Thomistic anthropology with another speculative construct of the human, much less with a speculative construct
which enjoys comparable consensus.

Something analogous has happened to the classical, philosophical understanding of God as essentially unchanging and unchangeable. As this
notion of the deity evolved philosophically it led to the idea that God
finds it metaphysically impossible to relate to the world.[24]

That such philosophical conceptions of God undercut theological claims
for creation, salvation, covenant, and God's ongoing, flexible providential care for His creatures passed unnoticed by more than one notable,
classical-minded Christian theologian. Contemporary process theology,
by contrast, has argued plausibly for the need to abandon these theologically indefensible, classical conceptions of God and replace them with a
rational understanding of deity which better approximates the Biblical
witness to God's action in the world.

The contemporary collapse of classical constructs of both humanity
and divinity has rendered Christological thinking hopelessly vague concerning two key Christological concepts. Vagueness engenders vagueness.
From a logical standpoint a vague concept eludes either verification or
falsification until it has received adequate clarification. The failure of contemporary theology to achieve a consensus concerning the meaning of
two key Christological terms—"humanity" and "divinity"—has left contemporary Christology equally vague on how to relate them. Instead of
facing these issues head-on, however, most recent Christologies have preferred to duck them.

The Second Christological Dead End

Contemporary Christology has reached a second theological dead end.
It has recognized the speculative indefensibility of the so-called "high"
Christologies which abounded during the middle ages. "High"
Christologies project illegitimately into Jesus' humanity traits proper to
His divinity. Often enough, "low" Christologies so emphasize the hu-
manity of Jesus that His divinity fades from view.

Perhaps nothing dramatizes the contrast between contemporary, historical Christologies and classical Christology more than contemporary
criticisms of the "high Christologies" popularized during the middle ages.
The very attempt to talk about "high" as opposed to "low" Christology
has itself led to considerable Christological confusion. Often one hears
"high" Christology defined as one which begins with Jesus' divinity and
"low" Christology as one which begins with His humanity; but in prac-

---

24. Alfred North Whitehead laid the systematic foundations for process theology's notion of God: see: Alfred North Whitehead, *Process and Reality*, edited by David Ray
Griffin and Donald W. Sherburne (New York, NY: Free Press, 1978).

tice things rarely sort out that neatly. More frequently, "high" Christologies stress Jesus' divinity at the expense of His humanity, while "low" Christologies stress Jesus' humanity at the expense of His divinity.

Some of the Christological claims made by Aquinas illustrate what theologians mean by a "high" Christology. During the middle ages, however, no one found the Angelic Doctor's Christology too "high." Its "high" Christological claims echoed things which other theologians were saying about the incarnate God. Because of Aquinas's extensive influence, however, his particular formulation of a medieval "high" Christology has come under fire more than those put forward by other medieval thinkers.

The "high" character of Aquinas's Christology echoes identifiable strains within the patristic and medieval traditions. As we have seen, Justin Martyr introduced the theologically questionable idea that one should interpret the *Logos* of the fourth gospel as a divine intelligence. Augustine popularized this fallacy in the west; and Aquinas, like most medieval theologians, accepted the authority of Augustine on this point and on other questionable theological points as well.

Moreover, as we have just seen, Aquinas partially Platonized Aristotelian anthropology by discovering in the human soul two purely spiritual powers of operation—the intellect and will, whose existence and formal objects demonstrated the human soul's essentially spiritual character and provided speculative grounds for belief in its survival after death.

In addition, as we have also seen, Aquinas conceived of these spiritual powers as having "Being" as their formal object. In Thomistic anthropology, the intellect grasps material sensible things as Being under the aspect of truth, while the will attains them as Being under the aspect of goodness. We have also seen that for Aquinas the essential orientation of intellect and will to Being implies their virtual infinity, since in Thomistic metaphysics Being as such exemplifies actual infinity and coincides ultimately with the reality of God.

In His Christology, Aquinas therefore found it unthinkable that the human intellect of Jesus could be personally united to a divine person whose ontological reality coincided with the intellect of God unless that human intellect from the first moment of its personal union with the divine experienced complete and total illumination. With many other medieval theologians, therefore, Aquinas argued that from the moment of His conception in the womb Jesus' human intellect enjoyed the "beatific vision," the objective contemplation of the totality of divine truth. In addition, Aquinas postulated the presence in Jesus of an infused "preternatural" knowledge which prepared Him for His messianic mission.

The antecedent possession of both of these more than natural forms of knowledge, however, left Jesus' ordinary human knowledge hard to explain. Aquinas did not deny that Jesus had to learn like every other human. Since, however, the beatific vision gave Jesus antecedent knowledge to the whole of truth, how could He with one and the same human mind learn naturally what he already knew supernaturally through immediate personal union with the *Logos*? This three-tiered understanding of Jesus' human knowledge illustrates well the allegedly "high" character of Thomistic Christology. (Thomas Aquinas, *Summa Theologiae*, III, ix-xi)

Viewed historically, Aquinas's account of Jesus' human knowing rooted itself remotely in the Christology of Hilary of Poitiers (310-367 a.d.), one of the most eloquent of the Latin fathers to oppose the Arian heresy. Hilary asserted unambiguously the divinity of Jesus; but he underlined that faith rhetorically by projecting into Jesus' humanity as many divine or quasi-divine traits as he could.[25] This rhetorical strategy had, more-over, a clear New Testament precedent. As we shall see, the gospel of John adopts an analogous narrative strategy in asserting the divinity of Jesus. That strategy raised but did not resolve the vexing Christological question of the *"communicatio idiomatum."* The phrase *"communicatio idiomatum"* designates a specific logical strategy for predicating divine and human traits of the person of the incarnate Word.

Contemporary Christology repudiates the graced divinization of Jesus' human consciousness as too "high" and as psychologically implausible. Karl Rahner, working within the Thomist tradition, suggested a specula-tive gambit for "lowering" medieval Christology by offering a more psy-chologically credible account of how Jesus' mind worked. Rahner pro-posed a different account of Jesus' *"scientia beata,"* or "blessed knowl-edge." (The term *"scientia beata"* refers to the way in which the personal union of the divine and human in Jesus transformed His human con-sciousness.)

---

25. Hilary claimed impassibility not only for the divinity but also for the humanity of Christ. (Hilary of Poitiers, *De Trin.*, X, 23). He also so "spiritualized" the humanity of Jesus that it had no need for food and drink. These rhetorical excesses express his concern to develop a Christology of the exalted Christ which would clearly counter the Arian denial of His divinity. (*Ibid.*, X, 35) Hilary did, however, allow Christ to grieve. (*De Synodis*, 49; *Tract. in Ps. 53*, 7; *De Trin.*, X, 55) Moreover, in speaking about the Word incarnate, Hilary tended to counter any statement about human weakness with a counter-statement about the divine glory present even in the mortal ministry of Jesus, not to mention in His paschal exaltation. That exaltation held the key to the incarnation for Hilary; for it embodied the saving ascent of humanity to God. (*De Trin.*, X, 7; *De Synod.*, 48; *Tract. in Ps. 68*, 25) Hilary characterized the pre-existent Word of God as "God before man (*Deus ante hominem*)," the kenotic Word as "both human and God (*homo et Deus*)," and the glorified Christ as "entirely hu-man, entirely God (*totus homo, totus Deus*)." Moreover, the term *"Deus* (God)" meant for Hilary "the divine fullness in all things (*Deus omnia in omnibus*)." (*De Trin.*, IX, 6) In his Christology, then, Hilary seems to have anticipated the medieval principal that "the soul of Christ has by grace what God has by nature."

Rahner argued, quite correctly in my judgment, that Jesus' *scientia beata* did not yield an objective knowledge of all divine truth from the first moment of His conception but transformed instead His subjective awareness of His own person. As a result, the human Jesus faced the challenge of "thematizing," or articulating, that personal awareness in an ongoing, gradual, historical manner by using the conceptual material available to Him in the culture of first-century Palestine.[26] Rahner's account of Jesus' human knowing has gained wide theological acceptance among contemporary theologians, both Catholic and Protestant.

The repudiation of "high" Christology has led to a spate of "low" Christologies. Unfortunately, the proliferation of contemporary "low" Christologies puts one in mind of the gradual drift into Arianism which took place in the first three centuries of the Christian era.

Among Protestant theologians, the Christologies of Friedrich Schliermacher (1768-1834) and of Paul Tillich (1885-1965) illustrate what contemporary theologians mean by a "low" Christology.

Schleiermacher's Christology blended German romantic philosophy, Enlightenment rationalism, and his own Pietistic upbringing. Schleiermacher divided his "doctrine of Christ" into the doctrine of the person of Jesus and the doctrine of His work. In what concerns the person of Jesus, Schleiermacher resisted any attempt to involve a divine person in the historical process. Instead, he suggested that God in Jesus has somehow (how remained obscure) produced a completely sinless human being who lacked both divine omniscience and divine omnipotence. Jesus possessed a humanly conditioned consciousness of God; but his sinlessness made him into a perfect ethical and religious model for other humans.

In effect, then, Schleiermacher rejected the Chalcedonian doctrine of the hypostatic union and in speaking of the relationship between the divine and human in Jesus settled for a totally redeemed human person. For Schleiermacher Jesus' saving work consists in the capacity his sinlessness has to evoke a similar work of divine grace in other human hearts.[27]

26. Cf. Gelpi, *Life and Light*, pp. 3-14.
27. Schleiermacher divided Christology into the doctrine of Jesus' person and into the doctrine of his work. He dissociated Christology from trinitarian theology and resisted any attempt to entangle divine eternity with history and time. Instead, he believed that God acted in Jesus to produce a perfectly sinless human person. As human Jesus possessed neither omnipotence nor omniscience. Rather, we discover the divine in him in the quality of his love. His divinely given sinlessness produced in him a new and perfect quality of God-consciousness. Jesus confronts us, therefore, as the perfect ideal we are called by God to become. True enough, we discover in Jesus a humanly conditioned God-consciousness. Since, however, his divinely given sinlessness ensured his total mastery of his lower powers, he nevertheless possessed the perfection of God-consciousness. That special God-consciousness constituted the presence of divinity in him. In his sinlessness, Jesus differed in no way from the first Adam.

Paul Tillich espoused an analogous position but on different philosophical grounds. An existential theologian, Tillich sought to transform the existentialist philosophy which developed in Europe in the wake of the two World Wars into the norm for authentic Christian discourse.

Like modern Transcendental Thomists, Tillich described the human person as open to infinite Being; but his theology of symbol moved this philosophical belief in heterodox directions. Tillich argued that because the infinite can never express itself within the realm of the finite, nothing like the incarnation of a divine person ever happened.

As a consequence, religious symbols of transcendence (as opposed to symbols of finite, historical religious realities) point to a reality they cannot in principle express. Tillich's Jesus called humans to a knowledge of God which eludes all objectification. Accordingly, Tillich rejected the notion of a "God-man" as contradictory and nonsensical. Moreover, having dispensed with the hypostatic union, Tillich, with courageous logical consistency denied the trinity as well.[28]

Schleiermacher rejected Chalcedonian Christology as derogating to the unity of the person of Jesus. The work of Christ consists in his ability to evoke in us through his sinlessness a work of divine grace analogous to the one God worked in him. Cf. Friedrich Schleiermacher, *The Christian Faith*, translated by R.H. Mackintosh and J.S. Stewart (Edinburgh: T. & T. Clark, 1928), pp. 355-342, 473-475. Cf. Emilio Britto, "Le rapport du Christ et du Saint-Esprit dans la 'Glaubenslehre' de Schleiermacher," *Ephemerides Theologicae Lovaniensis*, 66(1990), pp. 319-354.

28. Tillich conceded, of course, that Jesus really lived; but he deemed that theology had learned to distinguish between the empirically historical, the legendary, and the mythological elements in the New Testament witness to Jesus. It has also learned to trace the evolution of Christological symbols. Jesus brings us, however, "New Being" by overcoming the estrangement between God and humanity. Tillich's term "New Being" redefines in purely philosophical categories what an earlier theology called "faith." Jesus experienced real temptation just as we all do; but he overcame temptation by a free act of his will. He shared in the tragic element of human existence, knew betrayal by one of his intimate disciples. By embodying the "New Being" Jesus pointed in faith toward the transcendent reality of God and did so faithfully despite tragedy, rejection, and death. Thus, while not in any way incarnating God, he models for us a new way of existing in the world. Once we recognize that the mythic symbols used in the New Testament to speak about Jesus never express a literal truth, we can, then, penetrate to the authentic, "existential" meaning of the New Testament: namely, we can recognize that by faithfully embodying the "New Being" as a human person who knew the depth of human alienation and estrangement, Jesus put an end to the ambiguity which surrounds an alienated humanity's relationship with God.

In the end, Tillich offered an existential rendering of a Unitarian interpretation of the person and message of Jesus. He presented Jesus as a model of religious faith renamed and reinterpreted existentially as the "New Being." He denied, however, the reality of the incarnation, the doctrine of the hypostatic union, and the trinitarian nature of God which the incarnation reveals. Cf. Paul Tillich, "The Religious Symbol" in *Symbolism in Religion and Literature*, edited by Rollo May (New York, NY: George Braziller, 1960), pp. 75-94; *Systematic Theology* (3 vols.; Chicago, IL: University of Chicago Press, 1967), II, pp. 86-180.

One discovers the prototype of contemporary "low" Christologies in the kenotic Christologies which raised a storm of protest within the Lutheran church during the nineteenth century. Having embraced the confusing paradoxes of Hegelian logic, kenotic theologians tended to portray the incarnation as the negation of the divinity of the second person of the trinity. In portraying Jesus in a variety of speculative ways as less than divine, kenotic theology endorsed a theological understanding of the incarnation which reduced it to the graced presence of God in a human person rather than proclaimed it as the human incarnation of a divine person as such.[29]

Kenotic Christology finds a contemporary echo in the earlier Christology of Jürgen Moltmann. Like kenotic theologians, the earlier Moltmann approached the paschal mystery with a flawed, Hegelian, dialectical logic. The cross negates the divinity of both Father and Son. The Father abandons the dying Jesus as He hangs on the cross and by the act of abandonment ceases to be Father. The crucified Son despairs and for a time ceases to be Son. During the first Easter triduum, only the divine Breath holds (how?) the trinity together. Easter, however, negates the negation of Calvary and re-establishes paternal and filial relationships within the deity. Fortunately, Moltmann's more mature Christology abandons Hegelian dialectic for more Biblically based categories.[30]

Contemporary Catholic theology has also produced its own "low Christologies." Piet Schoonenberg has raised a barrage of objections to the Chalcedonian doctrine of the hypostatic union and has insisted that all Christology must begin with the assertion that in Jesus one encounters a human person who makes God present in a special way. Schoonenberg urges, therefore, the rehabilitation of an adoptionist[31] understanding of the presence of God in Jesus.[32]

Schoonenberg also prefers to deny the subsistent, or hypostatic, character of Jesus' divinity rather than that of his humanity. In other words,

---

29. Cf. Martin Breidert, *Die kenotische Christologie des 19. Jahrhunderts* (Gütersloh: Gütersloh Verlagenhaus Gerd Mohn, 1977).

30. Cf. Jürgen Moltmann, *The Crucified God*, translated by R.A. Wilson and John Bowden (New York, NY: Harper and Row, 1973); *The Trinity and the Kingdom*, translated by Margaret Kohl (San Francisco, CA: Harper and Row, 1981); *The Way of Jesus Christ: Christology in Messianic Dimensions*, translated by Margaret Kohl (San Francisco, CA: Harper & Row, 1990).

31. During the second century, adoptionist Christologies argued that Jesus has been born a human person like everyone else but at some point in time (usually on the occasion of his baptism) had experienced his adoption as Son of God through supernatural grace.

32. Cf. Piet Schoonenberg, *The Christ: A Study of the God-Man Relationship in the Whole of Creation and in Jesus Christ*, translated by Della Couling (New York, NY: Seabury, 1971).

Schoonenberg prefers to speak of the presence of God in Jesus rather than of Jesus as a divine person.[33]

Hans Küng's single-minded commitment to historical-critical method also commits him to "demythologizing" traditional Christological doctrine. Küng finds revelatory significance in Jesus but remains somewhat vague as to whether that significance includes belief in the hypostatic union. Küng questions the need to assert that the divine reality which manifested itself in Jesus existed in God from all eternity. Instead, Küng settles for saying that Jesus' relationship to God existed in God from the beginning and had its foundation in God.[34]

An orthodox "Spirit Christology" attempts to coordinate Christology and trinitarian theology in such a way as to give the Breath of God a personally active role both in the gracing of Jesus' human experience and in the life of the Church. David Coffey's Christology exemplifies such a Christology.[35] Walter Kasper's Christology moves in the direction of a Spirit Christology, although he treats Jesus' relation to the divine Breath almost as an afterthought.[36]

Roger Haight's "Spirit Christology," moves in a more heterodox direction. Haight argues correctly for the need to re-integrate the Holy Spirit into Christological thinking but seems to reduce the presence of God in Jesus to the extraordinary gracing of a human person. Haight's position resembles that of Geoffrey Lampe.[37]

In my judgment, Christologists need to abandon completely the logically vague and misleading distinction between "high" and "low"

---

33. Cf. Piet Schoonenberg, "From a Two-Nature Christology to a Christology of Presence," *Theological Folia of Villanova University, Speculative Studies, Vol II* (Villanova, PA: The Villanova University Press, 1975), pp. 219-243.

34. Cf. Hans Küng, *On Being a Christian*, translated by Edward Quinn (Garden City, NY.: Doubleday and Co., 1974).

35. Cf. Ralph Del Colle, *Christ and Spirit: Spirit Christology in Trinitarian Perspective* (New York, NY: Oxford University Press, 1994), pp. 91-140. Coffey undertakes a criticism of the traditional neo-scholastic doctrine that only in the incarnation does a single divine person act within salvation history. According to neo-scholastic doctrine, all other divine activity on the created universe flows from the divine substance through which all the divine persons act simultaneously. Such an interpretation of God's action on the world leaves no room for the action of the divine Breath as such. Instead of stressing the essential, or substantial, level of divine activity over the notional, or personal, level of divine activity, Coffey's Christology and trinitarian theology does the opposite. In making room for the personal action of the Breath within salvation history, Coffey recognizes the need to move beyond a traditional neo-scholastic account of both trinity and Christology.

36. Cf. Walter Kasper, *Jesus the Christ*, translated by V. Green (New York,NY: Paulist, 1977).

37. Cf. Roger Haight, S.J., "The Case for a Spirit Christology," *Theological Studies* (June, 1992), 53:257-287; John Wright, S.J., has taken significant exception to the position developed by Haight. Cf. John H. Wright, S.J., "Roger Haight's Spirit Christology," *Theological Studies* (December, 1992), 53:729-735. Cf. Del Colle, *op.cit.*, pp. 161-169.

Christology. Christology comes in only two forms: good Christology and bad Christology. Good Christology gives an account of the relationship between the divine and the human in the person of Jesus which expresses the shared faith of the Church. Bad Christology does not. Instead, it either sacrifices the divinity to the humanity or the humanity to the divinity. In other words, both "high" Christology and many "low" Christologies qualify as bad Christology.

A Third Dead End

The proliferation of "low" Christologies with its concomitant drift toward Arianism dramatizes a third dead end from which contemporary Christological thinking needs to extricate itself: namely, the academic dissociation of Christology from trinitarian theology. In order to understand how that dissociation occurred, one needs to reflect on the troubles which too often plague academic theological thinking.

Ever since the high middle ages, theological speculation in the West has tended to flourish in the groves of academe. In the twelfth century monastic theology correctly decried the separation of theology from spirituality which early academic scholasticism had already begun to effect.[38] The foundational Christology developed in this study seeks to suffuse academic theology with religious passion and with practical concern for living the gospel. In this sense it seeks to reconcile early medieval and scholastic theological concerns.

Contemporary liberation theology has mounted an analogous criticism of the academicization of theological thinking, although the perspective of liberation theologians differs notably from that of twelfth-century monastic intellectuals. Contemporary liberation theology views academic theology through the eyes of the oppressed majority of people living in the Third World. Liberation theologians have argued, quite correctly in my judgment, that the over-academicization of theology tends to make it morally and politically effete. Liberationists find academic theologians too concerned with "orthodoxy" and too little concerned with "orthopraxis." This dualistic split between theory and practice blinds academic theology to the moral and social consequences of Christological faith.

I find much merit in this criticism. When theology thrives in a predominantly academic environment, it tends to degenerate into a genteel conversation among intellectuals which largely ignores the practical problems confronting not only the Church but society as a whole. I find, for example, that academic theologians in this country often seem more willing to discuss the speculative pros and cons of Third-World liberation

38. Cf. Jean Leclercq, O.S.B., *The Love of Learning and the Desire for God: A Study of Monastic Culture*, translated by Catharine Nsrahi (New York, NY: Fordham University Press, 1961).

theologies than to face the serious justice issues raised by mainstream North American culture.

Academic preciousness also breeds a superficial faddishness: an overly academicized theology responds all too readily to the latest intellectual rage, especially to the latest speculative fad imported onto American campuses from Europe. The academy finds itself currently agog over the confusions of post-modernism.

In addition, much academic theology in this country systematically ignores the issues raised by the American intellectual tradition. Among Catholic speculative theologians especially, it rarely attempts to draw creatively on the North American philosophical tradition.

Not everything in our philosophical tradition has the same theological utility. One needs, for example, to distance oneself as a Christian from a Jamesean therapeutic individualism and from a naturalism closed to an encounter with God. Theology can, however, profit enormously from C.S. Peirce's systematic critique of the nominalistic caste of modern European philosophy. It can also profit from prophetic voices in the tradition which challenge the presuppositions of our Enlightenment culture. I refer to thinkers like Jonathan Edwards, Orestes Brownson, C.S. Peirce, Josiah Royce, Francis Ellingwood Abbot, and William Ernest Hocking. Cornel West's recent challenge to black liberation theology to re-appropriate the American pragmatic tradition addresses directly that kind of cultural ignorance to which I allude.[39]

By refusing to regard American philosophy as a major resource for developing a critical, inculturated theology, systematic theology in the United States often leaves many of its students all too vulnerable to the fallacies and ideologies which a sinfully flawed culture inculcates all too systematically.

The over-academicization of theology in the universities of the First World has also fostered the kind of intellectual specialization which characterizes thinking in technologically standardized cultures. Academic theology produces a flood of publications which exceeds anything most people want or need to read. As one scholar once wisely remarked: "Until one has mastered all the secondary literature in one's field one feels inadequate. Once one has mastered it, one feels cheated." Still, academic theology demands of academic theologians the professional mastery of the deluge of literature which the academy unleashes. One proves one's mastery, moreover, by contributing further to the inundation. Overwhelmed by the flood of print, finite academic minds tend to specialize.

While at one level, one can sympathize with the beleaguered academic faced with the stern imperative either to publish or to perish, the effects

---

39. See: Cornel West, *The American Evasion of Philosophy: A Genealogy of Pragmatism* (Madison, WI: University of Wisconsin Press, 1981).

of specialization can have a negative, fragmenting effect on theological consciousness. In what concerns systematic theology, for example, too much concern with analysis combines with over-specialization in order to undermine the inherently synthetic character of genuine religious thought.

As philosophy of religion in the Unites States has repeatedly insisted, genuine religious insight requires a synthetic grasp of reality. Theistic religion seeks to put one in a life-giving relationship with God, with oneself, with other people, and with the world. It therefore requires a unified way of thinking about all of these realities in their relationship to one another. The highly specialized, analytic methods espoused by most academic theologians, however, make the achievement of such an insight difficult, even impossible.

In what concerns contemporary Christology, analytic patterns of thought have combined with the exigencies of intellectual specialization in ways which re-enforce rather than challenge the Christomonism of the contemporary theology. Christomonism fails to situate Christological thinking within the context of Christian faith as a whole. One finds notable exceptions to this pattern as well as occasional protests against it. Nevertheless, analytic method and academic specialization have tended to isolate much of contemporary Christology from the trinitarian matrix of insights from which it emerged and which it seeks to illumine.

I am, then, suggesting that Karl Rahner had the right of it when he argued that the trinity constitutes the central, unifying mystery of Christian faith.[40] Balanced Christological thinking needs to situate itself within the trinitarian mystery which it reveals. All too frequently, however, contemporary Christologies fail to do that. The preoccupation with "low" Christology has especially served to re-enforce this unfortunate speculative tendency.

I have examined three of the speculative dead ends down which Christology has wandered. In the section which follows, I shall examine four paradigm shifts which also bedevil contemporary Christological thinking.

(IV)

Four major paradigm shifts in contemporary theological thinking place a new Christological consensus temporarily out of reach. A paradigm consists in a more or less organized way of posing questions and of attempting to reach an answer. The shift from Newtonian physics to relativity theory illustrates a paradigm shift in positive science. A paradigm

---

40. Cf. Rahner, *Schriften zur Theologie*, I, pp. 169-177, IV, pp. 138-154, 279-295; Cf. Gelpi, *Life and Light*, pp. 3-14.

differs from a model. Mathematical, imaginative, and scale models function within paradigms. Paradigm shifts propose new ways of thinking about reality. Paradigm shifts within theology demand that one develop a new approach to theological thinking.[41]

As I have already indicated, I count four paradigm shifts which pose a challenge to contemporary Christology: 1) the shift from metaphysical to historical thinking, 2) the shift from cultural colonialism to inculturated theological thinking, 3) the shift from sexist to gender-inclusive modes of thinking, 4) the shift from ecclesial triumphalism to dialogue with other churches and with other world religions. Let us consider each of these paradigm shifts in turn.

The Shift from Metaphysical to Historical Modes of Thinking

I have argued that contemporary theologians find it hard to replace classical notions of divinity and humanity with a new philosophical consensus. They find it difficult in part because they have in fact reached a kind of philosophical consensus on some issues; but that consensus has only complicated the contemporary Christological crisis instead of resolving it.

Contemporary theologians generally agree on the historically conditioned character of reality and of all human thinking.[42] This consensus reflects in no small measure the impact of Hegelian philosophy, of evolutionary theory, and of hermeneutics on contemporary theology, although an insistence on the historicity of Christian revelation also has sound Biblical inspiration.

Unfortunately, the historical analysis of any theological problem simply demonstrates that thinkers throughout the ages have approached it with from a variety of viewpoints and with a variety of methods. Historical analysis alone leaves one bereft of the speculative means for choosing one method or approach over another. As a result, the commitment to historical analysis leaves contemporary speculative theology impaled on the two horns of a cruel dilemma. On the one hand, the historically

---

41. For more on paradigm shifts, see: Thomas S. Kuhn, *The Structure of Scientific Revolutions* (Chicago, IL: University of Chicago Press, 1970); Ian Barbour, *Myths, Models, and Paradigms: A Comparative Study of Science and Religion* (San Francisco, CA: Harper & Row, 1976).

42. Most theologians would probably agree with Hans Küng on this point: cf. Hans Küng, *The Incarnation of God: An Introduction to Hegel's Thought as a Prolegomena to a Future Theology*, translated by J.R. Stevenson (New York, NY: Crossroad, 1987), pp. 448- 558. The Christology of Joseph Moingt exemplifies well the shift from ontological to historical discourse. In *L'homme qui vient de Dieu* (Paris: Editions du Cerf, 1993), Moingt first traces the historical evolution of patristic theological discourse and its culmination in the great Christological councils of the fourth and fifth centuries. He then re-grounds traditional Christological doctrine in an historical retrieval of the story of Jesus and of the paschal mystery.

conditioned character of all human activity makes the historical analysis of theological problems speculatively unavoidable. On the other hand, that analysis would seem to lead inevitably to an historical pluralism which all too easily degenerates into a relativism; and relativism makes systematic, theological thinking impossible.

The mounting scientific evidence in support of evolutionary theory only adds urgency to this dilemma. The fact that we live in an evolving universe makes a speculative return to classical modes of thinking impossible, since the essentialist character of classical thought, which constructs the world from fixed and unchanging essences, prevents it from providing a plausible account of cosmic evolution. In other words, the evidence of science only re-enforces the historical, developmental cast of modern theological thinking; but science alone lacks the means for moving beyond mere pluralism or for overcoming the temptation to relativism.

Hermeneutics elaborates a theory of interpretation. Much contemporary hermeneutics acquiesces in the presuppositions of Heideggerian existentialism. Unfortunately, Heideggerian existentialism equates Being with meaning. In the process, it slurs over a crucial distinction between meaning and significance. Events signify. The evaluative grasp of events endows them with meaning and so interprets them.

The equation of Being and meaning leaves all human thinking trapped in subjective intentionality. In the end, one can only interpret other interpretations. Without significant events to measure the truth of falsity of interpretations, therefore, one lacks finally any realistic criterion for choosing among interpretations.

The combined impact of historical, evolutionary, and hermeneutical thinking upon Christology poses, then, two clear challenges. First, theologians need to develop a thoroughly historical account of Christian revelation which avoids the pitfalls of historical relativism. Second, they need to coordinate their historical account of revealed truth with a philosophical understanding of the cosmos which interprets the validated scientific results of geology and anthropology. One might argue plausibly that, to date, no major Christologist has found an adequate way of responding with speculative adequacy to either of these challenges.

The different "quests" for the historical Jesus dramatize the impact of historical thinking on Christological speculation. The dawning of historical consciousness during the nineteenth century led scholars like H.S. Remarius, F.C. Baur, and D. Strauss to publish rationalistic, demythologizing, and ultimately contradictory "scientific" biographies of Jesus. Strauss himself acknowledged the failure of his own attempt.

W. Wrede in *The Messianic Secret* first unmasked some of the questionable assumptions which lay behind these early "biographies" of Jesus. Then Albert Schweitzer's *The Quest for the Historical Jesus* sounded the death knell of this phase of the modern historical reconstruction of Jesus' mortal ministry. Schweitzer catalogued in devastating detail the contradictions and tenuous assumptions which typified the first "quest for the historical Jesus."

The collapse of the first quest gave rise within modern Protestant scripture studies to a period of skepticism about the possibility of ever painting an historically accurate "scientific" portrait of Jesus and of His ministry, a skepticism which colored the early thought of a modern thinker like Rudoph Bultmann.[43]

Ernst Käsemann, however, in 1953 revived the quest in a paper entitled "The Problem of the Historical Jesus." While conceding that we cannot at a distance of two thousand years write a biography of Jesus, Käsemann questioned whether that fact justified total skepticism concerning Jesus' mortal ministry. He discovered historical and theological themes interwoven in the gospels; and he warned against the "Docetic"[44] consequences of separating faith in Jesus as exalted Lord from the actual career of Jesus. In support of this latter thesis, he pointed to the manifest intention of the gospels to link faith in Jesus' Lordship to His mortal ministry.

Initially Käsemann contented himself with establishing the historical authenticity of some sayings of Jesus preserved in the synoptics. Ernst Fuchs argued that one could also authenticate historically a number of Jesus' actions. Other major scholars—among them Günther Bornkamm, Hans Conzelmann, Herbert Braun, and Gerhard Ebeling—contributed significantly to re-opening scientific historical investigation into Jesus' life and ministry. Finally, in 1959 James M. Robinson gave this intellectual movement its name in his programmatic study: *The New Quest for the Historical Jesus.*[45]

Today we find a growing consensus among Biblical scholars concerning the principles which "authenticate" the sayings and actions of Jesus and some consensus about which teachings and deeds qualify as either certainly historical, or historical within a range of probability. Unfortunately, however, all the principles which govern the "new quest" require

---

43. Bultmann rejected any attempt to write an historical account of Jesus as He really lived and apart from the faith that people place in Him. Moreover, for Bultmann we have access to the Christ of faith only in the Church's proclamation. Even if one had complete knowledge of Jesus' teaching and deeds, they would not provide Christian faith with an adequate object. Only the risen Christ proclaimed in the New Testament does. In other words, Bultmann regarded the distinction between the "Jesus of history" and the "Christ of faith" as an unbridgeable chasm. Cf. Morris Ashcraft, *Rudolf Bultmann* (Waco, TX: Word Incorporated, 1972), pp. 35-7.

44. An early form of Gnosticism, Docetism reduced the humanity of Jesus to an illusion.

45. Cf. Michael L. Cook, S.J., *The Historical Jesus* (Chicago, IL: Thomas More Press, 1986).

prudential judgments in their implementation; and different scholars apply them differently. Moreover, virtually every new quester for the historical Jesus brings to the search a set of personal prejudices and assumptions which color his or her personal portrait of "the Jesus of history." As a consequence, the new quest has generated its own set of contradictory accounts of the mortal ministry of Jesus.

Moreover, the new quest itself has expanded beyond the attempt to "authenticate" specific words and sayings of Jesus. It now includes the attempt to reconstruct historically the social, political, and economic context within which Jesus conducted His ministry. Some call this expansion of the new quest the "third quest for the historical Jesus."[46]

The results of the new quest confront both contemporary Christologists and ordinary believers with a very thorny question. Since it seems unlikely that the new quest will ever produce unanimity among scholars, which version of the new quest ought one to endorse? Until one answers that question, one lacks adequate means to verify or falsify Christological theories.[47]

Clearly, the co-ordination of the results of the new quest with traditional Christological faith demands the development of something like an "empirical" theology. I do not use the term "empirical" in any narrowly scientific or nominalistic sense. The new quest does not qualify as "science" in the same way in which the mathematical sciences do; but it does qualify as scholarship. Moreover, as scholarship it proposes to provide Christological thinking with a plausible account of the "bare facts" about Jesus. Those facts, however, include a lot more than raw sense data, since they provide an interpretation not only of the events of Jesus' life but of the forces, the dynamisms, and the motives which caused them to evolve in the way they did.

A balanced and nuanced evaluation of the results of the new quest provides, then, an ongoing scholarly challenge to the formulation of a contemporary Christology. Moreover, the new quest lends a certain amount of instability to the human attempt to speak about Jesus, since the historical discovery of new facts or the legitimate re-evaluation of supposed facts about Him could in principle challenge any number of theological assertions about His person and ministry.

I have pondered the first paradigm shift which bedevils contemporary Christological thinking: namely, the shift from metaphysical to historical

---

46. Examples of the "third quest" would include: Richard A. Horsley with John S. Hanson, *Bandits, Prophets, and Messiahs: Popular Movements at the Time of Jesus* (New York, NY: Harper and Row, 1985); John Dominic Crossan, *The Historical Jesus: The Life of a Mediterranean Jewish Peasant* (San Francisco, CA: Harper & Row, 1991), pp. 1-224.

47. Cf. Roger Haight, S.J., "The Impact of Jesus Research on Christology," *Louvain Studies*, 21(1996), pp. 216-228.

thinking. I turn now to the second: namely, the shift from religious colonialism to theological inculturation.

From Cultural Colonialism to Inculturated Theology

The second Vatican council repudiated cultural colonialism as a legitimate strategy for evangelization. Instead, the council challenged the Church as a whole to develop a thoroughly inculturated evangelization. Inculturated evangelization needs to root itself in inculturated theological thinking.

Inculturated theological thinking demands the abandonment of a classical definition of the term "culture." A classical definition of culture canonizes a particular culture as normative for civilized living. It regards the canonized culture as superior and all other cultures as barbaric and inferior.

European colonialism thrived on a classical understanding of culture. European colonizers tended to assume the superiority of western culture to the culture of those they colonized. Not surprisingly, the evangelization which colonialism promoted tended to demand the Europeanization of non-Europeans as a condition for their Christianization.

As I have already indicated, the second Vatican council rejected cultural colonialism and called for the inculturation of all future evangelization. In the wake of Vatican II, however, the term "inculturation" not infrequently degenerated into a theological buzz word whose meaning often remained obscure. Pedro Arrupe contributed significantly to the clarification of the term when he suggested that it synthesizes two interrelated concerns: 1) the concern to communicate the gospel to people in images, attitudes, and concepts which reflect the culture in which they live and 2) the use of the gospel to challenge the sinfulness of any given culture and to call it both to self-reform and to gospel living.[48]

Since Vatican II, however, the attempt to inculturate theological thinking has raised other issues which only serve to complicate the contemporary Christological crisis. Chief among them rank the following questions: How far can one press the inculturation of theology? At what point does a narrow concern with the issues of a local church begin to dissociate it from the great Church and from its tradition? To put the same question in different words, at what point does narrow concern with the issues of a local Church tend to make it narrowly sectarian?

Some within the Church fear, and not without some cause, that the systematic pursuit of inculturated patterns of thinking will only erode further speculative consensus among Christian theologians. Will, for example, a Christology which fits the needs of Christians in the United

---

48. Cf. Pedro Arrupe, S.J., "On Inculturation," *Acta Romana Societatis Jesu* (1979), XVII, ii, p.257.

States have anything to say to Christians in India, in Africa, in Antarctica? Doesn't the espousal of inculturation as an ideal add to the relativizing tendencies of historical thinking another form of relativism: namely, cultural relativism?

Clearly, any contemporary Christology will need to devise an adequate method for pursuing a thoroughly inculturated understanding of the person and mission of Jesus while somehow avoiding the pitfalls of cultural relativism. I find it easy to excuse contemporary theologians and Christologists for confessing that to date they have formulated no clear solution to this incredibly complex problem. That fact, however, makes its resolution only the more pressing. Certainly, anyone who undertakes inculturated theological thinking needs to make sure that it advances in an ongoing and fruitful dialogue with the great Church and with its traditions. That means that inculturated theological thinking also needs to ensure theological dialogue among local churches and across cultures.

The failure to date of contemporary theologians to agree on such a method only dramatizes the challenge which cultural diversity poses for contemporary Christology and for theology in general. Moreover, until theologians formulate and agree on a method for dealing with cultural diversity, it will continue to erode theological consensus and raise the specter of cultural relativism.

I have examine the first two paradigm shifts in theological thinking. I turn now to the third.

From Triumphalism to the Dialogue among World Religions

A third paradigm shift in contemporary theology inhibits the formulation of a new Christological consensus: namely, the shift from triumphalistic to dialogic theology. The relatively small Integralist minority at Vatican II espoused a triumphalistic ecclesiology. Triumphalism confuses the ideals to which the Catholic church aspires with the thoroughly imperfect, often sinful reality of the living Catholic community.

Vatican II replaced such trimphalism with a truer, humbler vision of the Church as a pilgrim people whose blindness and sinfulness have contributed to its fragmentation by schism and doctrinal division. As an expression of penitence for these past failures, Vatican II committed the Catholic church to ecumenical dialogue. Moreover, the council expanded ecumenical dialogue to include dialogue with other world religions.

The shift from classical to historical forms of thinking has raised the specter of historical relativism. The shift from colonial to inculturated forms of thinking has raised the specter of cultural relativism. The incipient dialogue among world religions raises a different specter: that of religious relativism.

If one recognizes saving, revelatory significance in other religions besides Christianity, as the dialogue among world religions largely presupposes, what does that have to say about the traditional Christian claim to provide a normative insight into the practical demands of universal human salvation? As Christians enter into dialogue with other religious traditions, can they, for example, continue to assert that salvation comes to human kind "in no other name" than the name of Jesus? We stand only at the threshold of the dialogue among world religions; but already we find some theologians suggesting that the Christian entry into that dialogue demands soft-pedaling many traditional Christian Christological beliefs, including the belief that faith in Jesus Christ offers one privileged access to God's saving intentions for humankind.[49]

I have considered three of the four paradigm shifts which condition contemporary Christological thinking. Let us, then, consider the fourth and final shift.

From Sexist to Gender-Inclusive Theology

By calling prophetically into question the sexist bigotry of human culture, contemporary feminism is effecting another paradigm shift in theology: the shift from masculinist to gender-inclusive theological thinking. Feminist theology to date has failed to produce a systematic Christology, although it has, as we shall see, begun to develop a Jesusology. Nevertheless, feminist criticisms of the "masculinist" character of Christian theology engage Christological faith at a number of points.

The most radical strain in feminist theology regards Christianity as irredeemably patriarchal. It views faith in Jesus Christ as the worship of maleness. More moderate feminist theologians argue that women can find salvation and religious meaning within Christianity. Some moderate feminists discover within Jesus' prophetic ministry theological support for the feminist critique of sexism. Among Black women theologians, one also finds the emergence of a "womanist" approach to Christology which remains sensitive to feminist issues while criticizing them from the standpoint of Afro-American women.[50]

---

49. Cf. Paul Knitter, *No Other Name? A Critical Survey of Christian Attitudes Toward World Religions* (Maryknoll, NY: Orbis, 1986); John Hick, "Jesus and the World Religions," in *The Myth of God Incarnate*, edited by John Hick (Philadelphia, PA: Westminster, 1977), pp. 167-185. For a more successful attempt to advance dialogue among the world religions, see: Hans Küng, Josef van Ess, Heinrich von Stietencron, Heinz Bechert, *Christianity and World Religions: Paths to Dialogue*, translated by Peter Heinegg (New York, NY: Orbis, 1986); William M. Thompson, *The Jesus Debate: A Survey and Synthesis* (Mahwah, NJ: Paulist, 1985), pp. 385-394.

50. For a summary of key Christological issues raised by feminist theologians, see: William M. Thompson, *The Jesus Debate: A Survey and Synthesis* (New York, NY: Paulist, 1985), pp.375-382. For a thorough survey of feminist Christology and a Black womanist critique, see: Jacquelyn Grant, *White Women's Christ and Black Women's*

Feminism has, moreover, begun to formulate a kind of Jesusology. The title "Christ" designates Jesus as the messiah, the anointed of God. Christology devolves into Jesusology when it discourses about Jesus in abstraction from the paschal mystery, which reveals His divinity and, ultimately, His messianic dignity. To date, however, feminist "Christology" has shied away from Christological discourse as such, largely, I suspect out of a fear of divinizing masculinity. That same concern seems to motivate a feminist tendency to deal with Christological issues *in obliquo*, in studies dealing with other theological issues.

Elizabeth Schüssler-Fiorenza's *In Memory of Her*[51], for example, deals largely with ecclesiological issues. It argues, correctly in my judgment, that Jesus in proclaiming the kingdom envisioned an egalitarian community which blurred traditional gender distinctions. Schüssler-Fiorenza also argues that the apostolic church, in the course of defining itself as a community, progressively betrayed those ideals. *In Memory of Her*, then, discusses Jesusology largely in function of ecclesiology.

Elizabeth Johnson's *She Who Is* approaches Christological issues more directly. She argues that Jesus in His ministry revealed the feminine wisdom of God and that, in the Breath-inspired community which proceeds from His resurrection, one may imagine all three members of the trinity in feminine as well as in masculine terms. I deem both positions as arguable. Nevertheless, in my judgment, like Schüssler-Fiorenza, Johnson moves somewhat rapidly from issues in Jesusology to ecclesiological and trinitarian concerns. She would, in my judgment strengthen her argument considerably by a more systematic handling of the paschal mystery. She also needs to develop a scientifically validated, philosophical anthropology.

In *Jesus: Miriam's Child, Sophia's Prophet*, Schüssler-Fiorenza further develops the Jesusology which she sketched in *In Memory of Her*. In it she correctly argues for an Christian understanding of humanity which includes both women and men. Like Johnson, she presents Jesus as the revelation of the feminine wisdom of God. In dealing with the figure of Jesus, however, Schüssler-Fiorenza once again brackets the resurrection. She speaks of Jesus' career, of his execution, and of Christian interpreta-

---

Jesus: Feminist Christology and a Womanist Response (Atlanta, GA: Scholars Press, 1989); Mary Catherine Hiekert, O.P., "Feminist Theology: Key Religious Symbols: Christ and God" *Theological Studies*, 56(1995), pp. 341-352. Elizabeth A. Johnson's *She Who Is: The Mystery of God in Feminist Theological Discourse* (New York, NY: Crossroad, 1992) deals with a number of Christological issues from a feminist perspective by fails finally to elaborate a systematic doctrinal Christology. So does Elizabeth Schüssler-Fiorenza's *Jesus: Miriam Child, Sophia's Prophet: Critical Issues in Feminist Christology* (New York, NY: Continuum, 1994).

51. (New York, NY: Crossroad, 1983).

tions of Jesus' death; but she fails finally to deal adequately with the paschal mystery as such.

In addition, one finds in feminist theology criticisms of particular Christological doctrines, although not all feminist theologians endorse these critiques. Some feminists deride Jesus' death in obedience to the Father as "cosmic child abuse." Some see in the idea of atonement a supine acquiescence in suffering which rationalizes oppression, including the oppression of women.[52]

In summary, then, contemporary feminism calls into question narrowly sexist formulations of Christological doctrine; but it also provides some important resources for rethinking the mortal ministry of Jesus and the meaning of the paschal mystery. Clearly, any contemporary Christology needs to respond to both the challenges and the opportunities expressed in feminist theology.

So far in this chapter, I have reflected on two kinds of cultural impulses which have contributed to the contemporary crisis in Christology: Christological dead ends and paradigm shifts in contemporary theological thinking. In the following section, I shall reflect on a much broader cultural phenomenon but one which effectively undermines religious commitment in general and Christological faith in particular. I refer to the impact of secularism on religious beliefs, attitudes, and thought.

(V)

In the United States, secular culture fosters what Robert N. Bellah has aptly named "Enlightenment fundamentalism." Enlightenment fundamentalism transforms Enlightenment philosophy into an ideology by endowing even its least tenable doctrines with fallacious self-evidence. As I indicated above, "Enlightenment fundamentalism" thrives in both the academy and in American culture generally. It conditions some contemporary Christological thinking. It also contradicts the moral consequences of authentic Christological faith. As we shall see, moreover, those consequences constitute the full meaning of Christological doctrine.

Secularism and Enlightenment Fundamentalism

The eighteenth-century Enlightenment popularized a nominalistic, "empirical" British understanding of human knowing as well as a variety of political philosophies which inspired the revolutions of the eighteenth and nineteenth centuries.

In explaining human scientific knowledge Enlightenment philosophy reduced the grasp of reality nominalistically to the "empirical" awareness of individual, concrete, sensible things. In other words, in its analysis of

---

52. Cf. Mary Catherine Hilkert, O.P., "Feminist Theology: Key Religious Symbols: Christ and God," *Theological Studies*, 56(1995), pp. 341-352.

scientific forms of knowing Enlightenment epistemology denied in principle the existence of those realities which make scientific thinking possible: namely, the laws, or generalized tendencies, to act in predictable ways which science investigates. It therefore reduced "universals" to abstract concepts which the human mind imposes on reality. In the world of Enlightenment nominalism, nothing in reality corresponds to universal concepts. In effect, then, the Enlightenment popularized what C.S. Peirce aptly called "conceptual nominalism."[53]

In its political thinking Enlightenment philosophy held that a social contract among unrelated, atomic individuals creates the political order. Enlightenment political thinking therefore viewed all social relationships as accidental to the individual person and as artificially created through human convention. In the process Enlightenment political philosophy either overlooked or denied the fundamentally relational, social character of the human existence.

The Enlightenment also sought to bring religious belief under the complete control of scientific reason, nominalistically interpreted. Enlightenment rationalism therefore dismissed all revealed religion as superstitious and as grounded finally in unstable, untrustworthy, subjective human emotions. Moreover, by reducing the ultimate content of knowledge to discrete, concrete, sensible, individual things, Enlightenment philosophy rendered religious experience as unintelligible as scientific forms of knowing. I shall return to these themes in a later chapter.

In its "rational" understanding of God, the Enlightenment promoted a form of Deism: it asserted a creator God but held that God left humans to themselves to decide their own moral fates. In the end, Enlightenment rationalism reduced the content of religious belief to three basic philosophic tenets: the existence of a Deistic God, the immortality of the soul, and the universal norms of morality. For some Enlightenment thinkers the existence of a moral order implied also a system of rewards for virtue and punishments for vice after death.

Among the Christian churches the Enlightenment bore fruit in Unitarianism. In the American colonies, for example, it accelerated the erosion of religious consensus among local Congregational churches. Under the influence of Enlightenment forms of thought, liberal Congregational ministers began by denying the Calvinist doctrine of total human depravity and replaced it with an optimistic faith in the complete integrity of human nature. An integral humanity, they then argued, needs no redemption. The denial of the need for redemption, however, implied logically the denial of the need for a redeemer. The denial of a redeemer implied in turn the denial of the incarnation; and the denial of the incar-

53. Cf. C.S. Peirce, *Collected Papers*, edited by Charles Hartshorne and Paul Weiss (6 vols.; Cambridge, MA: Harvard University Press, 1931 ff.), 1.26-7.

nation entailed the denial of the trinity, which the incarnation reveals. By an inevitable logical progression, therefore, liberal Congregational theology transformed Christian faith into the rationalistic creed of the first American Unitarian churches.[54]

The philosophical presuppositions of the Enlightenment continue to inform much of modern culture. Those presuppositions also exhibit the same power in the twentieth century to transform traditional Christian beliefs as they did in the late eighteenth and early nineteenth centuries, especially when they lurk uncriticized within rational theological reflection.

Enlightenment fundamentalists in the academy prefer to ignore the fact that philosophical thinking in this country has already refuted the major speculative blunders of Enlightenment philosophy. Peircian realism mounts a devastating critique of Enlightenment nominalism, just as the political philosophy of Roberto Unger unmasks the folly of Enlightenment individualism.[55]

The philosophy of science also offers better ways of viewing the relationship of science and religion than the view popularized by Enlightenment fundamentalism. As Charles Peirce argued in the first part of this century and as Ian Barbour has demonstrated more recently, logic, properly interpreted, brings about the "wedding of religion and science." The human mind works analogously when it wrestles with religious and with scientific questions, because, after all, the same mind wrestles with both; and, when it thinks clearly, human reason employs similar patterns of inference in both areas of human speculation.[56]

In what concerns Christology, Enlightenment presuppositions very often lie at the basis of contemporary demands to "demythologize" Christian faith. They motivate, for example, Rudolph Bultmann's program for demythologizing the New Testament. Despite his existentialist philosophical aspirations, in what concerns the demythologization of the New Testament, Bultmann shows himself most concerned to placate "the modern scientific mind" by excluding from the content of Christian faith any notion of a divine intervention in history which disrupts the immanent, spatio-temporal chain of cause and effect studied by empirical science. In

54. Cf. Conrad Wright, *The Beginnings of Unitarianism in America* (New York: Putnam's, 1955).

55. For an examination of Peirce's refutation of the presuppositions of Enlightenment thinking, cf. Donald L. Gelpi, S.J., *The Turn to Experience in Contemporary Theology* (Mahwah, NJ: Paulist, 1994). For a critique of the individualistic presuppositions of Enlightenment political thinking, see: Roberto Mangabeira Unger, *Knowledge and Politics* (New York, NY: Free Press, 1975).

56. Cf. Peirce, *Collected Papers*, 1.616-677, 6.428-450; cf. Francis E. Reilly, *Charles Peirce's Theory of Scientific Method* (New York, NY: Fordham University Press, 1970; Ian Barbour, *Religion in an Age of Science* (San Francisco, CA: Harper & Row, 1990).

erecting the empirical sciences as the norm of religious belief, Bultmann, in my judgment, reverts uncritically to eighteenth-century patterns of thinking, even though Martin Heidegger rather than John Locke suggests to him most of the philosophical categories to which he reduces the meaning of divine revelation.[57]

Many of the presuppositions of Enlightenment fundamentalism also inspire the existential rationalism of Paul Tillich. Whatever the philosophy particular theologians may espouse, they subscribe more or less explicitly to the Enlightenment presuppositions whenever they accord to human reason the final judgment in determining the content of divine revelation. In the case of Tillich, his "theological" method of correlation erects his own version of existential philosophy into a theological norm of truth and credibility.

Tillich's method of correlation advances in three steps. The first step demands that one correlate the situation of contemporary Christians with the situation of Christians living in the first century. The second step requires the reduction of the Christian message of the New Testament to existential philosophical categories, even though Tillich, with manifest self-contradiction, also asserts that philosophy plays no role in systematic theology. Finally, one must correlate Tillich's existential restatement of

57. Bultmann, following Hiedegger, distinguished between history as event (*Historie*) and history as the meaning events acquire subsequently for those who live after them (*Geschichte*). Bultmann denied that history as event grounds Christian faith because he regarded all historical knowledge as ambiguous, as relative, and as a closed sequence of cause and effect which leaves no room for any unique elements. In acquiescing in this scientific view of history, Bultmann made his first serious departure from Heidegger's philosophy and tacitly endorsed an Enlightenment understanding of science. Having ruled out history viewed as event as the locus of divine self-disclosure, Bultmann discovered revelation in a history existentially meaningful to persons, i.e., in the proclamation of Christ by His disciples.

Bultmann defined myth as a story which expresses human understanding of being in the world. The New Testament mythic mind asserted that the origin and purpose of the world lies not in the world itself but beyond it, that humanity depends not only on the world but on mysterious, invisible powers, and that humanity can experience deliverance from those powers. New Testament mythic discourse, in other words, attempted to express other-worldly reality in this-worldly terms. The use of this-worldly language to express other-worldly realities objectified those other worldly realities in ways which rendered them obsolete to the "modern scientific mind." "Modern science" sees the world as a closed sequence of natural causes and effects and therefore finds Biblical language about transcendent cosmic powers unintelligible. Bultmann's program of demythololgization sought to respond to the challenge to New Testament faith posed by such "modern scientific thinking." Bultmann did not himself regard demythologization as subtracting from the New Testament message but as its interpretation in contemporary, existential language. In the process of formulating that interpretation, however, he assumed without proving the adequacy of existential philosophical language for expressing the kerygma, an adequacy his critics have correctly called into question. Cf. Ashcraft, *Rudolf Bultmann*, pp. 35-55.

the Christian message with religious reality. In other words, one puts the philosophical rabbit into the hat in step two and pulls it out in step three; for the last two steps of the method of correlation require that one employ Tillichian existentialism as a philosophical procrustean bed for measuring the content of Christian revelation.[58]

One also suspects that some form of Enlightenment fundamentalism has helped inspire the proliferation of "low" Christologies which seek in one way or another to present Jesus, not as the incarnation of a divine person, but as the most perfectly graced human ever to exist.

In this respect, Protestant process Christology exemplifies well the impact of Enlightenment fundamentalism on theological thinking. Whitehead insisted that philosophy must supply religion with the content of its faith. Protestant process theology has, on the whole, endorsed this methodological presupposition. It has, therefore, tended to use Whiteheadean cosmology as its norm for judging what in Christian faith qualifies as rationally credible. In Christology, it has produced a series of "low" Christologies which present Jesus as that human person who, to date, has responded most totally to God.[59]

While the Christology of Edward Schillebeeckx manages in my judgment to stand within the ballpark of orthodoxy (somewhere deep in left field), his Christological thinking too succumbs rather systematically to the presuppositions of Enlightenment fundamentalism, as we shall see in another chapter.

Individualism

In *Habits of the Heart*, Robert N. Bellah and his colleagues have anatomized the corrosive impact of individualism on mores in the United States, especially among the middle and upper classes.[60] Individualism differs from the legitimate recognition of human individuality and personal creativity. Instead, individualism gives fallacious ideological sanction to the Enlightenment belief that society consists of atomic individuals with only ephemeral and accidental relationships to one another.

---

58. Cf. Paul Tillich, *Systematic Theology* (3 vols.; Chicago, IL: University of Chicago Press, 1967), I, pp. 22-8, 60-76.
59. Cf. W. Norman Pittenger, *The Word Incarnate: A Study in the Doctrine of the Person of Christ* (London: James Nisbet, 1959); *Christology Reconsidered* (London: SCM Press, 1970); David R. Griffin, *A Process Christology* (Philadelphia, PA: Westminster, 1973); John B. Cobb, *Christ in a Pluralistic Age* (Philadelphia, PA: Westminster, 1975); Marjorie Hewett Suchocki, *God, Christ, Church: A Practical Guide to Process Theology* (New York, NY: Crossroad, 1982).
60. Cf. Robert N. Bellah, Richard Madsen, William M. Sullivan, Ann Swidler, and Stephen M. Tipton, *Habits of the Heart: Individualism and Commitment in American Life* (Berkeley, CA: University of California Press, 1985).

Two kinds of individualism subvert responsible moral commitment. Utilitarian individualism, which thrives especially in business and politics, justifies doing whatever one needs to do in order to "get ahead." "Getting ahead" means achieving success, wealth, and power over others. Expressive individualism romanticizes Enlightenment individualism by tricking people into believing that they possess an inner core self which they must protect at all costs from the encroaching demands of others. Expressive individualism thrives in popular culture and in the academy.

Individualism privatizes religious belief and practice. Privatized religion especially thrives among the middle and upper classes.

The Catholic Church in the nineteenth century established its extensive school system in order to keep immigrant Catholics in the fold of the Church and in order to help them move from the lower to the middle class. In both these goals Catholic education succeeded admirably. The bourgeoisification of American Catholics, however, had consequences which Catholic leaders in the last century probably did not foresee. With bourgeoisification also came secularization. With secularization came uncritical acquiescence in an ethos of individualism. When individualism privatizes religion, it deprives it of its prophetic voice. In the process, individualism transforms religious people and institutions into implicit supporters of the social, economic, and political *status quo*.

Individualism also personalizes religious faith in a way which deprives it of any normative claims. Because privatized religion acquiesces uncritically in the presuppositions of Enlightenment philosophy, it assumes that religious creeds express purely subjective and utterly arbitrary human emotions. Enlightenment fundamentalism discovers "objective truth" only in the results of positive science; and, as we have seen, Enlightenment fundamentalism interprets those results nominalistically, as the verification of scientific theories in sense data. When these philosophical fallacies infect religion, they promote popular religious relativism. Lacking "objective" scientific validation and symptomatic of arbitrary subjective impulses, religious faith becomes optional and any creed legitimate as long as it satisfies one personally and emotionally.

Finally, the individualistic privatization of religion subverts shared faith consciousness and the capacity of think religiously as a member of the Church. In what concerns Christological thinking, privatized theological thinking has, in my judgment, helped motivate the current drift into Arianism. One hears again and again the narcissistic refusal to believe in Jesus unless He is exactly like oneself.[61]

In its extreme expressions, an individualistic ethos so vitiates the conscience that it gives rise to practical atheism. The practical atheist pro-

---

61. Cf. Christopher Lasch, *The Culture of Narcissism: American Life in an Age of Diminished Expectations* (New York, NY: Warner Books, 1979).

fesses faith in God while living in ways which flout and contradict the practical demands of authentic religious faith. As we shall see in volume three, the practical demands of Christian faith define much of the speculative meaning of Christological doctrine.

Capitalism, for example, has an inherently aggressive character. It constantly seeks expanding markets. Aggression makes capitalism morally manipulative when it treats people like things, when it uses them to enhance capital gains without any regard for their personal rights. One can in principle mute the aggressiveness by placing the welfare of one's employees first, quality of product second, and turning a profit third. In the United States, however, capitalism consistently makes the maximization of profits the primary goal of big business. Quality of product comes second. The welfare of employees, last of all. When the maximization of profits combines with utilitarian individualism, together they render capitalism not only aggressive but viciously predatory. Predatory capitalism sacrifices people to the almighty dollar. It also justifies the ruthless exploitation of consumers in the name of institutionalized greed.

Predatory capitalism spawns consumerism. In consumerist societies, big money exploits the means of communication to create artificial human needs and to dupe people into regarding luxuries as necessities of life. Since luxuries enhance, not human life, but class superiority, consumerism re-enforces economic class distinctions as well as the divisive classist attitudes which they institutionalize.

Reaganomics promised to "get government off people's backs." In practice "getting government off people's backs" meant tax breaks for the rich and ruthless capitalism for everyone else. By eroding the middle class, Reaganomics began to turn this nation into a two-class society with a permanent under-class. In other words, Reaganomics led to ever deeper economic divisions in United States class structure. Racism and sexism only exacerbate the injustices of uncontrolled capitalism by institutionalizing other forms of oppression over and above economic exploitation.

In what concerns the nation as a whole, utilitarian individualism has spawned an ideology of "national security." That ideology convinced the American people and their leaders that this nation could do anything it needed to do in order to win the Cold War. An ethos of "national security" militarized life in the United States and created the military-industrial complex.

Our ensuing national preference for the violent solution of international crises finds an echo in the violence of our cities. The economic injustices spawned by Reaganomics also feeds violence in our streets. When people trapped in a permanent under-class with little or nothing to lose ascribe to an individualistic ethos, they can easily turn to crime as a way of "making it."

All of these forces in North American society contradict the gospel of Jesus Christ. To the extent that Christians endorse them, therefore, they stand convicted of practical atheism and Christological unbelief. Any inculturated Christology written in this country will, therefore, need to challenge nominal Christians to replace practical atheism with a life of committed discipleship. The second and third volumes of this study will especially address this complex set of issues.

In the course of the preceding pages, I have been trying to describe some of the major speculative motives which have contributed to the current Christological crisis. In the chapter which follows, I shall examine another important component of the current crisis: namely, the failure of contemporary theology to develop an adequate method for developing Christological doctrine.

Chapter 2
The Search for Christological Foundations

The preceding chapter began to document the fact of a contemporary Christological crisis by comparing and contrasting the Christological crisis of the fourth and fifth centuries with the current crisis in Christological thinking. This chapter examines some of the principal strategies which Christologists have proposed for resolving the current Christological crisis. Each strategy proposes a method for "regrounding" Christology. In each case the regrounding of Christology aspires to a new Christological consensus.

Four of these strategies envisage more than the current crisis in Christology, although they include it. The more comprehensive strategies offer a formula for regrounding the entire theological enterprise, including Christology. Other strategies focus on Christology as such but may or may not envisage the Christological crisis which I have just attempted to describe. These less ambitious strategies do, however, offer a specific method for pursuing Christology in a contemporary context.

In what follows I shall consider both kinds of strategies: both the more and the less comprehensive. As we shall see, each offers some insight into the kind of method which promises to resolve the current Christological crisis. For reasons I shall explain, however, none of the strategies which I shall examine in this chapter offers an adequate method for coping with that crisis. That methodological failure only compounds the crisis.

(I)

The following strategic proposals seek to reground the entire theological enterprise:

1) One can reground theology only by excluding all philosophical considerations from the theological enterprise and by rooting Christological discourse in faith and in faith alone.

2) One can reground theology by using Kantian logic in order to elaborate a necessary and universal metaphysical anthropology which defines the conditions for the possibility of Christian revelation ever happening.

3) One can reground theology by closing the hermeneutical circle.

4) One can reground theology in phenomenology and hermeneutics.

The following three strategies focus somewhat more narrowly on regrounding Christology as such:

5) One can reground Christology by summarizing the Christological insights of contemporary New Testament exegesis.

6) One can reground Christology by relating Christological thinking to contemporary personality sciences.

7) One can reground Christology by replacing rational with rhetorical analysis.

Before one can assess the relative adequacy of these methods, however, one needs to reflect on the relationship between adequacy and truth. To this reflection I turn in the paragraphs which follow.

All reasonable thinking, whether intuitive or rational, invokes norms of truth and norms of adequacy. In rational thought, for example, norms of truth apply to specific inferences and to the propositions which give them linguistic formulation. An illustration may help make this logical principle more concrete. When NASA released the first photographs of the planet earth taken from space, a group called "The Flat Earth Society" in England denounced the photographs as a hoax. One suspects that those who registered the protest did so with tongue in cheek. Nevertheless, the assertion "the earth is flat, not round" expresses an inference of the rational mind which can only qualify as either true or false. The earth cannot simultaneously have the shape of a flat pancake and of a ball.

A true inference applies to events in the sense in which one has defined its key terms. An inference applies to events when it interprets them correctly. A false inference fails to interpret events correctly. In other words, its key terms in the sense in which one has defined them fail to find exemplification in what occurs. As Columbus saw, if in fact the laws of nature have made the world round, then one will be able to reach the Orient by sailing west. As history evolved, events proved his inference correct. By a true proposition, then, I mean a validated inference which grasps the laws, the general tendencies, which explain events.

Adequacy, by contrast, does not measure particular inferences as such but the frames of reference in which one formulates those inferences and brings them to propositional expression. An adequate frame of reference will allow one to take into account all the data one needs to consider in order to make true and valid inferences about events. An inadequate frame of reference will either blind one to relevant data or prescribe ways of thinking about it which confuse rather than clarify human insight. Scientists, for example, abandoned alchemy when they realized that mathematical measurement and hypothetico-deductive methods of investigation yielded better results.

Each of the six strategies for regrounding Christology which I listed above suggests a frame of reference for dealing with Christological issues. In what follows, I shall argue that none of them allows one to deal with all of the issues one must face if one seeks to pursue Christological thinking in any kind of systematic way. Each strategy, however, has some merit; for each has correctly named some aspect of the methodological challenge which faces anyone who aspires to resolving the contemporary Christological crisis.

Let us, then, consider the strengths and weaknesses of each of these strategies in turn. I begin by examining those methods which seek to reground theology as a whole.

1) *One can reground theology only by excluding all philosophical consider-ations from the theological enterprise and by rooting Christological discourse in faith and in faith alone.*

The neo-orthodoxy of Karl Barth and of Emil Brunner pursues this strategy in an attempt to lay solid foundations for contemporary theol-ogy in general and for Christology in particular.[1] Neo- orthodoxy insists on the need for theology to advance in faith alone largely as a protest against the rationalizing tendencies of liberal Protestant theologians like Schleiermacher, Bultmann, and Tillich. Neo-orthodoxy, however, also rejects, with some justification, the inflated speculative claims which Catholic theologians have made for classical metaphysics.

The strength of the neo-orthodox strategy lies in its realization that, in whatever concerns the historical self-revelation of God, revelation does indeed stand in judgment upon any fallible philosophical hypothesis about the nature and activity of the deity. Neo-orthodoxy suffers, however, from several limitations which render it ultimately inadequate. In my judg-ment philosophy has traditionally played and ought to play a double role in theological thinking. In the systematic elaboration of theology, phi-losophy functions both *critically* and *constructively*. Let us reflect briefly on both of the contributions which philosophy makes to a systematic, speculative theology.

Philosophy has an important *critical* function to play within theology. Any sound and adequate Christian theology must deal not only with the Bible but with Christian tradition as well. One cannot, however, deal adequately with the development of Christian tradition without subject-ing to rigorous criticism the philosophical presuppositions which have colored its development. That criticism demands the capacity of think philosophically. As a consequence, philosophy will always have an im-portant role to play in the elaboration of a systematic Christian theology.

Even the brief survey of Christological thinking contained in the pre-ceding chapter should make it clear that ever since the second century theologians have invoked a variety of philosophical and scientific con-structs in discoursing about the human. If one denies philosophy a voice in theological discourse, then one also deprives oneself of the critical tools

---

1. Cf. Karl Barth, *Church Dogmatics*, translated by G.W. Bromley and F.T. Torrence (New York, NY: Scribner's Sons, 1956), I, ii, pp. 1-44.; Emil Brunner, *Dogmatics: Volume II: The Christian Doctrine of Creation and Redemption*, translated by Oliver Wohn (Philadelphia, PA: Westminster, 1952).

one needs to assess the truth or falsity of philosophically grounded theological assertions about the nature of the human or about any other created reality. One also discards all means of assessing the relative adequacy or inadequacy of the frames of reference in which those propositions arise.

Karl Barth's own theology exemplifies the hazards of excluding philosophical criticism from the theological enterprise. Barth's trinitarian theology, for example, gives evidence of a tacit acquiescence in the philosophical presuppositions of Augustinian trinitarian thinking. In Augustine's account of the trinity, a single substance grounds and unifies the trinity. Barth eschews the language of substance in speaking about the triune God. Nevertheless, in postulating that each of the divine persons manifests the reality of "Yahweh God," Barth's trinitarian thinking still moves more or less within an Augustinian frame of reference. A quasi-fourth reality within the Godhead underlies and grounds the reality of the divine persons. Barth's refusal to use critical philosophy in a systematic way leaves him, however, bereft of the speculative means to criticize the tacit philosophical presuppositions of his own thinking in a way which would free him to imagine other ways of unifying the trinity than the way pioneered by Augustine.

Besides facilitating an ongoing criticism of the philosophical presuppositions which lie at the basis of systematic theological thinking, philosophy also plays a *constructive role.* Divine revelation does not answer every question which theology has to face. Christology offers a clear illustration of this point.

As we have seen, every Christology needs to give an account of the relationship between the divine and the human in Jesus. In order to do that one must clarify what one means by divinity and by humanity. One must also clarify how they relate in the person of Jesus. That means that a doctrinal Christology which develops in tandem with trinitarian theology must elaborate a coherent account of person which applies not only to human persons but to the three divine persons and to one divine person who also incarnates full humanity. One will find no pat definitions of "humanity" or of "person" anywhere in the Bible.

On the other hand, the revelation of God enshrined in the New Testament certainly does pass judgment on every humanly concocted, philosophical conception of God. If, for example, a particular philosophy asserts that God's absolute perfection precludes in principle the possibility of God relating in any real way to the world, then the self-revelation of God in the new covenant demands its rejection. Such a philosophical conception of God simply does not interpret what God has disclosed to us about Himself in Jesus Christ. A covenanting God stands historically revealed as enjoying a complex saving relationship with the creatures with whom He enters into covenant.

Similarly, the Bible contains many stories about the human condition; but it contains no systematic rational anthropology. As a consequence, it leaves the meaning of "humanity" obscured in inferential vagueness. Any adequate doctrinal Christology needs to dispel that vagueness; for one can neither verify nor falsify a vague term inferentially until one clarifies it. The Bible also lacks any clear inferential elaboration of the meaning of another key Christological term: namely, "person."

As a consequence of Biblical vagueness concerning key Christological concepts, in formulating its account of "human" and of "person," a contemporary Christology needs to take into account valid philosophical reflections on human nature, on the human condition, and on the human experience of personal existence. Moreover, other sciences than philosophy investigate human life and personality. As a consequence, as Jean Piaget has correctly argued, one needs to verify or falsify philosophical hypotheses about the reality of the human in the results of close scientific investigations into human life and experience.[2]

Clearly, then, besides endowing theology with critical self-awareness, philosophy also has an important *constructive* role to play in the systematic formulation of Christian theology in general and of Christology in particular.

I find myself inclined to agree with Josiah Royce when he describes Christianity as a religion in search of a metaphysics. I also agree with his assertion that only a metaphysics of community can do justice to a Christian faith experience.[3]

The term "metaphysics" has meant many things to many people. I use it here to designate any rational attempt to formulate a fallible hypothesis about reality in general, a theory of the whole. Any theology which advances inferentially has need of such a theory. The synthetic character of religious insight requires it.

As we have seen, a genuine religious insight seeks to put one in a life-giving relationship with God, with oneself, with other persons, and with the world. If, therefore, one aspires to rational discourse about religious realities one must find a way of talking rationally about God, self, other persons, and the world. The formulation of such a theory requires the pursuit of metaphysics, in the sense in which I have defined it above.

In a later chapter of this volume, I shall argue that one can clarify what one means by the "humanity" of Jesus if one considers it as a developing human experience. As I have suggested above, not only philosophy but the social and personality sciences have important contributions to make

---

2. Cf. Jean Piaget, *Insights and Illusions of Philosophy*, translated by Wolfe Mays (New York, NY: World Publishing Company, 1971).
3. Cf. Josiah Royce, *The Problem of Christianity* (2 vols.; Chicago, IL: Henry Regnery Company, 1968).

to such an understanding of the human. If, however, one ambitions synthetic thinking, then one needs a frame or reference capable of *integrating* the disparate results of scientific investigations into human nature and the human condition. A successful theory of the whole will provide that integrating understanding.

A sound theory of the whole also has the capacity to *integrate* at an abstract level different but interrelated areas of theological speculation. As we have seen, Christology needs to take into account the insights of trinitarian theology and vice versa. Ultimately one needs to relate Christology to every other area of theological reflection: Church, grace, sacraments, eschatology, creation, etc. A theory of the whole which can interpret philosophically the results of all of these areas of theological speculation synthesizes the results of detailed theological investigations into divine revelation by situating those results in an over-arching, unifying philosophical frame of reference.

In the Christology which follows, I shall attempt to use philosophy both critically and constructively. Nevertheless, I also find myself sympathetic to the judgment made by Protestant neo-orthodoxy that Catholic theologians have in the past made intellectually inflated claims for the role of metaphysics within theology. To this problem I turn in considering the second strategy for regrounding contemporary Christology.

The second strategy makes the following suggestion:

2) *One can reground theology by using Kantian logic in order to elaborate a necessary and universal metaphysical anthropology which defines the conditions for the possibility of Christian revelation happening.* Anyone familiar with the theology of Karl Rahner will recognize in this strategy his method for regrounding theology.

Rahner not only places metaphysics at the heart of the theological enterprise, but he also defends a classical understanding of metaphysics. He believes that the human mind can reach a necessary, universal insight into the nature of reality. He also believes that the human mind can perform this prodigious feat by using Kantian logic. Indeed, he has made it clear that the attempt to use Kantian transcendental logic in a theological context distinguishes his theological method from that of most other theologians.

Kantian philosophy makes "the turn to the subject." It explores human subjectivity in the hope of discovering there the conditions for the possibility of human scientific knowing, of moral judgments, and of aesthetic experience. Kant never claimed that the turn to the subject yields a necessary, universal metaphysics. In fact, he thought that he had demonstrated speculatively the impossibility of ever doing such a metaphysics. Rahner, however, believes that one can use Kantian logic to formulate a metaphysics in the classical sense of the term.

Rahner's method demands that one stand within an experience of faith in order to explore the conditions for the possibility of divine revelation happening historically. Those conditions include the response of faith which the historical self-disclosure of God evokes. Rahner discovers the conditions he seeks in a metaphysical anthropology which he derives largely from the work of Joseph Maréchal, although Rahner's own thought also borrows some of its language and insights from the existential philosophy of Martin Heidegger.[4]

The details of Rahner's anthropology need not detain us at this point, since I am currently focusing on questions of method. I shall, however, reflect in more detail on some of the speculative inadequacies of Rahner's anthropology in a later chapter. Here it suffices to note the futility of using Kantian logic in order to prove anything, much less metaphysical conclusions which enjoy universality and necessity. In order to grasp that futility, one needs first to recall the cognitive claims of the kind of classical metaphysics which Rahner defended. Then one needs to understand why Kantian logic can never generate such a metaphysics.

Classical metaphysics claimed to yield a logically necessary and universal insight into the nature of reality. A sound insight into the workings of the rational mind, however, belies its capacity ever to achieve such an insight. One must formulate any hypothesis, including world-hypotheses about the nature of reality in general, before one knows for certain that one has taken all the relevant facts into account. The discovery of new data can, therefore, call even temporarily verified metaphysical hypotheses into question.

The human mind's capacity to construct different frames of reference also undercuts any human claim to have reached a necessary metaphysical insight; for one cannot guarantee that some mind more insightful than one's own might not create a more adequate way of thinking about reality in general than the way one espouses. When that happens, one may well have to revise one's metaphysical theory of the whole.

The fallibility of metaphysical hypotheses, however, does not prevent them from making a contribution to theological and to Christological thinking. As we have just seen, even only temporarily validated metaphysical insights into the nature of reality can help unify theological and Christological discourse in helpful ways by endowing it with the synthetic character to which every sound religious insight aspires. Any more adequate world hypothesis which replaces a discredited one must do the same job better.

Faith-derived categories also help synthesize religious insight; but they do so at a concrete, historical level. They disclose the specific kind of

---

4. For a critique of Rahner on these points, see: Donald L. Gelpi, S.J., *Grace as Transmuted Experience and Social Process*, pp. 67-94.

relationship which a self-revealing God wants us to have to Him, to one another, to ourselves, and to the world.

Any theological use made of a fallible metaphysical account of the real must insure that the metaphysics one employs enjoys the capacity to interpret the specific historical revelation it attempts to explain. One's metaphysical theory will succeed in that enterprise if its categories apply to revelatory events in the sense in which one defines them philosophically. Moreover, as we have also seen, any metaphysical theory of the whole will also need to interpret close scientific and scholarly studies of created reality.

Every philosophical metaphysics aspires, then, to universality. It will achieve universality if it can interpret the events of divine revelation, the validated results of close scientific and scholarly studies of created reality, and ordinary lived experience. No fallible world-hypothesis can, however, guarantee its own universality; for logical fallibility deprives it of any necessity.

Rahner, however, makes much more ambitious speculative claims for the metaphysical anthropology which subtends his entire theological enterprise. More specifically, he believes that by using Kantian logic one can achieve a necessary, universal insight into the nature of reality and that one can demonstrate one's position *a priori*.[5]

Had Rahner studied the inferential logic of C.S. Peirce, he would have realized that one can in fact prove nothing by using Kantian logic. Much less can that same logic establish necessary and universal truths *a priori*. Peirce studied the philosophy of Kant for several years, so intensively that by the end of this study he could recite long passages of Kant's *Critique of Pure Reason* by heart. He abandoned his study of Kant when he saw through the fallacies of Kantian philosophical method.[6]

Peirce's studies in logic had convinced him, correctly in my estimate, that in reasoning the human mind employs three irreducible kinds of inference. Every rational inference interrelates a rule, a case, and a result. A rule formulates a general principle, a generalized law or tendency operative in nature. A result names a fact or facts in need of rational explanation. A case classifies a result in a way which relates it to some rule.

The three forms of inference differ by the way in which they interrelate a rule, a case, and a result. Hypothetical inference concludes to a case; deductive inference to a result; inductive inference to a rule. Let us attempt to understand what this means.[7]

5. Cf. Karl Rahner, *Foundations of Christian Faith* (New York, NY: Seabury, 1978), pp. 1-176, 192-202.

6. Cf. Peirce, *Collected Papers*, 1.4-6.

7. *Ibid.*, 5.266-282. Cf. Francis E. Reilly, S.J., *Charles Peirce's Theory of Scientific Method* (New York, NY: Fordham University Press, 1970).

Hypothetical thinking results from creative mind-play. It engages intuitive rather than strictly rational forms of thinking. In the course of playing around with a set of unexplained facts, one formulates a hypothesis when one conceives a possible way of explaining those facts. In formulating an explanation, one must clarify the relevant facts in a way which relates them to some law which one assumes to obtain in reality.

In order to illustrate this point, let us consider the example of the young Columbus as he wrestled with the question of the actual shape of the earth. Columbus noticed that incoming ships appeared only gradually on the horizon. First the tops of the masts appeared, then more of the masts. Finally the entire ship swam into vision. Columbus argued that if the surface of the ocean were in fact flat, the ship's piecemeal appearance could never happen. Instead, the entire ship would appear in the distance and then become larger and larger. The fact that the ship appeared as it did suggested that the ocean has a curved rather than a flat surface. Moreover, a curved ocean surface suggested in turn that the earth has a round, not a flat, shape. In other words, in reasoning abductively, or hypothetically, Columbus re-categorized the traditional notion "earth" as "round" rather than "flat." His hypothetical inference concluded, therefore, to a case on the basis of a law which he assumed obtains in nature.

Deductive inference clarifies a formulated hypothesis by predicting its operational consequences. Thus, Columbus having inferred hypothetically the roundness of the earth argued deductively that its roundness meant that he could reach the Orient by sailing west rather than east.

Deductive inference concludes to a result. On the basis of the facts which have justified one's original hypothesis, one argues deductively that other facts not yet in evidence will become evident if the laws which one assumes to obtain in reality actually do so.

Inductive inference concludes to a rule. When, for example, ships finally circumnavigated the globe they proved decisively the truth of Columbus's original hypothesis about the roundness of the earth. In other words, the successful circumnavigation established that the laws of nature have in fact formed the earth into a round rather than a flat shape.

Peirce proved to his own logical satisfaction the reality and irreducibility of the three forms of inference. He stopped reading Kant when he realized that transcendental logic recognizes only one form of inference, namely, deductive inference. That insight convinced him, quite correctly, that Kant's analysis of human science, morality, and aesthetics produces in the last analysis only an unverified hypothesis about the way the human mind works. It presents the unproven hypothesis, however, as a verified conclusion. In other words, Kantian logic confuses a hypothesis, or abduction, with a verified conclusion, or induction, at the same time that it calls it a deduction. Peirce realized that if one wanted to adopt a formula for confused rational thinking one could hardly find one more muddled than Kantian, transcendental logic.

One can see the fallacies of that logic playing themselves out in Rahner's mature Christological thinking. The mature Rahner demands that one ground Christological thinking in *a priori* reasoning. *A priori* Christology allegedly yields an insight into the necessary and universal conditions for the possibility of the incarnation happening.

Having invoked Kantian logic in order to formulate an *a priori* Christology with necessary and universal claims, Rahner then concedes the legitimacy of approaching the Christological question *a posteriori*. By that he means using the results of the quests for the historical Jesus in order to flesh out the historical details of the metaphysical account of the incarnation which one has already established *necessarily and a priori*. In fact, Rahner's *a priori* Christology yields only an unverified hypothesis about the incarnation.[8]

The Christology which I shall propose avoids the fallacies of *a priori* metaphysical reasoning. I shall propose in a subsequent chapter a fallible hypothesis about the nature of the real, a fallible theory of the whole. I shall argue that if one adopts a realistic, triadic, construct of experience, then one can construct a logical, coherent, applicable, and adequate metaphysics of community. I shall try to show that such a metaphysics makes sense of Jesus' human development and of human development generally.

The uses of philosophy which I will make in the chapters which follow falls, then, somewhere between neo-orthodoxy, on the one hand, and the more classical understanding of metaphysical theology which Rahner defends. With Rahner and against neo-orthodoxy, I defend the utility and necessity of employing philosophical reasoning in Christological thinking. Against Rahner and with neo-orthodoxy, I reject as logically and methodologically inflated the claims of classical metaphysicians to have reached a universal insight into reality which enjoys *a priori* necessity.

In other words, I claim the middle ground cleared by Peirce's logic. Philosophical reasoning, like scientific, needs to espouse a contrite fallibilism. It may aspire to universality but can claim no necessity. It will, however, make a positive contribution to theology and to Christology if it can provide an integrating theory of the whole which interprets and helps contextualize both the historical events which reveal to us the reality of God and the results of scientific and scholarly investigations of finite, created things.[9]

8. Cf. Rahner, *Foundations*, pp. 235-320.
9. I agree with Jean-Luc Marion that in what concerns God-talk, God has the last word. I tend to agree too with his suggestion that onto-theology from Descartes to the present exhibits a self-referential, idolatrous character in virtue of its rationalism. Marion correctly criticizes rationalistic theology as bad theology. I tend to believe that the same rationalism exemplifies bad philosophy as well. Rationalistic idolatry in theol-

I have examined the pros and cons of two methods for regrounding theology as a whole, one proposed by Neo-orthodoxy and the other by Karl Rahner. I turn next to a third such method, the one developed and defended by liberation theologians.

3) One can reground theology by closing the hermeneutical circle. Anyone familiar with the development of contemporary theological thinking will recognize in this third strategy the formula for de-academicizing and de-privatizing theology proposed by liberation theologians.

In *The Liberation of Theology*, Juan Luis Segundo has, perhaps, given the clearest explanation of what "closing the hermeneutic circle" means. In order to close the hermeneutical circle, theological thinking must begin with the social analysis of a situation of manifest injustice. It must then search within the Christian tradition and within the Biblical witness for resources for resolving the injustices it confronts. One finally closes the hermeneutical circle when one transforms the insights born of faith and of social analysis into policies and strategies for either eliminating or attenuating injustice.[10]

The approach to Christology adopted in these pages concedes to liberation Christology the need for any theology to close the hermeneutical circle. No one can respond adequately to the current Christological crisis without deprivatizing Christological thinking. Deprivatizing Christology means demonstrating the capacity of Christological faith to help rectify unjust social situations. A socially, politically, and economically involved Christology de-academicizes theology by balancing a concern for orthodoxy with an equal and parallel concern for orthopraxis.

Indeed, in what follows I shall argue that orthopraxis provides the norms for orthodoxy provided one understands orthopraxis as Christian practice which embodies a sound, lived insight into the practical exigencies of an integral, five-fold conversion. Any doctrine which advances such a conversion counts as orthodox. Any doctrine which fails to advance such a conversion or even subverts it counts as heterodox.

The strategy for regrounding Christology which I shall propose in the next chapter recognizes, however, a limitation in just closing the hermeneutical circle. An adequate and balanced Christological method does

ogy roots itself in a philosophically indefensible logic and metaphysics. I find the logic of modern philosophical thought uniformly *a priori* in dealing with its own theories and with few exceptions nominalistic in matters metaphyicsal. I would suggest that the logic and metaphysics of experience developed in this study avoids Marion's censure and interprets philosophically the theological analogy of love which he seems to defend. Cf. Jean-Luc Marion, *God Without Being: Hors Texte*, translated by Thomas A Carlson (Chicago, IL: University of Chicago Press, 1991); J.-L. Marion *et al.*, *Analogie et dialectique: Essais de théologie fondametale* (Geneva: Labor et Fides, 1982); J.-L. Marion and A. de Benoist, *Avec ou sans dieu?* (Paris: Beauchesne, 1970).

10. Cf. Juan Luis Segundo, *The Liberation of Theology*, translated by John Drury (Maryknoll, NY: Orbis, 1982), pp.7-39.

indeed need to respond to the challenge which entrenched institutional injustice poses to Christological faith. It order to do that it needs to engage in social analysis. A fully adequate theological method needs, however, also to take into account the challenges which Christology makes to personal faith and personal religious transformation. In other words, besides "closing the hermeneutical circle," a balanced and fully adequate strategy for confronting the current Christological crisis needs to deal as well with the issues raised by the theological "turn to the subject."

Finally, an adequate contemporary Christological strategy needs to show the intimate connection between personal faith and the Christian search for social justice. The method which I shall suggest in the next chapter attempts to accomplish both of these goal simultaneously.

I have weighed the advantages and disadvantages of three of the methods currently proposed for regrounding theology. In the paragraphs which follow I shall reflect on a fourth such strategy: namely, the attempt to reground theology in phenomenology and hermeneutics.

A fourth strategy for regrounding theology in general and Christology in particular makes the following proposal: *4) One can reground theology by invoking the methods of phenomenology and hermeneutics.*

David Tracy has written extensively and insightfully about theological method. I find myself in fundamental agreement with much of what he has written. Nevertheless, because he focuses more on the philosophical presuppositions which lie at the basis of theological method, his writings often leave this reader at least still wondering about the concrete operational implications of his reflections.

One finds exceptions to this pattern, of course. In *A Blessed Rage for Order*, an early work, Tracy argues the following methodological theses:

1) The two principal sources for theology are Christian texts, on the one hand, and common human experience and language, on the other.

2) The theological task will involve a critical correlation of the results of the investigations of the two sources of theology.

3) The principal method of investigation of the source "common human experience and language" can be described as a phenomenology of the "religious dimension" present in everyday and scientific experience and language.

4) The principal method of investigation of "the Christian tradition" can be described as an historical and hermeneutical investigation of classical Christian texts.

5) To determine the truth-status of the results of one's investigation into the meaning of both common human experience and Christian texts, the theologian should employ an explicitly transcendental metaphysical mode of reflection.[11]

11. Cf. David Tracy, *Blessed Rage for Order: The New Pluralism in Theology* (New York, NY: Seabury Press, 1975).

The preceding theses make it clear that phenomenology and hermeneutics do not exhaust Tracy's methodological program for theology; but they do play a prominent role in it. I am focusing here on this aspect of his program because critical reflection on the theological tasks which he assigns these two philosophical disciplines promises to cast light on some of the operational procedures of foundational theological thinking.

One can hardly argue with Tracy's first two theses. Theology does use sacred texts in order to interpret human religious experience, and theologians do need to find some way of interrelating the two. One needs to clarify, however, what one means by both "texts" and "experience."

The third and fourth theses raise two important methodological questions. 1) Does phenomenology provide an adequate foundational tool for exploring human religious experience? 2) Does contemporary hermeneutics ground adequately the task of interpreting religious texts?

The fifth thesis also poses a challenge. I have already reflected in some detail on the some of its implications. Kantian transcendental method offers a formula for logical confusion and can establish the truth of nothing, including metaphysical truth. The collapse of Kantian transcendental logic does not, however, discredit the need for philosophy to engage in self-critical thinking. The fifth thesis forces one to ask, therefore: 3) What role does such self-critical reflection play in the construction of a theological metaphysics?

The answers to these questions will cast significant light on the foundational theological method which this study employs. Those answers also illumine one another. Let us then consider them in turn.

Phenomenology describes what appears in human experience, but phenomenological method requires that one suspend judgment concerning the ultimate reality of what one describes. In other words, phenomenology brackets the metaphysical question.

Phenomenology makes a significant contribution to the exploration of human experience in general and of religious experience in particular. A wide-ranging descriptive exploration of the complexities of human experience arms one against making facile explanatory generalizations about it.

One may, however, question whether phenomenology alone possesses the wherewithal to deal adequately with either experience in general or religious experience in particular. Here again I find the philosophy of C.S. Peirce extremely suggestive.[12]

---

12. I focus here on Tracy's method. One may, however, also question whether his phenomenological description of religious experience as a "limit situation" offers an adequate account of Christian religious experience. The characterization of religious experience as a "limit situation" accords well with apophatic theology. It suggests the otherness of the divine and its incomprehensibility. Cf. Tracy, *Blessed Rage for Order*, pp. 91-118.

Peirce held that philosophical thinking ought to begin with phenomenology but that the normative sciences ought to mediate between phenomenology and the formulation of a metaphysics. The normative sciences investigate the way human experience ought to develop. They therefore involve self-critical reflection. Peirce distinguished three normative sciences: aesthetics, ethics, and logic.

The normative science of *aesthetics* reflects on the kinds of affective and imaginative habits one ought to cultivate in order to appreciate the ideals which make life meaningful and worth living. The excellence, or inherent merit, of lived ideals elicits commitment to them. The experience of beauty perceives that excellence. We experience beauty when the affections and imagination grasp simultaneously both the goodness and truth of some reality.

The normative science of *ethics* studies what kinds of decisive habits one ought to cultivate so that one might live for the ideals to which one stands committed.

The normative science of *logic* studies what kinds of habits of thought one ought to cultivate so that one might think clearly about one's choices and about the realities with which one deals.[13]

Peirce argued, correctly in my estimation, that all three normative sciences yield the criteria needed for formulating a metaphysical theory of the whole. In other words, logic alone cannot supply the norms one needs for grasping reality; for, until one has dealt with disordered affectivity, one's metaphysical theory can all too easily substitute the rationalization of one's neuroses for a sound grasp of the real. Similarly, until one has put order into one's conscience, one's metaphysics can all too easily replace a sound grasp of reality with the rationalization of human selfishness. The formulation of a metaphysics does, of course, also demand clear thinking; but the dynamic relationship between thought and action and between responsible action and ultimate ideals means that the formulation of a metaphysical theory of the whole invokes other norms than just logical or methodological ones.

In the last analysis, however, incarnational religion takes one beyond apophatic thinking into the realm of analogy, as the Tracy himself insists in *The Analogical Imagination*.

Incarnational religion has a sacramental character because the events of revelation both reveal and conceal God. In revealing God they resemble the divine reality in some way. That requires affirmation. Because those same events conceal God they also point apophatically to God's difference from the revealing events themselves. God-talk which invokes simultaneously affirmation and negation to speak about the same reality employs analogous predication.

13. For an lucid exposition of the development of Peirce's theory of the normative sciences, see: Vincent G. Potter, S.J., *Charles S. Peirce On Norms and Ideals* (Worcester, MA: University of Massachusetts Press, 1967).

I have argued elsewhere for the convergence between Peirce's understanding of the relationship between the normative sciences and metaphysics, on the one hand, and Lonergan's understanding of the relationship between a strictly normative theory of conversion and doctrinal theology, on the other.[14] One enhances the convergence when one expands
Lonergan's original construct of conversion to include affective conversion in addition to intellectual, moral, and religious conversion.

Peirce's normative science of aesthetics suggests operational procedures
for exploring affective conversion. His normative science of ethics suggests operational procedures for exploring both forms of moral conversion. His science of logic suggests operational procedures for exploring
intellectual conversion. To the best of my knowledge Peirce never really
developed an account of religious conversion, which he probably felt lay
outside the field of logic in which he specialized. Here Lonergan's method
supplements Peirce.

As I have also argued elsewhere, one discovers another significant convergence between Peirce and Lonergan. Both recognized that strictly normative thinking provides the means to grasp reality. Peirce held that it
enables one to think metaphysically. Lonergan held that it enables one to
distinguish true from false doctrine.[15]

The preceding reflections render Tracy's third and fifth theses more
logically and operationally precise than he himself did. The strictly normative thinking which the pursuit of a foundational theology of conversion requires mediates between both the phenomenological exploration
of experience, on the one hand, and the formulation of a fallible theological metaphysics on the other. That same thinking enables one to distinguish true from false religious doctrine by identifying which doctrines
advance the conversion process and which do not.

Phenomenology alone, therefore, can never suffice for the theological
exploration of human experience in general and of religious experience
in particular. Their adequate exploration requires strictly normative thinking as well. Strictly normative thinking measures one's behavior
self-critically against principles, realities, and ideals which one has acknowledged as personally binding. In what follows, I shall also argue that
any adequate account of experience must in the end propose and validate
a metaphysics of experience.

No one, I believe, would seriously dispute Tracy's third thesis that understanding Christian texts requires some method of interpretation. That
method in turn needs to rest on some kind of epistemological foundation. Moreover, I find Tracy's own analysis of the religious classic in *The*

14. Cf. Donald L. Gelpi, S.J., *The Turn to Experience in Contemporary Theology* (Mahwah,
    NJ: Paulist, 1994), pp. 24-51.
15. Cf. Gelpi, *loc. cit.*

Analogical Imagination both sound and suggestive for reading the New Testament in ways which allow one to relate it to contemporary religious experience.[16]

Contemporary exegesis offers, of course, a menu of methods for reading religious texts: form criticism, redaction criticism, reader-response theory, literary criticism. In volumes two and three of this study I shall attempt a dialectical analysis of New Testament narrative Christology. That analysis will also take into account the insights of historical-critical exegesis. In what concerns foundational method, it probably suffices here to reflect in more detail on two points I have already made above.

First, any theory of interpretation which equates Being and meaning builds on philosophical sand. The contemporary equation of Being and meaning stems from the philosophy of Martin Heidegger; but the equation implicitly denies an extremely important distinction: namely, the distinction between meaning and significance. Since reality includes significance as well as meaning, any theory of reality which reduces Being to meaning fails to grasp Being with philosophical adequacy.

Events signify. By that I mean that they possess a dynamic relational structure which the human mind can grasp evaluatively. Minds endow significant events with meaning when they respond to them evaluatively. The significant structure of the event, moreover, measures the truth or falsity of the meaning with which the mind endows events. Symbolic acts of communication seek to express that meaning.

The failure to distinguish meaning and significance leads, it seems to me, in two unfortunate directions. First, it deprives the mind of any realistic check on the truth or falsity of different meanings. Why? Because if meaning and Being simply coincide, then one has nothing to interpret except other interpretations. As a consequence, one never moves beyond the phenomenological bracketing of the metaphysical question. In a world of pure meaning, one could predict that it will rain tomorrow; but one could never find out whether or not it did. If, as the equation of Being and meaning entails, the question of endowing significant events with meaning never arises, neither can the question of truth or falsity.

If reality and meaning simply coincide, then one can only interpret other interpretations. In such a universe, one can easily commit the blunder of regarding all reality as a text. One encounters the fallacy of universal textuality in some post-modern thinking. The fallacy rests on an inadequate semeiotic which reduces expressive and interpretive symbols to communications.

As we have seen, events signify. How, then, do events and communications differ? By the term "events" I mean physical processes like earth-

16. Cf. David Tracy, *The Analogical Imagination: Christian Theology and the Culture of Pluralism*, (New York, NY: Crossroad, 1981), pp. 99-229.

quakes, chemical changes, digestion, biological growth. Events consist of decisive actions and of the general laws which ground them; but they lack conscious intentionality.[17]

Communications also differ symbolically from interpretative symbols. Interpretative symbols consist of unexpressed evaluative responses and of the habits which ground them. In all its waking moments, the human mind is endowing events with meaning through sensation, emotion, memory, imagination, inference, and deliberation. But it attempts to communicate only a small portion of those evaluative responses to other minds. One may argue that human attempts to communicate condition unexpressed evaluative responses. I cheerfully concede the point; but, however conditioned, an unexpressed human evaluation differs in its se-meiotic structure from a communication because it involves only two variables: habits and evaluations. An interpretative symbol may also include decisions about how to respond evaluatively; but they do not contain decisions which impact one's surrounding environment. Communications do contain such decisions. Communications involve not only habits and evaluations but also decisive actions which seek to express to other minds one's evaluative response to events and to other acts of communication.

By the term "communication" I mean acts like writing, speaking, pointing, painting, ballet. Communications engage actions and tendencies; but in addition they express the more or less conscious intentionality of an intelligent mind in dialogue with other conscious minds. They exemplify, then, a symbolic act far more complex in its dynamic, constitutive structure than both expressive and interpretative symbols.

Any theory of signs which denies the difference between communications, on the one hand, and expressive and interpretative symbols, on the other, errs in a significant way. Texts exemplify human communications. By calling everything a text the fallacy of universal textuality asserts that all symbols exemplify a communication. That assertion errs with tragic speculative consequences.

The failure to distinguish expressive symbols from communications leads down the same philosophical dead end as the fallacious equation of Being and meaning, because in the end it leaves one with nothing to interpret except human intentional activity. If only texts exist, one can indeed interpret the intent of interpretations, or of interpretations of interpretations. One might even reach a true judgment about what someone actually said about events; but, without events to test the statement against, one could never reach a judgment about its truth or falsity. One could, for example, conclude that Descartes' espoused mechanism; but

17. I leave open the question whether or not events may contain unconscious intentionality.

one could never decide whether or not Cartesianism correctly interprets nature. Similarly, the failure to distinguish between communications and interpretative symbols entails the fallacious conclusion that humans find it as easy to read books as they do other minds. In fact, they do not. In a sound semeiotic, neither minds nor events function symbolically in the same way as humanly constructed texts; but the fallacy of universal textuality tries to persuade one that they do.

The fallacy of universal textuality rests on other fallacies as well. It implicitly denies the distinction between linguistic and non-linguistic signs; and it confounds intuitive and inferential thinking. Let us consider each of these fallacies in turn.

Linguistic symbols differ by their discursive character from presentational symbols. Language communicates through a succession of words syntactically arranged. Presentational art forms, like painting or sculpture, communicate simply by being what they are. The fallacy of universal textuality ignores this important semeiotic distinction.

One might call a painting a "text" metaphorically. Metaphor structures and enhances non-inferential, intuitive forms of thinking. Within the intuitive grasp of reality, metaphors communicate allusively, through free-floating fantasy and by suggesting an unspecified multiplicity of imaginative connotations.

In inferential thinking, however, precise definition replaces metaphor. Precise definition so circumscribes the meaning of a term that it necessarily connotes specific, predictable consequences. When, therefore, one uses a metaphor with unspecified connotations as though it were an definition, one inevitably lapses into rational vagueness. This the fallacy of universal textuality does by calling every reality a text. From a logical standpoint, however, one cannot verify a vague category until one has clarified it. In calling all signs texts, the fallacy of universal textuality proposes an inferential hypothesis whose vagueness renders it unverifiable. I have reflected in some detail on this particular fallacy because it currently enjoys a certain vogue in academic circles. The time has come, however, to bury it for good.

Tracy's most recent writings on method show a new openness to the concerns of liberation theology. That marks a significant advance in his thinking.[18] In one respect, however, I find Tracy's more mature theory of method less helpful than his earlier writings; for, when he suggests that theological method must take into account the kind of constituency for whom the theologian writes, he seems to me to confound method and rhetoric.[19]

18. Cf. David Tracy, *Plurality and Ambiguity: Hermeneutics, Religion, Hope* (San Francisco, CA: Harper & Row, 1987).
19. Cf. Tracy, *The Analogical Imagination*, pp. 3-98.

A method offers a set of recurrent and related operations which yield cumulative and progressive results. Theological method seeks to get at a true account of religious realities. Once one has applied one's method, one needs, of course, in publicizing the results to tailor one's explanation to the audience for whom one writes. Rhetorical concern with one's audience does not, however, enter into one's method as such. It begins to shape discourse only after the method has succeeded in uncovering the truth of the matter one is investigating. In other words, rhetoric takes over only after method has completed its work. Later in this chapter I shall reflect on the advantages and limitations of attempting a rhetorical Christology. Here it suffices to note that Tracy's blurring of this important distinction fails to advance theological method.

So far I have pondered the advantages and disadvantages of four proposals for regrounding theology as a whole and Christology in particular. The time has come to turn our attention to three other current strategies which focus somewhat more narrowly on Christology as such.

The revival of Biblical studies in Catholic theology has produced a spate of New Testament Christologies. These Christologies endorse, at least implicitly, the following methodological presupposition:

5) *One can reground Christology by summarizing the Christological insights of contemporary exegesis.*

This fifth strategy finds exemplification in a wide range of contemporary Christologies. Among Catholic theologians, Edward Schillebeeckx, Walter Kasper, Hans Küng, and Joseph Moignt all adopt this strategy.[20] Among Protestant theologians the work of Wolfhart Pannenberg exemplifies this fifth strategic approach to Christological thinking.[21] Although, as we have already seen, liberation theology proposes its own strategy for regrounding Christology, it also invokes this fifth strategy as well. Much of liberation Christology employs the results of the new quest for the historical Jesus in order to portray Him as a prophetic figure who protested social, economic, and political injustice in His own day. Liberation theology then uses this historical portrait of Jesus in order to justify its own prophetic denunciation of contemporary injustice.[22]

20. Cf. Edward Schillebeeckx, O.P., *Jesus: An Experiment in Christology*, translated by Hubert Hoskins (New York, NY: Crossroad, 1979); *Christ: The Experience of Jesus as Lord*, translated by John Bowden (New York, NY: Seabury, 1980); *Interim Report on the Books Jesus and Christ* (New York, NY: Crossroad, 1981); *Church: The Human Story of God*, translated by John Bowden (New York, NY: Crossroad, 1990); Hans Küng, *On Being a Christian*, translated by Edward Quinn (Garden City, NY: Doubleday and Co., 1974); Walter Kasper, *Jesus the Christ, translated by V. Green (New York, NY: Paulist/Burns & Oates*, 1984); Joseph Moignt, *L'homme qui vient de Dieu* (Paris: Les Editions du Cerf, 1993).

21. Cf. Wolfhart Pannenberg, *Jesus God and Man*, translated by Lewis L. Wilkins and Duane A. Priebe (London: SCM Press, 1973).

22. Cf. Leonardo Boff, *Jesus Christ Liberator: A Critical Christology for our Time*, translated by Patrick Hughes (Maryknoll, NY: Orbis, 1979); *Passion of Christ, Passion of*

The strength of this third strategy lies in the fact that it recognizes that contemporary Christology must take into account the results of contemporary Biblical and New Testament exegesis. The same strategy labors, however, under some fairly obvious limitations. Exegesis alone cannot begin to address the kinds of philosophical and doctrinal issues which post-biblical Christology raises. Moreover, even when they eschew some of the heterodox connotations of an excessively "low" Christology, contemporary biblically based Christologies usually end by giving short shrift to the post-biblical tradition.

The method which grounds contemporary New Testament Christology does not exclude metaphysical and philosophical thinking from Christological thinking in principle; but it does do it in practice. In practice, therefore, it falls under the same criticism as Neo-orthodox method. Any Christology which confronts the current Christological crisis needs, therefore, a more comprehensive philosophical frame of reference for thinking through the issues raised by post-biblical Christology.

In the next chapter I shall attempt to propose such a frame of reference. Here it suffices to note that, like the fifth strategy, the one which I shall defend acknowledges the contribution which biblical Christologies have made to the advancement of contemporary Christological thinking. At the same time, however, the method which I shall endorse seeks to make more ample room for dealing with the complex doctrinal questions raised by post-biblical Christological thinking.

Christological speculation in the United States has engendered two other methods: therapeutic method and rhetorical analysis. I close these dialectical reflections on method by weighing their blessings and woes.

Given the therapeutic caste of culture in the United States, it comes as no surprise that it has produced therapeutic Christological thinking. Therapeutic Christology rests on the following methodological assumption:

6) *One can reground Christology by relating Christological thinking to contemporary personality sciences.* Anyone familiar with the writings of Sebastian Moore will recognize in this fifth strategy a rough description

the World: The Facts, Their Interpretation, and Their Meaning Yesterday and Today (Maryknoll, NY: Orbis, 1987); Jon Sobrino, S.J., *Christology at the Crossroads: A Latin American Approach*, translated by John Drury (Maryknoll, NY: Orbis, 1978); *Jesus the Liberator: A Historical-Theological View*, translated by Paul Burns and Francis McDonaugh (Maryknoll, NY: Orbis, 1987); Juan Luis Segundo, S.J., *Faith and Ideologies*, translated by John Drury (New York, NY: Orbis, 1982); *The Historical Jesus of the Synoptics*, translated by John Drury (New York, NY: Orbis, 1985); *The Humanistic Christology of St. Paul*, edited and translated by John Drury (New York, NY: Orbis, 1986); *The Christ of the Ignatian Exercises*, translated by John Drury (New York, NY: Orbis, 1987); *An Evolutionary Approach to Jesus of Nazareth*, edited and translated by John Drury (New York, NY: Orbis, 1988).

of his Christological method. Moore's approach to Christology has the obvious advantage of addressing directly the therapeutic caste of middle-class American culture. Moreover, Moore relates Christological thinking skillfully to some of the more suggestive insights of clinical psychology and of the personality sciences.[23]

This sixth strategy, however, reverses the limitations of the method of liberation Christology. If closing the hermeneutical circle tends to stress situational analysis at the expense of attention to the human subject of faith, a purely therapeutic Christology fails to deal adequately with the challenge of social and institutional injustice.

In the strategy I shall propose in the chapter which follows, I shall, as I have already indicated, attempt to balance both of these legitimate Christological and theological concerns.

Christology in the United States has produced yet another strategy for regrounding Christology: namely, the rhetorical Christology of Franz Josef van Beeck. Rhetorical Christology rests on the following methodological principle:

7) *One can reground Christology by replacing rational with rhetorical analysis.*

Van Beeck has developed this particular strategy in *Christ Proclaimed*. His method has the freshness of any novel approach to traditional theological material. It acknowledges frankly the theological and Christological importance and claims of intuitive, non-rational forms of thought. It calls attention to the fact that rhetoric informs virtually every Christological statement and that one would do well to take that fact into account. It attempts to relate Christological thinking to the experience of conversion.

Rhetorical Christology invokes three kinds of rhetoric: a rhetoric of inclusion, a rhetoric of obedience, and a rhetoric of hope. The rhetoric of inclusion seeks to relate every human concern to the person of Jesus. The rhetoric of obedience induces personal commitment to the person of Jesus and purifies human striving of all self-assertiveness. The rhetoric of hope seeks to induce commitment to Jesus' cause.[24]

Rhetorical analysis alone, however, can never replace rational analysis in Christology or in any other branch of theology. The narrow pursuit of rhetorical analysis as an alternative to rational thinking leaves one no

---

23. Cf. Sebastian Moore, O.S.B., *The Crucified Jesus Is No Stranger* (New York, NY: Crossroad, 1977); *The Fire and the Rose Are One* (New York, NY: Seabury, 1980).

24. Cf. Franz Josef Van Beeck, *Christ Proclaimed* (New York, NY: Paulist, 1979). In *God Encountered* (San Francisco, CA: Harper & Row, 1988), van Beeck makes the shift from rhetorical analysis to systematic reflection on Christian worship. He discovers, moreover, a Christological orientation at the heart of shared Christian prayer. It remains to see whether the shift from rhetorical analysis to system building will modify van Beeck's Christology.

choice but to seek rhetorical solutions to speculative and rational issues. I find such a choice methodologically unacceptable. Honest rhetoric seeks to convince others of truths which one has validated by other means. Rhetoric alone, however, cannot validate those truths.

The strategy for confronting the contemporary Christological crisis which I shall propose attempts to balance a concern with intuitive, non-rational forms of religious thought with logical, rational reflection on religious issues. In the process it seeks to avoid a narrowly rhetorical approach to the resolution of the contemporary Christological crisis. It distinguishes between rhetorical and probative methods of thinking and restricts rhetorical analysis to persuasion and to literary analysis. In other words, sound theological method refuses to confuse rhetorical analysis with a validating demonstration.

Chapter 3
Foundational Theology and the RCIA

In chapter one I anatomized some cultural impulses which have helped generate the current crisis in Christology. I identified that crisis as widespread vagueness and confusion concerning key Christological terms: "humanity," "divinity," and "their relationship in the person of Jesus." Chapter two examined a different dimension of the same crisis: the failure of contemporary theology to develop an adequate method for coping with the current crisis.

In this chapter I shall explain the method which I shall employ in my own search for Christological foundations. The method which I shall propose builds on Bernard Lonergan's ground-breaking proposal for method in theology. I do not, however, endorse every aspect of Lonergan's theory of method.

In what follows, therefore, I shall first indicate which aspects of Lonergan's thought I endorse. I shall then indicate how my own pursuit of his method caused me to modify it. Third, I shall outline the operational procedures which will structure the argument which follows. Finally, I shall reflect on the pastoral relevance of a foundational Christology to the RCIA.

(I)

As I indicated in the preface to this volume, when I joined the faculty of the Jesuit School of Theology in Berkeley in 1973, I arrived with the express intention of testing Bernard Lonergan's account of theological method. That method, as I saw, claimed the ability to generate an inculturated theology. I wanted to see if it worked in a North American context.

I had decided to pursue Lonergan's method at the level of what he calls "foundational theology." Foundational thinking develops a strictly normative account of Christian conversion. Strictly normative thinking measures personal behavior against norms and ideals which one has personally interiorized.[1] As I have already indicated, the foundation which I lay for doing theology eschews all claims to *a priori* necessity and confesses a

---

1. Explanatory, rational thinking also claims a kind of normativity. Whenever I explain an event, I give an account of the kinds of laws, or conditioned tendencies, which govern its behavior. In other words, I can tell you the way reality ought to behave under specifiable conditions. The kind of "ought" with which explanatory thinking deals with differs, however, from the "ought" of strictly normative thinking. Strictly normative thinking adds to explanatory thinking self-conscious self-criticism.

contrite fallibilism. By "foundational theology" I mean a fallible, working hypothesis about how conversion ought to happen.

As my investigations into foundational thinking advanced I realized that I was in fact creating a new theological discipline, since no one, to the best of my knowledge, had ever attempted to elaborate in a systematic way the kind of strictly normative, interdisciplinary account of conversion for which Lonergan's method called. The novelty of what I was doing helped me understand why much of the theological community seemed to respond to my work with a kind of detached bafflement. My own limitations as a theologian no doubt contributed to that befuddlement; but I did not think that they explained it entirely.

I found several of Lonergan's insights into theological method particularly attractive. First of all, Lonergan's definition of "method" in general as a set of recurrent and related operations which yields cumulative and progressive results made eminent good sense to me.[2] I liked its practical, operational focus; and I liked its pragmatic justification. A set of operations which works proves its legitimacy by the very cumulative and progressive answers which it generates.

I also found Lonergan's theory of functional theological specialties extremely suggestive.[3] The four specialties which Lonergan calls mediating theology—namely, research, interpretation, history, and dialectics—seemed to me to describe accurately the best thinking of more traditional theologians. Research theologians provide the resources which other theologians need in order to work: archeological evidence, critical editions of sacred texts, grammars and dictionaries of sacred languages. Theological interpretation offers explanations of what sacred texts and religious activity originally meant and what they might mean to contemporary readers. History tells the story of a particular religious community. Dialectics deliberates about the issues and frames of reference operative in religious disputes.

Mediated theology ambitions theological reconstruction. Lonergan calls theological reconstruction mediated because it builds on the results of the ongoing retrieval of a tradition which mediating theology provides. Mediated theology also divides into four functional specialties: foundations, doctrines, systematics, and communications. Foundations formulates a strictly normative account of the conversion experience which authenticates a religious tradition. Doctrinal theology uses the norms which foundational thinking formulates in order to re-interpret the results of dialectical theology. The doctrinal theologian must decide which controverted doctrines foster integral conversion and which do not. Once doctrinal theologians have authenticated sound religious doctrines, the sys-

2. Cf. Bernard Lonergan, S.J., *Method in Theology* (New York, NY: Herder and Herder, 1972), pp. 4-5.   3. *Ibid.*, pp. 124-145.

tematic theologian shows how those doctrines relate to one another. Finally, the functional specialty of communications uses the insights of foundational theology in order to diagnose the breakdown of communications in a particular community; for that breakdown betrays a lack of initial or of ongoing conversion on the part of the community's members. Next, the communications theologian constructs a pastoral catechesis which summons hostile factions to the kind of integral conversion which will enable them re-enter into fruitful religious dialogue with others.

Among the functional specialties which concern themselves with the creative reformulation of a theological tradition, I found Lonergan's account of foundational thinking perhaps the most creative and suggestive. His attempt to ground revisionist theological thinking in a strictly normative account of conversion holds, in my judgment, great promise.

I realize that some people tend to bridle instinctively at the term "foundations." For many, foundational thinking connotes *a priori* reasoning which claims a fallacious universality. As a contrite fallibilist, I too reject such an understanding of foundational thinking. At the same time, I recognize that the work of theological reconstruction has to build on something. A fallible, working hypothesis about the normative demands of conversion offers the best foundation I have found for doing revisionist theology, since a working hypothesis beats one which does not work.

My fallibilism approved Lonergan's call for a healthy pluralism in thinking about conversion. I could well understand that one can legitimately approach an experience as complex as human conversion from a variety of points of view and with a variety of methods. I find, for example, that Lewis Rambo's study of conversion complements my own work.[4]

I especially appreciated the creativity of Lonergan's suggestion that conversion comes in many forms and need not occur exclusively in a religious context. Initially, Lonergan spoke of only three kinds of conversion: intellectual, moral, and religious.

Lonergan also correctly called for an interdisciplinary approach to conversion, one which draws simultaneously on philosophy, on theology, and on any other scientific and scholarly disciplines which shed light on the experience of conversion.[5] That too made sense. It appealed to my own endorsement of Peirce's fallibilism and confirmed Piaget's legitimate insights into the limitations of most classical and modern philosophical theories of knowledge.[6]

All these aspects of Lonergan's theory of method I heartily endorse. As my insight into the forms and dynamics of conversion has developed,

---

4. Cf. Lewis Rambo, *Understanding Religious Conversion* (New Haven, CT: Yale University Press, 1989). Rambo offers a lucid analysis of the social dynamics of conversion.
5. *Ibid.*, pp. 281-293.
6. Cf. Jean Piaget, *Insights and Illusions of Philosophy*, translated by Wolf Mays (New York, NY: World, 1971).

however, it has caused me to call into question other aspects of Lonergan's account of method in theology.

(II)

The more I reflected on the complexity of conversion, the more I recognized some significant oversights in Lonergan's reflections on foundational theological method. Robert Doran and I came quite independently to the conclusion that in speaking about conversion Lonergan gives short shrift to affective forms of human knowing. Doran developed a theory of "psychic conversion," while I developed an account of "affective conversion." We seem to mean, as far as I can tell, different things by "psychic conversion" and by "affective conversion"; but we both agree that one needs to build a strong affective component into the conversion process. That affective component makes a fourth form of conversion inevitable.[7]

Moreover, as I reflected on moral conversion, I saw the need to distinguish within it two forms of conversion: personal moral conversion and socio-political conversion.[8] These two forms of conversion relate to one another as do the two realms of personal and public morality to which they correspond. Personal morality judges human interpersonal relationships in the light of rights and duties, while public morality measures institutional justice or injustice by the norm of the common good.

The common good demands the creation of a social order 1) which allows all the members of the human community to benefit from the goods which make for humane living and 2) which allows all to contribute to the sum of those benefits. The two realms of personal and of public morality demand different kinds of commitment and invoke different, though interrelated, moral norms. They create, therefore, two distinct but interrelated realms of human moral consciousness and thus give rise to two distinct but interrelated kinds of moral conversion.

In addition, I recognized that one needs not only to explore each realm of conversion but also to give an account of how the different kinds of conversion mutually condition one another. I therefore began to reflect on what I called the dynamics and counterdynamics of conversion. By the dynamics of conversion I meant the ways in which different kinds of conversion transform one another positively by their presence. By the

---

7. Cf. Robert Doran, S.J., *Subject and Psyche: Ricoeur, Jung, and The Search for Foundations* (Washington, DC: University Press of America, 1977); *Psychic Conversion and Theological Foundations: Toward a Reorientation of the Human in Science* (Chico, CA: Scholars Press, 1981). Doran seems to mean by psychic conversion the clarification of disordered feelings by intellectual processes. While I concede that rational insight may contribute to both initial and ongoing affective conversion, I would see the evaluative processes involved as primarily intuitive, appreciative, and emotional. Affective conversion engages more judgments of feeling than inferential judgments.
8. Cf. Gelpi, *Grace as Transmuted Experience and Social Process*, pp. 97-139.

counterdynamics of conversion I meant the ways in which they distort one another negatively by their absence.

I also came to regard Lonergan's definition of conversion as inadequate. Lonergan defines the term "conversion" as a decision which creates an intentional horizon within human self-consciousness.[9] The definition accurately describes one dimension of conversion: namely, that every conversion creates a whole new evaluative frame of reference which transforms the way one perceives and relates to one's world. In my judgment, however, Lonergan's definition of conversion fails to express adequately the most fundamental dimension of every conversion experience, namely, that it involves a turning from and a turning to.

The Analogy of Conversion

The recognition of different kinds of conversion forces one think of conversion in analogous terms. Analogous realities simultaneously resemble one another and differ from one another. If all five experiences of turning qualify as conversions, in what do they resemble one another and in what to they differ?

It seemed to me that in every conversion experience one turns from irresponsible to responsible behavior in some realm of experience. Realms of experience differ in the kinds of habits which govern them.

Responsibility means accountability. Because conversion requires self-conscious, strictly normative thinking, converts stand accountable first of all to themselves because after conversion they measure their subsequent behavior by principles, norms, and ideals which they have interiorized as personally binding. I therefore define conversion as a decision to move from irresponsible to responsible living in some realm of human life and experience.

Converts also live accountable to others. Lonergan's endorsement of the Kantian turn to the subject prevented him from defining conversion in a manner which made clear its inherently social character. Lonergan defines a conversion as a decision which creates a horizon.[10] This definition correctly calls attention to the fact that conversion restructures individual intentionality; but conversion does more than that. Conversion has social as well as personal, individual consequences. Conversion never occurs in a vacuum. It occurs in community and in social dialogue with others. The notion of responsibility underscores conversion's inherently social character.

In religious conversion one also accounts responsibly to God. One can respond to the historical self-revelation of God authentically only on the terms which God sets. That means that one must respond to a self-revealing God in faith.

9. Cf. Lonergan, *Method in Theology*, pp. 130-132.   10. *Ibid.*, pp. 237-238.

If conversions resemble one another by embodying a turn from irresponsible to responsible behavior, how do they differ? Conversions differ from one another by focusing on different realms of experience and by invoking different norms in measuring human behavior. Realms of experience, as I have already suggested, differ according to the kinds of habits which govern them. The norms differ from one conversion to another because they correspond to the different kinds of habitual tendencies which shape the conversion in question.

Affective conversion deals with human intuitive responses. We respond intuitively with image and affect. Affective conversion also concerns itself with the unconscious, which also obeys the laws of intuitive thinking. Hence, affective conversion invokes two kinds of norms. It invokes norms of mental health in dealing with emotional dysfunction and with life-giving affective development; and affective conversion invokes aesthetic norms in the conscious cultivation of imaginative thinking.

Intellectual conversion deals with the truth or falsity of particular judgments and with the adequacy or inadequacy of the frames of reference in which one thinks. We humans grasp reality inferentially; but we also judge reality with our feelings. As a consequence, intellectual conversion concerns itself with both intuitive, imaginative perceptions of the real and with rational, inferential perceptions.

Both forms of moral conversion engage in deliberative thinking about decisions. Deliberation employs a disjunctive logic. It weighs the pros and cons of mutually exclusive concrete decisions. One can deliberate about adopting attitudes and beliefs, or one can deliberate about how best to respond to social and environmental impulses. Moral deliberation weighs such decisions in the light of realities, ideals, principles, and values which claim one ultimately and absolutely. An ultimate claim requires one not only to live for it but also, if necessary, to die for it. An absolute claim binds one in any circumstance.

Personal moral conversion focuses on interpersonal human interaction. Because personal moral conversion transforms the human conscience, it invokes prudential, ethical thinking. In judging human behavior, the personally converted measure conduct by human rights and duties. Rights and duties flow from the social character of human experience. They reflect the fact that finite and vulnerable humans can only live truly humane lives in mutual dependence and in community. Mutual interdependence in community creates the interpersonal claims which moralists call rights and duties. Properly understood, then, rights and duties free one to assess one's social and communal responsibilities realistically. Rights do not, as a bankrupt individualistic ethos claims, simply insulate one's subjective, personal preferences from interference by other persons or by social institutions.

Like personal moral conversion, socio-political conversion engages the human conscience. It, however, looks to public morality and to the search for a just human society. It therefore measures public policy and the institutions which public policy defines by the common good, The common good, as we have already seen, demands that every member of society have reasonable access to benefiting from the goods of a society and to contributing to those same shared goods.

Religious conversion responds to an historical self-disclosure of God. It therefore invokes norms of faith. Christian conversion exemplifies a particular kind of religious conversion.

Clarifying Foundational Method

As I pondered the five forms of conversion, I realized that one's construct of conversion will determine the kinds of operational procedures one employs in articulating a theology of conversion. Clearly both aesthetics and psychology have much to teach the contemporary student of affective conversion. In dealing with the intuitive perception of truth, the student of intellectual conversion will find illumination in aesthetics and in rhetorical, artistic, and literary criticism. Those same students will find considerable help in logic and in theories of method in dealing with the rational, inferential mind. Personal and social ethics will assist the student of the two forms of moral conversion. Finally, critical reflections on theological method will assist the student of religious conversion.

The strictly normative character of foundational thought determines, moreover, the way in which one asks foundational theological questions. Foundational questions always contain an "ought": How, for example, ought the gracing of experience to transform the conversion process? How ought the fully converted Christian to worship? How ought the fully converted Christian to relate to the triune God? A foundational Christology asks: How ought converted commitment to Jesus Christ in faith to transform every other aspect of conversion? As my work advanced, moreover, I realized that in developing a theology of conversion one can ask any theological question in a manner which engages strictly normative thinking.

Finally, I found Lonergan's method attractive for another reason. Of all the theological methods I had studied, it alone deliberately set out to promote inculturated theological thinking. Inculturated theological thinking attempts to examine the complex relationship between a religion and the culture in which that religion roots itself.[11] That means that besides the systematic historical retrieval of the religion in question, inculturated theological reflection must also retrieve the culture it attempts to assess

---

11. Cf. Lonergan, *Method*, pp. xi-xii. See also: Carl F. Starkloff, S.J., "Inculturation and Cultural Systems (Part One)," *Theological Studies*, 55(1994), pp. 66-81; "Inculturaltion and Cultural Systems (Part Two)," *Theological Studies*, 55(1994), pp. 274-294.

theologically. Moreover, I also realized that any theology of conversion has to deal with the impact of a given culture on religion.

(III)

As I attempted to wrestle with foundational method as Lonergan had described it, I realized that he had failed to give a clear or adequate account of the kinds of operations which must guide this kind of thinking. It made sense to say that an adequate theology of conversion must use categories derived from philosophy, from theology, and from other human disciplines which illumine the conversion experience. Lonergan, however, left one in the dark finally about how to coordinate the results of three very different ways of thinking about human life and reality.

As I indicated in the preface to this volume, I first made an initial assault on the complex question of interdisciplinary thinking in writing *Experiencing God.* I prolonged my experiment in interdisciplinary thinking in other volumes. In both *Inculturating North American Theology* and *The Turn to Experience in Contemporary Theology* I tried to articulate what I had learned from that earlier experiment about the coordination and interplay of categories in foundational thinking.[12]

The Coordination and Interplay of Categories

The coordination of categories deals with the way in which categories which derive from different disciplines interpret the realities to which they refer. One can legitimately employ four techniques for coordinating categories: agreement, complementarity, convergence, and dialectical reversal.

Categories agree when they say the same thing about the same reality. They complement one another when they say different but true things about the same reality. They converge when they say true things about two distinct but interrelated realities. When categories contradict one another they demand dialectical reversal, or the resolution of the contradiction.

Dialectical reversal can employ a variety of methods. It can endorse one set of categories as true and reject another as false. It can reject both as false and seek for another solution. It can endorse one set of categories as more adequate and reject another as less adequate. Finally, it can discover a partial truth in contradictory positions and seek for a more comprehensive frame of reference which reconciles all relevant counter-positions. The coordination of categories integrates insights achieved in diverse frames of reference into a unified theory of the whole.

12. Cf. Donald L. Gelpi, S.J., *Experiencing God: A Theology of Human* Emergence (Lanham, MD: University Press of America, 19870); *Inculturating North American Theology: An Experiment in Foundational Method* (Atlanta, GA: Scholars Press, 1988), pp. 147-176.

The interplay of categories engages the way different categories deriving from different disciplines interpret one another. Foundational thinking, as we have seen, requires the interplay of three kinds of categories: philosophical, theological, and scientific.

Philosophy uses language in order to reflect on lived experience as lived. Within foundational thinking *philosophical categories* seek to criticize, interpret, and contextualize the categories of theology and of the non-philosophical sciences which deal which human religious experience. Critical philosophy passes judgement on the truth or falsity, adequacy or inadequacy of the more or less tacit philosophical presuppositions which shape theological and scientific thinking. Philosophical categories interpret the results of theology and of the other sciences when they apply to them in the sense in which philosophy defines them. Constructive philosophy seeks to create a theory of the whole which contextualizes the results of detailed scientific and theological investigations into reality. This constructive philosophy does first by specifying the realms of experience which different theological and scientific disciplines address and then by showing their relationship to one another.   ·

Theological categories verify or falsify philosophical or scientific categories which speak about God. Theological categories judge the truth of falsity of such categories by their ability to interpret the historical self-revelation of God we have in fact received. Theological categories also transvalue philosophical and scientific categories by demanding that one re-interpret their connotations in the light of faith.

One transvalues an interpretation of reality when one transposes it from one frame of reference to another. When one does that, the new frame of reference endows one's interpretation with new connotations. The faith-motivated response to God's historical self-revelation creates a novel frame of reference which forces one to re-evaluate any merely natural perception of reality.

Both nature and grace designate processes. Natural processes advance in complete abstraction of the historical self-revelation of God. Graced processes respond to God's historical self-revelation on the terms God sets. Such processes qualify as graced because they put one into an unmerited, life-giving relationship with God.

Detailed *scientific investigations* verify or falsify philosophical and theological assertions about the nature of created reality. They also have the capacity to amplify philosophical and theological assertions about creation by expanding human insight into the way created things develop.

The coordination and interplay of categories will structure the foundational Christology developed in these pages. More specifically, the coordination and interplay of categories will validate in the results of positive science the metaphysics of experience which I shall employ in interpreting how divinity and humanity unite in Jesus Christ. Accordingly, in the second section of this volume, I shall show how a scientifically verified triadic construct of experience does in fact interpret Jesus' humanity. The Christology of hope and the narrative Christology which I shall present in subsequent volumes will explore the kinds of religious experience which doctrinal theology seeks to interpret. In volume three, I shall show that the same scientifically validated metaphysics of experience which interprets Jesus' humanity also interprets the religious experiences which give normative structure to Christological faith. That same metaphysics will, as a result, also correctly interpret how divinity and humanity unite in Jesus' person.

Here I note in passing that the capacity of a metaphysical theory to interpret ordinary lived experience, the results of focused, scientific and scholarly investigations of created reality, and the historical self-revelation of God constitutes that metaphysical theory's pragmatic meaning. Pragmatic logic asserts that the total number of operational consequences deducible from any given hypothesis constitutes the whole of that hypothesis's inferential meaning. Predictable operations include logical operations. In the case of a metaphysical hypothesis, logical operations constitute the whole of its pragmatic meaning. A metaphysical hypothesis predicts that a particular set of philosophical categories will have the capacity to interpret any reality whatever. One deduces the operational consequences of such an hypothesis by explicating its philosophical meaning. One then validates it by actually using it to interpret the results of ordinary, lived experience, scientific and scholarly investigations of created reality, and the events of divine self-revelation. The ongoing interpretative validation of a metaphysical theory turns it into a working hypothesis. A working metaphysical hypothesis certainly interprets some realities and could conceivably interpret any reality.

As I have already indicated, the formulation of a theology of conversion demands inculturated theological thinking. The more I attempted to pursue foundational thinking in a North American context, however, the more I saw that the kinds of issues raised by classical American philosophical thinkers demand a systematic revision of the epistemological presuppositions which lie at the basis of Lonergan's own theory of method.[13]

Logical fallibilism flows necessarily from Peirce's theory of inference, and logical fallibilism calls into question Lonergan's claim to have discovered an unrevisable starting place for philosophical thinking. So too does the distinction between explanatory and strictly normative thinking. Let us try to understand why.

---

13. Cf. Gelpi, *Grace as Transmuted Experience and Social Process*, pp. 1-40.

As I have argued above, Peirce's theory of inference, which makes eminent good sense to me, shows that at the precise point at which the human mind touches reality—namely, in hypothetical, abductive thinking and in verifying, inductive thinking—it remains radically fallible. In any question of complexity, one can never know with absolute certainty whether one has taken into account all the relevant data or that one has adopted the best possible frame of reference for dealing with the problem one faces. One can only judge whether or not one has done the best one can under limiting circumstances. As Peirce also saw both clearly and correctly, the human mind begins thinking about everything *in medias res*. It confronts the world with two kinds of beliefs: those it holds critically and those it holds uncritically.[14] Moreover, as I have already indicated, one does not begin philosophical thinking with critical reflection on one's own cognitive operations. Rather, one begins phenomenologically by describing whatever appears in experience. Then one invokes the normative sciences to build a bridge between phenomenology and metaphysics.

Let me emphasize once again, however, that fallibilism promotes measured optimism about the human mind's ability to understand reality truly. Fallibilism endorses both an epistemological and a metaphysical realism. In a realistic context, fallibilism measures the mind's likelihood of judging reality truly by its ability to admit that it might have erred when confronted with evidence which unmasks erroneous beliefs. Evidence would include overlooked, salient facts which call one's position into question, contradiction in one's stated position, or the emergence of a frame of reference which promises more fruitful results than the one which has heretofore guided one's inquiry.

Moreover, Peirce's notion of belief also prevents his fallibilism from degenerating into a skeptical relativism. By a belief, Peirce means, a proposition for whose consequences one is willing to take responsibility. This definition accords well with my own definition of conversion. Responsibility implies commitment. One stands committed to a belief until one has a sound reason for questioning it: some fact which contradicts it, contradiction between it and other personally held beliefs, or the emergence of a more adequate frame of reference for thinking about reality than the one to which one stands currently committed.[15]

Two other factors in Peirce's philosophy also precluded philosophical relativism: his critical common sensism and his conviction that, if the mind takes the time to think clearly about reality and if it tests out operationally the consequences of its hypotheses, then reality will teach us what it is by the way it behaves.

14. Cf. Gelpi, *Inculturating North American Theology*, pp.14-20.
15. Cf. Peirce, *Collected Papers*, 5.358-376, 388-410.

Critical common sensism holds that, if one takes doubt seriously, then, even if one subjects one's spontaneous beliefs to critical question, one discovers a certain number of them which one cannot seriously doubt. These critically held beliefs endow the rational mind with speculative stability. As Dewey saw, they help provide the means for resolving the truly problematic beliefs which perplex one.[16]

Similarly, Peirce also saw correctly that the clarification of one's rational ideas demands the systematic use of all three forms of inference. Clear thinking, in other words, requires the formulation of a hypothesis, the deductive clarification of its operational consequence, and its verification or falsification in events. An inductively verified hypothesis reveals the laws which ground the way events transpire. Falsified hypotheses fail to explain events.

In complex questions, of course, often one may verify a given proposition only within a range of probability. That fact tells one that one's thinking, while moving in the right direction, has yet to take into account all the factors which finally explain the realities one seeks to understand.

If, then, one takes the trouble to clarify the practical, operational consequences of one's hypothetical beliefs and if one subsequently tests them out against the actual behavior of the realities one is trying to understand, then the realities one confronts will disclose to one the laws, the tendencies, which they exemplify by the way in which they behave. By their behavior things will, then, teach one to think truly about them.

The distinction between strictly normative and explanatory thinking also calls into question any speculative claim to have found an unrevisable starting point for thinking, for the claim illegitimately blurs the distinction between the two forms of discourse. In contrast to description, explanation makes a kind of normative claim to the extent that an explanation articulates the laws which cause realities to behave in the ways in which they do. Strictly normative thinking, however, makes a different kind of normative claim. Strictly normative thinking enjoys self-conscious normativity because it measures one's own behavior against realities, principles, and ideals which one has interiorized as making binding claims on one's choices.

Lonergan invokes hypothetico-deductive logic in explaining perceived events, which he calls the "data of sense"; but he invokes Kantian, transcendental logic in dealing with strictly normative self-conscious thinking. He calls self-conscious thinking prior to its elucidation through transcendental logic "the data of consciousness." Kantian transcendental logic, as we have already seen, fallaciously treats univerified hypotheses as verified conclusions. In Lonergan's case this fallacy betrays him into treating his own fallible hypothesis about how one ought to think into a univer-

16. *Ibid.*, 5.438-463, 502-537.

sally valid explanation of how the mind works. Lonergan and all card-carrying Lonerganians assume as a consequence that anyone who reflects on his or her cognitive operations will find the very operations which Lonergan's hypothetical epistemology describes and in the very terms and relations in which he describes them. This logically questionable assumption ultimately grounds Lonergan's specious claim to have found an unrevisable starting point for all thinking. In fact, Lonergan's fallible account of human thinking needs significant revision at several points.

Expanding "Experience"

First of all, Lonergan uses the term "experience" far too restrictively. In explanatory thinking, it corresponds pretty much to Kant's sense manifold by providing the raw materials of knowledge. In self-critical thinking, it functions analogously, although, as we have seen, for Lonergan the "data of consciousness" differs from the "data of sense."

In fact, however, images, feelings, and the symbols which express them do more than provide the raw material for concrete and abstract judgments. Feelings judge reality in their own right, as accurately and as fallibly as the rational mind. That means that any sound epistemology needs to recognize two principles of judgment, not one, as Lonergan's does. We judge reality with our feelings; we also judge it rationally and inferentially. Moreover, any sound epistemology must also concern itself with the coordination of judgements of feeling and inferential judgments.

Second, Lonergan's theory of knowledge acquiesces, as I have already indicated, in Joseph Maréchal's theory of the virtual infinity of the human intellect. Close empirical studies of how human knowledge grows and develops fail, however, to verify belief in that virtual infinity.[17] Instead, they suggest that the human mind is born finite and remains finite throughout life.[18] Finite needs and interests motivate human cognitive activity, not some fictive insatiable desire to know. I shall return to this point in a later chapter.

Third, study of liberation theology has convinced me that one cannot ground an adequate account of conversion in the way in which Lonergan suggests. Like Rahner and Maréchal, Lonergan endorsed the Kantian "turn to subject." Narrow focus on the subject of conversion, however, blurred Lonergan's perception of a fundamental dimension of the experience of conversion. Lonergan, as we have seen, defined a conversion as a decision which creates a horizon, a wholly new frame of reference for self-critical

---

17. Cf. Lonergan, *Insight*, pp. 271-316.
18. Cf. Gelpi, *Inculturating North American Theology*, pp. 20-22; *Grace as Transmuted Experience and Social Process*, pp. 76-78.

thinking.[19] While this definition grasps an important dimension of conversion, it focuses too narrowly on the converting subject. The experience of conversion does more than expand the structure of subjective intentionality. It not only involves a turning from and a turning to; but that turning also requires social transformation in a social context. Moreover, as liberation theology has insisted, socio-political conversion especially involves a turning to the Others, to the marginal, the poor, the outcasts of society.[20] As a consequence, the systematic pursuit of foundational theology demands broader social and experiential grounding than the exploration of the intentional structures of individual human consciousness which the Kantian "turn to the subject" allows.

In other words, had Lonergan studied the philosophy of C.S. Peirce and of Josiah Royce, he would have realized that the pragmatic "turn to community" provides a better grounding for a theology of conversion than does the "turn to the subject." Pragmatic fallibilism requires the turn to community; for, if one grants the finitude and fallibility of the human mind, then in one's personal search for truth one requires the corrective of experiences and insights other than one's own. The search for truth has, then, a fundamentally dialogic character and requires commitment to a community of truth seekers who investigate the nature of reality in a shared and systematic way.[21]

As I reflected on the legitimate criticisms which the classical North American philosophical tradition makes of Lonergan's theory of knowledge, I realized that the pursuit of foundational theology, in Lonergan's sense of that term had forced me to distinguish his theory of method from his theory of knowledge. The fact, however, that a systematic pursuit of the method had forced me to criticize the theory of knowledge on which it rests only confirmed me in my conviction that Lonergan's theory of method was moving in the right direction; for any method worth its salt forces the one who uses it to criticize the presuppositions on which it rests.[22]

The Scope of Foundational Christology

In the course of pursuing foundational theology in a systematic way, I had, as I have indicated, learned to distinguish five forms of conversion and to articulate at least seven dynamics and seven counterdynamics within the conversion process as a whole. The more I reflected on the current Christological crisis in the light of that construct, the more it seemed to promise a fruitful methodological context for laying new, systematic foundations for contemporary Christological thinking.

19. Cf. Lonergan, *Method in Theology*, pp. 237-238.
20. Cf. Gelpi, *Inculturating North American Theology*, pp. 99-146.
21. Cf. Gelpi, *Experiencing God*, pp. 205-258.
22. Cf. Gelpi, *Inculturating North American Theology*, pp. 205-258.

I found myself sympathetic to Van Beeck's suggestion that theologians need to de-objectify Christology;[23] but, as I have already indicated, I found myself unconvinced that rhetorical analysis alone provides an adequate tool for effecting that de-objectification.

Two factors in the historical development of Christology had led to its objectification: the metaphysical claims of classical philosophical thought and the historicism of the modern mind. As we have seen, classical metaphysics promises the human mind something it cannot deliver: namely, a necessary, universal insight into the nature of the real. A necessary, universal insight resists revision. It claims to have grasped Being-as-such. By refusing to acknowledge the fallibility of metaphysical hypotheses, classical metaphysics naively objectifies its fallible theories as the fixed and unchangeable nature of the real. A Christology based on classical philosophical assumptions similarly objectifies its account of humanity, divinity, and their relationship in Jesus.

The collapse of classical forms of Christological thinking in the nineteenth and twentieth centuries did not produce a relational restatement of the Christological question. Rather, it replaced one objectification of Jesus Christ with another. It substituted for the objectifications of classic metaphysics the objectifications of history. Perhaps a story will illustrate my point.

In the early stages of research for this study, I was conducting a seminar in contemporary Christology and had assigned Schillebeeckx's *Jesus* as a text. Three quarters of the way through Schillebeeckx's summary of the new (or second) quest for the historical Jesus, one of my students asked: "Why do I find the gospels so interesting and this stuff so dull." "Because," I responded, "the gospels seek to tell the story of Jesus in a way which evokes your personal commitment to Him in faith, while this book attempts only to summarize 'objective,' historically verified assertions, the 'bare facts' about Jesus."

The regrounding of Christology in a relational account of an experience of conversion overcomes the objectifying tendencies of both classical metaphysics and of historical-critical method. A relational, experiential approach to Christology demands that one formulate a relational account of Jesus Christ from the beginning; for foundational thinking in the modest, fallibilistic sense in which I employ the term "foundational" must explore the way in which commitment to Jesus Christ in faith transforms every aspect of the human experience of conversion within community.

Relational thinking differs from relativistic thinking. Relativism questions the human mind's capacity to verify its beliefs in reality. A relational, social construct of experience, as we shall see in greater detail in a

23. Cf. Van Beeck, *Christ Proclaimed*, pp. 5-63.

later chapter, not only recognizes that one can understand nothing without interacting with it; but it also asserts that, if one takes the time to think clearly about reality, it will disclose its true identity to the inquiring mind by the way it behaves. In other words, the relational character of reality grounds epistemological realism rather than excludes it. It also advances theological thinking beyond all forms of relativism by grounding it in a defensible philosophical realism.

The regrounding of Christology in a theology of conversion demands that one ask the following strictly normative question: *How should commitment to Jesus Christ transform all the other non-religious, or secular, forms of conversion?* What does this reformulation of the Christological question imply? In order to understand its implications, one needs to reflect more in detail on the analogy of conversion and on the dynamics which structure an authentic conversion experience.

Conversion Dynamics

Lonergan had taught me to think of conversion analogously. In the preceding section I explained briefly what the analogy of conversion implies for the investigation of each form of conversion. As I reflected on the complexities of conversion, however, I came to realize that the existence of more than one kind of conversion had other important methodological consequences for the systematic pursuit of foundational thinking. Besides understanding human development within each kind of conversion, the foundational theologian also needs to ponder the dynamics and counterdynamics of conversion. The dynamics and counterdynamics of conversion name the ways in which the different forms of conversion condition one another. As I have already noted, by a dynamic of conversion, I mean the way in which one form of conversion strengthens and re-enforces another. By a counter-dynamic of conversion I mean the way in which the absence of one form of conversion tends to undermine and subvert another form of conversion.

Let us then begin to name some of the basic dynamics which give a positive structure to the total process of conversion. As we shall see, the two dynamics which Christian conversion contributes to the total process of conversion hold an important methodological key to the development of a foundational Christology.

The three dynamics which follow describe how three of the secular, or natural, forms of conversion re-enforce the other forms of conversion.

1) Affective conversion *animates* the other forms of conversion by promoting the ongoing healing of disordered affections and by sensitizing the human heart to the perception of beauty. The perception of beauty yields an affective, intuitive grasp of the simultaneous goodness and truth

of some reality. Affective conversion suffuses the other forms of conversion with hope, zest, and imaginative flexibility.

2) Intellectual conversion *informs* the other kinds of conversions by providing them with the means of distinguishing true from false beliefs and adequate from inadequate frames of reference for thinking about reality. Intellectual conversion therefore enables one to think more clearly and accurately about the practical exigencies of every from of conversion, including intellectual conversion itself.

3) The two forms of moral conversion *help orient* the other forms of conversion toward strictly ethical values and realities. A reality or value takes on a strictly ethical character when it makes ultimate or absolute claims. As we have seen, something claims one ultimately, when one stands willing not only to live for it but if necessary to die for it. Something claims one absolutely, when it requires one's commitment in all circumstances.

Affective, intellectual, moral, and theistic religious conversion all qualify as "personal conversion" in the sense that each requires converts to take adult responsibility for themselves and for the personal decisions which shape their subsequent human development.

"Personal conversion" contrasts with "socio-political conversion." Socio-political converts take responsibility, not simply for themselves and for their subsequent personal development, but also and especially for human institutions and for the decisions of those who give them shape. The socio-political convert stands therefore committed to collaborating with others in order to ensure that the social sanctions which shape human institutional life foster ongoing conversion and effect the common good. The distinction between personal and socio-political conversion grounds the fourth and fifth dynamics of conversion.

4) Socio-political conversion *deprivatizes* the four forms of personal conversion by dedicating them to the collaborative pursuit of a just social order. The commitment to social justice forces the socio-political convert to confront "the Others," the poor, the marginal, the outcast, as well as those whose beliefs, commitments, and life-styles differ from one's own. That ongoing confrontation poses emotional, intellectual, moral, and religious challenges which one ducks if one confines one's attention exclusively to the growth experiences which personal conversion demands.

5) The four forms of personal conversion *help authenticate* socio-political conversion by providing it with norms for evaluating disordered institutionalizations of human intercourse. Affective conversion yields important insights into the difference between institutionalized neurosis and psychosis, on the one hand, and healthy human customs of relating affectively, on the other. Intellectual conversion unmasks the lies, distortions, and inadequacies of deceptive ideologies. Ideologies seek to ratio-

nalize situations of injustice as part of the inevitable scheme of things. Personal moral conversion yields a sound insight into the personal rights and duties which unjust social structures violate. Christian conversion yields an insight into divine justice: i.e., into the way in which God desires humans to institutionalize their relationships to one another.[24]

The Two Dynamics of Christian Conversion

Finally, Christian conversion contributes the following two dynamics to the total process of conversion. 6) Initial Christian conversion mediates between affective and moral conversion. 7) Ongoing Christian conversion demands the transvaluation in faith of the other four forms of conversion. These two dynamics hold the methodological key to the operations which shape a foundational Christology. Let us ponder why they do so.

One form of conversion mediates between two others when it sets them in a relationship to one another which they would not otherwise have. Christian conversion begins in the heart, in the confrontation with those attitudes, commitments, and values which stand between oneself and one's commitment to God. Most frequently, disordered emotions block commitment to God in faith: resentment at the Church or at the hypocrisy of those who claim to believe, fear of an encounter with the Holy and of the demands it might make, guilt at having offended God, shameful self-hatred which makes it difficult to believe in the love and forgiveness of God. By bringing these disordered affections to healing in faith, Christian conversion transforms affective conversion into repentance.

As disordered negative emotions find healing, the sympathetic affections find greater scope to play. The imagination acquires new flexibility. One grows in a sensitivity to beauty. When, however, the divine excellence incarnate in Jesus and in people whose lives resemble His stirs the heart, one finds oneself loving divine beauty incarnate. That love motivates the commitment of discipleship; and the commitment of discipleship dedicates one to living in the image of Jesus and of those whose lives resemble His.

Inevitably, then, an initial commitment of faith in Jesus Christ also transforms the human conscience. Besides invoking natural prudential norms of right and wrong, the converted Christian conscience now also judges between good and evil in the light of the historical revelation of God's saving will for a sinful humanity. Moreover, growth in the ability to reach sound judgments of conscience in faith transforms natural prudence into the charism of discernment. The gift of discernment suffuses natural prudential thinking with prayerful receptivity to the divine Breath's illumination. Since both prudential judgments and judgments of dis-

24. Cf. Gelpi, *Grace as Transmuted Experience and Social Process*, pp. 97-139.

cernment engage a sense of the fitting and since one grasps the fitting with judgments of feeling rather than with inferential judgments, Christian conversion also establishes a new kind of relationship between affective and moral conversion.

Commitment to a life of discipleship has both a this-worldly and an other-worldly dimension. Commitment to proclaiming and establishing the reign of God anchors the Christian in this world; faith in the paschal mystery anchors the Christian in the world to come. These two worlds overlap and interpenetrate without completely coinciding. That interpenetration creates the eschaton, the last age of salvation. In the last age of salvation, one's work for the kingdom in this life begins one's participation in risen life with Christ, but full transformation in God comes only after death.

As we shall see in greater detail later on, life in the kingdom of God dedicates one to living as a child of God in Jesus' image. It requires one to trust in the Father's providential care in ways which free one to share one's bread, the physical supports of life with others. Christian sharing seeks to break down the barriers which separate people from one another by including the sinful, the marginal, the outcast, the oppressed in the active ambit of sharing. Christian sharing also expresses a mutual forgiveness which imitates the forgiveness of Christ. Christian forgiveness, therefore, extends even to love of enemies; and such forgiveness tests the authenticity of Christian prayer.[25]

The commitment of faith which results from initial conversion to Christ creates an all-embracing frame of reference which engages every dimension of human experience. It demands therefore that one judge all things in the light of that commitment. Re-evaluating things in the light of faith, things which one had previously known apart from faith, requires that one transvalue them. One transvalues one's perceptions of reality by transposing them from an old context into a new one which endows them with new connotations.

The transvaluation of the other forms of conversion in an ongoing Christian conversion supplies the second dynamic which Christian conversion contributes to the total process of conversion. A foundational Christology seeks to understand how commitment to Jesus Christ transforms affective, intellectual, personal moral, and socio-political conversion. It focuses, therefore, on the ongoing transvaluation of the natural forms of conversion in faith.[26]

A conversion occurs naturally when it happens in abstraction from the historical self-revelation of God and focuses exclusively on created reali-

---

25. *Ibid.*, pp. 41-66.
26. Because the counterdynamics of conversion do not contribute positively to the construction of a foundational Christology, I have not included them in the main text of

ties. Transvaluation happens when, having understood and appreciated some reality in one frame of reference, one finds oneself forced to re-evaluate it in the light of another frame of reference. The context of faith transvalues human natural perceptions in the light of God's historical self-revelation in Jesus Christ.

As Christian conversion transvalues affective conversion, it effects the healing in faith of disordered human desires and aspirations. In the process it gives birth to Christian hope. A foundational Christology of hope examines how commitment to Jesus Christ motivates Christian hope. It enables one therefore to distinguish false from true hopes, healthy from neurotic hopes, and oppressive from liberating hopes. At the same time, it teaches the human heart to long for the establishment of God's reign on earth as in heaven and for the ultimate redemption of all things in the second coming of Christ.

One cannot formulate a foundational Christology of hope, without confronting in a systematic way the claims of Pauline Christology; for hope in Jesus Christ lies at its heart. At the same time, a Christology of hope must examine the ways in which Christian apocalyptic, the Christian longing for the restoration of all things in Christ, also recreates and reshapes human longing for ultimate salvation. An exploration of the apocalyptic dimensions of Christian hope requires a reappropriation of the Christology enshrined in the book of Revelation. In the third part of this volume, I shall attempt to develop such a Christology of hope.

As we have seen, the human mind grasps reality both with judgments of feeling and with rational inferential judgments. A foundational Christology must explore how commitment to Jesus Christ transvalues imaginative perceptions of reality. That exploration engages the narrative Christologies enshrined in the gospels. In second volume of this study, I shall examine how faith in the Christ of the synoptic gospels transvalues human beliefs and the imaginative perception of reality; and, in the first part of the third volume, I shall examine the Beloved Disciple's narrative Christology.

this chapter. Let me, however, list them here. 1) The absence of affective conversion suffuses the other forms of conversion with neurotic rigidity and aesthetic obtuseness. 2) The absence of intellectual conversion suffuses the other forms of conversion with an inflexible fundamentalism. 3) The absence of personal moral conversion leaves the other forms of conversion in a state of partial ethical disorientation. 4) The absence of personal conversion leaves the socio- political convert without adequate norms for diagnosing social injustice. 5) The absence of socio-political conversion leaves all the other forms of conversion privatized. 6) The absence of initial Christian conversion leaves the other forms of conversion without any authentic, practical orientation to Jesus and to the action of His Breath. 7) The absence of ongoing Christian conversion betrays the initially converted Christian into replacing Christian hope, Christian faith, Christian love, the Christian search for justice, and Christian service with natural, secular, or sinful realities and values.

The theological virtue of faith engages the imagination; but it also transforms graciously the rational, inferential mind. Any foundational Christology must, therefore, also deal with the rational doctrines which ground commitment to Jesus. Foundational Christology needs, moreover, to develop criteria for distinguishing sound from unsound Christological doctrine and for understanding the relationship between the rational formulation of faith and its intuitive expressions. I shall address this question in section two of the third and final volume of this study. There I shall argue that the intuitive grasp of the divine in Christian hope and in narrative faith supply the doctrinal thinker with key criteria for distinguishing sound from unsound doctrine. Narrative and doctrinal Christology examine how faith in Jesus Christ transvalues intellectual conversion.

Finally, any fully adequate foundational Christology needs also to understand how commitment to Jesus Christ transforms the two forms of moral conversion: personal moral conversion and socio-political conversion. That requires the development of a practical Christology. To this question I shall turn in the final part of volume three. In it I shall examine how commitment to Jesus Christ requires not only the transformation of human interpersonal relationships but also the transformation of unjust social structures as well. Moreover, I shall argue that the moral consequences of Christological doctrines endow them with their full speculative meaning.

In this first section of the present volume I have reflected on the current Christological crisis and have proposed a method which promises to resolve that crisis, because if Lonergan and Peirce have the right of it, a foundational Christology will provide the norms for distinguishing between sound and unsound Christological doctrines. Sound doctrine will advance conversion; unsound doctrine will not.

In the second section of this first volume, I shall attempt to clarify one of the currently confused but key Christological categories. I refer to "the humanity of Jesus." I shall argue that in a contemporary, North American context one can legitimately conceive the humanity of Jesus as a finite, developing, human experience. Foundational method requires me to paint an interdisciplinary portrait of Jesus' humanity. Accordingly, I shall verify an experiential, philosophical construct of Jesus' humanity in the personal and social sciences and in the new quests for the historical Jesus.

In developing a systematic account of Jesus' humanity, I shall first examine some of the inadequate constructs of the human which Christologists have in the past invoked. I shall reject all dualistic and nominalistic constructs of the human, and I shall search for a middle ground between anthropological pessimism and anthropological optimism.

In the course of arguing for the legitimacy of understanding the humanity of Jesus philosophically as a finite, developing, socially conditioned human experience, I shall show that those who to date have attempted to make the theological "turn to experience" have done so poorly because they have acquiesced uncritically in a di-polar, individualistic, nominalistic construct of experience. I shall argue that only a realistic, social, triadic construct of experience promises to provide a verifiable and adequate philosophical understanding of this key term.

Philosophy alone, however, cannot offer an adequate contemporary account of the meaning of "the human." In addition, one needs to draw on relevant insights yielded by other scientific disciplines which examine the human condition: empirical, clinical, and social psychology; sociology; and anthropology. As we have seen, the results of these disciplines not only verify the truth of whatever philosophical construct of the human one may choose to defend; but they also expand that construct in greater developmental detail. Accordingly, after proposing a descriptive, philosophical construct of experience, I shall verify and amplify it in a preliminary manner in the results of the personality and social sciences. I shall at the same time ponder the Christological implications of the resulting construct of humanity.

Finally, any adequate, contemporary account of the humanity of Jesus must take into account the results of recent quests for the historical Jesus. In summarizing the results of those quests, I shall attempt to de-objectify them by contextualzing them in a thoroughly relational, social, philosophical construct of human experience.

An Adequate Method

The foundational strategy for regrounding Christology which I have just described takes into account all of the legitimate concerns of the other strategies which I have examined. At the same time, it supplies for their inadequacies.

With *Barth* my foundational method insists that one lay the grounds for reformulating Christology in faith; but it makes place nevertheless for both critical and constructive philosophical reflection in Christological thinking.

With *Rahner* my foundational method recognizes that laying the foundations for Christology requires the elaboration of a metaphysical anthropology; but it deprives that metaphysics of any claims to *a priori* necessity. Instead, it requires the metaphysical mind to confess to a contrite fallibilism.

With *Tracy* my foundational method recognizes that phenomenology plays an initial role in the philosophical exploration of a Christian experience of conversion; but it requires in addition that strictly normative thinking about experience mediate between a phenomenology and a metaphysics of experience.

With contemporary *New Testament Christologies* the foundational Christology which follows recognizes the need to take into account the results of contemporary exegesis; but it requires that one do so in the context of exploring the impact of commitment to Christ on all the different forms of conversion. It also grounds hermeneutics in a realistic metaphysics of experience rather than in the existential equation of Being and meaning. By distinguishing intuitive from rational forms of faith, moreover, the regrounding of Christology developed in these pages allows one to deal dialectically not only with New Testament theology but with post-Biblical Christological doctrinal development as well.

With *psychologizing Christologies*, the foundational Christology I shall develop in the following pages recognizes that commitment to Jesus Christ demands the transformation of human affectivity and of the human imagination. I shall argue that therapeutic Christology makes its best contribution to a practical Christology of personal moral conversion.

With *liberation Christology* the foundational Christology I shall propose requires that one "complete the hermeneutical circle." Foundational Christology concerns itself with the institutional consequences of Christological faith primarily, though not exclusively, in the course of examining the ways in which commitment to Christ transforms socio-political conversion.

Finally, the following approach to regrounding Christology recognizes the legitimacy of using *rhetorical analysis* in approaching Christological texts, but only where it applies. Rhetorical analysis will prove especially helpful in formulating a Christology of hope. It will not prove helpful in the verification of Christological doctrines, which requires other norms and methods.

So far I have examined the scope of the current Christological crisis. I have considered seven inadequate strategies for regrounding Christological faith. Finally, I have examined a new, more comprehensive strategy which promises to incorporate the best insights of inadequate methods at the same time that it corrects the inadequacies which mar them.

One final task remains. I need to explore the pastoral implications of the Christology which the following chapters will develop.

(IV)

It should not take a great deal of reflection to see that the regrounding of Christology in an adequate theology of conversion would have profound implications for the RCIA (The Rite of Christian Initiation of Adults). In *Committed Worship: A Sacramental Theology for Converting Christians* I began to lay systematic theological foundations for the work of the RCIA. Laying foundations for the RCIA differs from formulating a how-to-do-it catechesis for use in the restored catechumenate. If one applies Lonergan's theory of functional specialties to the work of the RCIA, the formulation of such a catechesis belongs to communications, not to foundational theology.

Foundational theology, however, provides the communications theologian with the norms and insights needed to construct such a catechetical program. For Lonergan, communications theology involves much more than popularization of academic theology. The communications theologian addresses pastoral situations in the Church in which communications have broken down. The breakdown of communications in the Christian community always betrays the lack of conversion at some level. The communications theologian needs therefore to use the insights into the demands of initial and ongoing conversion which foundational theology articulates in order to diagnose pastorally how the absence of conversion has fragmented a given Christian community or individual convert. One then needs to design a catechesis adapted to the persons and situation one confronts. That catechesis should summon all those it addresses to the kind of integral, five-fold conversion which will re-establish their communication with one another even as it restores constructive dialogue to the ongoing life of the Church.[27]

The foundational Christology developed in these pages seeks, then, to advance the work begun in *Committed Worship* by presenting a systematic, conversion-centered Christology which will provide those engaged in the RCIA with the diagnostic and foundational tools which they will need in order to call adult converts to integral conversion to Christ. The concrete, pastoral application of the results of the foundational investigation which follows must, however, lie in the hands of those who pursue communications theology as their peculiar functional theological specialty. For my part, I renounce any claim to professional competence in theological communications.

In so speaking, I do not intend to belie the pastoral importance of what follows but to underscore it. So far, the restoration of the catechumenate has advanced without adequate systematic reflection on the forms and dynamics of conversion. One can hardly blame those practically involved in the pastoral restoration of the catechumenate for this unfortunate lack; for, until foundational theologians supply them with the insights into conversion and with sound norms for conversion, those currently leading the RCIA lack the means for designing the kind of theologically grounded program which their converts need. *Committed Worship* together with this Christology and the trinitarian theology developed in *The Divine Mother* all attempt to advance theological reflection on the

---

27. Cf. Lonergan, *Method in Theology*, pp. 355-368.

foundations of Christian conversion and to do so in a manner which will make possible the responsible pastoral re-structuring of specific RCIA programs.

In *Committed Worship*, I argued that the pre-catechumenate ought to verify that converts have converted to Christ initially prior to their admission to the catechumenate. I also argued that the catechumenate itself ought to develop in adult converts an integral five-fold conversion. Advancement in a five-fold conversion requires that commitment to Christ transform and transvalue all the other forms of conversion. The catechumenate ought, then, to deal 1) with converts' affective relationship to Jesus, 2) with their intuitive, imaginative perceptions of Jesus, 3) with their rational beliefs about Jesus, 4) with the ways in which Jesus demands the transformation of their personal social relationships, and 5) with developing in converts a solid commitment to the prophetic Christian search for a truly just social order.

Any well-designed catechumenate begins, therefore, a life-long process of conversion which active participation in the shared faith-life of the Church ought to foster subsequently. As a consequence, a foundational Christology which addresses directly the needs of the RCIA will also address directly the developing faith-needs of any adult Christian; for the process of ongoing conversion never ends as long as we walk this earth. The doctrine of purgatory suggests that conversion even continues in the next life.

In focusing on the RCIA, I seek, then, to address the theological and pastoral needs of every believing adult Christian. In exploring how commitment to Christ transforms every aspect of the conversion process, I hope to invite and challenge all adult believers, both initial and ongoing converts, to confront the demands which ongoing conversion to Christ makes of them.

I recognize that in undertaking the regrounding of Christology, I have shouldered a burden which I may not have the strength to carry to the end. Should I fail, others, hopefully stronger and more capable than I, will undertake to complete the journey on which we are about to embark.

Chapter 4
On Misconceiving the Human

In the first section of this study, I reflected on the contemporary Christological crisis, on some of the cultural impulses which contributed to it, and on some possible strategies for responding to it. I then considered the method which structures the foundational Christology which I shall be developing in this and subsequent chapters. Finally, I reflected on the pastoral relevance of that method.

The present chapter begins to address one of the key issues raised by the contemporary crisis in Christology. As we have seen, a variety of historical causes have conspired to render a number of key Christological terms hopelessly vague. We find vagueness about the meaning of "humanity," of "divinity," and of "the relationship between the two in the person of Jesus Christ."

In the course of this study, I shall attempt to lend conceptual clarity to all these terms: "humanity," "divinity," "relationship," "person," "Jesus," and "Christ." In the present chapter and in the two which follow it, however, I shall focus on the first of these terms: namely, on "humanity." How, then, in a contemporary, North American context might one conceive the humanity of Jesus with philosophical and theological legitimacy? As we shall see, in responding to that question, I shall also have to clarify the terms "relationship," "person," and "Jesus."

In order to arrive at a sound understanding of "humanity" in a Christological context, one needs first to arm oneself against misleading and erroneous concepts of the human. In the present chapter, therefore, I shall survey dialectically[1] the way in which inadequate conceptions of the human have conditioned and often skewed Christological thinking. Having come to clarity about the blunders one needs to avoid in understanding human nature, I shall then in chapter five present the construct of the human which I shall employ in elaborating a contemporary, inculturated, foundational, North American Christology.

As we saw in the preceding chapter, the method for pursuing a foundational Christology requires that one employ three different kinds of cat-

---

1. As we have seen, dialectical theology compares and contrasts different theological frames of reference in order to identify areas of agreement and of disagreement together with their motives.

egories in its elaboration: philosophical categories, categories derived from theology, and categories derived from other sciences which study human religious experience. This chapter reflects on questionable philosophical and theological characterizations of humanity.

The argument of this chapter divides into four sections. In the first, I shall ponder dialectically the development of *Logos-anthrôpos* Christology during the patristic period. *Logos-anthrôpos* Christology helped create the theological consensus sanctioned at Chalcedon. *Logos- anthrôpos* Christology argued for the presence in Jesus of a complete and integral human nature. The development of *Logos-anthrôpos* Christology, however, has another important lesson to teach: to the extent that one espouses a dualistic anthropology, one finds it difficult to do full theological justice to the incarnation.

In the second part of this chapter, I shall examine dialectically the ways in which different philosophical constructs of humanity at the time of the Reformation colored classical Protestant and Catholic conceptions of the incarnation. Specifically, I shall call attention to the inadequacies which mar both an Augustinian and a Thomistic construct of the human. I shall focus on the Christological consequences of each construct.

In the third section of this chapter, I shall begin to probe the philosophical viability of conceiving humanity in general and the humanity of Jesus in particular as a developing human experience. I shall criticize "the turn to experience" in contemporary theology. This latest "turn" in contemporary theological thinking has attempted to use the category "experience" as a central, unifying, theological category. I shall argue, however, that the theological turn to experience has to date yielded confused and often negative Christological results, because those who have made it have acquiesced uncritically in a di-polar, nominalistic construct of experience which can explain neither the social nor the religious dimensions of human experience.

Finally, as I have already indicated, in chapter five I shall propose a philosophical alternative to the nominalistic understanding of experience which has to date fascinated contemporary theologians. I shall argue that only a triadic, realistic, social construct of experience promises to do justice to human experience in all of its dynamic social and religious complexity.

(I)

What, then, has the development of *Logos-anthrôpos* Christology to teach us today? To this question I turn in the paragraphs which follow.

As we saw in the preceding chapter, *Logos-sarx* Christology culminated in two important heresies: in subordinationism and in monophysitism. The defense of Nicea against both heresies engaged the best talents of the

Cappadocian fathers: Basil of Caesarea (329-379 a.d.), Gregory Nazianzus (330-390 a.d.), and Gregory of Nyssa (ca.334-ca.395 a.d). All three theologians developed a *Logos-anthrôpos* Christology. *Logos-anthrôpos* Christology insists that in the incarnation the second person of the trinity united Himself to a complete human nature and not just to a physical body.[2]

The dialectical analysis of the development of *Logos-anthrôpos* Christology has at least two important lessons to teach about the humanity of Jesus: 1) Any theological construct of the incarnation must vindicate the full and complete humanity of the incarnate Word. 2) One who understands Jesus' humanity in dualistic terms finds it difficult to do full theological justice to the incarnation. Let us examine how these insights surface historically in this strain of patristic Christological thinking.

Logos-anthrôpos Christology

During the pre-Nicene period, Origen of Alexandria (ca. 185-254 a.d.) laid the foundations for the development of a *Logos-anthrôpos* understanding of the incarnation. Origen asserted clearly and unambiguously the presence in Christ not just of a human body but of a human soul as well. Following Plato, Origen believed that the soul of Jesus, like every other human soul existed before the creation of His body. Moreover, in virtue of its union with the *Logos*, Jesus' human soul stands united to the *Logos* in a vision of perfect, spiritual love.[3] (Origen, *De Prin.*, II, 6, 3-8)

2. Although the Cappadocian fathers took the lead in developing a *Logos-anthrôpos* Christology, other thinkers, less well known than they, contributed to this movement in patristic thought.

   Epiphanius of Cyprus (d.403), for example, found a threefold reality in the incarnate Word: the Godhead of the Word which replaces the intelligence (*nous*) in Jesus, a human soul (*psychê*), and a human body (*sarx*). (Epiphanius of Cyprus, *Ancoratus*, 119) Epiphanius insisted on the completeness of the humanity which the divine Word assumed. This tripartite division of human nature into *nous*, *psychê*, and *sarx* reflected a Neo-Platonic anthropology.

   Pope Damasus (366-84 a.d.) also lent his support to the growth of a *Logos-anthrôpos* Christology. He rejected both Apollonarianism and adoptionism. The pope taught that in becoming human the *Logos* assumed a complete humanity, sin alone excepted. At the same time the Pope acknowledged only "one Christ," although he failed to offer an explanation for that unity. (*PL*, 13, 365B-357A). Cf. Grillmeier, *Christ in Christian Tradition*, I, pp. 349- 351.

   Didymus of Alexandria (313-98 a.d.) showed the influence of Origin on his thought when he insisted that the human soul of Christ did not share the immutability and impassibility of the *Logos* but suffered instead, not passion (*pathos*) in the sense of disordered and disorienting affections, but real though incipient emotions (*propatheia*). Moreover, he defended the basic soteriological principle: what is not assumed in the incarnation cannot be healed. (Cf. Grillmeier, *op.cit.*, pp. 362-363)

3. Origen failed to make a qualitative distinction between Jesus' *scientia beata*, the knowledge He enjoyed in virtue of His union with the *Logos*, and the graced vision of God enjoyed by the souls of the blessed. For Origen, Jesus' soul differs from the souls of

In his Christology Origen stressed the mediatorial character of the *Logos*, who exists in order to manifest the Father to humanity and in order to lead a fallen humanity back to the Father. Here the Platonic pattern of emanation from the One and return to the One inspired Origen's soteriology. (Origen, *Catena fragment.*, 2)

Origen also insisted on the mediatorial character of Jesus' soul. Just as the *Logos* mediates between the Father and us; so too, the human soul of Christ mediates between the rest of humanity and the *Logos*. It gives us access to the eternal wisdom present in the Logos.[4] (Origen, *Cant.*, III)

In the end, however, Origen's Platonism prevented him from doing the incarnation full justice, even though he recognized in the incarnation the novel contribution which Christianity makes to the human understanding of God. Scholars debate, for example, whether or not for Origen at some point the physical body of Jesus ceases to exist altogether.

As the confrontation with the Arians focused the attention of the defenders of Nicea on the inadequacies of a *Logos-sarx* construct of the incarnation, Origen's Christology, despite its limitations, did provide post-Nicene Christologists with a clear theological precedent for developing an alternative account of the incarnation, one which asserted the presence in Jesus of both a soul and a body.

The Cappadocian fathers laid the foundations for the more systematic development of a *Logos-anthrôpos* Christology. Basil of Caesarea mistrusted the philosophical rationalization of theology which had culminated in the Arian heresy. As a consequence, his Christology, like his pneumatology, tended to remain as close as possible to New Testament terminology. While fidelity to the New Testament witness kept his Christology orthodox, its lack of technical philosophical language also kept it from dealing with some of the thornier issues which preoccupied the two Gregories. In the end, therefore, Gregory of Nazianzus and Gregory of Nyssa offered more systematic accounts of the humanity of Jesus than Basil did.

In his Christology Basil showed more concern to distinguish the divine and human characteristics in the incarnate Word than to stress the unity of His person. We find in his writings a human Jesus who experiences suffering, growth, and ignorance (Basil, *Ep.*, 236). Basil distinguished physical and psychic sufferings and excluded from Jesus any psychic sufferings which result from perversity of will (Basil, *Ep.*, 261). Basil failed, however, to explore the soteriological implications of the presence of a human soul in Christ. His portrait of Jesus, concerned itself primarily with excluding all sin from Jesus' humanity.

graced believers primarily in the complete rational and volitional control which the *Logos* exercises over all of Jesus' human actions. (*Ibid.*, II, 4, 9) Origen, therefore, acknowledged the actual sinlessness of Christ, without, however, clearly asserting His inability to sin (*impeccabilitas*) (Origen, *Selecta in Psalmos*, in Ps. 4.5).

4. Cf. G. Aeby, *Les missions divines de saint Justin et Origène* (Freiburg: 1958), pp. 146-183.

Like his friend Basil, Gregory of Nazianzus also insisted against the monophysites on the presence of both divinity and a complete humanity in Jesus. He emphasized the unity of the two more explicitly than Basil, but neither thinker formulated an adequate theory of the unity in Christ.[5]

Gregory of Nazianzus inherited from Origen the idea of a complete human soul in Christ which mediates between the Godhead and the flesh (Gregory of Nazianzus, *Theological Orations*, 2, 23). Moreover, he began the process of extending into Christological speculation insights derived from trinitarian theology. Anti-Arian polemic had forced both Athanasius and the Cappadocians to distinguish the divinity common to the divine persons (*ousia*) from the particular reality of each member of the divine triad (*hypostasis*). Gregory saw the need to coordinate these technical theological terms with Christological thinking about the incarnation. In the process, he laid remote speculative foundations for the distinction between person and nature in the incarnate Word which Chalcedon would canonize. (Gregory of Nazianzus, *Theol. Or.*, 29,19). Gregory of Nyssa, as we shall soon see, developed this dimension of the first Gregory's thought even more systematically.

In his *Great Catechetical Oration*, Gregory of Nyssa sketched the main lines of his own Christological thinking. Against Apollinarius the second Gregory distinguished the duality of natures in the incarnate Word (Gregory of Nyssa, *Ant. adv. Apoll.* 18-19). More than either Basil or Gregory of Nazianzus, Gregory of Nyssa developed the role of the human soul of Christ in the economy of salvation. He insisted, for example, that Christ's death on the cross divides His human soul from His human body, but not the divinity from the humanity.[6] (*Ibid.*, 21, 26, 51, 55).

Moreover, Gregory envisaged the divine persons in dynamic terms, as three dynamic actualizations in the Godhead.[7] It comes as no surprise, therefore, that he also conceived the incarnation in dynamic terms, as the

5. By appealing to the Stoic notion of the "mixture" of two things that permeate one another while each retains it proper nature (e.g., fire and iron), both Gregories seemed to locate the unity of the incarnation in a "natural" process rather than in the person of the Son. Moreover, their Christology left vague the relationship between the divine and human substances in Christ, on the one hand, and his hypostatic, or personal, reality, on the other. Cf. Grillmeier, *op.cit.*, I, pp. 367-377.

6. Gregory of Nyssa also spoke of the reality born of the virgin as hypostatic. In the course of trinitarian debate, the term "*hypostasis,*" which originally meant "reality" had, of course, come to denote the particular reality of Father, Son, and Breath as opposed to the common divine reality (*ousia*) in which all three shared. Gregory in applying the same term to both the transcendent person of the Son and to His incarnate person not only linked trinitarian and Christological speculation more closely but also sharpened theological understanding of the kind of union the incarnation effects, namely, a personal (or hypostatic) one (*Ant. Adv. Apoll.*, 25).

7. Cf. Werner Jäger, *Gregor von Nyssas Lehre von Heiligen Geist* (Leiden: E.J.Brill, 1966), p. 14.

dynamic transformation of Jesus' humanity in His divinity, a transformation which the virginal conception of Christ begins. As a result of the transformation of the human reality of Jesus in His divinity, Gregory believed that we can understand the unique properties of His divinity and His humanity only by contemplating them in their unmingled state (Gregory of Nyssa, *Contr. Eunom.*, 5; *Ant. adv. Apoll.*, 54-5). Moreover, Gregory located the sufferings of the incarnate Son of God in His humanity alone, since the divinity enjoys total impassibility (Gregory of Nyssa, *Contr. Eunom.*, VI, 1-3).

Gregory of Nyssa also sharpened the distinction between *hypostasis* and nature in a letter once attributed to his brother Basil but now ascribed instead to Gregory himself. In it Gregory argued, with hints from Stoicism, that a universal needs to receive particularizing characteristics (*idiômata*) in order to exist. The *hypostasis* of the Word endows His humanity with those particularizing traits; or better still, the particularizing traits constitute the reality of the hypostasis (Ps.-Basil, *Ep.*, 38).

In so speaking Gregory transformed into personal traits the individualizing characteristics which in Stoic philosophy accrue to universal essences. For Gregory, then, the term "*hypostasis*" designated the confluence of the particularizing characteristics of each member of the trinity. They give a universal nature a face (*prosôpon*). These terminological shifts allowed Gregory to argue that in the incarnation divinity and humanity possess their own proper essential traits (*idiômata*) which the particularizing characteristics of the *hypostasis* of the Son render concrete (Gregory of Nyssa, *Ad Theoph. adv. Apoll.*, 126-7).

Gregory's language reflects the questionable essentialist presuppositions of both Platonic and Stoic philosophy. Nevertheless, he recognized that the distinction between divinity and humanity in Christ raises both metaphysical and logical questions about the *communicatio idiomatum*, or the relationship between divine and human traits in Jesus.

Two other fourth century thinkers, Evagrius of Ponticus and Nemesius of Emesa drew less successfully than the Cappadocians did on Origen's Christology in order to assert the incarnate Word's possession of a complete humanity. In the thought of Evagrius, the human soul of Jesus plays a more important role than the *Logos*. As a consequence, his Christology drifted in the direction of Arianism. Moreover, the substantial dualism which mars Platonic anthropology kept Nemesius from incorporating Jesus' body fully into the incarnation.[8]

8. While the Christology of the Cappadocians developed the more benign aspects of Origen's Christology, namely, its assertion of both a body and a soul in Christ's humanity, Evagrius Ponticus (c.345-399 or 400 a.d.), the disciple of both Basil and of Gregory of Nazianzus, showed less discrimination in his use of Origen.

Unlike Athanasius, he endorsed Origen's belief in the pre-existence of the soul of Christ. Like Origen Evagrius attributed a mediatorial function to the soul of Christ,

Western Developments

Hilary of Poitiers (d. 367) took up the anti-Arian crusade in the West. In matters Christological he confessed the unity of Christ but the duality of Godhead and manhood. He also acknowledged a human soul in Christ. He therefore professed himself an enemy of the *"tripartantes Christum"*: namely, of those who separate the divinity from the humanity of Christ and His human soul from His human body (Hilary of Poitiers, *De Trin.*, X, 19, 61-2). He also confessed the pre-existence of the Son (*Ibid.*, IX, 6).

Moreover, while Hilary's thought advanced beyond that of Athanasius in clearly affirming the presence in Christ of a human soul, he failed to exploit systematically the soteriological implications of that assertion. Moreover, what he said about the action of grace in Jesus' humanity tended to portray the latter more as an anomaly than as the pattern for Christian

which links together the *Logos* with its *sarx*. In the process he accented the dualistic connotations of Origen's Platonism. For Evagrius: "The flesh cannot by itself assume God; for our God is Wisdom (i.e., spiritual)....No being composed of the four elements is capable of receiving Him."

Evagrius did stress the visibility of the humanity of Christ against the Docetists. As in the case of Origen, however, one can legitimately question whether Evagrius gave full value to the whole of Jesus' humanity and whether the flesh of Jesus has eternal significance in the economy of salvation.

Evagrius also intellectualized the enlightenment which the incarnate Christ enjoyed. Moreover, in asserting that the human soul of Christ rather than the *Logos* as such becomes incarnate, Evagrius flirted with aspects of Arian Christology, particularly when he described the subject of the incarnation (i.e., the pre-existent soul of Christ) as a created spirit.

In the end, moreover, Evagrius so stressed the pre-existent soul of Christ that it played a more important role in the incarnation than the eternal *Logos*. The pre-existent soul of Christ even functions as the demiurge in his theology. As an intelligence (*nous*) enlightened by the *Logos*, the human soul of Christ mediates between us and the divine; but it rather than the *Logos* Himself descends into the underworld and ascends into heaven.

Nemesius of Emesa, another fourth-century thinker who developed an Origenist Christology illustrates the difficulty Christian thinkers found in using dualistic categories derived from Middle Platonism and Neo-Platonism in order to talk about the humanity of Jesus in a unified way. Nemesius rejected Apollinarianism clearly and decisively. He described the union of divinity and humanity as "real (*kat' ousian*)." Moreover, he attempted to provide a more unified account of the humanity of Jesus than he discovered in the Neo-Platonic sources which shaped his thought.

Against the Neo-Platonists Nemesius denied that soul and body become a composite being which is the subject of human emotion. For Nemesius, the soul, not the composite, initiates all human activity. Similarly, the soul suffers human emotions. He believed that the soul tends toward the body with a natural disposition.

In the end, however, in every human the soul and body remain independent realities which one should never confuse. By the same token, the only unity Nemesius found between the soul and body of Jesus amounts to a collaborative relationship between them. In the incarnation, the *Logos* pervades the body; but the body finally has no effect whatever on the *Logos*. Cf. Grillmeier, *op.cit.*, I, pp. 389-391.

salvation. For example, he claimed impassibility not only for the divinity but also for the graced humanity of Christ (Hilary of Poitiers, *De Trin.*, X, 23).

Hilary did, however, discover saving significance in the everlasting union of the humanity and the divinity of Christ. The glorified Christ reigns even in His humanity (*De Trin.*, XI, 49). In the glorified Christ both natures—divine and human—enter into the transcendent realm of the divine glory (*Ibid.*, IX, 9).

Among the Latin fathers, Jerome (d. 419 or 420 a.d.), in contrast to Hilary, drew a somewhat more realistic portrait of the humanity of Jesus. He acknowledged that Jesus had to assume both a human body and a human soul in order to save both. Moreover, he found in the humanity of Jesus the same capacity to suffer which besets every other human (Jerome, *Comm. in Isaiam XIV*, in 53:1-4). On occasion, Jerome even acknowledged the presence in Jesus of human passions, although by that he seems to have meant incipient passions (*propatheiai*), free of all sinful disorder. Jerome insisted, moreover, that passion never mastered Jesus and that for all His humanness the divinity shone through His sufferings and weakness (Jerome, *Comm. in Ev. Matth.* in 9:9). Jerome, however, did not develop as comprehensive a Christology as Hilary.[9]

Theodore of Mopsuestia (349-428 a.d.) developed a Christology which anticipated in many ways the Chalcedonian settlement. He divided the economy of salvation into two ages (*katastêseis*). The Old Testament narrates the first age and anticipates symbolically the salvation which the

---

9. Gaius Marius Victorinus (d. 362), converted to Christianity late in his life, but quickly joined the anti-Arian struggle. A Neo-Platonist prior to conversion, Victorinus introduced into His Christology elements of a Neo-Platonic *logos* philosophy. In the hierarchical world of Neo-Platonism, the universe comes to be through a series of emanations of degenerating ontological perfection. From the One emanates the Intelligence, from the Intelligence, the World Soul, from the World Soul individual souls, from Soul matter. In this universe of degenerating perfection the term "*logos*" designates a reality which exists on a more perfect plane of perfection and which functions as the pattern of another corresponding reality which exists on a lower plane of perfection. Thus, the eternal Intelligence, wherein reside all the forms of those things which exist in the material sensible universe, functions as the *logos* (the pattern, the rule) to which the World Soul must conform when the latter imparts schematic order to sensible world in which we live.

Victorinus imported this Neo-Platonic notion of the *logos* as rule into his Christology when he asserted that in the incarnation the divine *Logos* took to Himself not only a complete humanity with body and soul, but the *logos* of the human soul and the *logos* of the human body. In other words, He became the rule or pattern for the existence of all human souls and bodies (Gaius Marius Victorinus, *Adv. Arium*, III, 12, 26-8). Moreover, although some of his Christological rhetoric sounds adoptionist, Victorinus rejected in fact an adoptionist interpretation of the incarnation: "He did not assume a man, he became a man (*homo*)." (*Ibid.*, I, 22, 27-8; *Ad Phil.*, II, 6-8). Cf. Donald L. Gelpi, S.J., "The Plotinian *Logos* Doctrine," *Modern Schoolman*, 37(March 1960), pp. 163-177.

second age brings, the age of Christ. The age of Christ orients the entire history of salvation to an immortality in which Christians participate through their share in the divine Breath who inspires their eucharistic worship. The Breath of the risen Christ makes present, therefore, the gifts which the redeemed shall one day enjoy in their fullness in the life to come. Since, moreover, eternal life in God assimilates the redeemed to the risen Christ, Theodore found an eternal significance for the glorified humanity of the risen Jesus. (Theodore of Mopsuestia, *In Ev. Joh.*, III, 29; *Hom. cat.*, X, 18)

Theodore also recognized the threat of the monophysite heresy. (Theodore of Mopsuestia, *Hom. cat.*,V, 8). He realized that, if Christ in His humanity suffered physically, then His possession of physical life presupposed a human soul as the source of that life. Without a human soul Christ could neither die nor redeem the sins of the soul. Not only, therefore, did the *Logos* assume a human soul, but He delivered it from sin, made it master of its bodily sufferings, and brought it to immortality (Ibid., V, 11, 14, 19) Theodore denied that the *Logos* replaced the intelligence (*nous*) in the human soul of Christ, as some had asserted. Rather, through the grace of the incarnation the *Logos* ensures that human nature in its completeness triumphs over sin (*Ibid.*, V, 10).

The events which precipitated the council of Chalcedon began with an argument between Theodoret of Cyrus, on the one hand, and Eutyches, the monophysite Archimandrite of Constantinople. The conflict led to the trial of Eutyches for heresy. In the course of the proceedings, Flavian, the Patriarch of Constantinople, read a confession of faith which sought at one point to reconcile the Christological concerns of Alexandria and of Antioch. His creedal formulation of Christological faith asserted, among other things: "We acknowledge that Christ is from two natures after the incarnation, in one subsistent reality and person, confessing one Christ, one Son, one Lord."[10]

The assertion distinguished a before and an after in the incarnation: the pre-existent state of the *Logos* and His state after taking flesh. Moreover, in asserting that after the incarnation, Christ exists "from two natures," Flavian seems to have meant the same thing as the phrase "in two natures." Unfortunately, however, the phrase "from two natures" played into the hands of the monophysites, who, of course, interpreted it as blending two natures to form a third reality.

The theological turmoil in the east surrounding both Nestorius and Eutyches eventually drew the papacy into the debate. Pope Leo I (reigned 440-461 a.d.) responded with his *Tomus ad Flavianum* to which he appended Christological extracts from his other letters. In the *Tomus* Leo helped lay the foundations for the Chalcedonian settlement.

10. Cf. Grillmeier, *op.cit.*, I, pp. 523-524.

The *Tomus* ruled against Eutyches (vv. 1-15). It discussed the origin of the two natures in Christ from both the Christian creeds and from sacred scripture (vv. 16-53). It argued for the co-existence of the two natures of Christ in the unity of His person (vv.54-93). It discussed the mode of operation proper to each of the two natures in Christ (vv. 94-120). The *Tomus* also touched on the question of the *communicatio idiomatum* (vv. 121-76). In its discussion of the human operations of Jesus, the *Tomus* insisted that the man Jesus confronted God in freedom. Except in its discussion of Jesus' human freedom, the *Tomus* broke no new Christological ground; but it helped crystallize the emerging Christological consensus which would receive sanction at Chalcedon.

The Contribution of Chalcedon

The council of Chalcedon gave, then, official formulation to the theological consensus which the development of *Logos-anthrôpos* Christology had prepared. As we have seen, however, the council endorsed no particular philosophical conception of the humanity of Jesus. It asserted that humanity exists in Jesus in its perfection and that one finds the same humanity in other humans. In what concerns Jesus' humanity, therefore, He resembles us in all things except sin. Moreover, Chalcedon, as we have seen, explicitly condemned monophysitism by asserting that in the incarnate Word divinity and humanity exist "without confusion, without change, without division, without separation." Instead, the properties of both natures, the divine and the human, remain preserved co-existent and intact. (DS 302) In denying that the humanity of Jesus "changes," Chalcedon did not, assert its essential immutability. Rather it denied that the humanity and divinity blend into a third reality.

Clearly, in the Christological decree of Chalcedon, one encounters an attempt at doctrinal conciliation not only among warring theological schools but also between Christology and trinitarian theology. True, the council couched its teachings in historically conditioned categories. It did not, however, pretend to offer a fully developed Christology but a principle which should guide all future Christological catechesis and speculation. The principle demanded that, after Chalcedon, theologians recognize in the incarnate Christ a single subsistent reality: the Son of God, the second member of the divine triad, who after the incarnation exists in two complete, distinct, and unmixed natures: one divine and the other human. The council did not canonize any particular philosophical language for understanding this principle; instead, it enunciated general linguistic norms for any subsequent theological account of the mystery of the incarnation.

Dualism Once More

In the preceding chapter, I suggested that during the patristic period several assumptions of classical philosophical thought conspired to create confusion in Christological speculation. Those sources of confusion included the following: substantial dualism, operational dualism, cosmic dualism, essentialism, and the lack of a clear understanding of the term "person." As *Logos-anthrôpos* Christology evolved, the same confusing assumptions muddied its attempt to give adequate theological definition to Jesus' humanity.

As we saw in the preceding chapter, substantial dualism helped breed the monophysite heresy. The need to respond to the challenge of monophysitism, however, led *Logos-anthrôpos* Christology to offer a highly abstract philosophical definition of the humanity of Jesus. The theologians who developed a *Logos-anthrôpos* Christology saw clearly that monophysitism rooted itself in a *Logos-sarx* construct of the incarnation. That insight led the architects of the *Logos-anthrôpos* tradition to counter *Logos-sarx* Christology with a clear affirmation of the presence in Jesus of both a soul and a body.

In describing the humanity of Jesus as constituted of both body and soul, however, the *Logos-anthrôpos* tradition focused somewhat narrowly on the substantial constitution of that humanity. As the preceding brief dialectical analysis has tried to make clear, those who developed this tradition tended to assume that Jesus' human soul like His body had its own proper powers of operation. Nevertheless, the concern of the *Logos-anthrôpos* tradition to assert a complete human substance in Jesus did endow its understanding of His humanity with a high degree of philosophical abstractness. That Jesus possessed both a soul and a body asserts a truth but a philosophically vague and highly abstract one. Substantial dualism also made the philosophical and theological understanding of Jesus' humanity speculatively problematic whenever it endorsed, as Origen did, the Platonic notion that Jesus' soul, like all other souls, had existed in the pure realm of Spirit prior to its combination with a physical body.

Moreover, on occasion, the cosmic dualism which marred the classical Platonic tradition combined with substantial dualism in order to call into question the saving significance of Jesus' body. Cosmic dualism, as we saw, equates the realm of Spirit with the eternal, the real, the unchanging and characterizes the realm of matter as ephemeral, illusory, and mutable. The Platonization of Christian soteriology motivated the misleading assumption that salvation consists in "spiritualization," in assimilation to the eternal, the real, the unchangeable. This dualistic reading of the process of salvation seems to have led a Platonizing theologian like Origen to question the ultimate soteriological significance of Jesus' body.

As *Logos-anthrôpos* Christology evolved, cosmic dualism on occasion also distorted theological understanding of Jesus' humanity. For example, excessive concern to vindicate the divinity of Jesus over against the Arians led an anti-Arian like Hilary to project into the graced humanity of Jesus itself something akin to the metaphysical immutability of God. Hilary described the humanity of Jesus as "impassible"; but he attributed this quasi-divine trait, not to the humanity of Jesus, but to the action of supernatural grace. This kind of thinking laid the foundations for the so-called "high" Christologies of the middle ages.

Operational dualism colored the understanding of the humanity of Jesus which emerged from the *Logos-anthrôpos* tradition. We find operational dualism implicit in descriptions of the total victory of the spiritual powers of Jesus' soul over the unruly "lower," carnal passions. The architects of the *Logos-anthrôpos* tradition correctly recognized the need to exclude sinful passion[11] from Jesus. One may, however, legitimately question the more or less explicit operational dualism which tended to color their account of "higher," spiritual powers in Jesus' soul which exercised tight volitional control over the "lower," carnal powers rooted in the body.

The Lack of an Adequate Conception of Person

The development of *Logos-anthrôpos* Christology illustrates how the theological controversies of the fourth and fifth centuries forced patristic theologians to begin to hammer out an adequate language for talking about persons as persons. The defence of Nicea against the Arians forced Athanasius and the Cappadocians to distinguish clearly between the particular reality of Father, Son, and Breath, which they designated by the term "*hypostasis*," and the divinity common to all three members of the divine triad, which they designated by the term "*ousia*."

As the defenders of Nicea wrestled with the problem of devising adequate ways of talking about the co-presence of divinity and humanity in the incarnate Word, they also correctly saw the need to coordinate the technical trinitarian and Christological terms which they were in process of creating. Greek theology tended, however, to leave the meaning of technical theological terms like "*hypostasis*," "*ousia*," and "*physis*" conceptually vague. That very vagueness, however, invited conceptual clarification; and subsequent generations of theologians would attempt to supply it. By its calculated categorical vagueness, the Chalcedonian doctrine of the hypostatic union invited further doctrinal development.

---

11. In volume three, I shall follow Roberto Unger in defining "passion" as the affective perception of human interpersonal relationships. Those passions qualify as morally reprehensible or as sinful which prevent one from relating to other persons as persons. Wicked passions include the seven deadly sins. Faith, hope, and love exemplify life-giving passions.

Essentialism

Besides dualism, essentialism also marred the development of
Logos-anthrôpos Christology. The attempt of Cappadocian theology to
define the particularity of "person" and of "nature" had the advantage of
tacitly equating individuation with qualitative difference; but that same
attempt, as we have seen, also acquiesced uncritically in the essence fallacy.

Acceptance of the Chalcedonian doctrine of the hypostatic union, however, does not commit one to any particular philosophical understanding
of key terms like "nature (*physis*)" or "subsistent reality (*hypostasis*)." It
commits one even less to the questionable philosophical assumptions about
the humanity of Jesus which colored the theological thinking of those
who contributed to the eventual formulation of Chalcedon's Christological
creed.

In what concerns the humanity of Jesus, then, the development of
Logos-anthrôpos Christology poses a double challenge to any contemporary Christology. 1) Any viable contemporary construct of the incarnation must assert the fundamental insight of *Logos- anthrôpos* Christology:
namely, that Jesus possesses an complete and integral humanity. 2) In
formulating its understanding of the human, however, a contemporary
Christology needs to avoid the dualism and essentialism which distorted
the attempt of *Logos-anthrôpos* theologians to give a speculative account
of that humanity. It must also provide a more adequate understanding of
the term "person" than did patristic theology.

(II)

In the preceding section I reflected on the dialectical development of
Logos-anthrôpos Christology, on its strengths and limitations, and on the
contribution which it made to Chalcedonian Christology. I also reflected
on the challenges which this strain in patristic Christological speculation
poses to anyone interested in the contemporary regrounding of Christology.

Before I attempt to begin to lay systematic foundations for the contemporary reformulation of Christology, another controversy in the development of theological reflection on the humanity of Jesus deserves
critical attention. I refer to the contrasting philosophical and theological
accounts of humanity which divided Catholic and Protestant Christology
at the time of the Reformation.

Classical Protestant Anthropological Pessimism vs.
Catholic Anthropological Optimism

At the time of the Reformation, Protestants opted for a pessimistic,
Augustinian view of human nature, while the council of Trent opted for

the more hopeful account of human nature generally endorsed by medieval scholasticism. Since post-Tridentine Catholic theology showed a marked preference for Thomism, I shall in the present context reflect dialectically on the Christological consequences of opting for either an Augustinian or a Thomistic understanding of human nature.

As we shall see, Protestants and Catholics disagreed not only intellectually about the meaning of "human nature" but also attitudinally about its relative corruption. As a consequence, this particular Christological debate engages the heart as well as the head, emotions as well as inference.

Pessimism about human nature tends to spring from emotional deflation, while excessive optimism usually betrays emotional inflation.[12] Both deflation and inflation tend to distort one's perceptions of reality. In what follows, therefore, I shall suggest that the resolution of this particular Protestant-Catholic *contretemps* requires deeper affective conversion as well as the clear thinking which intellectual conversion demands.

I shall also argue that neither Augustinianism nor Thomism provides finally an adequate, verifiable philosophical understanding of humanity. Having rejected aspects of both positions, I shall then propose a middle ground between the two.

Immediately after his conversion, Augustine of Hippo (354-430 a.d.) found the idea of salvation through "angelization" attractive. An angelized version of salvation envisaged the eventual elimination of the body by its total spiritualization. With time, however, he learned as a Christian to recognize more positive value in physical creation. Nevertheless, ambivalent attitudes toward human sexuality did color his theological account of human nature.[13]

Augustine recognized that God had created human sexuality and sexual procreation and recognized them as naturally good in themselves. (Augustine, *De Nat. et Gra.*, II, iii-iv) The human fall from grace had, however, corrupted a naturally good reality. Prior to the fall, Augustine's operational dualism led him to imagine that all sensual impulses, even the erection and quiescence of the male sexual organ, obeyed the commands of the spiritual will. (*Ibid.*, II, xxxv) The original sin of Adam and Eve, however, had not only caused physical death. (Augustine, *De Pecc. Mer. et Rem.*, I, v, vi, ix) It had in fact corrupted human nature.

---

12. For a discussion of ego inflation and deflation, see: Edward F. Edinger, *Ego and Archetype: Individuation and the Religious Function of the Psyche* (Baltimore, MD: Penguin, 1973). For a theological contextualization of these clinical concepts, see: Donald L. Gelpi, S.J., *Experiencing God: A Theology of Human Emergence* (Lanham, MD: University Press of America, 1987), pp. 143-148.

13. For a nuanced and sympathetic reading of Augustine on the relationship between sexuality and society, see: Peter Brown, *The Body and Society: Men, Women, and Sexual Renunciation in Early Christianity* (New York, NY: Columbia University Press, 1988), pp. 387-427.

Sin darkens, confuses, and wounds human nature. (*De. Nat. et Gra.*, xxv) After sin, the body lusts against the spirit. (*Ibid.*, lvi; *De anim. et ejus Orig.*, I, ii) This lust of flesh against spirit Augustine called concupiscence. Wounded by concupiscence, the spiritual will can no longer command human passions or the activity of human sexual organs. (*De Nup. et Con.*, I, xxiii, xxvii; *De Pec. Mer. et ejus Rem.*, II, iv; *De Nat. et Gra.*, II, iv, xxv) Sinners beget sinners (*De Pec. Mer. et ejus Rem.*, III, vii), children who at birth possess a "depraved and polluted" human nature. (*De Nup. et Con.*, I, xxiii)

The corruption of human nature begun by the original sin of Adam and Eve and communicated through physical conception and birth deprives human nature of any natural capacity to act virtuously. Left to itself, therefore, human nature can only sin; virtuous action results only from the cooperation between nature and grace. (*De Pec. Mer. et ejus Rem.*, I, xxviii; *De Spir. et Lit.*, xxvii) Seeming natural virtue qualifies only as "splendid vice." (*Ibid.*, I, iii)

Augustine's dualistic, Platonic understanding of human nature prevented him from doing full speculative justice to Jesus' humanity. Nevertheless, since he regarded Jesus' graced human nature as sinless, Augustine's sense of human depravity did not color his Christology in a significant way. An Augustinian doctrine of depravity did, however, influence Luther's Christological thinking. More specifically, it colored his doctrine of the cross. Moreover, for Luther the reformer, the cross stands at the heart of the mystery of Christ.

Bedeviled by scruples as an Augustinian monk, Martin Luther (1483-1546 a.d.) drew systematically on the theology of the founder of his order in his attempt to make sense of his own religious experience. Augustinianism led the young Luther to find Platonism much more attractive than Aristotelianism. In addition, it caused him to interpret his own personal religious struggle in the light of Augustine's pessimistic reading of human nature. Only the "alien righteousness" of Christ which springs from faith and from the action of grace can keep the soul from sinning. (Martin Luther, *Works*, 31:297-302, 356) As a consequence, freedom of choice belongs properly only to God. The graced will chooses the good necessarily; the ungraced will chooses sin with the same necessity.[14] (*Ibid.*, 33:37-43, 64-68, 103, 107-108, 115, 184-185, 246, 270-274)

Luther believed that sin transforms a corrupt humanity into the enemies of God. As Jesus hangs on the cross, He substitutes for sinners by suffering in their stead. In His passion therefore a righteous Father vents upon His innocent Son the full force of His wrath against an utterly corrupt and sinful human race. The Son, for His part, freely throws Himself in the way of the Father's justly vindictive punishment of a sinful and

---

14. For the initial Roman response to Luther, see: *DS* 1451-1492.

depraved humanity. Luther laid heavy rhetorical stress on the sufferings of Christ's human soul, which in its dying agony endures not only the suffering of the cross but the very tortures of the damned. By thus "atoning" for sin, the Son both satisfies divine justice and reveals the love and forgiveness of God.[15]

Luther's nominalism led him to describe the gracing of the human soul as the "extrinsic imputation" of righteousness to a corrupt human nature. The same nominalistic cast of thought colored his Christology as well. Specifically it caused him to stress the utter and ineffable mystery present in the incarnation. The humanity of Jesus conceals rather than reveals God so that God can find humans in their sinfulness in order to offer them love, grace, and liberation from sin. The incarnation thus reveals the absolute transcendence and sovereign freedom of God.[16]

In the doctrinal section of this study, I shall return to a Lutheran doctrine of atonement when I consider the influence of medieval atonement Christology. Here it suffices to note the connection between Luther's understanding of the sinful depravity of human nature, on the one hand, and his Christology of the cross, on the other.

John Calvin (1509-1564 a.d.) endorsed both Luther's doctrine of natural depravity and its Christological consequences. Moreover, he went beyond Luther by insisting that the doctrine of natural depravity provided "the principal point of the argument" in the Christological section of the *Institutes*. (John Calvin, *Institutes of the Christian Religion*, II, ii, 1-24, iii, 1-24, iv, 1-8)

Calvin described "original sin" as "an hereditary depravity and corruption of our nature, diffused through all the parts of the soul, rendering us obnoxious to the Divine wrath, and producing in us those works which the Scripture calls 'the works of the flesh.'" (*Ibid.*, II, i, 1-9) As a consequence, everything which proceeds from human nature deserves divine condemnation.[17]

The abject corruption of human nature makes the incarnation necessary, since only by suffering the punishment which sin merited could Christ succor a ruined humanity and restore a fallen and utterly polluted world. In taking on flesh, the Son of God freely associated Himself with the vile and contemptible by assuming the likeness of sinful flesh. (*Ibid.*, II, ii, 1-7, xiii, 1-4, xiv, 1-8) In suffering the punishment for sin in our

---

15. Cf. Marc Lienhard, *Martin Luther's Christologisches Zeugnis: Entwicklung und Grundzeuge seiner Christologie* (Göttingen: Vanderhoeck & Ruprecht, 1973), pp. 37-97.

16. *Ibid.*, pp. 108-114.

17. William Thompson finds more convergence than hitherto presupposed between Calvin's understanding of justification and sanctification and the council of Trent's. Cf. William Thompson, "Viewing Justification through Calvin's Eyes," *Theological Studies*, 57(1996), pp. 447-466.

stead, the death of Christ enjoys expiatory, placatory, and satisfactory efficacy. (*Ibid.*, II, xvii, 1-5)

The young Luther's struggle with scrupulosity helped inspire his doctrine of human depravity. As the doctrine developed in Protestant circles, however, it drew on other affective and cultural sources. Augustine wrote and thought during the twilight of Graeco-Roman society. As a consequence, the world of social, moral, and political decadence in which he lived and wrote endowed his doctrine of human depravity both with its motivation and with its rhetorical plausibility.

A similar decadence helped both to inspire a classical Protestant doctrine of depravity and to endow it with a similar rhetorical plausibility. Classical Protestantism developed in the twilight of medieval culture and at the dawn of the modern era. Both the decadence and corruption of the medieval Church, on the one hand, and the violence and ruthless nationalism of Renaissance secular society, on the other, endowed Protestant diatribes against human depravity with the ring of truth. So did rage at the Church's apparent refusal to reform itself.

The Catholic church eventually did try to reform itself partly from a guilty conscience, partly in response to the Protestant challenge. The Church did so at the council of Trent (1545-1573 a.d). By the time Trent convened, however, Protestantism had already ossified into doctrinal rigidity, and the time for reconciliation had past.

Of all the Tridentine decrees, the Decree on Justification made the greatest effort to offer an olive branch of peace to the Protestants; but the document drew the line at calling human nature totally corrupt. Trent rejected the Augustinian pessimism of the Protestant reformers and defended human nature's capacity to choose freely and to perform some naturally good acts despite the weakness of the flesh which results from sin. (*DS* 1521, 1554-1558) At the same time, Trent agreed with Luther and Calvin that only the grace of Christ effects justification in the sight of God and that Christ alone causes redemption and the forgiveness of sins. (*DS* 1522-1523)

Trent also insisted that God justifies us without any antecedent merit on our part. Trent rejected, however, the "extrinsic" imputation of grace. Justification by faith does more than forgive sin. It effects the renovation of the human self, transforms us into heirs of eternal life, and changes us from God's enemies into God's friends. In justifying sinners, grace also transforms them and empowers them to act supernaturally. (*DS* 1526, 1528-1530)

A careful reading of Trent's decree concerning justification will reveal that the council refused to endorse any of the going philosophical constructs of human nature. Philosophical pluralism at the council made consensus on that subject impossible. Among the delegates one found Thomists, Augustinians, Scotists, and humanists.

Nevertheless, Trent did endorse in a general way the more optimistic conception of human nature proposed by medieval scholasticism. In what concerns God's saving action, medieval scholastic theology endorsed an Augustinian theology of the primacy of divine grace, but the medieval schoolmen grafted these Augustinian insights onto a different stock. The medieval scholastics eschewed on the whole Augustine's pessimism about human nature and affirmed instead human nature's ability to perform at least some morally good acts on its own. Only through grace, however, could one merit eternal salvation. On both of these points, Trent rejected Augustine and sided with the medieval scholastics.

The Thomism which came to dominate Catholic theology offered one way of systematizing these medieval beliefs. Far from discovering in human nature an utter depravity which closed it completely to the reality of God. Aquinas discovered within the spiritual powers of the human soul a natural longing for supernatural union with God.

Thomistic metaphysics conceives God as a pure act of Being unlimited by any potency and actually infinite in its perfection. (Thomas Aquinas, *Summa Theologiae*, I, v-vii, ix, x) It also equates Being with the formal objects of the two spiritual powers of intellect and will. (*Ibid.*, I, lxxix, lxxxii, lxxxiv, lxxxviii; I-II, iii, 47-48) This fixed, essential orientation of the spiritual powers of the soul to infinite Being as their natural end endows them with a virtual infinity. The intellect's formal object transforms it into an insatiable longing for truth and the will into an insatiable longing for goodness. (*Ibid.*, I, lxxxii-lxxxiii) Aquinas did not even hesitate to discover within human nature a natural desire for the beatific vision itself. (*Ibid.*, I-II, iii, 47-48, 51; v, 4)

Leo XIII's encyclical *Aeterni patris* (1879 a.d.) designated Thomism as the official philosophy of the Catholic church (*DS* 3135-3146) until the second Vatican Council dethroned it in favor of philosophical pluralism. As a consequence, all Catholic philosophers and systematic theologians in the first part of this century had to think *en bon thomiste*.

In the first part of the twentieth century, Joseph Maréchal, S.J. laid the speculative foundations for transcendental Thomism by blending a Thomistic metaphysics, anthropology, and theory of knowledge, on the one hand, with Kantian logic, on the other. Maréchal transformed the essential orientation of the human intellect toward Being into an active dynamism. Moreover, he called the attention of theologians to Aquinas's optimistic description of the human spirit as a "natural desire for the beatific vision."[18] Maréchal's work inspired Henri de Lubac's theology of

18. Cf. Joseph Maréchal, S.J., *Le point de départ de la métaphysique* (5 vols.; Louvain: Edition du Museum Lessianum, 1926-1947).

grace,[19] Karl Rahner's metaphysical anthropology,[20] and Bernard Lonergan's doctrine of the human intellect's unrestricted desire to know.[21]

No matter how formulated, however, the Thomistic doctrine of the virtual infinity of the human mind propounds an unverifiable, inflated understanding of the human intellect. The methodological presuppositions which ground this study require that all philosophical hypotheses acknowledge their fallibility and find their verification in closer, scientific studies of finite, created reality. Far from verifying the virtual infinity of the human mind and will, however, the evidence furnished by contemporary psychology points all in the opposite direction. Far from supporting the virtual infinity of human mental powers, contemporary psychology re-enforces belief in their radical and utter finitude.

Since belief in fixed, formal objects exemplifies the essence fallacy, it should come as no surprise that contemporary developmental psychology discovers in the human mind no such fixed and essential orientation of the human mind toward Being as such. Rather it suggests that the human mind consists of the finite number of intuitive and inferential habits of thinking which one has acquired in the course of a lifetime. For the human mind to enjoy an orientation to "Being as such" it needs schooling in Thomistic metaphysics; and even then its orientation results, not from some essential *a priori* dynamism of spirit but from the learned acquisition of a questionable metaphysical belief.

Studies of how the human mind develops give solid evidence that human thinking always moves from one limited frame of reference to another. Until humans reach the age of eighteen months, infant minds, though incredibly active, function purely at a sensory-motor level. During this period, while memories play a part in human cognitive activity, the child gives no operational evidence of a capacity to imagine a world which it does not sense directly. The intuitive imagination develops during the second year of life; but not until the age of eleven do most children exhibit a capacity to think abstractly. Once abstract thinking emerges, it moves within identifiable but thoroughly finite frames of reference: common sense, mathematics, positive science, philosophy, theology. Moreover, as we shall see in a later chapter, it would appear that not every human being develops the capacity to reason abstractly.[22]

Clinical psychology has also called attention to the finitude and specialization of the human ego. Ego consciousness develops gradually and incrementally in tension with both the needs of the unconscious and

19. Cf. Henri de Lubac, S.J., *Le mystère du surnaturel* (Paris: Aubier, 1965).

20. Cf. Karl Rahner, S.J., *Hörer des Wortes* (München: Kosel Verlag, 1936).

21. Cf. Lonergan, *Insight*, pp. 271-316, 348-364.

22. Cf. John H. Flavell, *The Developmental Psychology of Jean Piaget* (New York, NY: Van Nostrand, 1963); Hans G. Furth, *Piaget and Knowledge: Theoretical Foundations* (Englewood Cliffs, NJ: Prentice-Hall, 1969).

with social expectations. The Briggs-Myers test, moreover, has undertaken to investigate empirically the truth of Carl Jung's account of ego development, his theory of personality types.[23] The results of the Briggs-Myers test tend to document, not the virtual infinity of the human ego, but its functional specialization. In the course of a lifetime, the human ego cultivates different realms of experience and neglects others. In those areas it neglects, it manifests a spontaneous obtuseness. In addition, ego consciousness exhibits, not a spontaneous and insatiable desire for truth, but a deep and spontaneous inertia. It resists threatening insights and incorporates them slowly and reluctantly into its perception of things.

Other forms of cognitive testing tend to confirm the radical finitude of the human mind. IQ tests tend to establish the fact that some minds learn more quickly than others. At some point, moreover, every mind reaches the limit not only of what it can understand but even of what it wants to understand. Far from exhibiting an insatiable thirst for all truth, human cognition follows finite human needs and interests.

Thomistic anthropology defends, then, an inflated perception of the human. Augustinianism defends a deflated, disillusioned account of the human.

As we have seen, Augustinian pessimism bore Christological fruit in a classical Protestant theology of the cross. That theology draws on other sources as well; and we shall have occasion to examine them in the doctrinal section of this study. Here it suffices to note the connection between the way classical Protestantism viewed human nature and its interpretation of the saving role of Jesus Christ.

The example of Protestant Christology would, then, lead one to expect a reverse phenomenon in Catholic Christology: namely, that the inflated understanding of human nature propounded by Thomism would also have important and exaggerated Christological consequences, as indeed it does. As we have seen in the preceding chapter, it helped produce an inflated understanding of Jesus' human knowledge. More specifically, it provided Aquinas with a philosophical rationalization for the naive medieval assumption that the humanity of the incarnate Word must during His lifetime on earth possess by grace whatever the divinity possesses by nature. Aquinas, as we saw, believed that the immediate personal union of Jesus' human intellect with the object of its inbuilt, essential longing—namely, with infinite divine truth—explained why Jesus' human intellect enjoyed the beatific vision from the first moment of His conception. (Aquinas, *Summa Theologiae*, III, vii & viii)

23. Cf. Carl G. Jung, *Psychological Types*, translated by H.G. Baynes (Princeton: Bollingen, 1974); Allen W. Brownsword, *It Takes All Types!* (Fairfax, CA: Van Norman, 1987).

Beyond Both Inflation and Deflation

Unverifiable beliefs about the human spring from some other source than sound rational thinking. Pessimistic beliefs spring from a deflated ego, from a finite human consciousness overwhelmed by suffering and contradiction and incapable of appreciating the goodness of life. Overly optimistic beliefs spring from ego-inflation, from a human consciousness out of touch, sometimes dangerously so, with its own finitude, fallibility, and capacity for vicious behavior. The human mind which desires to cultivate healthy emotional perceptions of reality needs, then, to advance beyond both deflated and inflated images of itself to a more realistic assessment of its capacities and limitations.

Moreover, as we have just seen, both inflated and deflated conceptions of the human lead to questionable Christological doctrines. Any sound contemporary understanding of humanity in general and of Jesus' humanity in particular needs, then, to find a middle ground between inflated and deflated perceptions of the human.

Most Protestant theologians today would concede that an Augustinian doctrine of human depravity paints far too pessimistic a portrait of human nature, even though among fundamentalists one still finds echoes of the old rhetoric of depravity. Once Catholic theologians learn to eschew the folly of Kantian *a priori* logic (will that ever happen?), the evidence furnished by empirical studies of the way the human mind works ought to teach them a similar modesty concerning the overly optimistic, inflated claims which Thomism makes for the "spiritual powers" of the soul.[24]

Can theological anthropology find a realistic middle ground between anthropological pessimism and anthropological optimism? I believe that it can. I have come to believe that the American theological tradition claims that middle ground. One finds the position to which I refer articulated in the theology of Jonathan Edwards (1703-1758 a.d). I shall have occasion in the third volume of this study to consider in more detail Edwards's creative, aesthetic approach to Christological thinking. Here, however, I focus on an important aspect of his perception of human nature and of its relationship to divine grace.

Although Puritan theology (including that of Edwards) clung tenaciously to an Augustinian doctrine of predestination, the Puritan tradition very early nuanced a Calvinist doctrine of total depravity in a way

---

24. The internal contradictions which plague a Thomistic theory of knowledge also render it inherently incredible. Cf. Gelpi, *Experiencing God*, pp. 122-135; *Grace as Transmuted Experience and Social Process*, pp. 68-80. Moreover, since we clarify the meaning of rational beliefs by exploring their operational consequences, the extreme rationalism which Thomism has bred among theologians with its concomitant inability to deal adequately with appreciative forms of knowing provides further evidence of the intellectually inflated character of Thomistic perceptions of the human.

which better approximated a Tridentine understanding of the human. At least some Puritans held that human nature can indeed perform some naturally good acts but that, in whatever concerns human salvation, it remains utterly dependent on the grace of God.[25]

Edwards developed these Puritan insights in theologically suggestive ways. Edwards held that only God necessarily loves Himself because only the divine reality provides an adequate object for the divine will. His aesthetic metaphysics led him, however, to recognize a natural beauty in creation to which the human heart can respond spontaneously. He believed that self-love becomes vicious through selfish exclusivity, through narrow preoccupation with one's own private good. He also spoke of "compounded self-love," by which he seems to have meant a vicious, "enlightened" self-interest. Authentic self-love, however, must express true virtue, or "the cordial consent of being to Being in general." In other words, virtuous self-love subordinates the love of self to the universal, all-embracing will of God. One loves oneself and all other things with true virtue only when the divine will graciously orders one's natural preferences.[26] Benevolence to a large number of people, the approbation of a virtuous action, force of habit, natural pity, or the absence of moral evil in an action do not justify calling such things "true virtue," since they lack grounding in the gracious, transcendent love of God. On the other hand, such acts would not seem to qualify as vice in the strict sense.[27]

Edwards could in his own mind consistently defend the possibility of naturally good moral options and still defend a Calvinist doctrine of original sin because of the Ramist logic of supposition in which he seems to have acquiesced. The work of Pierre de la Ramée (1515-1572), Ramist logic and rhetoric blended humanistic and pedagogical concerns with a strong repudiation of Aristotle and of late scholastic patterns of thinking.[28]

When measured by contemporary logical standards, the "logic" of Ramée, who in academic circles adopted the Latin name of Ramus, produced a confused pedagogical popularization of the rhetorical and logical theory of his day. In his account of predication, Ramus, for example,

25. Cf. Perry Miller, *The New England Mind* (2 vols.; Boston, MA: Beacon, 1961), I, pp. 13-110, 239-299.
26. Cf. Norman Fiering, *Jonathan Edward's Moral Thought in Its British Context* (Chapel Hill, NC: The University of North Carolina Press, 1981), pp. 150-199; David D. Brand, *Profile of the Last Puritan: Jonathan Edwards, Self-Love, and the Dawn of the Beatific* (Atlanta, GA: Scholars Press, 1991), pp. 71-73.
27. Fiering, *op. cit.*, pp. 322-361.
28. Cf. Walter J. Ong, *Ramus, Method, and the Decay of Dialogue* (Cambridge, MA: Harvard, 1958); William Samuel Howell, *Logic and Rhetoric in England, 1500-1700* (New York, NY: Russell & Russell, 1961); Charles Waddington, *Ramus (Pierre de la Ramée: Sa vie, ses écrits, et ses opinions* (Paris: Librairie de Ch. Meyrueis, 1855); Charles Desamze, *P. Ramus: professeur au collège de France: Sa vie ses écrits, sa mort (1515-1572)* Geneva: Slatkine Reprints, 1970).

defended a logic of supposition. "Supposition" in Ramus has nothing to do with the formulation of a tentative hypothesis ("let us suppose that...."). Instead, "supposition" refers to the displacement of a subject by its predicate. The predicate replaces the reality of which it is predicated instead of revealing or disclosing it.[29] Using such a flawed logic, Edwards argued that unless true virtue, or graced cordial consent to the holiness of God, replaced not only sinful but even natural hopes, the latter would tend spontaneously to supplant the deity, transform themselves into idols, and so ultimately contribute to the overwhelming burden of original sin.[30]

I find the predestinationism, determinism, rigorism, and logical underpinnings of Edwards's thought seriously flawed. On the other hand, I agree with his characterization of human nature as finite and with his affirmation that, left to its own natural resources, human nature can indeed desire some naturally good things, but only limited, finite natural goods. Humans naturally and spontaneously love their own: members of their own family, tribe, or even nation. Left to itself, however, the human heart, as Edwards clearly saw, finds it morally difficult, even impossible, to love with the universal love to which the gospel of Christ calls us. We do not spontaneously love strangers. On the contrary, we fear them. We do not spontaneously love our enemies. On the contrary, we tend naturally to fear and hate them. We find it hard to forgive those who wrong us, much less to love them with the atoning love of Christ.[31] Military establishments institutionalize fear and aggression. Violent, militaristic societies like our own inculcate it. In Edwards's theology, only God loves universally by nature. Grace perfects and elevates human nature by teaching it to imitate the universality of divine love.

The fact that Stoic philosophy conceived the ideal of universal human benevolence does not in itself contradict the preceding hypothesis. Either the conception of that ideal flowed from the action of divine grace or it did not. If it did, that fact confirms the hypothesis. Even, however, if the ideal of universal human benevolence sprang from natural human aspiration, having an aspiration differs from actually living it. As I understand Edwards, he is arguing that without supernatural grace one cannot actually live in a way which embodies the universal divine benevolence incarnate in Jesus; and, on this point, I believe that he has the right of it. Indeed, experience teaches us all too well that even with divine grace we find loving with the atoning love of Christ difficult enough.

29. Cf. Ong, *op. cit.*, pp. 66-67; Stephen H. Daniel, *The Philosophy of Jonathan Edwards: A Study in Divine Semeiotics* (Bloomington, IN: Indiana University Pres, 1994), p. 85.

30. Daniel, *op. cit.*, pp. 131-152.

31. For a more detailed presentation of these insights, see: Donald L. Gelpi, S.J., ed., "Conversion: Beyond the Impasses of Individualism," in *Beyond Individualism: Toward A Retrieval of Moral Discourse in America* (Notre Dame, IN: University of Notre Dame Press, 1989), pp. 1-30.

Edwards wrote long before the development of the science of psychology, although one could argue that his *Treatise Concerning Religious Affections* ranks as one of the perennial classics in religious psychology and discernment.[32] As I have indicated, I personally reject the predestinationism, rigorism, and moral determinism which mars his understanding of the human as well as the flawed Ramist logic which underpins these positions. Nevertheless, in other respects, contemporary social and developmental psychology tend, in my judgment, to confirm Edwards's belief that only supernatural faith effectively motivates a genuinely universal human love. A personal anecdote may help illustrate this point.

During the late fifties, I taught high school in New Orleans. The city seethed at the time with racial bigotry. The Archbishop of New Orleans, Joseph Rummel, had quite correctly excommunicated several prominent Catholic racists, after years of trying to evoke from them some signs of repentance. I found more than half of my own students infected with racist prejudice.

In an attempt to understand better the roots of racist bigotry I read Gordon W. Allport's, *The Nature of Prejudice*. I found in it ample ammunition to use against the inbred bigotry of those I taught; but I also found in Allport's analysis of the judgment of prejudice a challenge to my own going philosophical creed.

I had just completed my philosophical studies in St. Louis, where Missouri-valley Thomism reigned supreme; and I regarded myself as a card-carrying Gilsonian Thomist. I therefore found troubling Allport's portrayal of judgments of prejudice as connatural to the human mind.[33] I sensed uneasily that, in some way, that contention called into question my own Thomistic beliefs about the spontaneous longing of the human spirit for infinite truth and goodness.

I had reason to feel troubled. Allport had put his finger on a fundamental fact about the human condition. The finitude and social conditioning of the human mind causes it to identify spontaneously with the "in-group" to which it belongs and to form overly generalized, stereotypical images and concepts of other social "out-groups" to which it does not belong but with which it has regular but superficial social contact. These stereotypical judgments ossify into bigotry when they resist revision despite clear factual evidence to the contrary. Moreover, bigotry devolves from deriding members of an out-group to social avoidance of them; and social avoidance degenerates into acts of overt hostility.[34]

---

32. Cf. Jonathan Edwards, *A Treatise Concerning Human Affections*, edited by John E. Smith (New Haven, CT: Yale University Press, 1959).

33. Cf. Gordon W. Allport, *The Nature of Prejudice* (New York, NY: Doubleday, 1958), pp. 1-79.   34. *Ibid.*, pp. 47-65

The fact that the human mind finds stereotypical thinking about the members of an out-group morally unavoidable tends, in my judgment, to support philosophical belief in its radical finitude and fallibility. All human thinking evolves within finite frames of reference more or less infected by both ego inertia and social prejudice. Judgments of prejudice institutionalize one such finite frame of reference into stereotypical, group perceptions of social aliens. Neurotic rigidity transforms those same stereotypes into entrenched prejudices. Extreme neurosis and even psychosis transform them into bigotry.

Allport documented the standard racial, ethnic, religious, and political prejudices of the dominant culture in the United States at the time when he wrote.[35] Not only did he insist on the learned character of social stereotyping, prejudice, and bigotry; but he argued persuasively for their moral inevitability given the socially conditioned character of human thinking.[36]

As I came to face the limitations and contradictions implicit in the Thomistic system I had learned, I eventually conceded that stereotypical, prejudiced, and bigoted thinking tends to support belief in the radical finitude and fallibility of the human mind. Moreover, after studying the theology of Edwards in the late seventies, I also concluded that the same phenomena tend to confirm his contention that the human heart, left to its own resources, finds it morally impossible to love universally.

The fragmentation of human society into in-groups and out-groups with superficial perceptions of one another makes personal fragmentation morally inevitable. Social conflict among groups commonly breeds prejudice and all too often bigotry. As prejudice and bigotry intensify, the fabric of any society unravels. As I learned, moreover, to confront my own racism, sexism, nationalism, and classism, I recognized how deeply inbred prejudicial stereotypes not only resist correction and reformulation but do so with remarkable intransigence.

Besides psychological studies of the nature of prejudice, developmental psychology also lends support to Edwards's contention that the human heart needs to learn to love universally. It does not do so spontaneously. James Fowler's studies of the stages of human cognitive development suggest that a universalizing faith, one which seeks to reconcile all things and persons in God, happens relatively rarely, usually in the case of genuinely saintly persons.[37]

35. *Ibid.*, pp. 83-296. For a history of bigotry in this country, see: Gustavus Myers, *The History of Bigotry in the United States*, edited and revised by Henry M. Christman (New York, NY: Capricorn, 1960).

36. Cf. Allport, *op. cit.*, pp. 273-368.

37. Cf. James Fowler, *Stages of Faith: The Psychology of Human Development and the Quest for Meaning* (San Francisco, CA: Harper and Row, 1976).

In the first part of this chapter, I reflected on the fact that any adequate, contemporary philosophical understanding of humanity needs to avoid the dualisms which plagued classical philosophical thought. In this second section, I have argued that in its portrait of the human condition, a sound Christology needs also to avoid the extremes of theological pessimism and of theological optimism. In order to avoid those extremes, one needs to come to terms with the emotional inflation and deflation which inspires them. In the section which follows, I shall begin to explore the ability of a contemporary philosophy of experience to provide the kind of philosophy of human nature for which we are searching.

(III)

I have argued that an sound contemporary Christology requires a philosophical understanding of human nature which avoids all the forms of dualism which distorted early Christological thinking. Such a Christology also needs a construct of the human which acknowledges the natural finitude of all human perceptions and desires. I have argued elsewhere that the classical philosophical tradition in the United States provides a rich resource for developing such a philosophy of the human, a resource left largely untapped by most Catholic systematic theologians in this country.

As the classical North American philosophical tradition evolved, it recognized the fallacious character of dualistic thinking and developed a strategy for avoiding it. The dualistic fallacy, as we have seen, misconceives interrelated realities in such a way as to render their relationship to one another subsequently obscure or unintelligible. As we have also seen, the dualistic fallacy and the essence fallacy tend to re-enforce one another in the speculative philosophical mind. The reification of contradictory essences like "spirit" and "matter," for example, has inspired a variety of dualisms, without, however, exhausting the dualistic fallacy's capacity for deception. Classical American philosophy calls into question subject-object dualism, the dualistic separation of matter from spirit, operational dualism, dualistic interpretations of the notion of substance, and the dualistic separation of the individual from society.[38]

Moreover, the philosophical tradition in this country gradually evolved a philosophical strategy for avoiding dualistic thinking. That strategy conceives reality as inherently relational in structure. It also develops a philosophical language which reflects the relational character of reality, including the fact of negative relationships.

In addition, classical American philosophers tend to insist on the radical finitude of the human mind. That insistence has inspired in turn a

---

38. Cf. Gelpi, *Grace as Transmuted Experience and Social Process*, pp. 1-11; *Inculturating North American Theology*, pp. 1-12.

relational construct of human reason. The classical American philosophical tradition has, since Peirce, tended to insist on the social, dialogic character of all human cognitive perceptions of reality and on the need for a logic of consequences in order to deal rationally with the dynamic, evolving, relational character of the real.[39]

Classical philosophical thought in this country has also tended to focus on the category "experience" as a central, unifying philosophical category. In some of its more recent formulations, it has even attempted to elaborate a metaphysics of experience which does justice to the relational, historical, evolving character of the real.

In the next chapter, I shall attempt to draw creatively on the North American philosophical tradition as a whole in order to develop a dynamic, relational, experiential construct of the human. Before I present that construct, however, another dialectical task faces us. We need to reflect on the speculative inadequacies which have marred the attempt of many contemporary theologians to use the term "experience" as a central, unifying category. A dialectical comparison of what these contemporary thinkers mean by "experience" will, as we shall see, uncover yet another fallacy which philosophical thinking about the meaning of the human needs to avoid: namely, the fallacy of nominalism.[40]

The Turn to Experience in Contemporary Theology

Contemporary speculative theologians in this country like to talk about the different "turns" which systematic theology has taken. We hear frequent references to "the turn to the subject" or to "the linguistic turn." Transcendental Thomism, with its strange wedding of Thomism and Kantianism, inspired "the turn to the subject." The attempt to exploit theologically the results of language analysis gave rise to "the linguistic turn."

Both the turn to the subject and the linguistic turn exemplify how systematic theologians come to take different speculative "turns." Christianity, as Josiah Royce saw clearly, exemplifies a religion in search of a metaphysics.[41] Systematic theology can take different "turns," therefore,

---

39. Cf. Gelpi, *Grace as Transmuted Experience and Social Process*, pp.22-29; *Inculturating North American Theology*, p. 13.
40. In what follows, I shall use the term "conceptual nominalism" in the same sense as C.S. Peirce. Peirce distinguished classical nominalism from conceptual nominalism. Classical nominalism reduces real generality to words, a mere *flatus vocis*. Conceptual nominalism recognizes the reality of universals but restricts their reality to human subjectivity. Peirce believed that most modern European philosophy falls into the fallacy of "conceptual nominalism." A realistic philosophy, by contrast, discovers real generality, or laws, in the very makeup of things. (Peirce, *Works*, 1.16-27, 5.53-65)
41. Cf. Josiah Royce, *The Problem of Christianity* (2 vols.; Chicago, IL: Regnery, 1968), I, pp. 420 ff.

as different theologians adopt different sets of philosophical presuppositions in their effort to construct a speculative theology.

The "turn to experience" in contemporary theology does the same thing. Those who make this "turn" adopt the term "experience" as a central, unifying category. In the process, they invoke a particular philosophical interpretation of the meaning of that term.

In a sense, Friedrich Schleiermacher first made the turn to experience in theology.[42] Among contemporary theologians, however, others have followed his example. In his attempt to elaborate New Testament foundations for Christology, Edward Schillebeeckx has clearly made the turn to experience. Process theology by adopting Alfred North Whitehead's metaphysics of experience makes the theological turn to experience even more systematically than Schillebeeckx. Liberation theology makes the turn to experience in its concern with "praxis." Moreover, certain strains in liberation theology explain the meaning of praxis in much the same way in which Schillebeeckx and process thought explains the meaning of experience.

In what follows, I shall argue that contemporary attempts to make the turn to experience all commit the same speculative blunder: namely, they adopt a nominalistic philosophical construct of experience which fails finally to explain the social character of experience. Nor can a nominalistic construct of experience account adequately for the fact of religious experience.

Experiential nominalism has colored two contemporary Christologies: that of Edward Schillebeeckx and of process Christology. I shall first examine the way each understands experience. I shall then contrast their position with the realistic philosophy of C.S. Peirce. Finally, I shall examine the Christological consequences of the first two positions.

How, then, does Edward Schillebeeckx make "the turn to experience." Schillebeeckx defines experience as "learning through direct contact with people and things." When we experience, we "assimilate perceptions." Assimilation means conceptual interpretation.[43]

"Experience" for Schillebeeckx has a temporal structure. It inherits from the past and projects plans for the future. Besides a temporal structure, "experience" also has a social structure. Language and social mores condition experience "from the outside." Moreover, Schillebeeckx concedes

---

42. In approaching religious experience, Schleiermacher focused on feeling and claimed to discover within human religious experience a feeling of absolute dependence unmediated by concept or image. Wayne Proudfoot correctly censures the characterization of a feeling described as "absolute," "dependent," and "unmediated" as contradictory. Cf. Wayne Proudfoot, *Religious Experience* (Berkeley, CA: University of California Press, 1985), pp. 1- 40.

43. Cf. Edward Schillebeeckx, O.P., *Christ: The Experience of Jesus as Lord.*, translated by John Bowen (New York, NY: Seabury), p. 30.

the finitude and fallibility of human experience.[44] Not only do we think in socially conditioned ways, but society defines our very identity as persons.[45]

Schillebeeckx defends a di-polar construct of "experience." "Experience" has a concrete, perceptual pole and an abstract, conceptual, interpretative pole. Schillebeeckx also calls the concrete pole of experience "praxis" and the conceptual pole of experience "thought."[46] "Praxis," or historical action, provides experience with objects for interpretation. Their conceptual interpretation endows experience with its "subjective" pole.[47]

In other words, like Immanuel Kant, Schillebeeckx endorses a British empiricist interpretation of the sensory pole of experience. It consists of concrete, individual perceptions. Schillebeeckx justifies this endorsement by acquiescing in the Enlightenment presupposition that in modern culture "the empirical *a priori* of science and technology" has replaced "the religious *a priori.*"[48]

In what concerns the conceptual pole of experience Schillebeeckx recognizes two radically different ways of interpreting "praxis": namely, reason and faith. Reason follows the methods of empirical science and of historical-critical method. Faith grasps the "depth dimension" of experience.[49]

Enlightenment fundamentalism also informs Schillebeeckx's interpretation of the way in which God functions in human experience. Schillebeeckx rules out the possibility of a "supernatural" encounter with God. By "supernatural" he seems to mean any encounter with God unmediated by praxis. He therefore also rules out any encounter with God through "inwardness."[50]

Since empirical science cannot demonstrate the existence of God, Schillebeeckx concludes that we have no rational demonstration of His existence. As a consequence, Schillebeeckx reduces the meaning of "God" to a limit concept, to an "unknown X" which defies definition by image and concept.[51]

The philosophy of Alfred North Whitehead inspires process theology. Whitehead makes the philosophical "turn to experience" when he formulates his "reformed subjectivist principle." That principle states that

44. *Ibid.*, pp.30-36.
45. *Ibid.*, pp.134-143. Schillebeeckx draws on social psychology in order to question the "closed" character of Kant's theory of knowledge. (Edward Schillebeeckx, O.P., *Church: The Human Story of God* (New York, NY: Crossroad, 1990), pp. 46-49.
46. Cf. Schillebeeckx, *Church, pp. 15-22.*
47. *Ibid.*, pp.37-38.
48. *Ibid.*, pp.46-53.
49. *Ibid.*, pp.23-28.
50. Cf. Edward Schillebeeckx, *Interim Report on the Books Jesus and Christ* (New York, NY: Crossroad, 1981), pp. 10-12; *Church*, pp. 55-56, 66-68.
51. Cf. Schillebeeckx, *Church*, pp.73-76.

"apart from the experiences of subjects there is nothing, nothing, nothing, bare nothingness."[52] By "the experiences of subjects" Whitehead does not mean that the subject which has an experience underlies it. Such a conception of "experience" belongs to the kind of substance philosophy which Whitehead rejects.[53] Rather, the subject *is* the experience. Each emerging subject consists of its own feelings, whether physical or conceptual. The feelings define and constitute the subject.[54] In a sense, Whitehead replaces the Cartesian "*cogito ergo sum*," with "I experience, therefore I am."

Whitehead, then, endorses the same di-polar construct of experience as Schillebeeckx. For both thinkers, "experience" consists of the subjective interrelation of concrete percepts and abstract concepts.[55]

Whitehead acknowledged his indebtedness to Henri Bergson and William James for his philosophical construct of experience.[56] George Santayana's *Skepticism and Animal Faith* also exerted significant philosophical influence on Whitehead's endorsement of a di-polar construct of experience.[57] Whitehead himself, however, also candidly derived his understanding of experience from Enlightenment sources: from the thought of John Locke, David Hume, and Immanuel Kant.[58] As we have seen, analogous philosophical sources inspired Schillebeeckx's di-polar philosophical construct of experience.[59]

I have examined the nominalistic conception of experience defended by both Schillebeeckx and process theology. I shall now examine its philo-

---

52. Cf. Alfred North Whitehead, *Process and Reality: Corrected Edition*, edited by David Ray Griffin and Donald W. Sherburne (New York, NY: Free Press, 1978), p. 167.

53. *Ibid.*, pp.28-29.

54. *Ibid.*, pp. 219 ff.; for Whitehead a "feeling" means a "positive prehension." He defines a "positive prehension" as a concrete fact of relatedness which contributes either physical concreteness or novel possibility to a specific occasion of experience. Every prehension includes three elements: the prehending subject itself, the datum it prehends, and the way it prehends it. Taken together the datum and mode of prehension constitute the prehending subject. (*Ibid.*, pp. 22-23, 26.)

55. *Ibid.*, pp. 48-51, 194. In Whitehead's system the "category of freedom and determination" insists on the subjectivity of experience. The "category of freedom and determination" requires that every occasion of experience be "internally determined and externally free." (*Ibid.*, p.27) In other words, as it defines its unique character each instance of experience creates itself totally and without any efficacious determination from outside itself.

56. *Ibid.*, p.xiii.

57. *Ibid.*, pp. 48-49, 52, 54, 81, 142-143, 152, 158.

58. *Ibid.*, p.130.

59. Nominalism even surfaces in Latin American liberation theology. As we have seen, Schillebeeckx uses the term "praxis" in order to designate the concrete, sensible pole of experience. In *Theology and Praxis: Epistemological Foundations*, Clodovis Boff develops a notion of "praxis" which has the same di-polar structure as does the term "experience" in the thought of both Schillebeeckx and Whitehead.

sophical inadequacies by contrasting it to the realistic construct of experience developed by C.S. Peirce.

Among North American philosophers, C.S. Peirce has, in my judgment, mounted the most telling criticism of Enlightenment nominalism. Peirce studied the debates which divided medieval nominalists and medieval realists. He sided with the realists and proclaimed his philosophy especially indebted to the realistic philosophy of John Duns Scotus.[60]

Peirce's realism, however, in contrast to the realism defended by most medievals, avoided the essence fallacy. Peirce defended the presence in things of real generality; but he did not mean by real generality a reified abstraction, idea, or essence. Instead, he meant the conditioned laws which ground and explain the behavior of things. Moreover, in the higher forms of life, Peirce recognized that those laws develop with a remarkable flexibility and plasticity.[61]

The di-polar construct of experience defended by Schillebeeckx and Whitehead derives in no small measure from the epistemology of Immanuel Kant. All three thinkers depict human cognitive activity as the subjective interrelation of concrete percepts and abstract concepts, even though Schillebeeckx recognizes, as we have seen, the "extrinsic" social conditioning of thought. A di-polar construct of experience equates existing reality with concrete, sensible, individual facts. Those facts exist as wholly determinate. They therefore lack any real generality. As a consequence, the human mind must impose universality subjectively on concrete sense data.

Peirce, a practicing scientist, saw clearly that such an understanding of human cognition can never explain the fact of scientific thinking; for science seeks to understand, not just concrete sensible facts, but the laws which render those facts intelligible. In a di-polar construct of experience, however, those laws have no real existence; only concrete sensible

---

By "praxis" Boff means "the *complexus of practices* oreintated (sic) to the transformation of society, the making of history." (Clodovis Boff, *Theology and Praxis: Epistemological Foundations*, translated by Robert Barr (New York, NY: Orbis, 1987), pp.5-6.) As his discussion of praxis develops, however, Boff eventually transforms it into a quasi-metaphysical term, not unlike Whitehead's metaphysical use of the term "experience." By "praxis" Boff means being, the concrete, facts, experience, history, life, the material. Theory functions within "praxis" as "theoretical praxis," or method. Theoretical praxis supplies the conceptual pole of historical praxis. (*Ibid.*, 195-197)

Like Schillebeeckx and Whitehead, then, Boff sees the interrelation of theoretical praxis and concrete, historical praxis as a subjective event. Reason, says Boff, echoing Kant, constructs its object with the result that the human mind has no cognitive access to the "thing-in-itself." (*Ibid.*, pp. 17, 29-34, 45-48, 71-2.) Theory, then, provides the concepts which transform subjectively the matter of praxis into the intelligible objects of thought. (*Ibid.*, pp. 213-216)

60. Cf. Peirce, *Collected Papers*, 1.6, 93-119, 180-212.
61. *Ibid.*, 6.246-271.

facts do. Far from explaining "empirical" scientific thinking, therefore, a di-polar construct of experience denies science access to the very realities it is trying to understand: namely, the laws of nature.

A di-polar construct of experience cannot explain scientific knowing because it peddles an indefensible "conceptual nominalism." It reduces generality to a subjective universal concept which the mind imposes on reality. In fact, as Peirce saw, the scientific mind grasps real generality inferentially when it performs an inductive inference.

Besides rendering scientific thinking unintelligible, the nominalistic fallacy leads to other philosophical dead ends. If, as those who defend a di-polar construct of experience contend, experience consists only in the subjective interrelation of concrete percepts and abstract concepts, then all thinking takes place exclusively between one's ears. As a consequence, a di-polar construct of experience lacks the conceptual means for talking about the social dimension of cognition. In other words, it has no categories for describing the very common human experience of one person talking to another person about some third reality.

In addition, a nominalistic philosophical construct of experience renders human religious experience unintelligible, as Kant saw clearly and as Schillebeeckx in some measure concedes. In a nominalistic, di-polar construct of experience reality consists exclusively of concrete sensible realities. One cannot, however, equate the reality of God with a concrete, sensible reality. God is not this rock, this tree, this chair, this Coca-Cola. As a consequence, in the world of nominalism God does not number among the realities one can experience; and the idea of "God" becomes an empty category, devoid of real significance or content. For Kant, therefore, God functions as one of the "ideals of reason." Schillebeeckx, as we have seen, reduces the notion of God to a "limit concept."

Theists like Whitehead and Schillebeeckx who espouse a nominalistic, di-polar construct of experience find themselves forced to look for God, not in the concrete, sensible pole of experience, but in its abstract conceptual pole. That search, for example, led Whitehead to espouse a philosophical ontologism. Whitehead believed that we have access within experience to the ideas in the mind of God. Since Whitehead's God functions as the ground of novel possibility, Whitehead equated religious experience with any experience of conceptual novelty.[62]

Human minds have enough difficulty understanding one another. That we have immediate cognitive access within experience to the mind of God, I find inherently improbable. Moreover, if one rejects the nominalistic presuppositions which underlie Whitehead's system, one need not, as we shall soon see, resort to ontologism in order to explain religious experience.

62. Cf. Whitehead, *Process and Reality*, pp. 26, 160-162.

Even if one were to concede to Whitehead his ontologistic account of religious experience, however, it falls woefully short of describing the complexity of religious experience as we know it. At the heart of religious experience lies a relationship to the transcendent reality of God. That relationship involves much more than having a novel idea.

Schillebeeckx too seeks to discover God in the conceptual pole of experience; but he does so on theological rather than on philosophical terms. Schillebeeckx distinguishes sharply between rational knowledge and faith. He therefore reduces the "encounter" with God to a subjective experience of having been graciously saved. Schillebeeckx believes that such an experience corresponds to a reality; but he fails to explain why in fact it does.

I have been arguing to the philosophical indefensibility of a nominalistic, di-polar construct of experience. I have urged three reasons for rejecting it: 1) It renders scientific explanation unintelligible. 2) It renders the social dimensions of human experience and cognition unintelligible. 3) It renders human religious experience unintelligible.

Other speculative woes, however, attend Whitehead's attempt to construct a philosophy of process on nominalistic presuppositions, largely because Whitehead develops his nominalistic construct of experience more systematically than Schillebeeckx. Among the chief woes must surely rank the fact that nominalism renders process itself unintelligible. In Whitehead's philosophy, "creativity" functions as the category of the "ultimate."[63] By "ultimacy," Whitehead seems to mean "universal predicability." Everything in the Whiteheadean cosmos must exemplify creativity.

Unfortunately, however, Whitehead's nominalism leaves him bereft of the philosophical means to explain how creativity happens. Having reduced reality to "experience" and "experience" to the subjective interrelation of concrete physical, feelings and abstract, conceptual feelings, Whitehead must explain why creativity results from the creative synthesis of these two types of feelings.

Whitehead concedes that conceptual feelings effect nothing. They function in Whitehead's world as pure possibility. They supposedly lure feeling. Physical feelings, however, function as perished facts, since, as each occasion of experience achieves physical concreteness, it ceases to exist. Perished facts, however, explain nothing; nor can they effect anything. The fact that I just punched a computer key may exist eternally as a truth in the mind of God, as Whitehead suggests; but it cannot effect or explain any other reality. It can only remain eternally what it is.

In other words, the juxtaposition within subjective experience of an eternally determinate fact and of a completely inefficacious possibility can only produce precisely that: the juxtaposition within experience of

63. *Ibid.*, pp. 20-22.

an eternally determinate fact and of an inefficacious possibility. Nothing creative results from that juxtaposition. In fact, nothing happens at all, for neither can do anything besides be what it is. One can try to lure a dead dog with the possibility of food, but it will not eat.

In other words, having excluded laws, or dynamic tendencies from his cosmos, Whitehead finds himself bereft of the philosophical means to explain the central category of his system: namely, creativity, or process.

Still other speculative woes result from Whitehead's endorsement of philosophical nominalism. 1) The atomicity of experience leaves him without any adequate explanation of motion or continuity. Indeed, Whitehead's universe denies the possibility of motion in principle.[64] 2) The reduction of the individual to a society of distinct but allegedly overlapping occasions of experience leaves Whitehead unable to offer an adequate account of personal continuity. In Whitehead's thought what people call an enduring object consists of a nexus of overlapping occasions of experience with a common element of form transferred serially from one member of the nexus to the other.[65] 3) The atomicity of experience plus Whitehead's reduction of relationship to a reified geometric grid (the extensive continuum) atomized by actual occasions of experience together leave him without the conceptual means to explain interpersonal relationship. In Whitehead's cosmos, one drop of experience can "prehend" another only as a perished fact. One relates to that fact in a utilitarian way as a datum for one's own processing; but such an experience falls woefully short of an I-Thou encounter. 4) Whitehead's reduction of what most people mean by an individual to an overlapping society of actual occasions of experience with a serial order leaves him without categories to interpret the genuinely social dimensions of experience. In the world of Whiteheadean "process," each atomic drop of experience remains impervious to outside social influence during its act of self-creation. As soon as it creates itself, however, it perishes.[66] In such a universe, one person

64. *Ibid.*, p. 73.
65. *Ibid.*, pp. 34-36.
66. For a more detailed discussion of these philosophical issues, see: Gelpi, *The Turn to Experience in Contemporary Theology*, Ch. III.

   In Whitehead's system each occasion of experience perishes within a fraction of a second. Hence, each occasion of experience incorporates within itself an immediate past to which it becomes present; but its immediate perishing makes it difficult to understand how it can experience a real future.

   The atomicity of experience reduces the "society" of actual occasions which constitute what most people mean by a subsisting individual to a series of overlapping occasions of experience. Some argue that the transference of the same subjective aim from one occasion of the same society to the next adequately accounts for the unity of the society. I find the argument unconvincing. Atomicity in Whitehead remains the ultimate fact. As in the case of motion, the transference of the same aim from one occasion of experience to the next could at best give only the illusion of continuity, not real continuity itself.

discoursing with another person about some third reality remains unthinkable.

The philosophical inadequacies of a nominalistic construct of experience would justify rejecting it as a helpful way for thinking any reality, including revealed reality. Unfortunately, however, those inadequacies have not prevented theologians from attempting to use a nominalistic construct of experience theologically. Before I undertake to elaborate an alternative, realistic construct of experience, therefore, I shall reflect on the negative Christological consequences of grounding the theological turn to experience in philosophical nominalism.[67]

Schillebeeckx's nominalistic, di-polar construct of experience structures his entire effort to lay systematic New Testament foundations for Christology. His first volume, *Jesus*, attempts to endow Christological faith with its concrete, perceptual content. In the first volume, Schillebeeckx uses the methods of redaction criticism in order to summarize somewhat conservatively the results of the second quest for the historical Jesus. His second volume, *Christ*, attempts to supply Christology with its conceptual content by comparing and contrasting New Testament theologies of grace. In his third volume, *Church*, he summarizes the first two volumes and appends miscellaneous reflections on the democratization of the Catholic church.

Schillebeeckx recognizes perfectly well that redaction criticism does not yield raw, sensible perceptions of Jesus of Nazareth but a theoretical reconstruction of the bare historical facts of His ministry. In *Jesus* therefore he attempts to summarize what one can say about the mortal ministry of Jesus either with certitude or with high probability. In the end, however, he believes that only the rational use of redaction criticism gives cognitive access to the "facts" about Jesus. In other words, he invokes the rational use of historical-critical method in order to supply Christological faith with its "perceptual content."[68]

As long as Schillebeeckx deals with bare historical facts about Jesus' mortal ministry, his method serves him well. When, however, he comes to discuss Jesus' resurrection, he reaches the limits both of his method and of his nominalistic construct of experience; for in the last analysis Schillebeeckx attempts to ground resurrection faith in the disciples' subjective experience of conversion, of having been "saved" by Jesus. Schillebeeckx does not deny the reality of the resurrection; nor, however, does he ground it in an experience of encounter with the risen Christ.[69]

---

67. For a more detailed philosophical and theological discussion of these issues, see: Donald L. Gelpi, S.J., *The Turn to Experience in Contemporary Theology* (Mahwah, NJ: Paulist Press, 1994).
68. Cf. Schillebeeckx, *Interim Report*, pp. 10-16, 20-35.
69. Cf. Schillebeeckx, *Interim Report*, pp. 93-99.

Pheme Perkins and Reginald Fuller have summarized the chief exegetical problems with Schillebeeckx's handling of the resurrection. They argue quite persuasively that: 1) Schillebeeckx's attempt to ground belief in an empty tomb in an annual tomb cult in Jerusalem has not a shred of evidence to support it. 2) One cannot get behind the appearances of the risen Christ to some more primitive religious datum, as Schillebeeckx seems to suggest. "He was seen" provides Christian faith in the resurrection with its most primitive datum. 3) The New Testament does not support Schillebeeckx's contention that the first Christians inferred the reality of the resurrection. On the contrary, throughout the New Testament the resurrection bursts in upon the disciples as something wholly unexpected, even incredible. 4) When Schillebeeckx suggests that the apostles deduced the reality of the resurrection from a subjective experience of conversion, he confuses effect with cause. In the New Testament those who saw the risen Christ experienced a conversion; but that conversion resulted from their encounter with the risen Christ, which preceded it causally.[70]

I find all of these criticisms sound. I only note here that Schillebeeckx's espousal of a nominalistic construct of experience ultimately motivates his inability to deal theologically with the Christian experience of the risen Christ. In the nominalistic world which Schillebeeckx inhabits, only concrete sensible facts can endow conceptual interpretations with content. Because he realizes that he cannot reduce the resurrection of Jesus to a concrete sense datum, Schillebeeckx finds himself forced to ground resurrection faith subjectively and conceptually: namely, in a subjective experience of conversion.

A Christology which cannot give an adequate theological account of the resurrection remains, however, fatally flawed; for Christian faith in Jesus as messiah and Lord grounds itself remotely in Jesus' mortal ministry but proximately and ultimately in the apostolic encounter with the risen Christ.[71] If in making the turn to experience, one endorses a philosophical construct of experience which forbids one to talk about an encounter with the risen Christ, then, one invokes philosophical reason in order to undercut the experiential basis for all Christological belief. One thinks, in other words, like an Enlightenment fundamentalist.

70. Cf. Reginald Fuller and Pheme Perkins, *Who is This Christ? Gospel Christianity and Contemporary Faith* (Philadelphia, PA: Fortress, 1983), pp. 28-37. For further criticisms of Schillebeeckx on the resurrection, see: Gerald O'Collins, *What Are They Saying About Jesus? Second Edition* (New York, NY: Paulist, 1983), pp. 57-63; *Jesus Risen: An Historical, Fundamental and Systematic examination of Christ's Resurrection* (New York, NY: Paulist, 1987).

71. Wolfhard Pannenberg correctly argues that resurrection faith must ground any attempt to formulate a Christological faith; see: Wolfhard Pannenberg, *Jesus God and Man*, translated by Lewis L. Wilkins and Duane A. Friebe (London: SCM Press, 1968).

Process theology in this country has produced several "Christologies." Like good Enlightenment fundamentalists, all of them approach Christology with the methodological assumption that Whitehead's cosmology supplies the basic content of Christian revelation.

Whitehead called his cosmology a philosophy of organism. In other words, "organism" provides Whitehead's system with its root metaphor. In Whitehead's cosmos, all realities relate organically, including God and the world. As a consequence, Whitehead's God needs the world in order to become God as much as the world needs God in order to become the world. Whitehead puts it this way: "It is as true to say that God creates the world, as that the world creates God."[72]

Process theology, therefore, reduces the experience of divine grace to what Whitehead calls "reversion," or the experience of creative novelty.[73] When reversion happens, a finite, spatio- temporal experience grasps, or "prehends," an idea in the mind of God which has yet to find concrete, physical embodiment in the experience in question. Since reversion supposedly explains creative advance, process theology equates the creation of the world with its gracing. The order of creation and the order of redemption fuse.

In process Christology, this theologically confused, naturalistic understanding of divine grace holds the key to the presence of God in Jesus. In the Jesus of process theology, one finds only a human being who cooperated with divine creativity more successfully than anybody else, at least to date.[74] In other words, process theology has so far managed to articulate nothing more than a Jesusology, not a Christology in the strict sense of the term. The "Christ" of process thought remains finally indistinguishable from the Jesus of Unitarian faith.[75]

In this chapter, I have undertaken to examine dialectically the inadequacies of several philosophical constructs of the human which theologians have invoked in formulating a Christology. This dialectical examination has served an important purpose: it has alerted us to the fact that serious philosophical inadequacies in one's understanding of the human

---

72. Cf. Whitehead, *Process and Reality*, p. 348.

73. *Ibid.*, pp. 26, 160-162.

74. Cf. W. Norman Pittenger, *The Word Incarnate: A Study of the Doctrine of the Person of Christ* (London: James Nisbit, 1959), pp. 100-236; *Christology Reconsidered* (London: SCM Press, 1970); David R. Griffin, *A Process Christology* (Philadelphia, PA: Westminster, 1973), pp. 9-24, 53-89; John B. Cobb, *Christ in a Pluralistic Age* (Philadelphia, PA: Westminster, 1975), pp. 62-95, 97-258; Marjorie Hewett Suchocki, *God, Christ, Church: A Practical Guide to Process Theology* (New York, NY: Crossroad, 1982), pp. 93-109.

75. Cf. Prescott B. Wintersteen, *Christology in American Unitarianism: An Anthology of Nineteenth and Twentieth Century Unitarian Theologians* (Boston, MA: The Unitarian Universalist Christian Fellowship, 1977).

tend to breed serious confusion in one's attempt to think the union of the divine and of the human in Jesus.

In the next chapter, I shall argue that the classical North American philosophical tradition offers the resources for constructing an experiential construct of humanity which avoids all of the philosophical fallacies rejected in this chapter. At the very least, therefore, it promises to bypass past philosophical blunders which have confused the theological attempt to understand the relationship of the divine and of the human in Jesus.

Chapter 5
Humanity As Experience

In the preceding chapter I reflected dialectically on three impulses in the development of Christology which throw light on the way not to understand Jesus' humanity. In this chapter I shall present a construct of the human which avoids all these pitfalls from the past. My construct avoids dualism by conceiving all reality as relational. It avoids essentialism by refusing to transform fallible human evaluative responses into metaphysical principles. It avoids Augustinian anthropological pessimism by conceding that humans can perform naturally good acts. It avoids over-optimism by insisting on the radical finitude of all human experience and of its natural loves. It avoids nominalism by presenting a realistic, triadic construct of experience which leaves it open to the possibility of religious experience.

This chapter, then, divides into three parts. The first part begins to explore the implications of defining reality realistically as experience. It offers a descriptive phenomenology of the three variables which give dynamic structure to the higher forms of experience. The first part of this chapter closes with a proposal for verifying a triadic construct of experience as a metaphysical category.

Part two begins to clarify the implications of defining experience in triadic, realistic, social terms. Part two ponders the personal character of human experience. It therefore begins to endow with logical precision the following key anthropological terms: "person," "consciousness," "autonomy," "freedom," "symbol," and "institution."

The third and final part of this chapter tests the construct of experience for its ability to avoid the fallacious conceptions of the human anatomized in the preceding chapter.

(I)

Like Whitehead's philosophy of organism, the construct of experience which I shall propose aspires to metaphysical universality. In other words, it suggests that any reality one encounters ought to exemplify an "experience" in the sense in which I shall define that term.

People trained in substance philosophy need to shift mental gears in order to equate the terms "reality" and "experience." In substance philosophy experiences can only modify substances accidentally. They do not define the "essence" of those substances. In a universe of substances, experiences exemplify psychological events, rather than subsistent reality. The metaphysical turn to experience, however, replaces substantialist thinking with functional thinking; and that shift allows one to re-conceive experience as a metaphysical category.

If one endorses some version of Whitehead's reformed subjectivist principle,[1] as I do, then anything which exists must exemplify experience. Moreover, in a world of emerging experiences, the essence of anything results, not from its "substantial form" but from its history. Things become what they are as experience evolves.

The metaphysics of experience which I shall propose, however, revises Whitehead's reformed subjectivist principle. It replaces Whitehead's di-polar, nominalistic construct of experience with a realistic, triadic, social construct of experience.

That substitution allows for a more adequate account of the social dimensions of experience. While Whitehead's subjectivist principle requires that each atomic occasion of experience create itself in causal isolation from any outside influence, the realistic, social construct of experience which I shall defend holds that each emerging experience creates itself in social dialogue with environing realities, including the all-encompassing reality of God.

My construct of experience also replaces the atomicity of Whiteheadean experience with Peirce's doctrine of synechism. Synechism holds for real continuity in development and grounds that continuity in the laws which cause and explain all evaluation and decision. Synechism also discovers in living things the capacity to develop new habits, new general tendencies.

In a synechistic view of the human, then, habit-taking accounts for continuity in development. The newly acquired habits do not, however, modify the emerging human self accidentally. Instead, they enter into the human self's developing, autonomously functioning, constitutive reality.

The transformation of experience from an accidental, psychological category into a metaphysical one universally applicable in intent also demands that one concede philosophically that the realities encountered in experience stand within experience itself, not outside it. If, as Kant did, one locates the objects of experience outside of experience, then one can never experience things themselves.

A realistic view of experience, one which affirms the human mind's ability to experience realities other than itself, requires therefore that experienced realities stand within an experience, not outside it. In that case the realities one experiences constitute the "what" of experience, and one's

---

1. Whitehead's reformed subjectivist principle asserts: "Apart from the experiences of subjects there is nothing, nothing, nothing, bare nothingness." The subject in question does not underlie experience. Instead it exemplifies and embodies experience. Cf. Alfred North Whitehead, *Process and Reality: An Essay in Cosmology*, edited by David Ray Griffin and Donald W. Sherburne (New York, NY: Macmillan, 1978), p. 167.

evaluative response to those realities constitutes the "how" of experience. In a metaphysics of experience the "what" and the "how" of experience define the two interrelated realms of reality, or Being.

Why ought one to endorse such a fallible metaphysical hypothesis? For the same reason one ought to endorse any fallible philosophical hypothesis: namely, that one finds it interesting and metaphysically promising. A promising metaphysical hypothesis interprets some realities, probably interprets others, and could conceivably interpret any reality whatever. Its promise makes it metaphysically interesting. By the end of this study, I would hope that the reader would have the wherewithal to decide whether or not to endorse at least tentatively the metaphysics of experience which I shall propose, develop, and test.

Every metaphysics systematically rationalizes some root metaphor for reality in general. Plato and Aristotle imagined reality as an idea. Aquinas imagined it as an act. Mechanists, fallaciously in my judgment, imagine reality as a machine. Whitehead imagined reality as an organism. I am suggesting that we begin to explore in a systematic way the logical consequences of imagining reality as experience.[2]

One begins to transform a root metaphor into a fallible metaphysical hypothesis by rendering it as a logical definition. I define an experience as "a process made up of relational elements called feelings."

The higher forms of experience exhibit three kinds of feelings: decisions, tendencies, and evaluations. Decisions define the realm of concrete actions, or facts. Tendencies define the realm of subsisting general habits, or laws; evaluations define the realm of particular qualities, or of essences.[3]

Evaluation

Let us, then, begin by exploring the realm of human evaluation. Human evaluative responses develop in a continuum which stretches from sensation to emotion, from emotion to imagination, from imagination to rational inference, from rational inference to deliberation.

Do sensations like sight, feeling, taste, touch, and smell qualify as evaluative responses? In Aristotelian anthropology, sensation belongs to the

2. For a discussion of the relationship between root metaphors and metaphysical (or "world") hypotheses, see: Stephen Pepper, *World Hypotheses: A Study in Evidence* (Berkeley, CA: University of California Press, 1948).

3. In a social, realistic, triadic construct of experience, both evaluations and decisions exemplify actions, but different kinds of actions. Evaluations exemplify both conscious and unconscious cognitive activity. Decisions exemplify actions with environmental impact. Either decisions affect one's own body, the environment from which every self emerges most immediately; or decisions have impact on one's body's surrounding environment. The latter create the social links among selves. Since decisions also create the habitual tendencies which shape experience, the kinds of decisions one takes define the kind of self one eventually becomes.

realm of cognition rather than to the realm of desire. Close scientific studies of sensation, however, call into question the artificial separation of sensation from emotion. Those studies reveal that sensations themselves have emotional coloring.[4] In the triadic construct of experience I am suggesting, affections function initially as emotionally colored modes of sensation. As we shall see, however, in the course of its development, affections also exercise a judgmental function.

A personal anecdote may help illustrate the emotive coloring of sensory experience. Years ago I taught high school in New Orleans. For some strange reason, someone had painted the walls of our recreation room red. The minister of our community, who cared for the house upkeep, blessedly decided to repaint the walls. He chose a light green as the color. A few weeks after we had begun using the repainted room, someone noticed that we were having half as many arguments as we had before the minister had the walls painted. We realized that at some unconscious level the redness of the walls had caused us to "see red."

Painters understand well the affective meaning of color. Georgia O'Keefe once remarked that she preferred paint to words as a medium of imaginative expression because colors communicate more precisely than words. Other forms of sensory awareness exhibit a similar emotional coloring. Emotions, then, even when sense-bound, disclose to us in a vague, initial way the tendencies inherent in the realities we sense.

As the affective element in sensation develops it expands to include the sympathetic and the negative emotions. Friendship, affection, romance, sympathy, compassion all exemplify sympathetic feelings. Shame, guilt, fear, anger, rage, panic all exemplify negative emotions.

When they express realistic responses to reality, negative responses make a positive contribution to experience as a whole. Realistic fear tells me that I am confronting a threatening reality stronger than myself. Anger tells me that I am confronting a threatening reality with which I can probably deal. Realistic guilt tells me I have done something I should not have done. Despite their potentially positive function, these emotions qualify as negative, because they function within intuitive perceptions of reality analogously to the way in which the adverb "not" functions in abstract speech.

Memory stores past experiences. Spontaneous memories resemble after-images in the senses, while reconstructed memories have more of an affinity for imaginative thinking. Children playing follow-the-leader practice imitative recall.

Imagination combines remembered images into new patterns of possibility. Both remembered and imagined images have emotional coloring.

---

4. Cf. Charles Hartshorne, *The Philosophy and Psychology of Sensation* (Chicago: University of Chicago Press, 1945).

Images associated with a given emotion, or affection, help clarify it. Dreams, for example, correctly understood, disclose the character of unconscious feelings. Painting, sculpture, dance, and the other arts transform human feelings about reality into clarifying images which disclose their meaning.

The perceptual link between image and emotion endows the latter with a double function within experience. Emotions, or affections yield initial perceptions of the tendencies present in the things we sense. Fear, for example, tells me that the rattler coiled on the ground in front of me could cause me harm. The sight of a friend fills me with joyful anticipation. As images and emotions interact within intuitive thinking, they clarify into judgments of feeling.

Natural[5] affective judgments divide initially into aesthetic and prudential judgments. I shall consider each in turn.

Aesthetic judgments of affection yield a felt, intuitive grasp of reality as beautiful, i.e., as simultaneously good and true. Within the act of artistic creation, aesthetic judgments tell artists whether or not they have shaped the medium in which they are working in ways which express their intuition of beauty. In the viewer and the critic, aesthetic judgments perceive and evaluate the significance of artistic and literary creations.

Prudential judgments of affection divide into practical and moral judgments. Practical judgments deal with pragmatic goods; prudential judgments deal with ethical goods.

The creative human imagination gives symbolic expression to aesthetic judgments of feeling in lyrics, narratives, dramas, dance, sculpture, painting. It gives expression to practical judgments in plans and projects. One uses the imagination in order to plan trips and business ventures, campaigns, and different kinds of strategies. Aesthetic judgments concern themselves with communicating to others an intuitive insight into reality. Practical judgments concern themselves with getting things done.

Prudential judgments of affection also take the form of judgments of conscience. Judgments of conscience measure human actions against realities, ideals, principles, and values which one has interiorized personally as making absolute and ultimate claims upon one's conduct. One affirms realities, ideals, principles, and values as morally ultimate when one stands willing not only to live for them but also, if necessary, to die for them. One affirms realities, ideals, principles, and values absolutely when one acknowledges their claim on one's conscience in all circumstances. The invocation of absolute and ultimate goods endows prudential thinking with a moral character.

---

5. As we shall see below, natural responses develop in complete abstraction from the historical self-revelation of God.

Judgments of affection can express only intuitive responses to reality. On occasion, however, they can also engage inferential forms of thought. Before one can reflect on such prudential forms of reasoning, however, one needs to understand how strictly rational, inferential thinking works.

I have been describing intuitive evaluations. All strictly rational, inferential thinking also begins intuitively. No one can tell a scientist, scholar, or philosopher how to come up with the right hypothesis. The hypothetical mind needs to play imaginatively with the data it is trying to explain.

Models mediate between intuitive and rational thought. For example, once atomic physicists decided to imagine the atom like a tiny solar system, they could begin making hypotheses about the way atoms act. Besides imaginative models, the rational mind can also employ mathematical models or scale models. Root metaphors provide imaginative models for metaphysical hypotheses.

Hypothetical, or abductive, inference begins intuitively, but it concludes rationally. A formulated hypothesis, as we have seen, offers a new way of categorizing inferentially data one desires to understand. Rational categories define the nature of things with logical precision. When, for example, Columbus decided to call the world "round" rather than "flat" he replaced one rational definition of the world with another. Moreover, as we have seen, rational categories offer conceptual definitions of things based on an assumption about the laws they obey: i.e., about the way they "ought" to behave under specifiable circumstances.

Deductive inference, as we have also seen, spells out the operational consequences of an hypothesis. It predicts that if one has guessed correctly the law or laws which ground one's categorization of reality, then other facts, not yet in evidence, will under specifiable conditions present themselves in experience. Columbus, for example, deduced from the roundness of the world that he could reach the Orient by sailing west.

Inductive inference verifies or falsifies an hypothesis by deciding whether or not the laws which ground it obtain in reality. Thus, the successful circumnavigation of the globe proved that Columbus had correctly assumed that the laws of nature had made the earth round, not flat.

Inferences exemplify complicated acts of reasoning. Linguistic propositions render those acts in a kind of verbal shorthand.

Aesthetic, practical, and prudential reasoning engage both intuitive judgments of emotion and inferential judgments. Architects, for example, need to understand the properties of the materials they use in building as well as the mathematics of stress; but they need creative imaginations in order to design truly beautiful buildings. If plumbers and fisher-folk expect to get the job done, they need to learn the rules of their trade; but they also need the intuitive insights of common sense. Ethical reasoning involves ideals and principles but it also demands a sound insight into the facts and forces ingredient in the moral situation which puzzles the conscience.

Aesthetic and prudential reasoning both advance primarily through prudential deliberation. The deliberating mind weighs the realistic advantages and disadvantages of contrasting evaluations and decisions. Even when the three forms of deliberative reasoning invoke inferential insights, because they deal with particular situations, they ordinarily reach a decision finally, not on the basis of an abstract inference, but on the basis of a sense of the fitting. A sense of the fitting yields a felt, appreciative insight[6] into the course of action appropriate to a given situation. In other words, in these three forms of reasoning the intuitive mind makes the final judgment, even though rational motives function suasively in one's choice of options.

Deliberative thinking engages all three variables which structure human experience. It seeks to build a bridge between the ideal and the real through the mediation of the actual. Let us try to understand what the preceding statement means.

Ideals exemplify conceptual possibilities, or the realm of value. Ideals open up a vision of the way reality ought develop under the best of circumstances.

Decisions make ideals actual because the evaluations a decision terminates define its character. Decisions also create new habits or re-enforce old ones. Decisions, therefore, also create personal and institutional modes of behavior; for institutions, as we shall soon see, consist of habitual patterns of publicly sanctioned group behavior.

Ideals exemplify possibilities; decisions, actualities; and tendencies, realities. By concretizing possibilities and transforming them into tendencies, decisions mediate between the ideal and the real. To put the same insight a bit more concretely, in all deliberative thinking, the human mind weighs alternative possibilities whose actualization through choice, or decision, promises to change the way in which people respond habitually to the world, to one another, or to both.

Aesthetic ideals seek to transform habitual modes of intuitive perception. Impressionists and luminists created works of art which sought to teach people to see light in a new way. Similarly, shifts in musical style sensitize people to new and different realms of auditory perception.

Practical ideals seek to reshape the environment in a way which will transform personal and social behavior. People build bridges to re-route

---

6. Bernard Meland has written extensively and often insightfully on appreciative forms of knowing. Cf. J.J. Mueller, *Faith and Appreciative Awareness: The Cultural Theology of Bernard Meland* (Washington, D.C.: University Press of America, 1981).

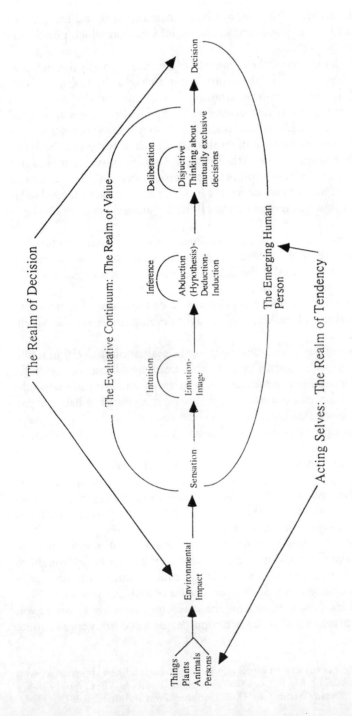

DIAGRAM 1: THE REALMS OF EXPERIENCE

traffic. They dig mines in order to extract and market commercially valuable ores.

Ethical ideals seek to realize a vision of human life and society which makes ultimate and absolute claims upon the conscience. Moral reasoning seeks to transform the way people perceive and respond to abiding personal and social responsibilities of ultimate significance.

Moral Deliberation

The dynamic structure of the human conscience illustrates well the way in which deliberative thinking works. In the formation of conscience, one needs first to reach clarity about the kinds of moral ideals to which one stands personally committed. As I have already explained, an ideal takes on a moral character, when one perceives it as not only worth living for but also, if necessary, worth dying for. It also takes on an moral character when it claims one in all circumstances. Moral ideals include a vision of interpersonal dealings marked by values like justice, truthfulness, and courage. Moral ideals would also include a vision of the common social good, i.e., of an institutional ordering of society which allows all its members to benefit from its shared goods and to contribute to those same shared goods.

The second step in the formation of conscience requires that one appreciate the values already inherent in any morally problematic situation before one regrets the ways in which they fall short of the moral ideal. A situation becomes morally problematic when it raises questions about correct conscientious behavior for which one has no ready answer. How, for example ought the United States to reform its medical care system in a just and equitable manner? How ought one to respond responsibly to the problems of environmental degradation, population explosion, and world hunger?

One cannot appreciate any situation unless one has also come to terms with those persons or forces within it which threaten one in any way. Threatening situations tend to evoke responses of anger, fear, guilt, or shame. In order to respond realistically to the challenge of a morally problematic situation one must make sure that such affective attitudes do not blind one to those elements in the situation genuinely worth conserving.

Failure to confront the threatening aspects of a moral situation freezes people in defensive rigidity, erodes communication, and eventually leads to the collapse of reasonable moral discourse. The national debate on health care under the Clinton administration illustrated how such a failure skews moral deliberation. Because the press and the public focused narrowly and rigidly on the cost of health care, they never got around to appreciating its benefits to the nation as a whole, and especially to the poor. Anxiety about higher taxes made it difficult to view the problem with either insight or compassion.

The third stage in the formation of conscience requires that one derive from one's ideals principles which will allow one to choose which course of action could best advance the situation toward the ethical ideals to which one stands committed. Commitment to a just social order would, for example, require that in dealing with an unjust social situation, one not resort to lies, deceit, or other unjust means for undoing the injustice.

The same commitment requires that one use one's imagination in order to devise policies and strategies for creating a situation of genuine equity. Hence, the fourth step of moral reasoning engages the creative imagination. One needs to deliberate creatively and imaginatively in order to decide how best to act in order to advance the moral situation the next possible step toward the ideals to which one stands committed. That step constitutes the fitting moral response to the concrete moral situation one faces.

In questions of interpersonal morality, often principles provide all one needs to reach such a decision. By that I mean that in relatively simple personal moral conflicts, one can often move directly from a principle which expresses the ideals to which one stands morally committed to a decision about which course of action conforms to that principle and promises to advance the situation in which one finds oneself closest to the realization of the ideals one would in principle like to see it embody.

The principle that one ought always to relate to other persons as persons ought, for example, to suffice to convince the conscience about the immorality of sexually abusing a child or of using another adult as a mere sex object. Given a situation, however, in which an adult has already sexually abused a child, the deliberating mind ponders the best means to minimize the evil consequences of the act for all those affected by it.

Complex problems in personal morality will probably force the people involved to agree in the future to certain patterns of behavior. Usually such agreements fall short of public policy statements. In dealing with questions of public morality, however, ordinarily one needs more than ideals and principles in order to resolve complex questions of conscience. Having derived from one's ideals principles which relate to a situation of serious social injustice, one often needs to transform those principles into public policies which promise to undo or at least to mitigate the injustice.

One then proceeds to transform policies into concrete strategies. Strategies offer practical plans of action for implementing policy. In other words, as the conscience struggles with complex situations of social injustice, one transforms ideals into principles, principles into policies, and policies into strategies. In this way, moral deliberation mediates between the social ideals to which one stands ultimately and absolutely committed and the situation one seeks to transform.

The ethical reasoning of the North American bishops in writing *Economic Justice for All*, their pastoral letter on the United States economy illustrates well how conscientious prudential reasoning works. The bishops began with a positive appreciation for the values which the United States economy embodies. They then regretted the shortcomings and injustices of the economic situation, which had worsened during the Reagan administration. They next derived from a Christian ideal of justice principles which ought to guide United States economic policy. They found the principle of preferential option for the poor especially relevant to the elimination of economic injustice. On the basis of that principle, they suggested specific policies for reforming United States economic institutions. Finally, they left it to those who deal directly with the economy to devise the concrete strategies which might begin to transforms those policies into more just social institutions.

In an experiential construct of the human, the mind engages in three kinds of thinking: intuitive, inferential, and deliberative. In all three forms of thinking the creative imagination plays a central and indispensable role. In intuitive thinking, the creative imagination gives rise to art, to literature, to ritual. In inferential thinking, the creative imagination formulates abductions. In deliberative thinking it bridges the gap between the ideal and the actual.

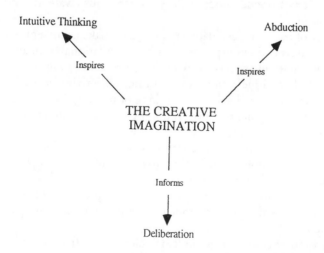

DIAGRAM II: THE CENTRALITY OF IMAGINATIVE CREATIVITY

The Evaluative Continuum

I have just described a complex spectrum of human evaluative responses. Every evaluative response enjoys particularity. In itself it exemplifies "particular suchness." Red is not giraffe is not triangle is not 52. Particular values become individual, universal, or general through use as predicates. I may intend by the term giraffe, this giraffe, all giraffes, or some giraffes. In other words, cognitive use transforms particular evaluative responses into intentional relationships.

Intentionality and connotation knit the realm of value together into a continuum of feeling. Affections link sensations with remembered and imaginative images. Imaginative thinking links intuitive and inferential thinking. Logical relations link one kind of inference to another. Both intuition and inference can inform prudential thinking. Rational inferential thinking has felt, intuitive connotations, just as intuitive thinking can have inferential connotations. Thus, the evaluative continuum stretches from sensation to memory to imagination to inference to deliberation.

Besides particularity and continuity, human evaluative responses enjoy presentational immediacy. By that I mean that through conscious evaluations, I become present to my world.

Human consciousness emerges with the ability to distinguish between one's own body and the realities in one's surrounding environment which act upon it and to which one responds. When that awareness fades we go to sleep; but a loud noise or a physical touch will waken us. On waking, we find our senses flooded once again with conscious awareness of the realities around us.

The ability of conscious evaluative responses to make us present to our world and it to us endows experience with "presentational immediacy." We have, therefore, no experience of a valueless presence to reality. Contrary to the Enlightenment myth of scientific "objectivity," the human mind has no experience of valueless thinking or judging. Even the most abstract scientific judgments endow the world with a certain kind of explanatory value.

Besides enjoying particularity, continuity, and presentational immediacy, human evaluations ground the experience of real as opposed to clock time. Let us reflect on how this occurs.

Presentational immediacy yields a sense of the present moment. As experience develops the present moment acquires temporal complexity and thickness.

The sensation of color, for example, which occurs a fraction of a second after light strikes the retina makes one visually present to one's world. The sensation of color, therefore, makes the past fact of light rays striking the retina present. Something analogous happens in other sensations.

As we respond emotionally to things, the vague sense of tendency present within sensation acquires initial imaginative clarity and therefore begins to endow sensory experience with a future. Fear of a coiled snake tells me vaguely that it might act in harmful ways. Longing speaks to me of possible future joy.

Imaginative thinking yields a clarified appreciative insight into the forces or tendencies vaguely disclosed by emotion. It therefore enhances one's sense of future possibility. When we focus our affections on the future we hope.

Judgments of affection, whether aesthetic, practical, or prudential, fix intuitive beliefs and shape attitudes toward one's world. Those attitudes help define the way in which one chooses habitually to be present to one's world.

Hypothetical thinking endows intuitive thinking with rational clarity and yields a heightened, though highly focused, sense of presence. Once I know that the dull ache in my tummy results from a stomach ulcer and not from heart burn or from cancer, I know how to deal with it. Clear rational definitions, however, often omit through abstraction more than they disclose consciously. Still, through hypothetical thinking, I become present to my world with a new conceptual vividness.

Deductive thinking transforms hypothetical presence into a future by anticipating its operational consequences. Inductive thinking transforms a rationally anticipated future into a present reality by either verifying or falsifying deductively anticipated consequences.

Prudential reasoning weighs alternative possible futures and decides which to actualize through decision.

Decisions

Every time I act decisively, I determine to do this rather than that. Decisions make experience concrete. They define the realm of fact. Concreteness, therefore, characterizes decision in the same way in which particularity characterizes value. Every value exemplifies particular suchness, while every decision embodies a this. Every this enjoys actuality, while in and of itself a value discloses only possibility. Every this differs from every other that.

Decisions express the evaluative processes they terminate and actualize. When they terminate emotions, decisions express joy, fear, sympathy, affection, rage, friendship, shame, guilt, sorrow, compassion. One can also decide either imaginatively or rationally. Imaginative actions terminate intuitive insights, while rational actions terminate inferences. In the dynamic flow of human experience, therefore, the realm of value defines the character of the realm of fact.

The connotations which link human evaluative responses can also make intuitive perceptions more or less rational and rational perceptions more or less intuitive and affect-laden. Given the connotative complexity of their evaluative responses, humans find it virtually impossible to decide from purely rational or from purely intuitive motives. Similarly, decisions can express conscious or unconscious motives; often they express some combination of the two.

Decisions whose impact extends beyond one's own body create the social bonds among acting selves. The persons and things which act upon me disclose themselves to me in acting. As we shall see, all decisive events signify something; but, because they can express conscious evaluative responses, actions can also function symbolically in human communication.

Tendency

Decisions also mediate between the first and third realms of experience, between evaluation and tendency. Every decision either creates a new habit of activity or re-enforces an old one. As long as I do not know what to believe about a person. I have no habitual way of responding to the individual in question. When I fix my beliefs about persons or things, by that decision I create within myself a tendency to act toward them in a specific way in the future. If, for example, I judge someone untrustworthy, I tend to disbelieve the things he or she says. Similarly, a burned child tends to fear fire. If I tend to act impulsively out of anxiety, every time I yield to impulse out of fear I re-enforce my tendency to respond that way.

Tendencies ground and explain actions, whether those actions take the form of evaluation or of decision. They ground actions by giving rise to them causally. They explain actions and evaluations when some mind grasps that causal relationship.

As we have seen, evaluations exemplify particularity and possibility. Decisions exemplify concreteness and actuality. They make experience this rather than that.

Tendencies, however, exemplify real generality. Human experience develops habits both of evaluation and of decision. The capacity to think mathematically differs, for example, from specific mathematical judgments. It constitutes a relatively permanent part of the mathematician's personality, whether the mathematician is solving equations or not. Professional harpsichordists enjoy the ability to play whether they perform or not. Habits, of course, can atrophy through disuse. That fact further dramatizes the link between decision and tendency.

The habitual tendencies which shape experience endow it with a general orientation to certain kinds of evaluative and decisive response. That general orientation endows experience with real generality, as opposed to conceptual particularity or decisive concreteness. Real generality orients experience toward its future.

Each realm of experience exhibits traits which define its constitutive character and prevent one from reducing one to the other. Particularity and possibility differ from concreteness and actuality. As a consequence, one must never confuse a decision with a value. In the same way, the traits which characterize value and decision differ from the real generality which characterizes a tendency.

Despite their irreducibility, however, the three realms of experience play constantly and dynamically into one another. Values define decisions which specify habits which give rise to other values and decisions. The human self emerges from that creative, dynamic interplay.

Every acting self consists, then, of a developing complex of habitual tendencies to react or to respond in specifiable ways. Since decisions create tendencies and since every human self exemplifies an organic complex of tendencies, one creates the kind of self one becomes in the course of a lifetime by the sum total of one's conscious and unconscious decisions. Moreover, one does so, not in splendid Cartesian isolation, as Whitehead has suggested, but in constant interaction with one's world and with other persons. That interaction endows the process of self-creation with its environmental and social character.

In the creation of the self, the creative human imagination once again plays a central and constitutive role. Indeed, imaginative creativity defines the human much more fundamentally than does abstract reasoning, since, as we have seen, it inspires all three forms of human evaluative response: intuition, inference, and deliberation. Moreover, as we shall soon see in greater detail, not every human person acquires the ability to reason abstractly. Instead of defining the human as a rational animal, we would do better to define the human as an imaginatively creative animal.

Every self-creating self emerges from an environment. The body provides finite selves with the immediate environment from which they emerge. The human body consists of elements appropriated from one's surrounding environment through ingesting them. Those elements one organizes largely unconsciously into a physical life-support system.

The body, however, anchors the self in a larger environment which may prove more or less nurturing, more or less threatening. When, however, the physical forces of nature threaten us they do so without malice. Earthquakes, hurricanes, drought may take a terrible toll on human life; but they act in oblivion of human suffering rather than with vindictiveness.

Communities of other persons potentially constitute the most significant and sustaining forces in the human environment. Those same communities can, however, act with immense destructiveness. Think, for example, of the Second World War, of the Nazi Holocaust, of the atomic incineration of civilians at Hiroshima and Nagasaki.

From Phenomenology to Metaphysics

I have in this section presented a phenomenology of human experience. One begins to change that phenomenology into a metaphysics when one concedes the existence, the being, the givenness of all three realms of experience.

In order to endow a triadic construct of experience with metaphysical applicability, however, one needs to make a plausible argument for the fact that the kinds of feelings which one discovers in human experience function in any reality whatever.

In *The Divine Mother* I argued for the legitimacy of conceiving the triune God as the supreme exemplification of a triadic, social experience. I shall not repeat that argument here, although I shall summarize it in the third volume of this study. Here I content myself with suggesting a speculative strategy for endowing the term "experience" with universal, metaphysical predicability. If the argument of *The Divine Mother* holds, then one can apply a triadic, realistic, social construct of experience both to humans and to God. In volume three, I shall show that a realistic, triadic metaphysics of experience can also interpret the historical incarnation of a divine person. There I shall argue that in Jesus one encounters the thoroughly human experience of being a divine person.

Can one also extend that same construct of experience to sub-human realities. The higher forms of animal life give behavioral evidence of the capacity to respond evaluatively and decisively. Dogs bark, growl, and wag their tails to express how they feel. They give evidence of dreaming. They can learn within fairly narrow limits. They give no evidence, however, of abstract inferential thinking, although tool-using animals like chimpanzees do seem to make simple, concrete inferences. Every animal counts as a developing self, although they do not exhibit the self-conscious responsibility which characterizes personal human selves.

Animals, like humans, respond both consciously and evaluatively to reality. Conscious evaluative response, however, shades off into the preconscious and the unconscious. We can recall preconscious experience. Unconscious evaluations, however, resist conscious recall.

How far into sub-human reality does unconscious evaluation extend? When a mollusk ingests food, does it feel that food unconsciously? Our stomachs know what to do with food even though the conscious mind has no awareness of the details of digestion.

Whitehead believed that we know with our bodies. His reformed subjectivist principle therefore extended unconscious evaluation to the most primitive kinds of physical events. Whiteheadean electrons and protons feel physical reality evaluatively.

Whitehead's di-polar construct of experience also forced him to extend evaluation into the smallest physical events, because Whitehead believed that any process which exemplifies novelty, including subatomic changes, must prehend an eternal object, or value, not yet ingredient in it.

The triadic construct of experience which I have just proposed lies under no such constraint. My construct leaves it to positive science to decide whether or not purely physical processes give evidence of evaluative discrimination. If they do, then the same three variables structure them as shape the higher forms of experience, albeit unconsciously.

If, on the other hand, physical processes lack an evaluative component, in a realistic, triadic metaphysics of experience they still count as experiences because they exemplify a process made up of relational elements called feelings. Unconscious feelings, to be sure, but dynamic and relational nevertheless. Without an evaluative component, however, purely physical processes would exemplify only two kinds of unconscious feelings: tendencies and decisions.

To argue exhaustively and systematically for the plausibility of applying to all reality the category "experience" in the sense in which I have defined it would take us far afield. In a Christological context, a metaphysics of human experience provides a possible way of understanding Jesus' humanity philosophically. In volume three, I shall show that one can interpret both the trinity and the incarnation in experiential metaphysical categories. I therefore rest content for the moment with indicating a general strategy for arguing the universal applicability and adequacy of a triadic construct of experience. Moreover, in the chapters which immediately follow this one, I shall demonstrate that a realistic, triadic, social construct of experience can indeed interpret the results of close empirical studies of the human.

In the first section of this chapter, I have, then, explored descriptively the shape of human experience and proposed a speculative strategy for transforming the category "experience" into a metaphysical category. In the section which follows I shall clarify deductively the meaning of the metaphysical hypothesis I have just proposed by examining some of its operational consequences. Specifically, I shall reflect on the way in which human experience becomes fully personal.

(II)

The preceding section outlined a particular construct of human experience. How in such a philosophical frame of reference does one understand personal human existence? The pragmatic logic which this study employs requires that one clarify any hypothesis, including a metaphysical one, by deducing its operational consequences. In order, therefore, to define the term "person" pragmatically, one needs to explore practically how a human experience becomes fully personal.

The Human Person

Any autonomously functioning reality qualifies as a self. Minerals, plants, and animals all exemplify selves. Minerals act on one another. Plants in addition grow and reproduce. Animals besides growing and reproducing also sense. More complex forms of animal life remember and think intuitively.

Some selves, however, also qualify as human persons. As acting selves human persons share some descriptive traits in common with animals. Let us then begin a descriptive exploration of personal behavior in an attempt to isolate those activities which characterize persons as such.

1) Human persons, like all selves, act autonomously. By that I mean that they initiate their own evaluations and decisions. Humans, moreover, experience autonomy as incommunicable. I can in a given circumstance refuse to act; but I cannot transfer to you my own power to decide. You cannot digest my food for me, learn for me, exercise in ways which will develop my body. In this respect humans differ in no way from plants, animals, or minerals.

2) Human persons, like all living things, also enjoy continuity of life. The self emerges from its history. As a consequence, some habits link the self one embodied at age two with the self one embodies at age sixty-two. The emerging human self, like other living selves, consists, then, of an autonomous developing complex of habitual responses. These habits do not modify the self accidentally. Rather they define its very reality.

3) The relational character of personal existence exemplifies the relational character of experience in general, which synthesizes three kinds of relationships, or feelings: conceptual (or intentional) relationships, factual (or decisive) relationships, and general (or habitual) relationships. Human persons relate conceptually, decisively, and habitually. The same three variables would seem to structure at least to some degree the higher forms of animal life.

4) Human persons enjoy the capacity for critical, creative, self-conscious activity. They can reflect on what they have done, learn from their mistakes, and modify their behavior in the light of such insights. Here one encounters distinctively personal behavior. All conscious animal life enjoys, of course, some measure of self-awareness. Animals, however, do not learn with the same facility as humans; nor do they exhibit the same kind of self-critical awareness which interiorizes ideals and norms and then measures subsequent behavior by them.

The relational character of experience makes all experience a transaction with a world. Human persons, however, become fully personal only in relationship to other persons. Children grow to mature adulthood in family environments which nurture such maturity in them. Human desire has a mimetic character: we imitate people we admire in the hope of resembling them. Mimesis motivates both collaboration and competition.[7]

5) Finally and most characteristically, human persons exhibit the capacity for conversion. One converts when one passes from irresponsible to responsible behavior in some realm of experience. Conversion personalizes human experience by endowing it with strictly normative, self-conscious responsibility.

When one converts, one comes of age as an adult person. The vital continuity which links the adult convert to the neonate and even to the foetus, however, makes the latter's life also personal. Children do not count as non-persons as pagan Graeco-Roman society falsely assumed. They qualify morally as persons precisely because they have the capacity and therefore the right to develop into fully mature adults. Children, therefore, count as immature persons in process of acquiring the full adult personality which comes only with an integral, five-fold conversion. Those who have yet to convert have all the rights of persons but remain infantile or adolescent in those areas of experience in which conversion has yet to occur.

Children, moreover, learn gradually and incrementally to take responsibility for themselves and for their lives. The process of initial conversion begins, therefore, with the earliest kinds of education and culminates in an initial conversion in which one finally decides to take full adult responsibility for one's person and one's world. Full adult conversion, moreover, always demands the transcendence of conventional wisdom, since conventional human wisdom always inculcates irresponsible behavior along with responsible conduct.

These reflections, therefore, warrant the conclusion that personal existence demands the capacity for self-conscious, fully responsible, social relationships with others like oneself. If, moreover, conversion personalizes experience, then the decisions which bring about initial and ongoing conversion give the notion of person its pragmatic meaning.

If fully responsible behavior personalizes human experience, in what does responsibility consist? Responsible people stand accountable to themselves, to other human persons, and ultimately to God. When I give myself an account of my own behavior, I measure it against norms, principles, ideals, and realities which I acknowledge as making claims upon me. When I give an account of myself to others I seek to justify the motives and

---

7. René Girard, in my judgment, over-exaggerates the competitive character of mimesis. People also imitate one another collaboratively. Think of most human education. Cf. René Girard, *Violence and the Sacred*, translated by Patrick Gregory (Baltimore, MD: The Johns Hopkins University Press, 1971).

social consequences of my choices. When I give an account of myself to a self-revealing, God I reflect on the adequacy or inadequacy of my response of faith.

Human persons can convert affectively, intellectually, morally, socio-politically, and religiously. In every act of conversion one takes a specific kind of responsibility for an identifiable realm of experience. The kind of responsibility one takes depends on the kind of norms which the convert invokes in measuring responsible activity in a given realm of experience.

The affectively converted, for example, commit themselves to cultivating healthy emotional and intuitive responses to reality. The relative health or pathology of emotional responses measures, therefore, the responsibility of affectively converted choices. Emotionally healthy people also cultivate sensitivity to beauty and excellence. Aesthetic norms, therefore, also measure responsible emotional development.

The intellectually converted measure both intuitive judgments of feeling and rational, inferential judgments by norms of truth and falsity, adequacy and inadequacy.

Those converted at a personal moral level measure their actions toward other persons by social rights and duties. Rights and duties flow, not from some fictive, reified *essentia humana*, but from the mutual interdependence of finite, needy persons within community.

Socio-politically converted persons measure the decisions which shape human institutions by the common good. The common good demands that all the members of society have reasonably ready access to its benefits and to the opportunity to contribute to those benefits.

Both forms of moral conversion—personal and socio-political—endow human experience with ultimacy by committing one to ideals, realities, and principles for which one stands willing not only to live but, if necessary, to die.

Theistic religious conversion also imbues the other forms of conversion with ultimacy by orienting the entire person to the ultimate reality of God; for the theistic religious convert responds to the historical self-revelation of God on the terms demanded by that revelation. Such a response exemplifies theistic, religious faith. Christian converts find God revealed normatively and historically in Jesus and in the sanctifying Breath who proceeds from Him.[8]

If the five forms of conversion personalize experience, then an insight into the dynamics of conversion makes the notion of personalization even more practical. By the dynamics of conversion I mean the way in which one form of conversion conditions another in positive, enhancing ways.

---

8. These descriptive traits correspond to the diagnostic definition of "person" which I developed in *The Divine Mother*. Cf. pp. 103-115.

One form of conversion enhances another when it fosters the kind of responsible living which the second conversion demands.

I have already discussed the dynamics and counterdynamics of conversion in the course of reflecting on foundational method. Here I simply identify them as laws which tend either to advance or to undermine the conversion process and with it the personalization of experience.

Conversion transforms one's conscious perceptions of reality by endowing them with responsible realism. Human personal consciousness, however, comes in two forms: individual and communal.

Individual personal consciousness grows by making distinctions and grasping the relationship between distinguished realities. For example, until one knows how to distinguish a sparrow from a finch, all finches look like sparrows. Similarly, once one has distinguished clearly between personal and public morality, one can begin to explore their relationship to one another.

Communal Consciousness

Communities grow in consciousness by much more complex processes of self-interpretation. For a community of any size and longevity to come to shared, communal awareness, it needs to do four things. First, it must reach a consensus about the significance of the events which found it and about the history which links it to those founding events. That consensus yields a shared sense of corporate identity. Second, on the basis of the shared sense of identity which historical self-understanding engenders, a community seeking full self-awareness needs to reach a consensus about the ultimate and proximate future it seeks to embody. Third, that same community must mobilize the gifts of all its members in the realization of the future to which it has committed itself. Finally, a community will grow in responsible shared awareness to the extent that its institutions foster an ongoing, integral, five-fold conversion in all its members. Just as the failure to make realistic distinctions and see real connections diminishes personal consciousness, so too the failure to realize the conditions for communal awareness reduces the shared awareness of communities.

By a symbol I mean anything which mediates the evaluative grasp of significance. The relational, triadic structure of experience endows it with a dynamic symbolic character. Three kinds of symbols function within experience so conceived: physical events (or expressive symbols), uncommunicated evaluations (or interpretative symbols), and communications (or decisive actions which seek to express conscious evaluations).

Physical events signify. By that I mean that they exhibit a dynamic relational structure capable of evaluative interpretation by reflective minds. The physical sciences study expressive symbols, like chemical and physical changes. Expressive symbols could well engage only decisions and the habitual tendencies which ground and explain them. As we have seen, a metaphysics of experience can leave open the question of an unconscious evaluative component in pre-organic processes until physical science solves it. Expressive symbols, however, certainly contain no conscious evaluative component.

Interpretive symbols include the whole gamut of unexpressed human evaluative responses. Humans seek to express in language acts only a relatively small portion of their evaluative responses. Virtually all of those responses, of course, exhibit some degree of social and linguistic conditioning; but, as long as one guards one's evaluative responses in the secrecy of one's heart and mind, those evaluations remain interpretative symbols rather than communications. Interpretative symbols engage evaluations and the habitual tendencies which ground and explain them. Psychology and epistemology both study interpretative symbols.

Communications seek to express in decisive activity some conscious evaluative response to reality. Gestures, artistic creation, speech all exemplify communications. Communications engage all three of the variables which shape experience: evaluations, actions, and tendencies. They embody not only a particular way of evaluating reality but also a particular way of rendering that evaluation symbolically so that others may understand it. Literary and artistic criticism, the social sciences, linguistics, aesthetics, logic, and semeiotic all study human communication. Communications engage two kinds of truth: 1) the truth about what one communicated and 2) whether what one communicated accurately interprets reality.

Communal self-awareness creates the symbolic matrix in which immature persons grow in consciousness and to which mature persons can contribute responsibly. Nevertheless, the historical character of personal and communal awareness makes both irreducibly finite. An individual can think only in the ways in which one has learned to think in the course of a finite lifetime. Similarly, communities with long histories share insights; but they also incarnate shared institutionalized biases, oversights, and errors.

Autonomy and Freedom

As we shall soon see, personal consciousness conditions and qualifies personal freedom. Before exploring that relationship, however, one needs to understand the distinction in relationship between autonomy and freedom.

Autonomy consists of the capacity to initiate activity of any kind, whether evaluative or decisive. Autonomy does not admit of degrees. Either one acts or not. Either John Wilkes Booth shot Abraham Lincoln, or someone else did. Autonomy roots itself in the realm of tendency, or real generality. Tendencies, or laws, cause the actions and evaluations which they therefore explain.

Freedom consists most fundamentally in the ability to act or not to act, to do this or that.; but as we shall see, conversion transforms elementary human freedom into liberty. By liberty, I mean the capacity to aspire to the beautiful, the true, and the good. Freedom, in contrast to autonomy, does admit of degrees. One can find oneself more or less free in different circumstances.

While freedom presupposes autonomy, it roots itself in a different realm of experience from autonomy. Freedom presupposes autonomy, because it consists in a specific way of acting. Without the power to act, one cannot act freely. Still, autonomy resides in the realm of tendency, or law, while freedom resides in the realm of evaluation, or quality, because freedom results ultimately from the capacity to distinguish conceptually, realistic alternatives for choice. The exercise of freedom thus engages deliberative thinking. In other words, the actual exercise of freedom involves autonomy because it consists in the autonomous decision to do this rather than that; but the deliberative thinking which precedes that choice specifies it and therefore makes it more or less free.

Identifiable variables condition freedom and therefore cause it to flicker, to wax and wane. Those variables number five: environmental, conceptual, perspectival, habitual, and decisive.

Environmental variables condition freedom. Some environments offer more realistic options than others; some offer different kinds of options from others. In New York city one may choose on any given night from among the concerts one wants to attend. No such options exist in St. Marys, Kansas. Environmental conditioning means that one can act freely only if one has enough control of one's environment to realize practically what one wants to do.

Conceptual variables also condition freedom. Because freedom results from the capacity to distinguish realistic alternatives for choice, the human capacity to make such distinctions will determine the degree to which one can act freely. The illiterate in the Library of Congress have no freedom to read the millions of volumes on the surrounding shelves, because the illiterate have never learned to distinguish one letter from another and to form them into words and sentences. Similarly, graded readers adapt their text to the learning child's ability to read: to the grammar and syntax which the child's mind has mastered.

Perspectival variables condition freedom. A person who can approach the same problem from a variety of frames of reference will experience greater freedom in solving it than one who cannot.

Habitual variables condition freedom. A concert violinist may decide whether or not to play the Bach chaconne. One who plays only the ukulele has no such option.

Decisive variables condition freedom. Decisions build into the character the habits of activity, the beliefs, and the frames of reference which condition choice. Decisions put one in either exciting or boring environments. Decisions also determine the quality of the satisfactions one cultivates. Ears which have listened only to rap music, for example, will not at first appreciate Palestrina's *Missa Papae Marcelli*.

Besides flickering, human freedom varies qualitatively. Joe Montana has cultivated the skills of a professional football quarterback, skills which few possess. On the field he enjoys a freedom which eludes the university professor placed in similar circumstances. On the other hand, the university professor exhibits a freedom of mastery in his or her field of specialization which eludes the professional athlete. Because both freedom and consciousness root themselves in the realm of evaluation, often the two flicker simultaneously.

One can distinguish three degrees of freedom: elementary freedom, responsible personal freedom, and the responsible search for a just social order free of personal and institutional oppression.

As I have already indicated, elementary human freedom marks the first degree of freedom. It consists in the ability to act or not to act, to do this and not that. Elementary human freedom, therefore, results from the ability in any given circumstance to conceive and to distinguish realistic alternatives for choice. The four forms of personal conversion—affective, intellectual, personal moral, and religious—transform elementary human freedom into responsible personal freedom by making elementary human freedom personally accountable, in the sense defined above.

Responsible personal freedom also endows elementary personal freedom with something like Augustinian *libertas*. By that I mean that the adult convert acquires the ability to aspire freely to the beautiful, the good, and the true. One aspires to beauty when one grasps the good and the true simultaneously with the affective, intuitive mind. The rational mind abstracts the good and the true from the experience of beauty and from one another. Inferential thinking deals with the true. Moral deliberation deals with the good, although the intuitive mind also deliberates about the best way to express the beautiful and the hypothesizing mind deliberates about the best way to formulate a truth. The religious convert responds with the whole person to some historical manifestation of divine excellence.

Socio-political conversion marks the third degree of human freedom. It deprivatizes responsible human freedom by transforming it into the responsible search for a just social order, one which embodies the common good. Since the realization of the common good gives all the members of a society relatively ready access both to its benefits as well as to the ability to contribute to those benefits, a just society enhances a community's collective freedom both to create and to enjoy. Socio-political conversion seeks to create environments which institutionalize responsible personal freedom and just social dealings.

Social Institutions

Social institutions endow with public sanction the habitual behavior of identifiable groups within communities. Institutions, therefore do not exist apart from the people who make them up. Communities, for example, which allow uncles and aunts to punish nieces and nephews institutionalize those family roles differently from communities which forbid such punishment. Transnational corporations institutionalize the world economy, often oppressively. Governments institutionalize the political lives of nations. Churches institutionalize the shared, public faith of religious communities.

Communities may institutionalize their life together in ways which either enhance or repress consciousness, whether personal or communal. Similarly, social institutions may either enhance or undermine all three forms of freedom. Communities which institutionalize the forms and dynamics of conversion simultaneously promote consciousness, responsibility, and freedom. Communities which institutionalize the counterdynamics of conversion undermine conversion. By discouraging conversion such communities both repress and distort consciousness, responsibility, and freedom. One may, therefore, measure the conversion of communities as such by the extent to which they have institutionalized the forms and dynamics of conversion.

An integral, five-fold conversion demands ongoing confrontation with all forms of institutional irresponsibility which subvert conversion and personalized living. Socio-political conversion deprivatizes attitudes, beliefs, and behavior. A deprivatized affective conversion promotes the eradication of institutionalized neurosis and psychosis as well as the creation of social forms of intercourse which foster shared, healthy, imaginative living. Deprivatized intellectual conversion demands the ongoing criticism of all errors, lies, and ideologies which fallaciously rationalize situations of injustice. Deprivatized personal moral conversion demands responsible institutionalized respect for personal rights and duties. Deprivatized Christian conversion demands that one measure the justice or injustice of all social institutions, both sacred and secular, by divine standards as well as by human prudential ones.

(III)

In the preceding section I have attempted to clarify the construct of human experience proposed in the first part of this chapter. I have done so by exploring the practical meaning of personal experience. In the course of doing so I have clarified three key Christological terms: "humanity," "person," and "relationship." In the present section, I shall begin to test the Christological adequacy of a triadic construct of experience by pondering its ability to avoid the fallacious conceptions of the human which in the past have confused Christological thinking.

Does the realistic, triadic, social construct of experience I have proposed avoid the fallacies of dualism, of essentialism, and of nominalism? In my judgment it does.

Avoiding Past Fallacies

Substantial dualism portrays humanity as two distinct and essentially different kinds of substances: one material, the other spiritual. In the preceding construct of experience, the terms "material" and "spiritual" do not even function. Instead, that construct insists on the dynamic relationship which unites the three variables which constitute the higher forms of experience. Evaluations define the character of decisions. Decisions give dynamic specificity to the habitual tendencies which they either create or re-enforce. Conditioned tendencies tend to produce predictable kinds of evaluations and decisions. Instead of possessing a fixed essence, emerging human selves define their character by the historical route of their evaluations and decisions.

Moreover, a social, realistic, triadic construct of experience understands subsistence, not as a substance existing in itself and not in another, but dynamically and functionally as the capacity to decide and evaluate autonomously. Since, too, the "what" of experience stands within it and helps define its specific character, the preceding construct of experience dispenses with the notion that anything can exist only "in itself." It therefore avoids any dualistic separation of subject from object. Experienced realities stand within experience. The way one evaluates them decides, not whether one will be present to them, but how.

Operational dualism grounds human activity in powers whose fixed essence results from their fixed formal objects. Typically, operational dualism divides human powers into the purely spiritual powers of intellect and will, on the one hand, and embodied, organic, sensory powers, on the other.

In the preceding construct of human experience, its powers evolve historically. They derive their character, not from an essentially fixed formal object, but from the kinds of decisions which give rise to them. In the preceding triadic construct of experience, the categories of "matter" and "spirit" no more function in the definition of the essential character of powers of activity than they do in defining substantial essences.

Moreover, the evaluative continuum which stretches from sensation through emotion, imagination, the three forms of inference, and deliberation discovers in human evaluative responses conceptual and intentional continuity rather than essential differentiation. The intentional continuities of evaluation disclose decisive social continuities and the dynamic continuities of tendency, or law. The grasp of negative conceptual relationship discloses distinctions between and among persons and things.

In a triadic construct of experience, therefore, one discovers three generic kinds of relationships. Conceptual relationships of intentional association link evaluations among themselves. Decisive, factual relations link one to one's environment and to other persons. Vectoral relations rooted in tendencies link the factual past dynamically to a possible future.

A triadic construct of experience avoids the essence fallacy by refusing to reify essences as principles of being. Rather essences function within experience as fallible modes of sensation and perception abstracted from the things they perceive and from the one who does the perceiving. Since "essences" in this sense reside in the experienced realm of value (or quality), they constitute the "how" of experience rather than the "what." They make us present to reality in particular ways.

Philosophical nominalism, as we have seen, runs into several dead ends. It cannot account for the scientific explanation of laws. It fails to do speculative justice to the social dimensions of experience. It makes a religious encounter with God unintelligible.

In the preceding realistic account of experience, by contrast, the scientific mind grasps laws inferentially and affirms their reality in inductive inference. The laws, moreover, which the scientific mind grasps inferentially, the intuitive mind grasps in judgments of affection. Moreover, instead of restricting experience to the subjective interrelation of percepts and concepts as conceptual nominalists do, the preceding construct of experience understands experience realistically as inherently social and symbolic.

A self-consistent nominalism reduces the concept of God to an empty category. While some theistic forms of nominalism claim to find God in the conceptual pole of experience, they tend to reduce religious experience either to an indefensible ontologism (i.e, to the immediate grasp of an idea in the mind of God) or to a purely "subjective" feeling without adequate "objective" grounding. In a triadic, realistic, social construct of experience, however, one experiences other selves and other persons when they act upon one efficaciously. One experiences the reality of God in the same way.

God touches human experience in two ways: directly, in solitary epiphanies which Ignatian spirituality calls "consolation without cause" or sacramentally[9] through the faith witness of others. In the latter case, one

---

9. I use the term "sacramental" here in the broad sense of an even which both reveals and conceals the reality of God.

senses that believers actually stand in a lived relationship with an alluring, world-transcending reality.

When God touches human experience efficaciously, one senses that
one stands in relationship to a reality which transcends all finite, created
reality. In a realistic construct of experience, one encounters the divine
reality as a personal vector, a self-conscious, purposeful, dynamic tendency which orients history toward transcendence. A social, realistic, triadic construct of experience can, then, make sense of the New Testament
experience of an encounter with the risen Christ. It can also interpret an
experience of the divine Breath whom one encounters in faith as a persuasive personal presence inviting the human heart to respond in faith to
the Christ event by prolonging Jesus' mission in space and time. I shall
begin to explore these experiences in the final section of this volume.

Whiteheadean nominalism portrays experience as developing in atomic
drops. A triadic, realistic, social construct of experience, by contrast,
grounds the experience of continuity within development in the realm of
tendency, or law. In opposition to Whiteheadean nominalism, triadic
realism need not, then, rule out the possibility of physical motion in
principle; nor need it reduce vital continuity to the transfer of a subjective aim from one atomic drop of experience to another. In other words,
a triadic construct of experience exemplifies what Peirce calls "synechism."
"Synechism" means a metaphysical theory about continuity: about real
continua, about social and environmental continuities, and about the
continuities linking creation and its creator.

While Whiteheadean nominalism cannot explain adequately human
interpersonal relationship, the preceding construct of experience defines
persons as autonomously functioning selves endowed with vital continuity and capable of entering into responsible, self-conscious relationships
with other selves similarly constituted. A triadic, realistic construct of
experience, therefore, makes ample speculative room both for interpersonal encounters and for the practical, utilitarian manipulation of things.
A social construct of experience can therefore appropriate all the valid
insights of Martin Buber's personalism.

The preceding philosophical construct of human experience rejects Augustinian pessimism about the human. It affirms with the medieval scholastics, with the council of Trent, and with most contemporary Protestant theologians that humans can perform some naturally good acts.

Since evaluative processes define the character of decisions which terminate them, purely natural decisions manifest ignorance of the historical self-revelation of God. Natural decisions respond to created goods.
Naturally motivated decisions create natural habits of evaluating and deciding. When naturally motivated decisions violate ideals, principles, realities, and values which make absolute and ultimate claims on the hu-

man conscience, they qualify as immoral. Since, however, they ignore the reality of God, they do not qualify as formally sinful. Sin embodies choices which deliberately contradict the will of God.

Decisions which respond consciously to the historical self-revelation of God on the terms which that revelation demands qualify as graced and proceed from faith. They qualify as graced for four reasons. First, the historical self-revelation of God and the consent to that self-revelation on God's terms establishes a relationship between God and humans which transcends anything which sinful humans can effect or merit on their own. Second, in everything which concerns that relationship, God holds the initiative and acts with sovereign freedom. Third, the relationship of faith creates a collaborative relationship between creature and creator in its struggle against sin, a relationship which empowers the creature to act in ways which surpass the power of human nature alone. Christians collaborate with God by prolonging Jesus' historical mission in time and space. When they love with the universal, atoning love of Christ, Christians do with the help of divine grace something which transcends the capacity of finite human love. Fourth, the relationship of faith discloses the divine excellence and beautifies believers by teaching them to appropriate God's universal benevolence.

The commitment of faith demands the transvaluation of all natural commitments. One transvalues a reality or value when, having understood it in one frame of reference, one sees it in the light of another frame of reference which endows it with new connotations and with new possibilities. One transvalues natural realities and values in faith by interpreting them in the light of God's historical self-revelation. Because a triadic, social, realistic construct of experience validates the possibility of naturally good acts as well as the possibility of graciously transformed human activity, it eschews Augustinian pessimism.

In its portrait of the human, a triadic, social, realistic construct of experience also eschews the inflated vision of human nature defended by Aquinas. It denies the virtual infinity of the human mind and will. Instead, it affirms the radical finitude and fallibility of all human evaluative responses. Even a human mind capable of endless development remains at any point in its growth actually finite. The human mind and heart remain finite because they always grasp reality within finite frames of reference which reflect the ways in which they have grown both consciously and unconsciously.

To err is human. Finite minds make mistakes because they lack the specific habits of thought which correctly anticipate the way in which reality behaves. Philosophical fallibilism recognizes that human minds can and do make mistakes. Philosophical fallibilism inculcates both intellectual humility and intellectual hope. It teaches the human mind to believe that, if it admits it might have erred, it has a better chance of reaching the truth than if it claims an inerrancy it does not in fact enjoy. Moreover, the intellectually converted fallibilist stands committed to shared systematic inquiry out of the conviction that the experiences and insights of others tend to enhance and correct one's own limited experiences and one's capacity to judge reality correctly, whether at an intuitive or inferential level.

The finitude of the human mind means that it enjoys no virtually infinite desire for truth, goodness, or reality, no natural desire for the beatific vision. It exhibits no unrestricted desire to know. Intellectual curiosity follows limited human needs and interests. It seeks to satisfy itself in limited human frames of reference. Only an encounter with the Holy, with the transcendent, self-revealing reality of God, creates the supernatural longing for graced transcendence. Left to itself, the human heart desires only the kind of self-transcendence embodied in natural growth.

As we shall see again in greater detail in subsequent volumes, only God loves all things by nature. Left to themselves, humans love their own; but they do not spontaneously love their enemies. On the contrary, the human heart tends to respond to enemies with a fear and a hatred which precludes love. The universalization of love results from the supernatural gracing of the human heart. Against Augustine, then, I would hold that human nature can perform some morally good acts. Against Aquinas, I would argue that, whatever the universality of its moral aspirations, human nature actually loves universally only when empowered to do so by the Breath of God.

Confrontation with radical human finitude, especially with the ultimate limitation of death, can raise the religious question. The religious question asks whether or not human life and existence has any ultimate meaning or significance.

Natural moral conversion endows human experience with an orientation to ultimate values, because the morally converted stand committed to give their lives, if necessary, for particular ideals, values, and realities, like one's family, one's friends, one's beloved, one's country. Since an orientation to ultimacy makes experience religious, natural moral conversion endows human experience with a natural religiosity.

Despite some points of similarity, natural moral conversion differs in important ways from theistic religious faith. A morally converted atheistic humanist could, for example, stand committed to live and, if necessary, to die for the sake of justice. Like natural moral conversion, theistic religious conversion also endows human experience with moral ultimacy; but by finding in God the source and ground of all ultimacy, theistic religious conversion reorients natural moral conversion to the transcendent reality of God.

Religious people answer the religious question positively. Religious people who remain both consciously and unconsciously atheistic can live naturally responsible moral lives but fail to relate to God in an attitude of faith. Religious people who identify the source of ultimate meaning and significance with God qualify as theists. Natural religion based on human reason and intuition can discover in created nature a revelation of the divine. Theists who respond to the historical self-revelation of God live graced lives of faith.

The construct of humanity which I am proposing refuses, then, to join Augustine in equating original sin with total human depravity. One sins whenever one deliberately makes a decision which one perceives as a violation of the divine will. Sin for Christians divides into personal sin and original sin. Personal sin designates the sum total of sinful choices taken by any given individual. Original sin designates the rest of human sinfulness: the personal sins of all other individuals, all human institutionalizations of sin, injustice, and oppression.[10]

A social, realistic, triadic structure of experience requires, then, that one view the reality of original sin perspectively. A perspectival account of original sin recognizes its qualitative diversity. Each of us experiences the corporate sinfulness of humanity from a different angle of vision, from a different human perspective defined by one's personal history. In a perspectival view of original sin, my personal sin contributes to your experience of original sin, and vice versa. Similarly, my connivance in corporate, institutional sin contributes to your experience of original sin, and vice versa. In other words, we experience original sin as qualitatively diverse because different people exemplify and different societies and cultures institutionalize different kinds of sinfulness

The fallibility and finitude of the human mind, its dependence on others for its initial beliefs and attitudes, and the mimetic character of human desire all combine in order to make the personal sin of one born into the world without the support of divine grace morally inevitable. Original sin corrupts us by shaping the environments from which we emerge. Those environments stand within us as experiences and inculcate in all kinds of subtle, more or less conscious ways many kinds of habitual behavior. One raised in a racist, sexist, anti-semitic culture will, therefore, tend to grow up despising Blacks, women, and Jews. One raised in an atmosphere of capitalistic greed will tend to acquiesce in a crudely selfish corporate ethic. One raised in an individualistic culture like ours will tend to perceive things individualistically. People who grow up in warring clans, tribes, and nations will tend to hate the enemy. Human

10. For a more detailed discussion of original and personal sin, see: Gelpi, *Committed Worship*, I, pp. 208-278.

minds dinned to acquiescence in lying ideologies will tend to consent with complacency to situations of rank injustice.

In such a social, perspectival view of original sin, it can also take different kinds of institutional shape in different epochs and cultures. Understanding original sin in the concrete, therefore, demands accurate social analysis illumined by religious faith.

Conclusion

I have only begun to test the Christological applicability and adequacy of a realistic, social, triadic construct of experience. In this chapter I have argued that it gives initial promise of avoiding some of the more obvious philosophical and doctrinal blunders of the past.

The method I adopted in chapter three requires, however, much more extensive testing than that. Besides avoiding past blunders, the construct of the human which I have proposed needs 1) to interpret the results of close scientific investigations of human life and experience. It also needs 2) to contextualize the results of those investigations; and it needs 3) to amplify its account of the human condition by incorporating into its account of humanity the validated insights of those natural sciences which study the human. In the three chapters which follow, I shall test the adequacy of a realistic, triadic, social construct of experience to respond to all three of these speculative demands.

In addition, once validated and amplified by the humane sciences, the construct of the human proposed in this chapter needs, if it expects to succeed as a Christological construct, to interpret the concrete, historical experience of Jesus of Nazareth insofar as one can reconstruct that experience in a scholarly way from the distance of two intervening centuries. I shall therefore also test the ability of the preceding construct to interpret and contextualize the results of the new quests for the historical Jesus.

Ultimately, of course, a triadic construct of experience must prove its Christological adequacy by its ability to make sense of the incarnation and of the trinity which the incarnation reveals. Dealing with that complex set of doctrinal question requires, however, an insight into the religious experiences which result from an encounter in faith with the risen Christ. I shall begin that exploration of those religious experiences in the final section of this volume and shall pursue it in the other two volumes of this study.

Chapter 6
Jesus' Personal Development

I am attempting to lay theological foundations for an inculturated North American Christology which addresses the conversion needs of adult Christians. In the process I am also seeking to resolve the contemporary crisis in Christology.

As we have seen, the resolution of the contemporary Christological crisis demands that one clarify what one means by humanity, by divinity, and by the relationship between the two in the person Jesus Christ. In this second section of volume one, I am focusing on the notion of humanity. In the section which follows I shall begin to consider how the paschal mystery transformed Christian perceptions of Jesus' humanity.

In what concerns the humanity of Jesus, the method adopted in chapter three requires that I take a multi-disciplinary approach to the understanding of human nature in general and of Jesus' human nature in particular. Philosophy, theology, and the other sciences which study the human each have a contribution to make to that understanding.

My construct of experience requires one to approach such a multi-disciplinary reconstruction of Jesus' human experience with fallibilistic caution. Twenty centuries of history divide us from the mortal ministry of Jesus. The humanity of people living in the first century of the Christian era bore some analogical resemblance to contemporary humanity. Nevertheless, times, circumstances, and cultures do change. Moreover, those changes, as we shall see, can and do affect the way specific human experiences develop. One ought not, then, to assume naively and automatically the right to transpose without qualification the results of twentieth-century investigations of human nature back into the first.

"Notes" for a Multidisciplinary Christology

As a consequence, in assessing the relevance of contemporary scientific and scholarly investigations of the human condition to understanding the person named Jesus, I shall take a methodological cue from an improbable source, namely, from textbook scholastic theology.[1] Like text-

---

1. Textbook theology written in the nineteenth and early twentieth centuries acquiesced methodologically in a decadent positivism which attempted to establish the truth of theological theses by proof-texting them in authoritative documents. It then embellished such proof-texting with rational corollaries.

   A thesis from one of the textbooks I examined when studying theology in St. Marys, Kansas, illustrates well the fallacies of text-book positivism. The author was arguing the thesis that one should regard the command of God to Adam and Eve not to eat the forbidden fruit as a positive precept and not as a natural law. The scriptural "argu-

book scholastics, I shall assign "notes" to any statement I make about Jesus' humanity.

The "notes" which I shall assign to specific statements about the man named Jesus of Nazareth will attempt to assess the degree of certitude with which one can predicate of Him contemporary philosophical and scientific assertions about human experience. In what follows, I shall assign these "notes" by using qualifying words like: certain, probable, plausible, possible, uncertain, improbable, implausible, impossible. Hence, before I begin the following interdisciplinary reflection on Jesus' humanity I need to clarify exactly what I mean by these qualifying notes.

The certain applicability of a proposition means in the present context that one can affirm something about Jesus without the shadow of a doubt. We can, for example, say with certainty that He was born and that He died by crucifixion.

Probable applicability means here that the preponderance of the evidence we possess favors the affirmation, even though one cannot rule out in principle that Jesus might have proved the exception rather than the rule. In what follows, for example, I shall regard it as probable that Jesus advanced through many of the same cognitive stages as other humans seem to do.

Plausible applicability means here that some evidence favors a given affirmation even though it also allows other interpretations as well. For example, in what follows I shall argue that James Fowler's stages of faith offer a plausible account of Jesus' personal religious development.

Possible applicability means that one cannot rule out an affirmation as impossible, but that relatively little evidence supports it. I would, for example, regard it as possible that John the Baptizer functioned as a male mentor for Jesus, although we know too little about their relationship to one another to move beyond possible affirmation.

Positive notes imply negative ones. If one can admit some affirmations as possible, one can rule other others as impossible. If one can verify some affirmations as plausible, one can deem others implausible. If one can affirm some hypotheses probably, one can rule out others as improb-

ment" went like this: in the Latin Vulgate translation of the Bible, a translation officially approved by the council of Trent, the Latin word "*praecepit*" renders the Hebrew verb which expresses God's command not the eat. Since the word "precept" comes etymologically from the Latin word "*praecepit*," this indicates that the divine command in question functioned as a positive precept and not as a natural law.

The human mind which can warp itself to such confused modes of thought will never understand either the Bible or the Christian tradition. Theologians have, therefore, long since buried text-book positivism. May it rest in peace.

Nevertheless, for all its hopeless confusions, text-book theology did one thing somewhat well. It attempted to assess the degree of certitude with which one could affirm any given theological thesis. Text book theology assigned "notes" to theses. The notes characterized different theses as defined doctrine, as theologically probable, as a common opinion, etc.

able. If one can assert some things as certain, one can regard others as uncertain.

Impossibility means here that one can exclude a particular affirmation about Jesus as having no applicability in His case. We know for certain, for example, that Jesus did not speak any form of the Chinese language.

Implausibility means here that the evidence weighs strongly against an assertion without, however, ruling it out in principle. I would deem it extremely implausible, for example, that Jesus ever read Aristotle.

Improbability means that the evidence calls into serious question one interpretation but without ruling it out altogether. Given the teachings of Jesus summarized in the New Testament, I find it improbable, for example, that Jesus' moral development would have rested on purely rational presuppositions. That conclusion, however, tells us nothing about the way Jesus did develop morally.

Uncertain means here that on a given issue we have no relevant evidence which would favor a judgment one way or another. We do not know, for example, how many people at any given moment affiliated themselves with the movement which Jesus headed.

I suspect (but cannot prove) that the new quests for the historical Jesus would reach scholarly consensus sooner if the questers employed either this set of "notes" or a better one.[2]

In the preceding chapter, I argued that human experience presents itself as simultaneously personal and social. This chapter will explore scientific and scholarly investigations of the human for the light they have to throw on personal development. The next chapter will examine the same sciences for the insight they yield into human social development. I shall also reflect on the possible Christological relevance of the theories which I shall examine. The construct of experience developed in chapter five also distinguished between natural human development and development in faith. Chapter eight will, therefore, examine the humane sciences for the light they have to throw on faith development in general and on Jesus' development in faith, in particular.

This chapter divides, then, into three sections. In the first I assess human cognitive development, in the second, human emotional development, and in the third human moral development.

(I)

In my judgment, much of contemporary developmental psychology both amplifies and tends to confirm the triadic construct of experience presented in the previous chapter.

---

2. E.P. Sanders takes a similar position; but his idiosyncratic way of approaching Jesus provides, in my judgment, a limited and sometimes problematic angle of vision on Jesus' person and ministry. Cf. E.P. Sanders, *Jesus and Judaism* (Philadelphia, PA: Fortress, 1985).

In his investigations of human cognitive development, Jean Piaget, the father of contemporary developmental psychology, discovered certain functional constants in the growth of human experience. He argued that as children mature, more complex behavioral structures tend to evolve from the more primitive. Biological constants, for example, provide the physical foundations for cognitive development. Those constants include the developing human organism with all of its functioning sub-units, its surrounding environment, and the modifications of behavior which result from interaction with that environment.

An analysis of biological growth reveals two basic operational constants: organization and adaptation. Biological organization produces the self-sustaining organic structures which constitute the human body. Adaptive activity relates the human body to its environment in ways which sustain and if possible enhance its own vital processes. Adaptation takes two basic forms: assimilation and accommodation.

Biological assimilation adapts the environment to the human body. The ingestion and assimilation of food and drink exemplify biological assimilation. Assimilation replaces what the human body expends through activity.

Biological accommodation produces adaptive growth: it modifies the organism in order to relate it in new ways to its surrounding environment. Professional rock climbers, for example, strengthen particular sets of muscles in preparation for the specific physical demands of a particular climb.

Piaget discovered in human cognition patterns of activity which correspond analogously to biological assimilation and adaptation. The human mind assimilates the things it knows when it interprets them within already familiar frames of reference. The human mind accommodates itself to reality when it recognizes its inability to deal with reality in familiar cognitive terms and reshapes its cognitive response to the demands of the real.[3]

If one reflects on Piaget's organic account of human cognition in the light of the of triadic construct of experience developed in the preceding chapter, then that construct can assimilate what Piaget has to say. Like Piaget it understands the relationship of the human self to its surrounding environment in transactional, organic terms. Like Piaget, it regards the body as a life support system created by the physical assimilation of elements in one's surrounding environment.

Piaget's analysis, however, also amplifies the account of experience sketched in the preceding chapter and in this sense requires its accommodation. That analysis calls explicit attention to certain dimensions of human cognitive behavior which the preceding philosophical construct ig-

3. Cf. Flavell, *The Developmental Psychology of Jean Piaget*, pp. 41-52.

nores. Specifically, Piaget's analysis of human cognitive behavior requires that a triadic philosophical account of human experience recognize more explicitly the analogies between human biological and cognitive behavior.

Can a triadic philosophical construct of experience also help contextualize Piaget's descriptive account of the generic traits of human cognitive behavior? I believe it can; but we need first to qualify that account.

At the heart of Piaget's theory of human cognition lies the notion of a "schema." The term "schema" designates a learned class of related evaluative responses. Schemata endow human cognitive responses with regularity and purpose.

Piaget's cognitive theory envisages the complexification of schemata. Simpler schemata lay the foundation for more complex cognitive responses. For example, a simple schema grounds the neonate's sucking instincts and instinctive manual prehension. More complex schemata ground the fantasies of the five-year-old or the mathematical inferences of the adolescent.[4]

Daniel Stern's studies of infant behavior suggest, however, a qualification of Piaget's theory of the schematization of human behavior. Piaget's system strictly speaking would require that the infant mind first develop different sensory schemata before it can acquire the ability to interrelate them. In other words, the infant mind would have to store up a certain number of visual schemata before it could relate them to motor schemata or to other kinds of cognitive response. Stern's studies, however, establish that the human infant emerges from the womb with an inbuilt ability to correlate input from different senses.

Stern suggests that this innate ability provides behavioral evidence for the presence within the neonate of something like the "common sense" of Aristotelian philosophy and of medieval scholasticism. By the "common sense" neither Aristotle nor the scholastics meant what people ordinarily mean by "horse sense," or the ability to relate sensibly and realistically to life. Rather, as a technical philosophical term, the "common sense" designates precisely the power to cross reference input from different sensory stimuli. Stern has shown that human infants possess such an ability at birth. Stern does not, however, consider the possibility that what he calls the common sense might have resulted from uterine learning.[5] Nor does Stern deny the cognitive schematization of human experience which

---

4. *Ibid.*, pp. 52-84.
5. Cf. Daniel N. Stern, *The Interpersonal World of the Infant: A View from Psychoanalysis and* Developmental Psychology (New York, NY: Harper/Collins Publishers, 1985). We shall return to the work of Daniel Stern when we reflect on the development of human self-awareness. Here, however, it suffices to note his qualification of Piaget's theory of schematic development.

Piaget describes. He questions rather the adequacy of Piaget's notion of schematization to account for all infantile cognitive behavior.

In a triadic, philosophical construct of human experience, the notion of "tendency" interprets Piaget's category of schema. Both terms designate learned generalized tendencies to act in regular, more or less predictable ways. The notion of tendency, however, also contextualizes Piaget's theory of schemata in two obvious ways.

First of all, by interpreting the idea of a schema, the notion of tendency establishes its relevance to the age-old debate between nominalists and realists. The empirically verifiable reality of developing cognitive schemata lends support to C.S. Peirce's twofold suggestion that scientific thinking presupposes philosophical belief in real generality and that philosophical realism explains the possibility of scientific thinking in a way in which philosophical nominalism never can.

Second, the philosophical concept "tendency," or "law," contextualizes Piaget's notion of a "schema" in a different way. Piaget's psychology focuses on human cognitive development. The term "schema" therefore has a narrower focus than the term "tendency." "Schema" designates primarily learned human evaluative responses, while the more general philosophical term "tendency" includes both evaluative and decisive responses, whether one acquires them consciously or not. In the very act of interpreting what Piaget means by "schema," therefore, the philosophical term "tendency" simultaneously reminds one of the need to contextualize Piaget's analysis of cognitive behavior in a broader philosophical theory of human activity which acknowledges the importance of both evaluative and decisive habits, or "schemata."

The fact that neonates also possess the ability to cross reference different kinds of sensory input suggests that this ability results from normal neurological development within the womb. One need not, then, interpret what Stern calls the infant's "common sense" in the manner of medieval scholasticism as a distinct sensory power with its fixed formal object. Like all other human powers, the ability to cross-reference different kinds of sensory input probably results from prenatal biological, neurological, and experiential development.

Stages of Cognitive Development

Piaget's psychology, however, amplifies a realistic philosophy of human experience most obviously in the detailed account it provides of human cognitive development. Piaget divides human cognitive development into three identifiable stages: the sensory-motor stage, the pre-operational stage, and the operational stage.

The sensory-motor stage extends from birth to approximately two years of age. During the sensory-motor period, the infantile mind begins to explore the evaluative realm of literal meaning. The pre-operational period extends from approximately the age of two until approximately the age of eleven. During this period the child exhibits the capacity for imaginative thinking and for concrete reasoning. The operational child, by contrast, exhibits the ability to think abstractly.

Piaget divides sensory-motor development into six stages. Let us examine each stage in turn.

For about a month, an infant engages in gross bodily movements. Instinctive responses like sucking and grasping gradually exhibit initial schematization. The child learns, for example, to differentiate nourishing and non-nourishing suckables.

Between one and four months, the infant begins to develop basic coordinated patterns of activity like thumb-sucking. Infants at this stage also wave their hands and feet and blow bubbles with their saliva. Piaget calls such operations primary, circular reactions. By "primary" he means that they center in the infant's own body. By "circular" he means that the pleasure they engender leads to their repetition.

Experiments in infantile behavior after Piaget's initial work suggest that the behavior of the infant's mother, as primary care giver, tends to condition primary circular operations. Mothers, for example, who jiggle their babies while they nurse encourage the infants to prolong the nursing period. Moreover, cultural conditioning can re-enforce certain patterns of infantile behavior. In the United States, for example, parents tend to value more behavior which expresses the infant's psychological responses.[6]

Between the ages of four and eight months, human infants make initial and futile efforts to keep interesting experiences going. After a rattle stops shaking, for example, the infant may begin to shake its arms and legs in an apparent attempt to prolong the entertainment. At this stage, the infant begins to exhibit what Piaget calls secondary circular reactions. The term "circular" means the same as in substage two: namely, that the activity tends to produce its own repetition. Piaget calls the reactions of this third substage secondary, however, because they focus on objects other than the infant's own body: a bell or rattle, the bar of the child's crib, etc.[7]

Between eight and twelve months, infants begin to exhibit goal oriented activity which engages secondary circular reactions. The child will, for example, try to get at a favorite toy as long as the child can see it behind some other obstacle. The child also begins to anticipate the consequences of the actions of others. Simply rising from one's chair, for example, may provoke infantile tears, whereas previously it took one's actual departure from the room. The child also treats visible objects as

---

6. Cf. Michael R. Cole and Sheila Cole, *The Development of Children* (New York, NY: W.H. Freeman and Company, 1989), pp. 165-168.

7. *Ibid.*, p. 189.

three dimensional and exhibits a nascent sense of concrete causality. The child, for example, now pushes aside an obstruction between it and a desired object and will try to make adults do for it what it cannot do itself.

Originally, Piaget contended that at substage four, the child still lacks any clear sense of object permanence. Subsequent work with infants, however, provides some evidence that at three and a half months infants realize that objects continue to exist when hidden. If so, then such awareness comes four and a half months sooner than Piaget suggested. Other experiments suggest, however, that babies who recognize the continued existence of hidden objects sooner than Piaget suggested quickly lose track of where to find them if distracted.[8]

Moreover, work with babies at this stage discloses other significant signs of cognitive development. Between seven and nine months, infants can recall persons and things without seeing them or some reminder of them. They also show signs of wariness when familiar objects do not correspond to their remembered image of them and when strangers approach. At this substage, infants begin to display signs of deep emotional attachment to primary care givers, try to make social contact with them, show distress at separation from them and joy at being reunited to them. Babbling begins to presage the emergence of speech.[9] Initially, however, infants seem to play with sound in the same way in which at an earlier stage of development they played with their saliva by making bubbles.

Between twelve and eighteen months, the child begins to exhibit a new capacity for creative improvisation which foreshadows the emergence of the creative imagination. Imitation takes on more control and precision. The child can remember hidden objects and search for them. Piaget calls such operations tertiary, circular reactions.[10] The term "tertiary" connotes the child's active exploration of the environment. The child exhibits a more developed sense of bodily position in space. The maturing infantile mind now studies changes in apparent size and shape, puts things inside containers and removes them. The child can amuse itself with activities like releasing a ball on an incline and watching it roll. The standing child releases its grasp of larger objects in order to sit down.

After eighteen months, the child exhibits an ability to discover new behavioral patterns accidentally and even to create them spontaneously. When, for example, in pushing a toy around the floor, the child encounters an obstruction, it can figure out how to remove the obstacle without experimenting. In other words, after eighteen months, the child begins to exhibit a novel capacity to represent things symbolically to itself through images. It can now imitate complex behavioral patterns in others with ease. It understands and has mastered the idea of the displacement of

8. *Ibid.*, p. 192.   9. *Ibid.*, pp.200-207.   10. *Ibid.*, pp. 216-217.

unseen objects. The child can now keep a running tab on its own bodily movements through space and react appropriately to unexpected obstacles to movement. Invisible sounds will lead the child to search for their source. The child now recalls past events as past. In other words, after eighteen months the normal human child begins to enter a world of fantasy and imagination, the world of intuitive thinking.[11]

Once a child develops the capacity to imagine a world, it enters into the phase of cognitive development which Piaget calls pre-operational. Thinking now exhibits a formally and explicitly representational character. Learned symbols shape the developing child's perceptions of the world.[12]

The pre-operational child manifests a spontaneous and innocent egocentrism. Innocent egocentrism makes it difficult at first for the human child to see things from the standpoint of others. Childish egocentric thinking tends to focus exclusively on a single striking quality of the child's own experience to the exclusion of any other. The narrow focus of experience makes it initially blind to balancing and compensating factors. The egocentric childish mind also remains oblivious of its own blindness and myopia.

The oversimplifications of innocent egocentric thinking trick the child repeatedly into blunders as it grapples with the complexity of its world. Thinking remains tied to concrete images. The primitive "inferences" of the childish mind tend to expect that what worked before will work again, despite altered circumstances. The pre-operational child still lacks the ability to deal with the abstract classification of things which marks the operational mind.

In the pre-operational child, memory plays a prominent role in realistic thinking. Memory functions differently in different circumstances. It enables the child to recognize things, to imitate the behavior of others, to link remembered images. As the evocative association of remembered images acquires more flexibility, it transforms itself into creative fantasy.[13]

Developmental psychologists after Piaget who have studied children of pre-school age question whether children develop the capacity for concrete reasoning with the uniformity which Piaget suggests. Some pre-school children exhibit one level of thinking in one experimental situation and another level of thinking in a different situation.

Defenders of Piaget's notion of uniform cognitive development in children argue that, if experimenters take care in dealing with pre-schoolers to correlate the logical structures of problems in concrete reasoning with

11. *Ibid.*, pp. 216-225. For a more detailed summary of the sensory-motor stages of cognitive development, see: Flavell, *op.cit.*, pp. 84-164.
12. Cf. Hans G. Furth, *Piaget and Knowledge: Theoretical Foundations* (Englewood Cliffs, NJ: Prentice-Hall, 1969), pp. 43-51, 164-201.
13. *Ibid.*, pp. 158 ff.

the developing child's different domains of knowledge, then one can observe the kind of synchronous development across stages for which Piaget argued.

Information processing theorists argue, however, that pre-schoolers simply function better in familiar situations and less well in unfamiliar ones. Biological theorists explain differences of cognitive ability among pre-schoolers by appealing to changes in brain structure. Still others argue that social expectations condition the way a child thinks. Finally, some discover a grain of truth in all of these suggestions and regard them as probably complementary rather than contradictory.[14]

By about the age of seven or eight a child's mind exhibits a more or less developed capacity for concrete reasoning. As yet, however, the young human mind cannot add or subtract abstract classes of things. It can grasp concrete spatio-temporal proximity and concrete temporal sequencing but cannot understand abstract symmetrical relationships. Thinking remains bound to the concrete and must master the properties of things one by one.

The capacity for hypothetical reasoning emerges at about the age of eleven. Now the child can classify things abstractly and without having to arrange them in clumps. Classifications take on a formally rational character. Between the ages of eleven and fifteen, the maturing human mind begins to exhibit the ability for abstract deductive thinking. The mind need not discover relations in things. It can conceive them abstractly. The young adolescent mind thinks about the future, about thinking itself, and beyond conventional limits.[15]

Experiments with adolescents again suggest that the human mind may not develop operational modes of thought with the kind of synchronic uniformity which Piaget originally envisaged. Some minds master more quickly than others the kinds of scientific problems which Piaget used in his original experiments. Interest, past experience, and cultural training all seem to condition the emergence of formal rational operations. Moreover, while cross-cultural studies tend to confirm that human minds achieve the ability to reason concretely in all cultures, in technologically unsophisticated cultures, what Piaget calls formal, operational thinking seems to emerge less frequently. Besides cultural context, language and the way one processes information tends to condition the ability to think abstractly.[16]

Verification and Amplification

Philosophical hypotheses, as we have seen, result from the activity of an adult human mind reflecting on the structure of gross, macroscopic

14. Cf. Cole and Cole, *op.cit.*, pp. 315-339.
15. Cf. Flavell, *op.cit.*, 202-236; Cole and Cole, *op.cit.*, p.561.
16. Cf. Cole and Cole, *op.cit.*, pp. 564-574.

experience. Scientific and scholarly hypotheses result from the focused investigation of a limited realm of human experience with prescribed empirical methods and, in the case of strictly scientific thinking, with the use of instruments and of mathematical measurement.

The philosophical construct of experience developed in the preceding chapter suggested that human evaluative responses develop in a continuum which stretches from sensation to abstract thinking. The affective coloring of sensory experience expands to yield affective perceptions of the tendencies present in sensed persons and things. As remembered images acquire flexibility, they transform themselves into imaginative intuitive thinking which judges reality affectively rather than abstractly and inferentially. Hypothetical inference begins imaginatively but culminates in the abstract, rational classification of reality. Deductive inference predicts the operational consequences of formulated hypotheses. Inductive inference verifies or falsifies those predicted consequences.

On the whole, the results of developmental psychology tend, in my judgment, both to verify and amplify this philosophical hypothesis. They verify it by discovering within human cognitive development the same kinds of experiences as the reflective philosophical mind discovers in its reflections on macroscopic experience.

Empirical studies of human thinking also tend confirm the existence of what our philosophical hypothesis calls an evaluative continuum in human cognition. Sensory motor thinking engages sensation, feeling, and memory. As memory develops from recognition to reconstruction and from reconstruction to evocation, it gradually transforms itself into fantasy. Fantasy, memory, feeling, and sensation all structure the realm of intuitive thinking which characterizes the pre-operational child. The development of habits of concrete reasoning prepares the human mind for abstract thinking, even though not every culture encourages the transition from concrete to abstract reasoning.

Scientific investigations of human cognitive development also tend to verify the philosophical suggestion that the human self emerges from its own history of biological, cognitive, and decisive behavior. Those same investigations also confirm that the human self consists of a developing but thoroughly finite complex of habitual ways of responding to reality. They also show that the complexification of human habitual response endows it with greater and greater flexibility.

Both Piaget's own work as well as subsequent qualifications of his original theories have, moreover, tended to re-enforce philosophical belief in the radical finitude of the human mind. The infantile mind begins with a few instinctive tendencies and gradually develops them into a more complex system of habits for dealing with itself and its environment. At no point, however, does the developing human mind give evidence of anything but a finite capacity to respond cognitively to its world. The fact, moreover, that the development of strictly operational thinking—i.e., of abstract, inductive inference—tends not to occur as often in largely oral and technologically underdeveloped cultures offers dramatic confirmation of human cognitive finitude.

Finally, the modifications of Piaget's theories suggested by subsequent research into human development also illustrate the importance of shared systematic inquiry as the best method for fixing inferential beliefs and for verifying inferential hypotheses. Those modifications tend, therefore, to confirm the social, dialogic construct of human reason proposed in the preceding chapter.

Empirical studies of human cognitive development not only offer evidence for verifying the philosophical construct of human experience suggested in the preceding chapter, but they also amplify it in significant ways. As the philosophical mind reflects on its own adult experience it can recognize the presence within it of all the different modes of thought which it has acquired in the course of its growth into adulthood. Philosophy alone, however, cannot reconstruct the growth processes which generate the adult human mind because it reflects on adult, macroscopic experience. As a consequence, philosophical thinking presupposes that the mind has completed the kinds of growth experiences which developmental psychology patiently documents. The accurate reconstruction of human developmental processes requires the kind of close empirical investigation of human cognitive growth which Piaget and other developmentalists have undertaken. Their empirical work provides us with an increasingly nuanced account of the probable stages which mark the human cognitive development in different cultural contexts.

Criticism

Studies of human development subsequent to Piaget have forced the amplification, modification, and qualification of his original theories. Such amplification, modification, and qualification tend to confirm the fallibilistic account of human inference suggested in the preceding chapter.

In the case of Piaget, his account of sensory motor development in children rested on a very narrow data base: namely, his observation of his own children. Predictably, more systematic investigations of the behavior of neonates and young infants have tended to uncover over-generalizations and oversimplifications in Piaget's original theory. Evidence began to turn up that infants exhibit awareness of the permanence of objects sooner than Piaget had anticipated. Developmental psychology after Piaget has also documented the fact that, while the schematization of experience which Piaget originally described does happen, it does not account for the whole of human cognitive development. Other variables—biological development, modes of information processing, social and cultural expectations—also shape the way the human mind grows and develops. Moreover, human development may not in all cases exhibit the kind of uniform, synchronous development across stages which Piaget originally envisaged.

In chapter three, I argued that philosophy has a critical task to perform in the construction of any systematic account of divine revelation. In any cross-disciplinary approach to human experience, philosophy also legitimately claims the right to criticize the tacit philosophical assumptions which lie at the basis of different scientific hypotheses.

In the case of Piaget, the construct of experience developed in chapter two calls into question the rationalistic bias implicit in his construct of human cognition. Piaget recognizes the reality of intuitive, imaginative modes of thought, but he does not regard the human mind as fully "operational" until it can reason abstractly and inferentially. In other words, in the terms which he chooses in order to describe human cognitive development, Piaget implies the inferiority of less than fully operational thinking. Rational, scientific thinking stands at the apex of human rationality and would seem to spell the difference between fully adult and immature patterns of thought.

The philosophy of experience developed in chapter two would question the legitimacy of those assumptions on three scores. First, it recognizes that the human mind grasps reality with two kinds of judgments: verified inferences and judgments of affection. Both ways of thinking qualify as human. Both give limited, fallible access to reality.

Second, the philosophy of experience which I have presented refuses to regard abstract, inferential thinking as inherently superior to intuitive, imaginative thinking. Each way of grasping the real has its advantages and disadvantages. Rational inferential thought does enhance the clarity, control, and precision with which one evaluates the reality; but it achieves logical precision precisely by narrowing its focus. The abstract theories of the rational, inferential mind leave out more reality than they disclose. In a world of developing experiences, one understands fully the "essence" of anything only by recapitulating its entire history. In other words, far from exhausting the reality of anything it claims to explain, inferential thinking in virtue of its analytic abstractness glosses over more reality than it illumines.

Intuitive, imaginative thinking, by contrast, precisely because it relies on free imaginative association yields a better sense of the organic wholeness of things than does the rational, technological mind. In other words, while inferential thought excels in analytic precision and conscious control, imaginative, intuitive insight excels in a synthetic, appreciative grasp of the real.

The radical finitude of the human mind demands that it oscillate between abstract inference and synthetic imagination if it expects to grasp reality in a more or less adequate manner. The holistic, synthetic character of intuitive thinking provides a healthy counterbalance to abstract, analytic, inferential thinking; and vice versa.

In other words, when one reads Piaget's account of human cognitive development in the light of the philosophy of experience developed in chapter two, that philosophy forces one to question Piaget's assumption that abstract, rational thinking outranks what he calls transductive, or pre-operational, thinking. Both yield a cognitive grasp of the real; each corrects the other's limitations in intellectually healthy ways.

Moreover, the fact that what Piaget calls fully operational thinking tends to emerge only in technologically advanced cultures also raises questions about its inherent superiority to what Piaget calls pre-operational thought. So does the fact that some human minds seem never to develop that particular skill at all.

The restriction of strictly operational reasoning to technological cultures suggests that the vast majority of human minds have never reached the level of full "operationality." Should one therefore characterize such minds as "sub-human" or "infantile"? I think not. Technological culture has its clear advantages, but it has its clear disadvantages as well, as the arms race, the threat of nuclear destruction, and the menace of planetary ecological disaster make plain. These massively evil consequences of abstract, technological thinking dramatize all too well the destructive potential inherent in a vicious abstractionism.

Moreover, even in technologized, rationalistic cultures, people do not live their lives at the level of abstract, scientific reasoning. Practical, prudential thinking claims the lion's share of human consciousness and provides a more typically human way of responding to reality than abstract, technological inference. C.S. Peirce made this point clearly and convincingly in his lectures on "Vitally Important Topics."[17] Madness, as G.K. Chesterton once wisely observed, consists in losing everything but one's reason.

I have been arguing that Piaget's researches into human cognitive development tend on the whole to validate the philosophical construct of experience proposed in chapter two. At the same time, that philosophical construct combines with subsequent empirical studies of Piaget's conclusions in order to challenge the tacit rationalism of Piaget's theoretical portrait of the human mind.

Consequences for Jesusology

Does the preceding validation, amplification, and criticism of Piaget's account of human cognitive development throw any light on the human-

17. Cf. Peirce, *Collected Papers*, 1.616-677.

ity of Jesus of Nazareth? I believe that it does, provided one approaches that humanity as dynamically human rather than simply as a concrete historical fact.

As we have seen, the dualistic caste of much of patristic thinking caused some of the fathers of the Church to exempt Jesus from the biological exigencies of human life. Such suggestions, however, flow from the self-deceptions of the dualistic fallacy and have not a shred of empirical or historical evidence to support them. In fact, the New Testament suggests the opposite: that Jesus ate and drank, grew and developed, assimilated food and eliminated waste like every other human being. (Mk 7:17-19; Mt 11:19, 15:17; Lk 2:52, 7:34)

If Jesus grew and developed biologically in the manner of other humans, then the same biological processes which ground and limit human cognitive responses grounded and limited His human cognitive development as well. His finite, biologically based human mind had both to assimilate His world and to adapt to it.

If, however, one can assert with high probability that Jesus' human mind grew and developed more or less in the manner of other human minds, then one can also assert that it very probably advanced through something very like the stages of cognitive development described above. In other words, at birth Jesus probably possessed a finite number of instinctive habits, the capacity to respond sensibly and emotionally, and the ability to correlate sensory input from different environmental sources. His finite, infantile mind gradually grew in cognitive complexity as it advanced through something like the six stages of sensory motor development which developmental psychology describes. At about the age of eight or nine, Jesus would very probably have developed the capacity for concrete reasoning, since this ability seems to develop in any culture.

Did Jesus have a fully operational adult mind? Before one can even attempt to answer this question, one needs to clarify its meaning. When interpreted in the light of the pragmatic maxim, the preceding question asks: If Jean Piaget administered to Jesus the kinds of tests which establish operational thinking in his theory of cognitive development, would Jesus have passed the test?

As we shall see in the chapter which follows, the new quests for the historical Jesus suggest that Jesus' mind developed in a largely agrarian and only partially literate culture.[18] As we shall also see in the following chapter, Jesus very probably spoke Aramaic as His first language. Although we know practically nothing for certain about education in Palestine during

18. Cf. Richard A. Horsley with John S. Hanson, *Bandits, Prophets, and Messiahs: Popular Movements at the Time of Jesus* (San Francisco, CA: Harper & Row, 1985); John Dominic Crossan, *The Historical Jesus: The Life of A Mediterranean Peasant* (San Francisco, CA: Harper & Row, 1991), pp. 3-88.

the first century, the New Testament suggests that Jesus could probably read the Old Testament and had enough facility in reading the Hebrew text in order to dispute with other rabbis.[19] As we shall also see later in this chapter, however, the teachings of Jesus preserved in the New Testament suggest that His own mode of public discourse resonated with the oral patterns of thinking of the illiterate peasantry. Jesus never wrote his teachings down. Those which the New Testament have preserved tend to take the form of story and of proverb. Both modes of thinking and reflection typify oral, pre-technological cultures.[20]

Nevertheless, Jesus' mind as we discover it expressed in His teachings also displayed a number of the traits which in developmental thinking accompany fully operational thinking: fascination with novel possibilities, with the future, and with advancing beyond the limits of human convention. Need such traits have flowed from the kind of abstract, inferential thinking which Piaget characterizes as "fully operational"? Not necessarily. The visionary dimensions of Jesus' teaching have much in common with the Jewish prophetic tradition. That tradition, however, gravitates toward imaginative rather than strictly inferential thinking.

As we shall see in chapter ten, one can make a plausible case for the fact that Jesus as the first born son of Mary and Joseph may well have received some secondary education, possibly in the synagogue of Nazareth.[21] We do not, however, know what shape education in a rural town like Nazareth would have taken in the first century.

The fact of education alone does not guarantee that the mind will develop the skills which Piaget regards as "operational" skills. The adults in predominately oral cultures educate their children, but those children do not necessarily develop Piaget's operational schemata. Nor would a study of the stories and concrete wisdom enshrined in the Old Testament have necessarily demanded the capacity to think with the abstract precision of the fully operational mind.

In other words, the evidence for Jesus' having developed fully operational patterns of thinking remains mixed. Moreover, the evidence we possess forces us to face the possibility that indeed He may not have thought operationally. That fact, however, would not make him any the less human but more typically human, since His patterns of thinking would then have conformed to the vast majority of the human race and to those which normal, adult humans seem to share in common. Moreover, in a social construct of the human, to think in culturally condi-

19. Cf. John P. Meier, *A Marginal Jew: Rethinking the Historical Jesus* (3 vols.; New York, NY: Doubleday, 1991), I, pp. 253-315.

20. Cf. Walter J. Ong, *Orality and Literacy: The Technologizing of the Word* (New York, NY: Methuen, 1982).

21. Cf. Meier, *op.cit.*, pp. 272-278, 316-332.

tioned and limited ways typifies all human thought and reflects its historical finitude.

To put the matter briefly and succinctly, if Jesus' humanity consisted of the human experience of a first-century Jewish artisan raised in a predominantly oral, agrarian culture but with the benefit of a rural, synagogue education, then we should not, within the philosophical presuppositions defended here, find it scandalous if he thought like a first-century Jewish artisan raised in a predominantly oral, agrarian culture, but with the benefit of a rural synagogue education.

Such a suggestion would have scandalized a medieval thinker habituated to thinking about humanity in *a priori*, essentialistic, and rationalistic terms. Many modern theological minds enjoy a similar habituation. Nevertheless, in asserting the possibility, even the plausibility, of the fact that Jesus never developed a mind which thought "operationally" in Piaget's technical sense of that term, I have asserted nothing different from the fourth gospel, which equates Jesus humanity with "flesh." By "flesh" the fourth evangelist meant humanity in all of its limitations, vulnerability, finitude, and mortality. Moreover, in making such a suggestion, I remind the reader of the technical sense in which I am using the terms "possibility" and "plausibility." Speaking personally and as a believing Christian, I find the notion that God in taking on a human experience would have embraced the human condition in all of its typical finitude not scandalous but endearing.

(II)

I have reflected on Jesus' human cognitive development. Humans, however, develop in other ways as well. The rationalistic bias of Piaget's thought diverted his attention from the question of human emotional development. Among developmentalists, however, the work of Eric Erickson has compensated for this oversight. What light, then, does Erickson's theory about the stages of emotional growth throw on our understanding of human experience in general and of the humanity of Jesus in particular?

Human Emotional Development

Among developmental psychologists, Eric Erickson has proposed an eight-stage theory of human emotional development. His construct of the human agrees in general with Piaget's. Both interpret human cognitive processes in organic, transactional terms. As a consequence, a triadic construct of experience interprets both theories.

Instead of describing uniform stages of cognitive development, however, Erickson speaks instead of a series of predictable emotional crises which humans have to face in the course of maturation, socialization, and senescence. The resolution of each crisis creates stable skills in the character which enable one to surmount similar challenges in the future with reasonable facility.[22]

In the first year of life children must learn to trust their primary care-givers. They must, for example, learn to tolerate their mother's occasional absence in the expectation that she has not totally abandoned them and will in fact return. Reasonable and realistic mistrust of circumstances serves everyone well at every stage of human development. When, however, mistrust dominates the infant's emotional responses, the infant begins to manifest signs of frustration, social withdrawal, suspicion, and lack of self-confidence.

Moreover, studies of infantile emotional development suggest that, when children attached to their parents suffer separation from them, they develop an indifference toward other people, an unhealthy attitude of "disattachment." The same studies suggest that infants feel an enormous need to have their mothers near them in the first year of life.[23]

The establishment of an ability to trust, prepares the infant to cope with the next crisis of emotional development. Erickson describes the next stage as the conflict between personal autonomy, on the one hand, and doubt and shame, on the other.

During the second year of life, small children are learning to control their own bodies: both their actions and biological functions. At the same time they are beginning to absorb adult standards of behavior. Repeated failure, especially when re-enforced by adult displeasure, buttresses infantile feelings of shame, self-hatred, and self-doubt. The crisis of autonomy vs. shame clusters around a variety of everyday activities like feeding oneself, getting dressed, taking a bath, going to the store, struggles with other toddlers, and toilet training.

As the capacity for autonomy grows, during the second year, toddlers grow in self-confidence and can tolerate separation from parents for longer periods of time. The interiorization of adult norms shows itself in the small child's initial sense of the way things "ought to be." Toddlers will, for example, try to clean up spills and correct other signs of visible disorder. By the end of the second year, most children exhibit reasonable control of their own bodily processes and enter the next stage of emotional challenge, the crisis of initiative vs. guilt.[24]

The mastery of autonomous control over their own bodies creates in children between the ages of three and six the ability to enjoy their own activity and achievements. At this age, children need the opportunity for purposeful, experimental exploration of their world. They also need to

---

22. For a summary of Erickson's stages, see: Eric Erickson, *Identity, Youth, and Crisis* (New York, NY: Norton, 1968); *Identity and the Life Cycle* (New York, NY: Norton, 1980).

23. Cf. Cole and Cole, *op.cit.*, pp. 228-229.   24. *Ibid.*, pp.237-238.

find joy and satisfaction in their own accomplishments. Without the opportunity to experiment and enjoy their achievements, children develop inhibiting and even crippling feelings of guilt when they attempt independent activity.[25]

The fourth stage of emotional development stretches from seven years to puberty and advances the process of socialization into the adult world. During the third stage, children need to enjoy and appreciate their own achievements. During stage four they need to experience adult and peer approval for their personal accomplishments. Unless they find such approval, children suffer from painful feelings of inferiority.[26]

Cross-cultural studies of the development of children show that schooling and culture condition in significant ways how children develop at this stage. In literate and semi-literate cultures, children must master skills like writing and record-keeping, notation systems, increased proficiency in reading, and basic mathematics. At this stage of growth, verbal exchanges and the honing of linguistic skills breed greater proficiency in problem solving. The same cross cultural studies do not suggest, however, that formal schooling produces general cognitive development at this stage, although the family environment and peer relations do affect learning in significant ways.[27]

Studies of human emotional development also suggest that children exhibit different degrees of self-confidence in different social situations. Pre-adolescent children with a high degree of self-confidence usually have parents who accept them and respect the child's individuality at the same time that they establish clear limits for the child's behavior. The establishment of limits aids the child's ability to define a clear sense of self.[28]

During adolescence, children need to establish a clear sense of social and personal identity. They need a clear sense of how they fit into their society, otherwise they lack a clear sense of who they are and of what they want to do with their lives.[29]

The growth spurt which adolescents experience also creates emotional problems of identity. Adolescent children need to integrate their own sexual drives into their maturing personalities. Besides developing healthy peer relationships, adolescents need to learn to relate to the adult worlds which they are about to enter. Typically, as adolescents confront the world of adult living, they find themselves attracted to or repelled by different kinds of ideology and idealism.[30]

Erickson holds that the successful resolution of the adolescent crisis of identity involves four important variables: 1) how the adolescent judges others; 2) how others judge the adolescent; 3) how the adolescent evaluates the judgments of others; and 4) the adolescent's ability to relate real-

25. *Ibid.*, p. 359.   26. *Ibid.*   27. *Ibid.*, pp. 438-473.
28. *Ibid.*, 508-509.   29. *Ibid.*, p. 359.   30. *Ibid.*, p. 575.

istically to social and cultural expectations in making judgments about others. In other words, personal perspective, the perspectives of others, and the expectations of society and of culture all shape identity formation during the period of adolescence.[31]

Contemporary adolescents in process of negotiating the identity crisis tend to fall into one of four categories: a) Identity achievers have determined their life-goals and are actively pursuing them; b) Foreclosers have accepted a social and personal identity without going through a period of indecision and turmoil. c) Those with moratoriums have postponed a decision about their adult identity. d) Those who suffer from identify diffusion have tried different identities and found that none of them fit.[32]

Young adults experience the need for intimate relations with others. When they fail to establish such relationships, they suffer from feelings of loneliness and isolation.

During middle age and before the onset of old age, adults need to find emotional satisfaction in their work and personal productivity. They also need to find fulfillment in nurturing the next generation. Frustration in both of these enterprises suffuses life with a sense of stagnant and pointless routine.

As old people face the prospect of senescence and dying, they need to assure themselves that their lives have had genuine meaning, otherwise they lapse into feelings of despair and self-recrimination over unaccomplished goals and ill-spent lives.[33]

Verification, Amplification, and Contextualization

The triadic, social construct of experience developed in the last chapter both interprets and contextualizes Erickson's theory of human emotional development. Like Erickson, it conceives human evaluative development in social, transactional terms. Like Erickson, it understands the emerging human self as a biologically conditioned, finite, social reality. The resolution of each stage of emotional development in Erickson involves not only evaluations and decisions but also the establishment of stable habits of emotional response which create the stability of character required to deal with the next stage of affective self-definition and consolidation. The philosophical category "tendency" interprets these character developments.

At the same time, Erickson's theory amplifies in significant ways the philosophical account of human experience sketched in the preceding chapter. It does so by describing in much greater detail the kinds of emotional crises which typically mark the different stages of human maturation and decline.

Erickson writes as a clinical psychiatrist rather than as an empirical psychologist. Although his theory lacks the more systematic data base

31. *Ibid.*, pp. 584-586.   32. *Ibid.*, p. 587.   33. *Ibid.*, p. 359.

which the empirical sciences of the human provide, it does attempt to take into account the results of cross-cultural studies of human emotional development. It therefore offers a plausible hypothesis about the way in which humans typically mature at an emotional level.

Finally, Erickson's thought avoids the rationalistic bias which skews Piaget's understanding of human cognitive development. It therefore does not invite the same kind of philosophical criticism.

Consequences for Jesusology

I am examining the results of clinical, empirical, and scholarly studies of human development for the light they throw on the experience of living as a human being. That examination has both a purely rational agenda and a theological agenda. At a purely rational level it seeks both to verify and amplify the philosophical construct of the human proposed in chapter five by testing it against the results of more focused studies of human life and development. At a theological level, I am attempting to assess in a preliminary way what a verified and amplified philosophical construct of humanity has to tell us about Jesus' human experience.

The fact that Erickson's construct of human affective development offers a plausible account of how humans in different cultures mature emotionally makes it also plausible that Jesus of Nazareth, in the course of his own personal development, would have had to pass through something like the stages of emotional growth which Erickson describes. We need, however, to qualify immediately even this tentative suggestion. Erickson's theory suggests that the process of socialization conditions in significant ways the manner in which human beings develop especially from stage four to stage eight. As we have already seen and shall see in more detail in the chapter which follows, the third quest for the historical Jesus can tell us something about the social and cultural context in which Jesus lived and grew; but it yields no detailed insight into his personal education and no detailed knowledge at all of the specific kinds of cultural factors which would have conditioned his personal emotional maturation.

Moreover, Jesus probably suffered crucifixion in His mid-thirties. On the presupposition that He had negotiated successfully the first five stages of human emotional development, at the time of His public ministry, He would, under Erickson's hypothesis, have been in the midst of the crisis of young adulthood. That means that during his ministry, He would have experienced vulnerability to personal loneliness and isolation.

Finally, the gospels make it virtually certain that Jesus not only foresaw His own death but interiorized it.[34] That makes at least plausible the possibility that, as a young adult he would also have had to face some-

---

34. Cf. Edward Schillebeeckx, *Jesus: An Experiment in Christology*. translated by Herbert Hoskins (New York, NY: Crossroad, 1979). pp. 274-294.

thing like the emotional crisis which confronts most people in old age: namely, the struggle between integrity and despair.

I would, then, deem it plausible that Jesus went through something like the first five stages of emotional development which Erickson describes. I would judge it equally plausible that at the time of his own public ministry He was dealing with issues of intimacy and isolation. I would also regard it as plausible that as Jesus approached death He would have had to struggle with feelings of integrity and despair. In the virtual absence of historical knowledge of Jesus' life prior to his public ministry, we can, however, only guess the concrete shape these crises might have taken for Him and the concrete way in which He might have resolved them. Here one can wander almost endlessly in the realm of unverifiable possibility.

(III)

I have pondered Jesus' plausible cognitive and emotional development. The third and final section of this chapter examines human moral development.

Among developmental psychologists, Jean Piaget, Lawrence Kohlberg, and William Damon have each produced theories about how the human conscience matures cognitively. Piaget's theory exhibits the same rationalistic bias as his theory of cognitive development, especially by its somewhat narrow focus on the way in which rules function within moral reasoning.

Piaget on Moral Development

According to Piaget, the first stage of cognitive moral development ends sometime between the ages of two and five. During this stage the child gives no evidence that it understands the meaning of rules or their relationship to conduct.[35] For Piaget, this first stage qualifies as more pre-moral than moral.

Sometime between two and five years of age, children begin to understand the notion of a rule. Other children play according to rules, and parents have rules which they expect the child to obey. At this primitive stage, the child gives no evidence of understanding that rules govern human social intercourse. Children at this stage seem to obey rules out of a desire to feel understood, accepted by others. The first stage of moral reasoning ends around the age of seven or eight.

At this initial, primitive stage of moral development, children seem to regard rules as simply given. They do not seem to understand that people make rules and can change them. Rules laid down by parents tend to enjoy an aura of noumenal mystery. As a consequence, very young children live by a heteronomous morality. In questions of personal decision,

---

35. Cf. Jean Piaget, *The Moral Judgment of the Child*, translated by Marjorie Gabain (New York, NY: Paulist, 1975), pp. 51-3.

very young children tend to rely rigidly on parental guidance and judgment. They tend to equate the best punishment with the most severe because it brings the surest conviction of guilt.[36]

According to Piaget, sometime around the age of seven or eight, children advance to the third level of ethical reasoning, which he describes as an ethics of cooperation. Children discover that children themselves can and do make the rules for play. They discover signs of fallibility in their parents and recognize that even parental rules have a sometimes questionable human origin. The developing child's discovery of a personal ability to make rules creates a new sense of responsibility concerning personal obedience to rules. The child now recognizes that because one can make the rules oneself, consent to abide by the rules, whoever makes them, brings with it a responsibility to obey. Children begin to negotiate with other children concerning the rules of play; but, once agreed upon, they expect everyone, including themselves, to conform.

During the period of moral cooperation, therefore, rules in the maturing child's eyes lose the sacred, given character which marked them at the second stage of development. Nevertheless, once children realize that personal consent to obey the rules brings with it the obligation to keep one's word, that realization enhances rather than undermines the child's sense of moral commitment.

Moreover, as the stage of cooperative morality develops, the child begins to exhibit a sense of moral proportionality in the violation of rules. In the early stages of cooperative moral thinking, children tend to insist on an egalitarian enforcement of a rule. The same punishment for its violation must fall upon everyone without exception. As the child's conscience matures, however, it also develops a more nuanced sense of equity in the application of rules as it takes into account the limitations of persons and of situations.[37]

For Piaget, the fully operational child enters a fourth stage of moral development: namely, the stage of codification. Around the age of eleven, as the child's capacity for abstract, inferential thinking grows, it increasingly generalizes, organizes, and institutionalizes the rules of moral conduct.[38]

Contextualization and Verification

The philosophical construct of experience presented in chapter two helps contextualize Piaget's theory of human moral development. That construct distinguishes between intuitive and inferential thinking, on the one hand, and prudential reasoning on the other. Intuitive and inferential reasoning interpret and explain. Prudential reasoning deliberates about concrete choices in an aesthetic, speculative, practical, or moral context.

36. *Ibid.*, pp. 57–61, 111–194.   37. *Ibid.*, pp. 199–279.   38. *Ibid.*, pp. 279–323.

Piaget, as we have seen, calls imaginative thinking "transductive" and abstract rational thinking "operational." Since moral reasoning differs from both forms of thinking, it defines in his theory a separate realm of human thought and discourse. Prudential moral reasoning provides, then, the correct philosophical context for evaluating Piaget's theory of human ethical development.

Moreover, to the extent that Piaget's account of human development recognizes and documents a realm of prudential moral reflection distinct from both imaginative thinking and inferential reasoning, it lends empirical verification to the philosophical notion of prudential reasoning as a distinctive realm of human evaluative response with its own distinctive habits, or "schemata."

Philosophical Criticism

The philosophy of experience defended in this study raises, however, serious questions about the philosophical presuppositions which lie at the basis of Piaget's construct of moral reasoning. As Lev Vygotsky has observed, Piaget made a sincere attempt to let the facts of human cognitive behavior dictate his interpretation of that behavior. Since, however, in any investigation one deals not just with raw facts but with interpreted facts, Piaget in the last analysis could not avoid making philosophical assumptions about the cognitive activities he described. Nor did he avoid philosophical assumptions in his formulation of the hypotheses which sought to explain those activities.[39]

As we have seen, a rationalistic bias led Piaget to misprize the importance of "transductive" thinking and to overrate the importance of "operational" thinking. Related assumptions mar his account of human moral development. Piaget's approach to moral reasoning betrays a certain Kantian bias. Like Kant Piaget models moral reasoning on theoretical reasoning, even though, with Kant, he also recognizes that they differ. Moreover, as in the case of Kantian ethics, Piaget gives disproportionate importance to the role which universal moral principles play in human prudential judgments.

The construct of prudential reasoning developed in chapter two would call into question the adequacy of such a construct of prudential moral reasoning. Rules and principles certainly function within moral deliberation; but the conscience ordinarily cannot deduce from universal principles the best solution to any complex ethical dilemma. Intuitive, imaginative thinking plays a much more important role in the deliberations of the mature conscience than Piaget's account of moral development seems to suggest.

39. Cf. Lev Vygotsky, *Thought and Language*, revised and edited by Alex Kozulin (Cambridge, MA: The MIT Press, 1988), pp. 40-47.

In other words, when one reflects on the philosophical presuppositions which shape Piaget's theory of human moral development in the light of the philosophy of experience developed in chapter two, one must question the adequacy of his conclusions. Like the philosophers of the Enlightenment, Piaget's assumption that human thinking culminates in abstract, empirical, scientific, reasoning led him, as Kant did, to assimilate moral thinking to scientific and to assume the normativity of something like Kantian deontological ethics.[40] The moral mind achieves adult maturity in Piaget's account when it begins universalizing and codifying the rules of human conduct.

In fact, however, moral thinking involves much more than the application of universal rules to concrete moral situations. It engages appreciative judgments of affecton which respect the concreteness and complexity of different ethical contexts. While the intuitive mind invokes principles relevant to the moral situations about which it deliberates, in the end it must make a creative judgment about how best to advance a conflicted moral situation as far as possible toward the embodiment of the kinds of ethical ideals to which one stands committed. Prudential deliberations yield, as we have seen, a sense of the fitting response to moral conflicts, all things considered.

At the same time, I personally find it plausible that games symbolize for children broader social relationships and that children need to learn to subordinate their social conduct to some mutually agreed upon social system of morality. Nevertheless, Piaget's Kantian bias seems to blind him to the complexity of moral reasoning, and his theory presupposes his rationalistic theory of cognitive development, a theory which gives short shrift to the intuitive grasp of reality. In the last analysis, therefore, his account of moral development offers only a plausible account of the way in which learned rules function in the moral deliberations of children, especially those raised in modern technological cultures.

Even in technological cultures, however, not everyone seems to achieve the level of scientific rationality which Piaget enthrones at the apex of human cognitive and moral development. Moreover, as we have seen, "operational" thinking in Piaget's understanding of that term does not seem to develop as frequently in pre-technological, oral cultures. As a consequence, one must in the last analysis question not only the philosophical adequacy but the universal applicability of Piaget's moral theory. Finally, we note that Piaget's focus on the cognitive dimensions of human moral development leaves open the question whether or not people actually follow the judgments of their consciences at any given stage of moral development.

40. Deontological ethics reduces ethical thinking to the nominalistic subsumption of concrete ethical situations under universal moral principles.

I have weighed the pros and cons of Piaget's account of human moral development. I turn now to the theories of Lawrence Kohlberg.

Kohlberg on Moral Development

Among developmental theorists, Lawrence Kohlberg has proposed the most comprehensive theory of cognitive moral development. Kohlberg built on the pioneering work of Piaget; but he also derived his developmental hypothesis from a variety of philosophical sources: notably from John Dewey, from John Rawls, and from social contract theory. From Dewey, for example, Kohlberg accepted the idea that human moral development advances through three general stages: a pre-conventional stage, a conventional stage, and a post-conventional stage. Each of Kohlberg's stages has two substages. Social contract theory provided the norms for Kohlberg's fifth stage. Kant's deontological ethics and Rawl's philosophy of justice colored stage six.[41]

Kohlberg characterizes the first sub-stage of pre-conventional moral development as heteronomous. During this first substage the child judges right and wrong according to rules which it accepts without question from others, especially from parents or from parental surrogates. The superiority of the moral authorities who legislate behavior combines with the fear of punishment in order to motivate obedience. At this stage, the child still tends to think with a spontaneous egocentrism which makes it difficult to understand the viewpoints of others or to take them into account.

At the second stage of pre-conventional development, the child's moral judgments still serve the child's own immediate interests; but the child now recognizes that others have the right to act according to their own individual interests and concerns. The "right" act means the "fair" act; and the maxim "You scratch my back, and I'll scratch yours" defines the meaning of fairness. Doing right signifies, then, serving one's own interests and needs in a world in which others also have legitimate personal interests and needs. Acknowledgement of the needs and interests of others creates in children a limited willingness to negotiate a balance of interests.

In Kohlberg's theory, one does not begin to make conventional moral judgments until one's mind is beginning to make the transition to fully "operational" thinking in Piaget's sense of that term. At the first substage of conventional morality, the conscience of the young adolescent moves in a world of mutual, interpersonal expectations, relationships, and social

---

41. For a summary of Kohlberg's stages, see: Lawrence Kohlberg, "The Cognitive-Developmental Approach to Moral Education," *Phi Delta Kappan*, LVI (June, 1975), pp. 670-677; D. Sholl, "The Contribution of Lawrence Kohlberg to Religious and Moral Development," *Religious Education*, LXVI (1971), pp. 364-372.

conformity. Doing right means now living up to what people expect of one in different social roles. Doing right means having good intentions, showing concern about others, and sustaining mutual relationships, like loyalty, trust, respect, or gratitude. The Golden Rule provides a basic maxim for judging right and wrong. One desires to act in ways which prove one's personal goodness in one's own eyes and in the eyes of others. One supports those authorities which re-enforce stereotypically good behavior. In making moral judgments one now values the preservation of mutual personal relationships.

By the time the young conscience advances to the second substage of conventional morality, it shows some mastery of formal operations. Doing right now means fulfilling the duties to which one has agreed. One supports the rule of law in judging moral situations, except in those cases in which laws conflict with other fixed social duties. Doing right also begins to mean contributing to society, to the group, to the institution to which one belongs. In one's moral judgments, one interiorizes the viewpoint of the social systems to which one belongs.

In the first substage of post-conventional morality, one espouses a social-contract ethics. The speculative mind has now consolidated its capacity for operational thinking. Doing right means taking into account the fact that other people defend a variety of values and opinions in moral matters. One recognizes the relativity of socially inculcated rules and values. One considers oneself bound by social obligations into which one enters freely and supports rules which encourage fidelity to such obligations. One believes that fidelity to one's social contracts promotes the good of all. The conscience assumes the standpoint of the rational individual who espouses rights and values personally and prior to social attachments.

At the second substage of post-conventional morality, the human conscience makes moral judgments on the basis of universal ethical principles. Doing right means following self-chosen universal principles of just conduct. Belief in the validity of universal moral principles motivates ethical choices. In making moral judgments one seeks to take the perspective of any rational individual who would judge the case in the light of universally just laws.[42]

Criticism and Contextualization
Kohlberg's theory labors under a number of methodological and philosophical difficulties. It acquiesces in the same kind of rationalistic presuppositions as Piaget. Moreover, the Kantianism implicit in Piaget's work comes to full and overt expression in Kohlberg's. Like Piaget, Kohlberg

---

42. Cf. Cole and Cole, *op.cit.*, pp. 486-487, 578.

believes that fully adult moral thinking ought to subsume concrete ethical situations under universal moral principles, especially under principles
of justice.

In testing out his hypothesis empirically, however, Kohlberg and others
have concluded that virtually no one ever reaches the sixth and highest
stage of "operational" moral reasoning. That fact suggests either that the
human conscience with fairly universal consistency fails to achieve the
full operational rationality to which Kohlberg destines it or that the conscience functions somewhat less rationally than he presupposes.[43]

Critics of Kohlberg have also justly faulted him for failing to take into
adequate account the role which feeling and imagination play in the judgments of the adult conscience. Those same critics call into question the
individualistic presuppositions which especially characterize the higher
stages of moral development.[44]

Carol Gilligan has criticized the implicit sexism of Kohlberg's research
techniques. Kohlberg studied only men when he attempted to verify his
theory of moral development. Gilligan argues that women on the whole
tend to resolve moral dilemmas on different presuppositions from those
suggested by Kohlberg. As a result, she objects that Kohlberg's hypothesis
does not paint a fair portrait of moral development among women.[45]

What, then, ought one to think of Kohlberg's theory of moral development? In my judgment, Kohlberg's work lends some plausibility to Dewey's
proposal that the human conscience advances through three discernible
stages of growth: pre-conventional morality, conventional morality, and
post-conventional morality. Like Piaget, Kohlberg has documented the
fact that infantile consciences exhibit a spontaneous and initially innocent egocentrism which the processes of socialization mute and gradually
transform. The fact, however, that Kohlberg's higher stages rest on questionable philosophical presuppositions renders them, in my judgment,
extremely problematic.

---

43. Cf. Lawrence Kohlberg, "The Claim to Moral Adequacy of a Highest Stage of Moral
Judgment," *The Journal of Philosophy*, LXX (October, 1973), pp. 630-646.
44. For a critique of individualism see: Robert N. Bellah, *et al.*, *Habits of the Heart:
Individualism and Commitment in American Life* (New York, NY: Capricorn, 1962);
Roberto Mangabeira Unger, *Knowledge and Politics* (New York, NY: Free Press, 1975);
Donald L. Gelpi, S.J., ed., *Beyond Individualism: Toward a Retrieval of Moral Dis-
course in America* (Notre Dame, IN: University of Notre Dame Press, 1989). For
Kohlberg on the higher stages of moral conceptualization, see Lawrence Kohlberg,
"The Claim to Moral Adequacy of a Highest Stage of Moral Judgment," *The Journal
of Philosophy*, LXX (October, 1973), p. 642.
45. Cf. Carol Gilligan, *In a Different Voice: Women's Conceptions of the Self and Morality*
(Cambridge, MA: Harvard University Press, 1982); "In a Different Voice: Women's
Conceptions of the Self and Morality," *Harvard Educational Review*, 47(1977), pp.
481-517.

Finally, even though Kohlberg offers a more detailed construct of human moral development than Piaget, his conclusions, like Piaget's, leave one in the dark as to whether or not people at any given stage of development actually make morally correct choices.

I have reflected on the strengths and limitations of two major theories of moral development. A third theory shows, in my judgment, greater promise. I refer to the work of William Damon.

William Damon on Human Moral Development

William Damon's theory of moral development avoids the problems which mar the two hypotheses which we have just examined.[46] Damon describes moral development as a facet of socialization. His theory correctly presupposes a social construct of the self. It also correctly recognizes the interplay of thought and action within human moral development. Damon believes, however, that practical moral reasoning about specific situations tends to lag behind theoretical moral reasoning, because the press of circumstances often forces a moral decision before the child has an opportunity to think things through. Damon also recognizes that cultural influences condition moral development in the young. Without endorsing cultural relativism, Damon confines his own generalizations to middle class children in the United States.[47]

In Damon's theory, children develop morally in six stages, as they do in Kohlberg's hypothesis. Damon, however, conceives the stages differently from Kohlberg. As in Kohlberg's theory, however, each stage divides into two substages.

The first stage in Damon's theory characterizes infantile moral development. In it the child's choices reflect personal desires. During both substages of stage one, children have yet to acquire the capacity for moral reasoning in the strict sense of that term. Damon therefore calls the first two substages "Level 0-A" and "Level 0-B."

Level 0-A characterizes the choices of children of four years and younger. Choices at this primitive stage simply express the desire that a certain act occur. Reasons for acting do nothing more than assert the child's own spontaneous desires. At substage one, for example, a child might argue that it deserves more ice cream because it likes ice cream and wants more.

Level 0-B characterizes the choices of children between the ages of four and five. At this stage, choices still reflect the child's spontaneous desires, but they acquire a new kind of justification based on external, observable traits like sex, size, age, etc. The childish mind reasons in a fluctuating, after-the-fact manner and still tends to act from self-serving motives. At this level of moral reasoning, for example, a child might argue that it

46. Cf. William Damon, *The Social World of the Child* (San Francisco, CA: Jossey-Bass, 1977).   47. *Ibid.*, pp. 1-23.

should get what it wants because he or she runs faster, is a boy (or girl), is taller, etc.

Damon's second stage brings the dawn of moral reasoning. Stage two also divides into two sub-stages: Level 1-A and Level 1-B.

Level 1-A characterizes the choices of children between the ages of five and seven. The moral negotiations of children now equate justice with fairness, and they define fairness as strict equality. The child now believes that all children should share and share alike, frequently because strict equality prevents fighting and unpleasant disputes.

Level 1-B characterizes the moral judgments of children between the ages of six and nine. At this level, moral negotiations begin to display a more nuanced sense of justice. The child now measures fairness by merit. The young conscience now proportions rewards to merit and punishments to guilt.

In Damon's third stage of moral development, children begin to recognize the concrete relativity of moral situations. Stage three divides into level 2-A and level 2-B

At Level 2-A, children define justice quantitatively. They recognize, however, that special human needs make special moral claims. The poor, the suffering, the destitute have the moral right to special consideration.

By age ten, children have advanced to level 2-B, Damon's final stage of moral development during childhood. The conscience now recognizes a qualitative difference among human moral claims. It understands that all people deserve their due. Given, however, the qualitative differences among persons and situations, "their due" can mean different things in different contexts.[48]

Verification, Contextualization, Amplification

Of the three explanations of human moral development, Damon's accords best with the notion of conscience developed in the preceding chapter. Damon underscores the social character of the self and the dialogic nature of human reasoning. He avoids endorsing the Kantianism, rationalism, and individualism which make the other two hypotheses problematic. Damon recognizes better than his two predecessors that moral reasoning involves more than the subsumption of problematic moral situations under universal rules. In Damon's account, as the human conscience matures it develops greater sensitivity to the complexity and qualitative differences present in concrete moral situations.

All three theorists recognize something like a pre-moral stage in human ethical reasoning. The spontaneous and initially innocent egocentrism of the human mind makes it difficult at first for children to under-

---

48. *Ibid.*, pp. 71-136. Cf. Cole and Cole, *op.cit.*, p. 489.

stand and therefore to take into account the viewpoints and needs of others.

Of the three theorists, Damon, in my judgment, gives the most plausible account of early moral development; but the applicability of Damon's theory remains an open question. He himself makes no claims of applicability beyond middle-class children in the United States.

Relevance for Jesusology

In attempting to assess the potential Christological relevance of contemporary theories of human moral development, one faces two interrelated problems, one doctrinal, the other historical. At a doctrinal level one must take into account the New Testament claim that Jesus resembled other humans in every respect except sin. From a doctrinal standpoint, therefore, Jesus in His humanity differed morally in significant ways from that of other human beings. I cannot deal adequately with the question of Jesus' sinlessness until I consider doctrinal Christology as such. Here I simply note that in its final formulation any Christology needs to deal with this doctrinal belief about Jesus.

Even if one concedes, however, that contemporary theories about human cognitive moral development do in fact have something to say about the way in which Jesus may have developed morally, one still faces the factual question, whether Jesus' conscience in fact grew humanly in the way in which contemporary developmental theories describe. Let us reflect on each of these problems in turn.

In what concerns the doctrine of Jesus' sinlessness, one should note that none of the preceding theories makes any judgment whatever about moral guilt or innocence. All three theories confine themselves to speculating about cognitive moral development, even though Damon concedes the interplay of thought and action in moral reasoning. All three theories agree in asserting that moral reasoning does advance in cognitive stages, even though they differ in their description of the nature of those stages. If Jesus had a human conscience, and He certainly did, I would regard it as certain that His human ability to make moral judgments developed.

If Jesus' human conscience developed in its ability to judge moral situations, then in its earlier stages it would have tended to invoke less adequate criteria than in its more mature stages. Doctrinal belief in Jesus' sinlessness makes no judgment in principle about the moral adequacy of the criteria which Jesus would have invoked at age two, age seven, or age eleven. It asserts, rather that at any given state of moral development Jesus would never have deliberately chosen anything which violated His human conscience. In other words, even if one asserts Jesus' sinlessness for doctrinal reasons, that fact does not preclude His cognitive moral maturation. Rather, His cognitive development means that as Jesus' conscience matured it invoked more and more sophisticated norms in making moral choices. Sinless moral growth would only require that at any given stage of growth, Jesus' conduct conformed to those norms to which He believed Himself humanly and conscientiously bound.

Did Jesus' conscience develop in the manner in which Piaget and Kohlberg suggest? Both theories, as we have seen, rest on questionable philosophical presuppositions derived largely from Enlightenment thinking. Those presuppositions render them, in my judgment, not only speculatively but historically implausible. I find it inherently improbable that a first-century, Palestinian, Jewish artisan living in a predominantly oral and religious culture would have developed the conscience of an eighteenth-century European *philosophe*.

Both Piaget's and Damon's theories of moral development abstract from religious considerations without necessarily excluding them. Kohlberg's theory, however, positively excludes religious variables from moral consideration. Eventually, Kohlberg expanded his theory to include a seventh, quasi-religious stage of moral development in which the conscience stands ready to suffer for the sake of justice. Since, however, stage six seems to exceed the capacity of most mortals, it seems on Kohlberg's developmental presuppositions morally impossible for anyone to reach stage seven.

Kohlberg's exclusion of religious motives from moral reasoning makes his theory particularly irrelevant to the issues raised by a systematic Jesusology. As we shall see, the New Testament portrays Jesus as proclaiming a morality of faith. That fact suggests a conscience thoroughly informed by religious realities and values. However Jesus' conscience evolved cognitively, Jesus' adult conscience seems to have ignored contemporary distinctions between the morally sacred and the morally secular.

The fact that both Piaget and Damon abstract from religious motivation also suggests that one should use extreme caution in projecting their theories onto the historical figure of Jesus. The fact, moreover, that all three developmental theorists cannot agree on a common construct of human moral development provides another good reason for not reifying any of the going theories historically.

Nevertheless, it seems probable to me that, as Jesus' matured in His ability to make moral judgments, He would have had to transcend the innocent egocentrism of the infantile conscience. Like other children, then, he would have had to learn to take into account the needs and interests of others. He would have had also to evolve more and more conceptually adequate criteria for making moral judgments.

Quite plausibly, moreover, both Piaget and Damon have named some of the human variables which conditioned the growth of Jesus' human conscience. I deem it plausible, for example, that He, like other children, found social symbolism in the rules of play, even though we have no way of knowing the specific kind of symbolism games may have held for Him. I also find it plausible that as Jesus' human mind developed the capacity for formal moral reasoning, however elementary, it would have struggled with questions of equity and reciprocity. I would judge it probable, even certain, that, as Jesus' conscience developed, it exhibited sensitivity to qualitative moral differences among persons and situations. Indeed, in His capacity to empathize with sinners, with aliens, with women, with outcasts, and with social expendables like lepers and beggars, the Jesus of the New Testament exhibits a conscience extraordinarily nuanced and empathetic in its assessment of moral individuals and moral situations.

Jesus' diatribes against moral legalism also make it clear that Jesus' adult conscience had advanced beyond conventional morality. Far from reducing moral reasoning to the subsumption of moral situations under universally applicable Kantian rules, however, the Jesus of the New Testament gives evidence of having placed a high ethical value on compassionate sensitivity to concrete persons and situations.

In this chapter I have weighed the contribution which contemporary developmental psychology makes to our understanding of personal cognitive, emotional, and moral development. Since the theories I have examined attempt to throw light on the human condition, I have also assessed their ability to throw light on Jesus' human development. I have argued for the plausibility of the fact that Jesus may have advanced through something like the cognitive and emotional stages described by Piaget and Erickson.

Moral developmental theories yield more meager results. Their questionable philosophical presuppositions and abstraction from the role which religion plays in forming the conscience raise serious questions about their applicability to Jesus. Yet, most probably, Jesus' conscience did develop cognitively; and Damon and Piaget have named some of the variables which, quite plausibly, conditioned His moral growth.

In the following chapter, I shall reflect on theories of human social development. As in this chapter, I shall assess their ability to verify and amplify a triadic, philosophical construct of experience; and I shall weigh their ability to illumine Jesus' social development.

Chapter 7
Jesus' Social Development

The preceding chapter examined developmental psychology for the light it has to throw on the complex processes of human personal growth. In the course of that examination, I have attempted to use the results of empirical investigations of human growth processes in order to verify and amplify the philosophical construct of experience sketched in chapter five. Moreover, where it seemed appropriate, I have also used that construct in order to criticize some of the tacit but questionable assumptions which motivate some developmental theories. Finally, I weighed what each developmental theory has to contribute to a contemporary Jesusology.

A triadic philosophical construct of experience requires that one understand human experience as simultaneously personal and social. In the present chapter, therefore, I shall examine several scientific theories about human social development. I shall assess their ability to verify and amplify the triadic construct of experience proposed in chapter five; and I shall assess what, if anything, they might contribute to understanding Jesus' human development.

This chapter divides into four parts. Part one weighs Daniel Stern's account of infantile interpersonal development. Part two examines how children interiorize linguistic thought patterns; and it also speculates about the kinds of linguistic patterns Jesus might plausibly have interiorized. Part three ponders patterns in human socialization. Part four considers male maturation.

(I)

Even though the developmental theories I have examined so far focus on personal growth processes, all of them presuppose the social character and conditioning of human experience. The theories examined in the last chapter have, however, focused on the growing individual as an individual. They predicted stages of personal intellectual, affective, and moral growth. Theories of human social growth stress by contrast the relational character of the self and speculate about its development with respect to other persons and social institutions.

Infantile Social Development

Among developmental theorists, Daniel Stern has insisted on the fundamentally social character of even early infantile development. Stern's close observations of infantile behavior convinced him that human infants begin very early to develop socially. He speaks of six stages in an infant's sense of social relatedness. The infant's initial vague sense of itself as emergent first develops into a social sense of a "core self." The core self then becomes a "subjective self" and finally a "verbal self." Two substages each define both the "core self" and the "subjective self." The "verbal self" emerges as the sixth and final stage.

After birth, infants possess a vague sense of self-awareness but a real one. This first stage of self-awareness takes the form of an alert inactivity, an absorption of surrounding events. These periods of attentiveness can last several minutes. Neonates also exhibit three kinds of behavior: they turn their heads, they suck, and they look at things. Nursing infants seem to recognize the smell of their mother's milk and to distinguish it from other smells. They also seek sensory stimulation and display apparently innate preferences for certain kinds of sensory stimuli, like sucking. Neonates learn to discriminate variant sensory experiences from invariant. Earliest lessons about the world seem to contain a strong affective component.[1]

The behavior of neonates gives evidence, therefore, of a vague sense of self-awareness which results from the effort to organize its experience. Indeed, the conscious organization of experience constitutes what Stern means by "the emergent sense of self." As I have already indicated, the child at birth already possesses the capacity to interrelate different kinds of sensory stimuli. The child also experiences the flux and surging of different emotions.[2]

At the age of two or three months, the behavior of infants takes a pronounced social turn. Stern characterizes the infant's new behavior as "more social: more regulated, more attentive, smarter." The infant displays greater bodily control and a more integrated body-consciousness. The child seems to own its own affectivity more, to exhibit a greater sense of the continuity of experience, and to display an awareness of other persons as other. At this first stage of core development, then, the child seems to define itself consciously over against the other as other in a manner which goes beyond the responses of the first two or three months.[3]

Four elements constitute the core self: 1) The child has a new sense of *self-agency*. It realizes that it can move or not move its own body. 2) The child exhibits a new sense of *self- coherence*. It seems to sense continuity in its own reality whether it acts or not. 3) The child displays affective responses to other persons. 4) The infant exhibits a vague sense of its own *self-history* at least in its ability to connect the past with the present.[4]

In Stern's theory each stage of infantile self-awareness presupposes and builds upon what precedes it. The core sense of self which the child de-

1. Cf. Daniel N. Stern, *The Interpersonal World of the Infant* (New York, NY: Harper/Collins, 1988), pp. 37-42. 2. *Ibid.*, p. 45-68.
3. *Ibid.*, p. 69 4. *Ibid.*, p. 71-99.

velops at three or four months continues to function in adult life. Indeed, the psychic health of adults presupposes it.[5]

Between the ages of approximately three and seven months, the core sense of self further evolves. An awareness of the other as other becomes an awareness of *being with* another self. In other words, the infant begins to understand the meaning of "we."

The infant begins to regulate its behavior with respect to the "other," usually with respect to its primary care-giver. In addition to regular routines of feeding, bathing, and clothing, think of simple games like "peek-a-boo" or "I gotcha."

Infants very early bond affectively with primary care-givers. As a result, the care-giver's activities help regulate the infant's attention; but the infant also has the capacity to direct its own attention. The remembered regularity of past interactions gradually transforms itself into the anticipation and evocation of possible companionship. During the first seven months, then, the infant acquires an initial sense of social bondedness.[6]

Between the seventh and ninth month, infants make a second quantum leap in social self-awareness: they discover that they have minds and that others have them as well. The infant responds to the intentional behavior of other persons with a new awareness that intentionality lies behind that behavior. Awareness of intentionality in others engages the infant's own experiences of desiring, excitement, and relationship. The child's responses acquire a new "feel," a new sense of conscious presence. In addition to being with others, the child now exhibits a new capacity for psychic intimacy: an openness to self-disclosure and interpenetration with other persons. In other words, the infant had discovered the realm of inter-subjective relatedness.[7]

At the first stage of inter-subjective self-awareness, the child shares experiences which do not require translation into language. The child, for example, recognizes the meaning of a gesture, like pointing. The child then begins pointing to things on its own. Besides gestures, the infant now seeks to communicate by posture, action, and nonverbal vocalizations which foreshadow the emergence of language. Instead of just seeking to influence the behavior of another, the child now tries to communicate with another mind.[8]

In addition, infants in the first stage of inter-subjective awareness learn to share affective states with other minds. The sharing of attitudes manifests itself in the activity of social-referencing. When encountering a baffling new situation, the infant now looks to the primary care-giver for indications of how to respond. If the parent smiles, the child will tend to smile and relate positively to the new challenge. If the parent shows fear,

5. *Ibid.*, p. 71   6. *Ibid.*, pp. 100-123.
7. *Ibid.*, pp. 124-127.   8. *Ibid.*, pp. 128-131.

the child will tend to react with apprehension and withdrawal. This primal ability to share affective attitudes gradually develops into the second stage of inter-subjective awareness, the stage of "affect attunement."[9]

With the emergence of affective inter-subjectivity, parents begin to relate differently to their infants. They begin to use language in emotionally charged ways which express to the infant that they share in the child's joy, excitement, pleasure. For example, as the infant joyfully bangs a toy on the ground, the mother might enter with both word and gesture into the play by nodding and repeating "Ka-bam, ka-bam" in rhythm with the child's act of banging. Or the primary care giver might match a child's smile of joy with a personal smile and an encouraging, "Yeah!" As in the first example, the parent's behavior uses a word which imitates the child's own affective state. This linguistic behavior toward the child expresses the fact that the care-giver shares the child's own affective response. From the child's standpoint, the parent's word functions as a potential linguistic symbol of that response.[10]

In these elementary linguistic interchanges between mother and child, the affective intensity of the parent modulates itself to match the infant's own affective responses. It imitates the rhythms and temporal beat of infantile activities which express the child's affective state. The time-span of the parent's behavior matches the time-span of the infant's. The parent's behavior imitates both physically and verbally what the child is doing rather than slavishly repeating it. For example, instead of moving her own arm to imitate the banging action of the infant, the mother in the example cited above, imitated the up-and-down movement of the infant's arm with an up-and-down movement of the head together with the rhythmic saying of the onomatopoeic word "ka-bam." Laboratory experiments make it clear that infants understand well the intentionality and symbolic character of these primitive acts of communication. The symbolic comprehension of affect attunement thus brings the infant to the threshold of language.[11]

The emergence of language effects the greatest transformation in the infant's sense of social self-awareness. It forces a distinction between the experience of life as lived and life as verbally constructed. Verbally constructed meaning lacks the immediacy of pre-verbal forms of communication and therefore teaches the child how to abstract consciously from immediate lived experience. The verbal child grasps intentionality through linguistic symbols rather than by the direct experience of the realities to which the concepts refer.[12]

Language transforms all the stages of emerging self-awareness which have preceded its emergence. Verbal children exhibit a new sense of self,

9. *Ibid.*, pp. 131-137.   10. *Ibid.*, pp. 138-145.
11. *Ibid.*, pp. 146-161.   12. *Ibid.*, pp. 162-165.

namely, a verbally mediated conceptual self-image. They display a new capacity for symbolically mediated play and fantasy. The verbalization of experience now enables the child to relate to others and share experiences with them in new ways. It therefore lends complexity, depth, and greater abstractness to the child's sense of "we." Language creates new possibilities for inter-subjective sharing.[13]

The distancing from immediate experience which language introduces into the child's emerging self-awareness has its dark side as well. While, on the positive side of the ledger, it creates new capacities for the symbolic exploration of experience, it also creates the capacity for the linguistic and conceptual distortion of experience. The new self-awareness which language brings creates a new capacity for self-deception which distances children from the immediacy of pre-linguistic experiences. Those earlier experiences sink into the preconscious and subconscious mind.[14]

Language theorists offer three kinds of explanations of the origins of language. Learning theory attributes the acquisition of language to nurture. Structuralist, innatist theory attributes it to an innate power of the psyche. Inter-actionist theory ascribes it to both nature and nurture.[15]

An inter-actionist approach would seem to offer the most comprehensive explanation. The spontaneous babbling and jargoning of infants at about the ages of three or four months clearly advances toward language; but infantile lalling needs to shape itself into language through interaction with speaking adults. Stern's theory of the origin of language develops inter-actionist thinking about the origin of language by identifying affect attunement as the experience which mediates between pre-linguistic and linguistic behavior in the child.

Verification, Contextualization, Amplification

Stern's theory of infantile social development accords well with the developmental, social construct of the self-suggested in chapter five. It not only tends to verify that construct; but it also amplifies it by giving a plausible, even probable account of the way children learn to speak. Stern describes the emergence of that social consciousness which makes both sensory motor thinking and all other symbolic development possible.

Stern's work also tends to verify the distinction made in chapter five among expressive symbols, interpretative symbols, and communications. The emergent infantile self needs to absorb events and to learn to interpret them as significant. At the same time, the interpretative symbols which mediate cognitive development initially develop quite independently of linguistic activity. The emergence of symbolic communication presupposes the infant's experience of its own intentional, conceptual

---

13. *Ibid.*, pp. 165-174.   14. *Ibid.*, pp. 174-182.
15. Cf. Cole and Cole, *op.cit.*, p. 274-278.

responses. It also presupposes the child's recognition of the reality of other minds than its own and its maturing desire to understand and commune with those minds.

Finally, Stern's account of the development of infantile self-awareness also lends indirect verification to the cognitive character of human affective responses. Indeed, if Stern has the right of it (and I suspect that he has), then affect attunement holds the key to the infant's transition from pre-linguistic to linguistic behavior.

Stern's close observation of infantile behavior yields, then, a highly plausible account of the growth of infantile self-awareness. His suggestion that affect attunement mediates the infant's transition to linguistic thought offers a suasive and highly plausible inter-actionist account of how children learn to speak. Cross cultural studies of the social interchange between infants and primary caretakers could conceivably transform Stern's hypothesis from a plausible to a probable one.

Implications for Jesusology

If, as the New Testament suggests, Jesus resembled other humans in every way but sin, then it seems at least plausible that His own infantile self-awareness would have developed much in the manner in which Stern describes. I also find it plausible that the affect attunement between Jesus and Mary would have mediated the baby Jesus's first stammerings in Aramaic.

(II)

Daniel Stern's work explains how children learn to speak. The work of Lev Vygotsky calls attention to the way in which language socializes the child's thought processes. Vygotsky criticizes Piaget for characterizing children's language as egocentric. Vygotsky finds such a characterization misleading and confusing because it fails to distinguish adequately between cognitive and linguistic development. Vygotsky correctly insists that language begins as social behavior. Only in the second stage of linguistic development, however, does language take on an egocentric character. The egocentric use of language, moreover, leads to the interiorization of linguistic thought patterns.

By linguistic egocentrism, Vygotsky seems to mean something quite different from the egocentric patterns of thinking which Piaget describes. Linguistic egocentrism refers to a stage in children's use of language. During it children "think out loud." They talk through their own thought processes, count on their fingers, etc. until they can think verbally without the need to speak. The interiorization of language transforms it into an "inner dialogue" within the mind of the thinker; but the mind, Vygotsky insists, internalizes a social behavior which it has learned.[16]

16. Cf. Lev Vygotsky, *Thought and Language*, revised and edited by Alex Kozulin (Cambridge, MA: The MIT Press, 1986).

Verification, Contextualization, Amplification

Vygotsky's qualification of Piaget re-enforces the distinction made in chapter five between interpretative symbols and communications. Interpretative symbols shape pre-linguistic cognitive development, while linguistic symbols count as communications. As the human mind internalizes the ability to think verbally it introjects socially acquired patterns of symbolic behavior. That introjection fuses linguistic and cognitive behavior but without effecting their total identity. The mind continues to have cognitive insights which it must subsequently verbalize in order to clarify and communicate them. Moreover, the limitations both of language itself and of the human mastery of its forms insure that even adult minds respond conceptually in ways which they can never fully or adequately verbalize. Sometimes those conceptual responses lie hidden in the pre-conscious or subconscious mind. Nevertheless, after the introjection of language, thinking, as Vygotsky suggests, acquires a linguistically conditioned character.

Finally, given the mimetic character of much human learning, Vygotsky's suggestion that language begins as social interaction makes good sense. I also find it highly probable that what he calls the egocentric use of language by children mediates their interiorization of linguistic patterns of thinking.

Implications for Jesusology

If one can understand the humanity of Jesus not only from the results of the new quests for the historical Jesus but also from scientific insights into the human, then I for one find it plausible that, as His social self-awareness matured, Jesus would have learned to interiorize the linguistic patterns of thinking which He acquired within His family in Nazareth.

(III)

I have reflected on the way in which Jesus, quite plausibly, learned to speak. Can one also formulate a plausible hypothesis about the kinds of linguistic patterns of thinking Jesus interiorized? To that question I turn next. In the paragraphs which follow I shall examine Walter Ong's insightful analysis of oral and literate patterns of thought.

Orality and Literacy

Stern makes a convincing case for the fact that the acquisition of language transforms infantile self-awareness. Vygotsky correctly insists that children need to learn to introject the linguistic symbols which they acquire through social interaction. The work of Walter Ong has called attention to the fact that the development of writing further transforms human consciousness itself.

Ong argues convincingly that people raised in literate cultures need to make a serious and difficult effort in order to understand how thinking in pre-literate, oral cultures advances. Writing never fully replaces orality; but as it dominates human communication, it transforms the human mind itself. The technologization of language in writing gives rise to what Ong calls "secondary orality." "Primary orality" designates the way language functions in purely oral cultures. "Secondary orality" designates the way orality functions in literate cultures.[17] How then does language function in cultures in which primary orality shapes human social interaction?

In primary oral cultures, people experience words as sound, as vocalization, as action. One cannot arrest sound. One cannot fix a spoken word to a page as one can a written one. Spoken words qualify as events. They strike the ear with the immediacy of something happening. As a consequence, in primary oral cultures, people tend to experience words as acts expressing power. They also experience the acquisition of words as the acquisition of power over the things they name.[18]

The absence of texts in primary oral cultures ties sustained thought to communication and to memory. Oral thinking uses a variety of linguistic patterns as mnemonic devices. Oral thinking employs heavily rhythmic, balanced language patterns. Repetitions and antitheses, alliterations and assonances, epithetic and proverbial expressions jog the memory and forge links between remembered thoughts and themes. Oral thinking contextualizes thought in standard thematic settings like assemblies, meals, duels, etc. Mnemonic patterns shape not only thought but even syntax.[19]

In primary oral cultures, proverbs and easily remembered formulaic sayings constitute the law. Thinking adds one idea to another usually without subordinating them to one another. Redundancy and repetition help the listening audience keep what they have heard in mind. Repetition ensures the preservation of the accumulated wisdom of the ages.

Oral thinking seeks to evoke an immediate response from living audiences. Variations in familiar narrative patterns apply old tales to new situations. The ability to apply familiar proverbs to novel and unfamiliar contexts manifests wisdom.[20]

Oral thinking stays close to the concrete world in which people live. As a consequence, it situates knowledge in the context of struggle. It dramatizes the conflict of ideas and embellishes the conflict with vituperation and diatribe instead of balancing the abstract pros and cons of theories. Rhetoric rather than logic tends to structure thinking.[21]

Instead of valuing distance and "objectivity," oral thinking seeks to evoke an empathetic communion with the realities about which one thinks.

17. Cf. Ong, *op.cit.*, pp. 1-15.   18. *Ibid.*, pp. 31-33.   19. *Ibid.*, pp. 33-34.
20. *Ibid.*, pp. 36-42.   21. *Ibid.*, pp. 42-45.

Oral thought lives in the present. It discards memories which no longer have vital relevance. The close bonding between oral thought and life keeps it concretely situational rather than abstract. Typically, people in oral cultures assign abstract figures concrete names. For example, they call a geometrical circle a plate, a moon, a bucket. Thinking remains tied closely to sensory experience. The oral mind resists speculation about things it has never sensed or experienced. It tends to regard verbal description for its own sake as a pointless waste of time and words.[22]

In the absence of texts which fix the word and freeze it, oral memorization tends to prefer adaptive to verbatim memory. Remembered wisdom seeks to illumine concrete situations: hence, as the situation changes so does the way in which one remembers the events which illumine it. Oral memory also has a high somatic component. One remembers by acting out the scene or truth one describes.[23]

Life in primary oral cultures fosters sensitivity to the way words function rhetorically and affectively and binds thought to persons rather than to objects or things. Thinking in such cultures takes on a shared, communal character. The oral imagination fastens on the memorable and therefore on figures of large, even of epic proportions. The spoken character of the word links thought to interiority: spoken words proceed out of the speaker and resonate in the hearts of hearers by illumining them. Since verbalized thinking happens rather than perdures, in oral cultures people tend to imagine the world as an ongoing process with the human event at its center. The interiorizing force of words links speech to the sacred and endows the sacred with a revelatory character.[24]

Narrative in primary oral cultures thrives on repetition. Plots tend toward simplicity: one find no evidence in oral cultures of epic-size or novel-size narratives. Epics like Homer's *Iliad* and *Odyssey* happen on the borderline between orality and literacy; and even they begin *in medias res* instead of exhibiting a clear beginning, middle, and end, as novels written in literate cultures tend to do. The simplicity of plot line in primary oral narratives finds a parallel in the "round," stereotypical portrayal of character. In primary oral narratives, characters tend not to exhibit the kind of psychological complexity which more typically characterizes written novels and short stories. Similarly, lyrics in primary oral cultures tend to brevity and to clear topical reference.[25]

The shift from oral to literate thinking effects not only a transformation in the way a culture communicates ideas but a revolution in consciousness itself.

The alphabet transforms spoken words into things, into unchanging marks for visual assimilation. Primary oral cultures tend to regard the

22. *Ibid.*, pp. 49-57.   23. *Ibid.*, pp. 57-68.
24. *Ibid.*, pp. 71-77.   25. *Ibid.*, pp. 139-155.

onset of literacy with suspicion. Initially writing performs very limited social functions. Special scribal classes cultivate the ability to read and write.[26]

Writing makes thinking solipsistic. It requires social withdrawal rather than social engagement. It distances thinking from concrete situations and introduces a new precision in verbalization. Writing enhances the analytic character of speech. It allows for revision, for afterthoughts, for the elimination of inconsistencies. Oral thinking allows for none of these things.

Writing also abstracts the meaning of words from a concrete spoken context. It standardizes speech and therefore tends to standardize as well interiorized speech, or thought. With the emergence of writing, grammar begins to develop in its own right without serving the need to recall ephemeral spoken words. Logic begins to replace rhetoric as the organizing principle of thought. Learned, scholarly languages, like academic Latin, further isolate thinking from living.[27]

In literate cultures, sight replaces hearing as the sense which communication addresses. Writing and its further technologization through print allows for the compilation of indices and of dictionaries, which presuppose and foster the standardization of meaning. This process of verbal and conceptual standardization eventually gives rise to scientific thinking. Print also allows for the ownership of words through copyright. Printing words allows for their fixation in definitive texts. Textual organization on a page helps define the parameters of thought and of expression. Print, then, endows thinking with a sense of fixity and closure alien to thought in primary oral cultures.[28]

Somewhat in the manner of the Homeric epics, the New Testament took written shape on the borderline between orality and literacy. Unlike Mohammed, Jesus never committed His teachings to writing. In my own judgment, that fact makes it highly probable that his human mind gravitated more to oral than to literary patterns of thinking. The fact that His disciples took so long to commit His teachings to writing suggests that their mind's too had interiorized oral rather than literary modes of thinking.

The way the evangelists write the story of Jesus reflects its rootedness in an oral tradition. They tell it in a way which seeks to evoke empathetic response and commitment from the reader. The evangelists prefer concrete narrative to abstract hypothesis as a mode of religious thought. They remember Jesus' words and actions adaptively and modify His memory in ways which makes it concretely relevant to shifting pastoral contexts. The gospels invite commitment not to abstract ideas but above all to the

26. *Ibid.*, pp. 96-101.   27. *Ibid.*, pp. 78-123.   28. *Ibid.*, pp. 79-138.

person of Jesus. Mnemonic devices link together sayings of Jesus which seem to have little logical connection to one another.

New Testament narrative paints an epic portrait of Jesus and a rounded, stereotypical portrait of His antagonists. The gospel narratives dramatize the agonistic conflict between their protagonist, Jesus, and His adversaries. In dealing with those adversaries, the gospels often gravitate toward invective and diatribe. Matthew and Luke preface their account of Jesus' public ministry with a highly theologized account of His birth; but when the time comes to tell the adult Jesus' story, like Mark and John, they immediately plunge *in medias res*.

Relevance for Jesusology

I find it at least plausible, if not probable, that the orality of New Testament thinking echoes in its own way the orality of Jesus' own thought patterns. The gospels suggest that Jesus related to His own proclamation of the kingdom with attitudes which reflect primary oral modes of thinking: His very proclamation of the kingdom made it real and present in His own eyes. He seems, therefore, to have looked upon His verbal proclamation as a religious event in its own right. (Mt 11:2-6; Lk 7:18-23)

Jesus seems to have gravitated to story as both a pattern of personal thinking and as a pedagogical device.[29] The parabolic character of those stories tied their meaning directly and concretely to the situation of those whom He addressed. His stories demanded commitment to the saving event unfolding in His own ministry of proclamation, healing, and deliverance. The brevity of Jesus' parables and their "rounded" portrayal of character also suggests their origin in and relevance to a predominantly oral culture.

Jesus' frequent use of proverbs dramatized His ability to apply conventional folk wisdom in new and surprising ways. The word He proclaimed He also embodied; and He seems to have expected His proclamation to resonate in the hearts of those to whom He spoke. His teachings expressed His own interiority and sought to evoke an immediate response in the depths of His hearers' hearts.

As we shall see in chapter ten, one can make a plausible case for the fact that Jesus received enough book learning to enable Him to read and expound the Torah; but both His mode of teaching as we find it in the New Testament and the very way in which the New Testament preserves that teaching make it highly plausible, if not probable, that His own thought patterns resonated spontaneously with the predominantly oral thought patterns of rural, first-century Palestine.

---

29. Cf. Joachim Jeremias, *The Parables of Jesus* (New York, NY: Scribner's, 1972).

(IV)

In the preceding sections of this chapter, I have examined plausible ways in which language conditioned Jesus' social awareness. The early socialization of children involves more, however, than language; and cross-cultural studies of socialization discover identifiable patterns within the socialization of the young.[30]

Social Development in Young Children

In all cultures, mothers function as the first primary care giver for infants and small children. Mothers in different cultural contexts tend to behave similarly toward infants and small children because the latter have predictable biological and social needs. Mothers in every culture feed and bathe their children, dress and undress them, play with them, toilet train them, teach them to talk. In all cultures, small children advance from a "lap" stage of care in infancy, to a "knee" stage as toddlers, to a "yard" stage in early childhood, and finally to a stage of formal schooling.

The style of mothering, however, shifts from culture to culture. In some cultures, mothers train children primarily by encouraging prosocial behavior. In others they tend by contrast to reprimand antisocial behavior. In still other more democratic cultures, mothers treat children in a more egalitarian way which encourages and rewards psychological interaction. Whatever the mother's cultural style, children initially learn to adapt their behavior to that of the primary care giver.[31]

For children in different cultures, peer relationships play at least as significant a role as parental relationships. Social interaction teaches children to expand their cognitive motives for acting. Those new motives manifest themselves in the way in which the child goes about seeking help, claiming attention, receiving comfort, playing, and relating to both adults and other children.

The social context conditions such cognitive development as children learn in different cultures. The social context also prescribes which rules script children's behavior. In every culture, however, children must deal with the scripting.

The demands of lap children makes nurture the dominant way in which others relate to the infant. Among toddling lap children and those still older, egoistic and prosocial dominance plays a significant role in the socialization process. As the child grows, however, egoistic dominance tends to rank second to sociability in peer interaction.

---

30. For a cross-cultural study of early social development in children, see: Beatrice Blyth Whiting and Carolyn Pope Edwards, *et al.*, *Children of Different Worlds: The Formation of Social Behavior* (Cambridge, MA: Harvard University Press, 1988).

31. *Ibid.*, pp. 266-268.

Girls tend to interact more with lap and younger children, in part because parents assign them the care of the young with greater frequency. Boys, as a consequence, tend to interact more with older children. Whatever the culture, parents seem to prefer child nurses between six and ten years. After the age of seven, boys rarely carry infants. Functioning as a child nurse incorporates the nursing child into the working family team.[32]

In different cultures, knee children exhibit a remarkable capacity for observation and imitation. They especially imitate other siblings. In all cultures, children exhibit dominance patterns in their social interaction. They tend to react to one another on the basis of size. Older children tend to dominate younger. Dominance takes either a prosocial or an egoistic form. Societies tend to sanction prosocial dominance as an appropriate part of the training of the young. Boys tend toward egoistic dominance more than girls, while girls tend toward prosocial dominance.

All cultures seem to find it difficult to deal with egoistic forms of childhood dominance. Some cultures attempt to suppress it, while others rest content with circumscribing it. Small children enter into dominance conflicts not only with siblings but with the children of other families. Schooling, of course, increases the possibility of dominance conflict.[33]

In different cultures, rough-and-tumble play among children need not express aggression or dominance. Often it expresses a kind of competitive sociability. Not infrequently, children themselves develop rules for regulating such play and preventing it from degenerating into egoistic dominance and aggression.[34]

Concern for gender identity seems to lead children in different cultures to prefer children of the same sex as playmates. Boys seem to exhibit more anxiety about gender identity than girls. Boys tend to distance themselves from home more than girls. Boys tend to enter more frequently into dominance struggles with their mothers than girls do. In cultures which stress the dominance of men over women, dominance conflicts between sons and mothers occur with greater prominence.[35]

In all cultures, the concrete shape of symbolic interaction increasingly modulates the behavior of children as they grow older. In different cultures, however, girls tend to get more practice in nurture and prosocial dominance than boys. Boys tend to receive more practice in egoistic dominance and challenge. As they mature, children tend to transfer these learned behaviors into their relationships with other children.[36]

Once children reach school age, education takes the form either of apprenticeship or of formal schooling. Apprentices relate differently to their teachers from school children; and the social organization of learning differs in apprenticeship from the social organization of formal school-

32. *Ibid.*, pp. 268-274.   33. *Ibid.*, pp. 274-276.   34. *Ibid.*, pp. 276.
35. *Ibid.*, pp. 276-277.   36. *Ibid.*, pp. 278-279.

ing. Apprentices learn in a one-on-one relationship to their teachers. Growth in practical skill rather than in theoretical abilities dominates the learning process. So too does direct imitation of the teacher. Formal schooling usually orients children toward literacy.[37]

Verification, Contextualization, Amplification

A triadic construct of experience insists on its social character. Cross-cultural studies of early childhood development verify that construct by giving a highly probable account of how the early stages of socialization advance in any given culture. The social and symbolic matrix of cultural life modulates the way human experience grows and develops; nevertheless, biological and social constants ensure analogous patterns of growth in quite different cultural contexts.

Cross-cultural studies of the growth of small children dramatize and underscore the social character of experience. They also amplify the philosophical construct of social experience developed in the preceding chapter by specifying the kinds of development which children of any culture will almost certainly face.

Relevance for Jesusology

In invoking cross-cultural studies of human development in order to amplify one's insight into the plausible development of Jesus' human experience, one still needs, of course, to take into account the historical distance which separates contemporary cross-cultural investigations from first century Palestine.

Nevertheless, in my judgment, Jesus would certainly have had to develop into the first-century Palestinian equivalent of a lap child, a knee child, a yard child, and finally a school-age child. I regard it as highly probable that, until He reached school age, His relationship to Mary would have played an extremely important role in His early maturation. I judge it as also highly probable that his father, Joseph, if still alive, would have taught his first-born son the skills of the family trade in an relationship of apprenticeship.

I deem it virtually certain that as the child Jesus grew, peer relationships would have shaped His social experience in significant ways. As the first-born son, he would have been cast in a role of social dominance with respect to His siblings.[38] From a strictly historical standpoint, however, we have no way of knowing how concretely He handled those relationships. As a boy, Jesus would certainly have had to learn to recognize His difference from girls. Once again, how exactly He handled the process of gender identification as a child remains an historical secret. As we shall see, however, the gospels suggest that he resisted gender stereotypes. It

37. Cf. Cole and Cole, *op.cit.*, pp. 450-451.   38. Cf. Meier, *op.cit.*, pp. 324-332.

would seem at least plausible that Jesus, as the first-born male, would have received some formal schooling in the Torah most likely in the synagogue at Nazareth.[39]

In this section I have considered plausible stages in Jesus' social development as a young child. The section which follows examines stages in the growth of human friendship.

(V)

Social development, of course, continues after childhood. R.L. Selman has studied patterns in the growth of friendship among the young. Selman has advanced the theory that the human capacity to see the world from the standpoint of other people advances in five stages. He has also suggested that the capacity to take the perspective of another has a close relationship to the capacity for friendship.

The Development of Friendship and Perspective Taking

Selman calls his first stage of development "Level 0," because during it children seem to operate from an egocentric and undifferentiated perspective. At this primitive stage, which lasts from about age three to age seven, children find it difficult to understand that others might interpret the same social experience or course of action from a perspective which differs from their own. During this first stage, children cultivate playmates of the moment. A "close friend" means a child who lives close by with whom one is playing.

"Level 1" lasts from about age four to age nine. The child now understands the fact that others' perspectives may differ from the child's own. Friendship now takes the form of "one way assistance." The child expects friends to acquiesce in the child's own wants and regards as a "close friend" another child who shares the same likes and dislikes.

"Level 2" spans the ages between six and twelve. In evaluating the perspective of other children the child now understands how his or her responses appear to other children. In other words, the child's perspective on social relationships exhibits both a self-reflective and a reciprocal character. Friendship now takes the form of "fair-weather" cooperation. The child now exhibits a more flexible willingness to adjust personal thoughts and actions to the expectations of others; but arguments impair that willingness and disrupt friendly relationships.

Between the ages of nine and fifteen, Selman believes that children enter into "Level 3," The youth can now step outside of an interpersonal relationship and view it from the perspective of a third party. As a consequence , the self-conscious character of social relationships moves beyond the reciprocity of Level 2 to a new kind of social mutuality. The

39. *Ibid.*, pp. 268-278.

young person now exhibits a capacity for intimate and mutually shared relationships with other persons and looks to friends in order to cultivate mutual intimacy and mutual support. Friendship exhibits a greater degree of commitment and now survives minor contretemps and even disagreements. Nevertheless, immature jealousy and possessiveness can mar or disrupt friendly relationships.

After twelve years of age, Selman's teenagers exhibit a capacity for in-depth, social relationships. The adolescent now sees both self and relationships as elements in a larger social whole and recognizes the claims which society as a whole can legitimately make. Friendship acquires an autonomous and interdependent character. Friends recognize explicitly their need for mutual support. Each friend has a sense of personal identity and accepts the need of the other to establish friendly relationships with a variety of people.[40]

Verification, Contextualization, Amplification

Selman's work verifies the fundamentally social character of human experience. It also suggests that the spontaneous egocentrism of biologically based life makes it necessary for children to grow into the capacity for fully mature, responsible, adult friendships. Selman's plausible account of social development from childhood to early adolescence amplifies a purely philosophical description of human experience by endowing the notion of self-emergence with social concreteness.

Relevance for Jesusology

Given the radical finitude of Jesus' human experience, I find it plausible that He too would have had to develop a capacity for mature adult friendships. I also find it plausible that He would have had to advance through something like the kinds of stages which Selman describes. Selman's stages in and of themselves prescind from the question of moral culpability in human relationships. They attempt, rather, to identify the kinds of growth processes through which children tend to pass as they mature in the capacity for deep interpersonal friendship.

The gospels suggest that Jesus developed the capacity to sustain a commitment of friendship even to those who abandoned, denied, and betrayed Him in His moment of direst need. (Mk 14:26-31, 43-52; Mt 26:30-35, 47-56; Lk 22:31-34, 47-54) That makes it at least plausible to suppose that in His relationship to His friends He had in fact developed an extraordinary capacity for fidelity.

---

40. Cf. R.L. Selman, *The Growth of Interpersonal Understanding: Development and Clinical Analysis* (New York, NY: Academic Press, 1980).

(VI)

I have presented plausible stages of human social development from earliest infancy to early adolescence. What of social development beyond adolescence? Here studies of male development offer some help. They also have potential significance for Jesusology, since Jesus belonged to the male sex.

Male Development

Studies of male development in the United States suggest that as men mature they tend to advance through predictable seasons of growth. These seasons mark stages in the process of biological maturation and senescence. The succession of "seasons" defines the shape of the life cycle in a way analogous to the seasons of the year.[41]

Studies of the life cycle of American men in different classes and professions suggests that a man's life typically advances through four such seasons. 1) The first season, childhood and adolescence, stretches from birth to about the age of twenty-two. 2) The second season, early adulthood, spans the ages between seventeen and forty-five. 3) The third season, middle adulthood, lasts from around age forty to age sixty-five. 4) The fourth and final season, late adulthood, lasts from about sixty to death.

The different stages in adult male development overlap. A new stage of growth begins as its predecessor begins to wind down.[42]

I have already considered in a fair amount of detail predictable growth processes in childhood and adolescence. What, then, of young adulthood?

During the period of young adulthood, men find themselves at the peak of their biological functioning. Indeed, the first signs that one has begun to pass one's physical prime, which occur around the age of forty, mark the transition to middle adulthood.

Young males experience the period of early adulthood as a time of considerable contradiction and stress. They experience instinctive adult male drives with full force and vigor, but in the first stage of young adulthood a young man still suffers from unresolved childhood conflicts.

During the twenties, young men also form a preliminary adult identity. They make preliminary choices concerning marriage, occupation, residence, and life style. They must, in a word, take their place within an adult world.

During the entire course of young adulthood, a man normally moves from the status of a "young adult" through a series of intermediate steps

---

41. Cf. Daniel J. Levinson, Charlotte N. Darrow, Edward B. Klein, Maria H. Levinson, Braxton McKee, *The Seasons of a Man's Life* (New York, NY: Ballentine Books, 1978), pp. 4-7.
42. *Ibid.*, pp.18-19.

until he reaches a kind of "senior" status in work, family, and community. If a man starts a family in his twenties, his children are usually reaching adolescence as he is making the transition to middle adulthood.[43]

The time of middle adulthood brings changes in biological and psychological functioning. Typically, in middle adulthood physical and sexual drives begin to ebb in men. Often middle adult males develop a greater capacity for intimacy. They get better in touch with their own affections and develop a deeper capacity for responsive friendship with both men and women. They begin to relate more compassionately to ageing parents and to exhibit greater understanding in dealing with the young. Physical decline begins to manifest itself in less active involvement in sports.

Typically, men tend to experience the onset of the midlife crisis as their first serious confrontation with their own mortality. As a consequence, middle adulthood also brings with it the opportunity to grow in wisdom, good judgment, largeness of mind, unsentimental compassion, widening of perspectives, and a tragic sense of life.[44]

During midlife, a man must deal with the next generation of young adults, who tend to regard him as part of the establishment. Middle-aged men tend also to relate differently to their careers. They commonly go through a time of career assessment. They wonder what they have accomplished with their lives and begin to question how they would like to spend their remaining years. Some feel trapped by the choices of young adulthood and feel the need to strike out in new directions.[45]

At about sixty, men begin to experience a new phase of physical decline which demands psychological and social adjustment as well. They must face their own mortality with new vividness as death and serious illness among peers reminds them of their own growing fragility. Late adulthood usually requires of men that they yield to others both power and authority. A man ceases to belong to the dominant generation. Aging men need to learn to strike a balance between social commitment and self-maintenance. As one faces increasing physical enfeeblement in late, late adulthood, one must come to terms with the meaning of one's own life.[46]

Jesus of Nazareth never experienced middle or late adulthood as a man. He died a violent death probably in His mid-thirties. Do studies of early adulthood among contemporary males throw any light on the kinds of growth experiences He might have had as a young adult?

Typically in the male life cycle, the period of young adulthood advances in three stages. First, between the ages of twenty-two and twenty-eight a young man enters the adult world. He ceases to count socially as a child or adolescent. As a consequence, he must choose an

43. *Ibid.*, pp. 21-23.   44. *Ibid.*, pp. 23-27.
45. *Ibid.*, pp. 27-33.   46. *Ibid.*, pp. 33-39.

occupation, decide his marital status, establish peer relations with other young adults, and determine the values and life style he will cultivate as an adult. In making these decisions, young men typically feel a tension. On the one hand, they want to keep their options open and maximize their alternatives; and, on the other hand, they feel the need to establish a stable life structure. They want to "make something of their lives."[47]

Contemporary studies of American males indicate that around the age of thirty they pass through a fairly stressful growth crisis. Often the choices made in the first stage of early adulthood begin to feel like entrapment. At midpoint in young adulthood, the young American male tends to find his life routine emotionally intolerable but seems incapable of working out a better routine.[48]

Typically, the crisis of thirty marks the transition to the last phase of early adult development. One may resolve the crisis of thirty in one of two ways. One can either decide to live one's life in the patterns one has chosen; or one can strike out in new directions. In either case, typically, around the age of thirty the young adult American male decides upon a personal enterprise which will allow him to "become his own man," either by achievement in his chosen work or profession or by creating a different niche for himself within the adult world.[49]

Relevance for Jesusology

To what extent can one extrapolate from the growth processes of young males in twentieth-century America to the experience of a young male in first century Palestine? At best one can do so with extreme tentativeness. The fact, however, that modern American men in different classes and walks of life seem to go through similar life crises at least suggests the possibility that the seasons of their lives reflect the kinds of adult experience which any growing male can expect to undergo. The fact that the different seasons correlate with stages of biological development and decline also argues for the plausibility of believing that they correspond to fairly common growth experiences.

I personally find the attempt to understand Jesus' humanity in the light of a theory of the seasons of ordinary male development at least suggestive. I would deem it certain that as a young Jewish male, Jesus in His teens or early twenties would have had to decide upon a career. The New Testament suggests that He in fact followed his father's trade as a practical workman.[50] Luke's story of the finding in the temple suggests at least the possibility that Jesus Himself would have preferred to study Torah at

47. *Ibid.*, pp. 56-58.   48. *Ibid.*, pp. 58-59.
49. *Ibid.* pp. 58-59.   50. Meier, *op.cit.*, pp.278-285.

the feet of the great rabbis in Jerusalem. (Lk 2:41-52) We do not know whom Jesus as a young man did or did not befriend; but, as we shall see in greater detail in chapter ten, he seems, in violation of normal social expectations, to have decided not to marry.[51]

Jesus probably died in His mid-thirties. His public ministry seems to have lasted only a few years at most. That ministry seems, moreover, to have begun with His decision to leave Nazareth in order to listen to the prophetic preaching of John the Baptizer in the deserts east of Jerusalem. Moreover, the little one can piece together concerning the chronology of His life suggests that He probably took that decision sometime after the age of thirty.

Did Jesus decide to abandon His father's trade in order to follow the Baptizer as a way of resolving the male crisis of the early thirties? The New Testament paints no detailed psychological portrait of Jesus and gives us no information whatever about the personal motives which might have led to His departure from Nazareth. If, however, young men in their early thirties do typically feel the need either to "make it" in their chosen career or to strike out in new directions, I find it at least interesting from a psychological standpoint that Jesus' decision to give a new direction to the course of His own life seems to have come in His early thirties. I also find it possible that His decision to seek out the Baptizer could have expressed at least in part an exceptional young man's need to escape entrapment in the familiar routines of village life in Nazareth.

I have been examining contemporary social psychology for the light it might have to throw on the typical stages of human social development. I have assessed the results of scientific investigations of human social maturation for their ability to confirm and to amplify the triadic, social construct of experience developed in the last chapter. I have also reflected on the potential light which such studies might throw on Jesus' development as human.

One final task remains. I need to examine typical stages in human religious development. In the following chapter, I shall reflect on James Fowler's theory of the stages of religious faith. As in the case of the other psychological theories which I have considered, I shall assess Fowler's work from two standpoints. I shall consider its ability to verify and to amplify a philosophical understanding of humanity as a developing experience. Having done so, I shall then also ponder the possible Christological relevance of Fowler's account of the stages of human development in the chapter which follows.

51. *Ibid.*, pp. 332-345.

Chapter 8
Jesus' Religious Development

The two preceding chapters have studied what contemporary scientific study of human development has to tell us about personal and social development. This chapter reflects on what developmental psychology suggests about the plausible stages of Jesus' religious development.

This chapter divides into two parts. In the first part, I shall summarize James Fowler's theory of cognitive religious development. I shall assess its ability to verify and amplify a triadic, philosophical construct of experience. Then I shall weigh its possible implications for Jesusology. In the second part of this chapter I shall summarize the tentative developmental portrait of Jesus which I have derived from scientific studies of human growth. I shall argue for its general plausibility only; but I deem a plausible account of Jesus' human growth better than nothing.

The therapeutic community in this country often finds it difficult to deal with human religious experience on its own terms. In the United States, Enlightenment fundamentalism combines with secularism and with the therapeutic caste of the culture to psychologize religious experience into triviality. I find it interesting, for example, that a standard text book on human development like *The Development of Children* seems to mention virtually every developmental theory currently proposed except that of James Fowler. Fowler has studied the stages of faith development, has coordinated his theory with those of other developmentalists, and has proposed at least as plausible an hypothesis as they. Nevertheless, in a standard text book on human development, his work goes completely unmentioned.

Fowler on Faith

Fowler's theory of the stages of faith focuses especially but not exclusively on its cognitive forms, on the ways in which human faith perceives and relates consciously to transcendent realities which make ultimate claims. Fowler defines religious faith as a "person's or group's way of responding to transcendent value and power as perceived and grasped through the forms of the cumulative religious tradition."[1] Fowler distinguishes faith from religion and from belief. Belief commits one to holding certain ideas, while faith designates the quality of a person, a fundamental orientation of the self. Religion organizes beliefs and practices about transcendent reality into traditions; but faith designates a deeper

---

1. Cf. James W. Fowler, *Stages of Faith: The Psychology of Human Development and the Quest for Meaning* (San Francisco, CA: Harper and Row, 1981), p. 9.

alignment of commitment and a resting of the heart in ultimate concern.[2] Faith sets one in a fundamental relationship to transcendence. It engages both heart and head; but faith thrives especially on an intuitive grasp of the real. It lives out of ritual, myth, symbol, story. Faith has a triadic structure which inserts one into communities of faith.[3]

Fowler regards the period of early infancy before the emergence of speech as a pre-stage of faith. The child gives no overt signs of religious experience. Nevertheless, infants do grow prodigiously in their first months and begin to form fundamental attitudes of trust, hope, love, and courage which significantly condition future faith development. Much of the concrete growing which infants do eludes empirical research; but we do know that abandonment, inconsistency, and depravation in an infant's environment can make an enormous difference in the quality of its future life and in the quality of its faith development as well.

In the pre-stage of faith, children need especially to establish a fundamental relationship of trust and mutuality with their primary care-givers. The failure to establish a relationship of mutuality and trust can, as we have seen, leave a child trapped in narcissistic shame and self-preoccupation; or it may lock the infant in patterns of isolation and failed mutuality.

The first stage of faith development typically spans the years three to seven. A child's sense of religious transcendence at this point exhibits a fluidity of ideas and images. Lacking any stable patterns of evaluative response, faith surfaces in an unrestrained fantasy uninhibited by logical thought.

In this early, fantasy-filled stage of faith, the child imitates the faith stance of adults with whom it has a primary relationship. Their example, moods, actions, and stories exert a powerful and permanent influence on the child's subsequent religious attitudes. This stage of faith endows later, more mature stages with long-lasting images and attitudes which exert both positive and negative influences on subsequent religious development. Early experiences of death, sex, and social taboos shape the infant's religious attitudes and may need sorting out at a more mature stage of religious development. At this first, infantile stage of faith, the child's religious self-awareness exhibits the innocent egocentrism which typifies infantile forms of knowing.

Infantile faith begins the process of orienting the imagination toward transcendence. It endows that imagination with powerful images which give initial formative shape to the child's sense of ultimate reality. Terrifying religious images can exert a destructive power over later religious attitudes as can the manipulation of an infant in order to re-enforce rigid emotional, moral, or doctrinal expectations.[4]

---

2. *Ibid.*, pp. 9-14.   3. *Ibid.*, pp. 15-39.   4. *Ibid.*, pp.199-121.

The child's need to introduce greater order into its perception of things eventually forces a transition to the second stage of faith. The second stage of faith spans the ages between seven years and the onset of adolescence. During this stage the child appropriates the religious stories, beliefs, and observances which incorporate it into a religious community of faith. Story above all gives religious meaning and coherence to the child's world. At this stage of religious development, the child accepts religious narratives, beliefs, and moral practices as literally true. The episodic, chaotic character of intuitive-projective faith acquires a linear, narrative construction which endows it with coherence and meaning. The child's imagination finds itself, however, possessed by the religious stories and by the anthropomorphic symbols of transcendence which structure them. Religious consciousness lacks the ability to step back from story, myth, and ritual in order to reflect critically upon them. It suffices for the time being that the received religious narratives, ritual acts, and modes of conduct endow faith with an element of coherence and stability.

While imaginative and narrative coherence give order to cognitive religious attitudes, the child needs eventually to distance personal faith from blind acquiescence in the literal truth of received religious traditions. Failure to advance to a more nuanced perception of religious truth and value can leave one trapped either in rigid fundamentalism and moral perfectionism or in an abasing sense of one's own evil which stems from the mistreatment, neglect, or apparent disfavor of others.

As a child's religious imagination matures, it needs to face the fact of conflict among the lessons which different religious stories teach. As the mind grows in its capacity to deal cognitively with its world, a maturing child may well experience disillusionment with its earliest religious instruction. An adolescent, as we have seen, also learns to understand the world increasingly from the perspective of other persons. All of these experiences normally conspire in order to advance the child to the next stage of religious cognitive development.[5]

Typically, one advances to the third stage of faith during adolescence. Fowler's researches suggest, however, that many adults never advance beyond stage three. As the adolescent moves on toward adulthood, faith provides the emerging young adult's life with a coherent orientation in the midst of increasingly complex human and social demands. Synthetic-conventional faith consolidates, synthesizes, and organizes mythic-literal faith. In the process, it gives an adolescent a stable religious identity through identification with the judgments and expectations of the religious community to which it belongs and of significant persons within that community.

5. *Ibid.* pp. 135-150.

Synthetic-conventional faith inculcates, then, a religion of social conformity to received religious beliefs, realities, and values. It transforms mythic-literal faith into a personal "ideology" but without yet inculcating critical reflection on the received religious wisdom which the adolescent is in process of interiorizing. At this third stage of faith, one acknowledges traditional religious authority and tends to accede to its demands without question. Because identification with a particular religious tradition now enters into one's very sense of identity, one tends to perceive those of other faiths as different kinds of persons.

At the third level of cognitive religious development, faith develops a new self-consciousness as the adolescent evolves a personal religious myth, a story of personal faith development which inserts the adolescent into his or her religious community and into its evolving story. A personal myth consolidates a personal sense of religious identity as the emerging young adult begins to face the uncertainties of an adult future.

Synthetic-conventional faith brings its own risks. A rigid sense of religious conformity can inhibit the emergence of a critical, fully adult religious faith and leave one trapped in traditional religious wisdom with both its insights into and distortions of religious reality. During adolescence, religious faith also exhibits an enhanced vulnerability to personal betrayal by persons whom one has come to trust. Personal betrayal and confrontation with the mystery of evil can raise doubts about the ultimate trustworthiness of that reality to which one looks for ultimate meaning and purpose in life.

Transition to the fourth stage of faith, when it does happen, typically results from a possible variety of causes. Serious disagreement among accepted religious authorities may alert one to the dangers of a religion of mere conformity. Officially sanctioned changes in traditional belief and practices can pose a similar challenge. In this culture at least, "leaving home" and the secure supports it provides for a conventional faith commitment often introduces the emerging young adult to the next stage of cognitive religious development.[6]

When a religious person advances to this fourth stage of faith, it can happen in late adolescence or young adulthood; but it can also take place as late as the mid-thirties or early forties. The fourth stage of faith marks a significant crisis in personal religious development. That crisis might result from a variety of causes: the need to assert one's religious individuality; conflict between conventional beliefs and practices, on the one hand, and deeply felt personal religious convictions, on the other; the abrasiveness of the constraints of traditional religion which inhibit one's ability to serve others in the ways in which one feels religiously called; the

6. *Ibid.*, pp. 151-173.

relativization of conventional faith by confrontation with alternative beliefs and attitudes.

The crisis to which individuative-reflexive faith seeks to respond tends to lead to two kinds of religious development. First, the developing believer now acknowledges the need to redefine his or her religious identity by a critical distancing from the received religious wisdom which defined one's identity at stage three. Second, in order to achieve a new personalized religious identity, the religious person now feels the need to formulate a personal religious vision which better defines one's experienced relationship to transcendent reality. One now differentiates one's personal religious stance from that of others instead of identifying with the accepted religious beliefs of the community to which one belongs. Both of these growth experiences—both the redefinition of one's religious self-identity and the formulation of a personal religious creed—play into one another. One experiences a new freedom to criticize received religious belief, wisdom, and practice.

The growth processes which mark the fourth stage of religious development bring with them their own risks. One runs the risk of over-individualizing one's religious view of the world, of over-assimilating religious reality to one's limited personal expectations. The collapse of conventional religion can leave one in a state of religious flux in which anarchic and disturbing voices trouble religious consciousness. Unresolved conflicts from one's past, the unleashing of new energies from deep within the self, and a sense of the sterility of many traditional religious forms of behavior signal a personal readiness for religious novelty and creativity. The need to resolve such conflicts can move one on to the next stage of religious cognitive development.

The fifth stage of faith resolves the crisis precipitated by stage four. In it one re-appropriates traditional religious beliefs, stories, rites, and traditions; but one endows them with new meanings which better express one's personal religious attitudes and commitments. At the stage of conjunctive faith one grapples with religious paradox and with the truth which seems to express itself in conflicting, even contradictory beliefs and attitudes. Faith now manifests a new openness to those who are religiously "other" than oneself. The religious search for a just social order now emancipates itself from the traditional expectations of tribe, class, religious community, or nation. Commitment to a personally meaningful religious cause tends to generate and sustain a religious sense of personal identity.

The religious imagination acquires an ironic character as one acknowledges the relativity of the received religious wisdom which at stage three tended to define one's whole religious identity and orientation. One now acknowledges the partiality and the distortions which mar that wisdom at the same time as one struggles to redefine oneself and one's religious world.

At stage five, however, one remains religiously divided. One experiences a tension between the religious world one knows and the religious vision to which one stands committed; but one still gropes for a way to unify the two. The tension which marks the fifth stage of religious cognitive development motivates a few exceptional individuals to advance to stage six.[7]

In the course of his publications, Fowler himself has groped for the right words to describe the sixth stage of faith, and understandably so; for the sixth stage of faith characterizes the exceptional, saintly religious person. In the fourth and fifth stages of faith, a religious person has begun to relate to transcendent reality with a new measure of human vulnerability. One no longer has a clear road map or fixed plan for how to confront the Ultimate. Those few who advance to the sixth stage of faith have, by contrast, achieved an integrated, personal religious vision of ultimate reality. At the same time, that vision exhibits a universal inclusiveness which eludes faith consciousness at stage five. At stage six, the person of faith incarnates and actualizes the vision of an universally welcoming and fulfilled human religious community. Such religious figures create what Fowler calls "zones of liberation from the social, political, economic, and ideological shackles" which oppress most humans. Their lives express a union with Ultimate Reality which unifies and transforms the world in ways which vested interest and the more religiously conventional tend to find threatening.

Those who have reached the sixth stage of faith not infrequently die as martyrs to their religious cause. People tend to honor them more after their deaths than while they actually lived. Nevertheless, their lives exhibit a special quality of religious lucidity, simplicity, and enhanced humanity which both attracts and challenges those who encounter them. Those few who achieve the sixth stage of faith love life intensely but hold their own lives loosely. They exhibit a capacity to relate empathetically to persons at any other stage of religious development and to members of any other faith tradition. Finally, the universal inclusiveness of the religious vision of stage six believers distinguishes their faith from the fanaticism of cults and from fundamentalistic zealotry.[8]

Verification, Contextualization, Amplification

Because he regards the response of faith as a commitment which engages the entire person, Fowler has made more of an effort than most developmentalists to coordinate his theory of faith development with other theories of cognitive, moral, and affective development.[9] I personally find considerable plausibility in Fowler's theory as a whole, and especially in the earliest stages.

7. *Ibid.*, pp. 184-198.   8. *Ibid.*, pp. 199-211.   9. *Ibid.*, pp. 37-116.

Of all the developmental theorists I have considered, Fowler's epistemological presuppositions show the greatest affinity for the construct of experience presented in chapter two. Fowler acknowledges a place for abstract rational thinking within the spectrum of human cognitive responses to reality; but he also understands well the role which intuitive forms of understanding play in human knowing. In Fowler's theory not only do imaginative forms of thinking yield a grasp of reality, but they yield privileged access to human religious insight. Fowler also appreciates the importance of shared religious consciousness and of the capacity of myth and ritual to mediate religious understanding. In all of these ways, his theory tends to verify the construct of experience defended in chapter two.

Fowler's insistence on the imaginative, mythic, and intuitive dimensions of religious faith provide a healthy counterbalance to the rationalistic assumptions of Piaget and especially of Kohlberg. Fowler seems to understand the differences which separate him from these two colleagues, but he has not, to the best of my knowledge, attempted to reconcile those differences philosophically. Moreover, Fowler's insistence on the importance of intuitive, appreciative forms of knowing encompasses Erickson's sensitivity to the need for emotional development but goes beyond Erickson in the cognitive claims which it makes for imaginative forms of understanding.

In its description of individuative-conjunctive faith, Fowler's theory suggests that adult believers ideally ought to advance beyond the stage of conventional religious faith. I find a parallel here with Kohlberg's insistence that personal moral development needs to move beyond the norms inculcated by conventional morality. Moreover, both theorists testify to the difficulty which people experience in making that crucial transition to adult moral and religious commitment.

One wonders, however, about the extent to which Fowler's account of individuative-conjunctive faith reflects the individualistic attitudes so prevalent in United States culture. Certainly North American individualists often make the transition from conventional religion to fully autonomous and responsible adult religious commitment very idiosyncratically, if they make the transition at all. Fowler recognizes the distortions which an excessive individualism could bring to the fourth stage of faith development. I suspect, however, that cross cultural studies of the transition from conventional to fully adult faith might modulate the growth processes which Fowler describes at stage four. I would expect the greatest modulations to occur in cultures which value shared communitarian values more than individual independence.

Nevertheless, like Fowler, I would regard stage four as an indispensable moment in the passage from infantile and adolescent faith to adult religious maturity. As we shall soon see, prior to stage four and to the transition to autonomous faith which it mediates, one cannot experience an adult religious conversion, even though, as Fowler himself insists, the transition to stage four alone does not guarantee that conversion will happen. I shall return to this insight below, in the course of considering whether Jesus underwent a religious conversion.

Implications for Jesusology

If one reads the New Testament in the light of Fowler's theory of human religious development, then the Jesus whom the evangelists describe, the Jesus of the public ministry, would seem to have achieved the sixth and highest stage of faith. Indeed, Fowler's description of stage six sounds a bit like a descriptive portrait of Jesus. Fowler himself cites Martin Luther King, Jr., Gandhi, and Mother Teresa of Calcutta as living examples of stage six.[10] His account of stage six also fits the Jesus of the gospels.

Jesus called the integrated religious vision which He proclaimed the reign of God. That vision sought to transform Israel into a community of radical inclusiveness, a community which welcomed the poor, the marginal, the sinful, and even the degraded of first-century Jewish society: the prostitutes, the beggars, and the lepers. The vision of the kingdom sought to create a "zone of liberation from the social, political, economic, and ideological shackles which oppress most humans." It did so by bringing into existence a religious community whose faith found embodiment in sharing the physical supports of life with the poorest and the least. In the kingdom the greatest have to act like the slaves of the weakest and the most vulnerable.[11]

The vision of the kingdom certainly threatened the vested power interests of Jesus' day. It threatened them to the point that they connived to discredit Him by having Him executed as a heretic and a criminal. Nevertheless, Jesus' religious vision endowed His life with a simplicity, lucidity, and availability which drew crowds to Him at the same time that it challenged those crowds to a radical transformation of their own hearts and of the world. Perhaps more than any other religious figure Jesus combined an intense passion for life transformed by faith in God with a selfless disregard for His own life. He seems also to have cherished and nurtured the least sign of religious faith in others.

Only one aspect of Jesus' ministry might lead one to question the universality of His religious vision: namely, the fact that he confined His own ministry to "the lost sheep of the house of Israel" and related only by way of exception to Samaritans and Gentiles.(Mt 10:5-8)

10. *Ibid.*, p. 201.
11. For a discussion of the moral demands which attend life in the kingdom, see: Donald L. Gelpi, S.J., "Breath-Baptism in the Synoptics" in *Studies on Pentecostal/Charismatic Experiences in History*, edited by Cecil M. Robeck (Peabody, MA: Hendrickson, 1984).

Only Matthew mentions explicitly the restricted focus of Jesus' ministry. Matthew wrote his gospel in the sub-apostolic age, when the Christian Church was transforming itself into a predominantly Gentile community; and I personally deem it unlikely that Matthew would have called attention to the restricted focus of Jesus' ministry in an increasingly Gentile Church unless the tradition about Jesus supported the claim. Moreover, I shall argue in chapter ten that embittered debates in the apostolic Church about the status of baptized Gentiles make it virtually certain that Jesus did not make Gentiles the primary target of His ministry. The Christian community began Jewish and evolved into a more universal community.

All the synoptic evangelists record Jesus' encounter with and endorsement of Gentiles of faith. (Mk 7:24-30; Mt 8:5-13, 15:21-28; Lk 7:1-10) Quite plausibly, those encounters may have led Jesus to make a more explicit place within the kingdom for believing Gentiles. If so, those encounters could have re-enforced the theme of universal salvation already present in Jesus' teaching. Indeed, I regard it as highly plausible, even probable, that the Jesus movement sought to challenge Israel to a quality and degree of faith which would allow it to serve as God's instrument for a universal salvation. The kingdom of God which Jesus preached enunciated His strategy for effecting the religious transformation of Israel. Jesus practiced, in Marcus Borg's felicitous phrase, a politics of holiness.[12]

The Jesus portrayed in the New Testament embodied the kind of universal faith which Fowler describes as the sixth and highest stage of human religious development. If we regard Jesus as an exemplar of the sixth stage of faith in Fowler's scheme, should we also assert that at some point in His own religious development He experienced a conversion? The question, "Did Jesus convert?" raises both psychological and theological issues. Let us consider the psychological issues first.

Fowler contrasts conversion and development. He describes development as an evolutionary change and conversion as a revolutionary change in faith.[13] I find that his definition, despite its abstractness, accords with the one which I have proposed. The definition which I have suggested names the specific kind of revolution which conversion effects: namely the passage from irresponsible to responsible behavior. Fowler, moreover, deals only with religious conversion, while the construct of conversion which I have developed recognizes in addition four forms of secular conversion.

Fowler argues, correctly in my opinion, that one must distinguish between conversion and the stages of faith which he describes. He supports

12. Cf. Marcus Borg, *Jesus: A New Vision* (San Francisco, CA: Harper & Row, 1982); *Jesus in Contemporary Scholarship* (Valley Forge, PA: Trinity Press International, 1994); *Meeting Jesus Again For the First Time* (San Francisco, CA: Harper & Row, 1994)
13. Cf. Fowler, *op. cit.*, p. 34.

this position with two arguments. First, people experience religious conversions without simultaneously progressing from one stage of faith to another. Second, one may progress from one stage of faith to another without experiencing religious conversion. Moreover, Fowler supports these two arguments with concrete examples.[14]

At the same time Fowler recognizes the possibility that conversion can stand in a dynamic relationship to the stages of faith. He recognizes that the experience of conversion can on occasion advance one from one stage of faith to another. He also concedes that the advancement to a new stage of faith could precipitate a religious conversion.

Fowler also argues, however, that certain kinds of conversion (for example, conversions which occur in a fundamentalistic context) might block one's advancement from one stage of faith to another. Moreover, once again, Fowler illustrates his position with concrete examples.[15]

The distinction between conversion and stage change in human religious development raises questions and doubts about whether Jesus converted; for the distinction suggests the illegitimacy of arguing from the fact of stage change to the fact of conversion.

Assessing the Psychological Issues

Fowler, in my judgment, correctly distinguishes between stages of faith and conversion. Nevertheless, I personally find it inconceivable that anyone could attain to the sixth stage of faith, which embodies outstanding personal holiness, without having at some point passed from conventional to fully mature and adult faith. Those who make such a transition successfully convert. In other words, I would regard a prior conversion experience as a precondition for any human achieving Fowler's sixth stage of faith consciousness.

I am not identifying the sixth stage with conversion. On the contrary, achieving heroic holiness under ordinary circumstances presupposes not only that an initial conversion has already occurred but that the individual in question has had time after converting initially to mature in sanctity.

In other words, from a psychological standpoint, I would regard it as morally impossible for Jesus first to have conceived and embodied the vision of the kingdom and then to have died for it without at some point in His life having taken full, adult responsibility for His relationship to God. That would mean that at some point He converted in the sense of conversion defined in chapter two. It also means that from a psychological standpoint He probably experienced that conversion some time before the events narrated in the gospels.

---

14. *Ibid.*, p. 285.   15. *Ibid.*, pp.285-286.

Psychological considerations aside, however, the question of Jesus' conversion also raises a number of theological issues. From a theological standpoint, one can convert from unbelief to belief or from a life of sin to the obedience of faith. Nevertheless, people raised in a religious environment, people who pass from infantile to adult faith as members of a believing religious community also experience conversion.

The definition of conversion given in chapter two applies to both kinds of conversion experience. I have defined conversion as the transition from irresponsible to responsible behavior in some realm of human experience. Irresponsible behavior can connote culpability, even sinful culpability; but it need not. The inability to act with full adult responsibility for oneself can also flow from immaturity. An infant at Fowler's stage one or stage two simply lacks the human wherewithal to take adult responsibility for its decisions.

In calling Jesus a convert, one need not imply His lack of faith. Rather one would simply assert that at some point in His own human religious development Jesus passed from conventional religious faith to an autonomous, adult faith in which He took full and mature responsibility for His relationship to the Father.

So understood, Jesus' conversion need not imply His personal repentance from sin. As I have already indicated, one cannot deal adequately with belief in Jesus' sinlessness until one considers the paschal mystery. One must, in other words, lay proper doctrinal foundations for assessing this traditional Christian belief. Here it suffices to note that the definition of conversion suggested in chapter two allows one to bracket the question of Jesus' sinlessness for the time being.

If Jesus did convert, when would He have grown religiously to the point that He could take full adult responsibility for His relationship to God? In order to take such responsibility, His human faith would have had to advance beyond conventional Jewish faith. The faith which Jesus proclaimed and embodied in the gospels certainly expresses more than conventional faith. Had Jesus settled for conventional faith He would have lived the life of a Pharisee, a Sadducee, an Essene, or of an ordinary Jewish peasant. He chose to do none of these.

In my judgment, Fowler's stage four marks the point at which conversion becomes humanly possible precisely because it marks the transition from conventional to a personally interiorized religious faith.

The transition from conventional religion to individuative-conjunctive faith need not, however, coincide with religious conversion. Authentic conversion demands a fully responsible adult religious commitment. One can, however, make the transition from conventional to individuative-conjunctive faith irresponsibly. One makes that transition irresponsibly when one substitutes for authentic religious faith an egotistical, idiosyncratic faith which has nothing to do with God's historical self-revelation. One thinks, for example, of the woman named Sheila described in *Habits of the Heart* who claimed to profess the religion of "Sheilaism." She had, apparently, advanced beyond conventional religion by substituting for it a kind of self-idolatry.[16]

I shall argue below that faith in the paschal mystery necessarily entails faith in Jesus' sinlessness. If so, then Jesus would have made the human transition from conventional to fully autonomous, adult religious faith as soon as He had matured sufficiently to take full and mature personal responsibility for His adult relationship to the Father. In this sense, Jesus' sinlessness demands His conversion, because not to have converted when He might have would have involved making a deliberately irresponsible choice before God. That a sinless Jesus could not do. In the case of a sinless Jesus, therefore, the transition from conventional faith to individuative-conjunctive faith and adult religious conversion would have coincided.

When did Jesus make that transition? Some have suggested that Jesus' baptismal experience at the Jordan coincided with His initial, adult conversion.[17] (Mk 1:9-11; Mt 3:13-17; Lk 3:21-22) I find the suggestion implausible. The gospel accounts of Jesus' messianic vision on the banks of the Jordan do not describe an initial conversion experience but His messianic commissioning. Moreover, given the degree of heroic sanctity which Jesus exhibits during His public ministry, I regard it as extremely probable, if not virtually certain, that, given the demands of growth into heroic holiness His initial conversion experience occurred much earlier.

The story of the finding in the temple in Luke suggests the possibility that already in early adolescence, Jesus had begun to experience God as *Abba*, Father. (Lk 2:41-52) Since Jesus' *Abba* experience, His sense of standing in an intimate, personal relationship to God as Father, lies at the heart of His highly personalized reading of Torah, I would find it at least plausible that already as a young adolescent He had begun to take personal responsibility for that relationship. If so, then we should understand His Jordan experience, not as His initial conversion, but as the crystallization of His adult faith into a sense of mission.

In the first part of this chapter I have used Fowler's theory of stages of religious cognitive development in order to verify and amplify the philosophical account of religious experience presented in chapter five. I have also pondered its potential contribution to Jesusology. In the section which follows, I shall summarize the tentative conclusions I have reached about Jesus' human development.

16. Cf. Bellah, *et al.*, *Habits of the Heart*, pp. 221, 235.
17. Cf. Donald P. Gray, "Was Jesus a Convert?" *Religion in Life* 43(winter, 1974), pp. 445-455.

(II)

In the last three chapters, I have argued that *on the whole* the results of developmental psychology tend to verify the philosophical construct of experience presented in chapter five. By that I do not mean that all developmental theorists endorse the philosophical position which I expounded in that chapter. I do mean that the triadic, realistic, social construct of experience which I have defended can interpret the results of empirical investigations into the normal stages of human development.

An Amplified Philosophical Construct

I have also argued that many of the theories of human development which I have examined amplify the philosophy of experience developed in chapter five. They do so by providing plausible, and in some cases even probable, accounts of the typical consolidation of habitual forms of behavior in different realms of human experience.

These developmental constructs amplify a philosophy of experience because they investigate empirically patterns of growth unavailable to philosophical reflection. The pursuit of philosophy presupposes a mature, adult mind. It therefore also presupposes that the kinds of growth experiences which create an adult mind have already happened. Philosophy reflects directly on lived, macroscopic experience, on an experience, therefore, which has already passed through the kinds of human development which developmental psychology studies. Philosophy uses no tools beyond language in its articulation of that experience. Any fully adequate theory of experience needs, therefore to amplify its philosophical insights by pondering the results of the empirical reconstruction of growth experiences to which the philosophical mind lacks immediate access.

I have also argued in this chapter that the philosophical construct of experience helps put the results of developmental psychology into perspective by providing an integrating frame of reference for contextualizing the latter's conclusions. That philosophical construct describes in broad strokes the dynamic shape of human experience in general, while developmental theories focus on a specific realm of experience. A philosophical construct of experience therefore allows one to locate the realm of experience which any given empirical theory decides to target within a more comprehensive descriptive and normative frame of reference.

Finally, I have tried to show in the preceding pages that the construct of experience developed in chapter two can, when necessary, criticize some of the questionable philosophical presuppositions which, on occasion, skew developmental theories. In the preceding analysis, for example, I called into question the Kantianism of both Piaget and Kohlberg.

Some may find the results of this dialogue between philosophy and developmental psychology disappointing. I have usually argued that the verification and amplification of a triadic, social construct of experience in developmental psychology yields on the whole plausible insights into the growth of experience. On occasion, I have argued for probability and only very rarely for certainty. Some, no doubt, would prefer certitude to mere probability or plausibility.

In my judgment, however, such certitude eludes us at this point. Jean Piaget for all practical purposes created the field of developmental psychology by devising methods for verifying empirically stages of human growth. The science of developmental psychology finds itself, as a consequence, in something like its own stage of infancy. Within a very short time, developmental psychology has accomplished an enormous amount; but I would regard none of its theories as immune to revision.

Only the naive would fail to recognize the cultural conditioning which attends any given theory of human development. The cross-cultural studies of development undertaken to date have as a consequence forced the modification of particular developmental schemes and will probably continue to do so. Moreover, the complexity of human growth makes it possible for a particular developmental theory to focus so narrowly on specific aspects of human experience that it ignores other variables which condition growth in the area it studies.

Both intra-cultural and cross-cultural studies of developmental processes promise, then, not only to modify many of the going developmental theories but to put them on a sounder empirical footing through needed qualification. Cross-cultural studies to date indicate that, despite their differences, cultures, like history, rhyme. By that I mean that culture modulates human growth in ways which introduce analogy, not total otherness, into human developmental patterns. Writing and printing, for example, seem to create abstract forms of consciousness which remain more generally unavailable in purely oral cultures. A clearer sense of the nature of the analogies which culture introduces into human developmental processes should lead to a more precise identification of those patterns of development which tend to appear in any culture.

In the end, therefore, one must settle for the fact that the philosophical construct of experience which I have proposed, even when verified and amplified in the results of developmental psychology, sometimes enjoys scientific probability but more often can claim only scientific plausibility. That may sound disappointing; but to the best of my knowledge, no one to date has ever attempted to develop a Christology based on a philosophical construct of the human which could make even that minimal scientific claim. Scientific probability or plausibility may not sound like much; but I for one deem working with a scientifically plausible philosophical construct of the human better than building a Christology on an implausible or patently false construct of humanity, as many Christologists have done.

In attempting to apply our philosophically verified and amplified construct of experience to Jesus, I suggested that only in a very few cases can one make certain judgments. In a handful of other cases one can draw probable conclusions. In most cases one must again settle for plausibility. By that I mean that some evidence supports a Jesusology amplified by the results of scientific studies of the human. At the same time the same evidence does not rule out other interpretations than the one I have suggested. Others, of course, might assess the evidence differently.

As the science of developmental psychology advances it may well warrant assertions about the humanity of Jesus which enjoy a higher degree of probability than I have here asserted. That will happen if cross-cultural studies of human developmental processes succeed in identifying predictable stages of growth common to humans in any culture. In that case, one could, in my judgment, assert that if Jesus developed like any other human being, as the New Testament suggests, then He too would very probably have passed through the same growth processes.

Developmental Conclusions About Jesus

Let me close by summarizing briefly the plausible conclusions I have drawn concerning Jesus' human development.

1) The same biological processes which underpin human development in other persons certainly grounded and limited Jesus' human cognitive development if He resembled us in all things but sin.

2) Jesus' human mind probably advanced through something analogous to the stages which Piaget describes. In His cognitive development, therefore, He probably advanced from sensory-motor thinking to transductive thinking and finally to concrete operations. One cannot, however, assert with the same probability that Jesus actually attained to the kind of thinking which Piaget calls operational. In other words, if Piaget had asked Jesus to solve the kinds of abstract puzzles which in his theory establish fully operational thinking, one cannot say whether Jesus would have passed the test or not. He could possibly have flunked.

3) One can plausibly suppose that Jesus would have passed through the first five stages of emotional development described by Erickson. At the time of His death, it also seems plausible to suppose that He was living at stage six and wrestling with issues of intimacy vs. isolation. As He faced His own death, He may have had to struggle with the issues of the final stage of emotional development in Erickson's scheme as He assessed the integrity of His own life.

4) In what concerns Jesus' personal moral development, one can plausibly suppose that the rules of children's games functioned for Him in His childhood as a symbol of larger social relationships. One can also

plausibly suppose that as He developed morally He acquired greater sensitivity to the complexity of human moral situations.

5) One can plausibly suppose that the infant Jesus developed something like the kind of social self-awareness described by Daniel Stern. In other words, He advanced from a vague sense of Himself as an emerging human self, to core self-awareness, then to subjective self-awareness, and finally to linguistic self-awareness. One can also plausibly suppose that affect attunement between Jesus and His mother Mary mediated His first stammering efforts in Aramaic.

6) One can plausibly suppose that Jesus, like other children, learned to interiorize the language patterns of His culture. One can also assert with high probability that He interiorized the oral patterns of thinking of His fellow Palestinian peasants.

7) In His social maturation Jesus almost certainly started as a lap child, graduated to the status of a knee child, and advanced to playing like a yard child. One can suppose that He almost certainly had to deal with questions of gender identity and peer dominance. One can also assert with plausibility that Jesus as a school-age child received some schooling in Torah possibly in the synagogue in Nazareth.

8) As He matured socially, one can plausibly suppose that Jesus advanced through something like the stages of social development described by Selman. Certainly, the Jesus of the gospels displays a truly extraordinary capacity for faithful friendship.

9) One can even imagine with some plausibility that the male crisis of the early thirties in part motivated Jesus' decision to abandon His father's trade in order to listen to the preaching of John the Baptizer.

10) One can plausibly assert that in His human religious development, Jesus advanced through something like all six stages of faith which Fowler describes. One can also assert with high probability, even certainty, that the Jesus of the gospels functioned at the sixth stage of faith and that at some time much earlier underwent a religious conversion in which He assumed for the first time full adult responsibility for His relationship to God.

In confronting the incarnation the human mind encounters the most profound of all religious mysteries. Developmental psychology can throw a dim and distant light on plausible aspects of Jesus human development. It can therefore help Jesusology to flesh out a philosophical construct of human experience. In the process, the results of developmental thinking clarify what one means by humanity in general and by Jesus' humanity in particular. In the last analysis, however, developmental psychology has nothing to say about the profound mystery of the incarnation or about the unique kind of religious awareness which it created in Jesus.

The new quests for the historical Jesus can, however, in some measure provide the kind of insight into Jesus which eludes any purely scientific study of human behavior. One final task remains, therefore, in this reflection on Jesus' humanity. I need to integrate into a verified and amplified construct of human experience the results of the new quests for the historical Jesus. Those results provide a partial insight into Jesus' uniquely personal religious vision. To a critical examination of the new quests I turn in the two chapters which follow.

Chapter 9
The World Jesus Entered

I am attempting to lay systematic foundations for an inculturated Christology which speaks to the needs of Christians converting in a North American culture. This section of the present study focuses on the humanity of Jesus. At this point, therefore, Jesusology rather than Christology provides the focus of interest. Christology as such, in addition to offering an account of Jesus' humanity must also deal with the paschal mystery. I shall begin to deal with the paschal mystery in the final section of this volume.

This chapter and the following one seek to verify and amplify other dimensions of the construct of experience presented in chapter five. As we have seen, every human self emerges from two kinds of environments. The self emerges most immediately from its own body, which it has constructed as a life-support for its own vital operations. Because, however, one must create one's own body from the larger surrounding environment, that environment provides the larger reality from which the self emerges.

As we also saw, every self constructs itself through interaction with its total environment. As a consequence, one's total environment serves as the arena in which a conditioned, flickering human consciousness exercises a conditioned, flickering human freedom.

The transactional character of the relationship between self and environment also transforms the process of self-creation into a collaborative enterprise. Far from creating oneself within a subjectivity impervious to outside influence, as Whiteheadean philosophy suggests, the act of self-creation results from the ongoing interaction of each self with its own body, with other selves, with the world, and ultimately with God. The confrontation with a hostile environment or with powerful enemies makes the process of social self-creation oppressive; but at no point does it cease to qualify as thoroughly social and transactional.

Besides enjoying environmental rootedness, a triadic experience develops over time. Its evaluative processes endow experience with a temporal structure. Its environmental rootedness endows it with a spatial structure. The evaluative presence of an experience to its environment therefore gives it a spatio-temporal character. The spatio-temporal development of human experience creates history. The present chapter examines therefore the results of scholarly attempts to reconstruct the personal history of Jesus of Nazareth.

I have not presented a triadic construct of experience out of some abstract philosophical interest but in order to test its ability to interpret the humanity of Jesus. Testing the Christological utility of triadic philosophical construct of experience once again demands cross-disciplinary thinking. Specifically, a philosophical construct will prove its Christological mettle if it can indeed interpret the results of the new quests for the historical Jesus, contextualize those results, and, if necessary, call into question any philosophical fallacies which may distort them.

As in the dialogue between philosophy and the developmental sciences, if our triadic construct of experience successfully interprets the results of the new quests, they in turn will amplify that construct. The two quests will do so in two ways. The third quest will specify the kind of environment which shaped and conditioned Jesus' developing human experience, while the new quest will supply specific information about the ways in which Jesus responded evaluatively and decisively to the situation in which He found Himself.

This chapter begins by summarizing the results of the so-called "third quest" for the historical Jesus. By the third quest I mean the attempt to expand the quest for the historical Jesus beyond a concern for authenticating His words and actions. The third quest seeks in addition to reconstruct historically the social, political, and economic environment which contextualizes Jesus' mortal ministry.

This chapter divides into three parts. In the first, I reflect on the accomplishments and limitations of the new quests for the historical Jesus. In the second, I examine Roman imperial rule and the *pax romana*. In the third, I focus on the world of first century Palestine into which Jesus was born.

In the following chapter, I shall summarize the results of the new quest for the historical Jesus. As we have already seen, the new quest attempts the historical reconstruction of Jesus' ministry by enunciating norms which allow one to sort out which elements in the New Testament witness constitute "authentic Jesus" and which do not. On the basis of those criteria, the new quest constructs a scholarly account of what we can at the distance of two-thousand years say about Jesus' words and actions.[1]

Before we launch our frail theological craft into the quagmire of first century history, however, we need to remind ourselves of the hazards of the journey on which we are about to embark. First of all, let me state quite plainly that I claim no credentials as a professional New Testament scholar. I pursue foundational theology in Lonergan's sense of the term. Every functional theological specialty must, of course, make use of the Bible as a whole. A foundational Christology must especially deal with the New Testament witness to Jesus. In using sacred Scripture, a foundational theologian needs, therefore, to take into account the results of con-

---

1. Cf. Marcus Borg, "Portraits of Jesus in North American Scholarship," *Harvard Theological Review* 84:1(1991), pp. 1-22.

temporary New Testament exegesis. A foundational use of Biblical texts goes beyond exegesis, however, by attempting to reflect systematically on the ways in which the Biblical witness ought to shape an authentic Christian conversion experience.

In what follows, therefore, I am attempting for the most part to trace a trail through the mountains of scholarly material which the new quests have raised. In summarizing the results of the new quests, I shall, moreover, keep in mind the pastoral focus of this study, namely, the RCIA. I shall present in capsule form the kind of historical information which an adult convert to Christianity needs to know in order to understand Jesus' mortal ministry and in order to situate His ministry in its historical context.

In referring to Jesus Himself I shall, moreover, continue to employ the "notes" I used in chapter seven. I shall therefore employ terms like "certain," "probable," " plausible," "possible," "impossible," "implausible," "improbable," and "uncertain" in the technical senses defined in that same chapter. In dealing with Jesus' own career I shall also indicate which criteria tend to validate the assertion in question.

Second, before one begins to examine the results of the new and third quests, one needs to acknowledge their scandal and limitations. By their scandal I mean their failure to date to produce a broader scholarly consensus concerning the scope and development of Jesus' mortal ministry. By the limitations of the new quests I mean the limited contribution which they make to Christology as a whole.

(I)

In his own recent foray into the quest for the historical Jesus, John Dominic Crossan begins by warning the reader that the new quest like the first quest has begun to degenerate into something like a bad scholarly joke. Despite a serious attempt to follow scholarly techniques which ensure the historical "objectivity" of its results, the new quest for the historical Jesus continues to pile up contradictory portraits of Jesus of Nazareth.[2] In my judgment, Crossan's own portrayal of Jesus' as "a peasant Jewish Cynic" only adds to the bad humor; but Crossan has made a substantial contribution to the third quest in his careful reconstruction of life in first century Palestine and in his assessment of aspects of Jesus' ministry and message.[3]

2. Cf. Crossan, *The Historical Jesus*, pp. xvii-xix; John P. Meier, "Dividing Lines in Jesus Research Today," *Interpretation*, 50(1996), pp. 355-372; Alfons Weiser, "Jesus und die neutestamentliche Theologie," *Zeitschrift für die Neutestamentliche Wissenschaft*, 87(1996), pp. 146-164; Klaus Berger, "Jesus als Nazoröer/ Naxiröer," *Novum Testamentum*, 38(1996), pp. 323-335.
3. Cf. Crossan, *op.cit.*, p. 422. In his more popular biography of Jesus, Crossan still has not got the joke. He still portrays Jesus as a Jewish Cynic, even though he puts more

The scandal of the new quest lies, then, in the fact that it has not to date produced more scholarly unanimity. Part of the scandal results from the fact that new questers for the historical Jesus all use historical-critical method in their attempt to reconstruct the Jesus of history. Historical-critical method has made a substantial contribution to our understanding of sacred Scripture; but to the extent that it acquiesces in an Enlightenment myth of scientific objectivity, it promises more than it can deliver. Not even the mathematical sciences think with the mythical "objectivity" to which the Enlightenment aspired. All thinking yields a more or less adequate, more or less verifiable interpretation of reality.

Historical-critical method, moreover, qualifies finally as scholarship rather than as empirical science in the strict sense of the term. It uses no mathematical measurement or tight experimental controls. Those who ply it as a method often do so with different assumptions about the texts which they are examining and about what those texts can and cannot say. As John P. Meier has insisted, since new questers for the historical Jesus cannot avoid assumptions, prejudices, and blind spots, they need as far as possible to subject their personal biases to critical assessment and to acknowledge them as conditioning their scholarly conclusions.[4] If more new questers followed his advice more systematically, they might achieve scholarly consensus sooner.

The new quest for the historical Jesus does not, then, yield "the real Jesus." It yields only a fallible, scholarly interpretation of Jesus' mortal ministry: a construct of a reality, not the reality itself. Moreover, since it seems unlikely that the scholarly world will ever reach complete unanimity concerning the correct account of Jesus' public activity, it also seems unlikely that the "historical Jesus" will ever become an object of Christian faith. In all likelihood, it will remain a theological construct of some, but limited, utility.[5]

Theological speculation has never saved anyone, although on occasion it can contribute something to salvation. Meier again has the right of it

rhetorical stress on the term "Jewish." The new stress, however, does not make Crossan's thesis any more credible.

   In his popular portrait of Jesus, Crossan does get a number of things right: the apocalyptic tone of John the Baptizer's ministry, the egalitarian character of Jesus' vision of the kingdom, Jesus' concern with both physical and social healing.

   At the same time Crossan shows an unfortunate persistence in pitting the New Testament against other historical sources. Moreover, Crossan approaches the pascal mystery with much the same kind of skepticism as nineteenth century questers for the historical Jesus. One suspects that his skepticism helps motivate his improbable portrait of Jesus, not as a Jewish Socrates, but as a Jewish Diogenes. Cf. John Dominic Crossan, *Jesus: A Revolutionary Biography* (San Francisco, CA: Harper & Row, 1994).

4. Cf. Meier, *A Marginal Jew*, pp. 1-14.
5. Cf. John P. Meier, "The Historical Jesus: Rethinking Some Concepts," *Theological Studies*, 51(1990), pp. 3-24.

when he insists that Christian faith terminates, not at the "historical Jesus" but at the person of Jesus. The "historical Jesus" can never substitute for the person of Jesus because the scholarly construct of a real person can never substitute for the person's reality. Faith terminates at the reality, not at a construct.

Nevertheless, within the theological enterprise, the new quests for the historical Jesus make a useful contribution to Christology as a whole. To the extent that the scholarly reconstruction of Jesus' mortal life and ministry produces even a modicum of consensus, it serves as a useful check against the uncritical assumptions about Him in which both individuals and faith communities all too often indulge. Christian faith roots itself in history. Hence, when the historical evidence does not support specific beliefs about or interpretations of Jesus, we need to take those beliefs and interpretations back to the drawing board.[6] We also need, of course, to deal critically with the claims of the new quests.

With these qualifications in mind, let us then begin to examine the results of the new quests for the light which they throw on the concrete humanity of the man called Jesus. We begin by examining the scholarly attempt to reconstruct the context in which Jesus lived and ministered.

(II)

We have very limited historical access to the details of ordinary life in the first century in general and to life in first-century Palestine in particular. Only fragmentary historical evidence has survived, almost all of it written by males who belonged to an elite social class. Even the meager evidence we have provides, then, a very limited angle of vision on the complex reality of first century life.

Our own personal and cultural biases also skew our ability to see the reality of the first century clearly. As we have already seen, people raised in twentieth-century, literate, technological cultures think differently and perceive reality differently from those raised in predominantly preliterate, oral cultures like first-century Palestine. Seeing beyond the cultural blinders we habitually wear takes effort even when we recognize our bias and want to transcend it. Indeed, much of the frustration which attends the new quests for the historical Jesus results from the attempt to apply methods of interpretation derived from literate, rationalistic twentieth century history to texts which developed on the borderline between oral and literate culture. Reading the New Testament on its own terms requires a capacity to think orally, a capacity which most scripture scholars find utterly alien. Nevertheless, through the mists of time and space, we can begin to glimpse

6. *Ibid.*, pp. 196-200.

some of the rough outlines of the social and cultural geography of first-century Palestine.[7]

The Roman Empire encompassed the Mediterranean basin but spread northward into Gaul and Germany, with far flung outposts in England. Life in the Empire followed pre-industrial, agrarian patterns.

In contemporary agrarian societies about sixty percent of the children die at birth, and ninety percent of those who survive die in their late forties. Moreover, in contemporary agrarian societies land means money. The rich tend to invest in large landed estates, while taxes tend to erode rather than to develop the tax base.[8] We have reason to think that life in the Roman Empire probably followed analogous patterns. Despite its predominantly agricultural character, the hierarchical social systems which emerged in the Mediterranean basin tended to come from the cities.

For over two thousand years, all the peoples of the Mediterranean have had written languages. In the first century, however, writing flourished primarily among the aristocratic elite and among the scribal class. The vast majority of the population remained illiterate.[9]

Bureaucracy, class, and honor codes have traditionally stratified the civilizations which emerged in the Mediterranean basin. Hierarchical codes of honor helped endow an agrarian and pastoral culture with a modicum of social stability.[10]

The hierarchical structure of Roman society institutionalized and perpetuated the extremes of social inequality. Roman society probably reproduced something like the same class structure as one finds in contemporary pastoral and agrarian societies.

Within the Roman Empire, the Ruling Class stood on the top rung of the social, political, and economic hierarchical ladder. They constituted a numerically small part of the populations (some estimate as small as five percent); but they probably controlled most of the national income (some estimate over fifty percent).

In the Roman empire, greed institutionalized itself primarily in landlordism. The Ruling Class acquired its wealth by taking it from others: from enemies conquered in war, or through taxes, or through economic and political manipulation. In politics, power tended to work through patronage, which in moments of political upheaval could make or break family fortunes.

The Retainer Class buttressed the power of the ruling, elite class. Like the Ruling Class it served, the Retainer Class also constituted only a numerically small portion of the population (perhaps five percent); but its

---

7. Cf. John K. Riches, "The Social World of Jesus," *Interpretation*, 50(1996), pp. 383-394; M. Eugene Boring, "The Third Quest and the Apostolic Faith," *Interpretation*, 59(1996), pp. 341-354.

8. Cf. Crossan, *op.cit.*, pp. 3-4.   9. *Ibid.*, p. 6.   10. *Ibid.*, pp. 11-12.

members occupied positions which gave them some degree of power and influence. The Retainer Class included the army (both the soldiers and its officers), governmental bureaucrats, and scribes. In the Roman Empire occupying armies besides fighting wars also functioned as a resident police force. Indeed, the Retainer Class as a whole, including professional bureaucrats, served to control the lower classes in the interests of an overlord. While the Ruling Class depended on the Retainer class as a whole in order to maintain control of the reins of power, it could dispense with and dispose of individual retainers without difficulty.

In Roman society, as in similar agrarian cultures, a relatively small merchant class developed especially in urban areas. The merchants controlled a considerable portion of the wealth which did not lie under direct control of the ruling elite. On occasion, the merchant class could also exert political power. In Roman society, the army seems to have taken little interest in economic issues.

As in other agrarian societies, the Roman priesthood, like the Retainer Class, also served primarily the interests of the ruling elite. They did so by lending divine sanction to the political and economic *status quo*. Emperor worship best exemplifies the client status of the priestly class, although priests and priestesses had other cultic functions in pagan worship.[11]

In ancient Roman society, the vast majority of the population belonged to the Peasant Class. Landed peasants fared better than those without property. The latter lived extremely marginal lives.

The Roman Empire exploited its peasant class systematically through taxation and military coercion. The system of exploitation effectively deprived the peasantry of all but the bare necessities of life.

The Artisan Class developed from the Peasant Class and probably stood slightly lower than the peasantry on the economic ladder. It too constituted only a small fraction of society (perhaps five percent). Jesus belonged to the artisan class.

Slaves occupied an ambiguous position within Roman society. Plantation slaves on the whole lived lives of misery, brutality, and degradation; but household slaves with humane masters could and did enjoy on occasion a more tolerable existence. The surviving epistolary literature suggests the possibility of even a measure of intimacy between master and trusted household slave.

The dregs of Roman society consisted of the Degraded Class, which included prostitutes and unskilled laborers, on the one hand, and the Expendables, on the other. As a subclass within the degraded class, the

---

11. Cf. Robin Lane Fox, *Pagans and Christians* (San Francisco, CA, Harper & Row, 1986); Jane Harrison, *Prolegomenon to the Study of Greek Religion* (New York, NY: Meridian, 1960).

Expendables included beggars, petty criminals, outlaws, and ostracized pariahs, like lepers.[12]

Jesus first saw the light of day during the so-called *Pax Romana*. This "Roman Peace" included, of course, wars with tribes in the provinces on the borders of the empire as well as the brutal suppression of all resistance or even protest by the armies which occupied the Empire's different provinces. "Roman peace" included as well the institutionalized violence of the hierarchical class structure, which subjected the vast majority of the population to ruthless exploitation. As one Roman writer put it: "*Faciunt desertam et vocant pacem.* (They make a desert and call it peace.)"

(III)

In order to understand the situation of first-century Palestine within the Roman empire, one needs to reflect on the reason for Jewish peasant unrest. The Jewish historian Josephus provides evidence that, among the provinces of the Roman empire, first-century Palestine seethed with an unrest and discontent which, in the century's second half, eventually erupted into the Jewish Wars. The Wars ended disastrously for the Jews with the fall of Jerusalem in the year 70 a.d.[13]

The unrest had deep-seated historical and religious roots. Under the leadership of heroic figures like Moses, Joshua, and others, Israel had come into existence as a peasant society free of any ruling over-class and covenanted with Yahweh as the guarantor of that freedom. The exodus created the Jewish people as a nation and Judaism as a religion. Every believing Jew knew that Israel became God's chosen people when God intervened in history in order to liberate them from slavery in the land of Egypt. Having liberated them, God then consecrated them to Himself by the Sinai covenant. Long after other nations had re-subjugated them, the memory of the exodus kept alive hope among the Jewish people that one day Israel would again know freedom from political and economic oppression.

Before the establishment of the monarchy under Saul, God reigned directly over Israel. David consolidated monarchical authority over the whole of Israel; and he entered the pages of Jewish history as the *messiah*, as God's anointed. Priestly and prophetic sanction of the Davidic monarchy endowed it with divine authority and transformed the king into one of the mediators between God and His chosen people. The Jewish peasantry did not, however, submit to monarchical rule without protest. David himself had to put down two revolts. Moreover, the oppressive extravagance of David's successor, Solomon, led the ten tribes to secede from the kingdom of Judah and to establish a separate monarchy.[14]

---

12. Cf. Crossan, *op. cit.*, pp.45-71.
13. Cf. Horsley and Hanson, *Bandits, Prophets, and Messiahs*, pp. 5-6.
14. *Ibid.*, pp. 6-7.

Especially in Israel, prophetic voices kept alive the ideals of pre-monarchical Judaism by denouncing the unbelief of the kings of Israel and by decrying the oppression and injustices which they inflicted on the ordinary folk, namely on the peasantry. Among the early ecstatic prophets, Elijah and Elisha opposed the word of God to monarchical idolatry and abuse. Amos and Hosea among the writing prophets continued the denunciation and foretold the collapse of the kingdom of Israel for its injustices and violations of its covenant with God. In the kingdom of Judah, Isaiah and Micah raised similar voices of protest.[15]

The Assyrians conquered the kingdom of Israel in 722 b.c.; and the weakened kingdom of Judah fell to the Babylonians in 587 b.c. Both events bore out the truth of prophetic denunciation of monarchical abuses and oppression of God's people. The prophet Jeremiah, whose denunciations fell impartially on the temple priesthood and on the Judean monarchy alike, saw in the fall of Jerusalem and in the destruction of its temple just retribution for the corporate sins of Judah and of its leaders.[16]

After the Persians conquered the Babylonians in 539 b.c., the Jewish exiles who returned from Babylon in the following year rebuilt Jerusalem and its temple. They laid its foundation stones in 537 b.c.

The returned exiles had Jewish governors; but they still remained politically subject to the Persian empire, which endured for two hundred years. Moreover, under the Persians, Jewish society exhibited sharp class divisions between the landed gentry and the peasantry whom the landed gentry manipulated and exploited. Under the Persians, hope that another anointed royal leader like David would appear and lead the Jews to political freedom from their oppressive conquerors faded for the time being. With the fading of royal aspirations, the temple priesthood assumed more and more political authority in Jerusalem, until the high priest in Jerusalem exercised significant control over the reins of national and political leadership.[17]

The Hellenizers

Alexander the Great conquered the Persians in 331 b.c. Conquest brought with it a cultural ideology. Alexander saw himself as the apostle of Hellenistic civilization. When Alexander died in 323 b.c. his generals divided his empire among them. In the third century before Christ the Ptolemies who governed in Egypt and southern Syria, also controlled Judea; but at the beginning of the second century, power passed from the Ptolemies to the Seleucids.

The Macedonian conquest of Persia introduced into Israel, therefore, Hellenizing tendencies which threatened the integrity of Jewish religious

15. *Ibid.*, pp. 7-8.   16. *Ibid.*, pp. 7-8.   17. *Ibid.*, pp. 8-9.

faith by pressuring Jews to abandon Torah piety for a paganized life-style. Both Alexander and his successors, for example, founded many Hellenistic cities in Palestine in which only the Greek speaking gentry enjoyed the rights of citizenship. As a consequence, Hebrews living in these cities found themselves living as aliens in their own land.

Although Jerusalem remained a Jewish city, Hellenistic rule transformed some of the priestly aristocracy in Jerusalem into agents of the government and its open collaborators. High priests collected taxes for their pagan rulers. Ordinary Jews, mostly the peasantry, saw their public and official representatives before God transformed into the toadies of Hellenizing pagans. Worse still, priestly collaboration with Gentile oppressors threatened the integrity of traditional Mosaic religion. The identification of the high priesthood with the rich aristocracy had already alienated them from the masses of the people. Willing priestly cooperation with proselytizing Gentiles would have only exacerbated their alienation from the common folk.[18]

Two decades after assuming political control in Palestine, the Seleucids found themselves in need of consolidating their power over their oriental provinces. In 175 b.c., after the ascent of Antiochus IV Epiphanes to power, the Seleucid government decided to achieve that end by stepping up its Hellenization campaign.

Members of the priestly aristocracy in Jerusalem scrambled to collaborate. Joshua, the brother of the high priest Onias III, deposed his brother by purchasing the position of high priest. Joshua paid Antiochus more than the usual three hundred talents of tribute which his brother paid. Joshua then took the Greek name Jason and offered Antiochus another one hundred and fifty talents to build a gymnasium in Jerusalem itself.

Jason also recruited other high priestly families in the enterprize of "modernizing" (i.e., Hellenizing) Jewish society. Members of these priestly families abandoned their service of the altar and actively participated in the Greek games. Because that meant that they had to appear in public naked, they disguised the marks of their circumcision so as to appear Greek. Since circumcision symbolized submission to the covenant, they equivalently declared themselves Gentiles in commitment.[19]

The priestly collaborators went even further. They consented to extend to Judea the government policy in Hellenistic cities of depriving Jews of the rights of citizenship. In effect, they agreed to replace the Torah as the operative constitution of the state with the new Greek cultural traditions. Jews in Judea, therefore, found themselves disenfranchised in their own land.

One ought not, however, to assume that all the members of the Jewish priesthood acted like the toadies of conquering Gentiles. The replacement of high priests by the conquerors of Palestine gives evidence that

18. *Ibid.*, pp. 10-11.   19. *Ibid.*, pp. 12-13.

some members of the Jewish priesthood did in fact resist Gentile influence and domination.

Menelaus, the leader of the radical Hellenizing faction, replaced Jason as high priest in the same way that Jason had ousted his brother Onias. Menelaus offered Antiochus Epiphanes three hundred more talents than Jason had. Jason found himself driven into exile across the Jordan. Once in office, Menelaus then proceeded to embezzle the temple treasuries and vessels, which the populace regarded as the religious patrimony of all the Jewish people. When word of this atrocity leaked out, popular blame fell on a certain Lysimachus who died at the hands of an outraged mob.[20]

When Antiochus Epiphanes returned from his first Egyptian campaign, Menelaus and the other Hellenizers greeted him warmly; but Antiochus outraged the populace by himself plundering the temple. A popular uprising forced Menelaus to barricade himself in the citadel in Jerusalem. Jason with about a thousand troops tried to take Jerusalem by force and regain power. Antiochus interpreted this action as a revolt and, after his second Egyptian campaign attacked Jerusalem, killed thousands of people, and sold many more Jews into slavery. Continued popular resistance provoked further punishment and led to the establishment of a military colony in Jerusalem. Undeterred the Jewish populace continued to resist the Hellenizers.

In 167 b.c. Antiochus in retaliation decreed the compulsory abandonment of Jewish customs. Jews had to prove their political loyalty by publicly violating the Torah under penalty of death.[21]

Apocalypticism and Revolt

The persecutions under Antiochus seem to have led to a surge of apocalypticism. The Greek word "*apokalypsis*" means "revelation." The revelations contained in apocalyptic writings of the period, however, sought to consolidate Jewish resistance to religious persecution and to suffuse it with the fervor of faith. Apocalyptic writers adopted a common strategy for hiding the real authorship of their subversive tracts. They attributed the revolutionary visions they popularized to ancient prophets from the past. The same strategy sought to endow those visions both with divine authority and with the authority of tradition. The apocalypticists sought to convince those who resisted religious persecution that God fought on their side.[22]

Eventually, resistance crystallized in the Maccabean Revolt (166-160 b.c.). The insurrection took its name from its military leader, Judas Maccabaeus ("The Hammer"). Judas, the third of five sons in a priestly family, the Hasmoneans, began resistance as bandits hiding in the wilderness, just as David had. They plundered and expropriated the estates of

20. *Ibid.*, pp. 13-15.   21. *Ibid.*, pp. 15-16.   22. *Ibid.*, pp. 16-20.

the Hellenizing aristocracy. Eventually they recaptured Jerusalem and purified the temple. In 160 b.c., however, the Seleucids defeated Judas and his peasant army and killed the great Jewish leader.

The revolt, however, taught the Seleucids to show greater respect for Jewish religious sensibilities. They recognized Judea as a semi-independent temple-state. Jonathan, one of the brothers of Judas, ruled as high priest and governor from 160 to 143 b.c.. Simon, another brother of Judas, succeeded Jonathan in 143 b.c. and subsequently had himself proclaimed high priest, military commander, and leader of the Jewish people in perpetuity. He thus established the Hasmonean dynasty which reigned for nearly a century. The Hasmonean family thus replaced as ruling high priests the descendants of Zadok, one of the high priests appointed by David to preside over temple worship.

As Hasmonean priestly rule evolved, it eventually dissociated itself from the Jewish peasantry whom it had originally led to semi-independence and replaced the peasant militia with mercenaries. Ironically, with time the Hasmonean state through a series of political compromises transformed itself into a petty, semi-Hellenized oriental regime indistinguishable from any other middle eastern vassal monarchy.[23]

Purists among the Jews reacted negatively to the political corruption of the priestly aristocracy, to the Hasmonean usurpation of priestly power, and to its corruption through compromise. We know something about two such movements: the Essenes and the Pharisees.

The Essenes, who established a community at Qumran in the deserts near the Dead Sea during the priesthood of Jonathan, promoted the strict and rigorous observance of Torah. Legalists and separatists, the Qumranites regarded as heterodox compromisers all Jews who settled for a less stringent interpretation of the Law than they. The Essenes resisted the Hasmonean priesthood as usurpers of priestly authority.

The community at Qumran practiced regular ritual baths, apparently as a way insuring its own purity as a religious community. The Essene monks saw themselves divinely commissioned to prepare the way for God's coming in apocalyptic judgment upon the Gentiles and upon unrighteous Jews. The Qumranites also conducted ritual banquets which anticipated the messianic banquet which they would attend when the Anointed One of Israel appeared to establish a "new covenant." That covenant would re-instate Mosaic religion in its original purity. The Essenes, moreover, established their own standards of purity, standards which marked their piety as not only rigoristic but idiosyncratic. Their dating of holy days, for example, differed from the calendar followed by the temple.

The Essene community at Qumran lasted about two hundred years, until the Roman armies, after conquering Jerusalem in the year 70 a.d.,

23. *Ibid.*, pp. 23-25.

advanced upon the final pocket of Jewish resistance at Massada. On their way to the siege of Massada, the Romans, with customary thoroughness, destroyed Qumran for good measure and probably used its members to construct the earthen ramp which eventually led to Massada's fall.[24]

The Pharisees responded to the Hasmonean priesthood differently from the Essenes. Based primarily in the Jewish laity, Pharisaism sought to re-instate fidelity to Mosaic religion within Jewish society as a whole. The Pharisees, therefore, eschewed the separatist attitudes of the Essenes. Instead, they sought to bring about a popular revival of Torah piety which would enshrine Mosaic religion once again at the heart of Judean life. The Pharisees also encouraged the interpretation of Torah in the light of unwritten oral traditions which eventually took literary shape in the Mishnah.

Because they sought to update and adapt Mosaic law to the lives of the people, the Pharisees found themselves popularly associated with the scribes, or lawyers, the professional class which studied the Law and helped adjudicate cases. Despite some similarities and overlapping, however, the two groups differed significantly. The lawyers functioned as an elite professional class, while the Pharisees embodied a broadly based renewal movement among the Jewish laity. Like the Essenes the Pharisees tended to regard the Hasmoneans as illegitimate usurpers.[25]

Hasmonean oppression led to a popular uprising under the brutal regime of Alexander Jannaeus (104-76 b.c.) Jannaeus put down the revolt with unprecedented cruelty. He first slaughtered the wives and children of eight hundred of his opponents before their very eyes and then crucified the rebels. The Pharisees may have helped foment the revolt. Certainly after the revolt failed, many Pharisees fled Judea until Jannaeus died. Under Queen Salome Alexandra, who succeeded Jannaeus in 76 b.c., the Pharisees enjoyed a brief period of political influence.

Conflict between the Pharisees and the Hasmoneans caused the latter to ally themselves with yet a third group in Palestinian Jewish society: namely, with the Sadducees. The Sadducees recognized Mosaic law alone as the basis of Jewish society; and they resisted the Pharisaical practice of interpreting the Law in the light of popular oral traditions. They thus absolved the people in general of the need to submit to the Pharisees' more rigorous interpretations of Torah. By aligning themselves with the Sadducees, the Hasmoneans effectively transformed the latter into the party of the ruling priestly aristocracy, although we have no reason to believe that all members of the high priesthood were Sadducees.[26]

24. *Ibid.*, pp. 25-26. Cf. Hartmut Stegemann, "Die Bedeutung der Qumranfunde für das Verständnis Jesu und der Frühen Christentum," *Bibel und Kirche*, 48:1(1993), pp. 10-19.

25. *Ibid.*, pp. 26-28.

26. *Ibid.*, pp. 28-29; cf. Brown, *The Death of the Messiah*, I, pp. 350-357.

Roman Conquest

Pompey conquered Palestine in 63 b.c. He besieged Jerusalem; and, when the city fell, he desecrated the temple. The Romans "liberated" and restored the Hellenistic cities established under Alexander the Great and his successors. The Hasmoneans had "re-Judaized" those cities and restored Jews within it to full citizenship. The Romans undid the work of the Hasmoneans and subjected all other territories they had conquered to tribute.

A generation of turmoil followed Pompey's conquest as different Hasmonean groups and factions struggled for dominance against rival Roman armies. War ravaged the land and further impoverished the peasants.

In putting down the last remnants of resistance, the conquering Romans acted with characteristic brutality and thoroughness. They burned and destroyed entire towns. They hacked to pieces the inhabitants, or crucified them, or sold them into slavery. History preserves a few accounts of typical Roman "pacification." At the fall of the town of Tarichean in Galilee, for example, several thousand Jewish men found themselves sold as slaves. After capturing the town of Sepphoris, the Romans burned it to the ground and sold all of its inhabitants into slavery. They then captured and crucified two thousand of the rebels. The Romans regarded such atrocities as standard policy. Needless to say, it did not endear them to those they subjugated.[27]

The aggressive young Jewish king Herod assisted the Romans in the subjugation of his own people. He subsequently ruled in Palestine as a client king of the Romans from 37 to 4 b.c. He maintained foreign mercenaries throughout the land who snuffed out the least sign of resistance. He consolidated his political power through military coercion and built a series of strategic fortresses throughout the land.

Among foreigners who did not know him first hand, Herod cultivated the image of a magnanimous builder and benefactor of his people. He rebuilt the temple in Jerusalem and endowed the city with a theater, an amphitheater, and a fortified royal fortress. (Today nothing remains of the Herodian temple but the Wailing Wall.) Herod even constructed entire cities like Caesarea Maritima and Sebaste, where he promoted the worship of the divine Augustus, the reigning Roman emperor. Herod also donated temples and public buildings in pagan cities like Athens, Sparta, and Rhodes.

Whatever his public image abroad, Herod's own people despised and feared him as a cruel tyrant. He financed his vast building programs with oppressive taxes ruthlessly extorted from the populace. He replaced the Hasmonean priestly aristocracy with other priestly families who toadied

27. *Ibid.*, pp. 30-31.

to his whims. Like the Hasmoneans these new priestly leaders could claim no Zadokite lineage.

Herod transformed his kingdom into a totalitarian police state. He outlawed all public gatherings and instituted an elaborate spy system. He met all resistance with cruel and ruthless public punishments and executions. The peasantry, who suffered most cruelly under Herod's tyranny, seethed with resentment.

Twice the Pharisees refused to take the oath of loyalty to a King they regarded as a "half-Jew" and puppet of the Roman oppressors. Under Herod, the Pharisees lost political power and devolved into a loosely federated religious brotherhood.

At the death of Herod, popular revolts broke out in every part of his kingdom. The Romans suppressed the uprisings with characteristic brutality.[28] Sometime toward the end of the reign of Herod the Great, possibly in the year 7 or 6 b.c., Jesus of Nazareth was born.

The Romans, after "re-pacifying" Palestine, divided Herod's kingdom among his three sons: Herod Antipas, Herod Archelaus, and Herod Philip. Herod Antipas ruled over Galilee and Perea. Archelaus ruled Judea and Samaria. Philip governed Itruria. After nine years of inept rule, however, the Romans deposed Archelaus; and the emperor appointed a governor, or prefect, to replace him.

The Roman prefecture in first-century Palestine divided into to two periods. The first period lasted until 41 a.d., when Herod Agrippa I assumed rule over Judea. The second period lasted until the Jewish wars in 70 a.d. The dishonesty and corruption of the post-Agrippa procurators inflamed Jewish nationalist sentiments and produced much more violence and political turmoil during the second Roman prefecture. The second prefecture boiled with discontent, terrorist attacks, and culminated in open revolt. Jesus lived during the first Roman prefecture. While hardly idyllic, by comparison with the second prefecture, the first advanced less violently.[29]

During the first Roman prefecture, Herod Antipas continued his father's patronage of Hellenistic culture. He rebuilt the city of Sepphoris, after the Romans destroyed it, a town not far from the Galilean town of Nazareth. Possibly, Jesus' father Joseph assisted in the rebuilding. Herod Antipas also founded the town of Tiberias on the Sea of Galilee as a center of Hellenistic culture.[30]

Under Roman rule many peasants lost effective access to the land. Those who continued to produce crops had to harvest a "surplus" reaped by the

28. *Ibid.*, pp. 30-34.
29. Cf. Raymond E. Brown, S.S., *The Death of the Messiah* (2 vols.; New York: Doubleday, 1994), I, pp. 677-679.
30. *Ibid.*, pp. 34-36.

Romans, by the aristocratic priesthood, and by the Herodian aristocracy. In fact, the collected "surpluses" left peasant families with little on which to survive.

As Jews, the peasantry also paid tithes to the temple. Those tithes, however, served not only to maintain God's house but also to keep the client priesthood in the rich life-style to which they had become accustomed. Temple taxes also helped to maintain the priests' landed estates. Temple taxes together with taxes levied by the Herodians only increased the already heavy burden of Roman taxation. That these taxes also served to buttress the power of the conquering Romans and of a priesthood and aristocracy who had sold their religious birthright for a mess of pagan pottage made the oppression rankle all the more.[31]

Popular Unrest

During the entire Roman occupation of Galilee until the destruction of Jerusalem in the year 70 a.d. Palestine seems to have heaved with growing unrest. Peasant protest took three forms: roving groups of bandits who preyed on the rich estates of the client Jewish nobility and of the client Jewish priesthood, prophetic religious leaders who stirred up apocalyptic yearnings, and periodic would-be bandit kings. The willingness of the Jewish peasantry to follow such problematic leaders testifies to their utter desperation. That willingness also testifies to deep religious commitment and to the popular impact of messianic longing.

Jewish messianic longing emerged from centuries of unrelenting conquest and oppression. It rooted itself in the divine promises enshrined in the Torah, in the prophets, and in Jewish history. Many of these promises had gone unfulfilled; but the Jewish people longed for the day when God would finally keep His word.

Apocalyptic messianism expressed as much hatred for conquerors like the Romans as it did for the corruption, venality, and complicity in oppression exhibited by the client Jewish aristocracy: the Herodians and the client, aristocratic priesthood. Devout Jews longed for a real leader like Moses, like David, like one of the great prophets of yore.

In the depths of their misery and oppression, the common people remembered God's promise to Abraham that he would father a vast people in whom all people would find blessing. (Gen 26:4; 28:14, 27-38) They recalled the promise of the dying Jacob that the scepter would never pass from Judah and from his offspring (Gen 49:10) and the prophecy of Balaam that a "star" would arise from Jacob who would bear the scepter of royalty and lead the people. (Num 24:17-19) They clung with tenacity to the promise that God would send another Moses, a second great lib-

31. *Ibid.*, pp. 48-63.

erator, whom all of Israel would obey. (Deut 18:15-19) The Jewish people needed a new "exodus" and yearned for its coming. (Am 5:15; 9:11-15)

Pre-exilic Hebrew prophets had foretold the coming of the day of the Lord, a day of judgment and of deliverance for Israel. (Am 5:15-17; 6:7; 7:17; 8:10, 13-14) An oppressed Jewish people longed for that "day": for the final establishment of the peaceable kingdom which the prophet Isaiah had foretold. (Is 2:2-4; 11:6-9; 29:18, 35-51, 67-68; 32:18)

In prophetic preaching sin leads to retribution, retribution to repentance, and repentance to redemption. (Jer 2:1-9; 3:12-17, 18-19; 4:1-4, 23-28; 6:9; 9: 12-16; 12:14-17; 15: 1-9; 16:14-15; 19:3-9; 22:10-19; 23:3-4, 14; 25:15-28; 29: 10-14; 30:3, 10-24; 31:31-34; 32:37; 46:27-28) Messianic longing fed itself on the hope that through repentance God's people might finally escape the terrible retribution they were suffering and experience deliverance and redemption once again. In the evolution of Jewish messianic piety, repentant hope would assume more and more of a self-righteous, dualistic character as scrupulous fidelity to the Law in apocalyptic Jewish conventicles combined with hatred for Gentile oppressors and contempt for their Hellenizing Jewish collaborators.[32]

The ancient messianic prophecies of Isaiah, which sprang from the prophet's passionate involvement with the fate of the Davidic monarchy, still awaited fulfillment in first century Palestine. As ordinary first-century Palestinian Jews listened to the words of the prophet at sabbath services, they yearned for the coming of Immanuel, the leader who would embody the very presence of God. (Is 6:13-16) They dreamed of the birth of the Davidic king called "Wonder Counselor, Mighty God, Eternal Father, Prince of Peace." (Is 9:1-7) They pined for the arrival of a Breath-filled leader who would sum up in his own person all the great charismatic leaders of Israel and whose coming would usher in an idyllic era of peace and prosperity. (Is 11:1-9)

During the period of exile and afterwards, the Deuteronomic history of Israel had enabled God's people to acknowledge the corporate guilt which had led to the destruction of the kingdoms of Israel and of Judah. That same history also fed messianic longing, as the poor recalled the prophecy of Nathan that God would establish the Davidic monarchy in perpetuity. (2 Sam 7:1-16) Prophets during and after the Babylonian exile echoed the prophecy of Nathan when they predicted the restoration of David's crown and the reunification of the kingdoms of Judah and of Israel under a single monarch. (Ez 11:18-21, 16:63; 20:32-38; 29:21; 37:22-25; Is 40:1-5; 41:17-20; 43:1-7, 16-21; 45:14-17; Zech 6:9-14; Mal 2:17-3:5)

---

32. Cf. Walter Smithals, *The Apocalyptic Movement: Introduction and Interpretation* (New York, NY: Abingdon, 1975).

The persecution under Antiochus Epiphanes had nourished among the Jewish people hope in the resurrection of the just, although Sadducees tended to sniff skeptically at the idea. (2 Mac 7:9-14, 22-23, 35-38) As messianic longing developed, it looked forward to an "end time" when God would finally fulfill all His promises to His people. After the end time the just would rise from the dead.

Among Jewish apocalyptic works, only the book of Daniel eventually found its way into the canon of Jewish scriptures. Written to shore up Jewish commitment during the persecution under Antiochus Epiphanes, the book of Daniel foresaw the destruction of Gentile kingdoms which oppress God's people and the simultaneous conferral of eternal sovereignty on a "Son of Man," a half-heavenly, half-human figure who probably symbolized Michael, the angelic protector of the Jewish people. (Dan 7:11-14)

The messiah made his literary debut in the apocalyptic book of Enoch whose earliest sections date from the end of the second century before Christ. In the visions of Enoch God inaugurates His final judgment of the world with "the birth pangs of the messiah," a period of conflict in which both demons and the unrighteous finally face divine judgment. (Enoch 1:3-9, 16:1-4; 19:1-2; 56:5-8; 58: 2-6; 62:1-6; 69:9-11) After vanquishing the wicked, the messiah ascends a throne of glory. (Enoch 45:3-6; 46:1-6; 48:2, 6-10; 63:11, 29; 69:26; 70:1; 71:7, 14; 90:17-38; 46) The Essenes too looked for the coming of messianic leaders who would lead Israel's conquest of her conquerors and betrayers.[33] (*Messianic Rule*, 11, 121; *Midrash on Last Days*, 1, 207, 246; *War Rule*, ii:125-126, 130, 139-140)

The historian Josephus suggests that peasant banditry increased sharply in Palestine during the two decades which preceded the fall of Jerusalem in 70 a.d. The fact, however, that the Romans crucified two bandits along with Jesus gives evidence that groups of peasant bandits roved the countryside during the tenure of Pontius Pilate. Because bandit groups preyed primarily on the client aristocracy, they probably enjoyed some support and connivance of the oppressed peasantry.

The Romans commonly punished captured bandits by burning them alive, by throwing them to the beasts, or by crucifying them. That the Romans felt the need to "set a public example" of the bandits by torturing them to death in the sight of others suggests that the authorities regarded the bandits as a significant problem. Bandit activity seeded the ground for the Jewish wars.[34]

33. Cf. Sigmund Mowinkel, *He That Cometh*, translated by G.W. Anderson, (New York, NY: Abingdon, 1954); Joseph Klausner, *The Messianic Idea in Israel*, translated by W.F. Stinespring (New York, NY: Macmillan, 1955); Rudolf Schnackenburg, *God's Rule and Kingdom*, translated by John Murray (New York, NY: Herder & Herder, 1963).

34. *Ibid.*, pp. 48-85; cf. Crossan, *op.cit.*, pp. 168-196; Brown, *op. cit.*, I, pp. 686-689.

Pontius Pilate executed Jesus of Nazareth as a messianic pretender. As the Jewish people moved inexorably toward the tragedy of the Jewish war in 70 a.d, other would-be kings would arise, no doubt indistinguishable from Jesus in Roman eyes. From time to time, this or that bandit leader would proclaim himself the anointed liberator of Israel.

The story of king David itself fed the political and military ambitions of these bandit chieftains. Before his election by the people as the king of Israel, David himself had lived the life of a fugitive, bandit leader playing a deadly game of hide-and-seek with the soldiers of king Saul.

In Deuteronomic history, the passage of the kingship from Saul to David had established its conditional character: God must anoint and choose His own ruler who would live in faithful obedience to the divine will. Both Saul's and David's popular election also made it clear that the people themselves had originally chosen their king. Moreover, the fact that David's line usurped the monarchy of Saul endowed the memory of the Jewish monarchy with a revolutionary character.[35]

After the death of Herod the Great, three peasant revolts followed upon the departure of Archelaus for Rome in 6 a.d., where he expected to press the case for his succeeding to his father's throne. All three revolutionary leaders presented themselves as messiahs: Judas, the son of a brigand chief named Ezekias; Simon, a former servant of King Herod; and an obscure shepherd named Athronges. Of the three, Athronges proved the hardest to subdue.[36]

During the ministry of Jesus, the memory of these messianic revolutionaries would have lingered fresh in the minds both of the Jewish peasantry and of their oppressors. In all probability, the Romans in condemning Jesus as a messianic pretender assimilated Him to them.

Besides roving bandits and royal pretenders, unrest among the Jewish peasantry living in Palestine during the first century found expression in popular prophetic movements. Prophetic leaders from among the people could invoke the sanction and precedent of history. After the conquest of the promised land, God in moments of national crisis had raised up charismatic judges of Israel from among the people. Elijah and Elisha, the great prophetic adversaries of the corrupt kings of Israel, had functioned as popular defenders of covenant religion. Popular messianic expectation therefore looked for the coming of a "prophet like Moses" who would once again mediate directly between the people and God and make a new exodus. (Deut 18:18)

Pharisaism failed to inspire prophetic visionaries. The voice of prophecy had also died among the aristocratic elite. Among the peasantry, how-

35. Cf. Horsley and Hanson, *op. cit.*, pp. 94-98; Crossan, *op. cit.*, pp. 198-266; Brown, *op. cit.*, I, pp. 682-684.
36. *Ibid.*, pp. 110-117.

ever, prophetic figures continued to emerge. While elite prophecy had in the past tended to culminate in written texts, peasant prophecy in first-century Palestine tended to culminate in action. After the governorship of Pontius Pilate (26-36 a.d.), two prophetic figures, one named Theudas and another called "the Egyptian," fomented revolutionary unrest prior to the Jewish Wars. Other popular prophetic voices joined theirs in inciting revolt against the Romans.[37]

During the governorship of Pontius Pilate a Samaritan prophet led a large armed throng of people up Mount Gerizim, where he promised to unearth the buried sacred vessels from its former temple. Pilate sent armed troops to block the prophet's expedition. The troops killed some and routed the others. They executed the leaders and those physically strongest among the captured.[38]

When John the Baptizer and Jesus began their prophetic ministries, it would appear probable that Pilate joined the priestly aristocracy in Jerusalem in monitoring their activities. Both the Romans and their client Jewish supporters had reason to fear peasant prophecy: prophets from among the peasantry spoke with a divine authority which threatened their own authority to the extent that it offered a credible religious alternative to it.

We are attempting to understand the humanity of Jesus as a finite, developing human experience. Every human experience emerges from a concrete historical environment. In the metaphysics of experience sketched in chapter two, the character of any reality results from its history. Within such a philosophical understanding of experience, anyone who seeks to understand the environment into which Jesus of Nazareth was born needs to ponder the historical forces which defined it.

In the historical experience of first-century Palestine, oppressive and rebellious actions, institutionalized faith and institutionalized oppression, religious visions and exploitative ideologies all blended to create a political and economic powder keg which eventually, during the second half of the century, exploded in a full-scale Jewish rebellion.

---

37. *Ibid.*, pp. 164-174; Brown, *op. cit.*, I, pp. 680-682, 684-686; John K. Levinson, "Did the Spirit Withdraw from Israel? An Evaluation of the Earliest Jewish Data," *New Testament Studies*, 43(1997), pp. 35-57.

38. Cf. Horsley and Hanson, *op. cit.*, pp. 160-172; Crossan, *op.cit.*, pp. 158-167.

Chapter 10
Jesus' Mortal Ministry

I have sketched the outlines of the volatile world into which Jesus was born. The time has come to focus on the man Jesus Himself and on the concrete shape of His experience, to the extent that we can glean it from history.

This chapter divides into seven parts. In the first, I explain the criteria which the new quest employs in authenticating words and actions of Jesus as historical. In the second, I summarize what one can piece together about Jesus' hidden life. In the third, I reconstruct the prophetic ministry of John the Baptizer. Part four examines Jesus' proclamation of the kingdom. Part five describes aspects of Jesus' religious experience. Part six examines how Jesus related to the various constituencies whom He confronted. The seventh and final section of this chapter reflects on the relevance to the RCIA of a cross-disciplinary portrait of Jesus.

(I)

Our principal historical sources for information about the life of Jesus remain the four Christian gospels. The rest of the New Testament offers only bits and pieces of information about Jesus. In secular historical writings about the period, we find only brief and fragmentary references to Jesus. None of it adds information not already contained in the four canonical gospels. The apocryphal gospels do not seem to offer a reliable historical source for reconstructing Jesus' life. The Christian apocrypha yield mostly pious fantasy. While other apocryphal sources rework materials present in the canonical gospels in order to serve the rhetorical and doctrinal needs either of rabbinic polemic or of Gnostic ideology.[1]

Criteria for Authenticating Jesus' Words and Actions

As we shall see in greater detail when we reflect on narrative Christology, the Christian evangelists did not set out to write a scholarly history of Jesus using modern critical methods. I have already suggested that the gospels took shape in the intersection between oral and literate culture.

---

1. Cf. John P. Meier, *A Marginal Jew: Rethinking the Historical Jesus.* (3 vols.; New York, NY: Doubleday, 1991), I, pp. 41-142. Not all new questers for the historical Jesus regard the apocryphal gospels as historically suspect. Crossan's work exemplifies an alternative view. He attempts to deal broadly with the "Jesus tradition." I concur with Meier in regarding this move as methodologically unsound. For a thematic culling of Christian apocryphal texts, see: J.K. Elliott, *The Apocryphal Jesus: Legends of the Early Church* (New York, NY: Oxford University Press, 1996).

Gospel narrative falls more or less within the parameters of first-century historiography, but the four evangelists wrote more like story-tellers than like contemporary scholarly historians. In the manner of story-tellers they adapted the saga of Jesus to the particular audience for whom they narrated it.

The new quest for the historical Jesus seeks to distill from gospel narrative assertions about Jesus which will pass muster before the court of contemporary scholarly opinion. Before pondering the results of the new quest, one would do well, therefore to reflect on the norms which new questers invoke in their attempt to certify words or actions of Jesus as "authentic." One needs to consider six norms: embarrassment, discontinuity, multiple attestation, coherence, rejection and execution, and the origination of Christianity.[2]

The criterion of embarrassment (or contradiction) regards as "authentic Jesus" information supplied by the evangelist which stands in tension with the image of Jesus which the evangelist would prefer to paint. This criterion argues that, if the evangelist records something about Jesus personally embarrassing in some way either to the evangelist himself or to the Christian community, then the embarrassing information communicates elements in the oral and written traditions which probably go back to Jesus Himself.

Jesus' baptism by John the Baptizer exemplifies the legitimate application of this first criterion. All four gospels suggest that the Christian community stood in an adversarial relationship with the disciples of John. All four evangelists go out of their way to portray Christian baptism as superior to Johannine. They argue their point polemically by asserting that John himself in prophecy had asserted its superiority to the baptism which he himself administered. (Mk 1:7-8; Mt 3:11-12; Lk 3:16-17; Jn 1:26-28, 32-34) In other words, the four evangelists clearly found it embarrassing that Jesus, the founder of Christianity, had actually submitted to Johannine baptism. The disciples of John very probably invoked that fact in support of the superiority of Johannine baptism. Nevertheless, all three synoptic evangelists record the fact of Jesus' baptism by John. The criterion of embarrassment argues that, given its embarrassing character, the evange-

---

2. For a summary of the first five criteria, see: Meier, *op.cit.*, I, pp. 168-177; Schillebeeckx, *Jesus*, pp. 88-98. For examples of a different approach to the criteria, see: Craig Evans, "Authenticity Criteria in Life of Jesus Research," *Christian Scholars Review*, 19(1989-1990), pp. 6-31; Dennis Polikov, "Method and Criteria for Historical Jesus Research," *Society of Biblical Literature Seminar Papers*, 26(1987), pp. 336-356. See also: Marcus J. Borg, "Portraits of Jesus in Contemporary North American Scholarship," *Harvard Theological Review*, 84(1991), pp. 1-22. For critical reflection on the limits of the new quest, see: C. Stephen Evans, *The Historical Christ and the Jesus of Faith: Incarnational Narrative as History* (New York, NY: Oxford University Press, 1996).

lists would never have recorded the fact of Jesus' baptism by John unless it actually happened. As a consequence, new questers for the historical Jesus generally regard Jesus' baptism as historically certain. (Mk 1:2-11; Mt 3:11-17; Lk 3:15-17, 3:21-22; Jn 1:24-27, 32-34)

Like all the criteria used by the new questers, this one requires prudential application. The way one uses it will, of course, depend on the theological reading one chooses to give this or that gospel. Many gospel texts, however, allow for a variety of interpretations. Differing interpretations of ambiguous texts will tend to modify any given exegete's reading of the gospel as a whole. As a consequence, not every new quester for the historical Jesus will employ this first norm in exactly the same way.

The criterion of discontinuity authenticates words or actions of Jesus which do not derive either from the Judaism of His time or from the early Christian Church. Some also call this norm the criterion of dissimilarity, originality, or dual irreducibility. Jesus' sweeping prohibition of oaths (Mt 5:34, 37), His rejection of voluntary fasting for His disciples (Mk 2:18-22; Mt 9:14-17; Lk 5:33-39), and His repudiation of Mosaic divorce practices (Mk 10:2-12, Lk 16:18) all exemplify this second criterion.

Once again one needs to use prudential balance in the invocation of this second norm. Its over-use would give the false impression that Jesus developed in an historical vacuum and that only words or actions of His at odds with common Jewish beliefs or with the faith of the apostolic Church qualify as "authentic Jesus." Too rigid an application of this second norm would, then, not only dissociate the figure of Jesus from the environment which shaped Him but would violate the sixth norm explained below. The sixth norm asserts that any historical portrait of Jesus must offer a plausible explanation of the fact that the movement which He started eventually developed into the Christian Church.

Different questers for the historical Jesus make different prudential use of the criterion of discontinuity. Indeed, they probably disagree most about its proper implementation.

The criterion of multiple attestation (sometimes called the criterion of the "cross section") argues that one can probably trace back to Jesus sayings or actions of His to which independent historical sources testify. This criterion acquires greater plausibility if the same historical motif appears in different kinds of literary sources and literary forms.

For example, new questers generally assert that Jesus proclaimed the kingdom of God not only because the theme of the kingdom surfaces in different contexts in all four gospels but also because Paul the apostle uses the term on occasion even though the notion of the kingdom does not have a prominent place in his own theological thinking. (1 Cor 4:20, 6:9-10, 15:24-5, 50; Gal 5:21) Similarly, in what follows, I shall argue that the criterion of multiple attestation authenticates the practical demands of discipleship propounded by the synoptic evangelists. I shall argue that those demands find an echo in Pauline moral teaching and in the letter of James.

Assessing multiple attestation within the synoptic tradition poses a more complex problem. The three synoptic gospels seem to have emerged from three different Christian communities. Certainly, each gospel addresses very different kinds of theological and pastoral issues. Most exegetes concede that Matthew and Luke probably used the gospel of Mark as a source.

Both evangelists edited Mark. Sometimes they omit significant portions of Mark or significant allusions in the Markan text. The relatively free editorial use which Matthew and Luke made of Mark transforms those sections of Mark which they reproduce with little or no change into something like an endorsement. Similarly, when all three synoptic gospels record the same traditions about Jesus, their agreement provides evidence that three different Christian communities endorsed those traditions as significant. Of course, the fact, of textual dependence within the synoptic tradition makes that endorsement less historically probative than a similar endorsement by both the synoptics and another independent tradition within the New Testament, like the Pauline tradition or the Johannine.

One faces an analogous situation in passages common to Matthew and Luke but not to Mark. Redaction criticism tends to attribute such passages to a literary source different from the synoptic tradition. Redaction criticism names that source "Q" after the German word "Quelle," which means source. Not all exegetes agree about the need to postulate Q as a synoptic source. If Q existed and provided a source for Matthew and Luke, they use it with an editorial freedom analogous to their citations of Mark. The fact, moreover, that Q would have developed prior to the synoptic tradition leads one to take material common to Q and to the synoptics with greater historical seriousness than material in Matthew and Luke derived from Mark.

Once again prudential judgment on the part of individual exegetes will cause them to apply the criterion of multiple attestation differently. Those, for example, who accept Q or the apocrypha as legitimate historical sources of information about Jesus will employ this norm differently from those who reject those sources.

The criterion of coherence argues that one may authenticate as historical, sayings or actions of Jesus which would appear compatible with sayings or actions authenticated by other criteria. Some call this fourth criterion the criterion of consistency or conformity. Clearly, the way in which any given quester for the historical Jesus will employ this fourth criterion will depend on the way in which the individual in question chooses to employ the other criteria. Since the other criteria allow for prudential variation in their application, *a fortiori* so does the fourth.

Nevertheless, careful use of this fourth norm can allow one to flesh out in greater detail one's historical portrait of Jesus, if not with certitude or even probability, then at least with some degree of plausibility. If, for example, one concedes that Jesus probably addressed a peasant audience attuned to oral patterns of thinking, then one must needs concede as well that Jesus' own teachings might not have enjoyed the kind of logical consistency which characterizes literate thought. In that case different sayings of His might well have reflected the influence both of the Old Testament wisdom tradition and of Jewish apocalyptic. One need not, then, force an artificial choice between Jesus the Jewish sage and Jesus the apocalyptic visionary. On different occasions Jesus could plausibly have sounded like both.

The fifth criterion, Jesus' rejection and execution, in a sense functions as a corollary of the criterion of coherence. It asserts that, since Jesus certainly died the death of crucifixion as a messianic pretender, any historically plausible account of Him must explain why he came to this end. This criterion would exclude, for example, any sentimentalized portrait of "gentle Jesus meek and mild." The real Jesus had to threaten the power structure of His day sufficiently for them to want to see Him die the discredited death of a criminal. This fifth criterion would also exclude any privatized account of the content of Jesus' religious teaching. Clearly, the kingdom He proclaimed threatened the principalities and powers of His day.

The sixth criterion has entered the literature only relatively recently. As I have already indicated, it serves to counterbalance any one-sided application of the criterion of discontinuity. Like the fifth criterion, it too functions as a kind of corollary to the criterion of coherence. It asserts that any historically plausible account of Jesus must explain, not only His rejection and death by crucifixion, but also how the movement He began could develop into the Christian Church.[3]

Let us, then, begin to assess the results of scholarly attempts to invoke these criteria in order to provide an account of "authentic Jesus." In the section which follows, I shall summarize what new questers glean from the meager evidence concerning Jesus' life in Nazareth before His baptism by John.

3. For the enunciation and application of this criterion, see: E.P. Sanders, *Jesus and Judaism* (Philadelphia, PA: Fortress, 1990). Unfortunately, in my judgment, Sander's minimalistic portrait of Jesus fails to meet adequately the criterion he enunciated. He argues that early Christian apocalypticism had its roots in Jesus' own apocalyptic tendencies and believes that Jesus at least spoke about the Twelve; but he ignores other important aspects of Jesus' teaching which link Him to the Church which took shape after His death.

(II)

Jesus of Nazareth was born probably in the last years of the reign of Herod the Great. Herod died in 4 b.c. That would suggest that Jesus was born somewhere around the year 6 or 7 b.c.

We do not know exactly where He was born. Both Matthew and Luke locate Jesus' birth in Bethlehem in Judea. (Mt 2:1-6; Lk 2:1-20) The highly symbolic character of the infancy narratives, however, leaves scholars loathe to apply the criterion of multiple attestation easily to these texts, especially since the location of Jesus' birth in Bethlehem, the city of David, clearly has theological motives. It points to Jesus as a Davidic messiah. Possibly, then, Jesus may have first seen the light of day in Nazareth.[4]

The "Hidden Life"

Jesus was certainly born into an ordinary Jewish peasant family. All three synoptic gospels insist that Jesus' own townspeople did not believe in Him. (Mk 6:1-6; Mt 13:53-58; Lk 4:16-30) Moreover, in the process of narrating this embarrassing fact they all insist that the completely pedestrian, ordinary character of Jesus' origins motivated the unbelief of the Nazarenes. The principle of embarrassment suggests that, when it comes to the pedestrian character of Jesus' origins and the skepticism of the Nazarenes, we take the synoptic gospels at their word.

Mary and Joseph called their firstborn child Jesus (*Yesua*), the same name as Moses' successor who led the conquest of the Promised Land. (Lk 2:7, 21) We have some indications that until the second century, Jewish parents liked the name and gave it rather frequently to their children. In the case of Jesus, people had to add the epithet "of Nazareth" in order to distinguish Him from all the other Jesuses living at the time. The name "Jesus (*Yesua*)" means "Yahweh saves."[5]

Other members of Jesus' family bore the names of significant people in the history of Israel. His human father, Joseph, bore the name of one of the twelve patriarchs. His mother, Mary (Miriam) bore the name of Moses's sister. Jesus' four brothers all bore patriarchal names similar to Joseph's: James (Jacob), Joses (Joseph), Simon (Simeon), and Jude (Judah). (Mt 13:55)

Prior to the Babylonian exile, it would seem that Jewish parents rarely assigned their children the names of the patriarchs; but, during the intertestamental period, assigning the names of major figures in Jewish history to Jewish children seems to have happened with greater frequency. The practice arose quite plausibly as a way of affirming Jewish historical, ethnic, and religious roots in the face of the Hellenizing campaigns of Gentile conquerors. The clustering of historically allusive names in Jesus'

---

4. Cf. Meier, *op.cit.*, I, p. 214-219, 407.   5. *Ibid.*, I, pp. 205-206.

family makes it also plausible to assume that his parents endorsed popular opposition to the Hellenizing tendencies of their Jewish leaders.[6]

Paul the apostle joins Matthew and Luke in affirming Jesus' Davidic lineage. Paul, moreover, is citing another source: namely, an early Christian creed. (Rom 1:4; Mt 18:1-25; Lk 2:1-7; cf. 2 Tim 2:8) The criterion of multiple attestation suggests that one ought to regard this assertion as factual. Luke further suggests that Elizabeth, and by implication, Mary, her cousin, both descended from the family of Aaron, the brother of Moses. (Lk 1:5) First century Jews, however, traced family descent patrilinearly. Joseph, then, belonged, as the synoptics assert, to the family of David.[7]

The New Testament asserts that Jesus had brothers. We can trace to the fourth century a tradition which interprets the Greek term for "brother (*adelphos*)" as meaning cousin. New questers for the historical Jesus, however, argue that the texts and language of the New Testament provide no basis for such an interpretation. In the New Testament, the term means either a full, blood brother or a half-brother. The apostle Paul seems to take it as factual that Jesus had brothers. (Gal 1:19; 1 Cor 9:5) By the criterion of multiple attestation, therefore, it would seem extremely probable, if not certain, that Jesus did in fact have brothers: four in number.[8] The same principle together with the criterion of embarrassment also allows one to assert as certain that during His lifetime His brothers put no more faith in Him and in His ministry than did the other villagers of Nazareth. (Mk 3:20-21; Jn 7:5)

Joseph certainly belonged to the artisan class; and most probably Jesus, as the first-born, (Lk 2:7) followed His father's trade. Moreover, the Greek term which the gospels use to designate Joseph's trade, namely, "*tektôn*," designates, not a "carpenter" in the specialized contemporary sense of that term, but something closer to a general handyman.[9] Joseph's trade would have securely anchored his family in the low end of the income bracket in first-century Palestine together with everything which low income implies: penny pinching, hard work, lower class status.

---

6. *Ibid.*, I, pp. 205-208. See also: Richard Bauckman, "The Brothers and Sisters of Jesus: An Epiphanian Response to John P. Meier," *Catholic Biblical Quarterly*, 56(1994), pp. 686-700.

7. *Ibid.*, I, pp. 216-219.

8. *Ibid.*, I, pp. 318-332. The new quest approaches all questions from the purely rational standpoint of scholarly historical method. Patristic and medieval piety popularized the notion that Mary remained a virgin after Jesus' birth. The results of the new quest call that pious belief into question. For a counter argument to the position of John P. Meier, which I have reproduced here, see: Richard Bauckman, "The Brothers and Sisters of Jesus: An Eipphanian Response to John P. Meier," *Catholic Biblical Quarterly*, 56(1994), pp. 686-700.

9. *Ibid.*, I, pp. 317, 278-285.

Joseph never appears in the gospel narratives, even though Jesus does in fact interact with His mother, Mary. Joseph's absence makes it plausible, even probable, that he did indeed die before Jesus began His public ministry, as Christian tradition has piously believed. Mary survived Jesus. (Acts 1:14; Jn 19:25) At the time of Jesus' death, she would have probably lived into her late forties or early fifties.[10]

History tells us extremely little about Jesus' formative years. We have no reason to suppose that Jesus spoke Latin. As an artisan, however, He may have had a working knowledge of *koinê* Greek so that He could deal with any Gentile customers who required His services. If, as seems plausible, Jesus, especially as first-born son, attended a synagogue, then he probably learned some Hebrew. It seems probable, moreover, that in His disputes with scribes and Pharisees, He would have had to exhibit some acquaintance with the original Hebrew texts of the Old Testament in order for them to take Him seriously as a teacher. It seems, then, at least plausible to believe that Jesus, in addition to Aramaic, spoke some Greek and could at least read Hebrew.

Jesus probably learned Aramaic as His first language and most probably spoke Aramaic by preference. He most probably taught for the most part in Aramaic and also prayed in Aramaic. We cannot, however, rule out the possibility that in His contacts with diaspora Jews, Jesus might have spoken *koinê* Greek.[11] One can also make a plausible argument for Jesus' ability to read and possibly to write (Lk 2:47; Jn 7:14), even though, as we have already seen, His teachings reflect a mind attuned to the thought patterns of a pre-literate, oral peasant culture.[12]

Under ordinary circumstances, young Jewish males in first century Palestine married. The New Testament refers more than once to Jesus' immediate family. Nowhere in the New Testament, however, do we find a reference to His having or having had a wife. The silence of the New Testament on this point makes it plausible to suppose that He did not marry. Since a celibate life-style went against normal social expectations, it seems equally plausible to suppose that a celibate Jesus would have chosen celibacy.[13]

Moreover, by the criterion of multiple attestation, we can assert that Jesus certainly repudiated Mosaic divorce practices. (Mk 10:2-9; Mt 19:3-9; Lk 16:18; 1 Cor 7:10-11) In Matthew's version of this particular teaching, the evangelist appends another saying of Jesus derived from a source unique to his gospel. In it Jesus refers to the option for celibacy as a form of self-castration. (Mt 19:10-12)

To refer to celibacy as self-castration would probably have shocked Jesus' hearers. Since no other evangelist associates this saying with Jesus' teach-

---

10. *Ibid.*, I, pp. 317-318.   11. *Ibid.*, I, pp. 253-268.
12. *Ibid.*, I, pp. 268-278.   13. *Ibid.*, I, pp. 332-345.

ing on divorce, it probably originated in another context. The New Testament in general does not hold up celibacy as a Christian ideal. The apostle Paul in arguing for celibacy as a Christian life style stands more as the exception than the rule. Moreover, in the course of his argument, Paul never calls celibacy self-castration. (1 Cor 7:7-8, 25-40) We know that Palestinian culture in the first century tolerated celibacy as an exception but did not encourage it. The criterion of discontinuity suggests, therefore, that Jesus Himself functioned as the source of Matthew's slightly shocking logion.

The criterion of coherence would also support such an interpretation. We know that Jesus' enemies slandered Him in a variety of ways; and the criterion of embarrassment suggests that one ought to take these slanders seriously as having historical roots. Jesus' enemies called Him illegitimate, demon-possessed, a glutton, and a drunkard. (Mk 3:20-22; Mt 11:16-19, 12:24-26; Lk 7:31-35, 11:15-18; Jn 8:41) Might they have also explained His option for celibacy by charging that He had castrated Himself? Might Jesus Himself have deliberately invoked the image for its shock value as a way of underscoring the radical demands of the kingdom? The criterion of coherence gives the suggestion an at least plausible ring.[14]

If we take this saying of Jesus as plausibly authentic and as a reference to his option for celibacy, then it suggests that He came to regard His option for celibacy as an expression of His own commitment to proclaiming God's reign. That would endow His practice of celibacy with a prophetic character, as Geza Vermes has suggested.[15]

Jesus did not belong to the tribe of Levi. He never in the course of His lifetime claimed priestly status. Nor did He function as a Levitical priest. We have no historical evidence which suggests that Jesus ordained any of His followers. Jesus lived His life and ministered as a Jewish layman with prophetic pretensions. Although people called Him "teacher (*rabbi*)," we have no reason to assume that He had formal rabbinic training; and, by the principle of multiple attestation, we have good reason to believe that He did not. (Mk 6:2; Mt 13:54; Jn 7:15) Given the subsequent theologization of Jesus in the letter to the Hebrews as the great high priest of the new covenant, and given the clericalized use which some have made of Jesus' priesthood, one needs to underscore Jesus' lay status if contemporary Christians expect to understand Him with historical accuracy.[16]

Jesus' lay status puts His conflict with the aristocratic temple priesthood in an important historical light. In that confrontation, a lower-class

14. *Ibid.*, I, pp. 343-345.
15. Cf. Geza Vermes, *Jesus the Jew: A Historian's Reading of the Gospels* (London: Collins, 1973), pp. 99-102.   16. Cf. Meier, *op. cit.*, I, pp. 345-349.

peasant defied a privileged aristocracy. A poor man challenged the rich and powerful. A prophet denounced a self-serving religious bureaucracy. A layman called to task a religiously compromised clerical establishment.[17]

Given the thinness of the evidence, it should come as no surprise that the new quest can only provide occasional glimpses into Jesus' formative years at Nazareth. That the new quest provides as much information as it does testifies to the ingenuity of new quest scholarship. In dealing with Jesus' public ministry, of course, the new quest stands on more solid ground; for the four gospels provide much more information to sift through its criteria.

(III)

News of the preaching of John the Baptizer seems to have motivated Jesus' departure from Nazareth. His contact with the Baptizer also seems to have helped consolidate his personal sense of religious mission. Any account of Jesus' public ministry must, then, begin with John's prophetic ministry.[18]

John the Baptizer

Luke's infancy narrative tells us that John lived in the desert before he began preaching and baptizing there. (Lk 1:80) One may, moreover, as Joseph Fitzmyer has suggested, make a plausible case for the fact that the Essenes who lived in the deserts near the Dead Sea educated John; for they did on occasion educate young Jewish boys in their monastery.[19]

It seems probable that John the Baptizer began his ministry of proclaiming a baptism for the forgiveness of sins either at the end of the year 27 a.d. or at the beginning of the year 28 a.d., in the "fifteenth year of the reign of Tiberius Caesar." (Lk 3:1) John "appeared" (Mk 1:4) in the deserts to the east of Jerusalem and baptized people in the river Jordan, the river which in the book of Joshua had parted to welcome the chosen people into the promised land just as the Red Sea had parted to deliver them from slavery. (Jos 3:1-4:9; Ex 14:5-15:21)

---

17. Cf. Hans Küng, *On Being a Christian*, translated by Edward Quinn (Garden City, N.Y.: Doubleday and Co., 1974), pp. 177-277. Schillebeeckx despairs of saying anything about Jesus' life prior to His ministry. Cf. Schillebeeckx, *Jesus*, pp.115-116. Meier, however, has demonstrated that Schillebeeckx need not be so skeptical. We can make some assertions about Jesus' early life. Cf. Meier, *op.cit.*, pp. 205-433.

18. Cf. Jerome Murphy-O'Connor, "John the Baptist and Jesus: History and Hypothesis," *New Testament Studies*, 36(1990), pp. 354-374.

19. Cf. Joseph A. Fitzmyer, "The Dead Sea Scrolls and Early Christianity," *Theology Digest*, 42(Winter, 1995), pp. 303-322; Hartmut Stegemann, "Die Bedeutung der Qumranfunde für das Verständnis Jesu und des Frühen Christentums," *Bibel und Kirche*, 48(1993), pp. 10-19.

John acted like a prophet and was perceived as one. He lived the life of a religious ascetic. He allegedly wore a camel skin cloak and a belt. Some liken his dress to that of Elijah, whose return would usher in the end time. (Mk 1:6; Mt 3:4) This assimilation has Christian theological motives; but nothing we know of first-century prophecy makes John's rough garments inherently impossible. Rough clothing went with the Baptizer's asceticism. If, moreover, as Luke's infancy narrative suggests, John abandoned the vocation of a temple priest for that of a desert prophet, his rough clothing could, possibly, have expressed a prophetic protest against the riches of the priestly aristocracy.[20] (Cf. Lk 1:5-25)

No matter how John dressed, the desert in which he prophesied probably stirred the apocalyptic imaginations of his contemporaries. Israel had entered into covenant with God during the desert sojourn which followed the exodus. When final salvation dawned, popular expectation looked for it to arise out of the desert. (Cf. Is 40:3-5)

The criterion of multiple attestation makes it historically certain that John proclaimed a message of impending judgment and called for national repentance. The evangelists all agree that he preached in the neighborhood of Jerusalem, probably along pilgrim routes to and from the Holy City, but that he did not preach in the city itself. Instead, he required that people come out into the desert in order to submit to the baptism which expressed their repentant readiness for the impending judgment of God.

At the heart of John's preaching, very probably lay a fundamental prophetic insight: mere racial descent from Abraham offers no protection from the impending divine judgment: only repentance and righteous living does. This message the criterion of multiple attestation validates as extremely probable, even certain. (Mk 1:4; Mt 3:7-10; Lk 3:7-9; Jn 1:19-28)

John's baptism identified those who received it as his disciples. Discipleship marked one out as a person who recognized the truth and the prophetic authority of the Baptizer and of his message. Discipleship also committed one to a life of prayer, righteous living, and of fasting in preparation for the coming judgment. The principle of multiple attestation also validates these aspects of John's ministry as extremely probable.[21] (Mk 2:18; Mt 9:14; Lk 5:33, 11:1-4)

Besides proclaiming repentance and righteous living as the only way of avoiding the impending judgment of God, the Baptizer seems to have

---

20. Cf. Meier, *A Marginal Jew*, II, pp. 42-56; F. Neirynck, "The First Synoptic Pericope: The Appearance of John the Baptist in Q?" *Ephemerides Theologicae Lovaniensis*, 72(1996), pp. 41-74.

21. Besides Mark, both Matthew and Luke drew on other sources in painting their portrait of the Baptizer.

developed other themes in his preaching. The evangelists show varying degrees of interest in preserving John's message. They all agree, however, on one point: that John foretold that another, more powerful than he himself, would come and baptize with a sanctifying divine Breath. Matthew and Luke add that "the coming one" would also baptize with fire. (Mk 1:7; Mt 3:11-12; Lk 3:15-17; Jn 1:24-28, 31-32) The image of fire as a symbol of a divine holiness which devours the unrepentant in judgment fits the tone of the Baptizer's preaching and may well represent a more primitive tradition concerning it.

The evangelists all cite this dimension of John's preaching as the Baptizer's personal testimony to Jesus' own superiority to John himself. Polemic and theological interests motivate the citation. The evangelists are most probably appealing to the Baptizer's own words in order to prove to his disciples Jesus' superiority to John.

I find it hardly probable, however, that the evangelists would have based their argument for Jesus' superiority on a prophecy of John which the evangelists themselves had fabricated out of whole cloth. The disciples of John would have found it far too easy to refute the citation as an argument, if John had said nothing of the sort. In all likelihood, then, John probably did see himself as inaugurating a movement of salvation in Israel which another would have to advance, especially after John's imprisonment by Herod.

Of all the evangelists, Luke shows the greatest concern to preserve John's teachings. To John's apocalyptic message of repentance and judgment and to his messianic prophecy of the coming of a mightier Breath-baptizer, Luke appends a sample of John's moral message. Besides inculcating prayer and fasting, Luke's John instructs his disciples in the demands of righteous living. They must share their physical possessions with the poor and avoid all exploitation and oppression of others. (Lk 3:10-14)

Two criteria support the historicity of Luke's account of the Baptizer's preaching: the criterion of coherence and the criterion of embarrassment. The criterion of coherence makes it at least probable that John in summoning others to repentance would have spelled out in some detail the moral conditions for repentance and the kind of righteousness he expected to find in his disciples.

The criterion of embarrassment, however, also supports such an interpretation of the Baptizer's preaching. Like the other evangelists, Luke finds himself embarrassed by the fact that Jesus submitted to John's baptism. He goes out of his way to separate Jesus' messianic commissioning in the power of the divine Breath from His baptism by John. In Luke, the commissioning does not happen until John has finished baptizing. Some exegetes argue that Luke deliberately leaves the identity of Jesus' baptizer vague, although the context certainly points to John. The temporal hiatus makes it clear, however, that John's baptism did not in any way effect the descent of the Breath, as Christian baptism does. (Lk 3:21-23)

Moreover, Luke in other ways downplays the narrative significance of the Baptizer. Luke makes Jesus' superiority to John a dominant theme in his infancy narrative. With Matthew he records Jesus' response to John's question about Jesus' own messianic identity. Like Matthew, Luke insists that, despite John's greatness, the least in the kingdom of God ranks higher than he. If any disciple of Jesus ranks higher than John, then *a fortiori* so does Jesus. (Lk 7:18-30; Mt 11:2- 15) Luke also edits out Mark's account of John's martyrdom by Herod. When he alludes to it, moreover, he subordinates it to the theme of Jesus' messianic identity. (Lk 9:9)

Nevertheless, despite his insistence on Jesus' utter superiority to John and despite his virtual elimination of the Baptizer from his account of Jesus' ministry, Luke not only records John's moral teaching in greater detail than the other synoptics but underscores the fact that it probably helped inspire Jesus' own moral message. Luke portrays John's proclamation of repentance, his moral teaching, and his messianic prophecy of the mightier Breath-baptizer as an "evangelization (*euêggelizeto*)" of the crowds who came to hear him.

In calling John's message "good news" Luke probably intended to suggest that the "good news" about the risen Jesus eventually fulfilled and replaced it. In the process, however, Luke also implicitly asserted the continuity between Jesus' message and John's. Moreover, Luke's account of John's moral message suggests that Jesus' own vision of the kingdom derived in part from the message of the Baptizer. As we shall see below, both Jesus and John stressed practical compassion for the poor and the avoidance of all exploitation and oppression.

In every other respect, Luke's gospel goes out of its way to minimize the role of John with respect to Jesus. The principle of embarrassment suggests, then, that Luke would probably not have insisted on the continuity between Jesus' moral teaching and John's unless the evangelist regarded that continuity as historical. In other words, the principle of embarrassment makes Luke's account of John's moral preaching and its continuity with Jesus' own message at least highly plausible, if not probable.

I have authenticated so far three major themes in the preaching of the Baptizer: national repentance as the only way to avoid an impending divine judgment, the preparatory character of John's mission and the coming of a mightier Breath-baptizer, and the moral demands of discipleship. Quite plausibly, those moral demands included conformity to the Baptizer's moral teaching, prayer, and fasting as expressions of one's readiness to face the divine judgment which approached.

To these three themes, all the synoptic evangelists add a fourth: John denounced the immorality of the Jewish client aristocracy in the person of Herod. Following Mark's somewhat inaccurate and legendary account of John's execution, all three evangelists assert that John attacked Herod's adulterous marriage and that the attack helped motivate John's arrest and imprisonment by Herod. Mark inaccurately identifies Herod's consort with his brother Philip's wife. (Mk 6:14-29; Mt 14:1-12; Lk 3:19-20, 9:7-9) Luke, however, states that, besides decrying Herod's adultery, the Baptizer mounted a much broader denunciation of Herod's immorality. Luke's Baptizer excoriates all the other wickedness which the client Jewish king had perpetrated (*peri pantôn hôn epoiêsen ponêrôn*). In Luke, then, John's arrest comes as a result of a general denunciation of Herod, one which includes, among other sins, his adulterous marriage. (Lk 3:19-20)

Since the Baptizer's summons to repentance probably targeted all of Israel, it would have included Herod and the client Jewish aristocracy, whom, as we have seen, the Pharisees regarded as "half-Jews." The criterion of coherence suggests, therefore, that we regard the Baptizer's general denunciation of Herod's immorality and oppressive acts as at least plausible. Moreover, a prophetic denunciation of Herod's crimes would accord well with Josephus's assertion that Herod arrested and executed John lest his preaching and popularity foment revolt. (Josephus, *Antiquities*, 18:116-119)

The Baptizer probably saw himself as summoning the whole nation of Israel to repentance. By positioning himself near Jerusalem, he also issued a religious challenge to the authority of the client, aristocratic priesthood. In other words, John's message challenged both branches of the client aristocracy: both the aristocratic priesthood and the Herodians; but John especially targeted Herod and implicitly the Herodians for special denunciation.

As we shall see, Jesus, for reasons which I shall discuss below, took exactly the opposite tactic. Throughout His ministry Jesus endorsed the prophetic character of John's ministry. That endorsement means that Jesus at least implicitly seconded John's attack on the Herodians. Jesus, however, focused His own prophetic attack on the client, aristocratic priesthood.

(IV)

As we have seen, other groups proclaimed religious messages in first century Palestine: peasant prophets and would-be messiahs, Pharisees and Essenes. Even the client priesthood proclaimed a message of religious compromise. None of these voices struck a responsive chord in the heart of Jesus of Nazareth; but the lone voice of the new "Elijah," the voice of this prophet of repentance and of immanent judgment, the voice of this teacher of compassion, of morality, and of justice, the voice which challenged the client temple priesthood and which denounced the immorality of the client Jewish aristocracy—this voice touched His heart with compelling force and caused Him to abandon his trade as a laborer in order to journey to the Judean deserts, where He submitted to the baptism which John proclaimed and administered. (Mk 1:9-11; Mt 3:13-17; Lk 3:21-22)

Jesus Baptized

As we have seen, all questers for the historical Jesus take it as certain that Jesus submitted to John's baptism. Like the others who submitted to John's baptism, Jesus by that act endorsed the kinds of things which the Baptizer was saying. We know nothing of the details of Jesus' religious development in Nazareth. We do, however, know this fact for certain. When the news of John and of his preaching reached Nazareth, Jesus not only welcomed it but left Nazareth in order to ally Himself with John and with his mission.[22]

We do not know how long Jesus maintained personal contact with John. It would appear that until the end of His life Jesus endorsed the prophetic character of John's ministry. The gospels give no indication, however, that the Baptizer ever formally endorsed Jesus as the "mightier one" who would succeed him. Matthew and Luke, following Q, suggest that John probably never endorsed Jesus and entered the kingdom. (Cf. Mt 11:11; Lk 7:28) The gospels also provide evidence of conflict between the first Christians and John's disciples. The principle of embarrassment would, then, endow Jesus' endorsement of John with high probability. It would also seem probable that John never returned the compliment.

Jesus' life-long endorsement of John also makes it plausible, even probable, that Jesus regarded the Baptizer's ministry as the first act in an unfolding drama of salvation and His own ministry as act two. (Mt 11:2-15, Lk 7:24-30) In Jesus' testimony to John, which Matthew and Luke derive independently from another source (Q), Jesus makes this point quite clearly. The principle of coherence also supports the historicity of this inference.

Can we say more about the relationship of Jesus to John? Very possibly. Scattered hints in the New Testament suggest the possibility that after His own baptism by John Jesus undertook a parallel baptismal ministry of His own. In what do these hints consist?

At the beginning of his gospel, Mark tells us that after His baptism by John, Jesus waited until John's arrest by Herod before He returned to Galilee and began to proclaim the reign of God. Matthew repeats this

---

22. Schillebeeckx chooses to write a minimalistic account of both John and Jesus. By that I mean that he restricts himself to things that one can say about both figures with either probability or certitude. Cf. Schillebeeckx, *Jesus*, pp. 107-136; Michael Grant, *Jesus: A Historian's Review of the Gospels* (New York, NY: Macmillan, 1977), pp. 8-29.

Markan assertion. (Mk 1:14; Mt 4:12) An extended application of the principle of embarrassment suggests that we regard this assertion by both Mark and Matthew as at least plausible. It does not contradict any of their theological presuppositions; but nothing else in the story of Jesus as either evangelist narrates it would suggest such an order of events. Except for this single verse in both gospels, one would have the impression that Jesus underwent John's baptism and then immediately began His Galilean ministry.

If Jesus remained in Judea after His baptism by John, then what was He doing? The gospel of John suggests that Jesus engaged in a baptismal ministry for a time but that He then abandoned baptizing, even though His disciples continued to do so. Some scribe seems to have inserted into the text of the fourth gospel the statement that Jesus at some time abandoned baptizing. One can only guess at the reason for the insertion. (Jn 3:22-23; 4:1-3) The synoptic account of Jesus' Galilean ministry leaves the impression that during it He never baptized.

One can make coherent sense out of these otherwise disconnected historical clues if Jesus, after His baptism by John, remained in Judea for a time and engaged in a parallel baptismal ministry of His own. Such activity would help explain the rivalry between His own disciples and John's to which the gospels occasionally allude. (Jn 3:26-27; Mt 9:14-17) Jesus Himself possibly saw His early baptismal ministry as an extension of and complement to that of John; but, even so, it would come as no surprise if John's disciples from the very start perceived Jesus as the Baptizer's rival.[23]

I personally find it plausible, that Jesus, after His baptism by John undertook a parallel but independent baptismal ministry of His own in Judea until John's arrest. If so, once John stopped baptizing Jesus too could conceivably have stopped as well. Certainly, apart from the early baptismal activity at which the gospel of John hints, we find no evidence that Jesus during His own proclamation of the kingdom used baptism as a sign of discipleship. Instead, he required of the inner circle of disciples who traveled with Him the willingness to give their possessions to the poor and live on alms.

Moreover, as we have seen, Jesus probably regarded His own ministry as the second act in a drama of salvation which included John's baptismal ministry as the first act. If so, then the principle of coherence makes it also plausible to suppose that after John's arrest Jesus decided that the Johannine phase of God's saving action had ended and that the time had come for Him to inaugurate His own proper ministry. With John si-

---

23. Cf. Jerome Murphy O'Connor, "John the Baptist and Jesus: History and Hypothesis," *New Testament Studies*, 36(1990), pp. 359-374; Ben F. Meyer, "'Phases' in Jesus' Mission," *Gregorianum*, 73(1992), pp. 5-17.

lenced, Jesus too, quite possibly, ceased baptizing and began instead proclaiming the arrival of God's reign in His own person and ministry.[24]

Proclaiming the Reign of God

During His Galilean ministry Jesus certainly proclaimed the reign of God. On that point all new questers agree, although they disagree about what we can know concerning Jesus' intention in proclaiming God's reign. Certainly, however, in Jesus' preaching the "reign of God" had the same centrality as the immanence of a divine judgment of wrath and condemnation had in the Baptizer's preaching.

The gospels call Jesus' message "good news," although Jesus' enemies clearly failed to appreciate its goodness. In teaching Jesus targeted especially the poor, the suffering, the marginal, the sinful, the expendable. (Mt 5:3-12, 11:4-6; Lk 6:20-26, 7:18-23) Jesus warned that those who rejected His message would have to face a stern divine judgment; but, He also seems to have believed that, in His very proclamation of the reign of God, salvation itself was dawning. (Mt 3:2, 4:17, 10: 7, 12:28, 21:31; Mk 1:15, 9:1; Lk 4:27, 11:20, 17:20-21) He also saw His own ministry as beginning the establishment of the divine reign, even though its final and full establishment lay in the approaching eschatological future. (Mt 6:10, 7:21, 16:28, 25:34, 40, 26:29; Mk 9:1, 12:34, 14:25; Lk 7:28, 9:27, 10:9, 11, 11:2, 12:32, 18:29, 22:16)

In my judgment, the criterion of multiple attestation makes these two aspects of God's reign certain. By "these two aspects of God's reign," I mean the fact that the kingdom represents the gratuitous eruption of divine salvation in a sinful world and the fact that it must still come in its fullness, even though it has already begun to arrive in Jesus and in His very proclamation of the kingdom.[25]

24. Cf. Ben F. Meyer, *The Aims of Jesus* (London: SCM Press, 1979), pp. 122-128. Not all new questers would agree that Jesus' baptized at all; cf. Küng, *op.cit.*, pp. 278-342; Gerhard Lohfink, "Die Not der Exegese mit der Reich-Gottes-Verkündigung Jesu," *Theologische Quartalschrift*, 168:1(1988), pp. 1-15. Meier suggests that Jesus never abandoned baptizing and finds in His baptismal ministry the origins of Christian baptism. If, however, as the Johannine scribe suggests, Jesus allowed His disciples to administer a baptism of repentance after He Himself had abandoned the practice, the baptismal activity of the disciples would just as plausibly explain the origins of Christian baptism. (Cf. Meier, *op.cit.*, II, pp. 116-130) For reflections on Jesus' relationship to John, see: Josef Ernst, "Johannes der Täufer und Jesus von Nazareth in historischen Sicht," *New Testament Studies*, 43(1997), pp. 161-183. Although written before the publication of N.T. Wright's *Jesus and the Victory of God* (Minneapolis, MI: Fortress, 1996), the following summary portrait of Jesus' ministry seems to me to converge with Wright's, without, of course, attempting his attention to historical context and exegetical detail.

25. Meier, *A Marginal Jew*, pp. 129-132, II, 237-454; Gerd Thiessen, "Jesusbewegung as charismatische Wertrevolution," *New Testament Studies*, 35(1989), pp. 343-360; A.M. Okori, "El Reino de Dios en le Ministerio de Jesús, *Revista Biblica*, 57(1995), pp. 19-28.

In His proclamation of God's reign, Jesus echoed the Baptizer's message of repentance and taught His disciples to do the same; but He gave repentance new meaning by proclaiming it in the context of the kingdom. For the Baptizer, "repent" seems to have meant: renounce sin, reform your lives, or else stand under the terrible, scalding judgment of divine wrath. By "repent" Jesus seems to have meant: accept the salvation which is already present in Me and in what I am saying and doing.

The new context of God's already dawning eschatological reign transformed the message of repentance into "good news" because it changed salvation from something which one gains through repentance into the acceptance of God's free gift of forgiveness. Jesus' table fellowship with sinners dramatized this dimension of His message, even though it caused Him to run afoul of some Pharisees. (Mk 1:14-15, 2:5-10, 15-17, 6:12; Mt 4:12-17, 3:8, 9:2-6, 10-13, 11:20, 21, 12:41, 18:27-35, 26:28; Lk 3:3, 5:20-24, 29-32, 7:47-49, 8, 5:32, 10:13, 11:32, 13:3, 5, 15:7, 10, 16:30, 23:34) Once again, the criterion of multiple attestation endorses this dimension of Jesus' ministry as certain.

Jesus, however, did set a fundamental moral condition for experiencing God's saving forgiveness: one cannot expect to receive the free gift of divine forgiveness unless one imitates God's own commitment to forgive others universally and gratuitously. (Mk 11:25-26; Mt 6:12-15, 18:21-35; Lk 11:4, 17:3-4) Universal forgiveness demands love of one's enemies. (Mt 6:44; Lk 6:27-28) The criteria of multiple attestation and of discontinuity also endow this aspect of Jesus' ministry with certainty.

The apostolic Church echoed Jesus' proclamation but in the new context created by the paschal mystery. The divine forgiveness which Jesus had proclaimed and embodied in His table fellowship with sinners took on new meaning in the light of Jesus' death, resurrection, and mission of the divine Breath. (Jn 20:23; Acts 2:38, 5:31, 8:22, 10:43, 13:30, 26:18; Eph 1:7; Col 1:14; Heb 9:22, 10:18; Jam 5:15; 1 Jn 9, 1:12)

Paradoxically, therefore, both the principle of discontinuity and the principle of Christian origins sanction Jesus' proclamation of divine forgiveness. The principle of Christian origins sanctions it because the apostolic Church's proclamation of divine forgiveness roots itself ultimately in Jesus' proclamation of God's forgiveness. The principle of discontinuity authenticates this aspect of Jesus' ministry because His message of divine forgiveness occurs in a different context and has different connotations from apostolic preaching. In Jesus' preaching, accepting God's forgiveness expresses faith in the fact that His ministry makes the reign of God a present, saving reality to which people can respond. In apostolic preaching, the acceptance of divine forgiveness expresses primarily faith in the paschal mystery.

The kingdom which Jesus proclaimed offered an alternative to the oppressive social structures under which the vast number of Palestinian Jews lived. It also challenged the disciples to resist those same forces of oppression in non-violent ways.[26]

The criterion of discontinuity authenticates Jesus' doctrine of love of enemies as historically certain. It also authenticates His demand for unlimited forgiveness. We find neither precept in the Old Testament. Nor does it seem likely that the first Christians would have invented them, if Jesus had not taught them. (Mt 5:44-48, 18:21-22; Lk 6:27-36, 17:3-4)

Love of enemies, however, does not mean passive acquiescence in violence, even though it does commit one to responding to violence in a non-violent way.[27] (Cf. Mt 5:39) In the confrontation with violence, Jesus offered a middle course, a third way, between fight and flight.

Jesus' instruction to His disciples to "go the second mile" illustrates how the third way works. (Mt 5:41) Roman law allowed soldiers on the march to force civilians to carry their baggage, but only for a mile. Any soldier who forced someone to "go an extra mile" would, then, have risked disciplinary punishment, possibly flogging. In limiting the distance to a mile, Roman law sought to mitigate the burden which occupying armies put upon local residents without, however, eliminating it. Anyone who followed Jesus' advice to offer spontaneously to carry a soldier's baggage for an extra mile would have put the soldier on the spot and forced him to see a routine act of oppression in a new light; for it would have forced him to recognize in the person who made the suggestion more than a beast of burden.

One can find a similar intent at the basis of "turning the other cheek." (Mt 5:39) A blow on the right cheek means a back-handed slap with the right hand: the contemptuous gesture of a superior to a subordinate. In turning the other cheek, the subordinate would do something utterly surprising which would force the superior to confront the subordinate as a person and to face his or her own brutality in abusing those who cannot retaliate.

"Giving away one's shirt" also illustrates the same strategy of non-violent resistance. Only a person of extreme miserliness would, under Jewish law, sue a person for his cloak. The Torah in fact required that before sunset one must return a cloak taken from a poor person as security for a debt. (Ex 22:25-27; Deut 24:10-13, 17) For a poor person to give his shirt as well in a public courtroom to someone miserly enough to sue him for his cloak would only make an open spectacle of the other person's greed and evoke public ridicule.[28]

---

26. Cf. Wink, *Engaging the Powers*, pp. 175-193.
27. Cf. Wink, *Confronting the Powers*, p. 185-186.
28. *Ibid.*, pp. 175-179.

In other words, in these counsels to powerless peasants about how to deal with violence and oppression from others, Jesus is not advising craven submission but the creative use of the imagination in order 1) to discover an alternative to countering violence with violence, 2) to assert one's dignity as a person, and 3) to invite one's oppressor to move beyond coercion to a different understanding of human relationships.[29]

If one grants the authenticity of Jesus' teachings about love of enemies and about mutual forgiveness, the principle of coherence would, in my judgment, tend to endow such a reading of the preceding maxims with considerable probability. So would the principle of discontinuity, since one finds nothing parallel in first-century Palestinian Judaism.

Most questers for the historical Jesus also take as historically certain that Jesus called God *Abba* and experienced God as Father. Some feminists question whether Jesus did in fact call God "*Abba*"; but in my judgment they have yet to come up with a convincing argument to support their skepticism.[30]

---

29. *Ibid.*, pp. 186-187.
30. Mary Rose D'Angelo has, for example, questioned whether we can with any certainty attribute the use of *Abba* to Jesus and suggests that the term enters the text of the New Testament because Christians in the communities of Paul and Mark used the term as an ectatic expression of empowerment, akin to glossolalia. She speculates that Paul may have gotten the term from Syrian communities He knew. She also finds the term "father" used in Rabbinic literature when one addresses God either as a refuge in time of persecution or in begging forgiveness. Finally, she argues that if Jesus used the term "Father," He more likely intended it to subvert Roman imperial order rather than to express any kind of intimate relationship. D'Angelo correctly censures sentimentalizing the meaning of "*Abba*"; but in my judgment, none of her key arguments conclude.

Although the Aramaic term "*Abba*" appears only three times in the New Testament, in every instance, the author, whether Mark or Paul, makes it the equivalent of the Greek term "*ho pater*," as D'Angelo implicitly concedes. Mark wrote in *koinê* Greek; and the Greek term for Father, which he equates with "*Abba*" (Mk 14:36) appears on the lips of Jesus. It comes, however, as no surprise that an Aramaic term would appear only rarely in the lips of Jesus in a text in which He speaks *koinê* Greek. That it appears at all on Jesus' lips in a Greek text has, in my judgment, far greater significance. Its appearance suggests that the evangelist wanted the reader to know the precise term which Jesus Himself used in addressing the Father.

The texts of the New Testament give no justification for assimilating the Christian use of the term "*Abba*" in prayer to ecstatic glossolalic utterance. Rather, they suggest that the Spirit of the risen Christ draws one into Jesus' own experience of God as "*Abba*." In other words, the Christian addresses God as "*Abba*" because Jesus, the prototypical Son of God and paradigm of Christian transformation in the Breath, addressed God in that way. That the term originated in Christian communities in Syria and gained popularity out of a Christian love of esoteric ways of talking to God seems far less likely than that the usage originated in the religious experience and teachings of Jesus.

Rabbinic use of the term "*Abba*" postdates Jesus. If it suggests anything, rabbinic use of "*Abba*" suggests that Jesus may have derived it from a Hasidic upbringing. As

One finds from time too time overly sentimentalized readings of the meaning of the term "*Abba*." A familiar term of address used by a child in speaking to its father, the term "*Abba*" does not connote automatically everything which contemporary Americans mean by "Daddy." The term on Jesus' lips did, however, invite His hearers to share in His own experience of a reverential, childlike, personal trust in God as universal Father. In my judgment, the criteria of multiple attestation and of coherence put this fact beyond serious question. (Mt 6:25-34; Lk 12:22-31) Moreover, trust in the Father binds one to Him in petitionary prayer and in unconditioned trust. (Mk 11:23-25, 14:35-39; Mt 6:9-11, 18:19, 21:18-22, 26:39-44; Lk 11:2-4, 22:40-42) Jesus seems to have demanded not only unconditioned trust in the Father but unconditioned and total love as well.[31] (Mk 12:28-34; Mt 22:34-40; Lk 10:25-29)

Besides mutual forgiveness, unconditioned trust in the Father, and unconditioned love of the Father, Jesus required of His disciples an interiorization of the most fundamental demands of Torah piety. He required a purity of intention (Mk 7:14-23; Mt 15:10-11) irreconcilable with religious hypocrisy, formalism, and legalism. (Mk 2:23-3:6, 7:1-13, 12:38-40; Mt 12:1-8, 15:1-9, 23:6; Lk 6:1-5, 20:45-47)

If, as seems at least plausible, Jesus waited until John's arrest to begin His proclamation of God's reign, then it also seems likely that He had no illusions from the beginning about the personal risks He was running in taking up the Baptizer's fallen prophetic banner. In the exercise of His own prophetic ministry, He seems to have anticipated rejection and even death as a matter of course.[32] (Mk 6:4; Mt 13:57; Lk 4:24, 13:33) Jesus quite possibly demanded a similar kind of commitment of His disciples. Certainly, Jesus Himself saw the reign of God as a reality not only worth living for but also, if necessary, worth dying for. (Mk 8:34-9:1, 10:35-40; Mt 16:24-28, 20:20-23; Lk 9:23-27; Jn 16:1-4)

As we have seen, baptism by John marked one out as living in repentant readiness for divine judgment. As we have also seen, quite plausibly,

we shall see, however, Jesus endowed the term with a depth and range of religious significance unknown in rabbinic literature.

31. Schillebeeckx questions whether Jesus ever cited the Great Commandment, since concern with ranking this or that commandment as greatest characterized the piety of diaspora Judaism more than that of Palestinian Judaism. (Schillebeeckx, *Jesus*, pp. 249-256) I find his argument unconvincing. Nothing sealed off Palestinian Judaism from influences from the diaspora. Moreover, even if one concedes that concern with the greatest commandment characterized diaspora piety, I find it entirely plausible that a diaspora Jew on pilgrimage to Jerusalem might have posed the question to Jesus in His final ministry in the Holy City. Both Mark and Matthew locate the incident in the context of Jesus' final Jerusalem ministry. (Mk 12:28-34; Mt 22:34-40) Luke puts it in the journey discourse, but for clear theological reasons. Luke wants to underscore that the two Great Commandments constitute fundamental demands of discipleship.

32. Cf. Brown, *The Death of the Messiah*, II, pp. 1468-1491.

Jesus may have engaged in a baptismal ministry parallel to John's until the latter's imprisonment; but, if so, it would appear at least plausible that He abandoned baptizing once He began to proclaim the reign of God, even though His disciples continued the practice. Once Jesus' own proper ministry began, He demanded more than repentance and a ritual bath of the close inner circle of disciples who traveled in His retinue. Close discipleship demanded the willingness to sell one's possessions and give them to the poor. (Mk 10:21-31; Mt 19:21-30; Lk 18:22-30)

Detachment from one's possessions expressed trust in the Father's providential care. (Mt 6:25-34; Lk 12:22-31) The disciples had to recognize that hoarding wealth in the manner of the client Jewish aristocracy poses one of the greatest obstacles to entering the kingdom. (Mk 10:21-31; Mt 19:21-38; Lk 18:22-30) Those who follow Jesus must avoid the hypocrisy of those who pray long prayers while ignoring the needs of the poor and the defenseless. (Mk 12:38-40, Lk 20:45-47) Instead the disciples of Jesus must practice open hospitality to the poor, the marginal, the oppressed, the socially expendable, even sinners. (Mk 2:14-17, 9:37; Mt 9:9-13, 18:5, 25:31-46; Lk 5:27-32, Lk 9:48)

Moreover, sharing the physical supports of life with others on the basis of need and not just of merit ought to express a mutual forgiveness which imitates God's own love for sinners. (Mk 2:15-17, Mt 6:43-48, 9:10-13, Lk 5:27-28, 6:27-35) In addition, mutual forgiveness must authenticate the disciples' prayer. (Mk 11:25; Mt 6:9-15; Lk 7:3-4, 17:1-4)

Jesus probably saw the reign of God as standing the class structure of first-century Palestinian society on its head. Those whom society regards of least value and importance must in the kingdom of God count as the greatest. (Mk 9:34-35; Mt 18:1-4, 20:16, Lk 9:46-48, 13:24) The rich and the powerful must transform themselves into willing slaves (*douloi*) of those in need. (Mk 10:13-16, 41-44; Mt 19:3, 20:24-28; Lk 10:15-17, 18:30, 22:24-27) Besides serving one another in an attitude of humility which imitates Jesus' own (Mt 12:28-30), the disciples must scrupulously avoid giving scandal to one another. (Mk 9:42-50; Mt 18:7-10; Lk 7:1-2)

The Parables

In his ground-breaking study of the parables, Joachim Jeremias has argued persuasively and, in my judgment, correctly, that one can trace most of the parables back to Jesus. He has also identified important thematic patterns in the parables.[33]

Jesus, quite plausibly, used stories in order to proclaim the reign of God because in oral cultures especially stories provide an attractive way

---

33. Cf. Joachim Jeremias, *The Parables of Jesus*, translated by S.H. Hooke (New York, NY: Scribner's, 1972). For an excellent scholarly and pastoral reading of the parables, see: John R. Donahue, S.J., *The Gospel in Parable* (Philadelphia, PA: Fortress, 1988).

of teaching.[34] Parables, however, function as a special kind of story. Within the narrative spectrum, parables stand at the opposite end of the scale from myths. Myths create a world of reality and value in which people ordinarily live. Parables seek to subvert the familiar world in which people ordinarily live in order to open them to a new vision of life and of society. The parables of Jesus sought to effect the same subversive end by opening people's hearts to the vision of the kingdom.

What message did the parables convey?

1) They conveyed, first of all, a message of realized eschatology. In His parables, Jesus challenged those who heard Him to recognize that the reign of God had already arrived in Him and in His ministry.

2) Jesus employed parables apologetically. He assured His hearers that despite the apparent humility of its beginnings—a rag-tag peasant prophet with a gaggle of largely peasant disciples—God's reign upon earth would nevertheless inevitably arrive because God wills it and will accomplish it. The parables, in other words, express the mysterious presence of a kingdom whose full realization lies in a future saving and vindicating act of God.

3) Jesus also used the parables to proclaim the gratuitous mercy and forgiveness of God toward sinners. In effect, then, He challenged His hearers to recognize that His very proclamation of divine forgiveness made that forgiveness a present reality.

4) Echoing the message of the Baptizer, Jesus also told parables in order to proclaim the immanent judgment of God. In the parables of judgment, He warned that unless Israel heeded Him and His message, it faced immanent catastrophe. He particularly excoriated the leaders of Israel, especially the temple priesthood but implicitly the Herodians as well, for leading God's people down a path of compromise which could only end in national disaster.

5) In some parables Jesus warned His hearers that time was running out, that they must choose either for or against Him and the divine reign He proclaimed.

6) Jesus also created parables for prophetic purposes, in order to demand that His hearers recognize the signs of the times and assent to the saving work which God was accomplishing in Him.

7) In some parables, Jesus also underscored the unconditional character of the moral demands of life in the kingdom and of the way of discipleship. Such parables taught those who had already chosen the way of discipleship to stay rooted in the absolute security of the Father's providential care. Parables of discipleship also made it clear that commitment to the kingdom or opposition to it marks a fundamental dividing line which makes the difference between salvation and perdition.[35]

34. Cf. Ong, *op.cit.*, pp. 139-147.   35. Cf. Jeremias, *op.cit.*, pp. 115-229.

Historical critical method has so accustomed exegetes to focus on iso-
lated sayings of Jesus that they tend to overlook that the ethics of faith
sketched above and placed by the synoptic evangelists on Jesus' lips displays a remarkable coherence and originality. Its originality, like all human originality, consists in the novel and unique way in which Jesus re-
combined elements from His religious tradition in a new kind of moral
synthesis. He endowed that moral synthesis with additional novelty by
filtering it through His own experience of God as *Abba* (Father). No
contemporary of Jesus proclaimed such a religious vision. In other words,
when we situate in the religious context of first-century Palestine Jesus'
unique vision of the kingdom and of the moral constraints it imposes,
the principle of discontinuity endows that vision with historical certainty.
All the synoptic evangelists assert that Jesus required consent to this value
system as a condition for discipleship. Entering the kingdom, meant,
therefore, learning to live as a child of God in Jesus' own image.

One also finds echoes of Jesus' moral and religious vision in other New
Testament documents. In the exhortation which closes the letter to the
Romans, for example, Paul cites the willingness to live by this fundamen-
tal ethics of discipleship as the proof that one shares the Breath of Christ
and possesses the "newness of mind" which She inspires. (Mk 4:31-35;
Mt 12:46-50; Lk 8:19-21; Rom 8:14-30, 12:1-21, 13:8-14; 1 Cor
2:10-16) One also finds echoes of the same value system in the letter of
James. (Jam 1:9-11, 2:1-9, 15-16, 13-18)

Other criteria also certify the historicity of Jesus' vision of the kingdom. The criteria of multiple attestation and of Christian origins both
put Jesus' understanding of discipleship beyond historical question. The
criterion of multiple attestation justifies it because both the synoptic and
Pauline traditions testify to it. The principle of Christian origins also
validates the historicity of Jesus' religious vision: in Acts the willingness
to live the ethics of discipleship which Jesus lived and proclaimed serves
as the most fundamental mark of Breath-baptism and of Christian commitment. (Acts 2:37-47, 5:32-35)

In proclaiming the reign of God, Jesus held up to His disciples a profoundly egalitarian vision of human society. He seems to have chosen the
Twelve as the foundations of the new Israel He was summoning prophetically into existence.[36] (Mk 3:13-19; Mt 10:1-4; Lk 6:16) His choice
of the Twelve exemplifies a prophetic gesture, not an ordination. We have
no historical evidence that Jesus ever ordained anyone, whether male or

---

36. Cf. Nicholas T. Wright, "Jesus, Israel, and the Cross," *Society of Biblical Literature
Seminar Papers*, 24(1985), pp. 75-95; Ida Raming, "'Die zwölf Apostel waren
Männer....' Stereotype Einwande gegen die Frauenordination und ihre tiefere
Ursachen," *Orientierung: Katholische Blätter für Weltanschauliche Information*, 56:12
(June 30, 1992), pp. 143-146.

female. The symbolic choice of the Twelve also makes it highly probable, if not certain, that Jesus saw in the reign of God a vision of the kind of Israel which God desired when He gave Israel the Torah. If so, then in all probability, Jesus also saw the vision of the kingdom as fulfilling the deep intent of Torah piety. (Mt 5:20-48)

Jesus certainly repudiated Mosaic divorce practices, and in doing so appealed to God's true intent in creating marriage. (Mk 10:1-12; Mt 19:1-19; 1 Cor 7:10-11) The historical certainty of that act makes it also at least plausible, if not probable, that Jesus reserved to Himself the prophetic right to judge which regulations of the Law expressed God's real intent and which did not.[37] Plausibility here derives from the criterion of coherence.

I have considered some of the major themes in Jesus' proclamation of the God's reign. In the section which follows, I shall attempt to glean from the gospels some insight into Jesus' religious experience.

(V)

The gospels do not provide us with a detailed psychological portrait of Jesus; but we can, on the basis of the information which they supply about Him, draw some conclusions about His personal religious experience.

Jesus' Prayer

The gospels give us some evidence that Jesus liked to get away from the press of the crowds in order to spend time in solitude. Moreover, they suggest that at least on occasion He used these times for personal prayer. (Mk 1:35, 6:46; Mt 14:23, 32-34; Lk 3:21, 5:16, 6:12-16, 9:18, 28-29, 22:41-45)

Jesus prayed, and He taught His disciples that they should pray. Indeed, He encouraged the disciples to approach the Father with both astonishing boldness and with utter confidence. (Mk 11:24; Mt 7:7-11; Lk 11:5-13, 18:1-5) Both Matthew and Luke cite the Our Father as the paradigm of Christian prayer, although Luke's shorter version probably reproduces the more accurate rendering of the prayer as Jesus taught it. (Mt 6:9-13, Lk 11:2-4) The criterion of multiple attestation makes it virtually certain, then, that Jesus placed high value on prayer.[38]

Jesus Himself probably attended synagogue worship on a regular basis like any other devout Jewish layman. During His public ministry, He seems to have used the synagogue regularly but not exclusively as a forum

---

37. In my judgment, Schillebeeckx fails to do justice to the moral demands of life in the kingdom of God. Cf. Schillebeeckx, *Jesus*, pp. 136-178, 228-268; Grant, *op.cit.*, pp.45-61, 78-94.

38. Cf. Meier, *op.cit.*, II, pp. 291-302.

for proclaiming the kingdom. (Mk 1:21-22, 39, 3:1-6, 6:1-2; Mt 9:35, 12:9-14, 13:21-22, 53-54; Lk 4:16-32, 44, 6:6-11, 13:10)

Jesus' zeal for the temple as a house of prayer motivated in part His protest against the commercialization of temple worship by the priestly aristocracy. (Mk 11:15-17; Mt 21:12-13; Lk 19:45-48; Jn 3:13-22) As we shall see in greater detail later, His attack on the vendors and money changers in the temple expressed, not antipathy to the temple as such, but a profound sense of its holiness combined with a revulsion at the ways in which the aristocratic priestly caste used God's house for their own economic advantage.

The synoptic evangelists do not, however, speak frequently about Jesus' personal prayer. They all record Jesus' prayer in the garden of Gethsemane before His arrest and passion. (Mk 14:32-42; Mt 24:37-41; Lk 21:34-36) All the evangelists, including John, portray Jesus as praying at some time. (Jn 11:39, 17:1-26) Of the four evangelists, however, only Luke stresses the fact that Jesus prayed regularly. (Lk 3:21, 5:16, 6:12; 9:18, 28-36, 11:1, 22:41-45, 23:34, 46)

When, moreover, it comes to describing Jesus' prayer, the synoptic evangelists manifest even more reticence. I find it at least possible that their reticence goes back to Jesus Himself. He apparently viewed ostentatious public prayer with genuine repugnance and counseled His disciples not to cultivate the practice. (Mk 12:40, Mt:6:5-15; Lk 20:47) Instead, in praying to the Father they should seek solitude and anonymity. (Mt 6:5-15) Only Matthew records this last saying of Jesus. If, however, one invokes the principle of coherence in order to authenticate it, then one can also plausibly suppose that Jesus practiced what He preached and kept the content of His own communion with the Father to Himself.

In other words, while the gospel tradition as a whole does not describe Jesus' personal prayer in any detail, a convergence of evidence makes it virtually certain that He did in fact cultivate a personal prayer life.[39] I myself find the strongest evidence that Jesus prayed in His teachings on prayer, especially when one reads those teachings in the light of His evident revulsion in the face of religious hypocrisy. (Mk 11:15-19; Mt 21:12-13, 23:13-36; Lk 11:37-52, 19:45-48) Given Jesus' dislike of hypocrisy, I find it implausible that Jesus would have urged His disciples to pray as insistently as He did unless He Himself cultivated some kind of personal prayer life.

Jesus' Abba Experience

The researches of Geza Vermes make a possible case for the fact that Jesus' roots in the Jewish Hasidic tradition may have taught Him to call

---

39. This account of Jesus' religious experience derives largely from: James Dunn, *Jesus and the Spirit* (Philadelphia, PA: Westminster, 1975), pp. 15-21.

God *Abba*.[40] Jesus, however, endowed the term with a depth and complexity of personal meaning which finds no parallel in Hasidism.

For Jesus the term "*Abba* (Father)" connoted God's personal care and authority, on the one hand, and His right to absolute love and unconditioned obedience, on the other. (Mk 12:28-34, 14:36; Mt 6:25-34, 7:21, 11:25, 12:50, 22:34-40, 26:39, 42; Lk 2:49, 10:25-29, 12:22-34, 22:49, 23:34, 46) Quite possibly, either on the occasion of His baptism by John in the river Jordan or shortly thereafter Jesus' sense of relating to God as *Abba* began to mature into a personal sense of religious mission. (Mk 1:9-11: Mt 3:13-17; Lk 3:21-22) Nevertheless, the highly theologized character of the gospel accounts of Jesus' baptism make it impossible to know what exactly He experienced at the moment of His baptism.

More significantly still, the fact that Jesus most probably regarded anyone who submitted to the demands of life in the kingdom as a sister or brother (Mk 3:31-35, Mt 12:46-50, Lk 8:19-21) links His experience of God as Father to the His vision of the divine reign. So does the first petition of the Our Father. (Mt 6:9-23; Lk 11:2-4) Very probably, then, in calling people to the obedience of faith which the kingdom required, Jesus was summoning them to live as brothers and sisters united in the family of God.

Certainly, Jesus' own sense of relating to God as *Abba* at some point crystallized into a driving sense of mission, of having been sent by the Father to proclaim the divine reign. Moreover, that fact also makes it highly probable that Jesus regarded His own relationship to the Father as the paradigm for living as a child of God. (Cf., for example, Mt 11:25-30; Lk 10:21-22)[41] We find no parallel use of "*Abba* (Father)" in Jewish Hasidism.

Jesus and the Breath of God

The synoptic tradition asserts clearly that Jesus' sense of standing in a special relationship to the Father and of having been commissioned by the Father to proclaim God's reign derived from His enlightenment by the Breath of God. (Mk 1:9-11, 14-15; Mt 3:13-17, 4:12-17; Lk 3:21-22, 4:21-22)

The principle of multiple attestation makes it virtually certain that Jesus' contemporaries who responded sympathetically to Him regarded Him as a prophet. The same principle makes it extremely probable that Jesus' Himself claimed prophetic inspiration. (Mk 11:32; Mt 14:5, 21:46; Lk 7:16, 39, 22:64, 24:19) Since in the Old Testament the Breath of God

---

40. Cf. Vermes, *op.cit.*, pp. 210-213.
41. While these texts give evidence of some reworking in the light of the paschal mystery, the kernel of what they assert could, quite plausibly, go back to Jesus Himself. See, Dunn, *op.cit.*, pp. 26-34.

functions as the ordinary source of prophetic inspiration, it seems at least probable that Jesus and those who believed in Him would have attributed His own prophetic inspiration to the divine Breath.[42]

Assaulting Satan's Kingdom

Moreover, Jesus' sense of speaking and acting under the inspiration of God's Breath seems to have inspired His own sense of eschatological awareness. In Matthew's account of the controversy over Beelzebul, for example, Jesus claims to exorcise by the power of the Breath of God (in Luke, by the finger of God) and points to that fact as justifying His claim that the reign of God is already coming to realization in what He is doing.[43] (Mt 12:22-37)

I regard it as probable that at least some of Jesus' adversaries would have conceded that His healings and exorcisms gave evidence of the fact that some preternatural force, some "spirit" or "breath," empowered Him to do the things that He did. Since they could not deny the reality of the "breath" which inspired Him, they tried by discredit Jesus by calling it an "evil breath," or demon.[44] Moreover, as we have seen, the principle of embarrassment counsels that we take the slanders about Jesus which the gospels record with historical seriousness.

42. Cf. John O'Donnell, S.J., "In Him and Over Him: The Holy Spirit in the Life of Jesus," *Gregorianum*, 70(1989), pp. 25-45.

43. In Luke's version of the story, Jesus claims to cast out demons through the finger of God. (Lk 11:20) Mark in his account of the controversy over Beelzebul does not cite any saying of Jesus which points to His exorcisms as a sign of the coming reign of God. (Mk 3:22-30) The saying, therefore, probably derives from a source common to Matthew (Mt 12:25-30) and to Luke (Q).

Meier argues that Luke cites the more authentic version of this saying (Cf. Meier, *op.cit.*, II, pp. 404-430); but one can read the evidence in more than one way. Matthew cites the term "Breath" even though She plays a less prominent role theologically in his gospel than She does in Luke's. Since Matthew does not stress the role of the Breath in the way in which Luke does, it seems unlikely that in quoting from a written source of Jesus' sayings that Matthew would have changed "finger" to Breath.

Luke, on the other hand, despite his frequent references to the Breath's action in Jesus, has fairly clear theological motives for changing "Breath" to "finger." The change in Luke alludes to the Exodus and implicitly to the theme of universality which also plays a prominent role in His gospel. In the story of the Exodus the Gentile sorcerers of Pharaoh recognize that Moses performs signs through the "finger of God." Luke seems to want to portray these Gentile sorcerers as more insightful than Jesus' adversaries. This Mosaic allusion also develops another prominent theme, for Luke portrays Jesus as the prophet like Moses promised in Deuteronomy. (Cf. Acts 3:21-24; Ex 8:15; Dt 18:18-19)

As a matter of fact, we shall probably never know which version of this saying can claim the greater authenticity. They could both go back to Jesus, who very probably regarded His exorcisms as evidence that God's kingdom had already arrived in His ministry. (Cf. Meier, *op. cit.*, II, pp. 404-428)

44. For a more detailed exegetical discussion of these points, see: Dunn, *op.cit.*, pp. 46-63.

In this context, I also find it highly probable, that, if Jesus Himself saw in His exorcisms evidence that the reign of God was already coming to realization in His proclamation of the kingdom (Cf. Mt 11:2-6; Lk 7:18-23), then, just as probably, He also saw the proclamation of the kingdom as a struggle between God's reign and that of Satan, whose power for evil finds embodiment in the principalities and powers of this world: i.e. in institutions like the client Jerusalem priesthood and the Roman empire.[45] In other words, the principle of coherence also makes it plausible, even probable, that He regarded the Breath which inspired His own prophetic ministry as God-sent and holy and as the opposite of the personal and institutional demonic forces which opposed the kingdom. Hence, the principle of discontinuity makes Jesus' mode of exorcism at least probable.[46]

Here, moreover, one should note that Jesus did not exorcise in the way in which other exorcists of His day did. They would almost certainly have invoked the name of God in exorcising. Jesus, however, seems to have ordered the demons to depart with a direct personal command. His style of exorcism differed too from that of His disciples who invoked Jesus' name in exorcising.[47]

(VI)

I have described Jesus' relationship to the Baptizer, His vision of the kingdom, and aspects of His religious experience. In the present section, I shall reflect on the ways in which Jesus related to the different constituencies who confronted Him.

Jesus and the Gentiles

The gospel of Matthew asserts that Jesus confined His ministry only to "the lost sheep of the house of Israel." (Mt 10:5-6) While only Matthew records this saying of Jesus, we have three reasons to regard it as literally true.

1) The gospels record only occasional contacts between Jesus, on the one hand, and Gentiles and Samaritans, on the other. Moreover, in these encounters the Gentiles or Samaritans take the initiative. (Mk 7:24-30; Mt 8:5-13, 15:21-28; Lk 7:1-10, 10:51-56, 17:11-19; Jn 4:1-42, 12:20-22)

2) The gospels seem to have taken literary shape for the most part in the sub-apostolic era, when the Christian community was in process of transforming itself into the Gentile Church. Had Jesus regularly con-

---

45. Cf. Walter Wink, *Naming the Powers: The Invisible Forces That Determine Human Existence* (Philadelphia, PA: Fortress, 1984).
46. Cf. Grant, *op.cit.*, pp. 30-44.
47. Cf. Meier, *A Marginal Jew*, II, p. 406.

sorted with Gentiles, the evangelists would almost certainly have recorded these edifying incidents. The paucity of encounters between Jesus and Gentiles which the gospels record probably results from the fact that such encounters in fact rarely happened.

3) The criterion of Christian origins also supports the authenticity of Mt 10:5-6. If Jesus had explicitly extended His own ministry to the Gentiles, it seems unlikely that the apostolic Church would have found itself as bitterly divided as it did on the issue of their degree of admissability into the "new Israel."[48]

Nevertheless, the few encounters between Jesus and faith-filled Gentiles which the gospels record also make it plausible to suppose that those encounters caused Jesus to develop the universalist strain in His own preaching by making a place for the Gentiles within the kingdom when it came to final and full realization. Both Matthew and Luke depict Jesus predicting the eventual gathering of the nations into the divine reign He was in process of proclaiming. (Mt 8:10-11; Lk 13:28-30) Since the two evangelists derive this saying from a third source (Q), the criterion of multiple attestation suggests that we accord it very plausible, even probable, authenticity. The same criterion also makes it plausible, even probable, that Jesus acknowledged the hostility which Palestinian Jews of His time felt toward the Samaritans as both enemies and heretics but that He Himself did not endorse those same hostile feelings. (Lk 10:29-37; 17:11-19; Jn 4:1-42)

These reflections also shed plausible light on the purpose of the movement Jesus headed. The choice of the Twelve suggests that in proclaiming God's reign, Jesus was seeking to bring into existence a "new Israel" whose obedience to the demands of life in the kingdom expressed the deep intent of Torah piety. Jesus seems to have believed that only by heeding His message could Israel avoid national disaster. His inclusion of the Gentiles in the kingdom suggests the possibility that He may have hoped that Israel's submission to the kingdom would transform it into God's instrument for effecting a universal salvation.

Jesus' Disciples

At the time of Jesus, rabbis probably did not ordinarily call their disciples. If their activity conformed to later rabbinic practice, they probably waited for disciples to seek them out. Nor do we find evidence in the New Testament that those who proclaimed the risen Christ called individual disciples in the personal, prophetic, and peremptory way in which Jesus on occasion does in the New Testament. (Mk 1:16-20, 2:14; Mt 4:18-22, 8:18-22, 9:9; Lk 5:4-11, 27-28, 10:57-62; Jn 1:43) The criteria

---

48. Cf. Raymond E. Brown and John P. Meier, *Antioch and Rome: New Testament Cradles of Catholic Christianity* (Ramsey, NJ: Paulist, 1983), pp. 1-9.

of multiple attestation and of discontinuity make it, then, extremely probable, if not certain, that Jesus called at least some of His disciples. Given His own prophetic sense of mission, the criterion of coherence also makes it probable to suppose that, at least on occasion, Jesus issued that call in something like the prophetic way in which the New Testament describes.

The gospels also give us at least plausible reason to suppose that Jesus in relating to His disciples engaged in another kind of activity which set Him apart from other teachers: namely, He showed Himself willing to teach women as well as men. The story of Martha and Mary makes this point clearly. In the story, Martha rebukes Mary for leaving her to do the "womanly" chores involved in getting dinner on the table, while Mary engages in the "unwomanly" activity of sitting at the feet of a male rabbi. Jesus empathizes with Martha's anxiety about getting dinner on the table, but He gives Mary His unqualified endorsement for desiring instead to listen to His teaching about God's reign.(Lk 11:38-42)

Luke alone records the story about Martha and Mary; but all three synoptic gospels testify to the fact that Jesus included women in the entourage which traveled around with Him. Both Mark and Matthew record the fact that these women "followed" Jesus from Galilee to Jerusalem. The phrase "followed Jesus" suggests a relation of discipleship as does the presence of the women at Jesus' execution. (Mt 27:55-56, Mk 15:40-41)

Some of the women who traveled with Jesus belonged to the aristocracy and contributed money to Jesus' support. (Lk 8:1-3) Jewish piety would have smiled upon rich women who undertook to help support this or that rabbi; but that they would have traveled around with Him would have deeply shocked first century Jewish sensibilities. Once again, the principle of embarrassment suggests that, unless Jesus actually engaged in such socially shocking behavior, the evangelist would not have attributed it to Him on his own initiative. If the rich women in question believed in Jesus enough to contribute in significant ways to His financial support, then it seems at least plausible that they also followed Him as disciples.

Finally, the fact that Jesus treated women in a manner which contrasted with the behavior of other Jewish men would also help explain the enhanced role which women seem to have played in the apostolic church.[49] In other words, the criterion of Christian origins also sanctions regarding this facet of Jesus' ministry as extremely probable, even certain.

In my judgment, the criterion of multiple attestation combines with the criterion of Christian origins in order to make the selection of the Twelve by Jesus historically certain. All the synoptic gospels record the

49. Cf. Elizabeth Meier Tetlow, *Women and Ministry in the New Testament: Called to Serve* (Lanham, MD: University Press of America, 1980); Cary Catherine Hilkert, "Women Preaching the Gospel," *Theology Digest*, 33:4 (winter, 1986), pp. 423-440.

call of the Twelve and indicate that Jesus involved them more actively than the other disciples in His own ministry of proclamation. (Mk 3:13-19; Mt 10:1-4; Lk 6:12-14) The gospel of John also describes the Twelve as a distinctive group among the disciples. (Jn 6:13, 67) In Acts, the Twelve already function as an established leadership group within the Jerusalem community. (Acts 1:12-26) The Pauline tradition records how "the Twelve" became apostles by seeing the risen Christ, even though at the time the Twelve numbered only eleven. (1 Cor 15:5) The Book of Revelation also alludes to the Twelve apostles as the foundation stones of the heavenly Jerusalem.[50] (Rev 21:14)

The fact that the lists of the names of the Twelve exhibit minor variations does not disprove the historicity of their call. Rather it points to the fact that the New Testament recorded an oral tradition which lacked the textual fixity of written documents.

The gospel of Mark indicates that Jesus gave nicknames to three disciples: Simon, whom He nicknamed "the Rock" and the two brothers James and John, whom He nicknamed "the Sons of Thunder." (Mk 3:16-17) Matthew and Luke in listing the names of the Twelve also record Simon's nickname. The fourth gospel offers similar testimony. (Mt 10:2; Lk 6:14; cf. Jn 1:42; Gal 2:9, 1 Cor 5)

Moreover, the synoptic gospels give us some reason to suppose a special relationship between Jesus, on the one hand, and Peter, James, and John, on the other. In all the synoptic gospels, Jesus calls them among His first disciples. (Mk 1:16-20; Mt 4:18-21; Lk 5:1-11) Their names lead all three lists of the Twelve. (Mk 3:17; Mt 10:2; Lk 6:14) Jesus chooses them to accompany Him to the top of the mount of Transfiguration. (Mk 9:2-8; Mt 17:1; Lk 9:28-36) Mark also has Peter, James, and John witness the raising of the daughter of Jairus. (Mk 5:37) Mark and Matthew make these three disciples privileged companions to Jesus' prayer in Gethsemane. (Mk 14:33; Mt 26:37) Luke, probably because he wants to portray Jesus as the model of prayer for all the disciples, omits any special reference to Peter, James, and John in his account of Jesus' prayer in the garden. (Lk 22:40-46)

As we shall see, Mark ties his gospel together by a complex network of allusive references. His references to Peter, James, and John serve such a narrative purpose. They link together the cure of Peter's mother-in-law, the raising of Jairus' daughter, the transfiguration, the eschatological discourse, and the agony in the garden as events which mutually illumine one another. (Mk 1:16-20, 29, 5:37, 9:2, 13:3, 14:33) Given the special allusive use Mark makes of these three disciples, I find it more plausible

50. Cf. John P. Meier, "The Circle of the Twelve: Did It Exist During Jesus' Public Ministry?" *Journal of Biblical Literature*, 116(1997), pp. 635-672.

to suppose that a narrative tradition about their special relationship to Jesus inspired his literary conceit than vice versa.

Quite plausibly, then, Jesus had a special friendship for Peter, James, and John. Possibly, He gave the sons of Zebedee the ironic nickname "Sons of Thunder" because they tended to respond with thud and blunder. Only Mark records the nickname given to James and John. I find it plausible, however, to suppose that Mark actually found this nickname in the tradition, since it seems unlikely that the evangelist would have invented this trivial and ironic detail on his own. Nothing else Mark says about James and John gives the nickname particular credence, although Mark does portray James and John as even more ambitious than the other ten. (Mk 10:35-41) Luke, however, at the beginning of the journey discourse describes James and John asking Jesus whether they should act like new Elijahs and call down fire from heaven to consume the Samaritan village which refused them hospitality. (Lk 9:51-56; cf. 2 King 1:10-12) Luke makes no mention of James and John's ironic nickname; but the story gives it some plausibility.

Did a similar irony motivate calling Simon "the Rock?" "The Rock's" impetuosity, to which the gospel's all testify, renders the suggestion plausible (Mk 9:5, 14:29; Mt 14:28-29, 17:4, 26:33-35, 58; Lk 5:8-10, 33, 22:54; Jn 13:36, 18:10-11, 18:15, 21:7), although Peter in all the gospels also exercises a leadership function among the disciples even before the resurrection. As we shall see when we reflect upon narrative Christology, Matthew for his own theological reasons transforms the image of "the Rock" into one of ecclesial stability. (Mt 16:18) On the lips of Jesus, however, it may possibly have sought through ironic humor to evoke from Peter a more stable leadership than his behavior tended to exhibit.

The principle of multiple attestation makes it at least plausible that Peter confessed Jesus as the messiah at some time during the latter's ministry. (Mk 8:27-29; Mt 16:13-16; Lk 9:18-20) Moreover, as Jesus sensed the inevitability of His own coming death, Peter almost certainly tried to dissuade Him from submitting to martyrdom. The synoptic accounts of their argument suggest a sharp disagreement between Jesus and Peter. Given the stature which Peter enjoyed in the Christian community at the time when the gospels took shape, the criterion of embarrassment makes it difficult to imagine that the evangelists would have recorded that Jesus had actually called Peter "Satan" unless the bitterness of their argument made the epithet plausible. (Mk 8:32-33; Mt 16:22-23)

The two criteria of multiple attestation and of embarrassment also combine in order to make the fact that Peter denied Jesus certain. The principle of multiple attestation makes it also probable that Jesus foresaw abandonment by His disciples during the passion.[51] (Mk 14:27-34, 66-68;

51. Cf. Raymond E. Brown, S.S., *The Death of the Messiah*, I, pp. 139-145.

Mt 26:31-35, 69-75; Lk 22:31-34, 54-62; Jn 13: 36-38, 18:15-18, 25-27)
These predictions suggest that Jesus had no illusions about the reliability
of His disciples in a moment of real crisis.[52]

The same criteria also make the treachery of Judas certain. (Mk 3:19,
14:10, 43; Mt 10:4, 26:14, 25, 47, 27:3; Lk 6:16, 22:3, 47-48; Acts
1:16, 23, 25; Jn 6:71, 13:2, 26, 29, 14:22, 18:2-5) The fact that all the
evangelists testify that Judas, one of the twelve, betrayed Jesus engages
the criterion of multiple attestation. The criterion of embarrassment argues that the evangelists would not have recalled that one of the privileged Twelve, whom Jesus had hand-picked, ended by betraying Him
unless the treachery actually happened.

Only the fourth gospel hints at a possible motive for the treachery. The
fourth evangelist asserts that, as Jesus moved toward Calvary, Judas had
begun to steal from the common purse, which he held in trust. (Jn 12:4-6)
In other words, the fourth gospel makes it historically possible that as
Jesus' final violent confrontation with the chief priests approached, Judas's
desire to distance himself from the coming debacle eroded any faith he
had put in Jesus and in His doctrine of sharing with the poor as an expression of faith in God. Instead, Judas, who kept the common purse, tried
to recoup his losses by stealing from it. Finally, Judas effectively distanced
himself from Jesus in the eyes of the authorities by betraying Him.

The above scenario remains, however, extremely speculative. Given the
diversity of traditions about Judas, we shall probably never know why he
betrayed Jesus. That he did act the traitor we do know. We can also assert
with high probability that he received money for his treachery. He very
probably assisted the high priests in planning Jesus' clandestine arrest.
He probably pointed Jesus out to the arresting party. Very probably, his
own death followed shortly after's Jesus' crucifixion; but given the contradictory accounts of how it happened we cannot say with any probability how Judas died. The Christian community, however, saw in his death
God's judgment upon him for his treachery. The name Iscariot possibly
puzzled the evangelists as much as it does modern scholars.[53]

Jesus and the Pharisees

We have no detailed knowledge of Palestinian Pharisaism at the time of
Jesus. The principle of multiple attestation makes it at least probable,
however, that Jesus responded negatively at least to certain aspects of
Pharisaical piety. The name "Pharisees" meant "Separated Ones." Quite
possibly, opponents of the Pharisees coined the name as a slur. The name
alluded to the fact that the Pharisees avoided social contact with Gen-

---

52. *Ibid.*, I, pp. 610-626.
53. Cf. Brown, *The Death of the Messiah*, I, pp. 652-660, II, pp. 1394-1418.

tiles, with unclean persons, with sinners, and with Jews less observant of the Law than they.

In the time of Jesus, Pharisaism, as we have seen, represented a movement of piety among devout lay Jews who sought to preserve fidelity to the Law by interpreting it in the light of oral traditions which they regarded as an added guarantee of righteous conduct. This practice especially separated the Palestinian Pharisees from the Jewish peasantry, from "the people of the land."

The gospels tend to use the Pharisees symbolically in order to castigate legalistic, judgmental, hypocritical tendencies in the Christian communities they address. The record of a previous oral tradition, the gospels tend to portray the Pharisees in bold adversarial strokes which reflect the predilection of oral narrative for diatribe.

One finds, however, occasional hints in the gospels that Jesus' own relationship to the Pharisees may have exhibited a bit more nuance. While the gospels almost always portray Jesus' relationship to the Pharisees in negative, confrontational terms, one finds in Luke the story of benign Pharisees who go out of their way to warn Jesus to flee the district because Herod has decided on His death. (Lk 13:31) Moreover, in His adversarial confrontations with the Pharisees in the gospel narratives, Jesus does not always respond with the same degree of negativity.[54] Finally, Jesus sided with the Pharisees and against the Sadducees in proclaiming the resurrection of the body. (Mk 12:18-27; Mt 22:23-33; Lk 20:27-40)

In my judgment, the principle of multiple attestation makes it at least probable that the stories of confrontation between Jesus, on the one hand, and some scribes and some Pharisees, on the other, did have an historical foundation in His ministry. Both the synoptic and Johannine traditions bear witness to hostile confrontations between Jesus and some Pharisees. Moreover, the synoptic gospels, in my judgment, also give a plausible account of the kinds of issues which led Jesus to condemn and antagonize His Pharisaical adversaries. Those reasons include the following: 1) the Pharisees' subversion of what Jesus perceived as the true intent of the Law through the needless multiplication of non-binding regulations and through legalistic rationalization (Mk 7:1-13; Mt 15:1-19); 2) the failure of at least some Pharisees to perceive that Jesus' sabbath healings fulfilled the purpose of the Sabbath (doing good) rather than violated it (Mk 3:1-6; Mt 12:9-14; Lk 6:6-11, 14:3); 3) the Pharisees' judgmental condemnation of the "laxer" piety of the "people of the land" whose cause Jesus especially championed (Mk 2:23-28; Mt 12:1-8; Lk 6:1-5); 4) the scandal of both scribes and Pharisees at Jesus' table fellowship with sinners and at His proclamation of the forgiveness of sins even to public sinners (Mk 2:1-2, 2:13-17; Mt 9:1-13; Lk 5:17-32); 5) the failure on

---

54. Compare, for example, Lk 7:36-50 and Lk 11:37-44.

the whole of the scribes and Pharisees to respond to Jesus with the kind of repentance and faith which He demanded (Mk 8:11-12; Mt 16:1-4)

Jesus and Herod

The synoptic gospels suggest that at some point in His public ministry, possibly toward the end of it, Jesus lived in some ways like an outlaw. Mark states, for example, that, after the death of John the Baptizer at the hands of Herod, Jesus deemed it expedient to leave Palestine in order to seek public anonymity in the territory of Tyre. (Mk 7:24) One wonders whether to trust Mark's chronology on this point; but all the synoptic gospels testify that Herod Antipas, after imprisoning and eventually be-heading John, showed an unusual degree of interest in Jesus and in His public activity.[55] (Mk 6:14-29; Mt 14:1-2; Lk 9:7-9)

Mark tells us that even during His Galilean ministry, the Herodians wanted Jesus dead. (Mk 3:6) Luke, as we have seen, tells of rumors reaching Jesus that Herod sought His death. (Lk 13:31) According to Mark, during His final Jerusalem ministry, Herodians seem to have joined His other enemies in conniving against Him. (Mk 12:13-17)

Moreover, if Jesus, as we have seen, publicly linked His own ministry to that of John and if He endorsed the prophetic character of the Baptizer's ministry, then He also at least implicitly endorsed John's public attack on Herod. As we have also seen, Luke with support from Josephus makes it plausible to suppose that John attacked more than Herod's sexual self-indulgence and that the Baptizer mounted a prophetic broadside against "all the wicked things" Herod had done. (Lk 3:19) Everything else we know about Herod suggests that he did wickedness aplenty and that he would not have taken kindly to criticism on Jesus' part any more than he tolerated it in the case of the Baptizer.

Those who think that the cleansing of the temple may have taken place earlier than the synoptics indicate do so in part because they believe this public act of defiance would have transformed Jesus into the focus of popular messianic expectations. They argue that this development would help explain why he left Palestine for Gentile territory and why the crowds had to seek Him out in desert places.[56] The antipathy of Herod and the Herodians, an antipathy rooted in Jesus' public endorsement of John and of the Baptizer's prophetic denunciation of Herod could, however, quite plausibly explain such behavior just as well.[57]

Jesus and the Crowds

Most new questers for the historical Jesus would today concede as his-torically certain that Jesus engaged in a ministry of faith healing and of

---

55. Cf. Albert Nolan, *Jesus Before Christianity* (New York, NY: Orbis, 1978), p.105; Grant, *op.cit.*, pp. 129-131.

56. *Ibid.*, pp. 101-106.   57. Cf. Grant, *op.cit.*, pp. 129-131.

exorcism. Jesus performed miracles and drove out demons. The criterion of embarrassment, for example, makes it unlikely that both Luke and the author of the canonical ending of Mark would have described as a former demoniac a person in the community of the stature of Mary Magdalene unless Jesus had in fact exorcised her. (Cf. Lk 8:2-3; Mk 16:9; See also Mt 27:56, 61, 28; Mk 15:40, 47, 16:1, 9; Lk 24:10; Jn 19:25, 20:1, 11, 16, 18) The criterion of multiple attestation makes it equally certain that curiosity about His teaching, on the one hand, and the desire for healing and deliverance, on the other, at least on occasion drew large numbers of people to Jesus. (Mk 2:4, 13, 3:9, 20, 32, 4:1, 5:21, 24, 27, 6:34, 45, 8:1, 9:14, 10:1, 46; Mt 4:25, 8:1, 18, 13:2, 14:4, 15:30, 19:2, 20:29, 21:8; Lk 5:15, 29, 6:17, 7:11, 21, 8:4, 30, 9:37, 14:25; Jn 6:2, 5, 11:19, 45, 12:9, 11-12)

The fact that Jesus exorcised and healed miraculously endowed His ministry with a charismatic power which distinguished it dramatically from the ministry of John the Baptizer. Moreover, the saying of Jesus which both Matthew and Luke derive from Q provides a plausible list of the kinds of healings which Jesus worked. He cured deafness, muteness, physical deformity, and leprosy. On occasion, He raised the dead. (Mt 11:2-6; Lk 7:18-23)

The same saying makes it also virtually certain that Jesus saw an intimate connection between His proclamation of the kingdom, on the one hand, and His exorcisms and miracles of healing on the other. Both aspects of His ministry revealed the kingdom as a reality already germinally present. Moreover, as we shall see below, Jesus probably also saw in His exorcisms and miracles a sign that His ministry marked the dawning of the messianic age, even though He rejected Davidic messianism.[58]

Vermes argues with considerable plausibility that, when people approached Jesus as a wonder-worker, they tended to address Him as "Lord."[59] The criterion of multiple attestation also makes it certain that some people in crowds who flocked to Jesus regarded Him as a prophet.[60] (Mk 6:4, 15, 14:65; Mt 13:57, 21:11, 46, 26:68; Lk 4:24, 7:16, 39, 13:33, 22:64, 24:19; Jn 4:19, 44, 7:52, 9:17)

The criterion of multiple attestation also makes it virtually certain that Jesus in the course of His public ministry became the focus of popular messianic expectations. (Mk 8:27-30, 11:9-10, 14:61-2, 15:32; Mt 16:13-20, 21:9, 26:63-64; Lk 9:18-22, 19:38, 22:67-70, 24:21: Jn 1:41, 6:15, 7:26-27, 31, 41-42, 10:24) The gospels suggest, however, that Jesus

58. For a thorough account of the historicity of Jesus' exorcisms and miracles, see: Meier, *op. cit.*, II, pp. 509-1038. See also: Franz Mussner, *The Miracles of Jesus: An Introduction*, translated by Albert Wimmer (Notre Dame, IN: University of Notre Dame Press, 1968); Gerd Thiessen "Jesusbewegung as charismatische Wertrevolution," *New Testament Studies*, 35(1989), pp. 343-360.

59. Cf. Vermes, *op.cit.*, pp. 122-126.   60. *Ibid.*, pp. 86-99.

responded to this particular popular perception of Him and of His ministry with ambiguity and on occasion even with negativity.

All the synoptic gospels portray Jesus reacting negatively to Davidic messianism. The role of warrior-king contradicted Jesus' doctrine of non-violent resistance to evil and oppression. It seems probable that Peter at some point during Jesus' career confessed Him as the messiah. Moreover, I find it at least possible that Jesus on that occasion forbade His disciples to tell anyone the content of Peter's confession, even though Jesus' command may originate in Mark's desire to portray Him as a secret messiah. (Mk 8:30; Mt 16:20; Lk 9:21) One may, however, invoke the principle of consistency to argue that Jesus' reservations about Davidic messianism made Him loathe to proclaim Himself the messiah in an overt way.

The synoptics also suggest that after Peter's confession, the disciples' attempt to cast Jesus in the role of a Davidic messiah collided directly both with Jesus' vision of the kingdom and with His own sense that His prophetic destiny made it inevitable that He would have to die for the truth which He proclaimed. (Mk 8:31-9:1, 30-32, 9:33-37, 10:32-40; Mt 16:21-28, 17:22-23, 18:1-4, 20:17-23; Lk 9:18-27, 43-45, 9:46-50, 18:31-34; Acts 1:6) In my judgment, the criteria of multiple attestation and of embarrassment make this conflict between Jesus and the disciples extremely probable.

Moreover, all the gospels suggest that in His teachings Jesus resisted playing the part of a Davidic king. (Mk 12:35-37; Mt 22:41-46; Lk 20:41-44; Jn 6:15) All the gospels nevertheless proclaim Jesus as the Messiah. (Mk 9:9-11, 8:27-30; Mt 2:1-6, 4:1-11, 16:13-20; Lk 1:67-79, 2:11, 24-32, 4:1-13, 9:18-21; Jn 11:27) By the criterion of embarrassment, then, the fact that they also record His reservations concerning Davidic messianism would seem to make those reservations historically certain. (Mk 12:35-37; Mt 4:8-11, 22:41-46; Lk 4:11-13, 20:41-44) Matthew and Luke both suggest, not without plausibility, that Jesus Himself regarded the attempt to replace the kingdom of God with Davidic messianism as the equivalent of idolatry. (Mt 4:8-10; Lk 4:5-8)

The fact remains, however, that Jesus died on the cross as one who made messianic claims and therefore as a criminal who sought to subvert the Roman empire. The principle of multiple attestation makes both the fact of the crucifixion and the reason for it certain. (Mk 15:26; Mt 27:37; Lk 23:35-38; Jn 19:17-22)

Although the synoptic gospels give highly theologized accounts of Jesus' trial before the Sanhedrin, those accounts make it possible, perhaps plausible, that in the course of His interrogation Jesus' enemies forced Him to say something which they could construe as a messianic claim. (Mk 14:61-62; Mt 26:63-65)

I shall reflect on Jesus' interrogation in more detail below. At this point we need to ask: can one trace Jesus' death as the messiah to something more than the possibility of a chance admission in the course of His trial? The way in which one answers that question depends on the way in which one chooses to interpret the triumphal entry into Jerusalem and the cleansing of the temple.

Here we face several interrelated questions. When did the cleansing of the temple happen? Did it embody a prophetic gesture? Did the triumphal entry into Jerusalem embody a prophetic gesture? If it did, had it any relationship to the cleansing of the temple? Let us reflect on each of these questions in turn.

First of all, did the cleansing of the temple follow close upon the triumphal entry, as the synoptics suggest; or did it happen earlier in Jesus' ministry, as the gospel of John seems to assert? (Mk 11:1-14; Mt 21:1-22; Lk 19:40-48; Jn 2:13-25) If the cleansing happened earlier, then one can argue that for explanatory reasons the synoptic evangelists located it later, in Jesus' final Jerusalem ministry, as a way of calling attention to the close connection between this event and His death on the cross. On the other hand, one can also make a strong case for the fact that the fourth gospel's displacement of the cleansing of the temple to earlier in Jesus' ministry results from a final redactor's editing of that gospel.

Exegetes generally concede that the original text of the fourth gospel underwent final editing as the hand of a redactor or of several redactors. Moreover, the text of the fourth gospel as we posses it suggests that a redactor, for theological reasons, did in fact displace other material from the end of Jesus' life to earlier in His public ministry. For example, it seems at least plausible, if not probable, that the final redactor transformed the fourth evangelist's original account of the institution of the eucharist into the second part of the Bread-of-Life discourse. (Jn 6:51-58) If so, theological motives would almost certainly have led the final redactor to transform the institution narrative into a doctrinal disquisition on the real presence of Christ in the eucharist. Denial of Jesus' real eucharistic presence, as we shall see in the doctrinal section of this study, numbered among the heterodox beliefs which the fourth gospel especially addresses. That Jesus would have discoursed during His public ministry about His real presence in a eucharist He had yet to institute enjoys, of course, practically no historical plausibility, even though the bread-of-life discourse in the fourth teaches some important theological truths.

Similarly, in the original gospel, Jesus' encounter with Nicodemus probably followed the events narrated at Tabernacles. (Jn 3:1-21; 7:14-8:15) The two pericopes develop similar theological themes; and Nicodemus's reference to the "many signs" Jesus has done (Jn 3:3) makes no sense where it now occurs, since Jesus has in fact performed only one rather private miracle. Moreover, the clandestine visit of Nicodemus to Jesus at night contrasts dramatically with the cured blind man's implicit acknowledgement of Jesus as the light of the world. (Jn 9:1-4, 35-37)

Analogous theological motives could also explain the temporal displacement of the cleansing of the temple to the Cana-to-Cana section of the fourth gospel. Let us try to understand those motives.

In John's gospel Jesus performs His first "sign," or revelatory miracle, at Cana of Galilee. (Jn 2:1-12) Later in the gospel, Jesus performs a second miracle at Cana. (Jn 4:43-54) The two signs at Cana function literarily as a Biblical inclusion and mark off the events they bracket as a thematic unit of text.

In the fourth gospel's Book of Signs, the evangelist elucidates the meaning of most of the signs Jesus works with an extended discourse from the lips of Jesus Himself. Three signs lack such a discourse: the two miracles at Cana and the last sign, the raising of Lazarus. The last sign reveals Jesus as the resurrection and the life. (Jn 11:25) This last sign receives its elucidation from the entire Book of Glory which follows it. The Book of Glory narrates the paschal mystery: Jesus death, resurrection, and sending of the Holy Breath as the living water which slakes human thirst for everlasting life. (Jn 3:5-8, 4:10-14, 7:37-39, 20:19-23) In an analogous manner, instead of a discourse, the events bracketed between the two Cana miracles elucidate the meaning of the first sign.

The first sign reveals Jesus as the divine bridegroom who will give the messianic wine in eschatological abundance when the hour of His glorification will come. (Jn 2:1-12) The wine of the eucharist which Jesus will later give fulfills the promise of messianic wine. (Jn 6:53-58) Moreover, eucharistic worship in Spirit and truth fulfills temple worship. (Jn 4:21-24, 6:63-66)

The Cana-to-Cana section of John develops all these themes. The final witness of John the Baptizer occurs in the Cana-to-Cana section. It explicitly identifies Jesus as the divine bridegroom. (Jn 3:22-36) The cleansing of the temple together with Jesus' dialogue with the Samaritan woman introduce the idea of the purification of worship which Jesus will effect when through the gift of His eucharistic body and blood He empowers believers to worship God in Breath and truth. (Jn 2:13-25, 3:5-8, 4:21-24, 6:53-71)

Given the theological contribution which the cleansing of the temple makes to the Cana-to-Cana section of the fourth gospel, I find it at least plausible, even probable, that the gospel's final redactor displaced the cleansing of the temple from Jesus' final Jerusalem ministry, where it probably first occurred, to the Cana-to-Cana section of the gospel. The redactor would have done so as a way of linking this incident to the full significance of the first sign which Jesus gives the disciples in that gospel. I shall develop these insights in greater detail when I consider the fourth gospel in the doctrinal section of this study.

Two other theological motives could also have led the final redactor of the gospel to displace the cleansing of the temple from its original temporal position in Jesus' final ministry to the Cana-to-Cana section of the Book of Signs: 1) The displacement allows the final redactor to portray the raising of Lazarus rather than the cleansing of the temple as the chief motive which led the chief priests to decide upon Jesus' death. (Jn 11:45-54) 2) The three Passovers which the fourth gospel narrates—the Passover in which Jesus cleanses the temple, the Passover at which He gives the Bread-of-Life discourse, and the final Passover at which He dies—from a theological standpoint all coalesce into a single Passover which all three events fulfill. Why? Because, viewed theologically, the first two Passovers both illumine the meaning of the final one. Moreover, taken together they all reveal how Jesus fulfills and replaces the meaning of the Jewish feast of Passover as a liturgical event. The theological coalescence of the three Passovers links the first two to the third. That means that in the fourth gospel even the displaced account of the cleansing of the temple continues to throw light on the reason for Jesus' death; but it plays a less dramatic explanatory role than it does in the synoptic tradition.

For all these reasons, I find it more plausible to suppose that the synoptic gospels correctly date the cleansing of the temple when they locate it in the early days of Jesus' final Jerusalem ministry.[61]

In driving the money changers from the temple, Jesus performed a prophetic gesture. In my judgment, the criterion of multiple attestation makes it probable that the commercialization of temple worship motivated Jesus' prophetic act. In the synoptic accounts, Jesus justifies His action by condemning the transformation of His Father's house from a house of prayer into a "den of robbers." (Mk 11:17; Mt 21:13; Lk 19:46) John's gospel uses different words but makes fundamentally the same point. John's Jesus rebukes the vendors and money changers for turning His Father's house into a "market."[62] (Jn 2:16-17)

In attacking the vendors and money changers Jesus attacked the chief priests who profited from their presence in the temple. Certainly in both the synoptic and Johannine traditions, the chief priests perceive His action as an attack on their authority. (Mk 11:18-19; Mt 20:15-16; Lk 19:47-20:8; Jn 2:18) In this context, I find it interesting to note that in narrating the story of the widow who gave everything she owned in order to pay the temple tax, all the synoptic evangelists link her act to Jesus' excoriation of the hypocrisy of Jewish leaders who pretend piety while devouring the meager resources of orphans and widows. The widow who

---

61. suggestion in no way calls into question the fact that most of Jesus' public actions elude chronological dating.   62. Cf. Grant, *op.cit.*, pp. 144-152.

gives her last coin to the temple functions, for all her generosity, more as a victim than as a model.[63] (Mk 12:38-44; Lk 20:45-21:1-4)

In other words, one can best understand the symbolism of Jesus' prophetic attack on the vendors and money changers when one situates His assault into the larger economic and political context which the third quest for the historical Jesus is in process of reconstructing. One also needs to interpret Jesus' action in the light of the revolutionary social and economic demands of the divine reign which He proclaimed.

As we have seen, in proclaiming the kingdom Jesus was calling for an egalitarian restructuring of Palestinian Jewish society. That restructuring required the rich to obliterate class structures by sharing their wealth with the poor, the marginal, the outcast, even with sinners. The temple priesthood belonged to the aristocracy. Given the other things we know about Jesus, the criterion of coherence makes it not at all surprising that He would have viewed with revulsion the use of the temple as a means of lining the pockets of rich priests at the expense of a marginally surviving peasantry. Such a use of "His Father's house" would almost certainly, in my judgment, have struck Him as something like an ultimate in religious hypocrisy.

Did Jesus' cleansing of the temple symbolize its coming destruction, as E.P. Sanders has insisted?[64] Jesus prophetic gesture in the temple recalled a similar prophecy against the temple uttered by Jeremiah the prophet. Jeremiah prophesied the destruction of the temple in Jerusalem as a divine punishment for Jewish idolatry and injustice. When Jesus prophesied the temple's destruction, He too probably saw the priest's abuse of God's house for the sake of economic exploitation of the poor as one of the reasons for the coming disaster. If so, then, Jesus' cleansing of the temple quite plausibly also connoted its destruction.

If one concedes the fact that the cleansing of the temple almost certainly embodied a prophetic attack on the commercialization of worship by the high priestly aristocracy, might one regard the triumphal entry into Jerusalem as another prophetic gesture which Jesus orchestrated as a way of contextualizing and inaugurating His final confrontation with the temple priesthood? In my judgment, one can make a highly probable case for the fact that He did.

---

63. In the fourth gospel's account of this incident "the Jews" challenge Jesus for His action. As we shall see, however, the term "the Jews" in John has a variety of meanings; but in this instance it refers to the chief priests.

64. Cf. E.P. Sanders, *Jesus and Judaism* (Philadelphia, PA: Fortress, 1985), p. 70. For an alternative view see: Craig A. Evans, "Jesus' Action in the Temple: Cleansing or Portent of Destruction," *Catholic Biblical Quarterly*, 51(1989), pp. 237-270. See also: Dale C. Allison Jr., "Jesus and the Covenant: A Response to E.P. Sanders," *Journal for the Study of the New Testament*, 29(1987), pp. 57-78.

Vermes suggests that Jesus probably entered Jerusalem riding on a donkey because He found it a more convenient mode of transportation than walking. Only later did the disciples realize that Jesus' procession fulfilled the prophecy of Zechariah 9:9.[65] Vermes, however, concedes that others interpret the triumphal entry differently. They argue that Jesus' use of the donkey as a mode of transportation did not simply happen accidentally. Instead, Jesus deliberately orchestrated His entry into Jerusalem as a fulfillment of Zech 9:9.

I find the second explanation the more plausible of the two. Vermes's suggestion rests on pure conjecture; while the second explanation has some foundation in the New Testament narratives of this event. Certainly, in the synoptic accounts of the triumphal entry Jesus does not just happen upon a donkey. He sends the disciples to collect the animals, a donkey and its colt, in order that He can ride the donkey into Jerusalem. (Mk 11:1-6; Mt 21:1-3; Lk 19:28-32)

The disciples who go to collect the animals find everything exactly as Jesus told them they would. Mark tells this particular narrative detail in a way which suggests that Jesus possessed a kind of preternatural knowledge of future events. In Mark's narrative, Jesus' foreknowledge implicitly depicts Him as the master of events, even of the events which led to His own death. Both Matthew and Luke seem to endorse Mark on this particular theological point.

Another possible explanation of Jesus' foreknowledge, however, occurs to the more skeptical, historical mind, although it remains just that, only a possibility. I mean that the entire matter could have been prearranged. In any case, the synoptic tradition suggests that Jesus in His triumphal entry used the animals in a calculated way.[66]

Might the calculation have expressed symbolic intent? The prophetic character of the cleansing of the temple endows this interpretation with plausibility. If in cleansing the temple Jesus performed a prophetic gesture, then the principle of coherence makes it plausible to suppose that in orchestrating the triumphal entry He performed another such gesture.

In Mark's account of Jesus' final Jerusalem ministry, the chief priests seem to put both events on a par: when they finally confront Jesus, they want to know by what authority He does "these things." (Mk 11:28) When read in context, the "things" in question would seem to refer not only to the cleansing of the temple but to the triumphal entry as well. Matthew and Luke follow Mark on this point. (Mt 21:23; Lk 20:2) The Johannine tradition also echoes the same priestly challenge. (Jn 2:13-22) In other words, the principle of multiple attestation makes it plausible to

---

65. Cf. Vermes, *op.cit.*, p. 145.
66. Cf. Brent Kinman, "Jesus' 'Triumphal Entry' in the Light of Pilate's," *New Testament Studies*, 40(1994), pp. 442-448.

suppose that the chief priests saw in both the triumphal entry and the cleansing of the temple prophetic acts which challenged their religious authority.

If, then, Jesus orchestrated the events of the triumphal entry in the way in which the synoptics suggest, I also find it at least plausible that He did so in order to fulfill the prophecy of Zechariah 9:9. If so, then the triumphal entry, viewed as a deliberate prophetic gesture, made qualified messianic claims. Zechariah 9:9 describes a king entering Jerusalem in victory; but instead of riding a war horse, he rides a donkey, a humble beast of burden commonly used by the peasantry. Riding the donkey symbolizes the fact that the king comes as a king of peace and not of war.

In other words, it seems to me at least plausible, even probable, that Jesus deliberately orchestrated the triumphal entry in a way which made messianic claims, but He did so in qualified terms which He found acceptable. By orchestrating the triumphal entry as a fulfillment of Zech 9:9, Jesus was asserting that He was indeed entering Jerusalem as its messianic king, but not as the bone-crushing Davidic messiah of popular expectation. Rather he came as the embodiment of a non-violent kingdom of peace, a kingdom which demanded repentance from the whole of Israel, including its religious leaders in Jerusalem.

In such an interpretation, the prophetic gesture of the triumphal entry would provide the context for understanding the prophetic gesture of the cleansing of the temple. The assault on the vendors and money changers simply spelled out in detail the kind of repentance which the reign of God demanded of the high priestly aristocracy: namely, they must repent of using the temple in order to exploit and oppress the poor. The criterion of rejection and execution also lends support to such an interpretation of Jesus' actions.

Such a interpretation of the triumphal entry finds added support from a narrative detail supplied by Luke. In Luke's version of the triumphal entry, Pharisees confront Jesus and urge Him to silence the disciples who are proclaiming Him "the King who comes in the name of the Lord." Jesus refuses to do anything of the kind. Instead, He replies: "If these were silent, the very stones would cry out." (Lk 19:38-40) In other words, Luke's Jesus regards the disciples' proclamation of His messianic identity during the triumphal entry as a truth which nothing, not even He, can suppress. Whether one finds here a historical fact or a theological gloss remains anyone's guess.

If one accepts the plausibility of interpreting the triumphal entry as a prophetic gesture which made qualified messianic claims, then one should also note that Jesus seems to have allowed Himself this messianic claim at a point in His public career when He expected that it would lead, not to his coronation as a Davidic king, but to His repudiation by the leaders of the people as a false prophet and ultimately to His own death. Moreover,

Jesus would have made His messianic claim in a way which would have allowed others to put upon His action whatever interpretation they chose.[67]

Jesus and the Chief Priests

In considering Jesus' response to the messianic expectations of the crowds, I began to reflect on the final confrontation between Him and the temple priesthood. Mark suggests that even during Jesus' Galilean ministry, the authorities in Jerusalem kept a weather eye cocked on Him and His activities. Mark notes that during Jesus' ministry in Galilee a group of scribes, possibly a delegation from the temple priesthood, came from Jerusalem with the express intent of undermining Jesus' ministry by sowing the rumor that He cast out demons in the power of Beelzebul. (Mk 3:22)

When we interpret this assertion in the light of other things we already know about Jesus and John the Baptizer, the principle of coherence endows it with considerable probability. As we have seen, the geographical proximity of the Baptizer's prophetic ministry to Jerusalem would have posed a threat to the religious hegemony of the temple priesthood. As a prophet, John offered the people another way of relating to God than through the authority of the temple priests. That threat when combined with Jesus' public association with and endorsement of John would have given the temple priests reason enough not only to keep their eyes on Him but also to discredit His prophetic authority if they could.

The synoptic gospels suggest that no formal confrontation between Jesus and the temple priests occurred until Jesus' final Jerusalem ministry. Certainly, the synoptic evangelists locate temporally all the stories of those direct confrontations during that ministry. The gospel of John, however, suggests a different temporal scenario. The fourth gospel depicts a series of confrontations between Jesus and the temple priests which occurred when Jesus went in pilgrimage to Jerusalem for other feasts than the Passover at which He died. One finds slight synoptic support for this Johannine scenario in Luke's suggestion that even Jesus' early ministry included Judea. (Lk 4:42-44) Might Luke refer to an early baptismal ministry? Matthew supplies another possibly supportive fragment: the evangelist notes that the crowds which flocked to Jesus during His Galilean ministry also came from Judea and Jerusalem. (Mt 4:25)

In my judgment, by the principle of multiple attestation, the supportive testimony of Luke and Matthew endows the Johannine account of Jesus' conflict with the temple priesthood with at most historical possibility.

The synoptic gospels also give a plausible account of the issues which divided Jesus from the temple priesthood. I have already considered two of them: 1) the challenge which even a qualified messianic claim would

67. Cf. Grant, *op.cit.*, pp. 95-108, 142-144.

have made to the political authority of the high priestly caste and 2) Jesus' cleansing of the temple and public denunciation of the priests' self-ish and oppressive use of the temple and of the temple taxes.

To these two issues we need to add others to which the synoptic gospels testify. 3) Jesus endorsed the prophetic authority of John the Baptizer, claimed a similar prophetic authority for Himself, and publicly reproached the temple priests for failing to hear the prophetic call to repentance which John first voiced and which Jesus' proclamation of the kingdom pro-longed (Mk 11:27-33; Mt 21:23-27; Lk 20:1-8). 4) Jesus not only proph-esied the destruction of the temple but laid principal responsibility for the impending demolition of the holy city and its temple to the corrupt leadership of the temple priests and of the Sanhedrin. (Mk 12:1-12, 13:1-2; Mt 21:33-36, 24:1-2; Lk 20:9-19, 21:5-6) 5) Jesus publicly reproached the party of the high priests, the Saducees, for denying the resurrection of the body and for misinterpreting the Torah on this point. (Mk 12:18-27; Mt 22:23-33; Lk 20:17-40)

The fourth gospel, as we shall see in the doctrinal section of this study, makes the divinity of Jesus the principal issue which divided Jesus from the temple priests. That Jesus would have proclaimed His own pre-existent divinity in the explicit way He does in the gospel of John strikes me as historically implausible, even though the Johannine Jesus in doing so enunciates a profound truth of Christian faith.

In what concerns Jesus' prophecy of the destruction of Jerusalem and of its temple, one probably encounters an echo of the theme of imma-nent judgment which characterized the Baptizer's preaching. Jesus' proph-ecy, however, could also have expressed more than eschatological reli-gious fervor. The third quest for the historical Jesus has made it clear that the seething rebellion which eventually boiled over in the Jewish wars had already reached a significant simmer during Jesus' lifetime. Jesus may well have had the political shrewdness to realize that unless His people put their own religious house in order and used the considerable resources of the client aristocracy—of both the Herodians and the high priesthood in Jerusalem—in order to right the blatant injustices in Palestinian soci-ety, then Palestinian Judaism stood on a collision course with the con-quering Romans.

Just as possibly, Jesus could also have possessed the political shrewdness to foresee that such a confrontation could only end in a debacle for the Jews and that the disaster would parallel the Babylonian conquest of Judea and of Jerusalem. The Babylonians had razed both Jerusalem and its temple. The Romans routinely obliterated those cities which resisted them.

I find it, then, at least plausible to imagine that Jesus, with political and historical realism, recognized that, unless the religious leaders of Palestin-ian Judaism heard and responded to the political, economic, and social revolution demanded by the reign of God which He proclaimed and embodied, then the Herodian temple, which survives today only as the Wailing Wall in Jerusalem, would suffer the same historical fate at Roman hands as the temple of Solomon had suffered at the hands of the Babylonians. If so, then Jesus prophesied shrewdly.

The Temptations of Jesus

The synoptic accounts of Jesus' mortal ministry all begin with His temptation in the desert. (Mk 1:12-13; Mt 4:1-17; Lk 4:1-13) Matthew and Luke draw on a third source (Q) in order to elaborate Mark's brief but highly symbolic account of this incident. As we shall see in considering narrative Christology, all three accounts of Jesus' desert temptations have clear theological motives: they seek to portray Jesus as the incarnation of a new Israel undergoing the prototypical temptations which any member of that new Israel can expect to encounter in a life of discipleship. The symbolic and highly theologized character of the desert temptations leaves one wondering whether the incident they describe ever occurred as such.

In Matthew's and Luke's account, Jesus experiences three specific temptations. He finds Himself tempted in the accomplishment of His messianic mission to trust in Himself rather than in God, to set conditions on His willingness to trust God, and to replace the kingdom of God which He proclaimed with a kingdom of law and coercive violence.

Whether or not Jesus encountered these temptations in a solitary encounter with Satan in the deserts of Judea, one can make a plausible case for the fact that He did indeed encounter them as He drew toward the end of His mortal ministry. As we have seen, after Peter's profession of Jesus' messianic identity, Jesus probably entered into a period of conflict with His disciples concerning the scope and purpose of His mission. Several of His disciples, as we have seen, seem to have regarded Him as a Davidic messiah who would rally the troops and lead Israel to military and political domination of her hated enemies and oppressors. In Jesus' confrontation with Peter, the latter sought to dissuade Him from facing death in Jerusalem. It would appear at least possible that Peter regarded death by martyrdom as inappropriate for a Davidic messiah.

The New Testament suggests the possibility that others too may have sought to persuade Jesus to use military means to establish the kingdom He proclaimed. In the fourth gospel's account of the multiplication of the loaves, the crowds, awed by the miracle, seek to crown Jesus king. He foils their attempt, however, by fleeing into the hills. (Jn 6:15) If, as seems virtually certain, Jesus did indeed become the focus of popular messianic expectations (Lk 24:21), then it seems also probable that He would have felt pressure from those expectations to abandon the non-violent course on which He had embarked and follow the militaristic path which other would-be messiahs had taken.

As Jesus moved quite deliberately toward a final confrontation with the Jerusalem priesthood, a confrontation which He apparently expected to culminate in His own death, might He not, humanly speaking, have felt the attractiveness of avoiding death by imitating the first David and Judas Maccabeus? Might He not have felt the allure of replacing personal martyrdom with a strategic throw of the military dice? I find the suggestion at least plausible.

Moreover, the synoptic accounts of Jesus' prayer in the garden of Gethsemane all portray Jesus, in the face of betrayal and death, wrestling with His relationship to the Father. As we shall see in the section of this study which deals with narrative Christology, all the synoptic evangelists use narrative strategies in order to affirm Jesus' divinity. That they would portray Him as troubled in His relationship to the Father on the very eve of His martyrdom calls attention in dramatic ways to Jesus' humanity and vulnerability. Given the fact that the evangelists all defend Jesus' divinity, the criterion of embarrassment makes it at least probable that they would not have called attention to His weakness in Gethsemane unless He actually felt it. The fourth gospel, which makes not only the divinity of Jesus but His divine pre-existence one of its central doctrinal concerns, finds the hint of weakness in Jesus so scandalous that the Beloved Disciple only alludes in a very cryptic way to His agony in the garden. (Mk 14:32-42; Mt 26:36-46; Lk 22:40-45; Jn 18:1-11) One senses here a parallel with the way in which the four gospels treat Jesus' baptism by John.

The principle of multiple attestation also makes it virtually certain that as Jesus approached death He wrestled with His relationship to the Father out of repugnance for the ordeal which confronted him. We find echoes of the synoptic account of Jesus' prayer in Gethsemane in the gospel of John. (Mk 14:32-34; Mt 26:36-38; Lk 22:40; Jn 12:27a, 18:1) Moreover, the letter to the Hebrews also testifies to Jesus' struggle with the Father in the face of martyrdom, even though Hebrews does not draw directly either on the synoptic or the Johannine tradition. (Heb 5:7-10) In other words, the New Testament points to a widespread tradition among the first Christians that Jesus faced His approaching death with repugnance, wrestled with the Father in prayer about its necessity, but accepted it in obedience to the Father's will.[68]

The picture of Jesus on the threshold of death wrestling with the Father about the necessity of submitting to His impending martyrdom gives, in my judgment, historical plausibility to the first two desert temptations recorded by Matthew. Did Jesus in the garden feel humanly tempted to trust in Himself rather than in the Father? Did He feel humanly tempted to set conditions on His obedience to the Father's will? Did He feel humanly tempted to say to the Father, "I will obey You, if only You do not

68. Cf. Brown, *The Death of the Messiah*, I, pp. 216-234.

ask me to suffer the hideous injustice of condemnation and death?" I find the suggestion at least plausible and the impulse profoundly human.

In other words, whether or not one regards Jesus' desert temptations as historical, one has plausible, perhaps even probable, grounds for asserting that, especially toward the end of His mortal ministry, as He faced human failure and martyrdom, Jesus did indeed experience the kinds of temptations which Matthew and Luke describe in His desert confrontation with Satan.

The Last Supper

The synoptic, the Johannine, and the Pauline traditions all testify to the fact that Jesus before His passion shared one final meal with His close disciples. (Mk 14:12-25; Mt 26:17-29; Lk 22:7-23; Jn 13:1-32; 1 Cor 11:23-25) The criterion of multiple attestation therefore puts the fact of the supper beyond question.

The synoptic and Johannine traditions both attest that on that occasion Jesus predicted His betrayal by one of the disciples present at the meal. (Mk 14:17-21; Mt 20:20-25; Lk 22:22-23; Jn 13:21-30) As we have seen, He also predicted Peter's denial. (Mk 14:30-31; Mt 26:30-35; Lk 22:31-34; Jn 13:36-38) The principle of multiple attestation would, then, make both predictions at least highly probable.

The synoptic and the Pauline traditions both testify that at some point during the supper, Jesus took some bread, blessed it, broke it, and gave it to His disciples while calling it His body. He also took a cup of wine, blessed it, and gave it to them to share while calling it His covenant blood. (Mk 14:22-25; Mt 26:26-29; Lk 22:14-23; 1 Cor 11:23-25)

The synoptic and Pauline traditions each exhibit minor variations in their account of the precise words Jesus used in performing these two prophetic gestures. That fact has led some new questers for the historical Jesus to attribute Jesus' eucharistic words to the Christian community rather than to Jesus.

In my judgment this kind of skepticism represents a misapplication of the criterion of discontinuity and violates the criterion of Christian origins. The notion that the Christian community made up Jesus' eucharistic words and actions out of whole cloth fails, finally, to explain the strong similarities in the different New Testament institution accounts. If Jesus' eucharistic words had no historical precedent, one would expect more radical disagreement in the different accounts of what He did or did not do at that final meal.

The four accounts of the institution of the eucharist which we possess all agree, however, that Jesus took, blessed, broke, and then gave some bread to His disciples. They all agree that in doing so He referred to the bread as His body. All the accounts mention that Jesus also took and blessed a cup of wine, then passed it among His disciples while telling them to drink of it and while calling it His covenant blood. In my judgment the criteria of multiple attestation and of Christian origins would put these basic words and actions of Jesus beyond serious historical doubt.

The differences in detail which one finds in the four New Testament versions of the origin of the eucharist receive their most plausible explanation from the fact that the New Testament records oral traditions. Oral traditions, as we have seen, do not prize textual fixity in the way in which literary traditions do. Instead, the oral mind remembers past events adaptively. In dealing with oral traditions, it makes no sense to demand of them the same kind of accuracy as one might expect from literary or scholarly history.

The eucharistic words and actions of Jesus at the last supper give us, moreover, our clearest historical clue to the way He approached His own death. The prophetic gift of His body to His disciples as food makes it plausible to suppose that He died hoping that His death, the breaking of His body, would somehow function as a source of life for His disciples. The prophetic gift of wine as His covenant blood, also makes it plausible that He died hoping that His death would somehow deepen and consolidate His disciples' own commitment to God, that it would reseal their covenant with God like the rite of atonement.[69]

Jesus' "Trial" Before the Priests

The apostle Paul (1 Cor 11:23) joins both the synoptic and the Johannine traditions in asserting that the Jewish authorities in Jerusalem arrested Jesus at night. By the principle of multiple attestation, then, they very probably did.[70] By the same principle, Jesus probably suffered physical abuse at the hand of his captors on the night of His arrest. (Mk 14:65; Mt 26:67-68; Lk 22:63-65; Jn 18:22-23)

Both the synoptic and Johannine traditions also make it very probable that Jesus' prophetic assault on the temple provided one of its major reasons for His arrest and a major issue in His "trial."[71] (Mk 14:55-59; Mt 26:59-63; Jn 11:47-48) All three synoptic evangelists also indicate, again with plausibility, that the issue of Jesus' messianic claims figured prominently in His confrontation with His Jewish judges. (Mk 14:60-62; Mt 26:62-63; Lk 22:66-71) I also deem it at least plausible that at some point in His trial Jesus may have been made to assert something which

---

69. Cf. Schillebeeckx, *Jesus*, pp.274-312; cf. Joachim Jeremias, *The Eucharistic Words of Jesus*, translated by Norman Perrin (New York, NY: Scribners, 1966). Cf. John P. Galvin, "Jesus' Approach to Death: An Examination of Some Recent Studies," *Theological Studies*, 41(1980), pp. 713-744.

70. Cf. Brown, *The Death of the Messiah*, I, p. 417.

71. For an assessment of the textual evidence in support of this assertion, see: Brown, *The Death of the Messiah*, I, pp, 454-460.

His enemies could construe as a messianic claim. (Mk 14:62-65; Mt 24:64-67; Lk 22:67-70) Certainly, in no gospel does Jesus deny outright His messianic dignity, not even during His trial.

Mark, Matthew, and John attest that the high priest took the initiative in persuading the Sanhedrin to condemn Jesus. The same three gospels make it clear that Jesus' enemies among the Jerusalem priests regarded Him as a blasphemer. Mark and Matthew make blasphemy the motive for Jesus' condemnation. (Mk 14:60-61; Matt 26:62-63; Jn 11:49-53)

Nowhere in the gospels does Jesus use the name of God blasphemously. Raymond Brown, however, argues for the possibility that Jesus identified with the apocalyptic figure of the Son of Man and that His enemies might well have construed this claim as blasphemous. In addition, Brown makes a convincing argument that Jesus' adversaries might well have viewed the total impact of His ministry as making blasphemous claims. Brown cites the following factors in Jesus' ministry in support of this claim:

1) Jesus spoke with great authority and by His frequent use of the double "Amen" demanded assent to His message.

2) Jesus proclaimed the forgiveness of sins and by his association with sinners exempted Himself from the standards of holiness imposed by religious authorities.

3) Jesus performed miracles and claimed that they made God's reign present in His person and ministry.

4) Jesus either implied or stated that God would judge people on the basis of their response to His proclamation of the divine reign. Other Jews proclaimed that God acted in history; but Jesus claimed that His ministry offered Israel a unique opportunity for salvation, one that had never come before and would never come again. As a consequence, Jesus' summons to submit to God's reign exhibited an eschatological newness which went beyond former prophetic calls to repentance.

5) Jesus claimed the right and authority to pass judgment on and revise the Law in accord with the needs of the eschatological moment which He proclaimed and embodied. He therefore implicitly claimed more authority for His message than for the Torah.

6) Jesus, a layman, indicated that rejection of His message would lead to the destruction of the very house of God.

7) Jesus claimed the sanction of no external authority. He therefore centered the right to say and do what He did in His own person.

8) Jesus claimed to relate to God as *Abba*. He therefore also claimed to be God's Son.[72]

Schillebeeckx proposes that the Sanhedrin referred Jesus' case to Pilate because they agreed on the need to get rid of Him but could not agree on

---

72. Cf. Brown, *The Death of the Messiah*, I, pp.480-482, 506-514, 536-547.

the grounds for doing so.[73] Schillebeeckx makes no use of the fourth gospel in his somewhat conservative portrait of "the historical Jesus."

The gospel of John suggests, however, that the Sanhedrin agreed upon Jesus death prior to His arrest. In John's gospel, on the night of Jesus' arrest, Annas, the father-in-law of the high priest Caiphas, interrogates Him informally prior to His deliverance into the hands of Caiphas. (Jn 18:19-24) In the fourth gospel, Pilate presides over Jesus' formal trial.

Both Brown and Meier suggest that Jesus probably underwent an interrogation at the hands of some Jerusalem officials but that He probably never had the benefit of a full and formal trial before the entire Sanhedrin.[74] I find their suggestion more plausible than Schillebeeckx's. If the Sanhedrin in plenary session had already decided on Jesus' death, Mark and Matthew in describing Jesus' trial by the Sanhedrin on the night of His arrest may, for the sake of narrative simplicity, have conflated that event with Jesus' interrogation by representatives of the Sanhedrin. After interrogation, the high priests certainly handed Jesus over to the Roman governor, Pontius Pilate.

Jesus and Pilate

Contemporary commentators on the passion accounts in the fourth gospel often suggest that the four evangelists paint a more appealing portrait of Pontius Pilate than one finds in the other occasional references to him in Josephus. These commentators seem to suggest that since Pilate acted with uniform ruthlessness and cruelty, he almost certainly did the same when asked by the chief priests to pass judgment upon Jesus.[75] Certainly, the four evangelists go out of their way to assign to the chief priests and the Sanhedrin principal blame for Jesus death; and they all portray Pilate as the chief priests' reluctant collaborator.

Without a doubt, Pilate could act cruelly on occasion; but the evidence does not support the portrait of him as a uniformly ruthless and blood-stained tyrant. Certainly, in his first major crisis as Roman prefect Pilate either relented or vacillated. On another occasion, he displayed some capacity for limited restraint. In both cases, Pilate found himself faced with a potentially explosive situation which engaged the deep religious feelings of the Jewish people.

73. Cf. Schillebeeckx, *Jesus*, pp. 312-318.
74. Cf. Meier, *A Marginal Jew*, I, p. 407; Brown, *The Death of the Messiah*, I, pp. 423-426. If the Sanhedrin decided on Jesus' death in a plenary session and only interrogated Him informally on the night of His arrest, then Mark and the other synoptic evangelists may well have collapsed the two proceedings into one for reasons of catechetical and narrative simplicity.
75. Crossan's handling of Pilate illustrates this tendency. Crossan's determination to discredit the historicity of the gospel accounts of Jesus' trial leads Crossan to portray Pilate as a "specialist" in crowd control (Crossan, *Jesus: A Revolutionary Biography*, p. 141), even though the very texts he cites concerning Pilate's handling of crowds shows him as vacillating and inconsistent, despite a certain penchant for brutality.

On the first of these occasions, in 26 a.d., Pilate, under orders from the emperor Tiberius, had standards bearing Caesar's image brought into Jerusalem. His action violated Jewish religious sensibilities because Jewish law forbade the erection of graven images in the Holy City. Pilate at the time was staying in Caesarea. A huge throng of people sought him out there and begged him to respect their ancestral laws and order the standards removed. When he refused, the crowd staged a sit-in for six days at the house where Pilate was staying.

On the sixth day, Pilate called a tribunal and pretended to sit in judgment on the crowd's request. Instead, Pilate at a pre-arranged signal had the protesters treacherously surrounded by armed troops. He told the people that they must accept the presence of the images of Caesar in the Holy City or die on the swords of the Roman soldiers. He then gave the order for the soldiers to unsheathe their swords.

The assembled Jews responded by bearing their throats and extending their necks to receive the sword's fatal blow. Confronted with a degree of religious commitment which he probably regarded as sheer fanaticism, Pilate either vacillated or relented. Certainly, he ordered the standards removed from Jerusalem. (Josephus, *The Jewish Wars*, 2.169-174)

In his first administrative crisis, Pilate showed himself culturally and religiously obtuse. He certainly threatened violence; but he did not order it. Instead, he seems to have recognized that he had underestimated the insult which his action offered to Jewish religious sensibilities and relented.

Between 29 and 31 a.d., Pilate had imperial coins minted in Judea depicting instruments of pagan sacrifice: a dipper shaped ladle for pouring wine in libation sacrifices and a bent staff for auguring. Herod the Great had minted similar coins; and Pilate's action probably exemplified standard Roman procedure rather than a calculated insult to Jewish religious sensibilities. We have no evidence that the minting gave rise to any form of religious protest.[76]

On another occasion, Pilate used dissimulation and treachery in dealing with a popular protest. He had taken money from the temple treasury in order to build an aqueduct which transported water into Jerusalem. Jews regarded the temple treasure as the religious patrimony of the nation. Pilate, for his part, probably regarded his action as benefiting the people of Jerusalem.

Thousands of indignant Jewish protesters assembled at the governor's tribunal in order to protest his action. Pilate had Roman soldiers disguised as civilians and armed with clubs infiltrate the crowd. Then, from his tribunal Pilate gave a pre-arranged signal. The soldiers attacked the crowds with clubs and dispersed the protest. Apparently Pilate had wanted

76. Brown, *op. cit.*, I, pp. 699-700.

the crowd dispersed; but, once the soldiers started bludgeoning the un-armed crowd, they got carried away. Many Jews perished, beaten or trampled to death. Besides the protesters, the dead included curious by-standers. (*Ibid.*, 2.176-177; *Antiquities*, 18.60-62) On this occasion, Pilate may have underestimated the brutality of his soldiers. He did nothing to stop the slaughter; but, faced with a riot, he may have lost control of events.[77]

The gospel of Luke reports that Pilate had killed a number of Galileans, probably on pilgrimage to Jerusalem, as they were offering their sacri-fices. (Lk 13:1-2) No other writer of the period mentions this incident. We do not know the circumstances of the slaughter; nor does Luke pro-vide information about Pilate's motives or his degree of actual involve-ment in the incident. Quite possibly, it contributed to the enmity be-tween Pilate and Herod Antipas, the prefect of Galilee.[78]

Possibly in the year 31 a.d. Pilate dedicated some golden ornamental shields in the Herodian palace in Jerusalem. Pilate seems to have learned something from his first administrative crisis. The shields bore no graven images; but they did have writing on them and may have referred to the "divine Augustus." A large delegation of Herodian princes protested to Pilate that his action infringed upon Jewish religious traditions. When Pilate refused to remove the shields, the princes appealed to the emperor, who decided in their favor. The emperor Tiberius rebuked Pilate and ordered the shields removed. We have no way of knowing how seriously the emperor regarded the incident.[79]

Pilate's first crisis involved a purely symbolic, religious act: namely, the introduction of graven images into a space sacred to the Jews. The erec-tion of the images violated Jewish law; but, like virtually every religious act in theocratic first century Palestine, the introduction of the images of Caesar had political significance as well. In dedicating the golden shields about five years afterwards, Pilate may have attempted a political end run: having failed to introduce the emperor's image into Jerusalem, he may have tried to introduce non-visual symbols of imperial veneration into the Jewish capitol. Pilate's action upset the Herodian aristocracy; but it seems not to have evoked popular protest. I find it at least possible that Pilate resisted the Herodian princes and allowed the emperor to decide the matter because he expected that, as the object of emperor worship, Tiberius would look upon Pilate's action with complacency, even if the emperor decided in favor of the Herodian princes.

Pilate's minting of coins seems not to have provoked any popular un-rest. In provoking the riot over the aqueduct, Pilate again acted like a

77. Cf. Horsley and Hansen, *op.cit.*, pp. 38-39.
78. Cf. Brown, *The Death of the Messiah*, I, p. 701.
79. *Ibid.*, I, pp. 702.

typical imperial bureaucrat. Initially, at least, the governor did nothing of direct religious significance; nor did his action directly engage the emperor as the incident of the standards had. Instead, it would appear that, as governor, Pilate routinely ordered an aqueduct built for the benefit of the people of Jerusalem. With, no doubt, the connivance of the temple priests, the prefect paid for the aqueduct with temple funds. In so acting, Pilate once again misread popular Jewish religious sensibilities. The prefect, however, may well have regarded temple funds as religiously compromised as the priests who almost certainly supplied them. In the profanation of the Galilean sacrifices, Luke presents Pilate as culpable but provides no means of assessing the degree of his culpability.

Pilate ruled in Judea for ten years in all, from 26 to 36 a.d. During that entire time Caiphas presided as high priest. The fact that Pilate never removed Caiphas suggests that the two had worked out at least a *modus vivendi*, perhaps a mutually profitable relationship.

Pilate's military action in 36 a.d. against the Samaritan prophet who led an armed band to rediscover the site of the Samaritan temple on Mount Gerazim proved the Roman prefect's political undoing. As we have seen, Pilate sent armed troops to prevent the ascent of the mountain with bloody consequences. When the Samaritan authorities protested the ensuing slaughter and executions to the Syrian legate, they argued that Pilate had attacked, not rebels, but a group of refugees. The legate found in favor of the Samaritans.

The Jerusalem priests hated the Samaritans and regarded the ancient temple on Gerazim as an upstart rival to the Jerusalem temple. Did Caiphas persuade Pilate to prevent the possible rediscovery of the site of the Gerazim temple? Did the Syrian legate pass judgment against Pilate on the merits of the case or for political reasons? We shall never know the answer to either question. In the end, Pilate found himself packed off to Rome to explain his action to the emperor Tiberius. The latter's death made any explanation unnecessary and probably saved Pilate's neck.[80] (Josephus, *The Jewish Wars*, 18.88-89)

These incidents allow one to nuance somewhat common scholarly portraits of "the historical Pilate." One finds him described as a bloody tyrant and as a master of mob control. Neither description fits the facts. The Pilate who confronts us through the mists of the centuries seems to bear the lineaments of a fairly typical Roman career bureaucrat who obtusely offended Jewish religious sensibilities on occasion. Nevertheless, the length of Pilate's reign and his apparent ability to get on with the high priest in most matters does not suggest a tenure regularly marked by wanton atrocities or political abuse. On occasion, Pilate even undertook

80. Cf. Horsley and Hansen, *op.cit.*, pp. 160-172; Crossan, *The Historical Jesus*, pp. 160-162.

projects, like the aqueduct, which benefitted the Jewish people. While capable of oppressive acts of violence on some occasions, on others Pilate vacillated. He showed a reluctant restraint in dealing with Jewish religious sensibilities.

When faced at the beginning of his term with what must have appeared to him fanatic Jewish religious commitment, Pilate even countermanded the order of an emperor in order to avoid violating Jewish religious sensibilities. Did Pilate sense a similar "fanaticism" in Jesus, who believed that God was calling Him to lay down His life for the religious vision He proclaimed? As a Roman governor, Pilate would almost certainly have felt reluctant to pass judgment in any case which he regarded as raising primarily religious issues. (Cf. Acts 18:15)

Jesus' trial probably took place in the Herodian palace on the western hill of first-century Jerusalem rather than in the fortress Antonia. We have no detailed information about how the Romans administered their provinces legally during the first century. One may, however, plausibly assume that from a legal standpoint, Pilate would have approached Jesus' case more as a hearing than as a formal, legal trial. Very probably, as a Roman judge, Pilate would have wanted to know the political implications of Jesus' activities and whether He posed a genuine threat to Roman authority. By the principle of multiple attestation, Pilate probably recognized that the chief priests desired Jesus' death for religious reasons of their own; but he acceded to their request under pressure and ordered Jesus crucified.[81] (Mk 15:6-15; Mt 27:15-26; Lk 23:13-25; Jn 18:38-19:16)

Pilate had Jesus crucified as a messianic pretender. Jesus probably died in the year 30 a.d. He had probably lived about thirty-six years. He public ministry had probably lasted a little over two years.[82]

By the principle of multiple attestation, Joseph of Aramathea very probably obtained from Pilate permission to bury Jesus. Joseph probably belonged to the Sanhedrin at the time. Luke and John call Him a disciple of Jesus; Mark and Luke do not. Possibly, he did convert later to Christianity and was venerated in the community for his act of piety in burying Jesus. (Mk 15:42-45; Mt 27:57-58; Lk 23:50-52; Jn 19:38) Moreover, some archeological evidence indicates that on occasion at least the crucified could receive private burial.

The principle of congruity also renders the action of both Joseph and of Pilate plausible. If, as seems probable, the Sanhedrin condemned Jesus to die illegally and in His absence, then, quite plausibly, some members of that body with more sensitive consciences, like Joseph, took exception to that illegal and immoral act. (Cf. Jn 7:50-52) If so, then it would

81. Cf. Brown, *The Death of the Messiah*, I, pp. 705-722.
82. Cf. Meier, *op.cit.*, p. 407; cf. Grant, *op.cit.*, pp. 153-168.

appear at least possible that Joseph undertook to bury Jesus in part as a gesture of atonement for an act of legalized murder. Mark, who records the earliest traditions about Joseph presents him, not as a disciple, but as a pious Jew. (Mk 15:43) If, moreover, as seems probable, Pilate realized that the chief priest had sought Jesus' death on religious grounds, resentment at their manipulative tactics during Jesus' trial might well have inclined him to look benignly on Joseph's request.[83]

(VII)

In reflecting on the method which structures this study, I indicated that I have opted for a foundational Christology because I believe that the attempt to develop a systematic Christology in the context of a theology of conversion addresses the pastoral needs of the RCIA and of any adult Christian desirous of deepening in an ongoing adult conversion to Christ.

Any contemporary Christology needs to propose not only a plausible account of Jesus' humanity but an inculturated one as well. I have chosen to approach the humanity of Jesus as a finite, developing, human experience in part because such an understanding of humanity fits the way American philosophy has tended to portray the human. Moreover, I have found from experience that people in this country tend to respond positively to such a philosophical construct of the human.

More than utility, however, has motivated my choice of philosophical categories for describing Jesus as human. I regard the realistic, triadic, social construct of experience which I have expounded as philosophically sound.

I have also attempted to demonstrate its scientific plausibility. Contemporary Christians in this country need a way of thinking about humanity which accords with the results of the social and personality sciences which play such an important part in our culture. If a particular philosophical construct of the human contradicts what scientific investigations of the human teach us, then, quite correctly contemporary Americans usually refuse to take it seriously. I would hope, therefore, that adult Christians in this country would find an experiential approach to Jesus' humanity which I have sketched at least initially credible.

In the second and third volumes of this study I shall reflect on the four gospels in a way which will, I hope, assist converting adults to pray them. The new quest for the historical Jesus yields, however, only the "bare facts" about Jesus. Converting adults may well find only the bare facts spiritually thin broth by comparison with the gospels.

In my judgment, however, all contemporary converting adults need to acquaint themselves with the results of the new quests, if only in order to assure themselves of the solid historical roots of Christian faith. More-

---

83. Cf. Brown, *The Death of the Messiah*, II, pp. 1205-1283.

over, studying the new quests promises another significant pastoral benefit. It challenges people to deal with naive presuppositions and latent
fundamentalism in their approach to Jesus.[84]

Needless to say, anyone designing a series of Christological presenta-
tions for an RCIA group would have to decide how technical an understanding of these issues any particular individual may need. Those with
philosophical and scientific backgrounds may well profit from an exploration of the technicalities of the preceding discussion in considerable
detail. Others might find the results of the preceding discussion helpful
without going very deeply into the philosophical, scientific, and methodological implications of thinking about Jesus as a finite, developing, human experience. A thorough theological grounding of the RCIA, however, has to take into account the learning needs of both kinds of people.

Moreover, a sound catechesis needs to address every dimension of conversion. It must therefore challenge people to intellectual conversion in
religious matters. Christians need to love God not only with all their
hearts but also with all their minds. That means that both foundational
Christology and the catechesis it inspires need to deal with the speculative issues which Christology raises. Those who conduct the RCIA need,
therefore, to educate themselves to those issues if they desire to avoid
disseminating a fundamentalistic piety or doctrinal error.

Conclusion

I would hope, therefore, in the preceding chapters to have laid speculative foundations for a sound Jesusology. I shall reflect on doctrinal
Christology in the third volume of this study. At that point I shall return
to the issues discussed in this section; for in dealing with Christological
doctrine one must, as we have seen, give an account, not only of Jesus'
humanity but of His divinity and of the relationship between the two in
His person.

One cannot, however, deal adequately with these doctrinal issues until
one has examined the Christian experience of the paschal mystery. To
that experience and to the ways in which it grounds Christological knowing I shall turn in the section which follows.

---

84. Cf. James T. Dillon, "The Historical Character of Jesus and Its Pedagogic Uses,"
Journal of Christian Education, 73(April, 1982), pp. 44-45.

Chapter 11
The Dynamic Shape of Christian Hope

So far, in my constructive attempt to understand the humanity of Jesus I have not engaged in Christological thinking as such. A speculative account of Jesus' humanity which prescinds from His divinity and from the relationship between divinity and humanity in Jesus yields a Jesusology, not a Christology as such. Unfortunately, many so called "low Christologies" never really advance beyond Jesusology. Not only do they fail to develop a philosophically adequate and scientifically plausible account of Jesus' humanity; but, as we have seen, they too often end by portraying Jesus as the most perfectly redeemed of all creatures. In other words, not only do they reduce Christology fallaciously to Jesusology; but they also confuse Christology with Mariology. Mariology gave systematic expression to popular Marian piety by portraying Mary, the mother of Jesus, not Jesus Himself, as the most perfectly redeemed of all creatures.

The time has come to abandon Jesusology for Christological thinking as such. One advances beyond Jesusology as soon as one begins to reflect on Christian faith in the light of the paschal mystery. The experience of the paschal mystery transformed the way in which Jesus' disciples perceived His person and mission. It also inspired their calling Him "Lord (*Adonai*)."

The foundational Christology which I am defending rests on a metaphysics of experience. That metaphysics requires that one approach every Christological question experientially, including the question of Jesus' divinity. In what follows, therefore, I shall probe the kinds of experiences which led the first Christians to proclaim as divine Jesus, the failed prophet from Nazareth, whom Pontius Pilate crucified as a criminal and a subversive. Since faith in the divinity of Jesus rooted itself initially in the paschal mystery, in the encounter with the crucified and risen Christ, I shall examine what the New Testament witness has to tell us about that encounter.

In probing the experiential shape of the Paschal mystery, the kerygmatic Christology of Paul the apostle holds a privileged place. Paul stands out from other New Testament theologians of the Paschal mystery in two important ways.

1) Paul personally saw the risen Christ. If one accepts the first letter of Peter as authentic, then it too counts as a document written by someone who saw the risen Christ. Not all exegetes, of course, endorse first Peter's authenticity. Even if one defends its authenticity, however, Peter's letter differs from Paul's epistles in that it fails to discourse extensively about the meaning of resurrection.

2) Paul stands out among New Testament writers precisely because he not only saw the risen Christ but also in several of his letters reflected in considerable detail about the theological significance of Jesus' resurrection. One cannot, of course, assume that everything which Paul has to say about the risen Christ directly describes His encounter with the glorified Jesus. On the other hand, one can argue plausibly that a Pauline theology of resurrection would not have directly contradicted that encounter. Certainly, I, for one, find it inherently improbable that, on so central and important a topic, one for which Paul suffered horribly and eventually gave his life, the apostle would have set out deliberately to deceive those to whom he preached.

In other words, we have good reason to believe that what Paul has to say about Jesus' resurrection at least does not contradict the apostle's experience of the risen Christ. Even more, we have good reason to believe that what Paul has to say about Jesus' resurrection in some way reflects the apostle's personal encounter with the risen Jesus. As a consequence, Paul's testimony to the resurrection promises to yield a significant insight into both the experience and the significance of Jesus' resurrection.

In examining Pauline kerygmatic Christology, I shall attempt to take into account the results of contemporary Pauline exegesis. Foundational theology, however, approaches the texts of the New Testament in a specific theological context. It ponders those texts for the light which they throw on a Christian conversion experience. The way in which one chooses to interpret the forms and dynamics of Christian conversion provides any given foundational Christology with its basic presuppositions. As a consequence, before I begin to examine Pauline Christology for the insight it yields into the experience of the Paschal mystery, I shall recall those dynamics of a Christian conversion experience which Pauline Christology especially illumines.

In what follows I shall argue that Paul developed an eschatological Christology of hope. Before one examines that Christology, therefore, one needs to understand how the experience of conversion gives rise to Christian hope. Understanding this complex dimension of Christian conversion creates a speculative context within which to integrate Paul's account of the paschal mystery.

By "Christological hope" I mean a religious hope which roots itself in the entire paschal mystery: namely, in the death and resurrection of Jesus and in His mission of the Holy Breath. A foundational account of Christian hope reflects, therefore, on how commitment in justifying faith to the realities revealed in the paschal mystery transforms human hope.

In this and subsequent chapters I shall argue eight foundational theses concerning Paul's kerygmatic Christology of hope. I shall devote one chapter to each thesis.

1) This chapter examines the ways in which commitment to the risen Christ transvalues natural human hopes. It provides an experiential, foundational context for a Pauline Christology of hope. In the present chapter I shall argue the following thesis: *Christological hope heals, perfects, and elevates natural and sinful human hopes.*

2) Chapter twelve begins to examine Paul's theology of the paschal mystery. This chapter probes the experiential foundations of Paul's "gospel," of his special way of proclaiming Christ. Here I shall examine some of the more obvious linguistic strategies which Paul employs for asserting the divinity of Jesus. I shall relate those strategies to Paul's encounter with the glorified Jesus. Chapter twelve, then, argues the following thesis: *Christological hope roots itself in the fact that in His resurrection, Jesus stands revealed as a "life-giving Breath."*

3) Chapter thirteen completes Paul's vision of the paschal mystery by examining the apostle's understanding of the saving power of Jesus' death. It attempts to show that for Paul the death of Jesus and His resurrection function as reverse sides of the same saving eschatological event. Chapter thirteen argues the following thesis: *Because on the cross Jesus died to sin, Christological hope roots itself in moral conformity to Him in the power of His Breath.*

4) Chapter fourteen begins to explore in greater detail the practical, saving consequences of the paschal mystery. It examines Paul's proclamation of Jesus as the last Adam. That proclamation insists on the universal scope of the salvation which the risen Christ brings. In the process, chapter fourteen invokes pragmatic logic in order to clarify the theses presented in chapters twelve and thirteen. Chapter fourteen argues the following thesis: *Christological hope roots itself in the fact that in Jesus God has revealed His desire to save all people through the paschal mystery.*

5) Chapter fifteen reflects on the apostle's testimony to the reality of the resurrection and to the fact that it transformed the whole of Jesus' humanity. This chapter expands an understanding of the consequences of Jesus' saving death, resurrection, and mission of the Breath by showing that it encompasses physical creation. In this section I propose the following foundational thesis: *Christological hope roots itself in the double fact that Jesus' resurrection transformed Him totally, even in the physical dimension of His humanity and that resurrection in His image therefore promises to transform in a similar manner those who believe in Him.*

6) Chapter sixteen deals with Paul's doctrine of the Christian community as the body of Christ. The argument of this chapter further explicitates, therefore, the physical consequences of the resurrection, since Paul, in portraying the Christian community as the risen Christ's body, is asserting that through the action of the charism-dispensing Breath, the risen Christ acts through the Christian community in order to extend the practical saving consequences of the resurrection to the rest of the physical universe. I shall first examine the origins of Paul's theological perception of the Christian community as the body of Christ. Then I shall reflect on the ways in which the letters to the Colossians and to the Ephesians deepen and expand this aspect of Pauline Christological teaching. Chapter sixteen argues the following thesis: *Christological hope roots itself in the present experience of the saving, charismatic activity of the risen Christ's Breath in the Christian community, because that activity transforms the Church into Christ's instrument for advancing a universal, even cosmic, salvation.*

7) Chapter seventeen probes the eschatological context of Pauline Christology. It will serve as a transition to the last two chapters of this volume. They examine the apocalyptic Christology of the book of Revelation. Apocalyptic Christology, as we shall see, expresses Christian hope as it confronts the principalities and powers of this world. In what concerns Pauline apocalyptic Christology, chapter seventeen argues the following thesis: *Christological hope expresses itself in the fact that those whom the risen Christ is in process of saving through the action of His Breath yearn for His second coming as the vindication of their present commitment to Him and as the final, full realization of their union with Christ in God.*

8) Chapter eighteen summarizes the results of this foundational analysis of a Pauline Christology of hope and relates it to the graced transformation of human hopes described in this chapter. Chapter eighteen examines how the kind of Christological hope which Paul describes heals, perfects, and elevates natural and sinful human hopes. It argues the following thesis: *A sound understanding of the Christological dimensions of hope makes it clear that foundational Christology reflects on a unique kind of knowing: namely, the knowledge of Jesus Christ which results from practical assimilation to Him in faith through the power of His Breath.*

This eleventh chapter divides into two parts. The first part recalls the two dynamics which Christian conversion contributes to the total process of conversion. The second part describes the way in which these two dynamics effect the graced transformation of natural and sinful human hopes.

(I)

This chapter argues the following thesis: *Christological hope heals, perfects, and elevates natural and sinful human hopes.* Proving this thesis requires that one understand how it relates to the construct of experience and to the model of conversion developed in chapter five. In chapter five I presented the philosophical construct of humanity which this study endorses. I argued that one can legitimately understand humanity as a developing, environmentally rooted, social experience. I also suggested that only a realistic, triadic philosophical construct of experience can take into account both the social and religious dimensions of religious experience.

In the course of reflecting on human religious experience, I described in an extremely schematic and preliminary way five forms of conversion: affective conversion, intellectual conversion, religious conversion, personal moral conversion, and socio-political conversion. I also identified seven dynamics and counterdynamics within the conversion process.

This chapter focuses on a specific aspect of a Christian conversion: namely, on the life-long growth in Christian hope. I take this focus because it promises to provide a necessary experiential context for understanding a Pauline Christology of hope. In order to understand how Christian hope grows and develops, however, one must first reflect in greater detail on the two dynamics which Christian conversion contributes to the total process of conversion.

By a dynamic of conversion I mean the way in which different forms of conversion condition one another in positive ways within the total process of conversion. Christian conversion contributes two dynamics to the conversion process: 1) Christian conversion mediates between affective conversion, on the one hand, and the two forms of moral conversion: personal and socio-political, on the other. 2) Christian conversion transvalues the other four forms of conversion. The first of these two dynamics grounds the experience of initial conversion. The second grounds the experience of ongoing conversion.

As we have seen, Christian conversion begins in the heart and culminates in a moral commitment rooted in faith. Christian conversion begins in the heart because it demands that humans face and bring to repentance before God all the emotional obstacles to living a life of faith in the God revealed by Jesus and by His indwelling Breath.

Under ordinary circumstances, repressed negative emotions pose the greatest obstacles to religious commitment. Shame teaches us humans to despise ourselves and convinces us that no one, not even God, can love us. Fear and anxiety make us cringe and avoid the sacrifices which faith in God demands. Rage at the hypocrisy of self-styled believers or at injustices in the Church alienates us from God and from any community which professes to believe in God. Guilt suffuses the encounter with God with terror of divine retribution.

Until we face these emotional obstacles to faith and bring them to some measure of conscious healing, we humans find it difficult, even impossible to convert. Affective conversion, as we have seen, seeks to heal disordered emotions through any created means available. Natural conversion remains, however, untouched by religious transcendence. Christian conversion, therefore, creates a new context for converting affectively, a context of transcendent, justifying religious faith. Christian converts must reach emotional honesty with themselves before God. Emotional self-confrontation before God transforms affective conversion into repentance.

The healing of negative emotions allows the positive emotions—like love, friendship, affection, appreciation, sympathy—much fuller play. The liberation of the positive affections enhances the human capacity for aesthetic experience. We have an aesthetic experience when we perceive the excellence inherent in persons and things as beautiful. An aesthetic response to the excellence incarnate in Jesus and in people whose lives resemble His exercises a spontaneous attraction over the human heart. That attraction motivates the consent of justifying faith.

Commitment in faith to Jesus demands as its consequence commitment to a life of discipleship. The disciples of Jesus accept the reign of God which He proclaimed and submit to the moral conditions of life in God's kingdom. That commitment transforms the human conscience. It endows it with faith-derived norms for making moral judgments in the interrelated realms of personal and public morality.

As an ethics of discipleship transforms personal moral conversion and the conduct which it inspires, discipleship teaches the conscience to embrace a life of Christian charity. As an ethics of discipleship transforms socio-political conversion, practical faith transforms the practice of public morality into the Christian search for a just social order. Finally, the charism of discernment changes the way in which the human conscience functions by transforming natural prudence into the gift of discernment.

Initial conversion, moreover, gives rise to a global commitment of faith which opens every aspect of human experience to the transforming action of the divine Breath. Foundational theology calls such a faith commitment justifying faith because it conforms the Christian conscience and the Christian conduct which flows from judgments of conscience to the divine will incarnate in Jesus. Initial conversion grounds and makes possible the experience of ongoing conversion; for commitment in faith to Christ claims one entirely: heart; mind; conscience; as well as public, institutional relationships. It demands that all these dimensions of the self conform to the demands of life in God's kingdom.

The second dynamic of Christian conversion requires the ongoing transformation and transvaluation of all the other kinds of conversion. One transvalues something when, having perceived it in one frame of reference, one begins to understand it in a new frame of reference which endows it with novel connotations and consequences. Commitment in faith to the divine realities revealed in the paschal mystery provides the context for transvaluing in faith affective, intellectual, personal moral, and socio-political conversion.

When over the course of a lifetime justifying Christological faith transvalues human affective perceptions of the future, it infuses into the heart the supernatural virtue of hope. When that same justifying faith transvalues the intuitive and inferential perceptions of reality which intellectual conversion validates, then Christological faith effects the ongoing infusion of the supernatural virtue of faith. When Christological faith transvalues the prudential deliberations of the conscience about personal rights and duties, then justifying Christological faith infuses progressively the supernatural virtue of charity. When Christological faith transvalues the responsible human search for a just social order, then that same faith transforms natural justice into the graced establishment of the kingdom of God on earth.

In subsequent volumes, I shall reflect on the relationship between Christological faith and the Christian cultivation of the theological virtues of faith and of charity together with the Christian search for institutional justice. The final section of the present volume focuses on Christian hope and examines its relationship to Christological commitment. The section which follows describes in a preliminary way the infusion of Christian hope which results from the ongoing transformation of human affectivity by a global, justifying commitment of faith.

(II)

As Christian conversion transforms affective conversion, it transvalues both human emotions and the human imagination. Image and affect interplay constantly in the course of human emotional development. When image and affect conceive a desirable future, that perception qualifies as hope.

Natural hopes respond in necessary and legitimate ways to the excellence and good capable of embodiment in finite, created realities; but natural hopes prescind completely from the historical self-revelation of God. They remain narrowly concerned only with the future realization of some created good. I may for example hope for a good job, for a hot meal, for a scholarship to school, for a society without violence, for a chance to develop my human gifts and talents. When one hopes naturally, one ambitions through dint of personal effort transforming some finite, created possibility into a reality.

Initial conversion teaches one to view all these perfectly legitimate human hopes in the light of the gospel. In the process, an initial Christian conversion endows natural aspirations with new meaning, with new connotations by opening human hope to transcendent divine realities. In other words, an initial Christian conversion inaugurates the ongoing transvaluation in faith of natural human hopes. This life-long process of transvaluation corresponds to what an earlier theology called the infusion of the supernatural virtue of hope.

In reflecting on the dynamic shape of human experience, I argued in chapter five for the radical finitude of all human perceptions and evaluations. Affective perceptions exhibit the same kind of finitude. When we focus our finite, natural, affective perceptions of the future, we hope.

The finitude of human hope circumscribes its scope. We hope good things spontaneously for ourselves, our families, our friends; but those who lie outside the immediate ambit of day-to-day living quickly fade from interest. Whatever hopes the human heart may have for humanity as a whole, if indeed it experiences such hopes, rarely advance beyond day-dreams or futile velleities.

The finitude of human experience affects natural hopes in other ways. All human hope roots itself in human affectivity; but all human affectivity exhibits neurotic biases. In the early days of psychotherapy, clinical psychological theory regarded neurosis as a pathology. With time, however, the universal prevalence of neurosis—the fact that everybody responds neurotically—led clinical psychologists to strike neurosis from the list of emotional illnesses. Instead, they came to regard neurosis as natural and as endemic to the human condition.

Pathological or not, neurotic hopes do bend out of shape human aspirations for the future. Neurosis tends to transform natural human hopes into pipe dreams, as reality refuses persistently to conform to our neurotically skewed and unrealistic perceptions of the way in which it ought to behave. Even when we succeed in realizing our neurotic aspirations, we end by institutionalizing our own warped and often egocentric perceptions of the shape the world ought to exhibit.

Natural human hopes give rise to natural, human institutions which can and do manifest all the limitations and neurotic (even psychotic) biases of the psyches from which they proceed. Healthy hopes, of course, breed healthy and life-giving human institutions: healthy families, healthy communities, healthy work-places, healthy laws, a politics free of bigotry. Neurotic and psychotic human hopes, however, produce the opposite kinds of institution.

Affective conversion, for example, nurtures healthy family relationships, but its absence produces dysfunctional families crippled by addiction and marred by marital violence. The members of affectively converted communities can regulate their lives in ways which encourage ongoing emotional healing; but communities can also make tabu any attempt to deal corporately with neurotic prejudices and pathological bigotry. People can create work places which value and encourage the creativity and input of all laborers; but in the United States, given the passion of business to maximize profits, people often prefer to institutionalize greed, class inequality, and oppression. Our laws can serve the ends of justice; but too often they also serve the ends of racism, individualism, sexism, classism, militarism, anti-Semitism, homophobia, and corporate, captialistic greed. Moreover, long standing forms of institutional injustice spawn and inculcate faith in obfuscating ideologies which rationalize the inevitability of human oppression. Institutionalized, ideological lying also skews human hope. The real problem of truth in contemporary society arises not so much from the possibility of human error as from lies systematically inculcated and popularized through the malicious manipulation of the media.

The theological virtue of hope seeks to heal, perfect, and elevate natural human hopes. Christian hope elevates natural human hope by focusing it on the God revealed in Jesus Christ and in the divine Breath who proceeds from Him.

Christian hope heals natural hopes by bringing them to repentant confrontation in faith and by opening the disorders of the human heart to the healing influence of God's sanctifying Breath. Christian hope perfects human hope by universalizing it, by teaching the human heart to expand to include all those whom God loves. The love of God revealed in Christ, however, excludes no one, embraces all, especially the poor, the marginal, the suffering, the sinner, the heretic, the socially expendable.

Moreover, Christian hope teaches the human heart to yearn for a world which incarnates only healthy, life-giving aspirations and goals. Christian hope, therefore, pits the human heart against all institutional embodiments of neurosis, psychosis, and injustice. It also dedicates one to eradicating the lies which rationalize sick and destructive social institutions.

Left to itself, the human heart yearns for created realities. The saving intervention of God in human history, however, creates the possibility of a future filled with realities which transcend anything which mere created nature can accomplish. In Christ, God reveals His desire to enter into a relationship of loving union with His creatures. The gift of His Breath begins to effect that union. By revealing Himself to us in Christ God transforms Himself into the saving future of the human race. Natural hope, then, perceives the future as an inefficacious possibility, either alluring or threatening. Christian hope perceives the future as a transforming divine reality.

Christian hope therefore elevates natural hopes by focusing them on supernatural realities and possibilities. One relates to the world-transcending reality of God supernaturally when one responds to His historical self-revelation and gratuitous self-communication to sinners on the terms which that revelation and self-communication demand. Since God freely and gratuitously creates any supernatural relationship through His free, gratuitous, saving interventions in human history, in all such relationships God holds and maintains the initiative. Any saving divine initiative demands a response from those it touches. That response must conform to God's saving purposes.

Natural hopes express the finitude of the human heart. Left to itself, the human heart can long for limited goods for itself and for others. Christian hope perfects human hope by universalizing it. It teaches the human heart to yearn for the good of all people and for a universe healed of all sin and injustice. In universalizing human hope, Christian hope perfects it. We become more perfectly human when our hopes exclude no other person, when they aspire after the day when the entire human family will find itself reconciled and unified in God. Human hope becomes more perfectly human too when it acknowledges the inherent excellence of all created things and when it longs for a world purified of all injustice, exploitation, and division.

The graced perfecting of human hope presupposes personal openness to the reality of God. Christian commitment demands such openness; but genuine religious openness to the saving action of God can occur in other religious contexts. So can the graced perfecting of human aspirations. Buddhism, for example, inculcates a compassionate hope for all created things.

Longing for universal reconciliation can, of course, take on a utopian character. The reality of the cross, however, endows Christian hope with a sober realism. While authentic Christian hope yearns for an end to sin and suffering, it never closes its eyes to the perennial tragedy of the human condition. Rather that tragedy anchors Christian hope in God as the only savior and as the ultimate perfecter of our hopes.

Christian hope becomes Christological hope when one focuses on the ways in which commitment to Jesus Christ in justifying faith informs and motivates such hope. In the following chapters I shall begin to explore in greater detail the Christological dimensions of the theological virtue of hope. As we shall see, Christological hope responds to the creative and saving possibilities revealed in the paschal mystery, in the death and resurrection of Jesus, and in His sending of the Holy Breath.

If Christological faith transvalues natural hopes, then, *a fortiori* it also has the power to heal, perfect, and elevate sinful hopes as well. Sinful hopes focus the heart on evils which contradict the will of God. Initial and ongoing repentance brings sinful hopes to healing. As the heart learns to appropriate Jesus' own aspirations, hope for the kingdom perfects and universalizes sinful hopes, while hope in the resurrection, in perfect and total transformation in God after death, elevates them.

This chapter has sketched a foundational account of Christian hope. In the chapter which follows, I shall begin to examine the foundational implications of a Pauline Christology of hope.

Chapter 12
A Life-Giving Breath

In the preceding chapter I suggested a foundational context for approaching a Pauline kerygmatic Christology of hope. In this and in subsequent chapters I shall present aspects of that Christology. Finally, in chapter eighteen I shall reflect on the ways in which Paul's Christological insights continue to transvalue contemporary Christian hope.

I have characterized Pauline kerygmatic Christology as a Christology of hope. The term "kerygmatic" needs little justification. The term "kerygmatic" designates the apostles' proclamation of the risen Christ; and that Pauline Christology surely does. Paul develops His Christological insights in the course of proclaiming the risen Christ to those to whom he writes. The phrase "Christology of hope" may, however, need some arguing.

In my judgment, the eschatological and apocalyptic flavor of Pauline Christology justifies calling it a "Christology of hope." As we shall see in volume two, narrative Christology reinterprets the entire ministry of Jesus in the light of the paschal mystery. The surviving Pauline letters, which alone give one contemporary access to the apostle's thought, display little concern with Jesus' mortal ministry. Instead, Paul's proclamation of the risen Christ concentrates on the paschal mystery itself. That concentration gives Pauline Christology its eschatological and apocalyptic tone. Paul discourses at some length on Jesus' death on the cross; but he does so because it sees Jesus' death and resurrection as reverse sides of one and the same revelatory mystery. Together they establish the eschaton, the last age of salvation; and the eschaton makes the saving future a present divine reality. Because Pauline Christology focuses rhetorically on the paschal mystery as the privileged, eschatological moment for understanding the saving reality of Jesus Christ and because the salvation which the paschal mystery initiates engages the present but lies ultimately in the future, Pauline Christology discourses at length about how the death and resurrection of Jesus have in fact reoriented human history to a completely new, transcendent future. In this complex sense, then, Paul's Christology does qualify as primarily a Christology of hope.[1]

Pauline Christology deals, of course, with doctrinal issues, but primarily with beliefs about the eschaton. Eschatological, Christian hope engages doctrine, moreover, because it perceives the future, not just as an alluring or threatening possibility, but as the transforming reality of the

1. Cf. Wolfgang Weiss, "Glaube-Liebe-Hoffnung. Zu der Trias bei Paulus," *Zeitschrift für die Neutestamentliche Wissenschaft*, 84(1993), pp. 196-217.

Breath of Christ drawing those who believe deeper and deeper into the mystery of God.

In this chapter, I shall argue the following thesis: *Christological hope roots itself in the fact that in His resurrection, Jesus stands revealed as a "life-giving Breath."* The argument divides into five parts.

Part one examines the divine origin of Paul's ministry. Part two explains Paul's identification of the risen Christ with the Breath who proceeds from Him in 1 Cor 15:45. Parts three, four, and five reflect on passages in other Pauline letters which make analogous assertions. The relevant passages occur in second Corinthians, in Philippians, and in Romans.

(I)

In approaching the letters of Paul the apostle, contemporary Christians need to remind themselves that Paul did not develop his theology in the systematic way in which some contemporary speculative theologians do. One finds a remarkable coherence in Paul's religious vision; but the apostle's few surviving letters suggest that his theology developed situationally and pastorally rather than systematically. Indeed, Paul seems to have distrusted the systematizing tendencies of pagan philosophers. (1 Cor 1:17-2:16)

In the course of his letters, however, Paul did reflect extensively on the mystery of Christ. In what follows, therefore, I shall trace through some of the themes which lend coherence to the apostle's Christological reflections. Instead of trying to force Paul's thought into some pre-conceived Christological scheme, however, I shall attempt to stay close to the argument and context of each of his letters.[2]

The term "apostle (*apostolos*)" means an official representative, one sent with authorization to speak in the name of another person. In alluding to his apostolic commissioning to bear witness to the risen Christ, Paul habitually ascribes the source of His commissioning to the Father and to Jesus.[3] (1 Cor 1:1; 2 Cor 1:1; cf. Eph 1:1-2; Col 1:1-2)

---

2. Cf. Jouette M. Bassler, "Paul's Theology: Whence and Whither? A Synthesis (of sorts) of the Theology of Philemon, 1 Thessalonians, Philippians, Galatians, and 1 Corinthians" in *SBL Seminar Papers*, edited by David J. Lull (Atlanta, GA: Scholars Press, 1989), pp. 412-423.

3. Cf. Simon Legasse, *Paul apôtre* (Paris: Editions du Cerf, 1991); Sherman E. Johnson, *Paul the Apostle and His Cities* (Wilmington, DL: Michael Glazier, 1987); Philip A. Cunningham, *The Jewish Apostle to the Gentiles: Paul as He Saw Himself* (Mystic CT: Twenty-Third Publications, 1986); Günther Bornkamm, *Paulus* (Stuttgart: Verlag W. Kohlhammer, 1970); Jürgen Becker, *Paul, Apostle to the Gentiles* translated by O.C. Dean, Jr. (Louisville, KY: Westminster, 1993); Lucas Grollenberg, *Paul* (London: SCM Press, 1978); Richard Longeneker, *The Ministry and Message of Paul* (Grand Rapids, MI: Zondervan, 1971); Alan Segal, *Paul the Convert: The Apostolate and Apostasy of Saul the Pharisee* (New Haven, CT: Yale University Press, 1990). For a review of recent Pauline studies, see: Noel Aletti, S.J., "Bulletin d'exegèse du Nouveau Testament: Bulletin Paulinien," *Recherches de Science Religieuse*, 81(1993), pp. 275-298.

On occasion Paul refers ironically to his apostolic commissioning as a type of slavery (Rom 1:1; Phil 1:1-2); but this metaphorical allusion only underscores through understatement the apostle's authority to speak in the name of the risen Jesus. In calling himself a "slave of Jesus Christ (*doulos Christou Iêsou*)" Paul assimilates himself to great Hebrew leaders whom the Old Testament called the "slaves of Yahweh." (Ps 27:9, 31:17, 89:51; 2 Kngs 18:12; Judg 2:8; Ps 105:42) In other words, the title uses ironic understatement in order to assert that as an apostle Paul has special leadership responsibilities. At the same time, it reminds both the apostle and his community that true leadership incarnates service to all, especially to the smallest and neediest. The title "slave of Jesus Christ" also contains other ironies; for it connotes the unique freedom which comes from knowing Christ Jesus.[4] (Gal 5:13-15; 1 Cor 7:22-4)

In the epilogue to Romans, Paul describes his apostolic ministry as priestly. He calls himself "a cultic minister (*leitourgos*) of Christ Jesus to the Gentiles, serving as a priest (*hieorourgounta*) of the gospel of God, so that the offering of the Gentiles may be acceptable, sanctified by the Holy Breath." (Rom 15:15-16) Paul conceived his apostolic ministry primarily as proclamation rather than as cultic leadership (1 Cor 1:14-17) Here, therefore, he applies cultic terminology metaphorically to his kerygmatic ministry of announcing the good news.

In doing so, however, Paul places the proclamation of the gospel on a par with a formal act of divine worship. His apostolic vocation has all the sacredness of the levitical priest who serves in the temple of God. Instead of leading a ritual sacrifice, however, Paul through the action of the Holy Breath, transforms those who listen to his message into a living sacrifice to God. The obedience of faith accomplishes efficaciously what temple sacrifices only symbolize ritually, namely, the reconciliation of sinners to God. In so speaking, however, Paul proclaims, not his own accomplishments, but the work which Christ has accomplished through Him in converting the pagans.[5] (Rom 15:17-8)

Without a doubt, then, Paul regarded his apostolic witness to the risen Christ as a sacred responsibility. In the letter to the Romans, he describes his apostolic ministry as an act of worship which springs from the center of his very self (*ho latreuo en tô pneumati mou*). (Rom 1:9) Similarly, in the first letter to the Corinthians, Paul describes those who proclaim the gospel, himself included, as "stewards (*oikonomoi*)" of divine mysteries. (1 Cor 4:1)

---

4. Cf. Brian J. Dodd, "Christ's Slave, People Pleasers, and Galatians," *Zeitschrift für die Neutestamentlische Wissenschaft*, 42(1996), pp. 90-104.
5. Cf. *New Jerome Biblical Commentary*, edited by Raymond Brown, Joseph A. Fitzmyer, and Roland Murphy (Englewood Cliffs, NJ: Prentice Hall, 1990), 51:128. In subsequent references I shall refer to this edition as *NJBC*.

In the letter to the Galatians, Paul insists not only on the divine origin of his mission but also on the divine origin of the message which he proclaims. The letter to the Galatians finds Paul in open, even bitter, conflict with the extreme right wing in the apostolic Church, namely, with those who held that Gentile Christians had to submit not only to baptism but to circumcision as well.[6]

In that context, Paul's salutation in Galatians once again vindicates the divine origin of his apostolic authority. Paul holds his right to speak as an apostle "not from humans nor through any human but through Jesus Christ and God the Father who raised Him from the dead." (Gal 1:1)

In the preceding text, Paul opposes the entire human race both individually and collectively to Jesus Christ and God the Father, an opposition all the more striking in that Paul in no way denies the humanity of Jesus. In Romans, that humanity makes Jesus superior to all sub-human creation (Rom 8:18-19); but, in second Thessalonians, Paul portrays Jesus as superior to angelic principalities and powers, a prerogative proper to God alone. (2 Th 1:7; Gal 4:1-7; 1 Cor 6:3; Rom 8:38) Here, in the first verse of Galatians, in opposing Jesus to humans both individually and collectively, Paul locates Him in the same divine realm which the Father occupies. In other words, Paul's divine apostolic commissioning flows simultaneously from God the Father and from Jesus Christ as from a single, conjoined, divine source. Moreover, Paul alludes in this same verse to the resurrection of Jesus as that event which reveals that He, Jesus, shares a divine authority on a par with the Father. As we shall see, Paul

---

6. The apostolic Church divided into four factions. They disagreed about the role of Gentile Christians in the new Israel which Jesus had begun. The most conservative group, represented by James and other members of the Jerusalem community, advocated full observance of the Mosaic Law for all Christians.

   To the left of this faction but still to the right of center stood "Petrine" Christians, who did not require Gentiles to submit to circumcision but did demand that they keep some Jewish observances. They insisted especially on Gentile observance of certain dietary laws. In the Petrine churches, Gentile Christians occupied much the same position as "God-fearing" Gentiles who converted to Judaism.

   Paul stood to the left of center in the apostolic Church. Paul held that baptism and faith in Jesus sufficed to make one a Christian, that Gentile Christians ought not to submit to circumcision, and that they need not observe Jewish dietary laws. Paul, however, recognized abiding revelatory significance in the divine election of the Jewish people. Paul, moreover, seems to have believed that anyone who underwent circumcision accepted the responsibility of abiding by the demands of Torah piety.

   Hellenizing Christians occupied the left-wing in the apostolic Church. They saw no abiding significance in Jewish cults and feasts and believed that faith in Jesus and in the paschal mystery had replaced all that. The letter to the Hebrews and the fourth gospel express this strain in early Christian thinking. Cf. Raymond E. Brown and John P. Meier, *Antioch and Rome: New Testament Cradles of Catholic Christianity* (New York, NY: Paulist, 1983)

will use other rhetorical strategies as well in order to situate the risen Christ in the realm of the divine.

Paul further authenticates the divine source of his apostolic authority by appealing to the divine origin and sanction of the very message he preaches. Paul's gospel has "no human origin (*ouk estin kata anthrôpon*)." Paul received it "not from a human (*oude....para anthrôpou*)" but directly "through a revelation of Jesus Christ (*di' apocalypseôs Iêsou Christou*)." (Gal 1:11-2) The revelation of which Paul speaks has Jesus Christ as both its source and its content.

A contemporary of Jesus, Paul probably never met face to face the prophet from Nazareth. Paul the convert had to learn from others details of Jesus' life. Here, however, he insists that he derives both the authority and the basic content of the gospel he preaches directly from a revelation of Jesus Christ. (Acts 9:1-9) While the revelation to which Paul alludes could include other religious experiences besides his personal encounter with the risen Christ, it certainly includes that encounter. Indeed, Paul insists in first Corinthians that without the risen Christ everything else he might say crumbles into vanity and futility. (1 Cor 15:1-18) When read in context, Paul's phrase in Galatians, "a revelation of Jesus Christ," also implicitly refers to the fact that the Father "raised" Jesus "from the dead." (Cf. Gal 1:1)

In tracing his message to the risen Christ whom he had encountered personally, Paul supplies an important hermeneutical key for understanding why his Christology roots itself so centrally in the paschal mystery. Paul is claiming that, whatever else he may teach, all his most fundamental Christological insights derive so directly and immediately from the his personal encounter with the risen Christ that he needs no other human to teach them to him. In the risen Jesus, God has revealed to Paul personally and directly the gospel which the apostle proclaims.[7]

Moreover, as the letter to the Galatians unfolds, Paul testifies eloquently to the difference which the encounter with the risen Jesus made in his relationship to God. He insists that the encounter transformed Him from a self-righteous Pharisee, single-mindedly dedicated to strict observance of the Law and to the persecution of Christian heretics, into a disciple of Jesus Christ and into an apostle consecrated to proclaiming the good news of the resurrection to others. (Gal 1:13-17) One finds similar testimonies in other Pauline letters. (1 Cor 15:1-19; 2 Cor 5:16-21, 11:21-29) From a faith rooted in Torah Paul passed to a faith rooted in the person of

---

7. Cf. Joseph Plevnik, "The Center of Pauline Theology," *Catholic Biblical Quarterly*, 51(1989), pp. 461-478; Scott Gambril Sinclair, *Jesus Christ According to Paul* (Berkeley, CA: Bibal Press, 1988); Wolfgang Schrage, "Der gekreuzigte und aufweckte Herr: Zur *theologia crucis* und *theologia resurrectionis* bei Paulus," *Zeitschrift für Theologie und Kirche*, 94(1997), pp. 25-38.

Jesus. From religious self-righteousness, Paul came to experience a righteousness rooted in the free gift of divine grace made to Him in and through the knowledge of Christ and of His resurrection.[8] (Phil 3:2-11)

How then did the apostle Paul experience the risen Christ? To this question I turn in the section which follows.

(II)

The first letter to the Corinthians contains perhaps, Paul's most sustained reflection on the saving significance of Jesus' resurrection.

Jesus' Resurrection Appearances

Paul's reflections on the meaning of resurrection in first Corinthians occur in a specific pastoral context. Some members of the Corinthian community called into question the possibility of bodily resurrection. Paul chides the Corinthians for their doubts and reminds them that faith in Jesus' resurrection lies at the heart of the shared faith of all Christians. Indeed, Jesus' resurrection provides the kerygma with its central message:

> For I delivered to you as of first importance that Christ died for our sins in accordance with the scriptures and that He was buried and that He was raised on the third day in accordance with the scriptures and that He appeared (*ophthê*) to Cephas and then to the Twelve. (1 Cor 15:3-5)

In asserting that Christ died for our sins, Paul portrays Jesus' death as an atoning sacrifice which remits sin. I shall reflect in greater detail on the saving significance of Jesus' death in the next chapter.

In stating that Jesus died "according to the scriptures," Paul probably alludes to the last of the servant songs in third Isaiah, which describes the reconciling suffering and death of the servant of the Lord. (Is 53:1-10) Christ's burial underscores the reality of His death.

In proclaiming that Christ "was raised from the dead on the third day according to the scriptures," Paul alludes to Hos 6:2. In Hosea, the phrase

---

8. Cf. Joseph A. Fitzmyer, *To Advance the Gospel* (New York, NY: Crossroad, pp. 149-161; John William Beaudean, Jr. *Paul's Theology of Preaching* (Macon, GA: Mercer University Press, 1988). For the divine Breath's importance in empowerment for apostolic mission, see: P.J. Gräbe, "*Dynamis* (in the Sense of Power) As a Pneumatological Concept in the Main Pauline Letters," *Biblische Zeitschrift*, 36(1992), pp. 226-235. See also: Alberto Viciano, "Das Bild des Apostels Paulus im Kommentar zu dem Paulinischen Breifen des Theodoret von Kyros," *Zeitschrift für die Neutestamentliche Wissenschaft*, 83(1992), pp. 138-142; Victor Paul Furnish, "On Putting Paul in His Place," *Journal of Biblical Literature*, 113(1994), pp. 3-17; William O. Walker, Jr. "Why Paul Went to Jerusalem: The Interpretation of Galatians 2:1-5," *Catholic Biblical Quarterly*, 54(1992), pp. 503-510; Michael Winger, "Tradition, Revelation, and Gospel: A Study in Galatians," *Journal for the Study of the New Testament*, 53(1994), pp. 65-86.

"the third day" means "before long." Paul could mean "the third day" quite literally; but quite possibly he also regards "the third day" symbolically as the day of salvation.

The appearances of the risen Lord to selected witnesses revealed in an initial manner the transformation which the resurrection effected in Jesus. In stating that the risen one "appeared (*ophthê*)" Paul uses the passive voice. The risen Jesus "was seen" in an encounter. Paul thus portrays the resurrection experiences as the self-manifestation of the risen Jesus and hence as an event which happened to those who saw Him.

Paul clearly regards the appearances of the risen Christ which he catalogues as sufficiently authoritative to ground the Corinthians' shared belief in the resurrection. In drawing up the list, Paul parallels the Lord's inaugural appearance to Cephas with His final appearance to Paul himself. (1 Cor 15:5, 8; cf. Lk 24:34) Paul, moreover, regards the tardiness with which he joined the ranks of the apostles as a sign that he did not deserve that responsibility, since, before encountering the risen Christ, he had persecuted the Church of God.[9] (1 Cor 15:9; cf. Gal 1:15- 2:10; Eph 3:1-13)

Between Cephas, the apostle of the Jews, and himself, the apostle of the Gentiles (Gal 2:8), Paul lists numerous other witnesses to the risen Christ: the Twelve;[10] more than five hundred brethren who saw the Lord at the same time, many of whom still live, even as Paul writes; James, the head of the mother church in Jerusalem; and then all the apostles. (1 Cor 15:5-8) In the course of naming these members of the original apostolic college, Paul makes it clear that the risen Jesus appeared not just to individuals, like Paul, Cephas, and James, but also to entire groups, like the more than five hundred brethren who saw Him at once. In other words, the early Christian kerygma grounded faith in the risen Christ not just in individual encounter experiences but also in the shared encounter between groups of people and the risen Jesus.

In stating that Jesus appeared to "James, then all the apostles," Paul eases rhetorically the transition from resurrection encounters between Jesus and His own disciples, on the one hand, to His "untimely" appearance to Paul himself, on the other. Like Paul, James, "the brother of the Lord," (Gal 1:19) had not, apparently, numbered among Jesus' disciples prior to His death and resurrection. (Cf. Acts 1:21-2) Paul nevertheless includes

---

9. Cf. Jerome Murphy-O'Connor, O.P., "Tradition and Redaction in 1 Cor 15:3-7," *Catholic Biblical Quarterly*, 43(1981), pp. 582-589; Markus Schäfer, "Paulus, 'Fehlgeburt' oder 'unvernünftiges Kind': Eine Interpretation zu 1 Kor 15,8," *Zeitschrift für die Neutestamentliche Wissenschaft*, 85(1994), pp. 207-217.

10. Paul uses the symbolic phrase "the Twelve" to designate Jesus' most intimate companions, even though at the time of the resurrection appearances, they numbered only eleven: the original twelve, minus Judas. Paul's language suggests that "the Twelve" had through usage become a consecrated title among the disciples of Jesus.

himself among "the other apostles" who saw the risen Lord, although he leaves their actual number vague.

Paul supplies no dates for any of these apparitions, even though he modestly puts himself chronologically last and calls himself the least of the apostles. Paul, however, leaves no doubt whatever that he belongs to the privileged circle of apostolic witnesses whose personal encounter with the risen Jesus grounds and authenticates the official kerygma which they all proclaim. "Whether it was I or they, so we preach and so you believed." (1 Cor 15:11) Indeed, he claims (by the grace of God) to have worked harder in spreading the good news than any of the other apostles.[11] (1 Cor 15:8-11)

The Truth and Significance of Jesus' Resurrection

Having warned the Corinthians that their doubts about the resurrection contradict the shared faith of all other Christians, Paul next mounts a series of arguments to convince doubters of the kerygma's truth. In the course of elaborating his argument Paul paints a complex and dynamic picture of Jesus' resurrection.[12]

Paul clearly asserts that Jesus Himself rose, that He experienced the resurrection as a personal transformation. Christ has been raised. God has raised Him from the dead. (1 Cor 15:12-15, 20; cf. 1 Cor 15:3-5)

Christ rises from the dead, however, not simply as an individual but as "the first fruits of those who have fallen asleep." (1 Cor 15:20) Christ, therefore, rises from the dead in an utterly unique manner which distinguishes His resurrection from those whom He will raise on the last day, because Jesus' resurrection possesses a distinctive and unique efficacy. It begins the final eschatological age of the world, an age which the resurrection of "those who belong to Christ" will one day complete. Jesus' resurrection functions, therefore, as the efficacious cause and unique prototype of all other resurrections. (1 Cor 15:23)

---

11. Cf. William F. Orr and James Arthur Walther, *1 Corinthians* (New York, NY: Doubleday, 19760, pp.316-23; F.F. Bruce, *1 and 2 Corinthians* (London: Oliphants, 1971), pp. 137-45; Fredrik Willem Groscheide, *Commentary on the First Epistle to the Corinthians* (Grand Rapids, MI: Eerdmans, 1953), pp. 346-54; Lucien Cerfaux, *Christ in the Theology of St. Paul*, translated by Gregory Webb and Alan Walker (New York, NY: Herder and Herder, 1959), pp. 71-91; Martinus C. De Boer, "The Composition of 1 Corinthians," *New Testament Studies*, 40(1990), pp. 229-245..

12. For a discussion of the logic of Paul's argumentation, see: Theodor G. Bucher, "Die logische argumentation in 1. Korinther 15,12-20," *Biblica*, 55(1974), pp. 465-486; Michael Bachmann, " Zur Gedankenfürung in Kor. 15, 12 ff." *Theologische Zeitschrift*, 55(1978), pp. 265-276; Theodor G. Bucher, "Nochmals zur Beweisfürung in 1 Korinther 15, 12-20," *Theologische Zeitschrift*, 36(1980), pp. 129-152; Wolfgang Lehrage, "1 Korinther 15, 1-11" in *Resurrection du Christ et des Chretiens (1 Co 15)*, edited by Lorenzo De Lorenzi *et al.* (Rome: Abbaye de S. Paul, 1985), pp. 20-62.

The resurrection reveals Jesus Christ's universal dominion over all creation, a dominion which the Bible reserves for God alone. Jesus, however, exercises His universal dominion in submission to the Father. In
speaking of the Son's submission to the Father, Paul here as elsewhere
invokes dispensational categories of thought by deriving his understanding of the Son's relation to the Father from the story of Jesus' ministry
and, specifically, from Jesus' utter submission to the Father's will, even to
the point of accepting death on a cross. (Cf. Phil 2:8) Jesus' death in
obedience to the Father reveals that in all things the Son related obedi-
entially to the Father.

In raising Jesus from the dead, the Father subjects everything to Him,
except the Father's own personal reality. The Son of God can thus serve as
the Father's instrument for reconciling "all things" to the Father, in order
"that God may be all in all."[13] (1 Cor 15:27-28)

In His final coming, moreover, Christ will reveal the scope and might
of His universal dominion by "neutralizing every rule and every authority and every power," i.e., by rendering impotent every personal and institutional embodiment of violent coercion and oppression contrived by
the demonic rulers of this age. (1 Cor 15:24) As Walter Wink has shown,
Paul is referring to cosmic forces of sin, oppression, and death which find
incarnation in concrete institutions and individuals at the same time that
their reality transcends any single incarnation.[14]

Last of all, Christ on His return will destroy death itself. (1 Cor 15:26)
He will destroy death by raising the dead to imperishable life and by
changing perishable human bodies into imperishable, pneumatic bodies.
(1 Cor 15:51-7) In destroying death itself, Christ will also destroy sin,
death's "sting," and the Law, which gives sin its "power."[15] (1 Cor 15:55-57)
Sin gives death its sting, apparently, by causing us to die in a state of
separation and alienation from God, while the Law gives sin its power by
heightening our awareness of sin without conferring the pneumatic power
to resist it.[16]

13. Viewed in dispensational terms, the term "all things (*panta*)" would seem to include
not only the whole of creation but also the divine Breath who makes the risen Lord
vitally present within creation. (Cf. 1 Cor 15:45) Cf. Uta Heil, "Theo-logische Interpretation von 1 Kor 15, 23-28," *Zeitschrift für die Neutestamentliche Wissenschaft*,
84(1993), pp. 27-35.

14. Cf. Walter Wink, *Naming the Powers: The Language of Power in the New Testament*
(Philadelphia, PA: Fortress, 1984); Cerfaux, *op. cit.*, pp. 99-106; Jean Noel Aletti,
"L'Argumentation de Paul et la position de Corinthiens" in *Resurrection du Christe et
des Chrétiens (1 Co 15)*, pp. 63-97; Maurice Cany, "Resurrection et seigneurie du
Christ, 1 Co 15,23-28," *Ibid.*, pp. 127-169.

15. Cf. Wink, *op.cit.*, 50-55.

16. Cf. Cerfaux, *op. cit.*, pp. 106-131; F.W. Horn, "1 Korinthen 15.56—ein exegetischer
Stachel,"*Zeitschrift für die Neutestamentliche Wissenschaft*, 82(1991), pp. 88-105; Harm
W. Hollander, "The Meaning of the Term "Law (*nomos*) in 1 Corinthians," *Novum
Testamentum*, 40(1998), pp. 117-135.

The uniquely efficacious character of Christ's resurrection transforms Him into the last Adam, the saving head of a new human race. Through sin the first Adam bequeathed death to all his descendants; the resurrection of the last Adam begins the universal resurrection. "For as in Adam all die, so also in Christ shall all be made alive." (1 Cor 15:21-2) I shall return to this theme below when I reflect on the universal scope of the salvation effected through the paschal mystery.

Because of its universal saving efficacy, Jesus' resurrection transformed Him into the last Adam by making Him into a "life-giving Breath (*pneuma zôopoioun*)." (1 Cor 15:45) In calling the risen Jesus a "life-giving Breath," Paul is asserting many things:

a) Jesus' personal transformation in the Breath of God culminated in His resurrection because it transformed Him totally, making His physical body into a pneumatic body suited to His new imperishable and heavenly mode of existence. (1 Cor 15:47-48)

b) The verb "became (*êgeneto*)" in the phrase "the last Adam became a life-giving Breath," invokes dispensational language. Dispensational language describes Christian revelation as an historical process. The verb "became (*êgeneto*)," however, also asserts a vital identity between the risen Jesus and God's Breath: in rising Jesus came to share a vital identity with the Breath of God. The risen Christ, endowed with a new pneumatic body, lives henceforth with a divine pneumatic life. (1 Cor 15:45-48)

As we shall see in greater detail below, the last Adam contrasts wih the first Adam. Both enjoy a certain absoluteness. One cannot go beyond the first Adam in the sexual generation of psychic human life. One cannot go beyond the last Adam in the communication of transcendent pneumatic life because only the risen Jesus baptizes with the divine Breath. The last Adam thus begins the *eschaton*, the last age of salvation, in which God, through the gift of the Breath, becomes the future of all who believe.

c) In calling the risen Christ a "life-giving Breath," Paul is also asserting a functional identity between the risen Christ and the Breath of God. Wherever She acts, the risen Christ acts, since we receive Her as the overflowing and transforming superabundance of Christ's risen life. (1 Cor 15:45-48) Hence, the term "life-giving (*zôopoioun*)" designates the risen Jesus as the efficacious source of the Breath. The same term also alludes to the beneficiaries of the divine, risen life which flows from the last Adam: namely, to those baptized in the name of Jesus Christ. (Cf. 1 Cor 6:9)

The term "life-giving (*zôopoioun*)," therefore, also connotes all those saving actions which Paul attributes to the Breath of Christ: sanctification through growth in hope, faith and love (2 Th 2:13-5); putting on the mind of Christ (1 Cor 2:16; Phil 2:1-11; Gal 3:27; 4:7); charismatic empowerment (1 Cor 12:1-14:19); liberation, especially from the constraints of the Law (Gal 5:33; 1 Cor 7:22-4); participation in the resurrection of Christ (1 Cor 15:51-8; 2 Th 2:13-15; Phil 3:10); participation in the cross of Christ and in His final eschatological struggle with evil.[17] (1 Th 1:6)

As we shall see in greater detail below, Jesus and the Breath enjoy both a functional and a vital identity. They enjoy a functional identity because Jesus' efficacious mission of the Breath entails that wherever She acts so does He. They enjoy a vital identity, because whoever shares the Breath of Christ shares Jesus' risen life by participating in the imperishable life of God.

The fact that Paul experienced the risen Christ as a "life-giving Breath" also implies Jesus' divinity. In the Old Testament "the Holy Breath" designates the immanent saving presence of the very reality of God. One experiences God's Breath as a source of empowering, divine enlightenment. The fact that Jesus functions as the source of a divine reality discloses, therefore, His divinity; for only God can send and communicate God to others. Any self-styled "Spirit Christology" which fails to build on this foundation builds on sand.

(III)

In the second letter to the Corinthians, Paul does not say that Jesus in His resurrection "became a life-giving Breath," but the apostle does use similar language to describe Jesus as Lord. In second Corinthians Paul speaks baldly of: "the Lord Who is the Breath." (2 Cor 3:18) Paul identifies the Lord with the Breath in the course of a long Christological digression which occurs during his defense to the Corinthian community of his apostolic authority over them.

Paul assimilates the apostle to burning incense offered to God. (2 Cor 2:14; cf. Sir 24:15) In the process of being consumed for the sake of the gospel, the apostle diffuses knowledge of God's saving action in Christ, the wisdom made manifest in Jesus. (1 Cor 1:24) This the apostle does through both verbal and lived testimony. (2 Cor 5:20, 4:10-1)

17. Cf. Cerfaux, *op.cit.*, pp. 284-294; Orr and Walther, *op.cit.*, pp. 323-41; Bruce, *op.cit.*, pp. 144-51; Groscheide, *op.cit.*, pp. 355-78; Robin Scroggs, *The Last Adam: A Study in Pauline Anthropology* (Philadelphia, PA: Fortress, 1966), pp. 92-112; C.K. Barrett, *From First Adam to Last: A Study in Pauline Theology* (New York, NY: Scribner's, 1966), pp. 68-91; James D.G. Dunn, "1 Corinthians 15:45—Last Adam, Life-Giving Spirit," in *Christ and Spirit in the New Testament*, edited by Barnabas Lindars and Stephen S. Smally (Cambridge: Cambridge University Press, 1973), pp. 127-141; Charles Kingsley Barrett, "The Significance of the Adam-Christ Typology for the Resurrection of the Dead: 1 Co 15, 20-22. 45-49," in *Resurrection du Christ et des Chrétiens (1 Co 15)*, pp. 99-126; Kurt Erlemann, "Der Geist als *arrabôn* (2 Kor 5,5) im Kontext der paulinischer Eschatologie," *Zeitschrift für die Neutestamentliche Wissenschaft*, 83(1992), pp. 202-223.

As the knowledge of Christ spreads like the aroma of incense, it effects God's judgment upon humanity. In the case of those who respond to the good news, the knowledge of Christ which the apostles diffuse has the sweet smell of a sacrifice acceptable to God. The sacrifice in question would seem to involve the self-sacrifice both of the apostle and of those who respond in faith to the apostle's message. In the case of those who reject the apostolic preaching, however, that sweet smell transforms itself into the stench of death, since they cut themselves off from the God of life who raises from the dead. (2 Cor 2:14-16) In other words, Paul's apostolic witness to the risen Christ brings about divine judgment by forcing the choice between belief in the risen Christ, on the one hand, and the refusal to believe, on the other.[18]

No human can qualify as either worthy of or equal to (*hikanos*) such a ministry. At best, the apostle can only seek to serve before God with sincerity as God's own chosen instrument and envoy by speaking the word of God without seeking to profit from it personally (Cor 2:17)

Forestalling an objection from the Corinthians that, in so speaking of the apostolate, Paul is indulging in self-glorification, Paul protests that he needs no letters of recommendation in dealing with the church at Corinth. The apostle has no need of such a letter because his Corinthian converts are themselves Paul's own letter of recommendation, a letter from Christ written through the action of His Breath in their hearts. Paul contrasts this mysterious pneumatic writing upon the heart with ink inscriptions on parchment or with inscriptions on tablets of stone. The contrast between stone inscriptions and pneumatic inscriptions on the heart alludes to Jeremiah's prophecy of a new covenant, inscribed in the hearts of God's people. (Jer 31:33) The contrast also echoes Paul's insistence that the Breath of Christ Herself functions as the law of Christian conduct and of the new covenant. (2 Cor 3:6; cf. Rom 7:6)

---

18. Elsewhere, in second Corinthians Paul assimilates the apostolic proclamation to a divine judgment. Paul's failure to convince others of the truth of "the light of the gospel of the glory of Christ who is the likeness of God (*eikôn tou Theou*)" only foreshadows their ultimate perdition.

> For what we preach is not ourselves, but Jesus Christ as Lord, with ourselves as your servants for Jesus' sake. For it is the God who said "Let light shine out of darkness," who has shone in our hearts to give the light of the knowledge of the glory of God in the face of Christ. (2 Cor 4:5-6)

> The God whose word caused physical light to shine at the dawn of creation has, in other words, effected a second and new creation through the light of faith effected by the Breath of the risen Christ. That faith flows from the divine Breath's action in the hearts of believers and orients them to God by giving them a share in the glorious life of the risen Christ. Those who reject this pneumatic life and light consign themselves to the darkness.

This allusion to the pneumatic character of the new covenant leads Paul into an extended Christological digression. In it Paul contrasts the old covenant, whose written letters brought death, with the glory of the new covenant: a glory sealed in the Breath of Christ, a glory which culminates in risen life with Jesus. Only God acting through Christ can seal such a covenant, Paul insists. God uses the apostles as instruments for effecting the new covenant. Of themselves the apostles lack all power to bring about such an effect. (2 Cor 3:4-6)

Paul describes the Mosaic covenant as 1) a "ministry of death" and "of condemnation" (2) written in letters upon stone, and 3) accompanied by a terrifying as well as a fading splendor. He then contrasts the Mosaic covenant with the new covenant sealed in Christ, which he describes 1) a "ministry of justification (*diakonia tês dikaiosounês*)" and 2) a covenant "of Breath (*pneumatos*)" and not of mere written letters 3) which therefore confers on the believer life through the action of God's Breath (*to de pneuma zôopoiei*). (2 Cor 3:4-11)

In speaking of the fading splendor of the mosaic covenant Paul alludes to the brightness shining from Moses's face after he spoke with God, a brightness which he hid from the Israelites by veiling his face. (Ex 34:29-35) Paul, however, embroiders the Exodus account of this incident in three ways.

1) He says both that Moses veiled the reflected divine splendor on his face and that the Hebrews could not bear to gaze upon it. That reluctance foreshadowed their present inability to recognize in Christ the fulfillment of the Mosaic covenant.(2 Cor 3:7, 12-15) The veil over Moses' face becomes, as the passage develops rhetorically, a metaphor for unbelief, a veil enshrouding the minds of Paul's Jewish contemporaries, a veil which only conversion to the Lord Jesus will lift. That conversion only Christ himself can effect through the action of the Breath.

2) Paul describes the splendor on Moses' face as a fading one and makes its ephemeral character into a symbol of the temporary and transitional purpose of the old covenant, since from the beginning God intended to replace it with the new covenant in Christ. (2 Cor 3:8, 10-11, 13)

3) Paul also contrasts the condemnation and bondage which resulted from the old Law with the justification and freedom effected by the Breath of Christ who seals the new covenant in the hearts of believers. (2 Cor 3:9, 16-17; cf. Gal 5:1-12)

In the present context, this digression's chief Christological significance lies in the strong identification which Paul makes between the risen Lord and the Breath of God.

Yes, to this day whenever Moses is read a veil lies over their minds; but when a person turns to the Lord the veil is removed. Now, the Lord is the Breath (*ho de Kyrios to pneuma estin*), and where the Breath of the Lord is, there is freedom. And we all with unveiled faces, reflecting (*katoptrizomenoi*) the glory of the Lord are being changed into His likeness from one degree of glory to another (*apo doxês eis doxan*); for this comes from the Lord who is the Breath (*kathaper apo kyrious pneumatos*). (2 Cor 3:15-8)

Over the centuries, Pauline scholars have found this passage a *crux interpretum.* They have differed in their interpretation of the term "Lord" (vv.16, 17, and 18); and they have offered different accounts of Paul's strong identification of the Lord with the Breath. The passage, however, echoes other Pauline texts which identify strongly the risen Lord with His Breath. (Cf. 1 Cor 15:45; cf. Rom 8:11)

In my opinion, when Paul in this passage uses the term "Lord," he intends it to mean what it ordinarily means in his letters: namely, the risen Lord, who in His resurrection became a "life-giving Breath." Those who hold for such an interpretation generally agree that Paul is speaking here of a functional identity between Jesus and the Breath: in other words, wherever the Breath of God is present and acts, the risen Christ is present and acting. Paul asserts such a functional identity; but he does not stop there.

As we have seen, the risen Lord and the Breath share an identity of life as well as a functional identity. Vital identity flows from the fact that whoever possesses the Breath of God possesses the risen life of Christ. Paul asserts that identity in the present passage by punning on the term "*katoptrizomenoi,*" which means at one level to contemplate and at another level to reflect. Those who contemplate the glory of the risen Christ reflect it back like a mirror, just as Moses's face reflected a lesser divine splendor. In other words, through a contemplative faith believers, who because of their faith stand before God with unveiled faces, participate in the glory of the risen Christ, a glory identical with the divine reality manifested to them in all its splendor. That participation transforms believers into images of the risen Christ by conforming them to Him in His glory.

Moreover, Paul describes the Christian's present participation in risen life and in the glory it imparts as both progressive and intensive, as advancement from one degree of glory to another. In other words, the vital identity between the risen Lord and the Breath He imparts stands historically revealed in the identity of risen and pneumatic life.[19]

19. Cf. Carol Stockhausen, *Moses' Veil and the Glory of the New Covenant: The Exegetical Substructure of II Cor. 3,1-4, 6* (Rome: Pontifical Biblical Institute, 1989); Victor Furnish, *II Corinthians* (New York, NY: Doubleday, 1984), pp. 201-242; Bruce, *op.cit.*, pp. 190-4; Cerfaux, *op.cit.*, pp. 344-352; *NJBC*, 82:61-66; Francois-Xavier Durrwell, "Pour une Christologie selon l'Esprit Saint," *Nouvelle Revue Théologique*, 114:5(September-October, 1992), pp. 653-677; Barrett, *From First Adam to Last*, pp. 46-67; Emily Wong, "The Lord is the Spirit (2 Cor 3, 17a)," *Ephemerides Theologicae Lovaniensis*, 61(1985), pp. 48-72; Seyoon Kim, "2 Cor 5:11-21 and the Origin of Paul's Conception of Reconciliation," *Novum Testamentum*, 39(1997), pp. 360-384.

The strong identification which Paul makes between the risen Lord and the sanctifying Breath throws light on the way in which the apostle experienced his own encounter with the risen Christ. Throughout the Bible, both Old and New Testaments, the Breath of God functions as a divine principle of empowering, saving enlightenment.[20] In describing the risen Christ as a "life- giving Breath," Paul, in my judgment, is implicitly asserting that he too experienced the encounter with the risen Christ as an empowering, divine enlightenment which effected in him a transforming religious conversion. The same empowering enlightenment commissioned Paul to testify to the saving fact of Jesus' resurrection, which reveals Him as the unique, mediating source of the saving Breath of God and therefore as divine.

In the section which follows, I shall examine the Christological hymn at the beginning of the letter to the Philippians. In it Paul asserts the divinity of Jesus with a different rhetorical strategy: namely, by identifying the human name of Jesus with the divine name. The apostle also asserts an inseparable, saving relationship between Jesus' death and resurrection.

(IV)

The risen Christ's functional and vital identity with the divine Breath provides one important way in which Paul asserts Jesus' divinity. In the letter to the Philippians, the apostle uses a different rhetorical strategy in order to identify Jesus with the deity: namely, Jesus' resurrection transforms a human name into the divine name and in the process reveals the man Jesus' divine Lordship. The apostle makes this assertion in the Christological hymn which he cites in the letter to the Philippians.

As in the case of other Pauline doctrinal assertions, this one occurs in a very specific pastoral context. Imprisoned, probably in Ephesus, Paul writes to thank the Philippians for contributing to his physical support during his prison ordeal.[21]

In reflecting on his own incarceration Paul asserts that it has been "for Christ," by which he means that his sufferings have encouraged others to

---

20. Cf. Donald L. Gelpi, S.J., *The Divine Mother: A Trinitarian Theology of the Holy Spirit* (Lanham, MD: University Press of America, 1984), pp.45-60; *God Breathes: The Spirit in the World* (Collegeville, MI: Michael Glazier/The Liturgical Press, 1988). See also: George T. Montague, *The Holy Spirit: Growth of a Biblical Tradition* (New York, NY: Paulist, 1976).

21. Scholars once tended to date Philippians as a late letter written during Paul's imprisonment in Rome, chiefly because of his references to the praetorian guard (Phil 1:13) and to the household of Caesar (Phil 4:22). These phrases, however, do not refer exclusively to a Roman context. More recent scholarship has tended to place the letter earlier, probably at Ephesus, whose prison had both a praetorian guard and slaves from the household of Caesar. Paul, then, would have written the letter, which reveals him still concerned about proselytizing Judaizers, (Phil 3:1) about the year 54 a.d., probably shortly before his first letter to the Corinthians.

proclaim the gospel boldly. (Phil 1:13-4) Some preach Christ out of envy and rivalry; others from good will. Paul, for his part, professes indifference to the motives of the envious, as long as they continue to proclaim Christ. (Phil 1:15-18) He also expresses confidence that, through the prayers of the Philippians and through the action of the Breath of Jesus Christ, the proclamation of the gospel will advance his own deliverance from prison. (Phil 1:19)

In a more personal testimony which dramatizes the extent to which Paul had interiorized the eschatological hope which he proclaims, the apostle expresses his indifference to living or dying as long as he gives honor to Christ in his own body. "For to me to live is Christ and to die is gain." (Phil 1:19-21) The gain in question involves more than just release from the sufferings of this life; for Paul assures the Philippians that he would prefer to "depart and be with Christ." (Phil 1:22) In other words, not only does Paul expect to survive death but to do so in a way which will consummate his present union with Christ. Faith in the risen Christ, therefore, empowers him to confront courageously the principalities and powers of this world, who have imprisoned him. His courage springs from his indifference to living or dying, or rather from his preference for death and perfect union with Christ.

In the end, however, Paul professes himself content to continue living in order to labor fruitfully among those who need him. He predicts that the Philippians will "glory in Christ" when Paul, after his release from prison, visits them again.[22] (Phil 1:25-6)

Paul's personal confidence and hope in the midst of suffering provides the rhetorical context for the exhortation which follows immediately. Whether or not Paul eventually visits the Philippians, they should continue to live in a manner "worthy of the gospel of Christ," united in spirit (*en heni pneumati*)," "of one mind (*mia psychê*)" in their fearless struggle against their adversaries; for like Paul, the Philippians too not only profess the gospel by their faith but are suffering for it. (Phil 1:27-30) Indeed, the Philippians will afford Paul the greatest "consolation in Christ" by their mutual love, shared faith, and humble, selfless concern for the interests of others. (Phil 1:1-4) By so living they will, like Paul, (Phil 1:8) appropriate the mind of Christ Jesus. (Phil 1:5)

The Christological Hymn in Philippians

A Christological hymn follows. It praises the "self-emptying" of Jesus Christ through His incarnation and death. It also asserts His subsequent exaltation in His very humanity to the status of the divine. Paul seems to

---

22. Cf. Samuel Vollenweider, "Die Waagschalen von Leben und Tod: Zum antiken Hintergrund von Phil 1, 21-26," *Zeitschrift für die Neutestamentlische Wissenschaft*, 85(1994), pp. 93- 115.

be quoting a hymn written by someone else, although he may have modified the original text for his own theological ends. Very likely, then, the hymn which Paul cites predates the letter to the Philippians and probably had a liturgical origin.[23]

The hymn begins by asserting that Jesus was "already existing (*hyparchôn*) in the form of God (*en morphê Theou*)" (Phil 2:6) before He emptied himself by becoming human.[24] One cannot know for certain whether Paul, in using the term "*morphê*" intends its technical philosophical mean-

23. Jerome Murphy O'Connor has attempted to explore the anthropological presuppositions of the original author of the hymn which Paul cites. His article, therefore, prescinds from what Paul, in citing the hymn, might have meant by it.

O'Connor's article summarizes well the contrasting, often contradictory, interpretations which exegetes have given to the hymn in Philippians. The article suggests that the original author of the hymn derived his understanding of Jesus' humanity from Hebrew wisdom literature. Hence, the hymn's author chose to portray Christ in the first stanza, not as pre-existent, but as "the Righteous Man" par excellence, who had every right "to be treated as if he were god, that is, to enjoy the incorruptibility in which Adam was created." Instead, he chose the mode of existence of a corruptible slave. Though thoroughly human Christ differed from other humans by his sinlessness. In virtue of his sinless suffering, God conferred on Him the title of *Kyrios* and made Him into the one before every knee must bow.

Even as an interpretation of the intent of the original hymn writer and not of Paul himself, O'Connor's argument seems to me to rest on a number of questionable pre-suppositions. Among them I would include the following: 1) New Testament Christological thinking began by focusing on the humanity of Jesus and only evolved subsequently into a focal concern with His divinity. 2) Hymn writers in the Pauline churches wrote liturgical hymns in order to solve Christological problems rather than to express a shared Christological faith. 3) The writer of the hymn in Philippians preferred to derive Christological categories from Old Testament wisdom literature rather than from the kerygma. Cf. Jerome Murphy-O'Connor, "Christological Anthropology in Phil II.6-11," *Revue Biblique*, 83(1976), pp. 25-50.

As for Paul's own understanding of the hymn's Christological significance, I find the position presented in this chapter more plausible than that suggested by O'Connor. The latter's reading of the hymn does not do justice, in my judgment, to the play on "*morphê*" and "*schêma*" in the hymn's language. It also misses the main point of the hymn: namely, that the free self-abasement of the pre-existent Son of God in taking flesh and dying on the cross had as its consequence the transformation of a human name "Jesus" into the divine name. The divinity of the name "Jesus" preoccupied the original hymn writer more than the title "*Kyrios*." As a consequence, the hymn makes more poetic sense if one sees the self-emptying of the pre-existent divine Son as seeking ultimately to transform a human name into a divine one. Cf. Ralph P. Martins, *Carmen Christi: Philippians 11.5-11 in Recent Interpretation and in the Setting of Early Christian Worship* (Cambridge: Cambridge University Press, 1967).

24. The hymn gives good evidence that the author of the fourth gospel did not invent the idea that the divine reality revealed in Jesus existed before its historical manifestation in Him. That the idea of pre-existence surfaces in a liturgical hymn which predates Philippians suggests that it had already achieved popular credence among the first Christians. Moreover, the fact that it surfaces in two other Christian hymns in the New Testament (Col 1:12-19, Jn 1:1-5, 9-14) suggests that belief in Jesus' pre-existence played a significant role in the worship of the apostolic church.

ing. In my opinion, he probably does not, since his mind gravitates to rabbinic rather than to Greek philosophical categories. What, then, does Paul mean by "*morphê*"?

In a subsequent passage in the same letter Paul again implicitly contrasts the term "*morphê*" with another Greek word "*schêma.*" (Cf. 1 Cor 7:31) "*Schêma*" in Paul's thought seems to designate the superficial, the passing, the ephemeral; "*morphê*," by contrast designates the abiding, constitutive reality of some person or thing. That, prior to the incarnation, Jesus Christ "already existed in the form of God" asserts, then, that before becoming human He already possessed the abiding, constitutive reality of God. As we shall see, however, when Paul compares "the form (*morphê*)" of the human with the "form of the divine," he deems the former a "*schêma.*" In other words, by comparison with the abiding reality of God, the abiding reality of humans qualifies as superficial, passing, and ephemeral.[25]

The hymn asserts that despite His pre-existence as divine, Jesus "did not consider likeness to God something to grasp (*ouk harpagmon êgêsato to einai hisa Theô*)" (Phil 2:6) The noun "*harpagmon*" means something seized or to be seized. Since the hymn has just asserted that Jesus already possessed the abiding, constitutive reality of God prior to becoming human, He could not have seized divinity as something exterior to himself. Hence, in the present context the phrase "*ouk harpagmon êgêsato*" probably has the colloquial meaning of not exploiting for selfish ends something one already possesses.[26]

25. Cf. George Montague, *The Living Thought of St. Paul: An Introduction to Pauline Theology Through Intensive Study of Key Texts* (Beverly Hills, CA: Benziger, 1976), pp. 51- 59; Alec Motyer, *The Message of Philippians* (Leicester: Inter-Varsity Press, 1984), pp.108- 109; Ralph P. Martins, *Philippians* (Grand Rapids, MI: Eerdmans, 1976), pp.94-96; Moises Silva, *Philippians* (Chicago, IL: Moody Press, 1988), pp.112-116; A. Boyde Luter, "Philippians and Chiasmus: Key to the Structure, Unity, and Theme Question," *New Testament Studies*, 41(1995), pp. 89-101; Teresa Yai-Chow Wong, "The Problem of Pre-existence in Philippians 2, 6-11,"*Ephemerides Theologicae Lovaniensis*, 62(1986), pp. 267-282.

26. Cf. Martin, *op.cit.*, pp.96-7; Silva, *op.cit.*, pp.116-8; Motyer, *op.cit.*, pp.110-1; *NJBC*, 82:48-50; N.T. Wright, "'*Harpagmos*' and the Meaning of Philippians 2:5-11," *Journal of Theological Studies*, 37(1986),, pp. 321-325.

Similar insights surface in second Corinthians. Paul's exhortation to the Corinthians to give generously to the collection for the poor of Jerusalem contains a few passing Christological references. Paul reminds the Corinthians: "For you know the grace of our Lord Jesus Christ, that, though He was rich, for your sake He became poor so that by His poverty you might become rich." (2 Cor 8:9)

Paul's reminder echoes the Christological hymn in the second chapter of Philippians. (Phil 2:6-7) There Paul described the self-emptying of Jesus in dispensational terms as changing the form of God for the form of a human and as dying on the cross. Paul invoked Jesus' selflessness in order to exhort to Philippians to relate to one another with a similar selfless love which would ensure their unity of minds and hearts. In second Corinthians, Paul calls attention to the utter gratuity of the gift of Christ's

Even though Paul uses different language from Genesis, the phrase "*ouk harpagmon êgêsato*" could possibly also have Adamic connotations. The poetic character of the hymn allows one to read it with an eye to literary allusion. In Genesis, Adam and Eve in their disobedient pride ate the forbidden fruit because they coveted becoming like God by learning to distinguish good from evil. (Gen 3:4-7) Adam and Eve, then, "grasped at" divinity as a reality alien to their own nature. As we have just seen, however, the pre-existent Jesus could not covet divinity as an alien possession, because He already possessed "the form of God." In Paul's Christological use of Adamic imagery, however, Christ functions as the reverse antitype to Adam. Christ and Adam do not, therefore, correspond point for point but by negation, as antitypes. Moreover, in Paul's thought the new Adam utterly transcends the old. (Rom 5:12-20)

One finds the same literary pattern in the Christological hymn in Philippians. The new Adam already possesses the divinity which the first Adam coveted as an alien good; but His humility and selflessness so utterly transcend the pride and selfishness of the first Adam that He even refuses to use for His own selfish advantage a good which He already possesses. Instead, "He emptied Himself by taking the form of a slave, being born in the likeness of humans." (Phil 2:6-7) In other words, the last Adam negates through transcendence the failure of the first Adam who illegitimately coveted a divinity which he did not possess.[27]

The phrase "form of a slave" clearly contrasts with the phrase "form of God" in a reverse parallel typical of Pauline Adamic imagery. Jesus, despite His unity with the divine reality, took on the abiding, constitutive reality of the human condition. The term "slave" portrays that condition as downward mobility. The heavenly Jesus exchanges the security of a divine mode of existence for a state of bondage to spiritual powers which ends finally in His death.

---

self-impoverishment in order to encourage the Corinthians to outdo themselves in generosity to the needy poor in Jerusalem.

27. T. Francis Glasson argues against an Adamic allusion in the Philippians hymn on the basis of the disproportion between what the pre-existent One abandoned and Eve's desire to be like a god distinguishing good from evil. The argument would hold if in Paul's application of Adamic imagery strict proportionality characterized the Christ and the first Adam. Instead, Paul habitually uses reverse proportionality in which the reality embodied in Jesus utterly transcends that exemplified in Adam. In that context the abandonment of divinity by the incarnate Son of God would utterly transcend Adamic longing for the godlike ability to discern good from evil. Adam sinned pridefully by exalting human perceptions of good and evil over the divine will. Jesus' obedience unto death negates that pride in a transcendent way and with transcendent saving consequences. Cf. T. Francis Glasson, "Two Notes on the Philippians Hymn (II. 6-11)," *New Testament Studies*, 21(1974-1975), pp. 133-139. In the fourth part of this chapter I shall consider in greater detail Paul's proclamation of Jesus as the last Adam.

Moreover, the term "slave" evokes the image of the innocent, suffering servant of second Isaiah, who gives himself over to death for the salvation of others. (Is 53:12) The "self-emptying" of God expresses itself, therefore, in the free choice of a powerless and vulnerable mode of existence. Paul, however, suggests that this powerlessness belongs to the more superficial realm of earthly existence by calling the "form of the human" a *"schêma"*: "being found in likeness as a human (*schêmati heuretheis hôs anthrôpos*)." (Phil 2:7b)

As the hymn proceeds, moreover, Jesus' humble self-emptying goes beyond the assumption of the human condition. After freely embracing the ephemeral human state (*kai schêmati heuretheis hos anthropos*), "He humbled Himself and became obedient unto death, even death on a cross." (Phil 2:8) Having owned human vulnerability and subjection to the powers of this world, in addition Jesus accepted the abysmal degradation of the cross but did so in humble obedience to the Father's will. The hymn here echoes something which all the gospels assert: namely, that Jesus not only accepted His death in advance but also came to regard it as an integral part of the mission He had received from His Father, quite plausibly as an aspect of His eschatological struggle against the forces of evil.[28]

With the utter and abysmal completion of Jesus' humble self-emptying, the reverse process begins. "Therefore God has highly exalted Him and bestowed on Him the name above every name." The Father in glorifying Jesus gives Him the divine name itself, the name "Lord." Jesus' prior self-emptying, His humble assumption of the form of a servant, has, therefore, the startling effect of demanding that in the eschatological age everyone must reverence a mere human name as the very name of God: "that at the name of Jesus every knee should bow, in heaven, and on earth and under the earth, and every tongue confess that Jesus Christ is Lord to the glory of God the Father." (Phil 2:9-11; cf. Phil 3:20-1) Every creature in the universe must now acknowledge as divine the human name of one condemned, degraded, and executed by the principalities and powers of this world. The resurrection therefore reverses the judgment of those principalities and powers and unmasks them in all their brutality and injustice. It also subjects the whole of creation to the risen Lord.

Here I would like to underscore the fact that in the climax of the hymn, every knee in heaven, on earth, and under the earth bends in adoration, not simply at the name Lord, but specifically at the human name "Jesus." The kenotic self-emptying of the divine reality which became incarnate in Jesus has as its historical and dispensational consequence the transfor-

---

28. Cf. Moises Silva, *Philippians* (Chicago, IL: Moody Press, 1988), pp.125-6; Alec Motyer, *The Message of Philippians* (Leichester: Inter-Varsity Press, 1984), pp. 112-118; Ralph P. Martins, *Philippians* (Grand Rapids, MI: Eerdmans, 1976), pp. 97-100.; Cerfaux, *op.cit.*, pp. 164-166.

mation of a human name, the name "Jesus," into the divine name itself. In the last age of salvation, "Jesus" names a divine reality.

An Old Testament theology of the divine name provides the key to the culminating verses of the hymn. In the Old Testament, a name designates the reality itself. (Ps 5:12, 7:18, 135:13; Is 29:23; Dt 28:58) Through Jesus' self-emptying, a human name now designates the reality of God. The name of God makes the divine reality present among those He has chosen. (Ex 3:13-16, 6:3) Now the name "Jesus" makes the divine reality present. The divine name designates the only adorable reality. (Cf. Ex 3:15) Now every knee bows in adoration at the human name of Jesus.

The fact that the first Christians invoked the name of Jesus as an equivalent of the divine name and did so with efficacious power gave experiential validation to belief in His Lordship. (Cf. Acts 3:6, 4:9-12; Ez 20:9) Of all the claims the first Christians made about Jesus, this one would almost certainly have struck devout Jews as most blasphemous. It may have motivated Paul's persecution of Palestinian Christians prior to his conversion.[29] (cf. Acts 4:17-18; 1 Cor 1:23)

In what concerns the hymn itself, Jesus' glorification in His humanity not only guarantees His universal adoration and divine sway but also contextualizes His humble self-emptying eschatologically. (Phil 2:16) Jesus' exaltation assures the Philippians a share in His glory if only they humble themselves as He did by serving both one another and God, even, if necessary, risking death in the process.[30] (Cf. Phil 2:30)

In this chapter I have pondered the ways in which Paul's identification of the risen Christ with the Breath He sends asserts, among other things, His divinity. Only one other parallel passage in the letters of Paul needs to claim our attention in this chapter: namely, the Christological creed

---

29. Cf. Montague, *The Living Thought of Saint Paul*, pp.3-4; Roselyne Dupont-Roc, "De l'hymne christologique à une vie de koinonia: étude sur la lettre aux Philippiens," *Estudios Biblicos*, 49(1991), pp. 451-472; Abdon Moreno Garcia, "Approximation al Sentido de Filipenses 2, 1-5," *Estudios Biblicos*, 47(1989), pp. 529-558.

30. Cf. Cerfaux, *op.cit.*, pp. 374-395; Silva, *op.cit.*, pp.126-33; Martin, *op.cit.*, pp.100-2; Motyer, *op.cit.*, pp.119-24; Fitzmyer, *To Advance the Gospel*, pp. 202-217; Alfred Hofius, *Der Christushymnus Philipper 2, 6-11* (Tübingen: J.C.B. Mohr, 1976); David M. Stanley, *Christ's Resurrection in Pauline Soteriology* (Analecta Biblica 13; Rome: Pontifical Biblical Institute, 1961), pp. 94-102; Frederic Manns, *Essais sur le Judéo-christianisme* (Jerusalem: Franciscan Printing Press, 1977), pp. 11-42; Shiela Briggs, "Can an Enslaved God Liberate? Hermeneutical Reflections on Philippians 2:6-11; *Semeia*, 49(1989), pp. 138-153; Jennings B. Reid, *Jesus: God's Emptiness, God's Fullness: The Christology of St. Paul* (Mahwah, NJ: Paulist, 1990), pp. 55-68; Jacques Scholsser, "La figure de Dieu selon l'epitre aux Philippiens," *New Testament Studies*, 41(1995), pp. 378-399; David Alan Black, "The Discourse Structure of Philippians: A Study in Textlinguistics," *Novum Testamentum*, 37(1995), pp. 16-49; Brendan Byrne, S.J., "Christ's Pre-Existence in Pauline Soteriology," *Theological Studies*, 58(1997), pp.308-330; Guiseppi Segalla, "Salvacion Cristologica Universel en Filipenses y 1 Pe," *Revista Biblica*, 59(1997), pp. 165-180.

which opens the letter to the Romans. There the apostle contrasts Jesus' divine status as Son, which His special relationship to the divine Breath reveals, with His human status as messiah and son of David. To this passage I turn in the section which follows.

(V)

In his salutation to the Christians in Rome, Paul describes the gospel he proclaims as the fulfillment of Old Testament prophecies about God's Son, "Jesus Christ Our Lord." Paul illustrates this point by incorporating an early Christian creedal formula into the message of his salutation.[31]

> He was born of the seed of David according to the flesh and He was constituted Son of God in power according to the Breath of sanctification through the resurrection of the dead, Jesus Christ our Lord. (Rom 1:3-4)

The creed in question contrasts Jesus' human descent "from the seed of David according to the flesh with His establishment as "Son of God in power according to the Breath of holiness through the resurrection from the dead." (Rom 1:3-4) Paul's allusion to Jesus' Davidic ancestry makes messianic claims; but by relegating that descent to the realm of the flesh Paul reduces it to relative insignificance in understanding Jesus' ultimate mission and status. The resurrection rather than physical descent establishes Jesus' authority; for by the resurrection He has been "established (*tou horisthentos*) Son of God," a title which both validates and transcends that of "messiah."[32]

31. Paul probably wrote the letter to the Romans sometime in the winter of 57 to 58 a.d. Cf. Kenneth Grayston, "Reading the Book 3. Paul's Letter to the Romans," *Expository Times*, 108(1996), pp. 68-71.

32. Contemporary exegetes tend to regard the letters to Timothy as deutero-Pauline. Each letter, however, also contains a very early Christological creedal formula, possibly a hymn.

We find the following formula in first Timothy:

> He was manifested in the flesh
>   vindicated in the Breath
>   seen by angels
> preached among the nations
>   believed in in the world
>   taken up in glory
>   (1 Tim 3:16)

One finds a certain parallelism of thought among the first, second, and third verses of each stanza. Jesus' earthly ministry mentioned in verse one finds a parallel in His proclamation to the nations mentioned in verse three, for that proclamation prolongs His ministry here on earth. The second verse finds a parallel in the fifth. The second verse refers to Jesus' vindication at God's hands by rising from the dead. He is vindicated "in the Breath" because by rising He stands revealed as a life-giving Breath. (1

The resurrection establishes Jesus divine Sonship "in power (*en dynamei*)." The phrase "in power" refers both to the source and consequences of the resurrection. The Father in raising the Son manifests His own power decisively; but the "Breath of holiness" manifests in turn the power of the risen Christ by effecting the sanctification of those who call upon His name. Paul's proclamation of Christ "in power" also alludes to the pneumatic inspiration of the apostle's own kerygmatic ministry. The parallelism between the phrases "according to the flesh (*kata sarka*)" and "according to the Breath of holiness (*kata pneuma hagiosynês*)" points to

Cor 15:45) Moreover, the Breath who proceeds from the risen Christ evokes the world's faith in Him described in verse five. Finally, the third verse parallels the sixth. The angels see the risen Christ when He ascends to heaven to share the glory of the Godhead.

The depth of the Christian mystery which this letter finds in this poetic creed includes, then, the incarnation and mortal ministry of Jesus as well as the paschal mystery. The paschal mystery has a triple focus. First, it vindicates the truth of Jesus' mortal ministry and of the religious vision He proclaimed. Second, it effects the universal salvation of the nations through the mission of the Breath of the risen Christ. Third, as risen savior, Christ now dwells in divine glory exercising universal sway over the world which He has saved.

Second Timothy cites another early creedal formula as an example of sound teaching:

> If we have died with [Him], we shall live with [Him]
> If we hold firm, we shall reign with [Him].
> If we deny [Him], He too will deny us.
> If we break faith, He remains faithful;
>   for He cannot deny Himself. (2 Tim 2:11-3)

The first verse of this second creedal formula resembles Rom 6:8. In order to share risen life with Christ, one must, like Him, die to sin in the baptismal bath and receive the Breath of the risen one, the victorious and unquenchable life which proceeds from Him. Steadfastness in that commitment ensures not only one's entry into the kingdom of God which Jesus proclaimed, but it even gives one a share in His saving dominion over all creation, a dominion firmly established in the paschal mystery but in process of full manifestation as the effects of the resurrection reveal Jesus' triumph over the principalities and powers which sought to destroy Him. Jesus' death reveals His unwavering divine fidelity to Himself and therefore to us. If we, confronted with the revelation of that fidelity, nevertheless choose to deny it in word or deed, then we leave Him no choice but to deny us. Otherwise, He would have to endorse our denial of Him and in the process deny Himself. Some see in verse 11 a reference to martyrdom; but one need not restrict the meaning of the text so narrowly.

Cf. Thomas D. Lea and Hayne P. Griffin, Jr., *1, 2 Timothy, Titus* (Nashville, TN: Broadman Press, 1992), pp. 124-127, 209-212; George W. Knight, *The Faithful Sayings in the Pastoral Letters* (Grand Rapids, MI: Baker Book House, 1979), pp. 102-136; Gordon D. Fee, *1 and 2 Timothy, Titus* (Peabody, MA: Hendrickson, 1988), pp. 92-95, 193-199; Martin Dibelius, *The Pastoral Epistles* (Philadelphia, PA: Fortress, 1972), pp. 60-63; 107-108; S. De Lestapio, S.J., *L'enigme des pastorales de Saint Paul* (Paris: Librairie Lecoffre, 1976); R. Alastair Campbell, "Identifying the Faithful Sayings in the Pastoral Epistles," *Journal for the Study of the New Testament*, 54(1994), pp. 73-86.

the person of the risen Jesus as the source of the Breath's sanctifying, pneumatic power. The risen Christ's establishment as Son of God in power also connotes His dominion over the principalities and powers of this world.[33] (Cf. Ps 2:7-11)

Finally, Jesus' "resurrection from the dead (*ex anastaseôs nekrôn*)" has both temporal and causal connotations. Not until His resurrection did Jesus stand decisively revealed as designated by God messianic Son of God. Moreover, the resurrection functions as the causal source of the divine power exercised by the risen Christ in the action of His "Breath of holiness."[34]

In the present chapter, I have argued the following thesis: *Christological hope roots itself in the fact that in the resurrection Jesus stands revealed as "a life-giving Breath."* Let me, then, summarize the main points of that argument. The resurrection endows the kerygma with its saving significance. Without the resurrection, no Breath. Without the Breath, no justification, no sanctification, no charismatic empowerment, no saving relationship with God, no share in the resurrection and glory of Jesus Christ. Paul therefore describes the risen Christ as a "life-giving Breath" not only because he experienced the encounter with the glorified Jesus as an empowering divine enlightenment but also because those who believe in the divine name of Jesus share a similar empowering divine enlightenment and have begun to experience pneumatic transformation in His image.

Even the texts we have examined so far make it clear, however, that for Paul the resurrection discloses only half of the paschal mystery. The death of Jesus discloses the other half. Moreover, together death and resurrection constitute a single saving event, for each derives some of its saving significance from the other. Hence, neither enjoys full intelligibility apart from the other.

How, then, did Paul understand the saving significance of Jesus' death? To this question I turn in the chapter which follows.

---

33. Cf. M.E. Boismard, "Constitué fils de Dieu (Rom. I,4)," *Revue Biblique*, 60(1953), pp. 5- 17; Fitzmyer, *To Advance the Gospel*, pp. 202-217; Stanley, *Christ's Resurrection in Pauline Soteriology*, pp. 160-166.

34. One finds other interesting Pauline parallels of Father and Son elsewhere in his letters. For example, in the greeting which opens both letters to the Thessalonians, Paul twice clearly parallels the two divine titles "God" and "Lord," reserving the first for the Father and the second for Jesus Christ, as he typically does throughout his letters. The title "Lord" places Jesus in the same divine realm as the Father, while the second title which Jesus bears, "Christ," connotes the messiah's intimate relationship to the Breath of God, as the prayer of blessing which follows in first Thessalonians makes clear. Moreover, the greeting in both letters portrays God "the Father and the Lord Jesus Christ" as the simultaneous source of "the grace and peace" which characterize the messianic age. Second Thessalonians repeats the phrase "God the Father and the Lord Jesus Christ" three times.(2 Th 1:1-2, 11-12, 2:16-17)

Chapter 13
Dying to Sin

In this chapter I shall argue the following thesis: *Because on the cross Jesus died to sin, Christological hope roots itself in moral conformity to Him in the power of His Breath.* This thesis completes the preliminary sketch of the paschal mystery begun in the preceding chapter. That mystery consists of three distinct but inseparable components: the death of Jesus, His resurrection, and the mission of His Breath. The preceding chapter pondered the intimate relationship in Pauline theology between resurrection and the sending of the Breath. This chapter presents the way in which Paul's Easter faith informs his perception of Jesus' death.

This chapter divides into three parts. The first part explains what Paul means when he asserts in second Corinthians that on the cross the innocent Jesus died to sin. Part two examines the arguments which Paul proposes in his letter to the Galatians in order to show that the Christian, who has died to sin with Christ, must also die to the Law. Part three shows how the letter to the Romans brings the insights discussed in parts one and two to something like systematic expression.

(I)

In his second letter to the Corinthians, Paul defends at some length both his apostolic authority and his conduct of the apostolate. In the course of that defense, Paul makes a startling statement. He says that in Jesus' crucifixion God made into "sin" one who had never sinned. (2 Cor 5:21) Let us try to understand this deliberately shocking statement in its context, because it contains a fundamental insight into Paul's understanding of the saving significance of Jesus' death as an integral component of the paschal mystery.

In second Corinthians Paul defends his conduct of his apostolate from critics at Corinth. Paul portrays his sufferings as an apostle as his participation in the death of Christ, a participation which brings risen life both to him and to those who respond to his message in faith. As in the case of the crucified Jesus, then, in Paul's very apostolate life triumphs over death: as Paul's sufferings spread the gospel, grace multiplies in more and more people to the glory of God. (2 Cor 4:7-15)

In his work for the spread of the gospel, Paul depicts himself as grasped, constrained, compelled by the love of Christ. (2 Cor 5:14) Here Christ functions as both the source and object of Paul's love.

Moreover, Christ's love for sinful humans stands supremely revealed in His cross and resurrection. Together they manifest the universal, saving will of God, who desires to impart the life of the risen Christ to all who believe in Him no matter who they might have formerly been. Those who accept a share in Christ's risen life begin to participate in His love by living thereafter "no longer for themselves but for Him who for their sake died and was raised." (2 Cor 5:15) Christ's saving love thus creates the believers' love for Christ as well as their love for one another in His name.

To those at Corinth who criticize Paul's conduct of the apostolate, the apostle responds that he rests content to leave all judgment concerning him and his ministry to the court of Christ, where "each one may receive good or evil, according to what he has done in the body." (2 Cor 5:10) Indeed, Paul himself refuses to judge anyone except in the light of Christ and of His redeeming love.

In this context, Paul asserts, almost as a theological aside, that God made the innocent crucified one into "sin." In order to understand what Paul means, one needs to ponder the passage in full:

> From now on, therefore, we regard no one according to the flesh (*kata sarka*); even though we once knew Christ according to the flesh (*kata sarka*), now we know Him thus no longer. Therefore if anyone is in Christ, such a one is a new creation (*kainê ktisis*); the old has passed away, behold the new has come. All this is from God, who reconciled us to Himself through Christ and gave us the ministry of reconciliation; that is, in Christ God was reconciling the world to Himself, not counting their trespasses against them, and entrusting to us for His own purpose the message of reconciliation. So we are ambassadors of Christ, God making His appeal through us. For our sake He made Him to be sin who knew no sin, so that in Him we might become the righteousness of God. Working together with Him, we entreat you not to accept the grace of God in vain. (2 Cor 5:16-6:1)

In refusing to judge anyone according to the flesh, Paul implicitly censures the fleshy character of the judgments which his adversaries in Corinth have passed on him. The apostle qualifies his censure of his opponents, however, by admitting his own former capacity for false judgment. The apostle recalls the time when he knew Christ only "according to the flesh." Paul thus implicitly reminds the Corinthians that prior to their conversion they too lived and judged according to the flesh.

Judgment "according to the flesh" refers simultaneously to the way one perceives a saving reality as well as to the limitations of one's perceptions. One judges according to the flesh when one does so without the enlightenment of the Breath of Christ. (1 Cor 1:17-2:5) When confronted with the saving acts of God, a fleshy judgment sees only the finite, the created, the human. It fails to discern the divine reality which graced persons and events disclose: namely, God graciously acting to save and redeem us in Christ.

The absence of pneumatic inspiration functions, therefore, like a pair of blinders cutting off one's perception of God's presence in Jesus and in those transformed in His Breath. Paul confesses that he once regarded Jesus as only a human reality even though he now acknowledges the saving, divine reality which Jesus' humanity discloses.

Paul cites his own bad example as a way of gently warning the Corinthians not to pass judgment on him according to the flesh. Implicitly, Paul is challenging the Corinthian community to judge his apostolate honestly in the light of Christ's illuminating Breath. If they do so, they will recognize in his apostolic commissioning God acting and commissioning Him in Christ to function as an instrument for reconciling sinners to God. By describing his ministry as one of reconciliation, Paul is, moreover, offering an olive branch to his adversaries in Corinth and urging them to reconciliation among themselves and with him.[1] (Cf. 2 Cor 6:1-2)

The divine reconciliation which God effected in Christ makes a new creation. Paul derives the term "new creation" from Jewish apocalyptic; but he re-interprets it in the light of the Christ event. In Jewish apocalyptic, the new creation replaces the old one vitiated by sin; for Paul, however, the paschal mystery has begun the new creation by transforming the old one in the redeeming love of Christ. (Cf. Rom 8:18-39) The gracious transformation of the old creation rather than its simple replacement, therefore, holds the key to a Pauline understanding of the new creation. One experiences the new creation in the graced capacity to judge all things with the redemptive love revealed in Christ (cf. Gal 6:14-5). One also experiences the new creation by accepting the divine offer of reconciliation with God which Paul as God's authorized ambassador proclaims.[2]

The cross reveals this redeeming, transforming love of God. In delivering His Son up to crucifixion, however, God "made Him to be sin who knew no sin." Here, with other New Testament writers, Paul asserts, first of all, Christ's sinlessness. (cf. Heb 4:15, 1 Pet 2:22, Jn 8:46, 1 Jn 3:5)

God made the sinless one "to be sin" by allowing Him to experience condemnation and death as a sinner. In the process, Christ identified totally with a sinful humanity and functioned as the servant of God, who through His sinless suffering and death reconciles a sinful people to God. (Is 53:4-9) By suffering this sinful injustice in sinless and atoning love,

---

1. Cf. John W. Fraser, "Paul's Knowledge of Jesus: II Corinthians V.16 Once More," *New Testament Studies* 17(1970-1971), pp. 293-313; J.L. Martin, "Epistemology at the Turn of the Ages," in *Christian History and Interpretation*, edited by W.R. Farmer, *et al.* (Cambridge: Cambridge University Press, 1967), pp. 269-287; Ferdinand Hahn, "Siehe, jetzt ist der Tag des Heils," *Evangelische Theologie*, 33(1973), pp. 244-253; Reimund Bieringer, "2 Kor 5,19 und die Versohnung der Welt,"*Ephemerides Theologicae Lovaniensis*, 63(1987), pp. 295-326.
2. Cf. Peter Stuhlmacher, "Erwœgungen zum ontologischen Charakter der *kainêktisis* bei Paulus," *Evangelische Theologie*, 27(1967), pp. 1-35.

Christ reveals to us God's determination to reconcile the world to Himself through His Son despite its sinfulness.

Moreover, through that same love Christ transformed His own death into a sacrifice of reconciliation which reveals the utter gratuity, the sheer "grace (*charis*)," of the salvation which He brings. For the Corinthians to refuse reconciliation with Paul would amount, then, to their rejection of the grace of reconciliation which they themselves have already received through Paul's own ministry.[3]

(II)

In the letter to the Galatians, Paul spells out in greater detail the saving significance of Jesus' death. There the apostle uses Jesus' innocent death to sin on the cross in order to argue that commitment to the crucified and risen Christ demands death to Law as well. By death to the Law Paul seems to mean that one no longer looks to the Law as a source of salvation.[4] As we shall see, Paul will urge the same point in Romans but with more temperate rhetoric than he does in Galatians.[5]

3. Cf. Cerfaux, *op.cit.*, pp. 132-150; Anthony Tyrrell Hanson, *The Paradox of the Cross in the Thought of St. Paul*, (Sheffield: JSOT Press, 1987); G.K. Beale, "The Old Testament Background of Reconciliation in 2 Corinthians 5-7 and Its Bearing on the Literary Problem of 1 Corinthians 6.14-7.1," *New Testament Studies*, 35(1989), pp. 550-581; Fitzmyer, *To Advance the Gospel*, pp. 162-185; Stanley, *Christ's Resurrection in Pauline Theology*, pp. 138-145; Margaret E. Thrall, "Salvation Proclaimed: 2 Corinthians 5:18-21; Reconciliation with God" *Expository Times*, 93(1981-1982), pp. 227-232; M.D. Hooker, "Interchange in Christ," *Journal of Theological Studies*, 22(1971), pp. 349-361; Otfried Hofius, "Erwägungen zur Gestalt und Herkunft des paulinschen Versonungsgedanken," *Zeitschrift für Theologie und Kirche*, 77(1980), pp. 186-198; Martin Hengel, *La crucifixion dans l'antiquité et la folie du message de la croix* (Paris: Editions du Cerf, 1981); Jan Lambrecht, S.J., "Paul's Appeal and the Obedience of Christ: The Line of Thought in 2 Corinthians 10,1-6," *Biblica*, 77(1996), pp. 398- 416.

4. The letter to the Galatians reveals Paul in open and angry conflict with the Judaizers. Although exegetes find Galatians hard to date, Paul probably wrote it around the year 54 a.d. Paul in high dudgeon wants his polemic letter read in all the "churches of Galatia." (Gal 1:2) He seems therefore to have conceived it as an open letter against his adversaries. Cf. Francois Refoule, "Approche de l'épitre aux Galates," *Lumière et Vie*, 192(1989), pp. 15-28; Ernst Heitsch, "Glossen zum Galaterbrief," *Zeitschrift für die Neutestamentlische Wissenschaft*, 86(1995), pp. 173-188.

5. The doctrinal section of the letter to the Romans closes, for example, with a long reflection on the role of Israel in the history of salvation. It contains several passages of Christological import. It begins with Paul's protestation "in Christ" that he would stand willing to be "accursed and cut off from Christ" if it would save his fellow Israelites. This startling assertion echoes the prayer of Moses in Exodus for the errant Israelites who have sinned by worshipping the golden calf. Moses asks God to blot him out of the book of the covenant along with his sinful brethren; but God refuses, saying only the sinner will suffer retribution for having rejected God. Moreover, in response to Moses' plea God promises to continue to lead a sinful Israel, but only through the intermediary of an angel. (Ex 32:32-5) By this allusion to Exodus, Paul

For Paul, then, Jesus Christ saves mortals from death by rising from the dead and sending His Breath as a source of imperishable, divine, risen life. Jesus saves us from sin by dying to all sin in the flesh and by sending His Breath to empower us to live sinlessly in His image. Finally, as we shall see in this section, Jesus saves us from the Law by enduring its unjust condemnation and by dramatizing its soteriological impotence through the gift of the Breath; for She empowers us to do everything which the Law commands without the power to effect. Indeed, She empowers us to do even more by conforming us to the love of Christ, which goes beyond the negative prohibitions of the Law.

tacitly equates union with Christ and having a part in a covenant with God. (Rom 9:1-3)

Paul continues:

> They are Israelites, and to them belong the sonship, the glory, the covenants, the giving of the law, the worship, and the promises; to them belong the patriarchs, and of their race, according to the flesh is Christ, who is over all, God (*ho ôn epi pantôn Theos*) forever blessed (*eulogêos*). Amen. (Rom 9:4-5)

Exegetes debate the punctuation of v. 5. Some would place the period after "Christ" and end the passage with a blessing: "God who is over all be forever blessed!" The Greek text, however, does not suggest such a reading, since grammatically, the word "blessed (*eulogêos*)" ought to precede "God (*ho Theos*)" in a blessing formula and does not. The translation given above has, moreover, genuine plausibility in that Paul uses a variety of other linguistic strategies to assert the divinity of Jesus.

Despite his yearning over his fellow Jews, Paul nevertheless asserts unequivocally that "Christ is the end (*telos*) of the Law, for the justification of all who believe." (Rom 10:4) Here again, exegetes debate the meaning of the noun "*telos*," which can mean here either "termination" or "cessation," on the one hand, or "purpose" or "goal," on the other. If one takes Christ as the temporal cessation of the Law, then Paul is asserting that He has put an end to the period of history in which humans strive to effect their own justification and that He has done so by the free gift of justification by faith. Such an interpretation has precedent in Paul's thought. (Cf. Gal 4:2-6)

In the verses immediately preceding this one, however, Paul has been speaking teleologically. He has been lamenting the mistaken purpose of the Jews who seek justification through works rather than through faith. In the verses which follow Paul refers to justifying faith as fulfilling the promise of the Law. (Rom 10:8-9) The context suggests, therefore, that Paul probably intended the term "*telos*" to carry teleological connotations. In that case Paul is asserting that Jesus fulfills the Law's purpose and that justification through faith accomplishes the true intent of the Law. Both a teleological and a temporal interpretation, however, fits within Pauline Christology. As a consequence, Paul may also have intended the ambiguity. (Cf. Rom 9:30-3)

Cf. Thomas Geer, "Paul and the Law in Recent Discussion," *Restoration Quarterly*, 31(1989), pp. 93-107; Otfried Hofius, "Das Evangelium und Israel: Erwägungen zu Römer 9-11," *Zeitschrift für Theologie und Kirche*, 83(1986), pp. 297-324; Frank Thielman, *Paul and the Law: A Contextual Approach* (Downers Grove, IL: Intervarsity Press, 1994); Heikki Rösersönen, *Paul and the Law* (Tübingen: Hohr, 1987); E.P. Sanders, *Paul, the Law and the Jewish People* (Philadelphia, PA: Fortress, 1983); R. David Kaylor, *Paul's Covenant Community: Jew and Gentile in Romans* (Atlanta, GA: John Knox Press, 1988).

As we have seen, Paul wrote the letter to the Galatians as a response to right wing Christians who had attempted to persuade his Gentile converts that in order to live as Christians they had to submit to circumcision and take on all the obligations of Torah. Paul regarded their religious zeal as seriously misdirected and interpreted it as an attack on Christian freedom. A tone of anger and outrage therefore suffuses the rhetoric of Galatians.

In Galatians, Paul discovers at the heart of Judaizing Christianity a fundamental and pernicious error: namely, the belief that the works of the Law, especially its ceremonial works, justify humans in the eyes of God rather than faith in Jesus Christ. (Gal 2:15-16) For Paul, anyone who assumes such a position "nullifies" Christ's death. (Gal 2:21) By "nullifying the death of Christ" Paul means denying its saving efficacy. (Cf. Rom 5:5-11, 6:1-11, 8:9-17)

Paul seeks to justify this position by a series of arguments. Paul argues from the need for conversion, from the meaning of Christian baptism, and from the Galatians' own experience of the Breath of Christ.

First, the apostle argues from the fact that Jews, like Gentiles, need evangelization and conversion to Christ. The very fact that "Jews by birth (*physei Iudaioi*)," who perform the works of the Law, still need justification by faith in Jesus[6] proves, that legal observances fail to liberate one from the human state of sinfulness until justifying faith in Jesus Christ can accomplish that. If those who already keep the Law still need justification though faith in Jesus Christ, then justification cannot come from keeping the Law.

Paul presses this point still further with a reduction to the absurd: if, as the Judaizers claim, those who have sought justification in Christ through faith and through baptism nevertheless remain sinners and need circumcision in order to enjoy justification in the eyes of God, then the realm of Christ and deliberate sin [literally, the service of sin (*hamartias diakonos*)] coincide. Paul rejects such a suggestion as nonsensical. (Gal 2:17)

The apostle therefore concludes that only faith in Christ absolves from sin. External legal observances leave the heart unchanged. They still leave one in the service of sin and prone to choose it deliberately.

Second, Paul argues against the Judaizers from the meaning of Christian baptism. The apostle uses himself as an example. Baptismal faith in Christ has identified Paul with one whom the Law itself crucified as a

---

6. Paul uses the phrase "in order that we might be justified from the faith of Christ (*ex pisteôs Christou*) and not from works of the law." The preposition "from (*ex*)" before both "the faith of Christ" and "the works of the Law" designates the causal source of the justification. In other words, faith effects justification causally, while the works of the Law do not. Since in the phrase "faith of Christ," "of Christ" exemplifies the objective genitive, it means "faith in Christ." (Gal 2:16)

sinner. If the Law condemned Jesus, then faith in Jesus demands that Paul die to the Law in order to live to God in Christ.

Paul insists enigmatically that he has already "died (*apethanon*) to the Law through the Law." The past tense—"died (*apethanon*)"—alludes to Paul's own baptism into Christ. (Gal 3:27; cf. Rom 6:3-10) Death to "the Law through the Law" results from His complete identification in baptismal faith with one whom the Law cast out and judged a sinner deserving of execution. Faith in a crucified savior demands, therefore, that one live not for the Law which condemned Him to death but for God, namely, for the God who reversed the judgment of the Law by raising Jesus from the dead.[7] (Gal 1:1-5)

Death with Christ through faith, death to both sin and the Law, and the moral death effected by Christian baptism all coincide because they coincided in Jesus to whom the Breath of God assimilates those who believe. Baptismal death to sin with Christ, therefore, bears fruit in present participation in risen life: for the living Christ now lives in Paul because of Paul's own living faith in "the Son of God who loved me and gave Himself up for me." (Gal 2:20; cf. 1:3-5) The Law effects no such saving consequences.

In Galatians, therefore, Pauline rhetoric poses a stark option between commitment to the ritual demands of the Law and commitment to Christ. The Son of God, in obedience to the Father, (Gal 1:4) freely chose to suffer condemnation by the Law. As a consequence, one must choose between faith in the crucified and the Law which condemned and crucified Him. The Son's condemnation by the Law leaves one no moral middle ground.[8] (Gal 2:18, 21)

7. Since in the present passage Paul is speaking autobiographically, his death "to the law through the law" could also have autobiographical connotations. He could be referring cryptically to the fact that his zeal for the law, to which he alludes in Gal 1:14, ultimately set him in opposition to Christ and to God through his persecution of Christians. At the same time, that same zeal set his feet on the road to Damascus where the God "who had called me through His grace was pleased to reveal His Son to me, in order that I might preach Him among the Gentiles." (Gal 1:15) Cf. Silvers Zedda, "'Morto alla legge mediate la legge'" (Gal 2, 19a): Testi autobiografico sulla conversion di san Paolo?" *Rivista Biblica*, 37(1989), pp. 81-95; Francois Vough, "Jean et Paul: Controverse sur la liberté," *Lumière et Vie*, 192(1989), pp. 45-63; Terence L. Donaldson, "Zealot and Convert: The Origin of Paul's Christ-Torah Antithesis," *Catholic Biblical Quarterly*, 51(1989), pp. 655-682; Bernard Lategan, "Is Paul Defending His Apostleship in Galatians?," *New Testament Studies*, 34(1988), pp. 411-450.

8. Paul re-enforces this central insight through other arguments. Like Paul anyone who lives by faith still lives in the flesh (Gal 2:20) and therefore still remains subject to human weakness and eventually to death itself. The full and final possession of life in Christ lies, therefore, somewhere in the future. (Gal 6:9) Paul himself, however, draws another conclusion from the fact that even believers continue to live in the flesh: for the Galatians to exchange justifying faith in the crucified and risen Christ for faith in the Law would betray them into swapping life in the Breath of Christ for life in the flesh alone. (Gal 3:3)

In a third and final attempt to clinch his argument rhetorically, Paul appeals to the Galatians' own experience of the Breath of the crucified and risen Christ. In making that appeal, Paul contrasts "the works of the Law (*ergôn nomou*)" with "the hearing of faith (*akoês pisteôs*)." (Gal 3:2, 5) Only by hearing the gospel preached and by responding to it in faith did the Galatians receive the Breath of God. Only through a gospel-inspired faith has the God who gives the Breath worked signs and miracles among them. (Gal 3:1-5; cf. 1 Cor 2:1-5; Rom 8:14-15)

In other words, the Galatians had experienced the manifest presence of God among them through the Breath's charismatic action long before Judaizing Christians persuaded them of their need for circumcision. Those signs and miracles confirmed the efficacy and reality of the Breath's saving presence in their midst. The fact that they already possessed corporately and manifestly the transforming Breath of God should, then, have convinced the Galatians that they have need for nothing else to unite them to God.[9]

The Breath makes baptized Christians into the heirs of God's promise by conforming them to Christ: the baptized have "put on Christ." By putting on Christ, Paul here means that the Holy Breath draws the baptized into Jesus' own *Abba* experience by teaching them to relate to the Father with the same reverential, childlike trust and obedience as He did.[10] (Gal 3:27-4:7)

Since, however, clothes also symbolize human social relationships, putting on Christ also connotes the transformation in faith of the way one relates to all other persons. The Law created the distinction between Jew and Gentile; but the fact that any baptized person—whether Jew or Greek,

9. Cf. Hans Dieter Betz, *Galatians: A Commentary on Paul's Letter to the Churches in Galatia* (Philadelphia, PA: Fortress, 1979), pp.113-136; Heinz Schürmann, *Jesu ureigener Tod* (Freiburg: Herder, 1975), pp. 97-120; Jean Noel Aletti, "L'acte de croire pour l'apôtre Paul, *Recherches de Science Religieuse*, 77(1989), 233-250; Sam K. Williams, "The Hearing of Faith: *akoêpisteôs* in Galatians 3," *New Testament Studies*, 35(1989), pp. 82-93; Paul-Gerhard Klumbies, "La liberté de penser Dieu autrement: Paul et la théologie," *Lumière et Vie*, 192(1989), pp. 65-72; Thomas R. Schreiner, "The Abolition and Fulfillment of the Law in Paul," *Journal for the Study of the New Testament*, 35(1989), pp. 47-74; J.S. Vos, "Die hermeneutischer Antinomie bei Paulus (Galater 3.11-12; Römer 10.5-10,)" *New Testament Studies*, 38(1992), pp. 254-270; In-Jyu Hong, "Does Paul Misrepresent the Jewish Law and Covenant in Gal. 3"1-14," *Novum Testamentum*, 36(1994), pp. 166-180; Michael Cranford, "The Possibility of Perfect Obedience: Paul and the Implied Premise in Galatians 3:10 and 5:3," *Novum Testamentum*, 36(1994), pp. 242-258; Dieter Sänger, "'Verflucht ist jeder der am Holze höngt'" (Gal 3, 13b): Zur Rezeption einer frühen antichristlischen Polemik," *Zeitschrift für die Neutestamentlische Wissenschaft*, 85(1994), pp. 279-285; Normand Bonneau, "The Logic of Paul's Argument on the Curse of the Law in Galatians," *Novum Testamentum*, 39(1997), pp.60-80.
10. Cf. Fitzmyer, "*Abba* and Jesus' Relation to God," in *A cause de l'évangile: mélanges offert à Dom Jacques Dupont* (Cerf: Publications de Saint-André, 1985), pp. 15-38.

slave or free, male or female—receives the same Breath and experiences the same conformity to Christ obliterates all such legal distinctions among persons by making all members of the new Israel offspring of Abraham through faith and heirs according to God's promise to Abraham to multiply his descendants. (Gal 3:23-29; cf. Gen 15:4-6)

In his final exhortation, Paul embellishes further his argument from the Galatians' experience of the baptismal Breath. In the process, he further clarifies what he means by putting on Christ. Paul reminds the Galatians that the Breath of Christ came to them as an empowering and liberating enlightenment: as "faith working through love." (Gal 5:1-25) While the Law offers only an external constraint which increases transgression instead of forgiving it, the Breath of Christ liberates by enabling the baptized to do what they could never do left to their own power: namely, avoid the sinful works of the flesh and cultivate the love, joy, peace, patience, kindness, goodness, faithfulness, gentleness, and self-control which the Breath of Jesus inspires. (Gal 5:16-23) The virtuous freedom which the Holy Breath instills makes external legal constraint superfluous. (Gal 5:23)

If, then, the Galatians look to the Law to justify them rather than to the baptismal Breath, they will sin grievously against the gospel and therefore forfeit the gift of the Breath-inspired faith which grounds all Christian hope for righteousness; for "all those who belong to Christ Jesus have crucified the flesh with its passions and desires."[11] (Gal 5:24; cf.Rom 2:25-9, 6:15-23, 9:30-3)

In this section, I have reflected on the way in which death to the Law extends Jesus' death to sin to the believing Christian community. In the section which follows, I shall examine how Paul expands and deepens these insights in his letter to the Christians in Rome.

(III)

In the letter to the Romans, Paul develops the preceding insights with greater leisure and depth.[12] Like Galatians, the letter to the Romans argues that justifying faith frees one from sin and death. After reflecting on

11. Cf. Lloyd Gaston, *Paul and the Torah* (Vancouver: University of British Columbia Press, 1987), pp. 64-79; Derek R. Moore-Crispin, "Galatians 4:1-9: The use and Abuse of Parallels," *Evangelical Quarterly*, 61(1989), pp. 203-223; Frank J. Matera, "The Culmination of Paul's Argument in Galatians: Gal 5.1-6.17," *Journal for the Study of the New Testament*, 32(1988), pp. 79-91; T.J. Leary, "Of Paul and Pork and Proselytes," *Novum Testamentum*, 35(1993), pp. 292-293; J.C. O'Neill, "The Holy Spirit and the Human Spirit in Galatians, Gal 5, 17," *Ephemerides Theologiae Lovaniensis*, 71(1995), pp. 107-117.

12. Cf. Klaus Haacker, "Der Römerbrief als Friedenmemorandum," *New Testament Studies*, 36(1990), pp. 25-41; Joel Marcus, "The Circumcision and the Uncircumcision in Rome," *New Testament Studies*, 35(1989), pp. 67-81.

these more fundamental liberations, Paul then begins to discuss the third liberation which faith in Christ accomplishes: freedom from the Law.

In Romans as in his other letters, Paul insists on the utter gratuity and superabundance of the mercy and forgiveness revealed in Christ. The more sin abounds, the greater the victory of divine grace. Paul then asks rhetorically whether such a faith justifies sinning in order to increase grace's victory.

He responds to his own question by reducing it to an absurdity. The fact that God graces us promiscuously in Christ gives us no leave to sin promiscuously so that grace might more abound. (Rom 6:1-2a) Paul demonstrates the absurdity of such a notion by appealing to the ethical commitment demanded by Christian baptism into the death of Jesus. In choosing to die in obedience to the Father's will, Jesus simultaneously died morally to sin. Since Christian baptism unites believers to Christ in His death, it demands of the baptized a moral death to sin which imitates the perfection of Jesus own sinless obedience to the Father. Adam bequeathed death to humanity through his sin of disobedience; Jesus by dying Adam's death in sinless obedience to the Father rises from the dead and transforms death to sin into risen life. Our obedience to God in the image of Jesus expresses our union with Christ within the paschal mystery, a union which therefore also guarantees our own share in His risen life. (Rom 6:1-4)

Death to sin with Christ frees one from slavery to sin, a state in which the Romans lived before they committed themselves to the gospel. Now their liberation from the slavery of sin has made them instead slaves of God in a process of sanctification which leads to eternal life. "For the wages of sin are death, but the free gift of God (*to de charisma tou Theou*) is eternal life in Christ Jesus our Lord."[13] (Rom 6:15-23)

---

13. Cf. *NJBC*, 51:62-9, 82:67-80; Cranfield, *Romans: A Shorter Commentary* (Grand Rapids, MI: Eerdmans, 1985), pp. 126-140; Lawrence Percy Akli, *The Pauline Concept of Baptism and New Life in Christ: The Dynamics of Christian Life According to St. Paul* (Rome: N. Domenici Pecheux, 1992); Jeffrey Reed, "Indicative and Imperative in Rom 6,21-22: The Rhetoric of Punctuation," *Biblica*, 74 (1993), pp. 244-257; Leander E. Keck, "'Jesus' in Romans,", *Journal of Biblical Literature*, 108(1989), pp. 443-460; Stanley K. Stowers, "*Ek pisteôs* and *dia pisteôs* in Romans 3:30," *Journal of Biblical Literature*, 108(1989), pp. 665- 674; S. Legasse, "Etre baptizé dans la mort du Christ," *Revue Biblique*, 98 (1991), pp. 544-559; James D.G. Dunn, "Salvation Proclaimed: Romans 6:1-11," *Expository Times*, 93(1981-1982), pp. 259-264; Günther Bornkamm, *Early Christian Experience* (New York, NY: Harper & Row, 1969), pp. 87-104; Florence A. Morgan, "Romans 6, 5a: United to a Death Like Christ's," *Ephemerides Theologiae Lovaniensis*, 59(1983), pp. 267-302; Karl Georg Kuhn, "Rm 6.7: *ho gar apothanon dedikaiontai apo tês harmatias*," *Zeitschrift für Neutestamentliche Wissenschaft*, 30 (1930), pp. 305-310; A.J.M. Wedderburn, "Hellenistic Christian Traditions in Romans 6?" *New Testament Studies*, 29 (1983), pp. 335-355; Heinrich Schlier, *Die Zeit der Kirche: Exegetische Aufsätze und Vortrage* (Freiburg: Herder, 1956), pp. 47-56; Werner Georg Kümmel, *Römer 7 und das Bild des Menschen im Neuen*

In Romans as in Galatians Paul argues that death to sin with Christ also implies death to the Law as a source of salvation. To make this point in Romans, Paul constructs a somewhat contrived rabbinic argument in which he likens the situation of a Jewish widow to that of the baptized Christian.

Under Jewish Law the death of a husband frees his widow from any further obligations to him. While her husband lived, marriage with another man would have made her an adulteress; but once her husband lies dead, the widow can, if she chooses, give herself to another man in marriage without guilt. "Likewise, my Brethren, you have died to the Law through the body of Christ, so that you may belong to another, to Him who has been raised from the dead in order that we may bear fruit for God." (Rom 7:1-4) Just as the first husband's death frees the wife from marriage obligations, so too the paschal mystery frees the Christian from the obligations of the Law.[14]

Paul's marital metaphor likens Christian baptism to a marriage covenant with Christ, the Lord and husband who now claims the believer's heart in a commitment of intimate love. (Cf. Rom 5:5, 8:31-39; Eph 5:21-22) Death to the Law "through the body of Christ" refers in the first instance to Jesus' execution under the condemnation of the Law. As in Galatians, commitment to the crucified frees one from subjection to the Law which condemned Him. (Cf. Gal 2:19-20, 3:10-14; Rom 6:4-6, 8:3)

The phrase "through the body of Christ" has, however, other connotations: baptismal death with Christ introduces one into His "mystical" body by giving one access to His sanctifying Breath. She, by empowering the Christian to "put on His mind," replaces the old, external Law written on tablets of stone with the law of the new covenant written on living hearts.[15] (Cf. Rom 8:1, 12:1-2; 1 Cor 2:10-16; 2 Cor 3:1-18; Gal 5:16-26)

The Law stands powerless to free one from "this body doomed to death," a body which, left to its own devices, submits so easily to sin. Through the Christ event, however, God can and does free the body-person from sin, death, and the Law. (Rom 8:7-25) The "law of the Spirit of life in Christ Jesus" frees the believing Christian from the condemnation of the

---

Testament, (Munich: Chr. Kaiser, 1974); Chrys Cargounis, "*Opsônion*: A Reconsideration of It Meaning," *Novum Testamentum*, 16 (1974) pp. 35-37. Cargounis argues that one should read Paul as asserting, not that "the wages of sin are death," but that "the provisions of sin are death." He therefore interprets Paul to mean that death offers sinners a poisonous, deadly fare which separates one from God. Whether one pays for sin with death or suffers death as a consequence of indulging in sin, the result remains the same.

14. Cf. John D. Earnshaw, "Reconsidering Paul's Marriage Analogy in Romans 7. 1-4," *New Testament Studies*, 40(1994), pp. 68-88.

15. Cf. *NJBC*, 51:70-2; Cranfield, *op.cit.*, pp.147-52.

Law of sin and death by teaching humans to live in the sinless Jesus' image. (Rom 8:1-2) The Breath of God frees one from death by functioning as a principle of resurrection. Those who share the divine Breath already share the risen life of Christ and can therefore look forward to bodily resurrection with Him. (Rom 8:9-11)

In all of this Paul echoes the arguments of second Corinthians and of Galatians. In Romans, however, the apostle insists more on the sacred character of the Law and on its divine origin. God gave the Law. It proved a Law of sin, however, because it heightened sin consciousness without giving the power to resist sin. By augmenting the awareness of sin without giving the power to shun it, the Law, despite its sacred character, ended by compounding the sinfulness of those who received it.[16] (Rom 7:7-20)

A Law of sin functions as a Law of death by condemning the sinner to receive the wages of sin. (Rom 6:23) These dire effects of the Law flow not from the Law itself but from "the flesh" in its weakness and proneness to sin without the gift of God's Breath.[17] (Rom 8:3)

In Romans, Paul ponders in greater detail the saving effects of Christ's death. More than in Galatians or in any other letter, he attempts to see the paschal mystery as a whole. As we have seen, at the heart of the paschal mystery lies the historical revelation of the risen Christ as a "life-giving Breath." In Romans, Paul's makes resurrection faith practical by requiring that those who confess the risen Christ die to sin in the power of His Breath just as Jesus Himself died to sin on the cross. Jesus died to sin on the cross because His death expressed the perfection of His obedience to the Father. Possession of the Breath of the risen Christ conforms believers to Him morally and so transforms them in His image. Present moral transformation in the image of Jesus and in the power of His Breath begins a process which culminates in final resurrection.

At the culmination of his argument in Romans, Paul meditates on the way in which God chose to overcome human sinfulness. "Sending His own Son in the likeness of sinful flesh and for sin, He condemned sin in the flesh, in order that the just requirement of the Law might be fulfilled in us, who walk not according to the flesh but according to the Breath." (Rom 8:3-4)

The phrase "His own Son" has a stronger meaning than "Son of God," for it heightens the close filial relationship of the Son to the Father. The fact, moreover, that the Father sends "His own Son" seems to place that relationship within the Godhead itself. (Cf. Phil 2:6-11)

16. Cf. David Hellholm, "Die argmetative Funktion von Römer 7.1-6," *New Testament Studies*, 43 (1997), pp. 385-411.

17. Cf.Fitzmyer, *To Advance the Gospel*, pp. 186-201; D.A. Campbell, "The Meaning of *pistis* and *nomos* in Paul: A Linguistic and Structural Perspective," *Journal of Biblical Literature*, 111 (1992), pp. 91-103.

God sends the Son in the "likeness of our sinful flesh." Paul recognizes the physical character of the incarnation; but he refrains from stating that Jesus assumed sinful flesh. Instead, the Son, who knew no sin, assumed a humanity like our own in that He was born like any human and lived subject to the Law. (cf. Gal 4:4; 2 Cor 5:21)

God sent His Son because He desired to do something about human sinfulness (Rom 8:3); for, through the Son's mission, God "condemned sin in the flesh." Since the Son did not possess sinful flesh, but only its likeness, when God condemns sin "in the flesh," He condemns it in us, in sinful humanity, not in His sinless Son. (Cf. 2 Cor 5:21) Moreover, in sending His Son, God did not rest content with condemning human sinfulness. Instead, through the Son He sent His Breath to take sin away. God, then, through the gift of the Breath of the risen Christ actively empowers Christians to live justified and righteous lives in the image of the sinless Christ.[18] (Rom 8:4-9a)

Possession of the Breath of the risen Christ joins the Christian to Him. It sets the hearts of believers on those realities and values whose love the Breath of Christ inspires: namely, on life and on peace. She dwells in believers as in a home and empowers them to overcome the longings of the flesh in ways in which the Law never could. (Rom 8:5-9)

Moreover, Paul calls the Breath of God, who orients us to the things of God, "the Breath of Christ." The risen Christ not only functions as the source of the Breath of God who dwells in us, but She incorporates us into Christ. She does so by giving us a share in His risen life and by conforming us morally to Him. Indeed in verses 9-11, Paul clearly equates "belonging to Christ" with "living in His Breath." He writes:

> But you are not in the flesh, you are in the Breath, if in fact the Breath of God dwells in you. Any one who does not have the Breath of Christ does not belong to Him. But if Christ is in you, although your bodies are dead because of sin, your spirits are alive because of righteousness. (Rom 8:10)

Here terms like "body," "flesh," and "spirit" designate the whole embodied person under different facets, or aspects. "Body" connotes finite, physical existence. "Flesh" connotes weakness, sinfulness, and proneness to death. "Spirit" designates the entire human person pneumatically transformed by God's Breath. The indwelling of the Breath incorporates believers into Christ and makes Christ present in them by inspiring the deeds of righteousness which manifest that presence.

Presence effects a mutual indwelling: Christians in Christ, Christ in Christians; Christians in the Breath, the Breath in Christians. Though condemned to physical death because of sin, believers have experienced a

18. Cf. Christian Scheutz, "'Nach dem Geist leben' (Röm 8,4)," *Theologisch-Praktische Quartalschrift*, 137 (1989), pp. 395-398.

transformation of their deepest centers of consciousness through their conformity to Christ and through their share in His righteousness. Attachment to Christ demands therefore personal transformation at the deepest levels of the self, a revitalization which empowers the Christian to live for God in an obedience which imitates the perfection of Jesus' sinless obedience.

Moreover, those who have experienced this profound transformation in the Breath of God and of Christ live in the confident, believing hope that their own transformation in God's Breath will culminate in their resurrection, as it had for Jesus; for in possessing the Breath of God they possess the same divine life principle which effected Jesus' resurrection, His total transformation in God. Indeed, God sends His Breath to believers precisely in order to prepare them to share risen life with Christ. (Rom 8:10-1)

If moral conformity to Christ culminates in resurrection, then Christians must always obey their Breath-inspired impulses, not the impulses of the flesh, which lead to death. Fidelity to their new, Breath-transformed reality guarantees their ultimate possession of risen life with Christ. (Rom 8:12-4; cf. Col 3:5-11) I note in passing that moral transformation in Jesus' image would culminate in resurrection makes sense if what people embody results from the kinds of choices they make in the course of a lifetime: i.e., if their history defines their essence, as the philosophical construct of experience expounded in chapter five proposes.[19]

Christians experience directly their own filial relationship to God as the Breath of Christ draws them both collectively and personally into Jesus' own *Abba* experience. The deep, pneumatic transformation of their human spirit in the Breath of Christ empowers them to address God with the same intimate name as Jesus Himself, to call God "*Abba*." Christians experience this transformation of their deepest selves as a liberation, not as slavery and constraint. That liberation also incorporates them into the family of God.

Since the divine Breath effects this incorporation, She lends divine sanction to the Christian's awareness of divine adoption. Moreover, the fact that God Himself is transforming those who believe, both women and men, into His "sons" makes all Christians into "heirs of God and coheirs with Christ."

---

19. Cf. Brendan Byrne, S.J., "Living out the Righteousness of God: The Contribution of Rom 6:1-8:13 to an Understanding of Paul's Ethical Presuppositions," *Catholic Biblical Quarterly* 43(1981), pp. 557-581; A.J. M. Wedderburn, *Baptism and Resurrection: Studies in Pauline Theology Against Its Greco-Roman Background* (Tübingen: Mohr, 1987); Wayne A. Meeks, "The Polymorphic Ethics of Paul the Apostle," *The Annual of the Society of Christian Ethics*, edited by D.M. Yeager (Washington, DC: Georgetown University Press, 1988), pp. 17-29.

Divine adoption also draws one into the passion of God's Son; but it gives the assurance that suffering leads to risen glory. (Rom 8:14-17; cf. Gal 4:7; I Cor 3:16-17) Indeed, the sufferings of this life pale to insignificance in comparison with glorious union with God which awaits his children.[20] (Rom 8:18)

In a Pauline vision of salvation, human liberation from sin and human participation in the glory of the risen Christ has cosmic consequences. (Rom 8:18-25) The sin of Adam had cosmic effects in that it caused God to curse the earth, thus transforming human labor into drudgery. Sinful acts impregnate creation with sinful, death-dealing impulses. God's curse subjected all creation to the dominion of sin and death. As a consequence, the Adamic reversal, the redemption from sin effected by Christ, must have cosmic implications as well. It must undo the cosmic consequences of Adam's sin.

In its present state of bondage, the whole of creation, infected by lethal, human sinfulness, writhes like a woman in labor vainly striving to give birth to life. Yet the God who subjected creation to this "futility" did so "in hope," (Rom 8:20) that is to say, with a view to the redemption finally accomplished in Jesus. Indeed, the Breath-inspired longing of Christians for their share in Jesus' bodily resurrection raises this cosmic birthing to consciousness and reveals its redemptive character. Creation will one day know freedom from its "bondage to decay."

Christians will experience final liberation from the reign of decadence in the final resurrection. On that day, all creation too will participate in "the glorious liberty of the children of God." (Rom 8:21) In what does that participation consist? Pauline hope envisages a universe freed finally from slavery to sin and from the constraint of death.

Christians, then, long for personal and cosmic redemption as the completion of the salvation they already know in Christ. Already children of God, they possess "the first-fruits of the Breath," a gift which guarantees their final redemption, as only life-giving union with God can.[21] (Rom 8:21-5)

The Breath who guarantees final resurrection also dwells in all believers in order to rectify the longings of their hearts. When we do not know for what we ought to pray, "the Breath intercedes for us with sighs too deep for words" and ensures that the prayers of God's saints conform to His

---

20. Cf. J.J. van Rensberg, "The Children of God in Romans 8," *Neotestamentica*, 15 (1981), pp. 139-179; A.J.M. Wedderburn, "Some Observations on Paul's Use of the Phrases 'In Christ' and 'with Christ,'" *Journal for the Study of the New Testament*, 25(1985), pp. 83-97.

21. Cf. John G. Gibbs, *Creation and Redemption: A Study in Pauline Theology* (Leiden: E.J. Brill, 1971), pp. 33-58; Anton Vötgle, *Das Neue Testament und die Zukunft des Kosmos* (Düsseldorf: Patmos Verlag, 1970), pp. 183-204.

mind. Once again, Paul makes a close link between the Breath of God and the mind of God.[22] (Rom 8:26-7; cf. 1 Cor 2:14-16)

Three realities, then, bear witness to the fact that the glory which awaits God's children utterly transcends the sufferings of this life: 1) the futile groaning of creation as it longs for deliverance from bondage to sin and death, 2) Christian longing for the final redemption of their bodies in risen glory, and 3) the Breath of God Herself who imparts a present share in risen life while rectifying human longing for redemption through conformity to Christ. The God-givenness of Christian hope—the fact that the divine Breath Herself inspires and therefore sanctions hope in the resurrection—makes the fulfillment of that hope a certainty by engaging the fidelity of God.

Under the purpose and providence of God, therefore, all things, even suffering and death, work finally for the good of those who love Him.[23] God not only foreknows those He calls, but in calling them He predestines them to transformation "in the image of His Son, so that He might be the firstborn among many brethren." (Rom 8:28-9)

The Christian's call to live as children of God in Jesus' image reveals, then, God's saving, predestining intent; for our calling effects our justification before God, and justification culminates in glorification with the risen Christ. (Rom 8:30; cf. Rom 5:1-5; 1 Th 2:13-5; Eph 1:3-23; Col 1:15-20) In other words, God the Father stands revealed in the paschal mystery as a God irrevocably committed to those whom He has called. Having not only sent us His own Son but even allowed Him to suffer for us the ignominy of the cross, God will withhold no good from those whom He loves. God's absolute commitment of love absolves in advance from any accusation of guilt those whom He has justified.

Nor need Christians ever fear the judgment of Christ, even though God has given all judgment into His hands. (2 Th 1:6-10; 1 Cor 2:4) Far from condemning us, Jesus has proved His commitment to us not only by laying down His life for us but also by rising in order to communicate to us the divine life which ensures our resurrection with Him. In addition, He pleads for His saints as He sits at the right hand of the Father, as

---

22. Cf. Ernst Käsemann, *Pauline Perspectives*, (Chatham: SCM Press, 1971), pp. 122-137. The divine Breath also authenticates prayer by ensuring that it expresses the believer's participation in Jesus' *Abba* experience. See: Julie L. Wu, "The Spirit's Intercession in Romans 8:26-27: An Exegetical Note," *Expository Times*, 105 (1993-1994), p. 13.

23. Divergence in the manuscript tradition has yielded three different readings of Rom 8:28. 1) God cooperates in all things with those who love Him in order to turn them to their good; 2) God makes all things conspire for the good of those who love Him; 3) All things work together for the good of those who love God. All three readings, however, assert the power of providence to turn all things, even evil, into good for those who love God. Cf. *NJBC*, 51:90.

the efficacious and saving invocation of His name reveals.[24] (Rom 8:31-34; cf. Rom 10:13; 1 Cor 1:2)

Christians, then, live in the conviction that nothing which they merely suffer can separate them from the love of God historically revealed in the unconditioned, death-defying, saving love of Christ. For those justified by the Breath of Jesus to experience separation from Him, they must choose that separation. No external sanction of the state or of any human authority can effect it: no eschatological tribulation (*thlipsis*), no constraining anguish (*stenochôria*), no persecution (*diôgmos*), no starvation (*limos*), no destitution or nakedness (*gymnotês*), no danger (*kindynos*), no threat of slaughter or execution (*machaira*).

Neither can any cosmic force separate us from Christ's love: neither death nor life (*oute thanatos oute zoê*), neither angels nor principalities

---

24. Cf. Cerfaux, *op. cit.*, pp. 209-210; Thomas Söding, "Gottesliebe bei Paulus," *Theologie und Glaube*, 79 (1989), pp. 219-242; Elsa Tamey, "Now No Condemnation: A Meditation on Romans 8," *Ecumenical Review*, 41(1981), pp. 446-453. One finds analogous insights in the second letter to the Corinthians. Contemporary exegesis suggests that second Corinthians consists of a fusion of several of Paul's letters to the Corinthian community. Certainly, this letter lacks literary unity. The precise way one dates the letter depends on whether or not one regards it as a single or a composite letter. (Cf. *NJBC*, 50:2-4; *HBC*, 1190-2.) The letter's content suggests that it was written reasonably close to the first letter to the Corinthians, possibly from Ephesus. Here I focus only on passages which contain Christological interest.

In defending himself against a charge of vacillation, Paul observes:

As surely as God is faithful, our word to you has not been Yes and No. For the Son of God, Jesus Christ, whom we preached among you, Silvanus, Timothy, and I, was not Yes and No; but in Him it is always Yes. For all the promises of God find their Yes in Him. That is why we utter the Amen through Him, to the glory of God. But it is God who establishes us with you in Christ, and has commissioned us; He has put His seal upon us and has given us His Breath in our hearts as a guarantee. (2 Cor 1:18-22)

In all that concerns his message, Paul proclaims himself utterly innocent of vacillation. As an apostle he proclaims Jesus Christ, the Son of God, as a divine "amen" to all the promises God the Father made through His prophets. Jesus fulfills and confirms those prophecies and reveals a God who is for us, a God who seeks our good and our salvation. (cf. Rom 8:31)

Moreover, when the assembled Christian community pronounces the word "amen" in its worship, it does so through Jesus Christ; for He has empowered the community to do so by fulfilling the divine promises. In saying "amen" to Jesus, the community simultaneously ratifies the divine promises He fulfills. In pronouncing the liturgical "amen," Christians glorify God the Father, the ultimate source of their salvation: they openly and joyfully acknowledge the wonders He has accomplished, His works which reveal to us His glory.

Christians can pronounce the "amen" of faith because God the Father established them on a firm foundation by incorporating them "into Christ (*eis Christon*)" when through the gift of the divine Breath the Father sealed them in baptism. That same divine Breath guarantees their final resurrection. Cf. Victor Paul Furnish, *II Corinthians* (New York, NY: Doubleday, 1984), pp. 132-50; Bruce, *op. cit.*, pp. 180-3.

(*oute aggeloi oute archai*), neither things present nor things to come (*oute enestôta oute mellonta*), no powers (*oute dynamei*s), neither height nor depth (*out hypsoma oute bathos*), not any other created thing (*oute ktsis hetera*).

Some of the items in these lists of cosmic forces impotent to separate us from Christ's love need special exegesis. The first list catalogues the violent means at the disposition of the state and of other potential enemies of the gospel in their attempt to drive a wedge between Christians and the love of Christ. The term "*thlipsis*" connotes tribulations which draw one into Jesus' own eschatological struggle with evil, a struggle which led Him to the cross. Because it heads the list of hardships inflicted on those who believe, the term endows the other trials which follow it with an eschatological coloring. They all qualify as instances of *thlipsis*, of the final eschatological confrontation with evil. As long as Christians only suffer these trials and continue to resist those forces instead of conniving with evil, not only do those same forces remain impotent to separate the saints from Jesus and His love; but Christians even triumph through their share in the eschatological suffering and victory of Christ.[25] (Rom 8:36-9)

Several of the specific cosmic forces which Paul names need explanation. In saying that neither life or death can separate us from the love of Christ, Paul seems to mean that it makes no difference whether one lives or dies: the saving love of Christ will still encompass those who believe in Him. Paul states this same idea quite explicitly in the final exhortation of Romans:

> None of us lives for self, and no one dies for self. If we live, we live for the Lord; and, if we die, we die for the Lord. Whether we live or whether we die, we belong to the Lord; for to that end Christ died and lived, so that He might be Lord of the dead and of the living. (Rom 14:7-9)

This later text underscores the ambivalence of the terms "life" and "death" in the final age of salvation. Neither life nor death as we experience them in this world has ultimate significance, because Christ, in dying and rising again, has made Himself Lord of both the living and the dead. Hence, union with the risen Christ both in this life and in the next has more importance than physical life or physical death in and of themselves. His Breath accomplishes that union.[26]

The term "rulers (*archai*)" can mean 1) the human agents of cosmic powers, 2) the powers themselves, or 3) both of the above acting in collu-

---

25. *Cf. NJBC*, 51:82-91; Cranfield, *op.cit.*, pp. 172-213; Barrett, *From First Adam to Last*, pp. 92-109.

26. Cf. W.C. Cotzer, "The Holy Spirit and the Eschatological View in Romans 8," *Neotestamentica*, 15(1981), pp. 180-198; Käsemann, *Pauline Perspectives*, pp. 32-59; James L. Jaquette, "Life and Death, *Adiophora*, and Paul's Rhetorical Strategies," *Novum Testamentum*, 38(1996), pp. 30-54.

sion with one another. Here, the term probably has the second meaning: namely, the evil powers themselves. Paul parallels the powers with angels. Whether the angels to whom he refers fight on the side of good or evil remains vague. Since, however, Paul is composing a list which includes every created reality, he probably wants to say that no spiritual reality, whether good or evil, can ever by any external means separate the faithful believer from Christ's love.

The terms "height" and "depth" derive from ancient astronomy and designate the top and bottom of the pillars which allegedly supported the heavens. Paul follows this all-encompassing spatial image with an all-encompassing temporal image: "things present" and "things to come." Taken together these spatial and temporal images assert that nothing which exists within space and time can separate believers from God's love in Christ.

Between his spatial imagery and his temporal imagery Paul inserts the term "powers (*dynameis*)," a generic New Testament term for the enemies of God, both preternatural and human.[27] By ending the list with the term "any other creature," however, Paul is asserting that all the enemies of God, even those of superhuman strength, finally count only as creatures made by God and therefore ultimately stand powerless before the victory of divine saving love.[28]

---

27. Cf. Wink, *op.cit.*, 17.

28. In Ephesians the love of Christ for His Church becomes an ideal to which the union of Christian spouses aspires. Christ by saving the Church has become its head. Paul here insists on the dynamic character of Christ's headship of the mystical body. He heads the body by actively saving it. Women should in a similar manner seek their salvation by freely subordinating themselves to their husbands. (Eph 5:22-24)

The husband, however, because he must relate to his wife as Christ relates to His body, the Church, should take no advantage of his wife's free subordination to him. Instead, like Christ, he must relate to his wife as her servant, willing to suffer anything, even death, for the sake of her sanctification, salvation, and ultimate glorification. He must serve her through encouraging a holy life, unsoiled by evil. (Eph 5:25-7)

The saving love of Christ has made the Church into His very body. In the same way husbands must love their wives as if the wives were their very body by nurturing and cherishing them. Indeed, as Gen 2:23 proclaims, she is "flesh of his flesh and bond of his bone." Moreover, the divine command that husband and wife become one flesh finds fulfillment in the transformation of the martial relationship through the mutual, Christlike love that spouses show toward one another. (Eph 5:23; cf. Gen 2:24-5)

Ephesians depicts the relationship of Christ, the divine bridegroom, to His bride the Church as a "great mystery." (Eph 5:32) Although the relationship of mutual love and service which Christian spouses must incarnate clearly participates in this mystery of divine love, Paul makes it clear that he is applying the term "mystery" to Christ's relation to His Church: "I am referring to Christ and to the Church." (Eph 5:32)

In one sense, Ephesians is only reiterating what Paul has said over and over again in many of his other letters: namely, that the incredible divine love revealed in the saving

This chapter has argued the following thesis: *Because on the cross, Jesus died to sin, Christological hope roots itself in moral conformity to Him in the power of His Breath.* As we have seen, Paul develops these insights most explicitly in the eighth chapter of Romans.

In many ways, the eighth chapter of Romans brings a Pauline Christology of hope to mature formulation. It places the paschal mystery at the heart of human salvation. In the process it endows Christian hope with personal, moral, social, and cosmic significance.

The same Christology of hope which Paul articulates in Romans also provides the context for understanding another Christological theme which Paul has developed earlier in the same letter: faith in Jesus as the last Adam. To this aspect of Pauline Christology I turn in the chapter which follows. In exploring in greater detail what Paul means by calling Jesus "the last Adam," I shall further explicitate the saving consequences of the paschal mystery which this chapter and the preceding chapter have together described.

death of Christ for sinners raises them up in glory and reconciles them to the Father. That love confronts us historically as the central religious mystery.

In Ephesians, as in Colossians, Paul is also saying something new about the central mystery of Christian faith by understanding it under the rubric of the *plêôma*. Implicitly, then, he is also portraying the day-to-day living of a marital commitment in mutual Christ-like service as building the *plêôma*. I shall discuss the Pauline *plêôma* in a subsequent chapter. Cf. Stephen Francis Miletic, *"One Flesh": Eph. 5.22-24, 5.31: Marriage and the New Creation* (Rome: Pontifical Biblical Institute, 1988); François Wessels, "Ephesians 5:21-23, 'Wives be subject to your husbands; husbands love your wives,'" *Journal of Theology for Southern Africa*, 67(1989), pp. 67-76; Albert Vanhoye, "Il 'grande misterio'; la lettura di Ef 5, 21-33 del neuvo documento pontifico [*Mulieris dignitatem*, 15.VIII.1988]," *Osservatore Romano*, Quad 9(1989), pp. 146-153.

Chapter 14
Universal Salvation in Christ

This chapter reflects on the scope of the salvation effected in the paschal mystery. In the following paragraphs I shall argue the following thesis: *Christological hope roots itself in the fact that in Jesus God has revealed His desire to save all people through the paschal mystery.* In the course of arguing this thesis, I shall examine in greater detail than in chapter twelve what Paul means when he designates Jesus as "the last Adam." I shall also develop in this and in subsequent chapters the lived, soteriological consequences of the paschal mystery. By the principles of pragmatic logic, a sound understanding of those consequences clarifies the paschal mystery's meaning.

This chapter divides into two parts. The first part examines Paul's reflections on universal salvation in Galatians. The second part ponders how he expands and deepens that same argument in the letter to the Romans.

(I)

When Paul names Jesus "the last Adam" he asserts that through Him God effects a salvation which encompasses the whole human race. In the letter to the Galatians, Paul lays the remote theological foundation for this belief by portraying the faith of Abram, prior to his circumcision, as the prototype of Christian faith.

In Genesis God promises that He will multiply the childless Abram's offspring until they number like the stars. Abram believes God's promise and experiences justification in virtue of His faith. (Gen 15:2-6) God subsequently changes Abram's name to Abraham when He enjoins the circumcision of Abraham and of his descendants. (Gen 17:1-9) Hence, in Paul's midrashic[1] argument, Abram's justification by faith preceded his circumcision.

In both Galatians and Romans Paul cites Abraham as a prototypical example of justifying faith. In both letters, Paul also sees in God's promises to Abraham a foreshadowing of the universality of the salvation effected in Christ. Paul, however, develops his argument somewhat differently in each letter.[2]

---

1. Rabbinic midrash adapted a Biblical text or narrative to the needs of a particular audience by reinterpreting it, often in the case of a event by modifying some narrative details.
2. Cf. G. Walter Hansen, *Abraham in Galatians: Epistolary and Rhetorical Contexts* (Sheffield: JSOT Press, 1989).

In Galatians, Paul reminds those to whom he writes that the Law curses those who violate it (Deut 27:23). It also curses specifically anyone who undergoes crucifixion. The Law therefore cursed Jesus who died on the cross. (Deut 21:23) This insistence on the curse of the Law, together with everything which it connotes in Galatians, fades from Paul's argument in Romans.

Paul also contrasts this double curse with the blessing promised Abraham whom faith justified before ever he underwent circumcision. Because of his justifying faith God promised Abraham that all nations would find blessing in him and in his offspring. (Gen 15:6, 18:18) Paul finds that promise fulfilled in the conversion of the Gentiles to Christ and in their justification by faith in Abraham's image.

Jesus, the offspring of Abraham, endured the curse of the Law for two reasons. First, He sought to redeem the Jews, whose guilt the knowledge of the Law had augmented. Second, in Christ God also sought to insure that the Gentiles need never experience the Law's curse. God gave the Law to increase human transgressions until Christ, through the gift of the Breath, would fulfill God's promises to Abraham by taking away the transgressions of Jew and Gentile alike. (Gal 3:6-14, 19, 22) God's promise to Abraham, therefore, finds its fulfillment in the universal salvation effected in the risen Jesus. Incorporation into Christ also incorporates one into the new Israel. It therefore makes the justified believer into a religious descendant of Abraham without the need for circumcision and the Law.[3]

The Law pales by comparison with the gift revealed in Christ. God gave the Law through both angelic and human mediation; but in the gift of the Breath, Christians encounter God immediately and directly. (Gal 3:19-20) The Law restrained human sinfulness the way a tutor restrains the waywardness of a child: through external discipline. Breath-inspired baptismal faith, however, transforms Christians from wayward children into the children and heirs of God, from minors, who pass their childhood under the authority and tutelage of slaves, to adults liberated from the need of such a tutor.

Paul is appealing rhetorically to the educational experience of a child of the first century who from the age of seven until he donned the toga of manhood had to submit to the authority and supervision of a slave called a tutor (*paidagogos*). As a consequence, until the child reached his majority, he spent much of his time in the company of slaves. The Law, Paul argues, tutored the Jews, who lived in the bondage of sin, until they came

---

3. Cf. R.G. Hamerton-Kelley, "Sacred Violence and The Curse of the Law (Galatians 3.13): The Death of Christ as Sacrificial Travesty," *New Testament Studies*, 36 (1990), pp. 98-118; Normand Bonneau, "The Logic of Paul's Argument on the Curse of the Law in Galatians 3:10-14," *Novum Testamentum*, 39 (1997), pp. 60-80.

of age religiously by putting on Christ through the liberating gift of His Breath.[4]

(II)

In the letter to the Romans, Paul embellishes the insights he sketches in a preliminary manner in Galatians. In the later letter, Paul argues that the "justice (*dikaiosunê*)" which God once revealed through the Law and the prophets "now" stands revealed "outside the Law....faith in Jesus Christ to all those who believe." (Rom 3:21-2) Instead of insisting on the curse of the Law as he had in Galatians, Paul now recognizes its ultimate saving intent.

By "now" Paul means the end time inaugurated by the death and resurrection of Jesus, "the acceptable time, the day of salvation." (cf. 2 Cor 6:2) The revelation of justice happens "outside the Law" during the end time through the action of the "Breath of holiness" who proceeds from the risen Christ and empowers the faith and righteous living even of uncircumcised Gentiles. The Breath of the risen Christ enables them through consent to the gospel to live in the newness of their minds. (Rom 8:1, 12:1-2)

Abraham believed that he would father countless multitudes; and that faith justified him in God's eyes before ever he was circumcised. (Rom 4:1-25) The same faith prefigures and finds fulfillment in the faith of Christians, both Jew and Gentile, who trust in "Him who raised from the dead Jesus our Lord, who was handed over for our sins and raised for our justification." (Rom 4:24-5) Jesus' deliverance to death for our sins reveals Him as the servant of God and His cross as an atoning sacrifice

---

4. Cf. Montague, *op.cit.*, p. 150; Augustin Grail, "Le baptème dans l'épitre aux Galates," *Revue Biblique*, 58 (1957), pp. 503-520; John Bligh, S.J., "Principalities and Powers," *Theological Studies*, 23 (1962), pp. 93-99; Albert Vanhoye, "Un médiateur des anges en Ga 3,19-20," *Biblica*, 59(1978), pp. 403-411; Barrett, *From First Adam to Last*, pp.22-45; Fitzmyer, *To Advance the Gospel*, pp. 236-246; Käsemann, *Pauline Perspectives*, pp. 79-101; T. David Gordon, "A Note on *paidagôgus* in Galatians 3. 24-25," *New Testament Studies*, 35 (1989), pp. 150-154; Michel Gillet, "Vivre sans loi," *Lumi`rre et Vie*, 192(1989), pp. 5-14; Linda L. Belleville, "'Under Law': Structural Analysis and the Pauline Concept of Law in Galatians 3.21-4," *Journal for the Study of the New Testament*, 26(1986), pp. 53-78; Sam K. Williams,"The Hearing of Faith: *Akoêpisteôs* in Galatians 3," *New Testament Studies*, 35 (1989), pp. 82-93; Joop Smit, "The Letter of Paul to the Galatians: A Deliberative Speech," *New Testament Studies*, 35 (1989), pp. 1-26; H.W. Hollander and J. Holleman, "The Relationship of Death, Sin, and Law in 1 Cor 15:56," *Novum Testamentum*, 35 (1993), pp. 270-291; Jean-Nöel Aletti, "L'acte de croire pour l'apôtre Paul," *Recherches de Science Religieuse*, 77(1989) pp. 233-250; Brian J.Dodd, "Paul's Paradogmatic "I" and 1 Corinthians 6:12," *Journal for the Study of the New Testament*, 59 (1995), pp. 38-58; Michael Cranford, "Abraham in Romans 8: The Father of All Who Believe," *New Testament Studies*, 41 (1995), pp. 71-88; Krister Stendahl, *Paul Among Jews and Gentiles* (Philadelphia, PA: Fortress, 1976).

which reconciles us to God. (cf. Is 51:11) The resurrection effects that reconciliation through the morally transforming, justifying faith inspired by the Breath of the risen Christ. Justifying faith finds living embodiment in confessing Christ in responsible obedience to the divine revelation made manifest in the paschal mystery.[5] (Rom 8:1-2)

Hence, only through faith in "our Lord Jesus Christ" does God judge us "righteous (*dikaiôthentes*)" and "at peace (*eirênên echômen*)" with Him.

> Through Him we have obtained access to this grace in which we stand, and we rejoice in our hope of sharing the glory of God. (Rom 5:2)

Justifying faith in the risen Christ and in the God who raised Him replaces the state of enmity with God, which resulted from sin, with a peace born of reconciliation through the forgiveness of sin. One possesses this reconciliation "through Christ," because His atoning death, resurrection, and mission of the Breath reveal the Father's plan of salvation. The present knowledge of the Father inspired by the Breath of the risen Christ even "now" introduces believers into the last age of salvation and orients them in hope to the full vision of God's glory with Christ in heaven.

The "grace (*charis*) in which we stand," moreover, grounds our hope for our ultimate vision of "the glory (*doxês*) of God" by ensuring our present participation in and reflection of that glory. (Cf. Rom 8:17-8, 21, 30, 15:7; 2 Cor 8:23) The "grace is which we now stand" leads to future glory because it unites us with God the Father through a love inspired by the Breath of the risen Christ. We experience that Breath as the principle of our own resurrection.[6] (Rom 5:5; cf. Rom 8:11)

---

5. Cf. Gaston, *Paul and the Torah*, pp. 45-63; Sam K. Williams, "The 'Righteousness of God" in Romans," *The Journal of Biblical Literature*, 99(1980), pp. 241-290; Luke Timothy Johnson, "Rom 3:21-26 and the Faith of Jesus," *Catholic Biblical Quarterly*, 44(1982), pp. 7- 90; Werner Georg Kummel, "*Paresis* und *endeixis*: Ein Beitrag zum Verständnis für paulinischen Rechtfertigungslehre," *Zeitschrift für Theologie und Kirche*, 49(1952), pp. 154- 167; Manfied Öming, "Ist Genesis 15,6 ein Beleg für die Anrechtung des Glaubens zür Gerichtigkeit?" 95(1983), pp. 182-197; Ulrich Wilckens, *Rechtfertigung als Freiheit: Paulusstudien* (Düsseldorf: Neukirchener Verlag, 1974), pp. 33-49; Peter F. Craffert, "Paul's Damascus Experience as Reflected in Galatians 1," *Scriptura*, 29(1989), pp. 36-47; Jan Lambrecht and Richard William Thompson, *Justification by Faith: The Implications of Romans 3:27-31* (Wilmington, DL: Michael Glazier, 1988); Ernesto Bravo, "La justification por la fé sola: Un enfoque nuevo para un viejo problem," *Revista Biblica*, 57(1989)pp. 11038; Stanley K. Stowers, "*Ek pisteôs* and *dia tê pisteôs* in Romans 3:30," *Journal of Biblical Literature*, 108(1989), pp. 665-674; Morna D. Hooker, "*Pistis Christou*," *New Testament Studies*, 35(1989), pp. 321-342; Edward Adams, "Abraham's Faith and Gentile Disobedience: Textual Links Between Romans 1 and 4," *Journal for the Study of the new Testament*, 65(1997), pp. 47-66.

6. Cf. Hendrikus Boers, "*Agapê* and *Charis* in Paul's Thought," *Catholic Biblical Quarterly*, 59(1997), pp. 393-413.

Christian hope motivates patience under suffering and the perseverance which patience inspires. (Rom 5:7) In other words, the present capacity to suffer without sinning inspires hope in ultimate perseverance.

Patient hope roots itself in the knowledge that Christ died for us while
we still lay in helpless bondage to sin. (Rom 5:6) Citing human reluctance to die even for a good person, not to mention sacrificing oneself for
an evil person, Paul observes: "But God shows His love for us in that
while we were yet sinners, Christ died for love of us." (Rom 5:7) God in
Christ did not even demand our prior repentance as a condition for acting to save us. Christ, the victim of human sin, died for sinners in their
sinfulness, loving them with an atoning, reconciling love. The unshak-
able love of the crucified Son of God reveals God's unconditioned commitment to a sinful humanity; and the sending of the Breath completes
the new covenant by empowering all sinners to "put on the mind" of the
sinless Christ. Christ died "at the appointed time (*kata kairon*)," at the
moment providentially decreed by the Father, a moment which establishes the "now," the saving, eschatological moment in which all Christians actually live. (Rom 5:6)

The fact that both Jews and Gentiles believe in Christ's atoning death
through the power of His resurrection and through their present share in
His risen life makes the ultimate fulfillment of their hope for risen glory
all the more certain; for justifying faith has transformed sinners from
God's enemies into His friends. Justification through the blood of Christ
therefore assures all believers that, as sharers in His risen life through the
gift of His Breath, they have no cause to fear the divine wrath; for God
reveals His wrath when He abandons hardened sinners to the consequences
of their own sinfulness. (Rom 1:18-27)

> Since, therefore, we are now justified by His blood, much more shall we be
> saved by Him from the wrath of God. For if, while we were enemies, we
> were reconciled to God by the death of His Son, much more, now that we
> are reconciled, shall we be saved by His life. Not only so, but we also
> rejoice in God, through our Lord Jesus Christ, through whom we have
> now received our reconciliation. (Rom 5:9-11)

All believers shall, then, be saved through possession of the fullness of
risen life which perfects their present union through faith with the living
God, the source of all life. The certainty of our hope for final salvation
also inspires our present joy in the presence of the God who is graciously
saving sinners from His own wrathful judgment.

Christian hope for salvation in Christ even frees all believers to boast
about their sufferings, their personal share in the cross of Christ; for the
patience and perseverance which such suffering inspires strengthen Chris-

tian hope for ultimate salvation.[7] (Rom 5:3-5, 11; cf. 1 Cor 4:8-13, 15:1-11; 2 Cor 1 3-11, 4:7-12, 5:14-21, 6:1-10, 11:21b-29, 12:1-10; Eph 2:11-22, Phil 3:17-21; Col 1:15-23)

In the course of the preceding argument, Paul has announced the central theme which he develops in the second part of Romans, namely, that the justified Christian, reconciled to God, will be saved by sharing through hope in Christ's risen life. He now proceeds to develop that theme by contrasting the status of the justified Christian with that of humanity prior to the coming of Christ. In the course of developing this contrast he portrays Christ as the last Adam, the new head of the entire human race. Christ becomes the last Adam by effecting the "Adamic reversal," by undoing the sin of the first Adam together with its consequences. This Christ accomplishes with a superabundance of grace which seeks to effect the salvation of all.

In both the Old and New Testaments, the figure of Adam has universalist connotations. The first Adam prefigures the entire human race, whom he fathers naturally. The second Adam redeems a lost humanity by re-creating it and re-unifying it through justifying faith and through the power of His Breath.

In Romans, Paul begins to develop his Adamic Christology with the following reflections:

> Therefore (*Dia touto*), as sin (*hê harmartia*) came into the world through one man and death through sin, and so death spread to all people, inasmuch as all sinned (*eph' hô pantes hêmarton*)—sin indeed was in the world before the Law was given, but sin is not counted where there is no law. Yet death reigned from Adam to Moses, even over those whose sins (*hamartêsantes*) were not like the transgression (*parabaseôs*) of Adam, who was a type of the one to come. (Rom 5:12-14)

The "therefore (*dia touto*)" which begins this passage probably refers globally and rhetorically to the entire preceding argument of Romans up to this point. Throughout his comparison of Adam and Christ, Paul will contrast the "one man," Adam, with the "one man," Christ. Since, however, in Gen 2-3, both Eve and Adam sin and subject themselves and their descendants to death, the emphasis on the "one man" underscores the Christocentric focus of the passage. Paul's midrashic imagination is re-reading the entire history of salvation in the light of the paschal mystery and of his experience of the risen Christ.[8]

---

7. Cf. Fitzmyer, *To Advance the Gospel*, pp. 162-185; Patricia M. McDonald, "Romans 5.1- 11 as A Rhetorical Bridge," *Journal for the Study of the New Testament*, 40 (1990), pp. 81-96.
8. Cf. A.J.M. Wedderburn, "The Theological Structure of Romans V.12," *New Testament Studies*, 19 (1972-1973), pp. 339-354.

Adam's disobedience introduces "sin (*hamartia*)" into the world. In personifying sin as a force which stands in opposition to God, Paul underscores its universal power and influence. Paul uses this rhetorical strategy so that he can contrast the corporate, collective character of "sin" with the stronger, universal power of the grace of Christ which undoes sin.

Sin brings death into the world: not just physical death but also separation from God, the source of life. In so speaking, Paul may be alluding to Wis 2:24: "Through the devil's envy death came into the world." Paul personifies both "sin" and "death (*thanatos*)" for the same rhetorical and dramatic ends. He desires to portray the entire human race when deprived of God's grace as living in bondage to both physical and spiritual death.

In the preceding passage, Paul enunciates for the first time in the pages of the Bible a clear causal connection between the sin of Adam and the sinful status of the rest of humanity. Moreover, once again, the assertion reflects the Christocentric tone of the passage. Universal solidarity in salvation with Christ implies a reverse solidarity in sin with Adam, the androgynous ancestor of all humans.[9]

Death spreads to all humanity "inasmuch as all people sinned (*eph' hô pantes hêmarton*)." Exegetes have offered a variety of interpretations of the phrase "*eph' hô*"; but the majority would today translate it as "since," "because," or "inasmuch as." If one accepts this interpretation, then Paul is attributing human subjection to death not only to the personal sin of Adam but to the corporate sinfulness of humanity as a whole. (Cf. Rom 2:12, 3:23; 1 Cor 6:18, 7:28, 36, 8:12, 15:34) The personal and communal sinfulness of every child of Adam stands, however, in causal connection with the primordial sin committed by humanity's father.[10]

In Romans, Paul divides the history of humanity into three periods: 1) from Adam to Moses, when sin reigned without the Law; 2) from Moses to Christ, when the Law judged human sinfulness (Gal 3:19; Rom 5:20); 3) from the coming of Christ to the *parousia*, the end time of history, when universal salvation dawns. One finds no such explicit theology of salvation history in Galatians.

---

9. The derivation of Eve from Adam makes the original Adam an androgynous figure. (Gen 2:18-24)

10. Nowhere in his writings, does Paul use the term "original sin" in order to describe the sin of Adam. That term would enter the Christian tradition through the coinage of Augustine of Hippo. Cf. *NJBC*, 82:81-111; Jean-Nöel Aletti, "Romans 5,12-21: Logique, sens et fonction," *Biblica*, 78 (1997), pp. 3-32; Akio Ito," Romans 2: A Deuteronomic Reading," *Journal for the Study of the New Testament*, 59 (1995), pp. 21-37; John W. Martens, "Romans 2.14-16: A Stoic Reading," *New Testament Studies*, 40 (1994), pp. 55-67; Paul Gerhard Klumbries, "Der Eine Gott des Paulus: Röm 3, 21-23 as Brennpunkt paulinscher Theologie," *Zeitschrift für die Neutestamentliche Wissenschaft*, 85(1994), pp. 192-206.

In characterizing the first period as a time of sin without the Law, Paul ignores the covenant with Noah and asserts only that God had yet to reveal the Mosaic covenant. (Cf. Gen 9:4-6)[11] Paul also explicitly contrasts the personal sins of Adam's descendants (*hamartêsantas*) with Adam's overt transgression (*parabaseôs*) of a specific divine precept. (cf. Gen 2:17, 3:17) In other words, while Adam transgressed a particular command of God, the rest of humanity, until the coming of Moses, sinned without having specifically revealed divine precepts to violate. The revelation of the Mosaic covenant heightens sin consciousness by teaching the conscience how it ought to act (Rom 5:20, Gal 3:19-20; cf. 2 Cor 3:7-11); but the Law does nothing to end the reign of sin, because it cannot transform the human heart in ways which empower sinless living.[12]

Having reflected on the sinful state of humanity before the coming of Christ, Paul begins to develop his theology of Jesus as the last Adam, the antitype to Adam the sinner. The figure of Jesus contrasts with that of Adam not only by reversing the effects of Adam's sin but by offering a gift which does much more.

> But the grace differed from the trespass. For if the many died through one man's trespass much more have the grace of God and the free gift in the grace of that one man Jesus Christ abounded for many. And the free gift is not like the effect of one man's sin. For the judgment following the one trespass brought condemnation; but the free gift following many trespasses brings justification. If, because of one man's trespass death reigned through that one man, much more will those who receive the abundance of grace and the gift of righteousness reign in life through the one man Jesus Christ. Then as one man's trespass led to condemnation for all, so one man's act of righteousness leads to acquittal and life for all. For as by one man's disobedience all were made sinners, so by one man's obedience many will be made righteous. Law came in, to increase the trespass; but where sin increased, grace has abounded all the more, so that as sin reigned in death, grace also might reign through righteousness to eternal life through Jesus Christ our Lord. (Rom 5:15-21)

Paul, as we have seen, reads the first sin through the lens of the paschal mystery and therefore repeatedly contrasts the sin of the "one man," Adam, with the redeeming grace of the "one man," Christ. Pauline reverse parallelism portrays Jesus as the author of the Adamic reversal: as the head of a new, pneumatic humanity and therefore as the source of universal sal-

---

11. Cf. Alan Segal, *Paul the Convert: The Apostolate and Apostasy of Saul the Pharisee* (New Haven, CT: Yale University Press, 1990), pp. 187-223.

12. Cf. Denis Byu-Duval, "La Traduzione di Rm 5, 12-14," *Rivista Biblica*, 38(1990), pp. 353- 373.

vation. Indeed, Paul uses the phrase "the many" (v. 15) elsewhere as he does here, to mean all.[13] (Cf. Rom 5:18, 12:5; 1 Cor 10:17)

As author of the Adamic reversal Christ effects a grace which far exceeds the enormity of the evil which has flowed from the sin of Adam. Paul contrasts the offense of Adam with the redeeming grace of Christ on several counts:

1) In the incarnation, death, and resurrection of His own Son, God has more than forgiven Adam's trespass and has given us in surpassing abundance a gift of inestimable value.

2) We all stand under the judgment of God not only because of Adam's offense but because of our own sins; but the grace of the "one man" Christ undoes all sin, both Adam's and our own.

3) The gift of endless life with God in Christ far exceeds the punishment of physical death and separation from God which resulted from Adam's sin. Sin made us into the enemies of God; but the grace and free justification accorded us through our share in Christ's life not only reconciles us to God but even empowers us to reign with Him.

4) The single sinful act of Adam brought all under the divine condemnation; the single righteous act of Christ brought justification to all through a share in His divine and risen life. Hence, what the disobedience of Adam did, the obedience of Christ more than undid.

With time the Law joined sin and death upon the stage of history. Personified as an historical force comparable to sin and death, the Law heightened sin consciousness and therefore also heightened human transgression. Nevertheless, the grace of Christ has also abounded far beyond the scope of our legally condemned transgressions. The reign of sin leading to death simply cannot compare with the reign of grace leading to our justification and ultimately to eternal life with Christ in God.[14]

---

13. Cf. Scroggs, *op.cit.*, pp. 76-82; G.E.B. Cranfield, "Some of the Problems in the Interpretation of Romans 5.12," *Scottish Journal of Theology*, 22 (1969), pp. 324-341; Chrys C. Caragounis, "Romans 5:15-16 in the context of 5:12-21: Contrast or Comparison," *New Testament Studies*, 31 (1985), pp. 142-148; Jean-Nöel Aletti, "La *dispotio* rhetorique dan les épitres pauliniennes," *New Testament Studies*, 38(1992), pp. 385-401; Rank Thielman, "The Coherence of Paul's View of the Law: The Evidence of First Corinthians," *New Testament Studies*, 38(1992), pp. 235-253.

14. Cf. *Cerfaux*, op.cit., *pp. 230-241; NJBC*, 51:51-61; Cranfield, *op. cit.*, pp. 98-125; Larry Kreitzer, "Christ and Second Adam in Paul," *Communio Viatorum*, 32(1989), pp. 55-104; Charles D. Myers, Jr. "Chiastic Inversion in the Argument of Romans 3-8," *Novum Testamentum*, 35(1993), pp. 30-47; Robert B. Sloan, "Paul and the Law: Why the Law Cannot Save," *Novum Testamentum*, 33 (1991), pp. 35-60; Giuseppi Segalla, "'L'obbedienza di fede': Tema della lettere ai Romani," *Rivista Biblica*, 36(1988), pp. 329-342; Romano Penna, "Il Problema della Legge nelle Lettere di S. Paolo," *Rivista Biblica*, 38 (1990), pp. 327-352; Carl Joachim Classen, "Paulus und die antike Rhetorik," *Zeitschrift für die Neutestamentliche Wissenschaft*, 82 (1991), pp. 1-33; Stephen Richer Bechtler, "Christ the *Telos* of the Law: The Goal of Romans 10:4," *Catholic Biblical Quarterly*, 56 (1994), pp. 288-308; Paul Trudinger, "An Autobio-

So far, I have attempted to argue three interrelated theses. 1) For Paul the resurrection reveals Jesus's divinity and saving power because it manifests Him as a "life-giving Breath." 2) The atoning death and resurrection function as reverse sides of the same mystery of divine, saving, reconciling love. 3) The salvation revealed in Christ extends to the entire human race. I need next to consider a fourth tenet: the reality of the resurrection and its capacity to save the entire body/person. This fourth Pauline theme also makes an important statement about the scope of the salvation effected in the paschal mystery: namely, it includes human physicality. To this theme I turn in the chapter which follows.

graphical Digression: A Note on Romans 7:7-25," *Expository Times*, 107 (1996), pp. 173-174; C.E.B., Cranfield, "Romans 6:1-14 Revisited," *Expository Times*, 106 (1994), pp. 40-43; James W. Aageson, "'Control' in Pauline Language and Culture: A Study of Rom 6," *New Testament Studies*, 42 (1996), pp. 75-89.

Chapter 15
Bodily Resurrrection

In this chapter I shall argue the following thesis: *Christological hope roots itself in the double fact that Jesus' resurrection transformed Him totally, even in the physical parts of His humanity and that resurrection promises to transform in a similar manner those who believe in Him.* In the preceding chapter I began to explore the universal saving consequences of Paul's understanding of the paschal mystery. This chapter begins to ponder the physical inclusiveness of salvation in Christ. Risen transformation in the Breath of Jesus encompasses the entire embodied self.

This chapter divides into three parts. In both Philippians and first Corinthians, Paul develops at some length his belief in the physical consequences of Jesus' resurrection. Part one examines the argument in Philippians. There the apostle speaks of Jesus' resurrection's saving efficacy, an efficacy which transforms the entire embodied person. Paul develops an analogous insight in first Corinthians. Part two examines that insight. As we shall see, Paul insists on the physical character of risen life in the course of censuring the Corinthian community for allowing serious public sinners to share in their eucharists. Part three analyzes a subsequent passage in the same letter. In it Paul again discourses at some length on the reality of bodily resurrection and on its centrality to Christian faith.

(I)

In the third section of his letter to the Philippians (Phil 3:1-4:7), Paul warns his Gentile Christians to keep an eye peeled for the Judaizers, whom he calls "dogs" and "deceitful workers." (Phil 3:2) Paul explains his motives for this stern warning: those who stand with him against the Judaizers belong to "the true circumcision, who worship in the Breath of God (*pneumati Theou*) and glory in Christ Jesus, and put no confidence in the flesh."[1] (Phil 3:3)

Paul knows that the Judaizers believe that he disparages the Torah. The apostle therefore forestalls any objection to his position from the standpoint of Jewish orthodoxy by appealing to his personal credentials as a former orthodox Jew and zealous Pharisee. He then justifies his opposition to the Judaizers by appealing to the total transformation of his own religious perceptions which resulted from his personal encounter with the risen Christ. That encounter and the enlightenment it effected in

---

1. Cf. Michael Tellebe, "The Sociological Factors Behind Philippians 3.1-11 and the Conflict at Philippi," *Journal for the Study of the New Testament*, 55(1994), pp. 97-121.

Paul now motivates the apostle's opposition to the circumcision of baptized Gentile Christians. Paul speaks as follows:

> But whatever gain I had, I counted as loss for the sake of Christ. Indeed, I count everything as loss because of the surpassing worth of knowing Christ Jesus my Lord. For his sake I have suffered the loss of all things, and count them as refuse, in order that I may gain Christ, and be found in Him, not having a righteousness of my own, based on law, but that which is through faith in Christ, the righteousness from God which depends on faith; that I may know Him and the power of His resurrection, and may share His sufferings, becoming like Him in His death, that if possible I may attain the resurrection from the dead. (Phil 3:8-11)

This powerful and moving testimony articulates the complex eschatological hope which Paul's "gospel" proclaims. The encounter with the risen Christ has turned Paul around. It has unmasked the sinfulness of the legalistic self-righteousness which he had cultivated as a Pharisee. That self-righteousness had betrayed him into persecuting those whom God had justified. The blasphemy to Jewish ears expressed in the first Christians' proclamation of the Lordship of Jesus had probably helped motivate Paul's persecution of the Church.[2] (Acts 7:54-60) Having seen the risen Lord, however, Paul the convert now regards all these earlier beliefs and actions not only as loss but even as so much refuse, garbage, dung (*skybala*) (Phil 3:7-8)

Paul has rejected an illusory "blameless righteousness under the Law" which he had once cultivated in proud self-reliance. (Phil 3:6, 9) Instead he has exchanged such religious self-deception for a faith which his former self-righteousness had made him deem blasphemous. Paul describes his new-found Christian faith in profoundly interpersonal language as "knowing Christ Jesus my Lord." (Phil 3:8) Faith in the person of Jesus as Lord and Christ, has replaced self-reliant, self-righteous trust in legal abstractions. Paul experiences this faith as the only true ground of "righteousness from God," (Phil 3:9) because it expresses "the power of His resurrection."[3] (Phil 3:10)

By the power of Jesus' resurrection Paul means, of course, that the resurrection manifests the power of God who in exalting Jesus bestowed on Him the name above all other names, as the Christological hymn in Philippians has just asserted. (Phil 2:9) In addition, however, the power of the resurrection effects the present transformation in Jesus' image of

---

2. Cf. George Montague, *The Living Thought of St. Paul* (Beverly Hills, CA: Benziger, 1976), pp. 3-4.

3. Paul's tentativeness about his share in the resurrection from the dead in verse 11 could express the apostle's reluctance to assert unequivocally that he had the courage to face martyrdom. Cf. Randall E. Ott, "If Possible I May Attain the Resurrection from the Dead," *Catholic Biblical Quarterly*, 57(1995), pp. 324-340.

all those who confess Him Christ and Lord. Moreover, that transformation grounds the Christian hope that suffering and dying in His image will also culminate in final resurrection in His image. (Phil 3:10-11) Indeed, the risen Lord will "change our lowly body to be like His glorious body, by the power which enables Him even to subject all things to Himself." (Phil 3:21)

The encounter with the risen Christ has convinced Paul of the bodily character not only of Jesus' resurrection but also of the resurrection of all those who rise in His image. Moreover, the power of the resurrection to transform human bodies in the image of the risen Christ manifests the Lord's universal dominion over all creation. That universal divine sway guarantees that He will one day "subject all things to Himself."

Paul never discusses Jesus' empty tomb in his surviving letters; but the apostle's insistence on the physicality of the resurrection accords well with belief in the empty tomb.[4] Theologians who assert that the New Testament never invokes the empty tomb as an argument for the resurrection ignore the fact that Luke puts such an argument on the lips of both Peter and Paul in Acts. The empty tomb alone does not prove the resurrection; but it provides an argument which supports and confirms the testimony of those who saw the risen Christ. Moreover, in Acts the argument occurs in speeches which typify early apostolic preaching. (Acts 2:29-36; 13:29-37)

Paul also experiences the power of the resurrection in the fact that Christ Jesus has taken possession of him and of his life. (Phil 3:12) Paul describes this experience of being commandeered by Christ as "the upward call of God in Christ Jesus." (Phil 3:14) That call makes Paul and the Philippians present members of the "commonwealth in heaven," (Phil 3:20), of the community of those who dwell now with God and Christ in "heaven." Together Paul and the Philippians look forward to the consummation of that social communion when the Lord Jesus Christ will return from heaven as savior to share His own risen glory with them.[5] (Phil 3:21)

The term "heaven" designates the mysterious realm of the divine rather than a geographical place in the modern sense of geographical. Moreover, the language of this final exhortation echoes in reverse imagery the language of the Christological hymn in chapter 2 of Philippians. There Christ, while already existing in the *form* of God, takes the *form* of a slave, in outward appearance (*schêmati*) found as a man. Here, the victorious Christ

---

4. Cf. Xavier Léon-Dufour, *Resurrection and the Message of Easter*, translated by R.N. Wilson (New York, NY: Holt, Reinhart, and Winston, 1971).
5. Cf. Silva, *op.cit.*, pp.178-98; Martin, *op.cit.*, pp.129-40; Motyer, *op. cit.*, pp.155-78; Jean Doignon, "Comment Hilaire de Poitiers a-t-il lü et compris le verset de Paul, Philippiens 3:21," *Vigilia Christianae*, 43 (1989), pp. 127-137.

takes the Christian's "lowly body (*sôma tes tapeinôseôs*)," changes its "appearance (*metaschematisei*)" into the "form (*symmorphon*)" of "his glorious body (*tô sômati tês doxês autou*)."[6] (Phil 3:20-21) One finds in the present text the same rhetorical play on the root meaning of "*morphê*" and "*schêma*" as in the Christological hymn. In both passages, "*morphê*" designates an abiding reality; "*schêma*," a passing, ephemeral reality.

While Paul vindicates the present power of the resurrection in his own life and in that of believers, he also makes it clear that the present manifestation of that power only anticipates its full revelation on the day of the Lord. Paul's longing for that final and full revelation motivates his present single-minded dedication to the gospel, his self-discipline, his lack of complacency. In addition, the risen Christ's power to raise from the dead manifests His divine authority and power over the whole of creation. I shall return to this last theme in the chapter which follows.[7]

In first Corinthians Paul develops a similar set of insights in two different contexts. Let us examine each of these contexts in turn.

(II)

In the second section of the first letter to the Corinthians (5:1-6:20), Paul deals with ethical abuses within the Corinthian community. In his argument, he refers twice to Christ.

In ordering the community to excommunicate the man living in public incest, Paul authorizes them to do so "with the power of the Lord Jesus (*te dynamei tou kyriou Iêsou*)." They must consign the unrepentant sinner to the power of Satan "for the destruction of his flesh, that his spirit may be saved in the day of the Lord Jesus." (1 Cor 5:4-5)

Satan personifies for Paul the forces of evil, both personal and corporate, which torment believers and put them to the test. (1 Cor 7:5; cf. 2 Cor 2:11) In handing over the unrepentant sinner to Satan, the community binds him with the divine authority of the name above every name. Paul, however, views this act of binding in an eschatological context which seeks ultimately the sinner's repentance, his death in the flesh to the sinful error of his ways, so that, in the deep center of his self-consciousness (1 Cor 2:11), he may survive Christ's final judgment. The "destruction of his flesh" means, then, not physical death but conversion of heart, repentance.

Paul also makes it clear that he is ordering this excommunication for the good of the community. That they should allow someone living in open incest to share in their eucharists compromises the integrity of their worship. When the community gathers in worship, they celebrate the passover of Christ, his own atoning death to sin. (1 Cor 5:7-8a; 11:26)

6. Cf. Montague, *op.cit.*, pp.68-9.
7. Cf. Montague, *op.cit.*, pp.59-68; Fitzmyer, *To Advance the Gospel*, pp. 202-217.

The Corinthians cannot consistently celebrate Christ's and their own death to sin while openly condoning a sin as serious as incest.

The Jewish seder, which the Christian eucharist fulfills, requires unleavened bread for its proper celebration. Paul endows the image of unleavened bread with moral and spiritual significance, when he identifies believers with the bread of the Christian passover celebration. The image suggests that those who consume the eucharistic bread, Christ's body and blood, (1 Cor 11:23-26) through eating become identified with the bread they eat: namely, with the sinless Christ.

The eucharist thus deepens the baptized Christian's identification with Christ. Washed, justified, and sanctified "in the name of the Lord Jesus Christ and in the Spirit of our God," (1 Cor 6:11), they have become members of Christ's own body. (1 Cor 8:12) Later in this same letter, Paul will denounce other eucharistic abuses as a failure "to discern the body." (1 Cor 11:29) By that he means that whoever sins against a member of the eucharistic community violates the body of Christ (1 Cor 8:12).

Paul therefore insists that he is disbarring the incestuous man from the eucharistic community because in their eucharists the Corinthians must purge out the old leaven of sin and celebrate the Christian passover with the unleavened bread of sincerity and truth. In this context, purging out the old leaven means most immediately the expulsion of public sinners from eucharistic communion; but it also signifies the degree of repentance required of any sincere and truthful celebration of the eucharistic passover meal. Those who share in the body and blood of Christ proclaim His death until He comes. (1 Cor 11:26) In order to make that proclamation in "sincerity" and "truth" they must each time they worship eucharistically die anew to sin as once they died to it in their baptism. (Rom 6:3-11)

By the term "body (*sôma*)," Paul means, not a part of a person, but the entire person viewed as corporeal. Precisely as corporeal realities, the Corinthians through baptism function as Christ's body, because by sharing in the baptismal Breath of Christ, they now live through the same divine, resurrected life which He possesses. (1 Cor 6:11, 15; 2 Cor 3:17-18) Paul underscores the corporeal character of the Corinthians' union with Christ by comparing it to sexual union. Joining oneself with a whore (*ho kollômenos tê pornê*) makes the two into one body (*hen sôma*), while joining oneself to the Lord (*ho de kollômenos tô kyriô*) makes one Breath (*hen pneuma*). Paul uses the same word to express sexual copulation as he does to express union with Christ; but he distinguishes the end result of the joining. Sexual joining produces one body; joining the body of Christ unites believers in His Breath.

The indwelling Breath of Christ transforms every baptized person, viewed precisely as a corporeal reality, into a temple, a dwelling place of

God. (1 Cor 6:19) The redeeming death of Christ purchases the human body and makes it into divine property. Since Christians through baptism now belong to God, they have renounced exclusive ownership of their very bodies. (1 Cor 6:19) In effect baptism makes believers into the slaves of God, who now owns them physically, not, however, to oppress but to liberate them. (1 Cor 7:22) As Paul will observe later in the same letter: "For one who is called in the Lord as a slave is a freedman of the Lord. Likewise one who is free when called is a slave of Christ. You were bought with a price. Do not become the slaves of humans." (1 Cor 7:22-24)

Worshippers gather in a temple in order to glorify God. Living, physical temples of God, Christians must "glorify God in your body" (1 Cor 6:20) by avoiding all forms of immorality. "For the body is not meant for immorality, but the body is for the Lord, and the Lord is for the body." (1 Cor 6:13) Immorality enslaves (1 Cor 6:12); but the Breath of Christ washes, sanctifies, justifies.[8] (1 Cor 6:11)

In asserting that "the body is.... for the Lord and the Lord for the body (*to de sôma ....tô kyriô kai, ho kyrios tô sômati*)," Paul asserts that the salvation which Christ brings encompasses one totally and includes the corporeal dimensions of human existence; but he says much more. By asserting that "the body is for the Lord and the Lord for the body," Paul is also testifying that God destines the human body for baptismal incorporation into the body of Christ and therefore into a eucharistic communion of believers united in His Breath. That incorporation destines the body for resurrection by giving it, through the indwelling of Christ's Breath, a present share in the Lord's risen life.

By the same token, the Lord is for the body because He became incarnate in order to die both morally and physically to sin by giving up His life in perfect obedience to the Father. His redeeming death claims our bodies for God, consecrates them into living temples of God's justifying, sanctifying Breath, whose empowering presence liberates us totally, even in our bodies, from slavery to sin.

The phrase "the body is....for the Lord and the Lord for the body" has, moreover, explicit ethical connotations. Paul makes this statement in the context of distinguishing the freedom Christ gives from moral licentiousness. (1 Cor 6:12) Apparently, some Corinthians felt that the freedom

8. Cf. R. Kempthorne, "Incest and the Body of Christ: A Study of 1 Corinthians VI.12-20," *New Testament Studies*, 14 (1967-1968), pp. 568-574; K. Romaniuk, "Exegèse du nouveau testament et ponctuation," *Novum Testamentum*, 23 (1981), pp. 199-205; Susan A. Ross, "'Then Honor God in Your Body' (1 cor 6:20): Feminist and Sacramental Theology of the Body," *Horizons*, 16(1989), pp. 7-27; Brain S. Rosner, "'*Ouchi mallon epenthêsate*": Corporate Responsibility in 1 Corinthians 2," *New Testament Studies*, 38(1992), pp. 470-473; Will Deming, "The Unity of 1 Corinthians 5-6," *Journal of Biblical Literature*, 115(1996), pp. 289- 312.

Christ brings means doing what comes naturally, in the same way that "food is for the stomach and the stomach for food (*ao brômata tê koila kai he koilia tois brômasin*)." (1 Cor 6:13)

Paul parallels rhetorically the maxim, "food is for the stomach and the stomach for food" with the new order established in Christ: "the body is for the Lord and the Lord for the body." Joined as they are to the body of Christ in the power of the Breath, the Corinthians can no longer follow every spontaneous sexual impulse. Instead, they must renounce the kind of sexual license which would betray them into joining a member of Christ to a whore.[9] (1 Cor 6:15; cf. Rom 6:1- 23)

In the passages I have just examined, Paul demonstrates the reality of resurrection by pointing to its saving, somatic consequences. Later in first Corinthians, he makes belief in the saving reality of the resurrection not only an object of Christian faith but its cornerstone. I shall examine how he does so in the section which follows.

(III)

Paul reflects most extensively on the saving significance and scope of Jesus' resurrection in the course of responding to doubts among the Corinthians concerning the possibility of a bodily resurrection. The doubts of Paul's Gentile converts almost certainly sprang from the dualistic pre-suppositions of Graeco-Roman culture. As we have seen, that dualism separates the human person into two essentially different kinds of parts: one, spiritual and indestructible; the other, physical and corruptible. The Corinthians probably had no difficulty in understanding that Christ had saved their incorruptible souls; but they seem to have questioned that divine salvation could even extend to bodies which rot in the grave. Paul responds by insisting that resurrection transforms the entire embodied person. It did so in the case of Jesus. It will do so in the case of those who will rise with Him.

Paul chides the Corinthians for questioning the possibility of bodily resurrection and constructs a *reductio ad absurdum* which advances in two steps. Paul then caps his argument rhetorically by responding to an objection raised by the Corinthians themselves.

1) If the Corinthians deny the possibility of bodily resurrection, then they also deny the possibility of Christ's resurrection. If they deny that Christ rose, then they deprive both Paul's central message to them and

---

9. Cf. Montague, *op.cit.*, 99-105; Orr and Walther, pp. 198-202; Bruce, *op.cit.*, pp.62-3; Groscheide, *op.cit.*, pp. 143-53; Jerome Murphy-O'Connor, O.P., "Corinthian Slogans in 1 Cor 6:12-20," *Catholic Biblical Quarterly*, 40(1978), pp. 391-396; Peter S. Zaas, "Catalogues and Context: 1 Corinthians 5 and 6," *New Testament Studies*, 34(1988), pp. 622-629; Bruce N. Fisk, "PORNEUEIN as Body Violation: The Unique Nature of Sexual Sin in 1 Corinthians 6:18," *New Testament Studies*, 42(1996), pp. 540-558.

their own faith of any real object. It follows, therefore, that: "If Christ has not been raised, your faith is futile and you are still in yours sins." (1 Cor 15:12-16; cf Rom 6:1-10; 2 Cor 5:14-21) Once again, the reality of the resurrection manifests itself in its effects: in the communication of the justifying, sanctifying Breath of the risen Christ.

2) If no one, including Christ, rises from the dead, then it also follows that dead Christians have perished and do not participate in the resurrection of Christ. (1 Cor 15:18) Here Paul implicitly asserts that dead Christians continue to live in the power of the divine Breath even as they wait for their final resurrection. In this particular text Paul leaves the fate of those who die in their sins problematic. As we shall see, however, in the describing the final judgment, Paul also asserts that even sinners must rise and confront in Jesus their divine judge.

3) Paul caps these arguments with a response to an apparent objection from the Corinthians. Some members of the community seem to have chided him for sacrificing himself to no good end in his apostolic work. Paul replies that he would not be expending himself so totally for the good of others unless the resurrection were in fact a reality. Paul prefaces his response with an enigmatic allusion to "baptism for the dead." (1 Cor 15:29-30)

Over the centuries scripture scholars have broken their heads trying to imagine what Paul might mean by "baptism for the dead." Predictably enough, the scholarly imagination has devised a bewildering list of incompatible translations for this obscure phrase. In the end, scholars may never reach an agreement about its meaning.

Jerome Murphy-O'Connor has, however, proposed perhaps the most plausible and coherent interpretation of this odd and atypical Pauline phrase. Murphy-O'Connor's suggestion draws on hints scattered throughout first Corinthians. Given, however, the slimness of the evidence, his hypothesis remains highly speculative, though ingenious and certainly possible.

Murphy-O'Connor suggests that the phrase exemplifies yet another Corinthian slogan. He argues with some plausibility that the phrase "baptism for the dead" originated in the pro-Apollos faction at Corinth. He describes this faction as Paul's main adversary in this section of first Corinthians and equates them with the proto-Gnostics who denied the possibility of resurrection.

Murphy-O'Connor believes that the proto-Gnostics probably defended a garbled version of Philonic theology which they had presumably learned from Apollos. The pro-Apollos partisans would have claimed privileged access to a wisdom so purely spiritual that it elevated them beyond the realm of the physical. They despised material reality as the realm of death. In Murphy-O'Connor's hypothesis, these spiritualists would have also characterized those who disagreed with them as "dead."

In other words, in Murphy-O'Connor's rendering of "baptism for the dead," Paul is responding to the objection of the Apollos faction that he is wasting his time and energy baptizing those who are "dead": i.e., those unenlightened, inferior types who remain blind to the true spiritual, anti-physical meaning of religious wisdom. Paul, as he does frequently in his letters, turns the tables on his adversaries by taking over their terminology and then endowing it with new meaning.

Paul replies ironically to his adversaries that those whom he baptizes are even deader than they suggest, since they will certainly die physically. Paul also concedes that he is "killing himself" in going around baptizing such people; but he suffers willingly the tribulations of the apostolate because the resurrection from the dead is in fact a reality. As for those who claim a privileged spiritual wisdom, in Paul's estimate, "some people have no knowledge of God. I say this to your shame."[10] (1 Cor 15:30-34)

Paul then attempts to name the basic misunderstanding which motivates the Corinthians' skepticism concerning resurrection: namely, they have confused resurrection with resuscitation. Just as a seed must die so that the plant may begin to live, so too the corpse consigned to the grave provides only a seed of the new pneumatic body which God will make for each person who rises from the dead.

> What you sow does not come to life unless it dies. And what you sow is not the body which is to be, but a bare kernel, perhaps of wheat or of some other grain. But God gives it a body as He has chosen, and to each kind of seed its own body. (1 Cor 15:36-8)

Paul argues from analogy. In the world as we know it, different living species have different kinds of bodies. Even among the heavenly bodies sun, moon, and stars differ in brilliance. In the same way, the risen, pneumatic body differs qualitatively from the animated physical bodies which we now possess. God must recreate our physical bodies by transforming them, not by resuscitating them. (1 Cor 15:39-41)

Paul then contrasts the body which we now possess with the new body which God will fashion for us in the image of Christ. He describes the body we now possess as sown in "perishability (*en phthora*)," "in dishonor (*en atimia*)," "in weakness (*en astheneia*)" and as only "animated (*psychikon*)." He describes the new body God will fashion for us as raised up "in imperishability (*en aphtharsia*)," "in honor (*en doxê*)," and "in strength (*en dynamei*)" because "pneumatic (*pneumatikon*)."

---

10. Cf. Jerome Murphy-O'Connor, O.P., "'Baptized for the Dead' (1 Cor 15:29). A Corinthian Slogan?" *Revue Biblique*, 88(1981), pp. 532-543. See also: B.M. Foschini, "Those Who Are Baptized for the Dead (1 Cor 15:29)," *Catholic Biblical Quarterly*, 12(1950), pp. 260-276, 379- 399, 13(1951), pp. 46-78, 172-98, 276-283; Joel R.

Paul is contrasting two orders of reality. In creation as we know it, living things perish; but those who belong to the new creation will participate in the imperishability of God. In this life we live in a state of dishonor as a result of our sinfulness; but in the eschatological age which the Jesus' resurrection begins, we share in the divine glory. In this life we display physical and moral weakness; the risen body, however, will participate in the strength of the risen Christ. We inherit animated bodies from the first Adam; we receive pneumatic bodies from the last Adam, Jesus Christ. We must, then, exchange a body made from dust (Gen 2:7), for a body which resembles the man of heaven in whose image God will recreate us.[11] (1 Cor 15:48-53)

Clearly, for Paul, denial of the reality of the resurrection involves more than the contradiction of a theological proposition. The reality of Jesus' resurrection manifests itself in the efficacy of its present saving consequences. One therefore who denies the resurrection simultaneously denies that the risen Christ continues to function efficaciously as a "life-giving Breath," as the source of pneumatic life which unites believers to God. That union ensures their present and future possession of imperishable divine life.

The efficacious, saving reality of the resurrection provides Christian faith, therefore, with its constitutive object. Without the resurrection, identification with Christ in His saving death has no life-giving consequences: it simply makes one inexpressibly miserable. It yields, not hope, but despair. Those, however, who possess the Breath of the risen Christ already live with the life of the glorified redeemer. They live in solidarity with those who have died in faith and continue to live with Christ in God, with those who await the final resurrection of the just.

Resurrection transforms the believer totally, just as it transformed Jesus totally. In transforming the human body, risen life changes it into a pneumatic, Breath-filled reality, utterly suffused with divine life.

Paul's testimony to the reality and physicality of the resurrection provides the correct context for understanding His theology of "the body of Christ" and its development in the letters to the Ephesians and to the Colossians. To this aspect of Pauline Christology I turn in the chapter which follows.

White, "'Baptized on Account of the Dead': The Meaning of 1 Corinthians 15:29 in its Context," *Journal of Biblical Literature*, 116(1997), pp. 487-499.

11. Cf. Montague, *op.cit.*, 135-45.; Orr and Walther, *op.cit.*, pp. 341-9; Bruce, *op.cit.*, pp. 151-3; Groscheide, *op.cit.*, pp. 379-89; Francois Altermath, *Du corps psychic au corps spirituelle* (Tübingen: J.C.B. Mohr, 1977), pp. 1-51; A.C. Perriman, "Paul and the Parousia: 1 Corinthians 15:50-57 and 2 Corinthians 5:1-5," *New Testament Studies*, 35 (1989), pp. 512-521; Karlheinz Müller, "Die Leiblichkeit des Heils: 1 Kor 15, 35-38" in *Resurrection du Christ et des chretiens (1 Co 15)*, edited by Lorenzo de Lorenzi (Rome: Abbaye de S. Paul, 1985), pp. 171-281; Gerhard Marcel Martin, "Körperbild und 'Leib Christi," *Evangelische Theologie*, 52 (1992), pp. 402-413; Andreas Lindemann, "Paulus und die kornithische Eschatologie," *New Testament Studies*, 37(1991), pp. 373-399; John Gillman, "Transformation in 1 Cor 15, 50-53," *Ephemerides Theologicae Lovaniensis*, 58 (1982), pp. 309-333.

Chapter 16
The Body of Christ and the Pleroma

In this chapter I shall argue the following thesis: *Christological hope roots itself in an experience of the saving charismatic activity of the risen Christ's Breath in the Christian community, because that activity transforms the Church into Christ's instrument for advancing a universal, even cosmic, salvation.* This chapter examines in greater detail the divine strategy for extending the saving consequences of the paschal mystery not only to the physical bodies of those who believe but to a physical cosmos impregnated with sin and distorted by it.

This chapter divides into four parts. Part one ponders the Christological connotations of the factional divisions in the church at Corinth. Part two deals with dietary discipline at Corinth. Paul situates the squabble over food in both a eucharistic and a Christological context. Part three examines the theological development of related Christological insights in the letter to the Colossians. Part four reflects on the way in which the letter to the Ephesians both echoes and deepens the Christological message of Colossians.

(I)

I have examined Paul's sense of the reality, universality, efficacy, and somatic character of the salvation effected in the paschal mystery: namely, in the death and resurrection of Jesus which together mediate the gift of His life-giving Breath. As we have seen, in Pauline Christology, the salvation which flows from the risen Christ encompasses not only the human body but also extends to the rest of physical creation. (Rom 8:18-25; cf. 1 Cor 15:42-50; 2 Cor 4:16-5:5; Gal 4:1-7) This sense of the all-encompassing, somatic, even cosmic character of the salvation wrought by Jesus' death, resurrection, and the communication of the divine Breath grounds and contextualizes a Pauline theology of "the whole Christ." To this aspect of Paul's Christology I now turn.

In first Corinthians, Paul first develops his theology of the Christian community as the body of Christ. He does so in the course of discussing the way in which the Breath's charisms ought to build up the local church. Factionalism at Corinth provides the context for understanding Paul's theology of the charisms; and Christological presuppositions underlie Paul's denunciation of factional strife. As we shall see, those presuppositions provide the context for understanding the full implications of his portrayal of the local community as the body of Christ.[1]

Very likely, Paul wrote his first letter to the Christians at Corinth from Ephesus, possibly a short time after his letter to the Philippians. The fragmentation and bickering among the Corinthians explains the sterner tone which Paul adopts in writing them.

In greeting the Corinthians, Paul describes himself as "called by the will of God to be an apostle of Christ Jesus." (1 Cor 1:1; cf 2 Cor 1:1; Gal 1:1; Eph 1:1, Col 1:1, 2 Tim 1:1) This initial assertion of the direct divine source of Paul's apostolic authority foreshadows the first part of the letter. There Paul will invoke that same authority both to scold the Corinthians for their sectarian tendencies and to summon them to mutual reconciliation.

A similar foreshadowing may lie behind Paul's reminder to the Corinthians in his salutation that they stand "called to be saints together with all those who in every place call on the name of Our Lord Jesus Christ, both their Lord and ours." (1 Cor 1:2) The call to Christian holiness and witness binds all the saints together in the same faith. It does not divide them. (Phil 2:10)

Paul next underscores the Corinthians' call to union in the brief prayer of blessing which opens the letter. God has called the Corinthians "into the fellowship of His Son, Jesus Christ our Lord." (1 Cor 1:9) The "grace given you in Christ" through gifts of speech and knowledge confirms this divine call to communion. Indeed, all the Breath's charisms advance "the testimony of Christ" at Corinth.

The phrase "testimony of Christ" could mean Jesus' testimony to the kingdom, or Paul's proclamation of Christ among the Corinthians, or the Corinthians' own testimony to Christ through their openness to the charisms of His Breath. (1 Cor 1:6) Quite possibly, Paul may have intended all three meanings.

In Paul's opening prayer, the apostle reminds the Corinthians that the grace of God already lavished on them also grounds their present eschatological longing for the final revelation of the Lord Jesus Christ. (1 Cor 1:7) That longing expresses their present trust that the Lord Jesus will insure that they will stand "blameless" at the day of judgment. (1 Cor 1:8)

Christ's call to live blameless lives, however, contrasts rhetorically with the sharp rebuke which follows immediately. Paul reproaches Corinthian factionalism "in the name of the Lord Jesus Christ (*dia tou onomatos tou kyriou hêmôn Iêsou Christou*)," with the authority, that is, of the name

1. Cf. David W.J. Gill, "Corinth: A Roman Colony in Achaea," *Biblische Zeitschrift*, 37(1933), pp. 259-264; David Wenham, "What Went Wrong at Corinth?" *Expository Times*, 108(1997), pp. 137-141.

above every name. (Phil 2:10) The dissensions at Corinth are destroying any union of mind and of judgment. (1 Cor 1:10) Faith in Christ, however, unites; it does not divide. (1 Cor 1:10)

Paul mentions four Corinthian factions at the beginning of his letter: a Pauline faction, a Petrine faction, a faction which claimed Apollos as its leader, and a faction which claimed to stand with Christ, apparently against the other factions. (1 Cor 1:10-12) We know very little of the positions espoused by the last two factions.[2]

Paul immediately situates the burgeoning factionalism at Corinth in a Christological context. The dissensions belie the Corinthians' professed faith in the crucified Christ, whom Paul proclaimed among them. Paul made that proclamation not with empty, rational, human rhetoric, but with the power which flows from the cross of Christ, a power manifested in the divine Breath's action among the Corinthians.[3] (1 Cor 1:17-18; cf. 1:4-7)

Having experienced the pneumatic power of God's word, the Corinthians, by yielding to dissension, have replaced the wisdom of the cross with human folly. (1 Cor 1:20-23) They need to rediscover authentic faith in Christ crucified, whom Paul calls "the power of God and the wisdom of God (*Christon Theou dynamis kai Theou sophian*)."[4] For the

---

2. Among the factions at Corinth, one group claims to be the party "of Christ." (1 Cor 1:12) Exegetes debate the position espoused by this group. Presumably, however, this faction opposed the teachings of Jesus to those of Paul, Peter, and Apollos. Cf. Montague, *op.cit.*, p. 89; Jay Shanor, "Paul as Master Builder: Construction Terms in First Corinthians," *New Testament Studies*, 34(1988), pp. 461-471; Settimo Cipriani, "'*Sapientia Crucis*' e sapienze 'Umana' in Paolo," *Rivista Biblica*, 36(1988), pp. 343-361.
3. Cf. Von Karlheinz Müller, "I Kor 1, 18-25: Die eschatologische-kyrotische Function der Verkündigung des Kreuzes," *Biblische Zeitschrift*, 10(1966). pp. 246-272.
4. Contemporary exegesis has correctly called attention to the fact that the New Testament at several points identifies Jesus Christ with divine wisdom. One needs, however, to take care not to read into the New Testament ideas which emerge only after its composition. In discussing Christ as the "Word" and "wisdom" of God, the fathers of the Church made philosophical and theological distinctions unknown to the authors of the New Testament.

One strain of patristic *Logos* Christology, for example, equates the *Logos* of St. John with the mind of God platonically conceived as the seat of the archetypal forms in which all created things participate. In the Latin tradition, this strain of Christological thinking culminates in the Christology and trinitarian theology of Augustine of Hippo. Because of Augustine's enormous influence on the western Church, his Christological ideas have on occasion also colored New Testament exegesis.

One finds, however, a second strain of patristic *Logos* Christology developed by Irenaeus, Tertullian, Basil of Caesarea, and Gregory of Nyssa. That strain interprets the *Logos* of St. John as the spoken rather than as the conceived Word of God. This second movement in patristic Christology tends to imagine the second person of the trinity as the one through whom the Father speaks and acts to save us. This strain also tends to remain closer to the Biblical witness by regarding the Holy Breath as the mind and wisdom of God.

foolishness of God (*to moron tou Theou*) is wiser than humans, and the weakness of God is stronger than humans." (1 Cor 1:24-5) Paul refers, of course, to the wisdom of dying to sin with Christ crucified and living reconciled to one another in the power of His Breath by professing the same hope, faith, and love.

The Breath of God communicates to the Corinthians the reconciling mind of Christ. (1 Cor 2:11-15; Phil 1:27-2:11) She comes to teach them to exchange a proud, self-reliant "wisdom" for the divine folly of the cross. (1 Cor 1:23-4) Before they converted, the ignorant Corinthians could not have plausibly claimed to possess even rational human wisdom. (1 Cor 1:26). That fact alone should convince them that any real wisdom which they do now possess comes from God "who is the source of your life in Christ, whom God made our wisdom, our righteousness, and sanctification, and redemption." (1 Cor 1:30)

When Paul calls Christ "our wisdom, our righteousness, and sanctification, and redemption," he employs dispensational rather than metaphysical language. The very fact that we possess wisdom, righteousness, sanctification, and redemption points to Christ as its efficacious source, as the one through whom God the Father acts to communicate these graces to us.

As a way of dramatizing the divine origin of the wisdom made manifest in Christ, Paul compares the ignorance of the Corinthians prior to their conversion with the "weakness....fear and trembling" with which he first proclaimed the gospel to them. Paul beset by human weakness proclaimed Christ to a bunch of nobodies. Paul's human weakness made it manifest that, when he proclaimed Christ, he announced no self-reliant, worldly philosophy. Instead, the apostle spoke "in demonstration of the Breath and of power (*en apodeixei pneumatos kai dynameos*)." In other words, the

---

The New Testament itself, however, never distinguishes between the conceived and the spoken Word of God, between conceived and articulated divine wisdom. Paul, specifically, never makes any such a distinction. Nor does he endorse Platonic metaphysics. In verses 11-16 of the second chapter of second Corinthians, Paul describes the Breath of God as a scrutinizing intelligence within God and as the "mind of Christ" in which all who possess the Holy Breath participate. Hence, if confronted with the distinction the fathers would later make between conceived and spoken word, Paul probably would have conceded that in calling Christ "the power of God and the wisdom of God," he was in fact, as he habitually does, using dispensational language to speak about Christ and not the metaphysical language of the fathers. In the crucified and risen Christ God has revealed His power and wisdom in eschatological fullness. Moreover, he has done so by sending us the Holy Breath of God, who endows the Godhead with a self-awareness analogous to human self-awareness. The divine Breathing comes to Christians to conform them to Christ by endowing them with His mind. (1 Cor 2:11-16; cf. Phil 2:5, Rom 12:2) Orr and Walther, *op.cit.*, pp. 152-165; Grosheide, *op.cit.*, pp. 43-55; Bruce, *op.cit.*, pp. 34-40. Cf. A. Feuillet, *Le Christ Sagesse de Dieu: d'après les épitres paulinniennes* (Paris: Librairie Lecoffre, 1966).

power of the God manifested in the action of Christ's Breath grounds the faith of the Corinthians rather than mere rational insight or argument. (1 Cor 2:4) Paul's identification of Breath and power re-enforces a dispensational interpretation of 1 Cor 1:24. Christ confronts the Corinthians as the power of God because He sends the Breath who acts powerfully in Paul himself and in those who open themselves to Her enlightenment.[5]

What kind of wisdom did Paul announce to the Corinthians? He proclaimed a crucified Lord and messiah who died on the cross to sin and rose in order to become the source of the divine Breath. She functions as the source of divine wisdom because within the Godhead She "comprehends the things of God (*ta tou Theou....egnôken*)." (1 Cor 2:11) In other words, She conceives the saving wisdom, the divine plan of salvation, fully and eschatologically revealed in a crucified and risen savior. The divine Breath also teaches believers "the mind of Christ (*noun Christou*)," (1 Cor 2:16) because, having inspired Jesus' mission, She now comes to the Church in order to conform it to Him. Jesus founds the faith She inspires as both its source and content. (1 Cor 3:11) Anyone who builds a community of faith on any other foundation will find that effort blasted by the consuming, purifying fire of divine judgment on the last day.[6] (1 Cor 3:12-15)

The wisdom embodied in the crucified savior reconciles sinners to God and to one another. Indeed, through Christ God has chosen to reconcile all creation to Himself. In possessing Christ the Corinthians possess all things: "the world or life or death or the present or the future." Christ in reconciling them to God has, through them and through all those who believe, also reconciled all things to God. (1 Cor 3:21-3) A reconciled community who serves as God's instrument of reconciliation has no room for factional divisions.

The Breath-inspired wisdom which Paul proclaims remains hidden from the "rulers (*archontes*) of this age." Had they recognized the reconciling divine wisdom incarnate in Jesus, they would never have crucified the "Lord of glory." (Cf. Ps 24:7-10) The term "Lord of glory" underscores the blindness of the "rulers of this age" whose hearts remained closed to the divine glory revealed in Jesus. The title "Lord of glory," however, also alludes to Ps 24:7-10, an entrance song in which Yahweh, surrounded by His angelic armies, battles victoriously for Israel. The title, therefore, also connotes Christ's ultimate eschatological victory.

---

5. Cf. Montague, *op.cit.*, 81-99; Ernesto Borghi, "Il Tema Sophia in 1 Cor 1-4," *Rivista Biblica*, 40(1992), pp. 421-458.
6. Cf. Orr and Walther, *op.cit.*, pp. 165-7; Grosheide, *op.cit.*, pp.69-75; Bruce, *op.cit.*, pp. 37- 40; Wendell Willis, "The 'Mind of Christ' in 1 Corinthians 2,16," *Biblica*, 70(1989), pp. 110-122; Elizabeth Stuart, "Love is....Paul," *Expository Times*, 102(1990-1991), pp. 264-266.

Exegetes debate whether the phrase "rulers of this age" refers to the human rulers who conspired to put Jesus to death (i.e., to the temple priesthood, Pilate, and Herod), to demonic powers alone, or to demonic powers which used human agents as their instrument. Paul almost certainly intended the third interpretation. In the New Testament, as we have seen, principalities and powers consist of cosmic forces corrupted by sin, personified by demons, and incarnate both in sinful human institutions and in those who lead and administer them.[7]

The Corinthians stray from the reconciling wisdom incarnate in the crucified and risen savior when they treat different apostles and teachers as the founders of independent sects. Instead, the bickering community needs to recognize that God has appointed every apostle and teacher as "servants (or assistants, *hypêretas*)" of the same Christ and as "stewards (*oikonomoi*)" of the same divine mysteries. (1 Cor 4:1, 8-13, 4:14-21) Christ unifies the apostolate as its source and message just as He unifies the Corinthian community by reconciling it to God.

(II)

Paul's discussion of the squabble between the meat eaters and vegetable eaters at Corinth clarifies some of the specific issues which divided that troubled community. This particular argument probably engaged the superstitious scruples of converted Gentiles who feared that eating meat sacrificed to idols might put them under the power of the god to whom the meat had been offered.[8]

In dealing with this issue, Paul once again begins by clarifying the pastoral issues as he sees them and then immediately contextualizes those issues Christologically. Since the problem arose in the context of the eucharistic love-feast, this time the apostle appeals to the unity which ought to characterize any authentic community of eucharistic worship.

In dealing pastorally with the conflict over food at Corinth, Paul finds no reason in principle why his Corinthian converts cannot eat animal flesh sold in the marketplace even though it comes from pagan sacrifices. Paul justifies this pastoral decision with two arguments. 1) The gods to whom pagans sacrifice do not exist. Hence, offering an animal to nothing signifies nothing. 2) The one God, the Father of Jesus, made all things and made them good. Moreover, the Father who has saved us in Christ, made all things through His Son, the Lord Jesus. The Corinthians should regard nothing given us by God through Jesus Christ as illicit. (1 Cor 8:4-6)

Paul next addresses the crisis of conscience experienced by the scrupulous vegetable eaters. Paul insists that even those who agree with him still

---

7. Cf. Wink, *Naming the Powers*, pp. 40-5.
8. Cf. Bruce N. Fisk, "Eating Meat Offered to Idols: Corinthian Behavior and Pauline Response in 1 Corinthians 8-10," *Trinity Journal*, 10(1989), pp. 49-70.

need to respect the consciences of those Christians who scruple at eating sacrificed meat. If the meat eaters force the vegetable eaters to violate their consciences by performing an act which the latter erroneously regard as sinful, then the meat eaters will end by scandalizing weaker Christians, persons "for whom Christ has died." (1 Cor 8:11) By leading the weaker members of Christ to violate their own consciences, the stronger Christians "sin against Christ."[9] (1 Cor 8:1-13)

Paul justifies forgoing food one could in principle legitimately eat by pointing out that he himself refrains from doing legitimate things when it benefits the community. He and Barnabas, for example, unlike the other apostles who receive financial support from the churches, freely and willingly support themselves financially in order to facilitate the work of evangelization. (1 Cor 9:1-14)

Here as elsewhere Paul urges his Christians to imitate him insofar as he imitates Christ. (Cf. 1 Cor 11:1) The Corinthians should deal with scrupulous members of the community in the same way in which Paul conducts his apostolic ministry, by relating to all in an attitude of humble service. (1 Cor 9:19) In proclaiming the gospel, Paul adapts himself flexibly to the needs of individuals and of groups. He respects the sensitivity of Jews, even to the point of obeying, when necessary, the prescriptions of the Hebrew Law, though he need not. In dealing with Gentiles, Paul continues to live obedient to God under "the law of Christ"; but he ignores the purely legal prescriptions of the Torah. (1 Cor 9:19-21) "To the

9. Cf. H. Giblin, S.J., "Three Monotheistic Texts in Paul," *The Catholic Biblical Quarterly*, 37(1975), pp. 529-537. The Corinthians were also squabbling, apparently, over whether the women at Corinth should prophesy without covering their heads. More recent exegesis finds in this minor debate about propriety in worship a concern with hair style rather than with wearing a head cover during eucharistic worship. Not every exegete accepts this interpretation; but, if one does, then, Paul finally resolves the issue by urging the Corinthian woman not to prophesy with unbound hair, which symbolized religious frenzy among first-century pagans and adultery among first-century Jews. (1 Cor 11:2-16) In the course of his argument Paul concedes that, among Christians, women and men relate to one another in mutual co-dependence. (1 Cor 11:11) His final and somewhat authoritarian resolution of this question reflects his historically conditioned, rabbinic sense of social propriety more than anything else.

Nevertheless, in the course of resolving this minor liturgical question Paul again invokes a Christological principle: Christ has God as His head, every man has Christ as his head, and every woman has her husband as her head. (1 Cor 11:3) In this context, the term "head (*kephalê*) could mean "source" or "fountainhead." The Christ sent by the Father has the Father as His source. In the Genesis account of creation, God makes woman from man, who therefore relates to her initially as her source. (1 Cor 11:9; cf. Gen 2:21-23) Since, however, as we have already seen, Paul has just asserted that God created all things through the Lord Jesus Christ, he here refers to Christ as the head of man, since God, in creating the first man, did so through Christ. (1 Cor 8:6) Headship, however, could also connote authority over someone else. Cf. Joseph A. Fitzmyer, S.J., "Another Look at *kephalê* in 1 Corinthians 11.3," *New Testament Studies*, 35(1989), pp. 503-511.

weak I become weak that I might win the weak. I have become all things to all people, that I might by all means save some." (I Cor 9:22) In dealing with the weaker and more scrupulous members of their community, the Corinthians would do well to imitate the apostle's example.[10]

As in dealing earlier with factionalism, Paul now puts the question of eating meat offered to idols in an even broader Christological context by comparing the situation of the Corinthians to that of the Hebrews during the exodus.

> I want you to know, brethren, that our fathers were all under the cloud, and all passed through the sea, and all were baptized into Moses in the cloud and in the sea, and all ate the same spiritual food and all drank the same spiritual drink. For they drank from the supernatural Rock which followed them, and the Rock was Christ. Nevertheless, with most of them God was not pleased; for they were overthrown in the wilderness. (1 Cor 10:1-5)

Paul describes the Exodus of the Hebrews in terms colored by the Christian experience of liberation in Christ. The waters of Christian initiation baptize believers "into Christ," (Gal 3:27; Rom 6:3) i.e., incorporate them into Him and into the Church. In the same way, the Hebrews led by the cloud of God's presence through the waters of the Red Sea experienced a "baptism into Moses," i.e., into the community he founded.

Just as the baptized Christians share in the same pneumatic food and drink of the eucharist, so too the Hebrews shared the same pneumatic (God-given) food called manna and drank the pneumatic (God-given) drink which flowed from the rock Moses struck at Meriba. In other words, dependence on God for physical sustenance unified Israel in its desert wanderings. All the more, then, participation in the eucharistic love feast should unify Christians.[11]

In the Old Testament the rock which gave water at Meriba did not follow the Hebrews around; but a Jewish legend based on Num 21:17 taught that it did. When Paul asserts that "the rock was Christ (*hê petra de ên ho Christos*)," he probably alludes to the peripatetic stone. (1 Cor 10:4) In so speaking Paul heightens the parallel between the situation of

---

10. Cf. Gerhard Dautzenberg, "Der Verzicht af das apostolische Unterhaltsrecht: Eine exegetische Untersuchung zu I Kor 9," *Biblica*, 50(1969), pp. 212-232; H. Chadwick, "'All Things to All Men,'" *New Testament Studies*, 1(1954), pp. 260-275; Richard A. Horseley, "Consciousness and Freedom Among the Corinthians: 1 Corinthians 8-10," *Catholic Biblical Quarterly*, 40(1978), pp. 574-589; Thomas Söding, "Starke und Schwache: Der Götzenopferstreit in 1 Kor 8-10 as Paradigma paulinischer Ethik," *Zeitschrift für die Neutestamentliche Wissenschaft*, 85(1944), pp. 69-92.

11. Cf. Gustave Martelet, "Sacrements, figure, et exhortation en 1 Cor. X, i-ii," *Recherche de Science Religieuse*, 44(1956), pp. 321-359, 515-559; J. Smit, "'Do not Be Idolators': Paul's Rhetoric in First Corinthians," *Novum Testamentum*, 39(1997), pp. 40-53.

the Corinthians and that of the Hebrews. Just as the rock in following the Hebrews provided a permanent source of God-given drink, so too Christians relate to Christ as the permanent source of the Breath-filled eucharistic bread and wine which they share.

Might the phrase "the rock was Christ" also imply Christ's pre-existence? Paul has already at the beginning of this section of the letter described the "one Lord Jesus Christ (*heis kyrios Iêsous Christos*)" as the one "through whom all things are and through whom we exist (*di' hou ta panta kai hêmeis di' autou*)." In other words Paul looks upon Christ as the one through whom the Father created everything. As co-creator with the Father, the Lord would have had to exist before "all things." Moreover, the Christological hymn in the letter to the Philippians, written at about the same time as the first letter to the Corinthians, asserts, as we have seen, Jesus' pre-existence. (Phil 2:6-7)

In asserting that "the rock was Christ," Paul is also making a statement about the soteriological continuity which links the Corinthians to their Hebrew forebears in faith. The God who creates all things through Christ also acts to save all through Christ. The same God, whom Jesus reveals as Father, intervened salvifically in the history of the Hebrews. In the paschal mystery, the Lord Jesus stands historically and eschatologically revealed as the one through whom the Father acts to create and to save. If God always acts salvifically through Christ, then He also did so in the past. The believing Christian differs from those who experienced Christ's saving action in former ages by experiencing Christ's saving action with an eschatological fullness which transcends anything God heretofore revealed.

Paul's midrashic rereading of the Hebrew exodus in the light of Christian experience has justification only if some kind of saving continuity links the two situations. Clearly, Paul believed that the salvation offered in Christ exceeds that proffered through Moses. Christian baptism supersedes baptism into Moses, just as the Christian eucharist supersedes the "God-given" bread and water given to the Hebrews. For both, however, Christ functions as the channel of God's saving action because the risen Lord stands historically revealed as the one through whom the Father acts to do whatever He does, whether He creates or whether He saves.[12]

---

12. Cf. Leonhard Goppelt, "Paul and Heilsgeschichte," translated by Mathias Rissi, *Interpretation*, 21(1967), pp. 315-326. Paul's midrashic rendering of the Exodus seeks to warn the Corinthians against spiritual complacency, idolatry, immorality, testing God, and grumbling. (1 Cor 10:6-10) In v. 14, Paul will focus his warning on idolatry. Since, however, he formulates his midrash as a way of contextualizing theologically the debate at Corinth over sacrificing food to idols, the apostle may well have intended all the sins he mentions in vv.6-10—spiritual complacency, testing God, idolatry, grumbling, immorality—to give the Corinthians pause. Those who recognize the legitimacy of eating food sacrificed to idols should not let their sense of

Paul has made his central point clearly and cumulatively: if God acted through Christ to baptize the Hebrews into Moses through His presence among them and through the waters of the exodus, if in addition God acted through Christ to give the Hebrews food and drink which foreshadowed the eucharist, and, if despite all these acts of God most of the Hebrews experienced God's rejection in the wilderness, then Christians living in the full revelation of Christ need to cultivate constant vigilance against all forms of temptation in the confident hope that, should temptation come, God will fortify them against it. In other words, Paul's elaborate midrash exhorts the Corinthians to live in hope and in practical, vigilant readiness for Christ's full and final revelation.[13] That same ecclesial readiness to meet final judgment contextualizes, then, the squabble between the meat eaters and the vegetable eaters.

In exhorting the community to eschatological vigilance, Paul implicitly chides the "strong" members of the community who do not scruple to eat meat sold in the marketplace. He challenges them to recognize that causing scandal to a weaker, more scrupulous Christian belies their readiness to face final judgment.[14] The meat eaters need to recognize that a perfectly legitimate concern motivates the exaggerated scruples of the vegetable eaters: namely, the repudiation of idolatry. (1 Cor 10:14) Paul, however, wants the Corinthians to deal with this issue like "sensible people (*phronimois*)," (1 Cor 10:15) rather than with rigid scrupulosity; but he does want them to face the issue.[15]

superiority to the scrupulous betray them into spiritual complacency. The abhorrence for idolatry which motivates the scruples of the vegetable eaters has solid foundation in the revelation. The debate between the two factions at Corinth had probably provoked a good deal of grumbling in the community. In 6:12-16, Paul had just warned the Corinthians against immorality, especially sexual immorality. Now, possibly, he recalls the sin in which the city of Corinth excelled as a way of undercutting any temptation to fall into spiritual complacency. Moreover, these sins—spiritual complacency, idolatry, immorality, and grumbling—all test God. Cf. James M. Scott, "Paul's Use of Deuteronomic Tradition," *Journal of Biblical Literature*, 112(1993), pp. 645-665.

13. Cf. Orr and Walther, *op.cit.*, pp. 244-9; Bruce, *op.cit.*, pp. 90-4; Groscheide, *op.cit.*, pp. 217-28.

14. Cf. Wayne A. Meeks, "'And Rose Up to Play': Midrash and Paranesis in 1 Corinthians 10:1- 22," *Journal for the Study of the New Testament*, 16(1982), pp. 64-78; Charles Perrot, "Les exemples du desert," *New Testament Studies*, 29(1983), pp. 437-452; Xavier Léon-Dufour, *Le partage du pain eucharistique selon le nouveau testament* (Paris: Éditions du Seuil, 1982), pp. 236-248; Gary D. Collier, "'That We might not Crave Evil'; The Structure and Argument of 1 Corinthians 10.1-13,"*Journal for the Study of the New Testament*, 55(1994), pp. 55-75.

15. Paul argues that any sensible person ought to realize that the purchase of meat once used in pagan sacrifice and now sold simply for profit differs from an act of demon worship as such. The sensible Corinthians should not, then, scruple to buy and eat such food; but they should refrain from eating it if in the process they cause a weaker member of the community to violate his or her conscience.

In exhorting his neophytes to focus on the basic intent of idolatrous worship, Paul again denies that "food offered to idols is anything, or that an idol is anything." (1 Cor 10:17) Here, however, the apostle acknowledges that, when pagans sacrifice food to idols, in fact they are worshipping demons. (1 Cor 10:20a)

In this context Paul once again finds the parallel between the old and the new Israel enlightening: under the Torah, those who ate the animals sacrificed to God participated in the altar and in the sacrifice offered on it. Those who eat the eucharistic bread and share the eucharistic cup similarly participate in the body and blood of Christ, and by implication in His sacrificial death. (1 Cor 10:16; cf. 11:26) Eucharistic participation unites the worshiping community by making it into the body of Christ enlivened by His Breath. (1 Cor 10:17; cf. 12:4-26) Active participation in the eucharist, therefore, precludes any active participation in demon worship, whether or not the gods which pagans worship actually exist or not.

Clearly, the factionalism at Corinth raises for Paul pastoral issues of both eucharistic and Christological significance. In dealing with the eucharistic issues, Paul provides the earliest Christian account of the last supper. Paul prefaces his account by reminding the Corinthians that this tradition comes directly from the Lord Jesus, not just from Paul.

> For I received from the Lord what I also delivered to you, that the Lord Jesus on the night when He was betrayed took bread, and when He had given thanks, He broke it, and said, "This is my body for you. Do this in memory of me." In the same way also the cup, after supper, saying "This cup is the new covenant in My blood. Do this, as often as you drink it, in remembrance of Me." For as often as you eat this bread and drink this cup, you proclaim the Lord's death until He comes. (1 Cor 11:23-6)

The eucharist solemnly proclaims Jesus' prophetic interpretation of the meaning of His own reconciling death. That proclamation occurs in an eschatological context: it expresses the community's longing for the Lord's final return in glory. In such a context of hope, the eucharistic community recalls and announces that before He died, Jesus asserted prophetically that He looked upon His death as His final self-gift to His disciples, as the ultimate expression of His love for them and forgiveness of them.

Why should they refrain from doing something legitimate? Because by emulating Paul's own self-restraint in dealing with the scrupulous, they will imitate Christ. (1 Cor 10:23-11:1) Paul, of course, recognized that Jesus never had to deal with the question troubling the Corinthians; but he trusts his Breath-inspired insight into the mind of Christ to yield a solution to this pastoral problem in conformity with the religious vision which Jesus lived and proclaimed. (Cf. Rom 14:5-12) Cf. Gordon D. Fee, "*Eidôlothula* Once Again: An Interpretation of 1 Corinthians 8-10," *Biblica*, 61(1980), pp. 172-197.

By giving His disciples His body as food and His blood as drink, He also expressed His confidence that His death would not only enliven the disciples but would abide as a source of life for them each time they remembered it. In referring to His blood as covenant blood, Jesus also voiced His hope that His death would somehow rededicate the disciples to God in covenanted commitment, as did the rite of atonement.

The Corinthians celebrated the eucharist in the context of an *agapê*, or love feast. Paul excoriates the Corinthians for the report that, when they gather for the love feast at which they share in the eucharist, factionalism prevents the free and impartial distribution of the food brought for the feast. As a result, some go in want while others eat and drink to excess. No meal marked by division and intemperance deserves the name "the Lord's supper," (1 Cor 11:20) because it embodies the opposite of the union in Christ which the Lord's supper symbolizes. (1 Cor 10:17)

By eating eucharistic bread and drinking the eucharistic cup in an unworthy manner, the Corinthians profane the body and blood of the Lord and transform a prayer of blessing into a divine judgment upon them for their hypocrisy and sinfulness. That judgment calls them to repentance and reform. (1 Cor 11:29-31) The Corinthians are sinning precisely because they share the eucharistic bread and eat the eucharistic cup without due self-examination and therefore "without discerning the body." One "discerns the body" by recognizing that participation in the eucharist makes those who do so members of Christ and therefore members of one another. (1 Cor 10:16-7; 12:) Hence, the only eucharistic celebration which deserves the name "the Lord's supper" embodies mutual reconciliation through living participation in Christ.[16] (Cf. 1 Cor 10:14- 22)

16. Cf. Montague, *op.cit.*, pp.115-122; Orr and Walther, *op.cit.*, pp. 265-75; Bruce, *op.cit.*, pp. 108-16; Groscheide, *op.cit.*, 263-77; Jerome Murphy- O'Connor, "Eucharist and Community in First Corinthians," *Worship*, 50(1976), pp. 370-385; Ernst Käsemann, *Essays on New Testament Themes*, translated by W.J. Montague (Philadelphia, PA: Fortress, 1982), pp. 108- 135; Léon-Dufour, *op.cit.*, pp. 248-265; C.L. Porter, "An Interpretation of Paul's Lord's Supper Texts," *Encounter Journal*, 50(1989), pp. 297-431; Duane Watson, "1 Corinthians 10:23-11:1 in the Light of Graeco-Roman Rhetoric: The Role of Rhetorical Questions," *Journal of Biblical Literature*, 108(1989), pp.301-318; Hyam Maccoby, "Paul and the Eucharist," *New Testament Studies*, 37(1991), pp. 247-267; R. Alastair Campbell, "Does Paul Acquiesce in Divisions at the Lord's Supper?" *Novum Testamentum*, 33(1991), pp. 61-70; Otfried Hofius, "'*To sôma to hyper hymôn*' 1 Kor 11,24,"*Zeitschrift für die Neutestamentliche Wissenschaft*, 80(1989), pp.80-88.
One finds some interesting eucharistic references in the letter to the Colossians:

> Let the word of Christ dwell in you richly, teaching and admonishing one another in all wisdom. With gratitude in your hearts, sing psalms, hymns, and Breath-filled song. Whatever you do in word or deed, do all in the name of the name of the Lord Jesus, giving thanks (*eucharistountes*) to God the Father through Him. (Col 3:16-7)

A charismatic prayer meeting at Corinth apparently followed upon the eucharistic meal and functioned as something like a eucharistic liturgy of the word. Paul's discussion of charismatic prayer in first Corinthians has, then, clear eucharistic presuppositions. Indeed, apart from those presuppositions, his discussion of the charisms makes very little sense. In the course of that discussion, Paul portrays the worshipping eucharistic community as the body of Christ. Paul's vision of a eucharistic community bound together in love through faith in the paschal mystery also informs, therefore, his theology of the Christian community as the functioning "body of Christ" in this world.

In his discussion of the charisms in first Corinthians, Paul explains that the unity which the Breath of Christ effects in the Corinthians results in part from the way in which they choose to use the diverse charisms which the divine Breath imparts to individuals within the community. The Breath of the one God inspires unity of faith. Nothing, therefore, which contradicts the Breath-inspired confession of Jesus as Lord can claim Her illu-

The term "*eucharistountes*" in verse 17 together with Paul's allusion to liturgical singing in verse 16 suggests that his exhortation to thankfulness has the Christian eucharist, the ultimate Christian act of thanksgiving, as its paradigm.

The first letter to the Corinthians gives us our most detailed glimpse of how the Pauline communities worshipped eucharistically. If we interpret the portrait of eucharistic worship depicted at Corinth as typical of the communities Paul founded, then eucharistic worship occurred at a plenary meeting of the community, which all members ordinarily attended. The eucharistic blessing of the bread and wine took place at a love feast to which each member of the community brought something to share with the other members of the community. A period of shared charismatic prayer then followed the eucharistic meal in which prayer, singing, prophecy, and teaching occurred. (Cf. 1 Cor 11:17-14:40)

In other words, in the Pauline churches the equivalent of what we now call the liturgy of the word apparently followed the eucharistic liturgy instead of preceding it. Moreover, the Pauline liturgy of the word apparently proceeded with much more shared, charismatic spontaneity than does the liturgy of the word as Christians currently experience it. Cf. Cheslyn Jones, Geoffrey Wainwright, and Edward Yarnold, S.J., eds., *The Study of Liturgy* (London: SPCK, 1978), pp. 150-162.

If we take these eucharists as the context for Paul's exhortation to thankfulness in Col 4:15-7, then, when he exhorts the Colossians to let the word of Christ dwell richly in them through mutual instruction and exhortation, he is in fact urging them to prolong in their daily lives the mutual instruction which takes place in the charismatic portion of their eucharists.

Paul also urges the Colossians to give thanks to the Father through the Son, a formula which would fit a eucharistic setting. Paul, however, seems to be speaking of more than eucharistic worship. He seems in fact to be suggesting to the Colossians that their shared eucharistic worship ought to suffuse their daily lives. The hymns of thanksgiving which they sing at the table of Christ should find an echo in their hearts all day long. This allusion to hymnic worship may also contain an invitation to the Colossians to ponder thankfully the Christological hymn on which Paul has been commenting and to take his exposition of its meaning as a model for the mutual instruction which they give one another. (Cf. Eph 5:15-20)

mination or sanction. (1 Cor 12:3; cf. Gal 3:26-9; Eph 2:11-22; Col 3:5-11)

Baptism, which communicates a share in the Breath of the risen Christ, incorporates the Christian into the one body of Christ. That incorporation introduces one into the egalitarian community which Jesus had proclaimed and inaugurated. It obliterates any distinction between Jew and Greek, slave and free person. In the same way, the Breath's charismatic inspirations seek to make each member of the community members of one another in the one body of Christ. (1 Cor 12:12-26) "Now you are the body of Christ and individually members of it." (1 Cor 12:27)

Organic membership in the body of Christ demands, that Christians recognize a certain "hierarchical" ordering in the way the Breath's charisms function within the community: "first apostles, second prophets, third teachers, then workers of miracles, then healers, helpers, administrators, and tongue speakers." (1 Cor 12:28-31) The Breath of Christ unites the community by inspiring a common faith which comes to practical expression in mutual charismatic ministry. She unites the community most effectively, however, in the bond of mutual love which She illumines and empowers.[17] (1 Cor 12:30-14:1)

Paul's charismatic theology echoes his theology of resurrection because in both the Breath of the risen Christ functions as a bond of divine life uniting the believing Christian community to the risen Lord. That vital bond grounds and explains the functional identity between the risen Christ and the inspirations of His Breath. Wherever She acts, He acts because He functions as Her unique and efficacious source. As a consequence, in the charismatic inspirations of the Holy Breath the glorified Christ in His glorified humanity unites Himself efficaciously to the believing Christian community. In the process, He transforms them into His body: into the physical instrument through which He acts, speaks, witnesses, heals, proclaims, ministers, prophesies, prays, and discerns.

Paul's charismatic theology engages both the reality and somatic character of the resurrection. The risen Christ in his glory possesses a "pneumatic" body, one totally transformed in the power of the Breath. Through the charismatic inspirations of His Breath, however, the risen Christ unites himself both vitally and functionally with the communities who confess Him and worship Him eucharsitically. That dynamic, vital union, which expresses itself in using the charisms to unify the Christian community, deepens the pneumatic transformation of the bodies of those who believe in Him. That transformation advances them up the road which leads to

17. Cf. Montague, *op.cit.*, 122-7; E. Earle Ellis, *Pauline Theology: Ministry and Society* (Grand Rapids, MI: Eerdmans, 1989); Willem van Unnik, "The Meaning of 1 Corinthians 12:31," *Novum Testamentum*, 35(1993), pp. 142-159.

final resurrection, to total, personal, corporeal transformation in the Breath of the risen Christ.[18]

I have examined the Christological foundations for Paul's theology of the Christian community as the body of Christ. In the next two sections of this chapter, I shall examine the ways in which the letters to the Colossians and to the Ephesians develop that theology.

(IV)

Those who defend the authenticity of the letter to the Colossians place it during Paul's captivity and Roman sojourn, between 61 and 63 a.d. Those who deny the authenticity tend to date it between 70 and 80 a.d. and attribute it to a disciple of Paul who used the apostle's name as a pseudonym.

Exegetes question the Pauline authorship of this letter because of significant shifts in vocabulary and because of its "untypically Pauline" use of the term "*ekklêsia*," which in four verses (1:18, 24; 2:19; and 3:15) refers to the Church universal rather than to local churches, as it does in other Pauline letters. Two verses of Colossians (4:15, 16) use the term "church" more typically to refer to local churches.

The sentence structure of Colossians also seems to some to belie Pauline authorship. The letter abounds in long and convoluted sentences which differ from the generally terser style of the Pauline letters whose authenticity everyone endorses. Even in the undisputed letters, however, one occasionally finds sentences of comparable complexity.

---

18. Paul also recognizes both celibacy and marriage as gifts, or charisms, of God's Holy Breath. (1 Co 7:7) Given, however, the shortness of the time, i.e., the likelihood, in Paul's opinion, that Jesus would return soon, (1 Cor 7:29), Paul recommends celibacy over marriage because it allows one to consecrate oneself single-mindedly to "the affairs of the Lord." Married people, by contrast, have to figure out both how to please the Lord by pleasing one another and how to serve God while still involved in worldly affairs. In other words, marital responsibilities would keep Paul from single-minded devotion to his apostolic ministry. (1 Cor 7:25-35) Paul, however, concedes that Christian marriage happens "in the Lord" (1 Cor 7:39) and insists that it commits one to a life of marital chastity and fidelity. (1 Cor 7:1-9) Cf. Montague, *op.cit.*, 105-10; John Koenig, *Charismata*: God's Gifts for God's People (Philadelphia, PA: Westminster, 1978); Robert Banks, *Paul's Idea of a Community* (Peabody, MA: Hendrickson, 1994); Vincent Branick, *The House Church in the Writings of Paul* (Wilmington, DL: Michael Glazier, 1989; Philippe Bacq, "Le prophetisme dans l'Écriture et dans l'Église," *Lumen Vitae*, 43(1988), pp. 173-183, 419-429; Eduard Schweizer, "On Distinguishing between Spirits," *Ecumenical Review*, 41(1989), pp. 406-414; Gregory W. Dawes, "'But if you can gain your freedom' (1 Corinthians 7:17-24), *Catholic Biblical Quarterly*, 52(1992), pp. 681-697; Enrique Nardoni, "The Concept of Charism in Paul," *Catholic Biblical Quarterly*, 55(1993), pp. 68-88; Rollen A. Mamsaran, "More Than an Opinion: Paul's Rhetorical Maxim in First Corinthians 7:25-26," *Catholic Biblical Quarterly*, 57(1995), pp. 531-541; Joop F.M. Smit, "Tongues and Prophecy: Deciphering 1 Cor 14,22," *Biblica*, 75(1994), pp. 175-190.

Colossians does refer to the risen Christ as the "head" of His body, the Church. This insight goes somewhat beyond anything one finds in the letters to the Corinthians.[19] (Col 1:18) There one finds talk of the local community as Christ's body; but in writing to the Corinthians, Paul never characterizes Christ as the head of the Church universal.

The same person can, of course, speak somewhat differently and use slightly different categories in different situations. We have no reason to believe that Paul's earlier letters, occasional writings for specific communities, exhaust his theological insight or vocabulary. As in the case of his other letters, Paul would, moreover, probably have dictated Colossians to a scribe (Col 5:18); and we do not know how much liberty a scribe might take in "polishing" the original author's style.

The anomalous use of the term "church (*ekklêsia*)" first occurs in Colossians in the Christological hymn which opens the letter. (Col 1: 18) The hymn, probably of liturgical origin, in all likelihood predates the letter. The other anomalous uses of this same term occur in the theological argument which follows the hymn and which elaborates on its insights. The letter cites the hymn for its relevance to the issues troubling the community at Colossae.

The anomalous use of the term "*ekklêsia*" does develop slightly the theology of Christ's body which Paul developed in first Corinthians. It does so by designating Christ explicitly as the of head the entire Church. In Paul's earlier letters the term "church" refers to a community in a specific place, not to the Church universal.

One may, however, find the notion of the Church universal implicit in Paul's more traditional usage; for a phrase like "the church at Thessalonika" implicitly asserts that the local church makes the wide church, the universal church, present in a particular place. One can, then, question just how drastic a shift in Pauline ecclesiology the new use of the term "*ekklêsia*" exemplifies.

One can say the same for the designation of the risen Christ as the head of his body, the Church. Every living, human body has a head. In speaking of Christ as the head of the Church Colossians simply draws out the obvious implications of the metaphor of the body of Christ which Paul developed in first Corinthians.

19. In Paul's letters the term "church (*ekklêsia*)" signifies the Christian community united in faith by the divine call and election. In first Thessalonians, for example, Paul applies the term to the primitive Christian communities in Judea. (1 Th 2:14; cf. Gal 1:21) Moreover, in the same letter Paul applies the term "church" to the community at Thessalonika "in God the Father and the Lord Jesus Christ." In other words, both God the Father and the Lord Jesus Christ have called and elected the united faith community of the Thessalonians. Moreover, that call and election establish a bond between the church, on the one hand, and both God the Father and the Lord Jesus Christ, on the other. (cf. 1 Th 3:8)

In addition, the letter to the Colossians addresses new and different adversaries who probably espoused an early form of Gnostic piety, a very primitive and somewhat chaotic kind of protognosticism which blended elements of Judaism, paganism, Christianity, magic, astrology, and mystery religions. Their eclectic piety probably rooted itself in diaspora Judaism. The very novelty of the problems at Colossae might well have influenced the way Paul chose to speak to this community.[20] Finally, those

20. Cf. D.L. Meland, "The Extent of the Pauline Corpus: A Multivariant Approach," *Journal for the Study of the New Testament*, 59(1995), pp. 61-92. Paul informs the Colossians that, through his ministry to the Gentiles, he has proclaimed "the mystery (*mysterion*) hidden from ages and generations, but now made manifest in His saints, to whom God chose to make known how great among the Gentiles are the riches of the glory of this mystery, which is Christ in you, the hope of glory." (Col 1:26-7; cf. 1 Cor 2:6-16; 2 Cor 4:1-12; Eph 3:1-13)

In contrast to mystery religions which proclaim and celebrate different mysteries, Christianity proclaims only one mystery, the mystery of Christ present in His Church. Christianity proclaims only one mystery, because it offers the same salvation to all, whether Jew or Gentile. A single, divine plan of salvation unifies all humanity and all history, a plan hidden from former generations in the mystery of God but now made manifest in the paschal mystery: in the death and resurrection of God's Son and in His presence in those who believe by the power of His Breath. God the Father, who decreed this mysterious plan, as always holds the initiative in revealing it to us through His Son. Paul proclaims this mystery ceaselessly, even while in chains, in the hope of bringing all people to perfection in Christ. Indeed, Paul commends the Colossians for living harmoniously and for the firmness of their faith in Christ. (Col 1:27-2:5)

At the same time that Paul urges the Colossians to pattern their whole lives on Christ Jesus the Lord, (Col 2:6), he also warns them against those who would seek to ensnare them "by philosophy and empty deceit, according to human tradition, according to the elements of the universe (*stoikeia tou kosmou*) and not according to Christ." (Col 2:8)

The phrase "*stoicheia tou kosmou*" also occurs in Gal 4:3, where Paul reminds the Galatians that prior to their conversion they lived enslaved to the "elements of the world." There the phrase seems to refer most obviously to the gods of polytheism. In Galatians, "*stoicheia tou kosmou*" also connotes the religious rituals common to both Jews and pagans, rituals devoid of the efficacy of the Breath of Christ.

In Colossians, the phrase "*stoicheia tou kosmou*" probably has similar, fairly broad connotations. Paul praises the faith of the community, but warns it against submitting to the needless, inefficacious, syncretistic religious practices of the protognostics in their midst. The protognostics are disseminating religious practices based on an empty philosophy which offers a false account of the elemental principles on which the universe is based.

In Colossians, then, "*stoicheia tou kosmou*" seems to mean roughly the same as the "*archai*," or principalities, or first causal principles, of the universe. To these "first principles" Paul opposes Christ, the one *archê* the single source of both the created universe and of human salvation, who exercises divine sovereign sway over all the principalities and powers of the universe. Cf. Wink, *op.cit.*, pp.67-77; *NJBC*, 54:21; Harris, *op. cit.*, 93-4. Walter Wink has suggested that one might well translate "*stoicheia tou kosmou*" as "the presuppositions of the domination system." See: Walter Wink, *Engaging the Powers: Discernment and Resistance in a World of Domination* (Minneapolis, MI: Fortress, 1992), p. 157. See also: Fred O. Francis and Wayne A. Meeks, *Con-*

who defend the authenticity of Colossians argue against the likelihood that a disciple of Paul could have mastered the apostle's theological vision as thoroughly as the author of this letter.

In discussing both Colossians and Ephesians, I shall for stylistic convenience refer to their author as Paul. In invoking Paul's name, I do not, however, intend to resolve the question of the authenticity of either letter.

The Christological Hymn in Colossians

The letter to the Colossians opens with a Christological hymn. Exegetes differ in their judgment about where the hymn begins. Some begin the hymn with verse twelve where Paul thanks God the Father for having translated the Colossians from "the power of darkness" and given them a place "in the kingdom of the Son of His love." The phrase "Son of His love" designates Jesus both as the special object of divine benevolence and as the one who reveals the perfection of the Father's love. By introducing the Colossians into the kingdom, the Father has also given them "a portion of the lot of the saints in light."[21] (Col 1:12-4)

We encounter here another relatively rare Pauline reference to the "kingdom of God" which Jesus had proclaimed. Here, however, Paul describes the saving work of Jesus in terms which suggest the struggle of light against darkness. The phrase "power of darkness" refers to the power of sin and of death; but it may have other connotations in the present contest.

The struggle between light and darkness finds important echoes in the theology of the fourth gospel. Quite possibly, Colossians invoked the image for much the same reason as John the evangelist. Both writers are probably battling against an early from of gnosticism. Gnostic religion promised a saving enlightenment, as did Christianity. Judged in the light of Christian faith, however, any enlightenment but a thoroughly incarnational enlightenment stands disclosed as darkness, not light.

The hymn which opens Colossians probably predates Paul's letter.[22] It asserts in its first stanza:

flict at Colossae: Revised Edition (Missoula, MT: Scholars Press, 1975); Richard E. DeMaris, The Collossian Controversy: Wisdom in Dispute at Colossae (Sheffield: Sheffield Academic Press, 1994); Roy Yates, "Colossians and Gnosis," Journal for the Study of the New Testament, 27(1986), pp. 49-68; James D.G. Dunn, "The Colossian Philosophy: A Confident Jewish Apologia," Biblica, 76(1995), pp. 153-181; Michael Goulder, "Colossians and Barbelo," New Testament Studies, 41(1995), pp. 601-619; Clinton E. Arnold, "Returning to the Domain of the Powers: Stoicheia as Evil Spirits in Galatians 4:39," Novum Testamentum, 38(1996), pp. 55-76.

21. Cf. P. Benoit, "Hagioi en Colossiens 1.2; Hommes ou anges" in Paul and Paulinism, edited by M.O. Hooker and S.G. Wilson (London: SPCK Press, 1982), pp. 82-99.

22. Cf. Bruce Vawter, C.M., "The Colossians Hymn and the Principle of Redaction," Catholic Biblical Quarterly, 33(1971), pp. 62-81; Jarl Fossum, "Colossians 1.15-18a in the Light of Jewish Mysticism and Gnosticism," New Testament Studies, 35(1989), pp. 183-201.

He is the image of the invisible God,
the first-born of all creation,
for in Him all things were created,
in heaven and on earth,
visible and invisible,
whether thrones or dominations or principalities or rulers—
all things were created through Him and for Him.
He is before all things,
and in Him all things cohere.
Now the Church is His body,
He is its head. (Col 1: 15-18a)

The first stanza blends creation motifs with soteriological ones. It begins by describing the Son of God as "the image of the unseen God (*eikôn tou Theou tou aoratou*)." Paul uses the same term, "image (*eikôn*)," when he describes Christians as images of God or of Christ (cf. Rom 8:29, 1 Cor 11:7, 15:49, 2 Cor 3:18) The term "image," however, could also echo Wis 7:26, which describes divine Wisdom as a "reflection of eternal light." In Colossians, the phrase "image of the invisible God" probably designates Jesus as the one who, in the divine dispensation, makes a wise, creating, and saving God concretely and historically visible and manifest.

The title "the firstborn of all creation (*prôtokos pases ktiseos*)" assimilates Christ to pre-existent, divine Wisdom, which Proverbs calls "the first-born of His (i.e., God's) ways." (Prov 8:22)" The phrase "firstborn of all creation" also finds an echo in the second stanza of the hymn, which designates Christ as "the beginning (*archê*), the firstborn from the dead (*prôtokos ex tôn nekrôn*)." (Col 1:15, 18; cf. Rom 8:29)

Since, moreover, the first stanza alludes to Christ's saving action (v. 18a) as well as to His creative power, the phrase "firstborn of creation" probably also has Adamic connotations. It points to Jesus as the last Adam, the one who recreates the world decisively by rising from the dead. (Cf. 1 Cor 15:20-28; 2 Cor 5:14-21; Rom 5:12-21) In all probability, the same phrase also connotes Davidic, and therefore messianic, dignity: Psalm 89, for example, calls David the "firstborn" of God, God's son and heir.

The hymn insists that all creation exists "in Him (*en auto*)" and was created "through Him (*di' autou*)" and "for Him (*eis autou*)." (Col 1:16) The assertion that all creation exists in the Son of God clearly places Him in the realm of the divine, since only God can encompass the whole of creation. It also asserts a panentheistic interpretation of the relationship between God and the world. (Cf. Acts 17:28, Jn 17:22-23)

Verse 17 makes the allusion to divinity more explicit by linking panentheism to the fact that the Son existed before creation. The present tense in the verb "is (*estin*)" can mean "is existing" and thus connote perpetual existence.

Verse 17 also gives the idea of panentheism a dynamic and, probably, a soteriological twist when it asserts: "and He is before all things and in Him all things cohere." The coherence of all things in the Son points to Him as the source of cosmic unity; but it also designates the Son as the single source of salvation, as the one whose saving death and resurrection ends the division caused by sin and reconciles the world to God (Col 1:19-20).

The assertion that the world was created "through Him" designates the Son of God as the one through whom the Father does whatever He does, not only in saving the world but in creating it as well. The Son, therefore, stands revealed as the one through whom the Father's eternal wisdom orders the universe.

The phrase "for Him" designates the Son along with the Father as not only the source but also as the goal of all created reality. This same phrase also has soteriological connotations, since only the saving death of Christ, His resurrection, and His mission of the Breath reconcile the whole world to God (Col 1:19-20). Only through Christ, then, can a sinful world attain the end for which God created it, namely, union with God through recreation in Christ.[23] (Rom 8:18-23; Phil 2: 9-11)

The hymn offers a brief catalogue of the creatures which exist in the Son: "all things in heaven and on earth (*panta en tois ouranois kai epi tês gês*), things visible and invisible (*ta horata kai ta aorata*) whether thrones (*thronoi*) or principalities (*kyriotêtes*) or rulers (*archai*)." (Col 1:16)

The phrase "things visible and things invisible" makes explicit an idea implied in the preceding phrase: "all things in heaven and on earth." The phrase invokes the New Testament myth of the powers. It portrays the creation as including not only human and subhuman creatures but invis-

---

23. Later in Colossians, Paul writes, "For in him dwells all the fullness of divinity (*pan to plerôma the theotêtos*) bodily (*sômatikôs*); you too will be filled (*peplêômenoi*) in Him, who is the head (*kephalê*) of every principality and power." (Col 2:9-10) The Christological hymn in Colossians proclaims that Christ possesses the fullness of divine creative and saving power. Here Paul makes the meaning of the hymn clear by speaking of the fullness of divinity, of Godhead, dwelling in Christ. Moreover, he insists that the divinity dwells in Christ in a bodily fashion (*sômatikôs*). (Cf. Col 1:19)

Paul's insistence on the physical character of the divine indwelling probably envisages the errors of the protognostics who found the incarnation of God repugnant. The phrase, however, implicitly echoes Paul's insistence elsewhere on the bodily character of the resurrection, since the divine indwelling in verse 9 looks to the risen Christ and not just to Jesus' mortal ministry. That Paul is thinking of the risen body of Christ becomes clearer in the verses which follow and which assimilate Christ's resurrection to that of His followers. The fact that the risen Christ possesses the fullness of divinity in a bodily fashion ensures that the Colossians too will be filled with divinity as a consequence of their existence in Christ as members of His body. Cf. Murray J. Harris, *Colossians and Philemon* (Grand Rapids, MI: Eerdmans, 1991), pp. 99-100; Harald van Broekhoven, "The Social Profiles in the Colossian Debate," *Journal for the Study of the New Testament*, 66(1997), pp. 73-90.

ible forces of cosmic scope, both for good and for evil, which take visible shape in the actions of individuals and of institutions.

The phrase "whether thrones or dominations or rulers" designates specific examples of these cosmic forces. The term "throne" designates a seat of human power which outlasts those who sit on it and which therefore also transcends the people who occupy it. The term "principalities" designates the realms over which the "thrones" hold sway, while the term "rulers" designates the agents through whom invisible cosmic powers act, those who sit upon the thrones and who reign over a given principality.[24]

All these visible and invisible realities, however, remain creatures only, all of them subject to the dominion of the Son in whom and for whom they exist and through whom they came to exist. In asserting that these thrones, principalities, and powers cohere only in the Son, the hymn seems to assert that they complement and build one another up only to the extent that they appropriate the Son's redemption and submit to His divine sway by serving rather than opposing God. (Col 1:19-20; cf. Eph 1:17-8)

In asserting that "He is the head of the body, the Church (*tês ekklêsias*)," the hymn develops Paul's earlier theology of the mystical body in a significant way. In both first Corinthians and Romans, Paul had referred to the Church as the body of Christ. (1 Cor 6:15, 10:16-7, 12:12-27; Rom 12:4-5) As we have seen, however, in those letters, the apostle did not designate Christ explicitly as the head of that body. In Colossians, the hymn develops the metaphor of Christ's body by giving the body a head. The extended metaphor interprets the relationship between Christ and the Church universal.[25] (Cf. Col 1:24,27, 2:17,19, 3:15)

The second stanza of the hymn begins to explore the meaning of Christ's headship over His Church. Stanza two asserts:

---

24. Cf. Wink, *Naming the Powers,* pp. 17-20; G.B. Caird, *Principalities and Powers* (Oxford: Oxford at Clarendon Press, 1956); Wesley Carr, *Angels and Principalities* (Cambridge: Cambridge University Press, 1981), pp. 47-85.

25. Later in Colossians, Paul argues that the rigorists, through their false teaching and false piety, have shown that they do not live united to Christ, the head of the Church, "from whom the whole body, nourished and knit together through its joints and ligaments, grows with a growth that comes from God." (Col 2:19) Instead of building up the body in unity, the protognostics sew dissension. They thus betray that their teachings and false piety come, not from Christ, but from the principalities and powers of this world. They promise a sham religious growth, not a growth which God inspires and sanctions. (Cf. Eph 4:11-6)

Appealing to the Colossians' baptismal death to "the elements of the world (*apo tôn stoicheiôn tou kosmou*)," Paul dismisses the false religious philosophy of the rigorists as "human doctrines and regulations (*ta entalmata kai didaskalias tôn anthropôn*)." (Col 2:22) As in Col 2:8, "the elements of the world" designates the sinful powers at work in everything which rationalizes or motivates the oppression they work. Cf. Käsemann, *Pauline Perspectives,* pp. 102-121.

> He is the beginning,
> the first born from the dead,
> that in everything He might be pre-eminent,
> for all the fullness was pleased to dwell in Him
> and to reconcile all things to Himself,
> whether on earth or in heaven,
> making peace by the blood of His cross. (Col 1:18b-20)

The statement that Christ is the beginning extends and develops earlier Pauline insights into the cosmic aspects of the salvation effected through the paschal mystery. (Cf. 1 Cor 15:20-8, 42-50; Rom 8:28-30; 2 Cor 5:14-21; Gal 6:15) In calling Christ the "beginning (*archê*)" the hymn puns triply on the term "*archê*." (v. 18b) As the source (*archê*) and goal of all the principalities and powers, Christ stands revealed as the primordial power (*archê*) which transcends mere worldly powers. As the first-born from the dead (*prôtotokos ek tôn nekrôn*), moreover, Christ also makes a new beginning (*archê*) by heading a new creation.[26]

---

26. The exhortatory section of Colossians urges that the baptized recognize that Christ has broken down all the traditional social barriers which have separated Jew from Greek, the circumcised from the uncircumcised, barbarian from Scythian, slave from free citizen. (Col 3:11) This social leveling has resulted from the fact that Christians, whatever their social origin or status, have stripped off their formal sinful habits and now live in the image of the one who created their new selves. Pauline egalitarianism claims to root itself in the egalitarianism which Jesus proclaimed and embodied.

Paul calls the former sinful habits of the Colossians "the old man (*ton palaion anthrôpon*)." The phrase has adamic connotations. The "old man" designates the Colossians as the sinful children of Adam. Having abandoned the sinful ways of the first Adam's progeny, they must live like the last Adam, the risen Christ. (Col 3:9-10)

In speaking of the image of the one who created the new man, Paul is referring to the Christological hymn in Col 1:15-20. The hymn described the Son of God as the one in whom, through whom, and for whom all things were created and as one who reconciles the whole of creation to God. The Colossians should, then, conform themselves to Christ and in the process to the Father who acts through Him both to create and save a sinful world. Paul's language even echoes that of the hymn: "There is only Christ: He is everything and in everything." (Col 3:11; cf. 5-11)

Paul then exhorts the Colossians to a variety of virtues, all of which describe aspects of Jesus' own character: sincere compassion, kindness and humility, gentleness and patience, mutual forgiveness. Paul makes it clear that these virtues imitate the mind of Christ by re-enforcing the exhortation to mutual forgiveness with an allusion to the forgiveness of Christ: "The Lord has forgiven you, now you must do the same." (Col 3:12-3)

Love must bind together all these virtues. "The peace of Christ" must reign in the hearts of the Colossians, the peace "to which you have been called in the one body (*en heni sômati*)." (Col 3:15) We find here another allusion to the Christological hymn in chapter 1. The hymn had described Christ as the head of His body the Church and as the source of its unity. In emphasizing the union which results from mutual commitment in the love of Christ, Paul again implicitly warns the Colossians to guard against the divisive influence of the protognostics.

Christ functions, on the one hand, as the creative source of all creation and therefore as the ruling head of all thrones, dominations, principalities, and powers. On the other hand, He also functions as the prototypical first-born in the new creation "so that He might become (*hina genêtai*) the one enjoying pre-eminence in all things (*en pasin autos prôteuôn*)." (v. 18b) The use of the verb "*genêtai*" underscores the dispensational cast of the hymn's thought: it looks not just to Christ's pre-existence as the creative source of all but to the process by which His pre-existent divine dignity together with His creative and redemptive power came to historical revelation.[27]

27. Cf. Rudolf Hoppe, *Der Triumph des Kreuzes: Studien zum Verhältnis des Kolosserbriefs zur paulinischen Kreuzestheologie* (Stuttgart: Katolisches Bibelwerk, 1994), pp. 146-225. Later in Colossians, Paul insists that anyone baptized into Christ need not bother any more with the principalities and powers of this world, because through His death and resurrection Christ has done away with the principalities and powers, has conquered them totally and decisively, and made of them a public mockery.

Assimilating baptism to circumcision, Paul calls Christian baptism "the circumcision of Christ." (Col 2:11) The phrase refers not to Jesus' own physical circumcision but to a pneumatic circumcision which joins one to Christ. Jewish circumcision physically removes the foreskin and binds one to observe the Law. The circumcision of Christ, by contrast, strips away the entire body of flesh by causing one to die to sin with Christ and to rise with Him to newness of life. This pneumatic transformation of the self effects the forgiveness of sin and inspires Christian confidence that God will raise from the dead all of those who believe in Christ. (Col 2:11-3; cf. Rom 2:18) No other passage in the New Testament makes such an explicit comparison between Christian baptism and circumcision, although, as always in comparing the realm of grace to that of the Law, Paul makes clear the superiority of Christian baptism to mere circumcision.

Col 2:13-5 assimilates the sinner's relationship to God to that of a debtor. In so speaking Paul echoes a familiar Biblical metaphor for sin, viz., a debt we owe to God. God cancels our debt of sin by taking the bond on which it is written and nailing it to the cross with Christ. Paul thus portrays the physical crucifixion of Jesus as the event which effects the forgiveness of sins. As we have seen, however, for Paul Jesus' physical death has a moral dimension as well: namely, His death to sin through the perfection of His obedience to the Father. His death also embodies the full expression of God's atoning love.

The perfect self-surrender of the Son to the Father through His death on the cross breaks the dominion of the principalities and powers at the very moment and in the very act in which they seemed to triumph over Him. Here the phrase "principalities and powers" refers both to the preternatural forces of evil which oppose God and to the human instruments whom they employ to accomplish their ends: in the case of Jesus, to Pilate and to the chief priests in Jerusalem.

By raising Jesus from the dead, God transforms the moment of His deepest abasement and death at the hands of the principalities and powers into a moment of absolute triumph over them by transferring dominion over all creation to His hands. As always, Paul sees the death and resurrection of Jesus as inseparable facets of the same saving event. Like a Roman general, the risen Christ now celebrates a triumph over the vanquished principalities and rulers, parading them in disgrace behind Him in His victory celebration.

The triumph of Christ over the principalities and rulers has freed all believers once and for all from any need to submit to enslavement by them. Paul relegates the regu-

The hymn then asserts that "in Him all the fullness was pleased to dwell (*en autô eudokêsen pan to plêrôma katoikêsai*)." (v. 19) Some translators render the term "all the fullness" as " the fullness of God"; but the Greek text has no such qualifying genitive. Here, "all the fullness" designates the plentitude of divine creative and saving power. The eternal Son possesses the fullness of divine creative power, since through Him the Father in His wisdom created all things. The incarnate Son's atoning death on the cross together with His resurrection insures that He enjoys the plentitude of saving power. As a consequence, the effects of His saving death penetrate the whole of creation.[28] (vv. 19-20)

In saying that the fullness "was pleased (*eudokêsen*)" to dwell in Christ, (v. 19) the hymn suggests that such indwelling expresses the divine good pleasure and providential dispensation. Moreover, that divine good pleasure desired that Christ reconcile all things "to himself (*eis auton*)." As a consequence, Christ's saving death unites "both heaven and earth [literally: "whether the things on the earth or the things in the heavens (*eite ta epi tês gês eite ta en tois ouranois*)]." Put archetypally, the death of Christ effects the *hieros gamos*, the saving union of heaven and earth, of the divine and the human. (Cf. Col 2:9)

The use of the term "*plêrôma*" in the Christological hymn differs significantly from its use in Gnostic literature. In Gnostic literature, the term has creative significance, the fullness of the heavenly powers which emanate from God. In Colossians, it has both creative and redemptive significance. Moreover, in Colossians redemption flows from the death of the incarnate God, a doctrine abhorrent to Gnostic modes of thought.

The Pauline *plêrôma* also differs from the Stoic. In Stoicism the *plêrôma* has pantheistic connotations: deity animates the cosmos and thus fills it. Colossians sees God's creative power as extending to all creation; but God does not animate the world as a quasi-soul. While Colossians recognizes that all things exist in God, its hymn eschews Stoic pantheism for a more Biblical panentheism. Moreover, Colossians links the ultimate union of

lations and ritual observances which the protognostic rigorists at Colossae were trying to impose on the Christians there to the worldly realm dominated by the very principalities and rulers whom Christ has conquered once and for all. The Colossians should turn a deaf ear to the rigorists' demand that they observe abstinence from certain food and drink as well as "annual festivals, new moons, or sabbaths." (Col 2:16, 20)

"These things," Paul writes, "were only a shadow of things to come: the body of Christ (*to sôma tou Christou*)." (Col 2:17) Paul puns here on the term "*sôma*," which here means both a physical body which casts a shadow and the pneumatic reality of the Church, the body of Christ. One should never confuse the reality of a physical body with the insubstantial shadow it casts. The ascetical and religious practices demanded by the Mosaic covenant resemble the insubstantial shadow cast by the reality of Christ's body, the Church.

28. Cf. N.T. Wright, "Poetry and Theology in Colossians 1.15-20," *New Testament Studies*, 36 (1990), pp. 444-468.

heaven and earth, of the divinity and creation, not to the created order of things but to the atoning, reconciling death of Christ. That death, because reconciling, exhibits the character of an atoning sacrifice.[29]

Paul makes immediate application of the hymn's Christology to the situation of the Colossians. Despite their former estrangement from God, Christ has reconciled them "in His body of flesh (*en tô sômati tes sarkos autou*) through death." (Col 1:22) In apparent opposition to the false teachers at Colossae, who seem to have found the union of God with a mortal, material body abhorrent, Paul insists not only on the physical character of the union but on the body's fleshy mortality as well. The Son through whom God created the world really had a body, really died, and really experienced human weakness. Moreover, Christ's physical death has saving significance: it reconciles a sinful people to God. (Col 1:21-3; cf. Gal 4:8-11; Eph 2:11-22)

Paul then applies the hymn to himself and portrays his imprisonment as his participation in the cross of Christ. Paul asserts, "Now I rejoice in my sufferings for your sake, and in my flesh (*en tês sarki mou*) I complete (*antanaplêro*) what is lacking in Christ's afflictions (*ta usterêmata tôn thlipseôn tou Christou*) for the sake of His body, that is, the Church (*hyper tou sômatos autou, ho estin hê ekklêsia*)."

Exegetes have debated what completion means in this context as well as the meaning of the phrase "Christ's afflictions." The hymn has just proclaimed Christ the one, who through His sufferings, has reconciled all things to God. When Paul speaks of "completion," he is not, then, asserting the redemptive insufficiency of Christ's passion. Moreover, Paul never uses the phrase "*thlipsis*" to designate the passion itself. Rather, it designates the hardships and sufferings of Christians as they are drawn into the passion of Christ as a consequence of proclaiming and living the gospel. (Cf. Rom 5:3, 8:35; 2 Cor 1:4-8, 2:4, 4:17, 6:4, 7:4) By the phrase "sufferings of Christ (*tôn thlipseôn tou Christou*)," then, Paul seems to mean the sufferings of Christians, of those who belong to Christ, or better the sufferings of Christ the head in His members. (Cf. Acts 9:5)

One finds an analogous use of the genitive of "Christ" in Col 2:11, where Paul speaks of "the circumcision of Christ" but means, not Jesus' own circumcision, but a metaphorical circumcision of the Christian community. In effect, then, Paul is saying here what he has said elsewhere: namely, his apostolate brings him tribulations (*thlipseis*) which draw him

29. Cf. Montague, *op.cit.*, 201.; Harris, *op.cit.*, pp. 28-55; Arthur G. Patzia, *Ephesians, Colossians, Philemon* (Peabody, MA: Hendrickson, 1984), pp. 27-35; *NJBC*, 54:12-3; Cerfaux, *op.cit.*, pp. 399-432; F.F. Bruce, "The 'Christ Hymn' of Colossians 1:15-20," Bibliotheca *Sacra*, 141(1984), pp. 99-111; Josef Ernst, *Plêrôma und Plêrôma Christi* (Regensberg: Verlag Friedrich Pustet, 1970), pp. 71-105; Deichgräber, *op. cit.*, pp. 78-82, 143-155; J. McCarthy, S.J., "Le Christ cosmique et l'âge de l'écologie: une lecture de Col 1, 15-20," *Nouvelle Revue Théologique*, 116(1994), pp. 27-47.

into the passion of Christ. In saying that he "completes what is wanting" in Christian suffering, Paul refers to the amount of suffering providentially allotted him by God as a member of Christ's body.[30]

The Christological hymn which begins the letter to the Colossians enunciates a number of themes which the body of the letter develops at greater length. The letter to the Ephesians develops similar Pauline themes. Like the Christology of Colossians, those themes deepen germinal insights present in Paul's earlier theology of Christ's body. Moreover, Ephesians takes more explicit account than does Colossians of how the charisms extend the Christian *plêrôma*. I shall, then, examine the Christology developed in the letter to the Ephesians in the section which follows.

(V)

Since the late second century, the Christian tradition has identified the letter we call "Ephesians" as intended for the church at Ephesus. The earliest manuscript traditions, however, omit the phrase "*en Ephesô*" from the first verse of chapter one. That fact has led more than one recent exegete to suggest that the author of the letter intended it as a circular letter probably to churches in Asia.

From the second to the late eighteenth century, no one questioned the Pauline authorship of this letter. Those who have since questioned the authenticity of Ephesians tend to question the authenticity of Colossians as well and for similar reasons. They point to differences of vocabulary from the undisputed Pauline letters. At one point the letter to the Ephesians seems to cite the letter to the Colossians; and the opponents of authenticity question the likelihood of Paul citing himself. Those who question the authenticity of Ephesians also base their argument in part on a denial of the authenticity of Colossians: they argue that the unauthentic Ephesians derives from the unauthentic Colossians.

Those who defend the authenticity of Ephesians once again argue that it seems unlikely that a disciple could have mastered Paul's thought as thoroughly as the author of this letter has. They point out that the slightly more convoluted style which one finds in this letter and in Colossians has occasional parallels in Paul's earlier writings. They also explain the similarity between the two letters by appealing to the similarity between Galatians and Romans. After having written a somewhat polemic letter

---

30. Cf. *NJBC*, 54:16; Patzia, *op. cit., pp. 40-1; Harris,* op. cit., pp. 65-7; Reid, *op. cit.,* pp. 31-54; Michael Cahill, "The Neglected Parallelism in Colossians 1, 24-25," *Ephemerides Theologiae Lovaniensis*, 68(1992), pp. 142-147; Roy Yates, "Colossians 2:15: Christ Triumphant," *New Testament Studies*, 37(1991), pp. 573-591; Michael Wolter, "Der Apostel und seine Gemeinde als Teilhaber am Leidengeschick Jesu Christi: Beobachtungen zur paulinischen Leidenstheologie," *New Testament Studies*, 36(1990), pp. 535-557; Roy Yates, "From Christology to Soteriology," *Expository Times*, 109 (1996), pp. 268-271.

to the Colossians, Paul could have decided to follow it up with a more irenic epistle which develops in greater detail issues he argued more vehemently in Colossians. If Paul wrote the letter as a circular letter instead of addressing it specifically to the Ephesian community, he might well have decided to address a cautionary tract to the other churches in Asia, trying to inoculate them as well against the aberrations beginning to surface at Colossae.

Those who defend the authenticity of the letter tend to date it from Paul's Roman captivity. Those who question the authenticity tend to place it later, between 80 and 100 a.d.[31]

Heaven and Earth United in Christ

A hymnic blessing, reminiscent of the hymn in Colossians, opens the letter to the Ephesians. Although the blessing has a rhapsodic quality, it has resisted the attempts of commentators to discover in it a clear verse structure.[32] It would seem therefore to flow from the pen of Paul himself rather than to have liturgical origins, even though Paul may have been working from a liturgical model in composing the blessing. A phrase-by-phrase commentary follows.

> Blessed be the God and Father of our Lord Jesus Christ, who has blessed us in Christ with every spiritual blessing in the heavens (*en tois epourianois*) for He chose us in Him before the world's foundation so that we might be holy (*hagious*) and blameless (*amômous*) before Him in love. (Eph 1:3-4)

The prayer in Ephesians imitates the traditional blessing formula found in the Old Testament, but it identifies the God of the Bible with the Father of Our Lord Jesus Christ. (Cf 2 Cor 1:3-1; Col 1:3-14)

The phrase "in Christ" in verse 3 would seem to have instrumental connotations: the Father has made Christ the channel of the blessing He has showered upon us. Elsewhere in Paul the phrase "in Christ" normally alludes to incorporation into Christ. While the two ideas do not coincide perfectly, neither do they differ totally. Saving incorporation into Christ presupposes that the Father in a sense uses the reality of Christ as the instrument of our salvation.

The phrase "*en tois epouranois*" could mean existing in heaven, coming from heaven, or leading to heaven. Paul could conceivably have intended all three meanings. The phrase "in the heavens" also connotes place, and it finds a parallel in Eph 3:10. There as here, however, instead of desig-

---

31. Cf. Rudolf Schnackenburg, "Ephesus: Entwicklung einer Gemeinde von Paulus zu Johannes," *Biblische Zeitschrift*, 36(1992), pp. 41-64; Valentina Conti, "Paolo ad Efeso," *Rivista Biblica*, 37(1989), pp. 283-303.

32. Cf. Jack T. Sanders, "Hymnic Elements in Ephesians 1-3," *Zeitschrift für Neutestamentliche Wissenschaft*, 56(1965), pp. 214-232.

nating heaven as a realm totally removed from earthly existence, the letter seems to assert that the Christ event has blurred any absolute distinction between heaven and earth. In the eschatological age created by the paschal mystery heavenly realities find earthly embodiment and earthly realities find themselves engaged with realities of heavenly origin.[33] (Cf Eph 1:10)

This interpretation finds re-enforcement in Paul's designation of the blessings of the eschatological age as "pneumatic." Those blessings have the Breath of God and of Christ as their origin. The Breath of God makes the transcendent reality of God immanent and salvifically active in this world; She gives those in this world a present share in the risen life of Christ with God.

Verse four begins an enumeration of the heavenly pneumatic blessings which God has heaped upon us in Christ. First of all, in Christ God has chosen us. Our election in Christ resembles the election of Israel. That election transformed Israel into God's own people bound to Him as He to them by covenant. Like the first Israel we belong to God and now live bound to obey Him.

God, however, has chosen the new Israel "in Christ." As in verse 3, the phrase "in Christ" once again has instrumental connotations. God has acted through Christ to bind us to Himself with a view to our justification and sanctification. The divine election justifies us by making us "blameless (*amômous*)" in the eyes of God. It also effects our pneumatic sanctification in Christlike love (*agapê*). The phrase "in Christ" also connotes the Church's existence in Christ through His indwelling Breath.

> He destined us [in love] through Jesus Christ for adoption to Himself (*eis huiothesian dia Iêsou Christou eis auton*) according to the good pleasure of His will for the praise of the glory of His grace (*eis epainon doxês tês charitos autou*) which He freely bestowed upon us in His beloved (*to egapamêno*). (Eph 1:5-6)

Since in Greek verses three to fourteen form a single sentence, the phrase "in love" can have either a forward or a backward reference. One can take it as identifying love with the source of Christian justification and sanctification in verse 4.; or one can take the same phrase as a designation of the motives of divine predestination. Both interpretations fit the pattern of Paul's thought. Moreover, given the rhapsodic, poetic character of this passage, the apostle could conceivably have intended the ambiguity, since the intuitive mind signifies by connotation rather than by analytic, rational precision.

The divine election mentioned in verse four takes on the character of a predestining decree in verse five. The idea of predestination adds to that

33. Cf. Wink, *Naming the Powers*, pp. 89-96; Edgar J. Goodspeed, *The Meaning of Ephesians* (Chicago, IL: University of Chicago Press, 1933), pp. 20-4.

of election the notion of a unifying divine intention which guides the entire course of salvation history. That saving intention expresses the free benevolence of a God who acts for our good. (Cf. Rom 8:28-31)

Moreover, verse five clarifies the nature of God's saving intention, which only the Christ event reveals clearly. In Christ the Father's election of those who believe in Christ stands revealed in their adoption as children and heirs of God (*eis huiothesian dia Iêsou Christou*). The Father adopts us "for Himself (*eis auton*)." Adoption expresses our acquisition by God. That acquisition which flows from our divine election.

The phrase "*dia Iêsou Christou* (through Jesus Christ)" underscores the instrumental role of Christ in our salvation. It also designates Jesus Christ (cf. Eph 1:6) as the model and paradigm for all God's adopted children. Because adoption expresses the saving intention of divine election, election seeks to incorporate those whom God chooses into the divine family so that they may live united as children of the same divine Father. (Cf. Eph 3:14-5)

God bestows upon us from free and unforced benevolence the supreme gift of divine adoption so that we might praise "the glory of His grace." The term "grace" underscores the gratuity and freedom with which the divine good pleasure claims us in Christ. The term "glory" designates the purpose of divine election and adoption: participation in the glory of the risen Christ through perfect union with God.

In designating Jesus Christ, the one through whom the Father elects, adopts, and glorifies us, as "the Beloved," Paul uses a term similar to that used by the voice from heaven which in the synoptic traditions speaks to Jesus after His baptism. (Cf. Mk 1:11; Mt 3:17; Lk 3:22) In the synoptics, the baptism of Jesus begins His historical revelation as the beloved Son of God, messiah, suffering servant, and beginning of a new Israel.

Might Paul during his Roman captivity (61-63 a.d.) have had access to some version of Mark, which some exegetes date as early as 64 a.d.? A later pseudonymous author could have had access to one or more of the synoptic gospels. In either case, one cannot prove here a deliberate allusion to Jesus' baptismal commissioning, even though such an allusion would fit the present context, as the reference to the redeeming blood of Christ in verse 7 suggests. In the synoptic accounts of Jesus' baptism, the voice from heaven designates Him not only the beloved Son of God but also the suffering servant whose innocent death will reconcile Israel to God. In the present context, however, we can only assert with certainty that the perception of Jesus as the beloved of God did not confine itself to the synoptic tradition.

In Him we have redemption through His blood the forgiveness of transgressions according to the riches of His grace which He lavished on us, having made known to us in all wisdom and understanding the mystery of

> His will, according to His purpose which He set forth in Him as a plan (*oiknomian*) for the fullness of the times (*tou plêrômatos tôn kairôn*) to recapitulate (*anakephalaiôsasthai*) all things in Christ, things in heaven and things on earth in Him (*ta epi tois ouranois kai ta epi tês gês en autô*). (Eph 1:7-10)

In Jewish worship sprinkled blood symbolized the bond of life uniting God and His people. Sin disrupts that bond and alienates us from God. When God redeems us through Christ, He gets us back, re-acquires us as His own people, because the blood of Christ has re-established the bond of life uniting us to the Father. Through the sprinkled blood of Christ, God forgives our transgressions with a superabundance of divine grace.

The superabundance of grace to which Paul alludes here recalls the overwhelming plentitude of grace brought by the new Adam in Rom 5:12-21. So too does the term "*anakephalaiôsasthai*," which designates Christ as the new head of the human race and therefore implicitly as the last Adam who reconciles all things in God.[34]

The redemption of a sinful humanity reveals the secret purpose of God's will, a purpose conceived with the fullness of divine wisdom and understanding. Its secrecy results from the fact that its revelation had to await Jesus' coming. The wisdom and understanding to which Paul refers belong to God. The same divine wisdom and all-encompassing insight which orders the universe also encompasses our salvation despite our sinfulness. Moreover, this mysterious divine good pleasure here has an ecclesiological focus: the transformation of Jew and Gentile into a single people chosen and elected by God. (cf. vv. 11-13)

The "fullness of the times (*tou plêrômatos tôn kairôn*)" designates the whole of the messianic age which in Paul's understanding brings earlier periods of history, the other "times," to a climax and a close. Moreover, the term "fullness" has an implicit reference to the final consummation of the work of redemption already begun in Christ. The term also endows the universal headship of Christ with the sense of plentitude. Not only does Christ make a new beginning; but He brings creation and all of history to its culminating fullness.

The unfolding of the secret mysterious intent of God reveals a divine plan (*oikonomia*) for saving us, a plan conceived out of the plentitude of divine wisdom and understanding. Christ embodies and sums up that plan, especially in the paschal mystery which reveals Him as the one divinely designated to head the new creation. His headship extends not only to earthly things but to heavenly realities as well. He therefore stands historically revealed as the *coincidencia oppositorum*, as the one who rec-

---

34. Cf. Markus Barth, *Ephesians* (Garden City, NY: Doubleday, 1974), pp. 76-113; *NJBC*, 55:16-7; Patzia, *op.cit.*, pp. 148-57.

onciles all polarities: heaven and earth, God and sinners, Jew and Gentile, as the concluding verses of the blessing make clear:

> In Him we also, predestined according to the purpose of Him who accomplishes all things according to the counsel of His will have been chosen by lot to live for the praise of His glory, being the first to hope in Christ. But, having heard the word of truth, the good news of your salvation and having believed in it, you too were sealed with the Holy Breath of the promise who is the pledge of our inheritance for the redemption of acquisition to the praise of His glory. (Eph 1:11-4)

The all-encompassing plan of God began to come to light with the election of the Jews as God's chosen people, as His "lot," His possession. Their election expressed the divine good pleasure which orders the course of human history. Divine election bound the people of God to live for Him, praising His revealed beauty. Moreover, through their messianic longings, the Jews, as a consequence of their special election by God, first hoped for the coming of Christ.

Now, however, by reconciling all things in Christ, God has redeemed the Gentiles too, claiming them as His own no less than the Jews. By redeeming them God acquires them as peculiarly His, as the enigmatic phrase "redemption of acquisition" indicates.[35]

The proof that the Gentiles too now belong to God's holy people lies in the fact that they too now possess God's Holy Breath. The phrase "the Breath of the promise" could mean the divine promise to pour out His Breath on all flesh. (Jl 3:1-5) It could also mean the Breath whose possession brings the promise of risen life in Christ. Paul may well have intended both meanings; but he certainly intended the latter, since the Gentiles have consented to the good news about Christ as both a word of truth and a promise of salvation.

Moreover, in designating the Jews as the first to hope in the messiah, Paul has implicitly designated the Gentiles as the second to hope in Him. In the messianic age, hope looks to the final coming of Christ, to the consummation of the work of redemption begun in Him through the universal resurrection of all who believe in Him. Like Christian Jews, Christian Gentiles possess the Breath of God and of the risen Christ as a

---

35. Cf. Deichgräber, *op. cit.*, pp. 64-67; J. Cambrier, "La bénédiction d'Eph 1.3-14," *Zeitschrift für Neutestamentliche Wissenschaft*, 54(1963), pp. 58-104; J. Coutts, "Ephesians 1.3-14 and 1 Peter 1.3-12," *New Testament Studies* 3(1956-1957), pp. 115-127; Stanislaus Lyonnet, S.J., "La bénédiction de Eph 1, 3-14 et son arrière-plan Judaique," in *A la rencontre de Dieu* (Le Puy: Editions Xavier Mappus, 1961), pp. 341-352; Pierre Grelot, "La structure d'Ephesiens 1, 3-14," *Revue Biblique*, 96(1989), pp. 193-209; Ch. Reynier, "La bénédiction en Ephesiens 1,3-14: Elections, filiation, redemption," *Nouvelle Revue Théologique*, 118(1996), pp. 182-199.

pledge of their inheritance, i.e., of their own full share in the risen glory of Christ. The glory of God which the Jews recognized and praised now stands fully revealed in the glory of the risen Lord.[36] (Cf 2 Cor 1:22)

An intercessory prayer follows the blessing which opens Ephesians. The prayer follows an introductory and transitional sentence which assures those to whom Paul writes of his constant prayer for them. (Eph 1:15) Paul addresses his petition to "the God of our Lord Jesus Christ, the Father of glory." (Eph 1:16) The phrase alludes to Jesus' proclamation of God as Father. The addition of the phrase "of glory" to the name "Father" designates the Father as possessor and source of the divine glory and as the object of the praise offered by both Jew and Gentile. (cf. Eph 1:12,14)

Paul begs the Father to give the Ephesians "a breath of wisdom and of revelation (*pneuma sophias kai apokalypseôs*) in the knowledge of Him, enlightening the eyes of your heart, so that you may know what hope comes from His call and how glorious the riches (*to ploutos tês doxês*) of his inheritance in His saints and how surpassing the greatness of His power toward those who believe." (Eph 1:16-19)

The "breath" to which Paul refers designates not so much the third member of the divine triad as the grace of wisdom and of divine revelation which She imparts. The enlightening wisdom Paul asks for has the character of a revelation (*apokalypseôs*) because it engages Christian hope in the resurrection, which will bring the self-disclosure of God to ultimate clarity and fullness. God will reveal Himself through a mighty act, a demonstration of His supreme power.

The final revelation of God's saving power already stands initially disclosed in the resurrection of Jesus. The Father has raised Him from the dead in order to seat Him at His own right hand in heaven "far above every ruler (*archês*) and authority (*exousias*) and power (*dynameôs*) and dominion (*kryiotêtos*) and every name named (*pantos onomatos onomazomenou*) not only in this age but in the age to come." (Eph 1:20-1) In exalting Jesus to His right hand in heaven, the Father confers upon Him divine authority over the whole of creation. The risen Lord now dwells in a realm which surpasses utterly the angelic hierarchies, the preternatural forces at work in the world and incarnate in social structures of domination. Christ possesses this divine power forever, not only in the world as we now know it but in the new age which the final resurrection will usher in. The subjection of all things under His feet thus reveals the universal scope of His messianic authority. (Cf. Ps 2:6)

Christic Fullness

Besides enjoying universal dominion, the risen Lord functions as "head of everything for the Church which is His body, the fullness of the one

36. Cf. Barth, *op.cit.*, pp.130-44.

who fills all in all (*to plêrôma tou ta panta en pasin plêroumenou*)." (Eph 1:22-3) Jesus stands at the head of all creation. His glorification has subjected every creature under His feet. Jesus' universal headship seeks to advance the mission of the Church, whom the risen Christ "fills." That infilling transforms the Church into Jesus' instrument for extending the divine fullness to all creation. The Church, then, in accomplishing its mission mediates the fullness of salvation to a sinful world, the fullness of Christic life.

Once again, one finds in Paul a very different understanding of the divine "fullness (*plêrôma*)" from that invoked in both Stoicism and Gnosticism. As we have seen in commenting on the Christological hymn which opens Colossians, the Stoics conceived the fullness pantheistically, as God animating the cosmos. The gnostics used the term "*plêrôma*" to designate the whole panoply of heavenly powers which proceed from God. As in Colossians, however, Paul uses the term "*plêrôma*" in a dynamic, soteriological sense. God pours divine fullness into Christ by exalting Him to His right hand in glory. Christ communicates His own fullness to the Church by sharing with it His own divine, risen life. The Church in turn mediates the saving fullness of God and of Christ to the cosmos, whose subjection to sinful futility requires its participation in the redemption of the saints. (Cf. Rom 8:18-25)

The redemptive process, therefore, incorporates all things into Christ by transforming them in the power of His resurrection. It discloses Christ as "the one who fills all in all." He exercises His universal divine sway for the sake of His body, the Church, ordering all things to their good and to their final salvation. (Cf. Rom 8:18) He extends His saving power into the cosmos in order to transform it into a new creation.[37]

Prior to their conversion the Ephesians lived sinful lives, "living according to the age of the world (*kata ton aiona tou kosmou*)." In other words, their sinfulness manifested the fact that they had not yet entered the final age of salvation, the graced fullness of the end time. Instead, they lived enslaved to the oppressive, divisive powers of this world. (Eph 2:1-2; cf. 1:23) They obeyed "the prince of power of the air, the spirit now at work in the sons of disobedience."

In the cosmology of Ephesians the demonic powers claim the air as their realm. The "ruler of power" who dominates them designates Satan, the enemy of Christ and of God, who acts in and through sinful humans, in the rebellious who refuse to acknowledge God's will. (Eph 2:2-3) More-

---

37. Cf. Barth, *op.cit.*, pp.145-210; Ernst, *op. cit.*, pp. 105-197; George Howard, "The Head/Body Metaphors of Ephesians," *New Testament Studies*, 20(1974), pp. 350-356; Roy Yates, "A Re-examination of Ephesians 1.23," *Expository Times*, 83(1972), pp. 146-151; Ignace de la Potterie, "Le Christ Plerôme de l'Église," *Biblica*, 98(1977), pp. 500-524; David Bosch, "Paul on Human Hopes," *Journal of Theology for Southern Africa*, 67(1989), pp. 3-16.

over, the juxtaposition of the "age (*aoina*) of this world" with the "prince of power" gives the term "*aiona*" the connotations of an evil power opposed to God. (Cf. Col 2:8-15)

In this sinful state the Ephesians found themselves objects of the divine anger along with the rest of sinful humanity. (Eph 2:3) As in the letter to the Romans, God manifests His anger against sin by allowing sinners to suffer the evil consequences of their own wicked choices. (Rom 1:18-27) Moreover, as in Romans, God by contrast reveals his surpassing love for us by calling us from our sinfulness back to life, to a loving union with Him which leads to endless risen life in God with Christ.

> [God] raised us up and seated us in Christ Jesus in the heavenly places so that He might show in the coming ages the surpassing riches of His grace through His goodness toward us in Christ Jesus. (Eph 2:6-7)

The Father raises the Ephesians with Christ. Here Paul, once again, conceives the resurrection and the sending of the Breath as two inseparable facets of one and the same event. God in raising Christ transforms Him into a life-giving Breath who imparts risen life to His disciples by sharing His Breath with them. As a consequence of their union with Him in baptism, they rise with him to new life. (Cf. 2 Cor 3:12-4:6)

Here, however, Ephesians goes even further and asserts that through our share in the resurrection the Father has already seated us with Christ Jesus in the heavenly places. Moreover, the letter is not merely referring to the fact that one day we will reign with Christ in heaven. Even now, God has made us take our seat with Christ in power at His right hand. This has already happened because the resurrection blurs any sharp distinction between the present condition of Christians and the fullness of the eschatological age.

The resurrection translates Christians into the realm of the divine where Christ reigns and where even now He gives them power over the principalities and powers who rule this world. Acting as instruments of the Christ who seeks to fill the universe with the transforming power of His resurrection, Christians do battle against these worldly powers. God, therefore, reveals to us the surpassing power of His goodness to us in Christ. He does so by translating us from death to life in Christ and by making us masters of the very powers of evil which once ruled us.[38] (Cf. Col 3:8-11)

All this God has given us even in our sinfulness in order to manifest that salvation comes to us as an utterly free and gratuitous gift. Only faith in that gift, the willingness to accept it as free and gratuitous, saves the sinner from the divine wrath. The divine plan of our salvation

---

38. Cf. Barth, *op.cit.*, pp. 236-8; Jacques Dupont, *Syn Christô: Union avec le Christ suivant Saint Paul* (Paris: Desclée, 1952).

(*oikonomian*) [Eph 1:10]) has thus ordered things in such a way as to manifest that we have in no way saved ourselves. The gift of salvation comes from God, not from spontaneous human initiative or striving. (Eph 2:8-9; cf. Rom 3:27-31)

The same gift of divine grace effects our moral transformation. God has "created [us] in Christ Jesus for good works, which God prepared beforehand so that we might walk in them." The Ephesians should, then, see themselves as God's handiwork (*poiêma*), as a divine artistic master-piece, as the splendor of the new creation in Christ. (Eph 2:9-10; cf. 1 Cor 1:29; 2 Cor 10:13)

Once sinful Gentiles "separated from Christ, alienated from the com-monwealth of Israel, and strangers to the covenant of promise, having no hope and without God in the world," the Ephesians now find themselves "brought near in the blood of Christ." (Eph 2:11-3) This bringing near negates all the former alienation which the Ephesians knew as Gentiles excluded by the Law. Members of Christ, they now possess citizenship in the new Israel, share in the promises of the new covenant, and through their union with God in this world look forward to the fullness of risen life with Christ.

The atoning, reconciling blood of Christ has effected this union, has re-established the bond of life between God and a sinful humanity. (Eph 2:13) Christ has not only reconciled the sinful Gentiles to God, but He has also reconciled Jew and Gentile to one another. He has united them in His body, the Church, and in the process has transformed them "into one new humanity (*eis hena kainon anthropon*)." (Eph 2:16; cf. Rom 5:12-21, 8:3; 1 Cor 15:21; 2 Cor 5:16-6:10)

Paul uses three powerful images to express the new union of Jew and Gentile which the blood of Christ effects. First, Christ has broken down the wall which in the Jerusalem temple separated the court of the Jews from the court of the Gentiles.[39] In the new Israel Jew and Gentile wor-ship God together.

Second, through the indwelling of His Breath, Christ has transformed both Jew and Gentile together into a living temple of worship. The apostles and prophets who lead the Church form its foundation stones. Christ serves as the cornerstone from which the entire building rises. In Him, "the whole structure is joined together and grows into a holy temple of the Lord; in whom you also are built into it for a dwelling place of God in the Breath." (Eph 2:14, 19-22)

Third, possession of the Breath, which makes the Christian commu-nity into God's household, also introduces believers into that household. (Eph 2:19) The image of the divine household connotes the new inti-

---

39. Cf. Barth, *op.cit.*, 283-7.

macy which comes from knowing God as "*Abba*" and from knowing other Christians as brothers and sisters.[40] (Cf. Rom 8:14-17)

Not only has Christ broken down the wall of separation between Jew and Gentile by transforming them into a single living temple of divine, pneumatic worship, but he has abolished "in His flesh the law of commandments and ordinances." (Eph 2:15) Christ has brought the Gentiles into the new Israel by Himself becoming an outcast from Israel, condemned by the Law of commandments and ordinances.

By condemning the source of all grace and reconciliation, the Law demonstrated once and for all its impotence to save a sinful humanity. Moreover, in dying on the cross under the curse of the Law, Jesus also died once and for all to sin, so that as risen Lord and life-giving Breath He could effect the graced transformation of Jew and Gentile together. (Cf. Rom 3:21-31, 6:1-10; Gal 3:10-4; 1 Cor 15:45, 2 Cor 4:1-6)

The Law had required that Jews separate themselves from the Gentiles. (Deut 12:29-14:2, 26:16) Now that God has revealed the risen Christ as the source of universal justification and salvation, the separation demanded by the Law has ceased to bind. As a consequence, Jew and Gentile find themselves united in a single, new Israel. Moreover, both have equal access to the Father through Christ in the saving power of His Breath. (Eph 2:22)

The reconciliation of all humanity to God in Christ gives concrete meaning to the messianic gift of peace. Christ first killed in His flesh the hostility which divided Jew from Gentile. Then He came proclaiming the good news of peace. (Eph 2:16-18) The proclamation which follows Christ's destruction of the hostility of the Law in His flesh refers, not to His mortal ministry, but to His resurrection as the source of the Breath Who unites and reconciles both Jew and Gentile in the one body of Christ.[41]

As an apostle, Paul has the privilege to announce this saving mystery of Christ in all its fullness to the Gentiles. (Eph 3:1-4; cf. Rom 11:33-6) The Breath of Christ uses both apostles and prophets in the Christian community in order to announce the same mystery as good news. The mystery counts as news, because not until the coming of Christ did God make manifest His secret, saving purposes. It counts as good news, because Christ effects a universal salvation which reveals God's saving intent in all its fullness. The pagans now share the same inheritance as Jews: participation in divine Sonship, membership in the body of Christ, and the promise of risen glory as their shared inheritance with Him. (Eph 3:6)

40. Cf. Antonio Gonzalez Lamdrid, *Ipse Est Pax Nostra: Estudio exegetico-teologico de Ef. 2.14-18* (Madrid: Instituto Francisco Suarez, 1973).

41. Cf. Barth, *op.cit.*, pp.290-322; Neil J McEleneu, C.S.P., "Conversion, Circumcision, and the Law," *New Testament Studies*, 20(1974), pp. 319-341; Peter Tachau, *"Einst" und "Jetzt" im Neuen Testament* (Göttingen: Vanderhoeck & Ruprecht, 1972).

As the apostolic bearer of this message Paul not only announces the infinite treasure of Christ, the inexhaustible gift of life in Him; but he also explains how God dispenses this mystery. (Eph 3:9) In a sense the entire letter to the Ephesians has described how God dispenses the mystery of Christ: namely, through the historical unfolding of the divine economy which reconciles all things in Him. Moreover, the prayer which closes this doctrinal section of the letter also describes in its own way how God dispenses universal salvation in Christ.

The concluding doxology explores four dimensions of the salvation accomplished in Christ:

1) God reveals Himself as universal Father and source of all paternal authority.(Eph 3:14-5) God reveals His universal paternity by drawing all those who confess Jesus Christ into His *Abba* experience. God thus transforms them into the members of a single human family. (Cf. Eph 2:19; Rom 8:14-17)

2) The Father through the Breath of the risen Christ also strengthens the inner selves (*eis ton esô anthrôpon*) of those who believe in Him. Though hidden from our eyes in infinite glory, the Father nevertheless condescends to enter into a relationship of intimacy with humans. Through faith Christ Himself dwells in our hearts; for we know Christ with an intimacy which results from transformation in His image through the power of His Breath. Transformation in the image of Christ makes charity the source and foundation of everything which those who believe in Him do. (Eph 3:16-17)

3) Saving transformation in Christ eventually empowers believers to experience "all the fullness of God (*pan to plêrôma tou Theou*)." The *plêrôma*, as we have seen, extends the saving consequences of the paschal mystery into the entire universe. (Eph 3:19) As a consequence, saving transformation in Christ empowers them to comprehend "the length and breadth, the height and depth." (Eph 3:18) Exegetes differ in their interpretation of these spatial images. Some see in them a reference to the temple in Jerusalem. I deem it more likely that Paul intends spatial images of the *plêrôma*, of the saving transformation of all things in Christ. Christians will comprehend the length, breadth, height, and depth when they witness the reconciliation of all things in Christ, everything in heaven and everything on earth. (Cf. Eph 1:10; Col 1:20)

The final transformation of all things in God through the saving power of Christ will bring to its culmination and consummation both God's saving presence in the world and the world's presence in God. The concrete shape which things will take in the new creation exceeds our wildest imaginings; because God can do infinitely more than anything we try to imagine. (Eph 3:20)

4) The infinite divine glory which the Father thus discloses draws from the saved the praise of His glory "from generation to generation, in the Church, and in Christ Jesus, for ever and ever." (Eph 3:20-1) Each succeeding generation adds to the confession of the glory revealed in Christ, as the Church serves as His instrument for effecting the *plêrôma*. Moreover, the glory thus made manifest knows no end.[42] (Cf. Col 1:9-14)

This plan for universal, even cosmic, salvation teaches the "rulers and powers in the heavenly places" a lesson which they need to learn: namely, how comprehensive and wise a plan of salvation God has conceived. God uses the Church to teach them this needed lesson by transforming it into His providential means of effecting the salvation of all. As a consequence, the Church, having entered the eschatological age does battle with worldly powers through confronting and confounding their human agents.[43] (Eph 3:10)

The exhortatory section of Ephesians begins with a plea for unity in the Holy Breath. Paul urges the Ephesians to make the universal reconciliation effected by Christ a reality in their midst through humility, meekness, patience, forbearance, and love. (Eph 4:1-3; cf. Col 3:12-5)

> One the body and one the Breath, just as you have been called in the one hope of your calling. One Lord, one faith, one baptism. One God and Father of all who is above all and through all and in all. (Eph 4:4-6)

The divine Breath who reconciles the Ephesians to one another also unites them to the rest of the Church in a single, living, organic reality: the body of Christ. Verses eight to seventeen make it clear that active, loving sharing of the charisms which Christ bestows creates the body of Christ. (Cf. 1 Cor 12:4-11, 27-31) In addition, verses 8-17 explicitly relate the theology of the charisms which Paul elaborated in first Corinthians to the realization of the *plêrôma*. Ephesians attributes their dispensation to the glorified Lord rather than to the Breath. In verse four, however, the letter links the Breath closely with the body of Christ, which in Corinthians the charism dispensing Breath creates. That would suggest that in attributing the distribution of the charisms to the Lord rather than to the Breath, Ephesians is envisaging the Lord as the source of the Breath who dispenses the charisms.

The deepening union of the Ephesians through the action of the Breath orients them to a common future: namely, to the salvation which is dawning in Christ. All look forward to risen life with the Lord, to final trans-

---

42. Cf. *NJBC*, 55:23; Barth, *op.cit.*, 366-97; Patzia, *op.cit.*, pp. 220-6.
43. Cf. Wink, *Naming the Powers*, pp. 89-96; Clinton E. Arnold, *Ephesians: Power and Magic: The Concept of Power in Ephesians in the Light of Its Historical Setting* (Cambridge: Cambridge University Press, 1998).

formation in God in His image. This hope rests upon the divine call which the Ephesians have received in the power of the one Breath who unites them in the body of Christ.

The affirmation of "one Lord" fits the central theme of Ephesians: that only through the Lord Jesus does the one God and Father bring about the *plêrôma*, the saving reconciliation of all things to God in Christ. One baptism conforms believers to that Lord by causing them to die with Him to sin, so that they might rise with Him in the power of His Breath. Moreover, the same baptismal commitment to the one and only Lord ensures the unity of the faith which Christians confess.

The God who sent the Lord into the world to accomplish its reconciliation stands historically revealed not only as the Father of Jesus but as universal Father. He exercises ultimate dominion "over all." His presence through and in all things portrays His relation to the world in panentheistic terms. Here, however, Pauline panentheism also has soteriological connotations. Christ must fill the universe with saving grace in order to restore it to the Father from whom it proceeds. Only then may the Father graciously permeate the world He has reconciled to Himself in Christ.

The Charisms Create the Plêrôma

Christ allots saving grace to each member of His body in the measure He deems fitting. Paul cites Ps 68:19 in order to underscore his point; but he does so in a way which differs from any existing Greek or Hebrew version of the psalm. Paul says: "Having ascended on high, He led captivity captive and gave gifts to humans." (Eph 4:8)

The noun "captivity" probably means "prisoners." Paul substitutes the abstract rhetorically for the concrete. To what captives does Paul refer? In all likelihood to the sovereignties, authorities, powers, and rulers over whom Christ triumphed in Eph 1:21; for Christ ascends into heaven as the universal Lord and sovereign of the universe.

The sending of the divine Breath from heaven to confer gifts to humans expresses, then, the Lord's Jesus's universal sovereign sway. Moreover, the charismatic action of the Breath now stands revealed as the means which the risen Lord has chosen in order to fill all things and so to accomplish the *plêrôma* by filling all things. (Eph 4:9-10) Through the outpouring of the charisms He is building His own body, "until we all arrive at the unity of the faith and love of the Son of God, at the mature man (*eis andra teleion*), at the measure of the stature of the fullness of Christ." (Eph 4:13) "The mature man" designates all humanity redeemed in Christ.

The gifts accomplish several saving effects. They unify the Church, Christ's body, in faith and in hope. As Paul had asserted in 1 Cor 13, the charisms yield only incipient insight, they furnish only an imperfect image of God, like the slightly distorted reflection of one's face in ancient mirrors. The charisms belong then to that period of the final age of salvation when the Church lives by faith and by hope rather than by sight, by face-to-face vision. (1 Cor 13:12-3) The unity of the Church in faith and in hope presupposes love, however, as the ultimate source of union with God in Christ. (Eph 4:16)

The gifts of the Breath build up the body of Christ; they bring it to adult maturity. They make Christ dwell in the Church in its fullness. They effect the *plêrôma* in the Church so that the Church in turn may serve as Christ's instrument for His filling all things. (Eph 4:10; cf. 1 Cor 12:4-13)

Ephesians, then, marks a significant development in a Pauline theology of the gifts principally by portraying the charisms as the providential means which Christ uses in order to effect the *plêrôma*. The charisms ensure the full and vital presence of Christ in His Church, a presence which the Church then communicates to the rest of the universe, so that Christ may restore and reconcile all things to the Father and so that the Father in His turn may exist through all and in all.

The Church, Christ's body, will have attained the *plêrôma*, the full maturity to which Christ has destined it, when it stands firm and unmoved in the face of error and malice, no longer "tossed to and fro and carried about with every wind of doctrine through human trickery and through cunning at the service of deceit." (Eph 4:14) The Church will reach full maturity in Christ when it speaks the truth in charity and lives united to Christ in everything which it does. Union with Christ the head will ensure the unity of the body itself, whose members will mutually support one another, impervious to all threats of fragmentation, for love binds the members to one another. From Christ:

the whole body, joined and knit together by every joint with which it is supplied, with each part working properly effects the body's growth for building itself up in love.[44] (Eph 4:16)

44. Cf. James M Efrid, *Christ, The Church, and the End: Studies in Colossians and Ephesians* (Valley Forge, PA: Judson Press, 1980); Stig Hanson, *The Unity of the Church in the New Testament: Colossians and Ephesians* (Lexington, KY: American Theological Library Association, 1963) Carol L. Stockhausen, *Letters in the Pauline Tradition* (Wilmington, DL: Michael Glazier, 1989), pp. 20-125; J.C. Kuby, *Ephesians, Baptism, and Pentecost* (London: SPCK, 1968); Ulrich Betz, *Einsein in Christus: Eine Einfürung in den Epheserbrief* (Kassel: J.G. Onicken, 1969); Koshi Usami, *Somatic Comprehension of Unity: The Church in Ephesians* (Rome: Biblical Institute Press, 1983); Claudio Basevi, "La Missione di Cristo et dei Cristiani nella Lettera agli Efesiani: Una Lettura di Ef 4,1-25," *Rivista Biblica*, 38(1990), pp. 27- 54; Trös Engberg-Pedersen, "Ephesians 5, 12-13: *elengchein* and Conversion in the New Testament," *Zeitschrift für die Neutestamentlische Wissenschaft*, 80(1989), pp. 89-110; Felice Montagnini, "Echi di Paranesi Culturale in Ef 4, 25-32, *Rivista Biblica*, 37(1989), pp. 257- 281.

One fundamental task still remains: namely, to reflect on the apocalyptic dimensions of Pauline Christology. To this aspect of Paul's Christological doctrine I turn in the chapter which follows.

As in first Corinthians, the proper use of the charisms presupposes a more fundamental conformity to Christ. The following of Christ demands that the Ephesians avoid the aimless kind of life which pagans lead: estranged from God, blunted in conscience, given to sexual profligacy and indecency. "You, however, did not so learn Christ, as you surely did hear Him and were instructed in Him, as the truth is in Jesus." (Eph 4:21) The final phrase, "as the truth is in Jesus," qualifies the hearing and instruction the Ephesians received by portraying Jesus as the embodied norm of divine truth. The Ephesians must, therefore, cultivate a spirit of universal friendship forgiving one another as Christ has forgiven them. (Eph 4:32) They must imitate God by living as His children in Jesus' image. This they will do by entering into Jesus' atoning sacrifice by sacrificing themselves for one another. (Eph 5:1-2)

Once the children of darkness because of their sinfulness, the Ephesians have now become "light in the Lord." (Eph 5:8) They will live an children of the light by allowing the illumination which comes from Christ to transform their conduct, consecrating them to "all goodness, justice, and truth." (Eph 5:9) Here as in verse four, truth includes truth of action and not just truth telling. The light of Christ bestows a power to discern and discriminate what truly pleases God. The living of Christ-like lives will, then, free the Ephesians to live open lives without the need to conceal anything. In the process they will live in the light by experiencing true divine illumination: "all things exposed to light become manifest; for everything illumined is light. Hence, it is said:

> Awake, O sleeper,
> arise from the dead,
> and Christ will give you light." (Eph 5:13-4)

Some strains of Gnostic piety would promise an illumination which so spiritualized one that even lives of licentiousness lack the power to diminish one's spiritual status. Paul by contrast insists on the morally transforming consequences of Christian enlightenment. Moreover, by citing what sounds like an early Christian baptismal hymn, Paul links this morally transforming enlightenment to Christian baptism, which teaches the Christian to die with Christ to sin.

Therefore do not be foolish, but understand what is the will of the Lord. Do not get drunk with wine, but be filled with the Breath, addressing one another in psalms and hymns, and Breath-filled songs, singing and making melody to the Lord with all your heart, always and for everything giving thanks in the name of our Lord Jesus Christ to God the Father. (Eph 5:17-20; cf. Col 3:12-7)

The Ephesians will grow in a discernment which allows them to recognize and live the will of Christ by becoming intoxicated with His Breath. They must allow that intoxication to express itself joyfully in their shared worship. As in Colossians, Paul seems to have eucharistic worship in mind, which, as we have seen, in the Pauline communities seems to have culminated in shared charismatic prayer. Moreover, as in Colossians, he urges the Ephesians to allow the joyful thanksgiving voiced in their Breath-filled songs to permeate their lives and to transform the entire day into a kind of eucharistic celebration. Their grateful adoration of God the Father through the Lord Jesus Christ and in the power of the Breath should become not just a way of worshipping but also a way of living.

Chapter 17
Apocalyptic Longing and the Antichrist

The second and third theses in this section of the present volume summarized Paul's theology of the paschal mystery. Thesis four pondered the universal scope of salvation in Christ. Thesis five and six examined the physical dimensions of salvation in Christ. They argued that the saving consequences of the paschal mystery encompass the whole embodied person and seek to eradicate the corrupting impact of sin upon the physical world.

The seventh thesis presented in this chapter explores in greater detail the temporal dimensions of Christian hope. It does so by examining the dynamic interplay between present longing for salvation and its final consummation. In this chapter I shall argue the following thesis: *Christological hope expresses itself in the fact that those whom the risen Christ is in process of saving through the action of His Breath yearn for His second coming as the vindication of their present commitment to Him and as the final, full realization of their union with God.*

Pauline Christology evolved in response to pastoral problems and needs in the communities with whom the apostle dealt. Paul developed the apocalyptic dimensions of his Christology most explicitly in his two earliest letters: namely, in first and second Thessalonians. The special focus on apocalyptic Christology in the earliest letters could, then, suggest that, as Paul's Gentile mission evolved, apocalyptic concerns receded as other kinds of Christological questions came to the fore. The delay of the second coming could also have dampened apocalyptic fervor.[1]

1. Col 3:1-4 contains a moral exhortation with apocalyptic overtones. The exhortation discusses the eschatological dimensions of dying and rising with Christ. By entering through baptism into the final age of salvation, the Colossians now live in this world but oriented to ultimate life in God. Now possessing God as their future, they should yearn for and ponder always the things of God—"the things above—and not the things of this world." The image of Christ seated at the right hand of God reminds the Colossians of his divinely sanctioned messianic authority, an authority conferred on Him by the God who raised Him from death and gave Him authority over all creation. (Cf. Eph 2:1-10)

One should not, however, understand "the things above" in a dualistic manner. The things of heaven and the lives the Colossians are actually leading interpenetrate and blend. The transcendent force and power of the risen Christ have taken hold of the Colossians to transform them in this present life in Jesus' image, as the exhortatory section of the letter which follows will make abundantly clear. (Cf. Col 3:5- 4:6) The eschaton encompasses both this world and the next. Instead of taking the Colossians out of the material universe, the transcendent, eschatological power of risen Christ transforms the Colossians' present as well as their future. Better still, in the eschaton the Colossians experience the future as God coming at them in the

This chapter divides into three parts. Part one discusses the authenticity of second Thessalonians and the chronological order of the two letters to the church at Thessalonika. Part two examines the apocalyptic Christology of second Thessalonians. Part three compares and contrasts the apocalyptic Christology of second Thessalonians with that of first Thessalonians.

(I)

While no one disputes the canonical authenticity of the first letter to the Thessalonians, exegetes remain divided on the issue of the Pauline authorship of second Thessalonians. Moreover other Pauline scholars challenge the authenticity of 1 Th 2:13-6, the only place in the surviving letters of Paul where he explicitly blames the Jews for Jesus' death and voices several other complaints against them. Even those who question that Paul wrote the second letter concede, however, that it belongs within a Pauline tradition in New Testament theology; and those who regard 1 Th 2:13-6 as pseudonymous attribute its insertion to a disciple of Paul.[2]

The Authenticity of Second Thessalonians

Those who question the Pauline authenticity of second Thessalonians do so largely because they claim that the letter displays characteristics of style significantly different from first Thessalonians. How significant a difference remains a question of debate.

Second Thessalonians addresses a community undergoing persecution. The letter also gives clear evidence of divisions in the community: doctri-

---

present transforming power of the risen Christ. They should, therefore, long for the completion of that transformation and ponder its implications for how that they live in this life.

Indeed, the exhortatory section which follows immediately makes it abundantly clear that setting one's heart on heavenly things means the present transformation of Christian conduct. The Colossians must extinguish within themselves all sinful impulses: all idolatry, all destructive, divisive behavior. Instead, they must cultivate all those virtues which bind them together in the love of Christ and which abolish all social distinctions among them. (Col 3:5-15; cf. Phil 2:1-11; Eph 5:3-14)

The hiddenness of the Colossians' life in Christ flows too from its eschatological character: from the fact that they already possess risen life with Christ but do not yet experience the fullness of that life. They know Christ as their life, as the efficacious source and incarnation of risen life. They should therefore long for the final and full revelation of the Christ who has triumphed over the elements of this world; for His final revelation will coincide with their own full participation in risen glory.

Cf. John R. Levinson, "2 Apoc. Bar. 48:42-52:7 and the Apocalyptic Dimension of Colossians 3:1-6," *Journal of Biblical Literature*, 108(1989), pp. 93-108; Edouard Delebecque, "Sur un problème de temps chez Saint Paul (Col 3:1-4)," *Biblica*, 70(1989), pp. 389-395.

2. Cf. Simon Legasse, "Paul et les Juifs d'après 1 Thessaloniciens 2,13-16," *Revue Biblique*, 104(1997), pp. 572-591.

nal disputes about whether or not the day of the Lord has already arrived divided the church at Thessalonika. Moreover, some members of the community had stopped working. Presumably, they did so because they believed that, if the day of the Lord had already arrived, burdensome work had become unnecessary. The idlers were apparently mooching off those who continued to work. (2 Th 3:11) In other words, second Thessalonians addresses a persecuted community divided over the timing of the second coming. That split conceivably sprang from an intensified chiliastic enthusiasm engendered in part by persecution and false prophecy.[3]

In his study of the letters to the Thessalonians Charles A. Wanamaker surveys the arguments contesting the authenticity of both second Thessalonians and of 1 Th 2:13-6 and finds them all wanting. Moreover, he has suggested that the textual difficulties which in the past have motivated scholarly doubts about the Pauline authorship of the letters to the Thessalonians all find resolution provided one reverses their chronological order.[4]

While exegetes have tended to endorse the traditional ordering of the two letters, I find Wanamaker's suggestion highly plausible. If he has the right of it, then Paul would have written two letters to the Thessalonians from Corinth in either 50 or 51 a.d. Paul's repeated longing to return to Thessalonika (1 Th 2:17-20) would have arisen from news that the Jewish community in Thessalonika was persecuting the fledgling Christian community. (1 Th 2:13-6) Paul also felt concern that, under the pressure of crisis, the new Christians, in an excess of chiliasm, had allowed false prophets and teachers to convince them that the day of the Lord had already arrived.

3. Cf. *NJBC*, 53:1-9; Montague, *op.cit.*, pp.28-9; James L. Mays, ed., *Harper's Biblical Commentary* (San Francisco, CA: Harper & Row, 1988), 1234 (hereafter abbreviated as *HBC*]; Leon Morris, *The Epistles of Paul to the Thessalonians: An Introduction and Commentary* (Grand Rapids, MI: Eerdmans, 1984); B. Rigaux, O.F.M., *Saint Paul: les epitres aux Thessaloniciens* (Paris: Librairie Lecoffre, 1956); R. Russell, "The Idle in 2 Thess 3.6-12: An Ecclesiological or a Social Problem," *New Testament Studies*, 34(1988), pp. 105-119; Jorge Sanchez Bosch, "La chronologie de la première aux Thessaloniciens et les relations de Paul avec d'autres églises," *New Testament Studies*, 37(1991), pp. 336-347; M.J.J. Menken, "Paradise Regained or Still Lost? Eschatology and Disorderly Behavior in 2 Thessalonians," *New Testament Studies*, 38(1992) pp. 271-289; Jerry L. Sumney, "The Bearing of a Pauline Rhetorical Pattern on the Integrity of 2 Thessalonians," *Zeitschrift für die Neutestamentlische Wissenschaft*, 81(1990), pp. 190-204.

4. Cf. Charles A. Wanamaker, *The Epistles to the Thessalonians: A Commentary on the Greek Text* (Grand Rapids, MI: Eerdmans, 1990), pp.17-45. See also: Burger A. Pearson, "1 Thessalonians 2:13-16: A Deutero-Pauline Interpolation," *Harvard Theological Review*, 64(1971), pp. 79-94; Hendricus Boers, "The Form Critical Study of Paul's Letters, I Thessalonians as a Case Study," *New Testament Studies*, 22(1975-1976), pp. 140-158.

Worse still, the Thessalonians were circulating among themselves a forged letter attributed to Paul, a letter which apparently supported the errors of the false prophets and teachers. (2 Th 2:1-2) Alarmed but unable to extricate himself from his work at Corinth, Paul wrote what we now call 2 Th, excoriating the persecutors of the community, (2 Th 1:5-12), encouraging the neophytes to remain steadfast in faith (2 Th 1:3-4: 2:13-3:5), correcting the false teaching circulating there, (2 Th 2:1-13) and disciplining the moochers (2 Th 3:6-14). He dispatched Timothy to Thessalonika with his first letter (2 Th) and with instructions to restore order.

When Timothy returned with the word that, despite persecution, the community had obediently accepted the first letter, Paul wrote a second, more irenic letter of encouragement in which he both acknowledged receipt of Timothy's report and expressed his satisfaction with the community's steadfastness and obedient acceptance of his directives (1 Th 1:2-4:12).

In this second letter, Paul also attempted to respond to two questions which Timothy himself had failed to answer to the satisfaction of the Thessalonians. First, did the death[5] of the some of the Christians at Thessalonika diminish the deceased Christians' chance of sharing fully in the final resurrection? (1 Th 4:13-18) Second, if the day of the Lord had not arrived already, when would it come? (1 Th 5:1-11).

After responding to both queries, Paul closed his second letter with an endorsement of the local leaders (who had mismanaged the original crisis but had now come into line with Paul's directives), with a warning to discern rather than to despise prophecy (even though false prophets had misled the community), and with a brief warning about keeping the moochers in line. (1 Th 5:12-28)

The following analysis adopts Wanamaker's hypothesis as plausible even though a certain linguistic confusion results, since the hypothesis makes second Thessalonians chronologically the first of the two letters and first Thessalonians chronologically the second.[6]

---

5. Did the people in question die at the hands of persecutors or, as seems more probable, from natural causes? The text gives no indication of the cause of death.

6. For an alternative assessment, see: Robert Jewett, *The Thessalonian Correspondence: Pauline Rhetoric and Millenarian Piety* (Philadelphia, PA: Fortress, 1986), pp. 24-30. See also: Reinhold Bohlen, "Die neue Diskussion um die Einheit des Thessalonischerbriefes: Eine Kurzinformation fuer die Verkündignugpraxis," *Trierer Theologische Zeitschrif,* 96(1987), pp. 313-317; Bruce Johanson, *To All the Brethren: A Text-Linguistic and Rhetorical Approach to 1 Thessalonians* (Stockholm: Almqvist & Wiskell International, 1987); Abraham Smith, *Comfort One Another: Restructuring the Rhetoric and Audience of 1 Thessalonians* (Louisville, KY: Westminster John Knox Press, 1995); Karl P. Donfried and I. Howard Marshall, *The Theology of the Shorter Pauline Letters* (Cambridge: Cambridge University Press, 1993), pp. 3-113; A.J. Malherbe, "'Pastoral Care' in the Thessalonian Church," *New Testament Studies*, 36(1990), pp. 375-391.

(II)

Despite the shift from more negative apocalyptic imagery in second Thessalonians to more positive imagery in first Thessalonians, one finds considerable coherence in both letters' account of the end time. For example, in second Thessalonians Paul promises divine retribution for those who persecute his neophytes; and in first Thessalonians the theme of retribution resurfaces in somewhat muted form. Other apocalyptic themes from the first chapter of second Thessalonians also find an echo in first Thessalonians: the divine, judgmental authority of the Lord Jesus; His vindication of believers; and His punishment of unbelief. While the tone of Paul's apocalyptic rhetoric contrasts in the two letters, in both the apostle portrays resurrection as perfect union with Christ. In first Thessalonians, the perfect and everlasting union with the Lord Jesus which the saints will enjoy after the second coming will consummate their present union with Jesus through faith. (1 Th 1:2-7; 4:13-18)

Second Thessalonians uses a reverse image in order to express an analogous idea. In second Thessalonians the punishing fires of judgment exclude unbelievers from a face-to-face encounter with the Lord, from the vision of divine glory, and from an experience of divine saving power. Second Thessalonians also speaks of resurrection as "the glorification of the name of the Lord Jesus in His saints and their glorification in Him." (2 Th 1:12) Glorification adds to union with God the idea of a public manifestation of divine power, presence, and splendor which vindicates the saints and confounds their enemies.

Both letters to the Thessalonians begin with prayers of blessing which contain some of the same soteriological themes. In both letters the Father appears as the ultimate object of Paul's prayer of thanksgiving. (1 Th 1:2; 2 Th 1:3) The prayer in second Thessalonians thanks the Father for many of the same things as will the opening prayer in first Thessalonians: the increasing faith and love of the Thessalonians and their steadfastness under persecution, the witness they give to the other churches, Paul's pride in their fidelity, their election by God the Father, their response of faith and good works which manifests their divine election. (1 Th 1:3-10; 2 Th 1:3-4, 11-12) Second Thessalonians, however, names these blessings somewhat cursorily and lacks the more genial tone of warm affection which characterizes the later letter. In second Thessalonians an anxious Paul cuts the blessing short in order to get right down to business.

Paul exhorts the Thessalonians to view the persecution which they are currently enduring in the light of God's final judgment. The apostle reminds his neophytes of the retribution which awaits their persecutors when Jesus returns as eschatological judge. The apostle consoles the beleaguered community with the thought that their steadfastness in suffering gives them reason to have confidence that they, not their persecutors, will inherit the kingdom of God and that "the righteous judgment of God" will grant relief from the afflictions which both he and the Thessalonians are currently experiencing. (2 Th 1:5-7)[7]

The Thessalonians, together with Paul, look forward to the second coming as their ultimate vindication. Their persecutors, however, can anticipate only divine anger and rejection. While first Thessalonians will depict the second coming primarily as the consummation of the loving union between the Lord Jesus and His saints, second Thessalonians thunders the retribution which the Lord Jesus will visit on His enemies and on the enemies of His followers.[8]

Second Thessalonians anticipates "the revelation of the Lord Jesus from heaven with mighty angels and in flaming fire (*en pyri phlogos*)." (2 Th 1:7-8) The "heaven" from which Jesus descends in final judgment designates the mysterious realm of the divine. The vast and mysterious realm of the physical heavens symbolizes this realm; but the heaven of which Paul speaks also finds proleptic embodiment in the Christian community.[9]

The phrase "mighty angels" (literally, "with angels of His power [*met' aggelôn dynameôs autou*]") insists even more strongly than first Thessalonians will on the power and authority which the Lord Jesus will exercise over the angels in His final revelation. In the Bible God alone possesses such power. In first Thessalonians, that divine power will manifest itself in a positive way, by uniting both dead and living Christians to the Lord Jesus; but, in second Thessalonians, the divine power invested in the angels brings retribution to the Thessalonians' enemies and persecutors.

Besides mighty angels, flaming fire also accompanies the Lord Jesus's final revelation. The phrase "in a fire of flame (*en puri phlogos*)" invokes the familiar Old Testament image of fire as a symbol of the divine holiness, a holiness which purifies believers but devours the enemies of God. Accordingly the fire inflicts "punishment (*ekdikesin*) on those who know not God and on those who refused to listen to the good news of the Lord Jesus Christ." (2 Th 1:8) They will pay "the penalty of eternal doom through exclusion from the presence of the Lord and the glory of His might."[10] (2 Th 1:8)

Troubled by the excessive chiliasm in Thessalonika, Paul in second Thessalonians expresses his concern that the community not be "quickly shaken in mind or excited." The apostle identifies the sources of the community's current confusion: 1) a "spirit (*pneumatos*)," apparently of

7. Cf. Wanamaker, *op.cit.*, pp.220-2.
8. Cf. A.L. Moore, *The Parousia in the New Testament* (Leiden: E.J. Brill, 1966).
9. Cf. Walter Wink, *Naming the Powers*, pp.118-48.
10. Cf. Jouette M. Bassler, "The Enigmatic Sign: 2 Thessalonians 1:5," *Catholic Biblical Quarterly*, 46(1984), pp. 496-510.

prophecy, 2) a "word (*logou*)," probably of teaching, and 3) "a letter claiming to be from us (*epistolês hôs di' hemôn*)." In other words, false prophecy, confused teaching, and rank forgery have muddied the waters in Thessalonika. (2 Th2:1-2)

In verse 3:17, Paul authenticates second Thessalonians with his own farewell and signature. He apparently wanted to certify this letter as genuine and to distinguish it from the forgeries troubling the community. Second Thessalonians gives no indication how the forgeries originated at Thessalonika.

Paul next states clearly the doctrinal issue which most concerns him: the false belief that the day of the Lord has already arrived. (2 Th 2:2). He denies this belief categorically and then appends supporting arguments from Christian apocalyptic.

In Jewish apocalyptic, mass apostasy often precedes the last day as one of the evils of the end time. (Cf. Jub 23:14-21; 2 Esd 5:1-2; 1 QpHab 2:1-3). Paul adapts this belief to Christian apocalyptic by requiring that mass apostasy occur before the second coming of Jesus. The fact that the apostasy has not yet occurred should prove to the Thessalonians that the second coming could not possibly have occurred already. (2 Th 2:3, 6)

The apocalyptic mind thinks narratively and intuitively. As a consequence, it personifies the forces of God and the forces of evil engaged in the cosmic struggle of the end time. Paul acquiesces in this tendency of apocalyptic thought by personifying the final apostasy as "the man of lawlessness (*ho anthrôpos tês anomias*)" and "the son of perdition (*ho huios tês apoleias*)." (2 Th 2:3) The title "son of perdition" designates the man of lawlessness as the special object of divine retribution.

The lawlessness fomented by the son of perdition takes two related forms: his opposition to divine worship and his blasphemous proclamation of himself as divine object of adoration. (2 Th 2:4) In speaking thus of the man of lawlessness, Paul alludes to the book of Daniel. There the Seleucid king, Antiochus Epiphanes (175-164 b.c.) erected the statue of Olympian Zeus, "the abomination of desolation," for adoration in the temple at Jerusalem. (Dn 11:36-7) In Pauline apocalyptic, however, the man of lawlessness outdoes the blasphemies of Antiochus Epiphanes by taking his seat in God's temple and demanding that others worship, not Zeus, but the man of lawlessness himself. The image, which has overtones of emperor worship, suggests that humanity's final apostasy from God will culminate in some form of overt human self-idolatry. The phrase "the temple of God" could allude to the worshipping Christian community. If so, then Paul is suggesting that the Anti-Christ will seek to subvert authentic Christian worship with the idolatrous worship of his own person.

The fact that some of the Thessalonians find themselves tempted to assent to false prophecy and teaching (2 Th 2:2) indicates that the power which the man of lawlessness symbolizes is already working in the world and among the Thessalonians themselves; but a mysterious force (*to katechon*) (2 Th 2:6) holds the evil power in check (2 Th 2:7-12). The following verse personalizes this retraining force and predicts its eventual withdrawal, so that the man of lawlessness can manifest himself in a false *parousia* which will seek to bring about the final apostasy of humanity from God.[11]

Only then will "the Lord" Himself finally appear. He will destroy the man of lawlessness, the Anti-Christ, with "the breath of His mouth (*tô pneumati tou stomatis autou*)." The image "the breath of His mouth" asserts the power of the Lord, who will snuff out the man of lawlessness with the ease of blowing out a candle. "The breath of His mouth" could also connote of the power of the Breath of God, who sanctifies the Thessalonians, inspires their practical love of the truth, and opposes unrighteousness and sin. (2 Th 2:13; cf. 1 Th 1:2-7, 5:4-8)

In the mean time, restraint of the forces of evil may create the illusion that they have disappeared. (2 Th 2:7). Eventually, however, evil will strike back during the final apostasy. Then "the lawless one (*ho anomos*)" will stand clearly revealed as the instrument of Satan, as a power opposed to God and to Christ. Despite false signs, wonders, and wicked deceptions, the lawless one will, however, succeed only in deceiving those destined for perdition. They will perish by their own choice because they refused to believe the truth and live it. Instead, they will take pleasure in unrighteousness. Because of the hardness of their hearts, God will abandon them to delusion and falsehood. (Cf. Rom 1:24) Then, the Lord Jesus will destroy the man of lawlessness by His appearing. (2 Th 2:8-12; cf. Rom 1:18-23; 1 Cor 15:20-9; Eph 6:10-7)

The Thessalonians, by contrast, as "the beloved of the Lord," as "the first fruits of God's election," stand committed by the power of the Holy Breath to live the truth. They therefore will share in the divine glory of the Lord Jesus Christ.[12] (2 Th 13-15)

The section which follows examines the more irenic apocalyptic Christology contained in the first letter to the Thessalonians.

---

11. Some interpret the restraining force as Satan, since the man of lawlessness acts as the former's instrument. If one takes the passage in this sense, then, it would assert that Satan is holding rebellion in check until the appropriate time. Others interpret the restraining force as God. (Cf. Is 66:9) I personally find the latter interpretation more plausible. Cf. Wanamaker, *op. cit.*, pp.249-54; J. Coppens, "Les deux obstacles au retour glorieux du Sauveur," *Ephemerides Theologicae Lovaniensis*, 46(1970), pp. 383-389; Roger D. Aus, "God's Plan and God's Power: Isaiah 66 and the Restraining Factor in 2 Thess. 2:6-7," *Journal of Biblical Literature*, 96(1977), pp. 537-553.

12. Cf. Andreas Schmidt, "Erwägungen zur Eschatologie des 2 Thessalonicher und des 2 Johannes," *New Testament Studies*, 38(1992), pp. 477-480; Maarten J.J. Menken, "Christology in 2 Thessalonians: A Transformation of Pauline Tradition," *Estudios Biblicos*, 54(1996), pp. 501-522.

(III)

As we have seen above, in bringing order back to the Thessalonian church, Timothy had apparently failed to respond to two questions put to him by the Thessalonians. First, the death of some members of the community, possibly as a result of persecution, had apparently caused the Thessalonians to wonder if the dead would share as fully in the final resurrection as those who still remained alive at the second coming. Second, having conceded that the day of the Lord had not yet arrived, they wondered when it would.[13]

In responding to the first question, Paul reminds the Thessalonians that hope in life beyond the grave distinguishes the Christian from the pagan. (1 Th 4:13) The reality of Jesus' death and resurrection grounds Christian hope that those who die "through Jesus (*dia tou Iêsou*)" will rise "with Him (*syn autô*)." (1 Th 4:14) The odd phrase "through Jesus" seems to mean that Jesus' death has transformed the deaths of Christians from annihilation into an act of "falling asleep (*tous koimêthentas*)." "Falling asleep" foreshadows the awakening which the Christian dead will one day experience at the second coming.

As for the Thessalonians' concern that Christians who have died might forfeit a full share in the resurrection of Jesus, Paul responds that death has no power to prevent deceased Christians from rising with Christ. Both the dead and those still living at the time of the second coming will experience the same union with the glorified Jesus. (1 Th 4: 15, 17); for resurrection will bring to perfection the union with the Lord which Christians experience in this life through the action of His Breath. (1 Th 1:2-6)

Paul re-enforces his answer rhetorically with a dramatic portrayal of the second coming. The vivid apocalyptic images make a clear statement about the resurrection for which Christians hope, even though they do not provide a literal depiction of the *parousia*.

First, Paul portrays the second coming as a sudden irruption of divine authority and power. The Lord Jesus "will descend from heaven with a summons of authority" sanctioned "by the voice of an archangel and by a trumpet of God." The Lord Jesus' ability to command archangels, who announce God's word solemnly to humans, manifests the divine authority with which He now summons to Himself both the living and the dead.

---

13. Interestingly enough, Paul brackets his response to these questions with two exhortations to moral fidelity to the demands of gospel living. (1 Th 4:1-8; 5:12-28) These exhortations especially the second, serve an important rhetorical purpose. They put the Thessalonians' two questions in context. Rather than yielding to anxiety about the dead or composing time-tables for the second coming, Christian hope in the *parousia* ought to commit the Thessalonians to faithful obedience to the moral demands of the gospel, since moral transformation in Jesus' image ensures their personal and collective share in the resurrection.

The trumpet blast has rich connotations in the Old Testament. There a trumpet assembles the faithful. (Ex 19: 13, 16, 19) It announces the "day of the Lord," a day of vindication and of judgment. (Zeph 1:16, Jl 2:1, 15) It proclaims the triumph of the messiah. (Zech 9:14) It begins the restoration of the true Israel. (Is 27:13) While all these allusions fit the Pauline text, whether Paul or not intended them all no one can tell.

In order to assure the Thessalonians that the dead will have no advantage over the living, Paul portrays them as responding with temporal priority to the Lord's divine summons. At the voice of the Lord, they will rise from the dead. (1 Th 4:16)

The power of Lord's summons also manifests itself in the fact that the Lord Jesus has no need to descend all the way to the earth in order to consummate the divine union to which all the saints look forward. Instead, His divine call draws both the risen Christians and those who are still alive upward into the air to meet Him "enveloped by clouds (*en nephaleis*)." Clouds symbolize the mysterious divine presence. The ascension into the clouds of both the risen Christians and those still alive symbolizes the final transforming union with God which both will experience at the second coming. That union will perfect their present graced condition.[14] (1 Th 4:17; cf. 1 Cor 15:12-28, 51-8; 2 Cor 4:13-5:5)

Paul makes no mention of the resurrection of sinners, although his allusion earlier in the letter to "the wrath to come" (1 Th 1: 10) recalls similar images from second Thessalonians and suggests that the divine judgment will encompass both saint and sinner. The absence of divine retribution from Paul's vision of the second coming in 1 Th 4:13-8 illustrates both the contextual character and the rhetorical intent of the apocalyptic images which the apostle uses in both letters. Those images address specific questions and concerns and simultaneously re-enforce Paul's central point: namely, that in the final resurrection the Lord has the divine authority and power to unite both living Christians and the risen dead to Himself in an unbreakable union. The images express the apostle's confident hope that the saving God revealed in the paschal mystery has the power to triumph finally and fully over the forces of death and of Anti-Christ.[15]

Having dealt with the first of the Thessalonians' concerns, Paul proceeds to deal with the second, namely, the time of the second coming. Paul tells the Thessalonians to forget about "times and seasons (*ton chronôn kai kairôn*)." In other words, they should stop making time-tables. No one knows when "the day of the Lord (*hê hêmera kyriou*)," the moment

14. Cf. A.J.F. Klijn, "1 Thessalonians 4:13-18 and Its Background in Apocalyptic Literature" in *Paul and Paulinism*, pp. 67-73; Joseph Plevnik, "The Parousia as Implication of Christ's Resurrection: An Exegesis of 1 Thess 4:13-18" in *Word and Spirit*, edited by Joseph Plevnik (Toronto: Regis College Press, 1975), pp. 199-277.
15. Cf. Cerfaux, *op.cit.*, pp. 37-43

when the Lord Jesus will judge both the nations and Israel, will arrive. It will surprise every one like a thief in the night. (1 Th 5:2).

Having insisted that even Christians live in ignorance of the day of judgment, Paul hastens to assure the Thessalonians that this ignorance should cause them no concern if they are living lives which express their expectant hope in the salvation which the Lord Jesus brings. In that context, Paul contrasts the way in which believers and unbelievers will experience the day of judgment. The Day of the Lord will visit sudden and inescapable destruction on the wicked. Their sufferings will surprise them all the more because of their complacency which will only intensify the darkness of their unbelief. They will find themselves suddenly enveloped in pain like a woman in childbirth (1 Th 5:3).

The Thessalonians, by contrast, look forward to the day of the Lord strengthened by the light of a faith which teaches them to live in constant and vigilant anticipation of that final day, whenever it comes. As a consequence, the Thessalonians can expect to experience the day of the Lord, not as a divine ambush, but as the fulfillment of all their deepest yearnings for salvation. Their practical fidelity to the gospel thus makes knowledge of "times and seasons" superfluous. (1 Th 1:10, 5:7)

Indeed, the breastplate of faith and hope, on the one hand, and the helmet of love, on the other, arm them against that final day, protect them from evil doing, prepare them for judgment (cf. Wis 5:17-20), and assure them of the salvation which the Lord Jesus will bring. He will save both those living Christians who watch in vigilance for His coming and those who have only "fallen asleep" in order to awaken at the sound of the Lord's summons from on high. (1 Th 5:9-10; 4:16)

The letter closes with an moral exhortation which reiterates the Thessalonians' need to live in vigilant hope of the second coming. They must respect their leaders lovingly for the faithful service which they render the community. They should admonish the idlers, encourage the wavering, help the weak, manifest a universal patience, repay evil with good, cultivate continual joy, and submit to God's will for them in Christ Jesus. They should encourage prophecy while subjecting it to discernment, holding to every good prophecy and rejecting everything evil. Their constant sanctification will keep them safe, "whole and blameless" at the second coming of the Lord Jesus Christ.[16](1 Th 5:12-23)

16. Cf. J. Christiansen Beker, *Paul's Apocalyptic Gospel: The Coming Triumph of God* (Philadelphia, PA: Fortress, 1982), pp. 29-54, 79-121; John M. Court, "Paul and the Apocalyptic Pattern" in *Paul and Paulinism*, pp. 57-66; B.N. Kaye, "Eschatology and Ethics in 1 and 2 Thessalonians," *Novum Testamentum*, 17(1975), pp. 47-57; B. Rigaux, "Tradition et redaction dans I Th V.1-10," *New Testament Studies*, 21(1974-1975), pp. 318-340; Hans Heinrich Schade, *Apokalyptische Christologie bei Paulus: Studien zum Zusammenhang von Christologie und Eschatologie in den Paulusbriefen* (Göttingen: Vanderhoeck & Ruprecht, 1981); Peter Arzt, *Bedrohtes Christsein: zu Eigeart und Func-*

I have reflected on the apocalyptic dimensions of Pauline Christology. One task remains in order to complete this account of a Pauline Christology of hope. In the chapter which follows I shall probe the ways in which a Pauline Christology of hope continues to inform a contemporary experience of Christian conversion.

tion eschatologisch bedrohliche Propozitionen in den echter Paulusbriefen (New York, NY: Peter Lang, 1992), Paul-Emile Langevin, S.J., "L'intervention de Dieu selon 1 Thes 5,23-24," *Science et Esprit*, 41(1989), pp. 71-92; A.C. Perriman, "Paul and the Parousia: 1 Corinthians 15.50-57 and 2 Corinthians 5.1-5," *New Testament Studies*, 35(1989), pp. 512-521; Helmut Merklein, "Der Theologe als Prophet: zum Funktion propehtischen Redens im theologischer Diskurs des Paulus," *New Testament Studies*, 38(1992), pp. 402-429; Frank D. Gilliard, "Paul and the Killing of the Prophets in 1 Thess 2:15," *Novum Testamentum*, 36(1994), pp. 259-270; Jean-Nöel Aletti, "L' apôtre Paul et la parousie de Jésus Christ. L' eschatologie paulienienne et ses enjeux," *Recherches de Science Religieuse*, 84(1996), pp. 11-14.

Chapter 18
Christological Knowing

In this final chapter on Pauline kerygmatic Christology, I shall attempt to argue the following thesis: *The realities disclosed to Christian hope require that foundational Christology reflect on a unique kind of knowing: namely, on the knowledge of Jesus Christ which results from practical assimilation to Him in faith through the power of His Breath.* This thesis draws on the insights of the preceding seven theses in order to identify the kind of religious experiences which provide foundational Christology with its proper object of study.

Several interrelated tasks confront us in the present chapter. First, a foundational account of Christian hope requires a re-interpretation of a Pauline Christology of hope in the light of the construct of experience developed in chapter two. I shall show that the realistic, triadic, social construct of experience which I have proposed does indeed interpret a Pauline account of Christological hope. That construct will interpret Christological hope successfully if its categories apply in the sense in which I have defined them to the human and religious realities disclosed to Christian hope.

In pondering a contemporary experience of Christian hope, I shall argue that contemporary converts to Christianity share analogously the same kind of hope as Paul describes because they experience the risen Christ in a manner analogous to the way in which the apostle himself did. In the course of my argument, I shall examine in greater detail than in chapter eleven the ways in which Christological hope heals, perfects, and elevates ordinary human hope.

In the course of what follows, I shall also argue that the fulfillment of Christian hope yields a unique kind of knowing: namely, the knowledge of Jesus Christ which comes through practical assimilation to Him in the power of His Breath. I shall call this kind of knowing Christological and shall show that it provides foundational Christology with its proper object of study.

Finally, having probed and understood the experiential foundations for Christological thinking, I shall argue that many contemporary "low" Christologies articulate at best a dwarfed and truncated version of Christian hope. At worst, they proclaim a Christology of discouragement and despair.

This chapter divides, then, into four parts. Part one interprets Christological hope in the light of the construct of experience developed in chapter five. It does so by exploring the analogies between contemporary and Pauline expressions of Christian hope. Part two reflects on the specific ways in which hope in Jesus Christ heals, perfects, and elevates natural and sinful hopes. Part three discusses Christological knowing as the proper object of foundational Christological thinking. Part four reflects on the ways in which excessively low Christologies betray Christian hope.

I have called Pauline [1] a Christology of hope. By now the reader should recognize that the strong eschatological and apocalyptic flavor of Pauline Christology justifies that designation. I have also called Pauline Christology kerygmatic because the paschal mystery transforms Jesus from the proclaimer of the kingdom to the one proclaimed by the Christian community.

By the paschal mystery I mean Jesus' death, resurrection, and mission of the Breath viewed as interrelated phases within one and the same complex, saving event. In Pauline Christology, the paschal mystery begins the eschaton, the last age of salvation precisely because it transforms human perceptions of the future. Left to their natural resources, humans perceive the future as either an alluring or a threatening set of possibilities. Those who believe in the risen Christ, however, experience the future as His Breath drawing one into the mystery of God by transforming them in the image of the crucified and risen Jesus.

The paschal mystery transforms the future of the entire human race. It brings a universal salvation, because God confers the Breath of the risen Christ on any person who confesses Him in repentant, justifying faith. The Breath's action transforms the entire embodied person and redeems the physical cosmos from the corrupting effects of sin by creating environments of saving grace. The Christian community serves as the charismatic instrument of the risen Christ by mediating His Breath to other persons and to the world.

Proximately, then, those who hope in Jesus Christ desire that the Breath of Jesus will transform Christians collectively and personally by teaching them to "put on His mind": to respond personally and ecclesially to God, to other persons, and to the world as sinlessly as He did. Ultimately, those who hope in Jesus Christ long for His second coming as the final completion of the work of salvation which the paschal mystery begins and therefore as the final and full consummation of their loving, Breath-inspired union with the Lord of glory.

I begin, then, by arguing that a metaphysics of experience successfully interprets a Pauline Christology of hope.

---

1. Cf. James D.G. Dunn, "Prolegomena to a Theology of Paul," *New Testament Studies*, 40(1994), pp. 407-432.

(I)

In chapter two I argued that some contemporary theologies which attempt to approach Christology by using experience as a central, unifying category fail finally because they acquiesce in a nominalistic philosophical construct of experience. Nominalism, especially when combined with subjectivism, makes both the social and religious dimensions of experience unthinkable. Conceptual nominalism makes the social dimensions of experience unthinkable by defining experience as the private, purely subjective interrelation of concrete percepts and abstract concepts. All forms of nominalism make the religious dimensions of experience unthinkable by reducing the content of experience to concrete sensible facts. We do experience God; and, when God touches us, that experience has an element of decisive facticity; but we do not and cannot boil the experience of God down to a concrete sensible fact.

In chapter two I argued that a social triadic construct of experience makes both the social and religious dimensions of experience thinkable. In reflecting on Jesus' social development, I attempted to show that the fundamental categories of a triadic, realistic construct of experience can, in the sense in which I define them philosophically, interpret human social relationships and human personal and social development; for, as we have seen, the pragmatic meaning of a metaphysical hypothesis plays itself out in acts of interpretation. The time has come to test the ability of these same philosophical categories to interpret, not just religious experience in general, but Christian religious experience in particular.

Christian religious experience roots itself, as Paul correctly saw, in the paschal mystery: in an experienced encounter with the crucified and risen Jesus as the saving source of the divine Breath. The writings of Paul provide, as we have seen, the clearest first-hand glimpse into what the encounter with the risen Christ entailed. Can the metaphysics of experience proposed in chapter two make sense of such a religious experience? I believe that it can.

Seeing the Risen Christ

In a triadic, realistic, metaphysics of experience, reality divides, not into act and potency, but into the what and the how of experience. The "what" of experience designates the realities encountered within experience. The "how" of experience designates the way in which one experiences those realities.

As we have seen, the what of experience divides into two distinct but interrelated realms: the realm of concrete action (fact, decision) and the realm of general tendency (law, vectoral dynamism). Things act decisively upon us, and we either react or respond to them whenever we make decisions. We experience decisions as facts: as concrete determinations which make reality this rather than that. We also experience autonomously functioning tendencies in our world. An autonomously functioning tendency, one which originates its own activity, qualifies as a "self." Selves divide into persons and things. Human persons exhibit the capacity for conversion. Things—minerals, plants, and animals—do not.

The way we respond to the persons and things which act upon us engages the whole spectrum of human evaluative responses from sensation to feeling to imagination to rational inference to prudential deliberation. Evaluative response endows experience with its how. Particular evaluations become universal, general, or individual through the intentional meaning we assign them in responding to the realities we experience.

In speaking of an encounter with the risen Christ, one must with Paul and with the rest of the New Testament distinguish between the experience of those who actually saw the risen Christ in a direct confrontation and the experience of those who know Him through faith only. Both experiences involve action and reaction, being touched by God and responding to God. Both experiences involve a personal encounter with God. They differ, however, in the way in which one comes to know the risen Christ.

Those who saw the risen Christ met Him, encountered Him, found themselves suddenly and unexpectedly confronted by Him. "He appeared." The apostles did not infer the existence of the risen Jesus with cool rationality, as Edward Schillebeeckx has falsely suggested. Those who met the risen Christ experienced that encounter as surprising, startling, and personally discombobulating. Far from flowing from dispassionate reason, the encounter blew their minds.

In that encounter the Risen One held the initiative. He revealed Himself to those who saw Him, to those to whom He appeared. He appeared, moreover, not just to individuals, but to groups of persons. In other words, the resurrection encounters exemplified both personal and shared experiences.

The encounter had a physical component. The risen Christ had a body: not a body like ours, but a "pneumatic" body; not a resuscitated body but a body completely suffused with divine life, so suffused indeed that it communicated that life to those who saw Him in the form of an empowering enlightenment. The physical encounter with the risen Christ endowed that religious experience with facticity. It functioned as both a divine touch and as a divine commissioning.

The letters of Paul and the Acts of the Apostles both give us good reason to regard the apostle as a mystic. Paul had visionary experiences;[2] but he also distinguished those visionary experiences from an encounter with the risen Jesus. (Cf. 2 Cor 12:1-6; 1 Cor 15:3-8) Moreover, as we have

2. Cf. Segal, *op.cit.*, pp. 34-71.

seen, Paul insisted on the bodily character of his encounter with the risen Christ even though he also insisted just as strongly that Jesus' transformed risen body differs from ordinary human bodies.

One fails, then, to do justice to either the what or the how of the apostles' encounter with the risen Christ if one reduces it to a purely visionary experience in the ordinary sense of that term. The precise character of the encounter with the risen Christ remains mysterious, even in the Pauline witness. Part of the mystery stems from its strange physicality. That physicality, however mysterious, endowed the encounter with the risen Christ with facticity. Those who saw the risen Christ interacted with Him. Since decisions bind experiences together socially, the encounter with the risen Christ had both an interpersonal and a social character.

Paul also describes the encounter with the risen Christ as an illumination, a conversion, a theophany. That illumination endowed the original encounter with the glorified Jesus with a vectoral thrust. It completely turned around those who experienced it and sent them forth to testify to others about the divine encounter which they had undergone. In other words, the encounter with the risen Lord effected in them a religious conversion which completely reoriented their lives.

Those who saw the risen Christ not only experienced simultaneously God's Breath; but they also experienced Her as emanating from and as mediated by the risen Christ. They experienced Her too as a saving impulse, as a dynamism, as a persuasive dynamism in their own lives and in the lives of others. They therefore experienced Christ's Breath as a persuasive vectoral thrust within human history originating in and leading into the transcendent reality of God eschatologically revealed in the risen Breath-baptizer. Paul identifies that empowering vectoral thrust and the human response to it with justifying faith, with sanctification, and with charismatic empowerment.

Faith, therefore, defines the how of the original apostolic experience of seeing the risen Christ. One responds to an historical self-revelation of God in faith when one responds on the terms God sets, in the ways in which the encounter with God demands. In the case of Paul, the apostle recognized that the risen Christ lives with and communicates to others divine life through the gift of His Breath. In the case of the apostle that gift required his personal consent in faith to the divinity and Lordship of Jesus. It also commissioned Him to proclaim both Jesus' Lordship and His divinity to others.

Those, therefore, who, like Paul, saw the risen Christ in an experience of encounter, through the very experience of conversion which that encounter mediated, simultaneously began to know the risen Christ in yet another way: namely, by practical assimilation to Him in the power of His Breath. In the case of Paul, the apostle clearly regarded the conversion he experienced in consequence of having seen the risen Christ as the paradigm for the conversion for which he looked in his neophytes. He repeatedly exhorted them to imitate him as he imitated Christ.[3] (2 Th 3:9; 1 Cor 9:1-4, 11:1; Gal 4:12)

By the practical imitation of Christ in the power of His Breath, one also comes to know Him. Moreover, assimilation to Jesus yields a deeper kind of knowing than the encounter with Him which the apostles experienced. The apostolic testimony to those encounters grounds and provides the context for interpreting personal assimilation to Jesus in the power of His Breath; but the increasingly unitive character of the latter form knowing gives it an enhanced depth.[4]

Those who know the risen Christ through faith also experience Him; but they do so in a way which both resembles and differs from the original encounter experiences of the apostles. By "the apostles" I mean the numerically limited group of people who originally encountered the risen Jesus face-to-face and were commissioned by the risen one to testify to that experience before others. One cannot equate the original apostolic college which founded the Church exclusively with the Twelve, as those who oppose the ordination of women habitually and fallaciously do. Others who saw the risen Christ functioned as apostles including not only Paul but also, quite possibly, Mary Magdalene, whom the fourth gospel describes as the apostle to the apostles, and other women as well. (Jn 20:17-18)

In a sense, Paul's converts also "encountered" the risen Christ. They did so, not face-to-face, but in the apostle's proclamation of the kerygma. They did not see the risen Christ in the same way in which Paul and the other apostolic witnesses had. They had no Damascus experience. Nevertheless, those who consented in faith to the kerygmatic proclamation of the paschal mystery did know the risen Christ in precisely the same way as the apostles did after the apparitions of the risen Jesus ceased. Both Paul and his converts knew Jesus Christ through conversion and assimilation to Him in the power of His Breath. After the apparitions of the risen Christ ceased, such assimilation constituted the only way in which one could come to know the risen Christ through faith.

One can call knowing through practical faith "connatural" as long as one allows connaturality to include the realm of the supernatural. Such knowing engages initially intuitive perceptions of divine saving activity;

---

3. Cf. David M. Stanley, S.J., "'Become Imitators of Me': The Pauline Conception of Apostolic Tradition," *Biblica*, 40(1959), pp. 859-877; Robert W. Scholla, "Into the Image of God: Pauline Eschatology and the Transformation of Believers," *Gregorianum*, 78(1997), pp. 33-54; Jan Lambrecht, S.J., "Paul's Appeal and the Obedience to Christ: The Line of Thought in 2 Corinthians 10,1-6," *Biblica*, 77(1996), pp. 398-416.

4. Cf. Donald L. Gelpi, S.J., *Experiencing God: A Theology of Human Emergence* (Lanham, MD: University Press of America, 1987), pp. 324-389.

and those perceptions must finally pass judgment on doctrinal formulations of Christological faith.

A realistic, triadic, social construct of experience can also interpret this dimension of a Christian faith experience. Converted assimilation to Jesus contains an element of facticity: one converts in response to the proclaimed word; and the proclaimed word impinges efficaciously on human experience through the words and actions of those who announce the kerygma. In addition, those who convert on hearing the gospel do so because in that proclamation they find themselves touched by God. They recognize in those who proclaim the risen Christ people in whom and through whom the Breath of God is acting in human history. As a consequence, they respond to the proclaimed word as God's word; and, as Paul insisted, they do so quite correctly.

Those who convert to Christ can also experience the touch of God in moments of solitude, in times of personal prayer. Such touches exhibit a greater immediacy than those mediated sacramentally through an encounter with persons of faith who witness to the risen Christ by living like Him. Both experiences, however,—both the direct touches of God in prayer and those mediated by the faith-witness of others—enjoy an element of facticity. As Saint Ignatius of Loyola says in his *Spiritual Exercises*, when God touches the human heart directly, that touch leaves one in no doubt concerning it actuality, origin, or character.[5]

The knowledge of the risen Christ which flows from faith also has a vectoral character. Paul calls it "putting on the mind of Christ," or assimilation to Him in the power of His Breath. The Breath of Christ assimilates believers to Jesus persuasively, through enlightenment, not through coercion. As a consequence, that assimilation requires our autonomous and creative, human collaboration. Because the Breath of God initiates and guides the assimilation, Christians who know the risen Christ in this way experience that knowledge as an ongoing, collaborative assimilation to the divine reality. The realization that such union remains only partial in this life inspires Christian longing to die and be with Christ. It also inspires Christian longing for the second coming, for the perfect consummation of the union of creation with God, for a world finally purified of sin and of death.

Finally, the vectoral character of knowing Jesus through assimilation to Him in the power of His Breath presupposes its evaluative form; for the mind of Jesus Christ, His way of perceiving the reality of God, of humanity, and of the world, defines the character of that assimilation's dynamic orientation. In other words, Christians experience Jesus in faith as the paradigm of total human transformation in God.

---

5. Cf. Ignatius Loyola, *The Spiritual Exercises* of St. Ignatius Loyola, edited by Luis J. Puhl, S.J. (Chicago, IL: Loyola University Press, 1951), # 336, p. 149.

The risen Lord possesses the plentitude of the divine Breath, because only He functions as Her saving source. Other human founders of religions left behind doctrines; but only Jesus became a life-giving Breath. That fact endows Christian revelation with its normative character which measures the truth or falsity, the adequacy or inadequacy of all religious doctrines.

Every other person who knows the risen Lord through assimilation to Him in the power of His Breath participates receptively and collaboratively in the power of Jesus' resurrection. In rising with Jesus, none of us makes anyone else rise. We respond to His Breath. We receive Her into our hearts and lives. *She* raises *us* up with Christ. We neither command nor send Her, however, because as creatures we cannot command God. Only the risen Lord can do that.

The experience of contemporary Christians accords with the Pauline witness when it regards knowledge of the risen Christ through assimilation to Him in the power of His Breath as, not just a personal, but especially as a corporate, ecclesial enterprise. In other words, Christians experience assimilation to Christ in faith as a social process mediated through shared, sanctifying memories; shared, sanctifying hopes; shared, sanctifying lives and through sharing the Breath's charisms.

Individual Christians share in limited ways in the Breath of the risen Jesus although no individual possesses Her totally. The Breath of God who dwelt personally in Jesus now dwells corporately in the Church as a whole; but she encompasses and transcends both individual believers and the Church as a community. As a consequence, one shares fully in the Breath of the risen Christ by participation in the life of His Body, His Church. One does so by growing in ecclesial and personal faith through sharing the Breath's charisms. *Ubi ecclesia ibi Spiritus; ubi Spiritus ibi ecclesia.*

Membership in the community of believers animated by the Breath of Christ yields to that community and to those who belong to it corporate, ecclesial access to His "mind." On this point too, the Pauline witness and contemporary faith experience concur. By the mind of Christ, Paul does not mean just His rational intellect, if indeed as a human Jesus possessed a fully "operational" mind in Piaget's sense of that term. Rather, the mind of Christ designates the full spectrum of human evaluative responses which constituted Jesus' response to God, to other humans, and to the world. In other words, it means the religious vision, the kingdom of God which Jesus proclaimed. That vision tells us how to respond to God, to one another, and to the World without telling us what to do.

As we have seen, the term "kingdom" does not play a central role in a Pauline Christology of hope. That Christology focuses more on the paschal mystery than on the mortal ministry of Jesus; and it concerns itself with the ecclesial consequences of faith and hope in the risen Christ. If, however, by the "kingdom" one means the religious vision of Jesus, then a Pauline Christology of hope does indeed concern itself with the reality of the kingdom, even though the apostle rarely uses that term. For Paul a life inspired by the Breath of the risen Christ demands fundamental conformity to the ethics of discipleship which Jesus, during His mortal ministry, lived and proclaimed.

One finds moral exhortations in all the letters of Paul. One must, however, look to the letter to the Romans to find a summary of basic Pauline moral doctrine. Paul probably wrote that letter to a community of Petrine Christians which he himself had not founded. Moreover, he wrote the letter in order to summarize and justify to that community his version of the "gospel." (Rom 1:14, 15:14-21) In the other Pauline letters, the moral exhortation which usually closes the letter addresses issues current in the community to which Paul is writing. In Romans, however, the moral exhortation which closes the letter attempts to provide the community at Rome with a summary of Pauline morality.

The exhortation begins by urging the Romans to live not by the sinful values of the world but "in the newness of the mind (*tê anakinosei tou nou*)." (Rom 12:2) By the newness of the mind, Paul means the moral vision inspired by the Breath of the risen Christ. (Rom 8:12) One also finds in the phrase "the newness of the mind" an echo of first Corinthians, where Paul names the divine Breath the "mind" of God and of Christ. By that Paul seems to mean that within the Godhead, the Breath functions as the cognitive link between Father and Son just as in the historical age of the Church She functions as the cognitive link between the Christian community and the risen Christ. She therefore gives privileged access to Jesus' mind.[6] (1 Cor 2:14-16)

The exhortation at the end of Romans divides between general exhortations, on the one hand, and the pastoral resolution of specific problems, on the other. Paul deals with two specific pastoral problems: first, how to relate to unconverted Gentiles (Rom 13:1-7) and, second, how to resolve the conflicts between the meat eaters and vegetable eaters. As we have seen, practical faith in the paschal mystery required of both meat eaters and vegetarians mutual tolerance, respect for one another's consciences, and mutual reconciliation in the same community of faith. (Rom 14:1-15:6)

As for the general exhortations at the end of Romans, they do not reproduce the exact words of Jesus, but they do echo His vision of the kingdom. Christians must love one another with a leveling love which creates a thoroughly egalitarian community. They must forgive the evil

6. Cf. Günter Haufer, "Das Geistmotiv in der paulinischen Ethik," *Zeitschrift für die Neutestamentliche Wissenschaft*, 85(1994), pp. 183-191.

they suffer and eschew revenge. They must share the physical supports of life, especially with the poor and the hungry. They must practice Christian hospitality and welcome into their homes anyone in need. (Rom 12:9-21)

Living as he does in the post-Pentecostal era, Paul expands Jesus' doctrine of sharing by including in his own moral vision the sharing, not just of bread and of the other physical supports of life, as Jesus had taught, but also the sharing of the Breath's charisms. (Rom 12:3-8) Given the shared faith experience of the apostolic Church, one may, in my judgment, recognize that theological expansion as legitimate.

Paul also indicates in the exhortation which closes Romans why those who live by the mind, or Breath, of Christ have no need of the Law; namely, through gospel living they already do what the Law requires and more. Those, therefore, who embody the moral vision of Jesus have no need of the negative or ceremonial prescriptions of the Law. (Rom 13:8-14)

The philosophical construct of experience which I defend in these pages interprets this fundamental Christian experience of putting on the mind of Christ in the power of His Breath. Christians living in "the newness of the mind" experience the Breath of Christ as a vectoral movement deep within their own hearts and in the shared charismatic witness of the Christian community. That community experiences Her as a dynamic impulse which persuasively, during the course of a life-time, conforms believers to Jesus by teaching them to embody collectively and personally the same religious and moral values as He lived and embodied. That experience has an evaluative component: growth in the same kind of feelings, attitudes, imaginative vision, and rational religious perceptions as Jesus himself. Living in "the newness of the mind" also has a factual component: the behavior of Christians which flows from and witnesses to the Breath's illumination. It has a vectoral component: the Breath Herself and the habits of practical faith which She inspires.

Experiencing the Eschaton

A realistic, triadic, social construct of experience also interprets a Pauline theology of resurrection. For Paul those who share in the Breath of Christ already possess risen life. In the construct of experience which I am defending, what one is results, not from some idea or essence fallaciously reified as a principle of being, but from one's history. We are in process of defining the kind of persons we will become. The human "essence" we are in process of creating results, then, in no small measure from our own moral and religious choices. Those who choose in response to the illumination of the Breath of the risen Christ experience their life stories as their own ongoing creation through the action of the Breath.

Believers co-create themselves with God by collaborating with God's touch and with the divine Breath's saving illumination. We experience that collaboration as our own persuasive penetration into the mystery of God. The more we deepen in loving union with God the more we desire the consummation of that union. In Pauline terms, we desire all the more our own final resurrection. In other words, the vectoral thrust of Christ's Breath re-orients human experience toward ultimate self-transcendence into the reality of God.

Those who live in the illumination of Christ's Breath, therefore, experience the future differently from those who live naturally. Those who live naturally must use their wits to create a future from a spectrum of alluring or threatening possibilities. When they respond naturally, humans use creative ingenuity in order to reorient their histories and situations toward life-giving, this-worldly possibilities.

For the Christian convert, however, God becomes the future through the saving illumination of the Breath of the risen Christ. Instead of experiencing the future as a configuration of empty possibilities, Christians experience the future in the onrush of God's Breath into their lives through the illumination and empowerment which that onrush brings. As Paul saw clearly, when we humans enter the eschatological age through baptism and the reception of Christ's Breath, God becomes our future. Moreover, that future sometimes comes at us with breath-taking speed.[7]

Each individual responds to the Breath of the risen Christ from a different angle of vision, from a different place within the historical process; but, for all, the goal of transformation in the Breath remains the same: practical exploration into the mystery of divine love incarnate in Jesus. In this sense everything which rises, which advances that exploration, does indeed converge. Nevertheless, the convergence allows for only analogous resemblance. Each individual Christian and each Christian community experiences the Breath's call in a way which responds to a particular historical situation. In becoming other Christ's, we prepare for ourselves different ways of sharing in the fullness of risen life.

In this section I have interpreted a Pauline kerygmatic Christology of hope in the light of a social, realistic, triadic construct of experience. I have in the process explored the analogy between Paul's religious hopes and those of contemporary Christians.

In the section which follows, I shall use Paul's kerygmatic Christology of hope, interpreted experientially, in order to describe how specifically hope in Jesus Christ heals, perfects, and elevates natural and sinful human hopes. In the course of that discussion I shall interpret a Pauline kerygmatic Christology of hope in the light of the construct of conversion which a triadic understanding of experience grounds.

7. Cf. Jürgen Moltmann, *The Theology of Hope*, translated by James W. Leitch (New York, NY: Harper & Row, 1965).

(II)

Before describing the graced dynamics of Christological hope, I first need to distinguish among three different theological meanings of the term "faith." Those distinctions allow one to situate the theological virtue of hope with respect to faith.

The experience of initial conversion to Christ gives rise to faith in its broadest meaning. Taken most broadly, the term "faith" designates the openness of the entire human person to transformation in God which initial religious conversion effects. Paul uses "faith" in this sense when at the beginning of Romans he asserts that the just person lives "by faith." (Rom 1:17) We call such faith justifying.

Second, one may also speak of the theological virtue of faith. In this second, more restricted sense, "faith" contrasts with hope and with love as three fundamental Christian ways of relating personally and ecclesially to God. Paul uses faith in this second sense in the first letter to the Corinthians. (1 Cor 13:13)

Third, "faith" may also mean the charism of faith. (Cf. 1 Cor 12:9) Those who possess the charism of faith live lives which embody in some special way trust in God's providential care over them. The Jesuit martyrs of the University of Central America lived lives informed by the charism of faith. So did Dorothy Day. So did Mother Teresa. So do all of those nameless Christians who in this bloody century of martyrs put their lives on the line for the sake of the gospel.[8]

Healing Human Hope

The notion of Christological hope implies the second sense of faith. It designates the theological virtue of hope as opposed to the theological virtues of faith and of charity. A global commitment of justifying faith (i.e., of "faith" in the broadest sense of the term) inaugurates the process of sanctification. As this global faith transforms and transvalues human affectivity, human intelligence, and human moral behavior it gives rise to the three theological virtues of hope, faith, and charity.

"Christological hope," therefore, transforms natural and sinful human hopes through commitment in global faith to Jesus Christ as savior, as Lord, and as a life-giving Breath. A foundational account of "Christological hope" calls attention to the specific ways in which commitment to Christ brings about that transformation.

Commitment to Jesus Christ provides believing Christians with practical norms for discriminating graced, natural, and sinful hopes. Gracious hopes embody the "mind of Christ" expressed both in His vision of the kingdom and in the hope with which He died on the cross. Gracious

---

8. For a more detailed foundational discussion of these sense of faith, see: Gelpi, *Committed Worship*, I, pp. 56-155, 126-128.

hopes long for resurrection and for total transformation in God in the image of Jesus. Sinful hopes contradict all these things. Natural hopes yearn for legitimate, finite, created goods but without any reference to Jesus and to the God whom He reveals.

Any vision of human life and society which contradicts the egalitarian vision of the kingdom which Jesus proclaimed and embodies counts as sinful. Hopes, therefore, which express human self-reliance as a deliberately chosen alternative to radical trust in the providence of God count as sinful. Hopes which embody greed, selfish sensuality, domination, and the coercive use power count as sinful. Hopes which express vindictive resentment, vengeance, violence of heart, the refusal to forgive count as sinful. Hopes which deliberately refuse to transcend this life and which reject life with Christ in God count as sinful. Hopes which incarnate religious hypocrisy count as sinful. Hopes which fail to embody the reconciling love which Jesus incarnated on the cross count as sinful.

Graced hopes, by contrast, incarnate the mind of Christ and the paschal mystery. Graced hopes long for the realization of God's will in this world and find the divine will normatively embodied in the sinless Jesus. Graced hopes draw us into the same kind of filial relationship to the Father as Jesus experienced. Graced hopes teach us to look to Jesus as the model of that relationship and to His Breath as its empowering inspiration. Graced hopes commit us to creating in this world a community of sharing which breaks down all the social barriers which separate people from one another. Graced hopes dedicate us to bringing hope to the hopeless. Graced hopes commit us to a life of mutual forgiveness in the image of Christ and to growth in a kind of prayer which embodies that forgiveness. Graced hopes measure present suffering in the light of the paschal mystery and of the world to come.

Commitment to Christ in global, justifying faith also provides us with the means for distinguishing between merely natural hope and gracious hope. Our hopes remain natural when they fall within the parameters of responsible behavior but remain completely untouched by faith in a self-revealing God. In other words, our hopes develop only naturally when they respond legitimately to others and to the world in which we live but when we aspire to a future circumscribed by this physical universe. When as humans we abstract completely from the historical self-revelation of God and hope for health, a good job, this-worldly fulfillment we hope naturally. A global commitment to Christ in faith demands that we transvalue all such hopes by viewing them in the light of Jesus and of the paschal mystery.

Moreover, in dealing with natural and with sinful hopes, we need to keep in mind that they take both personal and corporate form. The communities to which we belong school us to Christian hope, to natural fulfillment, or to sinful despair, either to a hope centered on God or to a hope centered only on this world.

We experience personal neurosis in part because we institutionalize neuroses which we subsequently interiorize; and neurosis distorts hope and makes it unrealistic. We also institutionalize sin. Capitalistic cultures which give top priority to maximizing profits value money more than people. As a consequence, they all too easily institutionalize and inculcate hopes motivated by sinful self-reliance, greed, and domination. In the United States we live in a gun culture, because as a people we have come to believe fallaciously that one can achieve peace and justice through violence. We believe that even though no war has ever produced a just peace. When people break our laws, we desire vindictively that they suffer and die. When they kill, we self-righteously and hypocritically try to undo the evil they have done by murdering them legally in electric chairs, in gas chambers, through lethal injections. In other words, because much of secular culture teaches us to believe that peace flows from the use of violence, many of our personal hopes imitate our national hopes in their lust for vengeance and for violent domination over others. Capitalistic greed, racism, sexism, chauvinism, homophobia, and all forms of bigoted human behavior also exemplify the institutionalization of disordered hopes.

Even when we do not aspire to a sinful future, how often does the future we would create for ourselves include God? Here the finitude of our lives and minds all too often betrays us into attempting to shape our futures by relying only on our limited natural resources. In the process, we forget about God and about the future to which God calls us in Christ.

Christological hope seeks to heal and transform both personal and corporate hopes, whether sinful or merely natural. Christological hope recognizes in the paschal mystery God's sanction of everything for which Jesus lived and died. Christological hope demands, therefore, that we like Jesus stand committed to obey God perfectly, that we stand willing to live and die for the same things as He. Obedience to the divine Breath in putting on the mind of Christ demands, then, both the transvaluation in faith of our personal hopes and the systematic reform of our corporate hopes.

Commitment in global faith to Jesus Christ also gives us access to a transcendent divine reality which heals sinful hopes and graciously transforms natural hope: namely, to the Breath of the risen Christ. Moreover, because the Holy Breath seeks the saving redemption not only of human hearts but of the world, She transforms believers, both personally and as a community of faith, into the risen Christ's instruments for redeeming and healing human corporate hopes.

Perfecting Human Hope

Besides healing natural and sinful hopes, Christological hope, hope motivated by a global, justifying faith in Jesus Christ, also perfects our spontaneous hopes by making them more human and more humane. Left to our own natural resources, our hopes reflect the finitude of the human condition. We find it easy to hope well for ourselves and for those close to us. Natural hopes encompass with some spontaneity one's family, friends, associates, even one's tribe or nation; but natural hopes often lack the moral stamina to hope well for all people. We do not spontaneously identify with the stranger, with the alien, or with our enemies. We do not tend to view them as our brother or sister, as members of the human family. We fear the stranger and the alien and therefore tend naturally to exclude or omit them from our hopes. We fear and hate our enemies and tend naturally to hope suffering and retribution for them.

Christological hope perfects natural hope by universalizing it. Those who hope in the image of Jesus Christ desire reconciliation with all people. They long for the salvation of all people. Christological hope teaches the human heart to yearn for the day when all people will relate as brothers and sisters in Christ. It demands that we love even our enemies and long for their salvation in Christ Jesus.

The religious vision of the kingdom which the paschal mystery endows with divine authoritative sanction universalizes Christian hope. Christian hope longs for the salvation of all people. Jesus seems to have dreamed of eventually including the Gentiles in God's just reign; and Paul's Gentile mission conducted under the inspiration of the Breath of the risen Christ began to transform that dream into a reality. In accepting a universal salvation, Christians simultaneously commit themselves to helping bring it about. Christians therefore hope the best for all other persons, including strangers and enemies. With Paul, they seek to become all things to all people.

If the universality of salvation in Christ perfects Christian hope, its physical and cosmic character politicizes it. Christian practice begins with the body: it seeks to insure that all people possess the wherewithal to lead a human as well as a graced life. Moreover, as Paul saw, purification of this world from sin sets the Christian community in prophetic opposition to the principalities and powers of this world, which take institutional shape in social, political, economic, and ecclesiastical oppression.

One has only to reflect on the deep-seated intransigence of racism, sexism, tribalism, nationalism, clericalism, and of every other "ism" which circumscribes human hope in order to recognize how difficult humans find it when left to themselves to expand their hopes to include everyone in principle and in practice. Left to ourselves we humans often find it hard enough to love all of our own relatives and in-laws.

When, however, we encounter persons of universal hope we acknowledge in them a perfection of humanity which we ourselves all too often lack. We celebrate nationally the yearnings of a Martin Luther King for a world healed of racial injustice. We admire and praise the hopes of a Mother Teresa to bring life to the otherwise expendable dregs of human society. We reverence the hopes of a Dorothy Day for a just social order which includes the poor, the marginal, and the outcast. We reverence the Christian character of Gahndi's hope for a society which renounces violence and builds on the solid rock of peace and justice. The hopes of all these people give evidence of having undergone universalization in the Breath of Christ. We recognize their longings as more perfectly human in their very universality. In allowing Christ's Breath to expand their hearts in hope to include everyone, even enemies, such people strike us as the living embodiment of the kind of hope every human ought to espouse.

We recognize the more perfect humanity of such saintly people; but left to our own natural resources, we find ourselves all too loathe to imitate them. We shrink from putting our lives on the line in order to achieve God's just social order. We fear the ghettoes which imprison the poor; and we tend if possible to avoid them. We long for a non-violent world but fear taking risks in order to achieve it. In other words, we tend to recognize spontaneously that the gracing of human hope perfects our very humanity; but, left to ourselves, we tend nevertheless to live content with a diminished mode of human existence.

Paradoxically, then, only the supernatural gracing of human hope fully humanizes it. The healing action of the Breath of the risen Christ humanizes hope by teaching it to imitate the universality of Jesus' longing for a world-order which excludes none and includes all, even the marginal and expendable, in an egalitarian community of sharing and of faith. Christological hope humanizes natural hopes by teaching them to recognize that in Christ all people stand united in the same family under God. Christological hope humanizes natural hopes by teaching them to include all persons in their well-wishing since they view every person as a sister or brother in the Lord.

Elevating Human Hope

Christological hope elevates human hope by focusing it on the paschal mystery. The paschal mystery expands the scope of human hope beyond this world. It teaches the human heart to long for the fulfillment of its hopes by perfect union with God in the image of the risen Christ; and it grounds that hope in the present experience of the transforming activity of His Breath.

In elevating Christian hope, the paschal mystery, as we have seen, blurs the distinction between time and eternity, between this life and the next, between historical existence and resurrected existence. A hope rooted in the paschal mystery does not find itself constrained as one does in dualistic frames of reference, to choose between this world and the next. Instead, Christological hope commits Christians to labor as Jesus did for the accomplishment of God's will here on earth in the power of His Breath. Moreover, Christians discover in that commitment the only sure ground for hope in the life to come, since a life dedicated to doing God's will on this earth makes the life to come a present, saving, transforming reality.

Christian piety and theology has so long acquiesced in the cosmic dualism inculcated by Greco-Roman culture that western Christians often find a Pauline understanding of the elevation of human hope hard to grasp. Paul, however, spoke out of a unique religious experience which falsified the theological use of philosophical dualisms; for those dualisms cannot finally make sense of a Christian experience of the paschal mystery and of the end time which it begins. Paul's diatribes against philosophy probably express his realization that the paschal mystery falsifies the dualistic ways of thinking which Greco-Roman philosophy systematically inculcated. If so, a metaphysics of experience, which eschews all forms of dualism, would, however, escape the apostle's censure.

The philosophical construct of experience defended in these pages has resources for interpreting the healing, perfecting, and elevating of human hopes through a global faith in Jesus Christ. It uses the categories of "transvaluation" and "transmutation" in order to do so.

"Transmutation" means change, but change conceived on an organic model. An experience undergoes transmutation when its inclusion of a novel variable forces the re-ordering of all the other relationships which define its reality and character. The notion of "transmutation" also conceives change aesthetically. One "transmutes" a picture, for example, when one adds to it a new patch of color. After the addition, one does not have the same old picture plus the new patch. Rather, one has a completely new picture because the addition affects the way in which all the other colors in the picture relate to it and to one another.

"Transvaluation" designates a transmutation in the realm of human cognitive response. One transvalues ways of perceiving oneself, others, or one's world when, having understood them in one frame of reference, one perceives them in a different frame of reference which requires one to re-evaluate their meaning and connotations. The shift from Newtonian to Einsteinian physics or from a classical view of nature to evolutionary theory, for example, transmuted in two different ways our scientific perceptions of natural processes.

Christological hope both transmutes and transvalues natural and sinful human hopes, whether those hopes take personal or institutional form. Christological hope transmutes human hopes by setting them in a novel relationship to historically revealed divine realities: namely, to the reality of Jesus Christ and to the Breath who proceeds from Him. Christian hope transvalues human hopes by demanding that we re-evaluate them in the light of Jesus' hopes and of the paschal mystery. The paschal mystery endows Jesus' human hopes with normative authority by revealing His divinity. Interpreted in the light of the paschal mystery Jesus' human hopes become God's own hopes for a sinful humanity.

A Unique Kind of Knowing

In the first section of this volume, I argued for the need to de-objectify Christology by conceiving it in relational terms and by approaching it with a pragmatic logic of relations and of consequences. The preceding analysis of the experience of Christian hope provides a strategy for doing precisely that. Christians hope to know Jesus Christ in a unique way: namely, through practical assimilation to Him in the power of His Breath. I call such knowing Christological knowing.

Christological knowing differs from mere knowledge about reality. We know about things when we become present to them through conscious evaluative responses. We organize such knowledge into art, literature, science, scholarship, and common sense. When, however, we know Jesus Christ in practical faith, that knowledge has a unitive character which transcends mere knowledge about things. We know Jesus Christologically when we allow the Breath of Christ to teach us ecclesially and personally to "put on His mind" by perceiving reality through His eyes and by responding practically to others and to our world as He did.

Christological knowing presupposes that the same divine principle of empowerment and illumination which transformed Jesus two thousand years ago is now transforming us who believe in Him ecclesially and personally. The New Testament identifies that principle as the Breath of the risen Christ. Since the resurrection reveals Jesus as "a life-giving Breath," He confronts us historically as the only one through whom the Father sends Her into the world in order to heal, perfect, and elevate sinful human hearts.

Christological knowing, therefore, graces the mimetic character of human learning through the imitation of Christ in a life of discipleship. Christological knowing not only assimilates believers practically to Jesus but binds them to Him through the common divine life which they and Jesus share. As Paul saw clearly, those who know the risen Jesus in faith become His body in this world. Through the community of the Breath-baptized, the risen Jesus continues to speak and act in order to establish the Father's just reign on earth as in heaven.[9]

9. Brian McDermott has correctly observed that no disciple of Jesus can relive His life; but discipleship does commit one to living in the image of Jesus by assimilating His

In this section, I have reflected on the way in which justifying faith in Jesus Christ heals, perfects, and elevates natural and sinful human hopes. In the next section I shall argue in greater detail that a sound insight into the dynamics of Christian hope allows one to identify the proper object of a foundational Christology. Foundational Christology reflects on the unique kind of knowledge of Jesus Christ which results from practical assimilation to Him in the power of His Breath.

(III)

Christological knowing embodies a unique kind of human knowing. It differs from all forms of purely speculative knowing because it flows directly from practical assimilation to Jesus in the power of the divine Breath who proceeds from Him. As a consequence, no purely theoretical investigation can grasp the kind of knowing on which Christological thinking seeks to reflect.

Christological knowing both resembles and differs from a more traditional understanding of graced, connatural knowledge. Like knowledge through connaturality it results from practical moral transformation in faith; but, unlike the traditional understanding of connatural knowledge, Christological knowing asserts the cognitive character of emotions and passions instead of reducing them to quasi-volitional impulses.

Christological knowing stands historically revealed as utterly unique in four different ways: 1) unique in its historical and transcendent source, 2) unique in its purpose and goal, 4) unique in its pattern, and 4) unique in its mode of accomplishment. Let us reflect on each of these modes of uniqueness in turn.

The world has seen many religious leaders. All the great world religions trace their origins to a human founder. None of them, however, rose from the dead as Jesus did. None therefore stands historically revealed as the divine source of God's saving Breath in the way in which Jesus does. All other authentic religious leaders, including the founders of all other religions, confront us only as converted sinners and as limited human recipients of the Breath of God. Only the risen Christ confronts us as Her saving source.

The apostle Paul insisted on the centrality of the paschal mystery to Christian faith, and rightly so. Only in the paschal mystery does the saving reality of God stand finally and fully revealed within human history.

sinless attitudes, His religious vision, His "mind," to use the Pauline phrase. When illumined by the same divine Breath as inspired Him, the synoptic gospels especially give access to His mind. In other words, the imitation of Christ presupposes the analogy of experience; and the analogy of experience allows Jesus to function as the paradigm of Christian behavior. We live His mind in circumstances other than those in which He lived and ministered. Cf. Brian McDermott, *Word Become Flesh: Dimensions of Christology* (Collegeville, MI: The Liturgical Press, 1995).

It stands revealed in human history because the history of Jesus begins the eschatological age and inaugurates the total transformation of human history in God. The uniqueness of Christological knowing flows from fact that in His resurrection Jesus of Nazareth "became a life-giving Breath." In His resurrection, therefore, He stand historically revealed as the unique, normative, divine source of transformation in the very Breath of God.

Christological knowing also stands historically revealed as unique in its goal or purpose. As the normative eschatological source of God's saving Breath, Jesus redefines and effectively re-orients the whole thrust of salvation history. One enters historically into the process of salvation to the extent that one allows the Breath of God to transform one in Jesus' image: not in the image of the Buddha, of Mohammed, of Lao Tzu, or of any other human religious figure but in the image of Jesus Christ.

Moreover, the incarnation alone reveals the inner social life of the deity. The resurrection in revealing Jesus' divinity transforms His *Abba* awareness into an historical revelation of the constitutive social life of the triune God. It also reveals that salvation consists in assimilation into the divine society.

The resurrection, moreover, in lending divine sanction to Jesus' life and ministry reveals it as the normative incarnation of the mind and saving intentions of God. Any other religious vision gives evidence of inspiration by His Breath to the extent that it conforms to His. To the extent that it diverges from Him or contradicts Him, it diverges from and contradicts the mind of God. In the resurrection, therefore, Jesus stands historically revealed paradigmatically as the normative human pattern of salvation. We stand finally in a life-giving relationship to God to the extent that His saving Breath conforms us to Him and draws us into His *Abba* experience.

Christological knowing stands also historically revealed as unique in its mode of accomplishment. Salvation consists in gracious transformation in the Breath of the risen Christ because the risen Christ stands revealed as the normative human embodiment of God, as indeed the only human embodiment of a divine person. Jesus incarnates in history the second divine person's relationship to both the Father and the Breath. In other words, He exemplifies the human experience of being a divine person. The incarnate Son of God also recreates humanity in sinless, graced perfection. Because sin partially dehumanizes us, the sinless Christ confronts us as more perfectly human than we.

The writers of the New Testament understood well the uniqueness and normativity of Christological knowing when they asserted that "in no other name in heaven or on earth" can humans find salvation. Paul understood well its uniqueness when he proclaimed that at the name of

Jesus every knee must bend on earth and under the earth and every tongue proclaim the human name of Jesus as the adorable name of God.

In this section I have discussed the uniqueness of Christological knowing. I have also argued that it provides foundational Christology with its proper object. In the section which follows I shall reflect on the doctrinal normativity of Christological knowing and ponder the relevance of a Pauline Christology of hope to the RCIA.

(IV)

Foundational Christology studies the way in which a global commitment in faith to Jesus Christ transforms the process of conversion. That commitment transforms the natural forms of conversion by inaugurating Christological knowing. Christological knowing, therefore, provides foundational Christology with it proper field of study.

Christological knowing, as we have seen, transforms affective conversion in part by suffusing human aspirations with supernatural hope; but Christological knowing also transforms the other forms of conversion. It infuses into intellectual conversion the supernatural virtue of faith. It changes personal moral conversion into the love of charity. It transforms socio-political conversion into the collaborative human effort to realize God's just kingdom on earth.

Christological knowing, practical assimilation to Jesus in the power of His Breath, also measures the soundness of Christological doctrines. Sound Christological doctrine fosters authentic Christological knowing. Unsound doctrine either fails to foster it or undermines it. In other words, one must judge the soundness or unsoundness of Christological doctrines by their practical consequences, by their capacity to foster practical assimilation to Jesus Christ in the power of His Breath.

As we shall see in the doctrinal section of this study other norms enter into the authentication of Christological doctrine, norms derived from intellectual, moral, affective, and socio-political conversion. Within Christian conversion, however, Christological knowing provides the religious norms.

I began this volume by pondering a variety of Christological doctrines. I cannot at this point enter into a detailed consideration of doctrinal Christology. Nevertheless, on the basis of what we have already understood about the paschal mystery, we can begin to rule out particular Christological doctrines as unsound. For example, any "Christology" which denies that Jesus in the paschal mystery confronts us as God in human form fails to measure up to the practical demands of genuine Christological knowing. If one denies the divinity of Jesus, one must also logically deny that He functions as the divine source of God's saving Breath. If Jesus does not send the Breath, then Christological knowing cannot happen; and Christology has nothing on which to reflect. In denying the divinity of Jesus' person one simultaneously denies the reality of the paschal mystery; and, as Paul saw both clearly and correctly, any denial of the paschal mystery guts the gospel of its central saving message.

As a consequence, all "low Christologies" which reduce Jesus to just another human person fail to measure up to the practical demands of Christological knowing. A Jesus who simply led an extraordinarily graced human life differs in no way from any other holy human person. Even if one asserts that He functioned as the passive recipient of God's Breath (not all low Christologies even go this far), in low Christologies which either deny or do not assert Jesus' personal divinity, He fails finally to function as the saving, divine source of God's Breath. No finite human person, however, including the Jesus of such low Christologies, has the divine power to effect universal human salvation. By the same token, any "Spirit Christology" which fails to include the paschal mystery in its account of Jesus' relationship to the Breath of God fails to measure up to the practical demands of Christological knowing.

In the doctrinal section of this study, I shall have occasion to explore in greater detail these and other doctrinal questions. The preceding observations, however, should suffice to illustrate how Christological knowing can measure the soundness or unsoundness of Christological doctrine.

These brief observations inspire, then, a kind of theological hope. By that I mean that they cause one to believe that foundational Christology has the means to resolve the current Christological crisis by enabling one to judge Christological orthodoxy in terms of its ability to advance or undermine Christian orthopraxis.

Relevance for the RCIA

I have undertaken this study as an attempt to lay systematic Christological foundations for the RCIA. In the final section of this chapter I have attempted to show that the construct of experience developed in chapter two mediates between a Pauline Christology of hope and the contemporary religious experience of Christian converts. Moreover, in this same section I have attempted to sketch some of the fundamental insights which Pauline Christology has to contribute to a contemporary catechesis aimed at adult Christian converts. As I have indicated, by "converts" I mean not only those experiencing an initial conversion to Christ but also those who are attempting to live out in responsible ways their life-long, ongoing conversion to Christ.

The theses which I have developed in the course of reflecting on Pauline Christology provide a practical program for converts who wish to grow in the Christological dimensions of hope. Through prayer, study, self-examination, and renewed commitment, they need to experience both personally and communally the ways in which commitment to Jesus Christ heals, perfects, and elevates their own natural and sinful human hopes. Through faith in the paschal mystery they need to grow in a Pauline experience of the risen Christ as a "life-giving Breath." They need to learn how death to sin with Christ and in the power of His Breath heals, perfects, and elevates their spontaneous human aspirations. They need to let the Breath of the risen Lord expand their limited natural hopes to embrace not only the rest of the human race but a sinful cosmos as well. Through active participation in a charismatic community of faith and of prayer, converts need to let the Breath of Christ make their graced hopes practical by discerning which gifts will enable them inspire humanity with hope in a world transformed in Christ. Through practical commitment to realizing God's just kingdom on earth, converts need to grow in a longing for Christ's second coming, i.e., for the final and total fulfillment of the work of salvation which He began. Finally, by growing in practical assimilation to Jesus, adult converts need to experience the uniqueness of Christological knowing in the sense described above.

Apocalyptic Christological Hope

We have, however, only begun to explore the full scope of Christological hope. As we have seen, a Pauline Christology of hope includes an apocalyptic strain; but the occasional and fragmentary character of Paul's writings leaves contemporary readers largely in the dark about the details of his apocalyptic vision. Nevertheless, even the writings we have make it plain that his Christological catechesis included much more than the scattered apocalyptic insights contained in his surviving letters.

One document in the New Testament does, however, reflect in considerable detail about the apocalyptic dimensions of Christological hope. I refer, of course, to the Book of Revelation. That book did not emerge from the Pauline tradition; but it does yield a detailed and unique insight into the Christological longings of those who first believed in Jesus Christ. Its inclusion in the canon of the New Testament endows it with a normativity for all believers. Moreover, more perhaps than any other document of the New Testament, the book of Revelation challenges converts to face the institutional, political, and economic consequences of Christian conversion.

In the final two chapters of this volume, therefore, I shall examine the apocalyptic Christology of the Book of Revelation. Moreover, I shall read it, not simply as an archaic historical anomaly, but as a Christian classic[10]: as a document with a surplus of meaning which continues to inspire and orient the hopes and aspirations of contemporary Christians.

10. I use the term "Christian classic" in the same sense as David Tracy. Cf. David Tracy, *The Analogical Imagination: Christian Theology and the Culture of Pluralism* (New York,NY: Crossroad, 1981), pp. 193-338.

Chapter 19
Apocalyptic Christology: The Book of Revelation

In the preceding chapters I considered the contribution which Pauline kerygmatic Christology has to make to a foundational theology of hope. Paul's theology includes an apocalyptic dimension, but in his surviving letters the apostle does not develop this aspect of his Christology in as much detail as he apparently did in instructing his neophytes.

In this chapter and in the next and final chapter, I shall explore in greater detail the apocalyptic dimension of Christological hope. I shall do so by examining the Christology of the book of Revelation. This chapter analyses the narrative structure of the book of Revelation. The following chapter reflects on Revelation as both Christian myth and Christian classic. The next chapter also ponders its contribution to a foundational theology of hope.

The reader may wonder why I am leading an expedition into an arcane and puzzling realm of New Testament Christology. Does first-century apocalypticism still have something to teach twentieth-century Christians? In my judgment it does. As I indicated at the end of the last chapter, more than any other book of the New Testament, Revelation makes it clear that those who hope in Jesus Christ set themselves up for a head-on collision with the principalities and powers of this world. By principalities and powers, I mean perennial and vast, even world-wide, institutional systems of injustice, unbelief, exploitation, and oppression.

This chapter divides into seven parts. Part one addresses the problem of access to the book of Revelation. By the problem of access I mean that contemporary readers often do not know how to read the book of Revelation. They find its imagery obscure, bizarre, and off-putting. In part one, I shall suggest a strategy for making the message of Revelation more intelligible to people living in the twentieth century. In a contemporary context, fundamentalist readings of Revelation pose one of the serious obstacles to understanding this puzzling text. I shall therefore propose a strategy for interpreting Revelation which avoids the pitfalls of fundamentalism.

Part two analyzes the introduction to Revelation. Part three explains the book's inaugural vision. Part four explains the Christological message of the seven letters to seven churches in Asia Minor. The rest of the book of Revelation consists of five cycles of visions. Part five examines the visions which accompany the breaking of the seals on the scroll of history. Part six considers the visions introduced by the blast of an angelic trumpet. The visions of the trumpets describe the cosmic woes which will precede final judgment. Part seven reflects on a cycle of visions which portray the coming of the messiah and the conflict between His Church and Satan. Part eight presents the visions of the bowls, which describe the retribution which God metes out to the Roman empire and its cohorts. Part nine describes visions of the last judgment and of the final victory of God over Satan.

I begin, then, by reflecting on the problem of access which the style of the book of Revelation raises for many contemporary Christians.

(I)

Most contemporary readers find the book of Revelation daunting. Many despair of deriving from this arcane text a meaningful message which speaks to contemporary Christian life and faith. The book teems with strange, violent, and disturbing visions of cosmic woe. It bristles with references to the Old Testament and alludes cryptically to popular first century religious beliefs. Even those who bother to look up the references or who try to understand the ancient religious legends often still find themselves baffled by the author's message and intent.

Fundamentalistic interpretations of Revelation abound. They, however, only compound the problem. Belief in the literal truth of every word in the Bible provides a sure formula for misunderstanding the meaning of the sacred text, especially a text as complex, symbolic, and obscure as the book of Revelation. The book of Revelation does not provide a newspaper account of the end of the world; and pretending that it does only popularizes false interpretations of its meaning, interpretations which make it even less accessible to contemporary Christians.

Both the alien thought patterns of Revelation and popular misinterpretations of its intent raise doubts about the ability of New Testament apocalyptic to speak to Christians living in a contemporary, rationalistic, technological culture. Nevertheless, I happen to believe that contemporary Christians have a lot to learn from this obscure and baffling book, if only they take the effort to approach it correctly. In what follows, I shall explain why I espouse this belief.

I propose a strategy for solving the problem of contemporary access to the message of Revelation. The strategy advances in four steps. First, contemporary Christians need to understand apocalyptic writing as a literary genre. Second, they need to situate the book of Revelation within apocalyptic literature as a whole. Third, they need to attend to Revelation's carefully crafted literary structure. Finally, they need to read Revelation as a Christian myth of the end time. Contemporary readers who employ such a strategy can, I believe, distil from the pages of Revelation important insights which continue to inform Christian hope and longing. In what follows I shall examine each of the preceding steps in turn.

Jewish Apocalyptic

How, then, did apocalyptic literature arise, and what was it trying to accomplish? As we saw in examining the world which Jesus entered, Jewish apocalyptic literature emerged during the intertestamental period. It expressed the religious longings of God's people for divine vindication and deliverance from Gentile oppression. In this sense all apocalyptic literature speaks to a fundamental and perennial aspect of the human condition: namely, human yearning for justice, for freedom, and for peace.

Opposition to political, social, religious, and economic oppression made apocalyptic literature subversive. Its subversive character helps explain its deliberately obscure, sometimes bizarre symbolism. Apocalyptic Jewish writers wanted fellow Jews "in the know" to understand what they were saying about their oppressors; but they did not want the oppressors themselves to recognize that Jews longed for their political, social, economic, and vital obliteration.

Of all the Jewish apocalyptic books, only the book of Daniel made it into the Old Testament canon. Besides Daniel, sections of the book of Enoch, predate the New Testament. Much of Jewish apocalypticism, however, developed cheek by jowl with Christianity. Moreover, as Jewish apocalyptic writing evolved, it adopted a number of characteristic literary and doctrinal conventions and doctrinal beliefs.[1]

Apocalyptic Jewish writers hid their identity from the authorities by attributing their works to famous Jewish prophets from the past. By ascribing their work to an established prophet, apocalyptic writers also hoped to endow their visions with divine authority and with the aura of tradition. Pseudonymous authorship served, then, two purposes simultaneously. It concealed the true identity of the author of a politically subversive religious tract; and pseudonymous authorship also tried to throw dust into the eyes of Jewish readers. Apocalyptic writers donned the mantle of tradition by attributing their tracts to acknowledged prophets in part because they wanted to disguise the disillusioned, heterodox interpretation of salvation history which they propounded. How, then, did an apocalyptic religious vision differ from more orthodox Jewish piety?

As we have already seen, the Greek word "*apokalypsis*" means "revelation." Jewish apocalyptic writing prophesied the future in visions. Apoca-

---

1. Cf. Leonard W. Thompson, *The Book of Revelation: Apocalypse and Empire* (Oxford: Oxford University Press, 1990), pp. 11-34; Walter Smithals, *The Apocalyptic Movement: Introduction and Interpretation* (New York, NY: Abingdon, 1975), pp. 10-39. See also: Andre Paul, "De l'apocalyptique a la théologie," *Recherches de Science Religieuse*, 80(1992), pp. 165- 186; Christopher R. Smith, "The Structure of the Book of Revelation in Light o Apocalyptic Literary Conventions, *Novum Testamentum*, 36(1994), pp. 373-393; Alexander Sand, "Jüdische und christliche Apokalyptic: Exegetische Fragen und Theologische Aspekte," *Renovatio: Zeitschrift für das Interdiziplinare Gesprach*, 54(1989), pp. 12-24.

lyptic authors dreamed terrifying dreams of cosmic judgment and destruction. They spoke the language of feeling, imagination, and hope; but they often voiced a hope warped by bitterness and despair.

At the heart of later Jewish apocalyptic lay a dualistic separation between "the present age" and "the age to come." Later apocalyptic thought looked upon "the present age," the age of sin and oppression in which they lived, as irredeemably corrupt. Satan, the prince of demons, presided over it. Moreover, so totally had he subjected to himself both the hearts of unbelievers and their sinful institutions, that he left God no choice but to wipe out "the present age," to obliterate it totally, and then to replace it with "the age to come," with a new and sinless creation. In the hearts of Jewish apocalyptic writers of the early centuries of the Christian era, then, hope of redeeming and transforming history had often died. Not even God, they felt, could redeem the present demonic epoch. He could only destroy it utterly and replace it with something else.

Traditional Jewish faith recognized human sinfulness; but it also confessed the saving presence of a God who transforms and redeems history. Despite human deviation from God's saving ends, God still retains the power to save humans from their own sinful folly. Hope in God's power to re-orient history to His own saving purposes lay, then, at the heart of traditional Jewish faith. As a consequence orthodox Judaism refused to endorse the extreme dualistic pessimism with which the apocalyptic imagination viewed the history of salvation.

Apocalyptic pessimism also gravitated toward historical determinism. The mounting debt of human sin and oppression made the final and terrible retribution against both the Gentiles and their compromised Jewish clients inevitable. Nothing, therefore, could prevent their utter annihilation

Apocalyptic piety tended to view "the present age" with self-righteous contempt. The members of apocalyptic conventicles saw themselves as a religious elite, as the remnant chosen by God for ultimate vindication when the final day of retribution dawned. Their stern judgment on less rigoristic Jews, whom they regarded as tepid and religiously flaccid, probably contributed to their marginality within the Jewish community.

Yearning for final vindication at God's hands gave rise to apocalyptic longing for the messianic end time. Apocalyptic writers described the coming of a variety of messianic figures who would serve as God's instrument for wreaking His vengeance on the enemies of the faithful remnant of His people. The arrival of the messiah would, then, usher in a time of intense political conflict cosmic in its proportions. In the course of that conflict, the forces of God would triumph decisively over the forces of Satan and of evil. Some apocalyptic writers referred to this final ordeal as "the birth pangs of the messiah."

The messiah's victory would inaugurate the "end time." During the end time, apocalyptic hope anticipated that God would restore political hegemony to His faithful apocalyptic elite. The end time would usher in an age of unparalleled peace and prosperity for the elect. The blessings of the end time would, moreover, finally fulfill God's promises to Israel. In a typical apocalyptic scenario, general resurrection and judgment terminated the end time and ushered in the new creation.[2]

Christian Apocalyptic

The book of Revelation which closes the New Testament exhibits some of the literary conventions of Jewish apocalyptic thought. It teems with visions of cosmic disaster and of divine judgment. It voices Christian resistance to the religious, political, and economic oppression of the Roman empire. Nevertheless, the book of Revelation also differs in significant ways from Jewish apocalyptic, especially in the latter's more mature literary expression. Let us try to understand those differences; for they provide a path of understanding into this perplexing New Testament document.[3]

Jewish apocalyptic writers hid their true identities behind pseudonymous authorship. The author of the book of Revelation, however, would have none of that. He identified himself by name: a Christian prophet called John. He also identified the place in which he received the visions which he subsequently crafted into the book of Revelation: namely, on the island of Patmos.[4]

John the prophet also insists on the Christian origin and character of what he wrote. In the first verse of the book of Revelation, John describes his book as a disclosure (*apokalypsis*) made to him by God and through Jesus Christ, a revelation of things which will happen "very soon." (Rev 1:1) John even takes an oath to attest that his prophecy contains "the word of God and the witness of Jesus Christ."[5] (Rev. 2)

Moreover, unlike most apocalyptic literature, John cast his vision in the form of a circular letter to seven churches in Asia Minor: Ephesus,

---

2. Cf. Smithals, op.cit., pp. 81-110. Thompson finds by contrast in the book of Revelation a tendency to blur boundaries rather than to sharpen them: cf. Thompson, *op.cit.*, pp. 74-91.

3. Cf. Hans Meitenhard, "The Millennial Hope in the Early Church," *Scottish Journal of Theology*, 6(1953), pp. 12-30; Johannes Irmiseher, "Die Bewertung der Johannesapokalypse in Byzenz," *Patristic and Byzantine Review*, 10(1991), pp. 25-31; John M. Court, "Reading the Book of Revelation," *Expository Times*, 108(1997), pp. 164-167.

4. Most contemporary exegetes hesitate, however, to identify the John who authored the book of Revelation with the apostle John or even with the "Beloved Disciple" who authored the fourth gospel.

5. For an analysis of the linguistic complexity of the book of Revelation, see: Thompson, *op.cit.*, pp. 37-52.

Smyrna, Pergamum, Thyatira, Sardis, Philadelphia, and Laodacea. (Rev 1:4, 11) The epistolary tone of Revelation provides a key to the book's purpose. John the prophet foresaw an immanent persecution of the churches, a persecution which the emperor Domitian[6] would soon launch. John wrote in order to prepare the Christian communities of Asia Minor for the ordeal which threatened them. In response to the threat of persecution, John summoned his fellow Christians to renewed repentance and to an expectant faith in the ultimate victory of Christ over their Roman oppressors.[7]

Numerology plays an important part in the book of Revelation.[8] As its letters and visions unfold, the number seven repeatedly symbolizes perfection, or completion. Geographically, the churches John addresses form a rough circle. In the ancient world circles too symbolized perfection of form. In John's apocalyptic imagination, the circle of cities, plus their number, seven, probably symbolized the Christian Church as a whole. If so, then, John would have intended his prophetic warning not only for the specific churches in Asia Minor to whom he wrote but for the entire Christian community. John interpreted the looming persecution as an act of judgment and as a sign of the immanent return of Jesus in final judgment. (Rev 1:3) Like the apocalyptic book of Daniel, which probably sought to prepare the Jewish community for persecution under Antiochus Epiphanes, Revelation sought to shore up Christian commitment in the face of an imperial persecution reminiscent of Nero's persecution of Roman Christians.

Despite its use of many traditional Jewish apocalyptic images, however, the book of Revelation manages to avoid the extreme historical pessimism which would characterize later Jewish apocalyptic. John's visions contain warnings aplenty about God's final judgment of the world. The prophet warns that intransigent lack of repentance and of faith will subject one to terrible eschatological retribution. Far from regarding history as unredeemable, however, the Christian prophet John insists that Jesus, the victorious Lamb who was slain and then rose to life, has already won the victory over Satan and over the sinful powers of this world.

Moreover, while John anticipates the visitation of divine judgment on the enemies of Christ at the hands of angels who accomplish the divine will, John never exhorts Christians to counter the violence of the Roman empire with their own violent resistance. Replete with violent imagery, the book of Revelation nevertheless preaches a message of non-violent

---

6. Titus Flavius Domitianus Augustus (51-96 a.d.) reigned as emperor from 81 to 96 a.d. John the prophet probably wrote the book of Revelation around 95 a.d.

7. For a brief assessment of Domitian's reign, see: Thompson, *op.cit.*, pp. 95-115.

8. Cf. Austin Farrer, *A Rebirth of Images: The Making of St. John's Apocalypse* (Westminster: Dacre Press, 1949), pp. 36-90, 245-260.

resistance to evil. Instead, Revelation prophesies that the victory of Christ has made the fall of the corrupt and sinful Roman empire inevitable. For John, the Jerusalem which will one day descend from heaven and supplant oppressive regimes like Rome is already in process of preparation in the faithful witness of Christian martyrs.

The prophet John, then, views the immediate Christian future with stark realism: it threatens persecution, suffering, torture, and death. Nevertheless, suffering for the faith will unite faithful Christians to the victorious Lamb and to the saints and martyrs who have gone before them. Even in the midst of suffering, Christian martyrs stand assured of their final triumph.

I have compared and contrasted the spirit of the book of Revelation with later Jewish apocalyptic writing. The time has come to examine the book itself in greater detail in an attempt to understand what it has to tell us about the apocalyptic dimensions of Christological hope.[9] To this task I turn in the section which follows.

(II)

Even though the author of Revelation claims to have received the fundamental content of his message in a vision (Rev 1:1-11), he has expended an enormous amount of imaginative energy in giving that vision systematic literary shape. Indeed, among the documents of the New Testament the book of Revelation stands out for its careful literary and stylistic crafting.

The Literary Structure of Revelation

After a prologue in which he announces the purpose and content of his book (Rev 1:1-8), John describes a vision of the glorified Jesus which he had on the island of Patmos. (Rev 1:9-20) I shall examine below the images with which John depicts the risen Christ. Here it suffices to note that each image not only links this inaugural vision to the seven prophetic messages which John sends to the churches of Asia Minor; but those same images tie together the inaugural vision, the seven letters, and the five cycles of visions which follow. In other words, the inaugural vision unifies imaginatively the entire work.

The letters to the churches sound more like prophetic oracles than epistles. Jesus dictates each message to the prophet John and prefaces each with the oracular phrase "I know...." In each message, John assesses the strengths and weaknesses of each of the communities to whom he writes. In the process, he warns each church of its need to repent and to

9. For a summary of the context and doctrine of the book of Revelation, see: Wilfrid J. Harrington, *Understanding the Apocalypse* (Washington, DC: Corpus Books, 1969). See also: Jacques Ellul, *Apocalypse: The Book of Revelation*, translated by George W. Schreiner (New York, NY: Crossroad, 1977), pp. 1-64.

prepare itself for the ordeal of persecution which threatens most imma-nently.[10] (Rev 2:1-3:22)

As we have seen, each cycle of visions which follows contains seven visions. Three of the cycles describe punishments of greater and greater cosmic scope and terror which God will visit upon unrepentant sinners. In every case, the suffering which people endure flows directly from their intransigent refusal to repent and believe in Jesus Christ. In other words, John eschews a deterministic reading of salvation history. The cataclysms of the end time result from deliberate and intransigent sinfulness

A central image unifies three cycles of visions. In the first, each break-ing of a seal on the scroll of history brings punishment to God's enemies as the prayers of the saints simultaneously advance the day of final judg-ment. In the second cycle, angelic trumpets announce the onset of that judgment. In the fourth cycle, angels empty bowls of divine wrath which bring the Roman empire crashing down to its final ruin.

The third and the fifth cycles of visions focus on historical events of eschatological significance. The third cycle describes in highly symbolic terms the first coming of Jesus as the messiah and the cataclysmic struggle between God and Satan which His coming inaugurates. The fifth cycle of visions describes Jesus' second coming and the final judgment. Be-tween the third and fifth cycle of visions, the visions of the bowls depict the fall of Rome.

In other words, John's visions seek to disclose the saving significance of God's saving action as salvation history advances toward final judgment. The story of Jesus forms an integral part of that history. His own eschatological victory over death empowers Him to support, protect, and save those who believe in Him, not only despite their sufferings, but through them.[11]

One finds, moreover, a rather straightforward rationale in the ordering of the cycles of visions. The vision of the letters prepares the churches for persecution. The visions of the seals contextualize the coming persecu-tion within the sweep of history. The visions of the trumpets announce the onset of divine judgment and the approach of the final judgment. The first cycle of eschatological visions portrays Jesus' initial victory over Satan and the victory of the martyrs during the coming persecution un-der Domitian. The visions of the bowls describe the visitation of divine retribution on Rome for spilling the blood of God's saints. Finally, the

---

10. For a description of the communities to whom John the Prophet wrote, see: Thomp-son, *op.cit.*, pp. 116-201. For another view of the purpose of Revelation, see: Alan Le Grys, "Conflict and Vengeance in the Book of Revelation," *Expository Times*, 104(1992-1993), pp. 76-80.

11. Cf. Robert Surridge, "Redemption in the Structure of Revelation," *Expository Times*, 101(1992-1993), pp. 231-235; F. Mondati, "La struttura generale dell' Apocalisse," *Rivista Biblica*, 35(1997), pp. 289-327.

last cycle of visions describes the last judgment and the replacement of Roman tyranny with the heavenly Jerusalem.

Let us, then, consider each literary segment of Revelation in turn. This section deals with the introduction, inaugural vision, and seven letters.

The Introduction

John addresses the seven churches in the name of "the one who is, who was, and who is to come." This elaboration of the divine name "Yahweh (I Am)" here designates God the Father, although later Jesus will also appropriate the same divine name. (Rev 1:4) As we shall also see below, in his inaugural vision of Jesus, John will apply to Him descriptive traits derived from the book of Daniel. Those descriptions identify Jesus with both of the Ancient of Days (Yahweh) and with the heavenly Son of Man.

John speaks in the name of the seven spirits, or angels, which stand in the Father's presence before His throne. (Rev 1:4) The seven angels also preside over the seven churches to whom John writes. Their presence before the throne of God symbolizes God's presence to the churches.[12]

Finally, John speaks in the name of "Jesus Christ, the faithful witness (*ho martys ho pistos*), the first-born from the dead (*prôtotokos tôn nekrôn*), and the ruler of the kings of the earth (*ho archôn tôn basileuôn tês gês*)." Jesus' witness transforms Him into the prototype of all Christian martyrs.[13] Jesus' resurrection validates the witness He bore to God and gives him divine authority over all earthly rulers, including, of course, the wicked Domitian. Because the risen Lord has power over earthly rulers, those for whom He died have nothing to fear from them.

Jesus Christ has proven His love for those who believe in Him by washing away their sins with His blood. We find here the already traditional New Testament assertion that Jesus by His atoning death reconciles repentant sinners to God. United with Christ they now share in His royal and priestly authority. Moreover, Jesus is coming soon as God's instrument of final judgment in order to vindicate His priestly people. He will appear on the clouds, like the Son of Man in the book of Daniel, and will triumph over all the kingdoms of this world and over those who serve them. (Dan 7:13) When humanity sees the one who was pierced through the side on the cross (Jn 19:37) they will be filled with grief over His death, thus fulfilling the prophecy of Zechariah 12:10-14. (Rev 1:5-7)

---

12. John may also have identified the seven spirits with the seven planets, which the ancients regarded as living beings. In Rev 4:5 John describes these angels as seven flaming lamps, a description that partially assimilates them to the heavenly lights.

13. Cf. Mitchell G. Reddish,"Martyr Christology in the Apocalypse," *Journal for the Study of the New Testament*, 33(1988), pp. 85-95; Charles Homer Giblin, S.J. "Recapitulation and the Literary Coherence of John's Apocalypse," *Catholic Biblical Quarterly*, 56(1994), pp. 81-95; Michelle V. Lee,"A Call to Martyrdom: Function as Method and Message in Revelation," *Novum Testamentum*, 40(1998), pp. 166-194.

The Introduction closes with a biblical inclusion, with a second reference to the God who is, who was, and who is to come. God Himself, the Alpha and Omega, the creator and goal of all things, the only God, who was, who is, and who is to come, attests to the truth of John's prophecy.[14] (Rev 1:8)

In this section I have considered the literary structure of Revelation and its introduction. The next section explains the prophet John's inaugural vision

(III)

John the prophet testifies that he had the vision which eventually took literary shape in the book of Revelation on a Sunday on the isle of Patmos, where he had been exiled for his proclamation of Christ. Seized by the Breath of prophecy, John hears a voice "like a loud trumpet" command him to write down all his visions and to send them to the seven churches. (Rev 1:9-11) The loudness of the voice suggests the irresistible authority and power of the one who speaks.[15]

The Inaugural Vision

John turns and confronts the risen Christ whom he describes in vivid allusive images which underscore His divine majesty and power. John sees one who resembles the "Son of Man" described in Dan 7:13, a human figure who like God comes riding the clouds of heaven. In the book of Daniel, God, the Ancient of Days, gives the Son of Man dominion over the kingdoms of the earth. John therefore confronts Jesus as one who holds sovereign sway over the thrones and empires of this world.[16]

Jesus wears a robe which signifies his priesthood and a golden girdle which symbolizes his royal authority. Like the Ancient of Days in Dan 7:9, the whiteness of His hair symbolizes His eternity. John's assimilation of the risen Christ to the Ancient of Days Himself (Yahweh) implicitly asserts His divinity.

The other symbolic details of the vision call attention to other aspects of Jesus' divine dignity and authority. Jesus' seven blazing eyes reveal His power to probe minds and hearts. The number seven symbolizes the omniscient perfection of His knowledge. (Cf. Rev 2:23) His bronze feet suggest His strength, permanence, everlastingness. (Cf. Dan 2:31-45) His

---

14. Cf. David Aune, *Prophecy in Early Christianity and in the Ancient Mediterranean World* (Grand Rapids, MI: Eerdmans, 1984), pp. 280-281.

15. Cf. M. Eugene Poring, "The Voice of Jesus in the Apocalypse of John," *Novum Testamentum*, 34(1992), pp. 334-359.

16. Some exegetes discover in Daniel's Son of Man Michael, the angel guardian of Israel. The action of the Ancient of Days therefore prophesies Israel's triumph over the kingdom's which oppress it.

voice sounds like the roar of the ocean and thus reveals His awesome power. (Rev 1:13-5)

Christ holds in his hands seven stars, which symbolize the angels who care for the seven churches to whom John is writing. The seven angels stand in the presence of God, who through them watches over the churches. Since the number seven symbolizes perfection, the angels probably represent Jesus' provident concern for His entire Church. By Jesus' side stands a lamp stand with seven candles which symbolize the churches themselves and, implicitly perhaps, the Church universal. (Rev 1:12, 16, 20)

From Jesus' mouth comes a sharp, two-edged sword, a symbol of the power of the divine, prophetic word of command which He now speaks. (Rev 1:16; cf. Wis 18:14-16) Jesus' all-seeing eyes and sword-like tongue will later effect judgment on His enemies. (Rev 19:11-16)

As Jesus continues to speak, His words suggest that the resurrection reveals His divine vitality as well as His divine judicial authority; for, having spoken in the person of God, Jesus announces: "I was dead and now I am to live for ever and ever; and I hold the keys of death and of the underworld." (Rev 1:18) The resurrection reveals Jesus' divine power over death and over the Satanic forces of evil. It also discloses that Jesus is "the Living One" who lives for ever and ever, the living God whom the Hebrews adore, the judge of all humanity.[17]

John's inaugural vision finds an echo in the letters to the churches of Asia Minor, as we shall see in the section which follows.

(IV)

Jesus commands John to write down the visions which he is about to witness. First, however, Jesus dictates a "letter" to the angel of each of the seven churches. The "letters," as we have seen, seek to prepare the churches for the coming trial and judgment which they face. As I have already indicated, the "letters" lack the literary form of letters in the ancient world and consist instead of prophetic utterances of encouragement and rebuke. Each "letter" closes with the claim that it expresses the prophetic Breath which fell upon John and in whose power he experiences his visions. (Rev 1:10, 2:7, 11, 17, 29, 3:6, 13, 22) The Breath speaks to the churches in the prophetic words which Jesus Himself dictates to John. In other words, John portrays Breath-inspired prophecy as the words of Jesus Himself. (Cf. Rev 19:10)

Admonitions to the Angels of the Churches

Jesus addresses the letters to the angels of the churches. Although some exegetes identify the angels of the churches with their presbyter-bishops,

---

17. Cf. G.K. Beale, "The Interpretation Problem of Rev. 1:19," *Novum Testamentum*, 34(1992), pp. 360-386.

Walter Wink has suggested with plausibility that one ought to interpret the "angels" in the light of a New Testament myth of the powers. New Testament angels and demons personify human institutions and the people who make them up. Demons personify sinful human institutions which inculcate an ethos of evil, corruption, and oppression. The angels of the churches, by contrast, symbolize the particular ethos which characterizes a local community's response to the gospel, a response which blends both faith and weakness, both commitment and compromise.

The letters themselves lend such an interpretation plausibility. Each epistolary prophecy does indeed dissect the strengths and weaknesses incarnate in the faith response of the communities to which John writes. Jesus addresses each letter not to the community itself but to the church's angel, but the issues raised concern the community as a whole.[18]

Many of the letters begin with an allusion to one of the descriptive traits which John has just ascribed symbolically to Jesus in the inaugural vision. Occasionally, the epistolary prophecies open with an allusion to some other messianic characteristic derived from the Old Testament. In either case, the images portray Jesus as divine messianic judge. They therefore underscore the divine authority of the prophetic letter which He sends each of the churches.

The body of each letter begins with the oracular phrase "I know...." The phrase expresses the prophetic character of the message which follows it. Some also see in the oracular tone of the letters rhetorical similarity to imperial edicts. Each letter ends with an allusion to a detail from one of the visions which John will describe as the rest of his book unfolds. These allusions to subsequent visions stress the transcendent reward which awaits those who persevere in the true faith.

The allusions make it clear that John regards the letters as integral to the message of the book of Revelation as a whole. The letters contain seven formulaic exhortations to heed the prophetic Breath's message. All of them close with an exhortation to victorious conquest. The exhortation alludes to the conflict between the Christian churches and the Roman empire. Those who win the victory suffer a martyr's death at imperial hands rather than deny the faith.

Finally, in the manner of the Hebrew prophets, the letters insist that human choices have ultimate consequences. They promise reward to the virtuous and fitting retribution to unrepentant sinners.[19]

18. Cf. Wink, *Unmasking the Powers*, pp. 69-89.
19. Cf. Aune, *op. cit.*, pp. 276-279; Ferdinand Hahn, "Die Sendenschreiben der Johannes Apokalypse: Ein Beitrag zur Bestimmung prophetische Redeformen," *Tradition und Glaube: Das frühe Christentum in seiner Umwelt*, edited by Gert Jeremias, Heinz-Wolfgang Kuhn, and Hartmut Stegemann (Göttingen: Vanderhoecht & Ruprecht, 1971), pp. 355-394; D.E. Aune, "The Form and Function of the Proclamation to the Seven Churches (Revelation 2-3)," *New Testament Studies*, 36(1990),

For example, to the angel of Ephesus, Jesus speaks as the one "who holds the seven stars in his right hand, who walks among the seven golden lamp stands." (Rev 2:1) In other words, Jesus in addressing the Ephesians invokes His authority over the churches, symbolized by the angels He holds in His hand. The fact that Jesus moves among the lampstands which symbolize the churches asserts His presence in the midst of the communities which profess faith in Him.

At the end of the same letter, Jesus promises to feed those who obey Him from the tree of life. The tree of life had, of course, grown in Eden, (Gen 2:9); but in the heavenly Jerusalem later disclosed to John at the end of Revelation trees of life line the river of life which issues from the throne of God and of the Lamb. The river of life-giving water flows down the center of the heavenly street. These wonderful trees bear fruit every month, yielding an endless abundance of life, and their leaves heal the nations. (Rev. 22:2) The letter thus promises to the Ephesians that those who triumph over persecution will one day dwell with Jesus in the heavenly Jerusalem and enjoy endless healing and life.

In the letter to the angel of Smyrna, Jesus speaks with the divine authority of the risen Lord, as "the first and last, as the one who died and came to life." (Rev 2:8) Since the Smyrnans face arrest and possible martyrdom, the designation of Jesus as the one who died and rose again implicitly exhorts them to confess the gospel even in the face of death, since the risen Lord has power to restore one to life. (Rev 2:9-10)

At the end of the letter, Jesus promises that, if the Smyrnans endure persecution victoriously, they need not fear the second death, the burning lake of sulphur into which those who do not belong to Christ, will, at the end of the book of Revelation, find themselves hurled after their final judgment. (Rev 20:14-5, 21:8) Those martyrs spared the second death also enjoy the dignity of priests of God and of Christ, with whom they will reign for the thousand years which will precede Satan's final overthrow. (Rev 20:6) Revelation views the Christian community as priestly (Rev 5:10), but martyrs share in a special way in Jesus' priestly sacrifice on the cross. In other words, faith in the paschal mystery, fear of final damnation, and confidence in their call to celebrate the heavenly liturgy with the risen Christ all shore up the Smyrnans commitment in the face of the coming physical ordeal.

In addressing the angel of Pergamum, Jesus speaks at the beginning of the letter as the one who wields the sharp, double-edged sword, i.e., as the one who has authority to speak the divine commands and execute divine judgment. (Rev 2:12) To those who endure victoriously despite persecution, Jesus promises at the end of the letter the hidden manna and

pp. 182-204; Anne Enroth, "The Hearing Formula in the Book of Revelation," *New Testament Studies*, 36(1996), pp. 598-608.

a white stone with a new name written on it, a name known only to the person who receives the stone. (Rev 2:17) The hidden manna recalls the heavenly food on which the Israelites fed in their desert sojourn. In Jewish apocalyptic, the renewal of the gift of manna characterized the messianic age. (Cf. 2 Apoc. Bar 28:8) The hidden manna could also have eucharistic connotations; but its gift clearly expresses full participation in the benefits which the messianic age brings. The image of the stone comes from popular magic. The stone in question, an amulet, gives power in virtue of the secret name inscribed upon it, most likely the name of the Jesus, the risen Lord; for later, in the course of his visions John will see the messiah ride to victory with a name written on Him known only to Himself. (Rev 19:12) Clearly, reverence for Jesus' divine messianic and judicial authority, confidence in the victorious power of His name, and longing for a full share in the blessings of the messianic age must stiffen resolve at Pergamum to face without flinching the coming persecution.

To the angel of Thyatira Jesus speaks at the beginning of His letter as the who has eyes like burning flame and feet like burnished bronze. The eschatological judge's flaming eyes read the secrets of the heart with divine omniscience; and His bronze feet symbolize strength, endurance, and permanence. (Rev 2:18, 23)

At the end of the letter Jesus promises to those who endure faithfully until His second coming that they will share in His divinely given authority over the nations and that he will give them the Morning Star. (Rev 2:26-9) In Rev 22:16, Jesus identifies Himself as the Morning Star. Jesus' the gift of Himself to His beloved friends assures their final loving union with Him in risen glory. In other words, the realization that one can hide nothing from Jesus, the divine judge, trust in His abiding strength, and the promise of everlasting friendship with Him will stiffen the resolve of the church at Thyatira.

To the angel of Sardis Jesus speaks at the beginning of the letter as the one who holds the seven spirits of God symbolized by the seven stars. Jesus exercises divine authority over the angels who guard the churches and, therefore, over the churches themselves. Moreover, as we have seen, the churches probably symbolize the Church as a whole. (Rev 3:1)

At the end of the letter Jesus promises to those who endure faithfully until His second coming that they will wear white robes. The white robes signify that they will join the numberless throng of faithful and innocent martyrs who later in Revelation celebrate the victory of God and of the Lamb. (Rev 7:9-10) The whiteness of the victors' robes symbolizes their own innocent triumph over sin. Jesus also promises not to blot their names from the Book of Life which will be opened before God on the day of final judgment. (Rev 20:12) Moreover, Jesus assures them that on judgment day He will speak for them in the presence of the Father and of His angels. (Rev 3:5) All these things encourage the church at Sardis to stand firm.

To the angel of Philadelphia Jesus speaks at the beginning of the letter as messianic judge, as the one "who has the key of David, who opens and no one shall shut, who shuts and no one shall open." (Rev 3:7) This text refers to Is 22:22, where a newly appointed steward receives exclusive personal access to the king. Possession of the key of David, therefore, designates Jesus as the sole mediator, the only one who gives us access to the Father.

At the end of the letter, Jesus promises to those who endure faithfully until His second coming that they shall dwell forever as living pillars in the heavenly sanctuary. Later in Revelation the reader learns that the heavenly Jerusalem will have no temple. Instead, God and the Lamb themselves function as the temple through their illuminative indwelling in the saints. As pillars in the heavenly sanctuary the redeemed will, then, know immediate, personal union with God.

They shall also bear inscribed upon them the name of God and the name of the heavenly Jerusalem whose descent from heaven will climax John's vision of the end time. (Rev 21:1-22:7) Bearing the divine name marks them as belonging to God; bearing the name of the heavenly Jerusalem marks them as its citizens.

Finally, at the beginning of the letter to the angel of Laodacea, Jesus designates Himself as "the Amen, the faithful and true witness (*ho martys ho pistis kai alêthinos*), the source of God's creation (*hê archê tês ktiseôs tou Theou*)." (Rev 3:14) The title "Amen" refers to Is 65:16, where it means "truth." Jesus' witness (*martys*) refers to His crucifixion as His ultimate testimony to the truth and as the prototype of Christian martyrdom. Just how Jesus functions as the source, the beginning of creation remains ambiguous. The phrase "source of God's creation" could designate Jesus as the beginning of the new creation. It could also present Him, at least implicitly, as co-creator with the Father.

At the end of the letter, Jesus promises to those who endure victoriously until the second coming that He will share with them His throne, just as He shares His Father's throne. Before the descent of the heavenly Jerusalem, John will see those who have borne faithful witness to Christ mounting thrones of judgment and reigning with Him during the millennium which precedes Satan's final overthrow. Moreover, from the throne of God and of the Lamb the water of life which flows through the heavenly Jerusalem takes its origen. (Rev 20:4, 11, 22:1-2) Like the martyred Jesus, Christian martyrs will judge their sinful persecutors and share in endless life.

As part of His exhortation to the Laodiceans, Jesus says: "Behold, I stand at the door and knock; if any one hears my voice and opens the door, I will come in to him and eat with him, and he with me." (Rev 3:20) The exhortation alludes to the final coming and to the messiah's victory banquet. The exhortation also endorses the kind of Christian hospitality which welcomes the stranger as Christ Himself. Dining with Jesus also has eucharistic connotations.[20]

If, as seems at least plausible, the prophet John wanted the seven churches to function as a symbol of the Church as a whole, then each of the promises made at the end of each letter applies in a sense to all Christians, just as the symbols of divine authority and of promise invoked at the beginning of each letter shape the Christological faith of all Christians. The prophetic words which Jesus speaks to the churches, like the post-exilic Jewish oracles of salvation and of judgment which they resemble, contain praise, censure, calls to repentance, warnings of judgment, and promises of salvation. The exhortations themselves seem to have no particular Christological significance other than the need for repentance and renewed commitment if the churches hope to survive the coming ordeal and live ready to confront the messianic judge at His second coming. The Christological images which frame the letters explicitate the context of Christological faith in which the seven churches must read the letters.[21]

This section has examined the introductory parts of Revelation. The sections which follow meditate on the cycles of visions which elaborate the book's message.

(V)

After dictating the letters, Jesus summons John to enter into heaven and view the future. Seized anew by the Breath of prophecy, John is transported through a door into the awesome presence of God seated on His throne, from which lightning flashes and thunder peals with apocalyptic power and authority. Before Him the seven spirits of the seven churches flame like burning lamps. The presence of the spirits symbolizes the Father's presence to the Church of His Son. A sea like glass separates John from the throne of God. (Rev 4:1-6)

The Figures Around the Throne

Grouped around the throne John sees four angels whose description he derives from Ezekiel: a six-winged lion, bull, human, and eagle. (Ezk 1:5-21) These angels have charge of the universe, of the four corners of the world. They symbolize the Father's universal cosmic authority over all creation, for these four angels will soon inaugurate the woes which

---

20. Cf. Ellul, *op.cit.*, pp. 123-143; Harrington, *op.cit.*, pp. 71-104.
21. Cf. Christine Trevett, "The Other Letters to the Churches of Asia: Apocalypse and Ignatius of Antioch," *Journal for the Study of the New Testament*, 37(1989), pp. 117-135.

will begin to afflict the enemies of God throughout the earth. These initial natural woes inflicted by angels who preside over nature occur during the course of history and differ in cosmic scope and intensity from "the birth pangs of the messiah" which characterize the end time. The four angels have eyes on the inside and outside of their wings, a symbol of the divine omniscience whose decrees they execute.

Besides the four angels, twenty-four elders who surround the throne of God like the courtiers who wait upon the emperor and like concelebrating presbyters around their bishop. They worship God constantly with the trishagion described in Is 6:3. Some believe that the twenty-four elders, who help lead the heavenly liturgy recall the twenty-four ranks in the levitical priesthood. The elders could also symbolize the elect.[22] (Rev 4:1-11; cf. 1 Ch 24:1-9)

God holds in His right hand a scroll with seven seals which contains the future events which John will soon witness. John weeps when he hears that no one in heaven or on earth can open the scroll and read it. John's tears of disappointment indicate his deep longing to learn the events of the end time. One of the elders, however, consoles him with the words that only one person has the power to open the scroll and reveal the future: Jesus, the Lion of Judah, the Root of David, can do it in virtue of his victory. (Rev 4:5)

Once again, linking messianic titles like Lion of Judah and Root of David to Jesus' victorious resurrection from the grave indicates that His glorification transforms Him into the messiah. His authority as messiah and divine judge of the universe empowers Him to break the seals which keep the historical future hidden. In breaking the seal, Jesus reveals the content of the scroll. As history unfolds, sword, famine, plague, and wild beasts kill God's enemies, while the saints yearn ever more impatiently for the second coming.

The figure of Jesus now enters the vision in the shape of "a Lamb standing as though it had been slain." (Rev 5:6) That the slain Lamb stands and acts symbolizes His possession of risen life. The slain Lamb also identifies the risen Christ with the passover lamb, as the one whose death seals a new covenant between God and humanity. (Cf. Jn 1:29; Ex 12:1-13) The image of the slain Lamb also identifies the risen Christ with the suffering servant who goes to His atoning death with the docility of a lamb. (Is 53:7) In other words, the paschal mystery—Jesus' death and resurrection—seals the new covenant and reconciles the saints to God.

---

22. Cf. Pierre Prigent, *Apocalypse et liturgie* (Neuchatel: Editions Delachaux et Nestle, 1964); L.W. Hurtado, "Revelation 4-5 in the Light of Jewish Apocalyptic Analogies," *Journal for the Study of the New Testament*, 25(1985), pp. 105-124; Robert G. Hall, "Living Creatures in the Midst of the Throne: Another Look at Revelation 4.6," *New Testament Studies*, 36(1990), pp. 609-613.

Like the Christ of the inaugural vision, the Lamb possesses seven eyes which John identifies as the seven spirits of God sent into all the earth. The seven eyes signify perfect knowledge, omniscience. The identification of the eyes with the seven angels suggests the providential efficacy with which the divine knowledge rules the world and the churches.

The Lamb also has seven horns. The horns on the Lamb link the image to the victorious Lamb of Jewish apocalyptic literature. The horns function as the animal's weapons. Since the number seven exemplifies a perfect number, the seven horns could also symbolize divine, omnipotent power over the enemies of God; and, indeed, as John's visions unfold the slain but living Lamb will execute terrible judgment upon His enemies and upon the enemies of His saints.

As the Lamb advances and takes the scroll from God's right hand, the four angelic animals prostrate themselves before Him in worship, as do the twenty-four elders. Their worship acknowledges His divinity. Each of them holds a golden bowl filled with the prayers of the saints, since the judgment which Jesus is about the wreak upon His enemies fulfills the prayers of His persecuted and suffering Church.

The angelic animals and elders also hold harps and begin a paean of praise to the Lamb echoed first by all the angelic choirs and then by the whole of creation. This act of cosmic adoration, which the elders and the angelic animals sanction with an "Amen," underscores the Lamb's divine right and authority to preside over the course of salvation history. (Rev 5:7-14)

The four angelic animals and the elders chant:

> Worthy are You to take the scroll and open its seals,
> for You were slain and by your blood
> ransomed people for God
> from every tribe and tongue and people and nation,
> and you have made them into a kingdom for our God and priests,
> and they shall rule upon the earth. (Rev 5:9-11)

The hymn to the Lamb parallels the worship which the four angelic animals and the elders have already offered to God the Father. The elders have sung two hymns to God the Father. The first echoes the song of the angels in Is 6;3. (Rev 4:8) The second hymn extols the Father for creating all things by His will. (Rev 4:11)

The first hymn to the Lamb praises Him for His redemptive death which undoes the effect of sin and effects a universal salvation. That universal salvation encompasses "every tribe and tongue and people and nation." The Lamb's redemption makes the redeemed share in His priestly office and transforms them into a kingdom by giving them authority to share in the Lamb's universal reign. The first hymn to the Lamb stresses, then, His redemptive activity which transforms Him into the Lord of history.

A second hymn to the Lamb follows in which the elders acknowledge that His death gives Him to right to receive "power and wealth and wisdom and might and honor and glory and blessing." (Rev 5:12) In other words, the Lamb deserves divine worship. A third hymn then follows which offers equal adoration to both the Father and the Lamb:

> To the one seated on the throne and to the Lamb
> be blessing and honor and glory and might forever and ever!
>
> (Rev 5:13)

The progression of the hymns implicitly asserts that the Lamb's redemptive victory reveals His co-adorability with the Father.[23]

The Visions of the Seals

The Lamb begins breaking the seals which allow the scroll of history to unfold. In the visions which accompany the breaking of the seals, the Lamb acts in part through angelic intermediaries. As the Lamb breaks each of the first four seals, the four angelic animals who have charge of the four corners of the earth send out four riders on horseback to afflict the earth. The riders symbolize death by sword, famine, plague, and wild beasts. (Rev 6:1-8) They execute Jesus' judgment on His sinful and unrepentant enemies.

The image of Jesus sending affliction upon the earth jars the sensibilities of many contemporary Christians; and, indeed, the image in some ways fits the triumphant messiah of Jewish apocalyptic better than it does Jesus. To tell the truth, however, this imaginative warning against divine punishment does have a foundation in Jesus' teachings in the gospels. There Jesus warns against the dreadful consequences of hardness of heart and of the persistent refusal of His message. (Cf. Mt 24:1-25:46; Mk 13:1-37; Lk 21:38)

The breaking of the fifth seal reveals that history includes more than the punishment of intransigent sin. As the Lamb breaks the fifth seal, His act discloses all those who have already shed their blood for the word of God gathered beneath the heavenly altar. Among these martyrs the prophet John includes those killed in the persecution under Nero. (Cf. Rev 11:1-13) The heavenly altar suggests the altar described in the letter to the Hebrews and revealed to Moses atop Mount Sinai. The heavenly altar provided Moses with the pattern for the Hebrew altar of sacrifice. (Heb 8:5; Ex 25:1-27:8) The presence of the martyrs beneath the altar suggests their inability as yet to share fully in the heavenly liturgy.

---

23. Cf. Ellul, *op.cit.*, pp. 100-124.

They complain at God's slowness to visit retribution on those who murder His servants; but they receive white robes which symbolize their own innocent and joyful victory over sin and death. With the robes comes an exhortation to patience, because their number remains as yet incomplete. The slaughter of the saints will continue on earth. (Rev 6:9-11) Only when the slaughter ends will the heavenly Jerusalem descend and all God's holy ones join in the celestial liturgy.

The complaint of the martyrs in heaven, however, receives an immediate response with the breaking of the sixth seal. It ushers in cosmic signs of the beginning of the end time: the moon turns to blood, stars fall from the sky like ripe figs in a high wind, the sky disappears like a rolled up scroll. (Rev 6:12-4) Despite the fact that God seems to delay judgment, the prayers of the saints are in fact hastening the day of its coming. In a sense, the rest of the book of Revelation narrates the divine response to the martyrs' prayer.[24]

These cosmic disasters produce terror in God's enemies as the rich and powerful join whole populations of people in caves and mountains which they hope will hide them from the wrath of the Lamb. (Rev 6:15-7) The disasters produce terror, but no repentance.

The breaking of the sixth seal further qualifies the disasters which the Lamb is visiting upon the earth. These events of judgment do not touch the saints. As God's enemies swarm into hiding, an angel of God intervenes to hold back the visitation of further cosmic disasters until he has sealed the foreheads of the servants of God. In Rev 14:1, we shall learn that the angel has sealed their foreheads with the name of the Father and of the Lamb. This sealing protects and prepares the saints for the onset of final judgment which will commence after the great silence which greets the breaking of the seventh seal.

The sealing of the saints recalls the sealing of those who have avoided idolatry in Ezk 9. The seal does not protect the saints from facing suffering and death. It does, however, protect them in the midst of both; and it shelters them from the disasters of the end time, which plague only those who freely refuse to repent. (Ex 12:1-33)

Later we shall learn of the martyrdom of those signed. (Rev 6:9-11, 14:1-5, 20: 4) Clothed in martyrs' white robes, they will praise God and the Lamb for their final triumph over the forces of evil. Clad in the white robes which mark them as people purified from sin through the blood of the Lamb, they will rejoice in His glorification and victory. By extending His special protection to them, God has promised, then, to gather them into His heavenly sanctuary, where they will never again know hunger or thirst, sun or scorching wind and where God will wipe all tears from their

24. Cf. John Paul Heil, "The Fifth Seal as a Key to the Book of Revelation," *Biblica*, 74(1993), pp. 220-243.

eyes. (Rev 7:5-17) Later, at the moment when the martyrs face their ordeal of suffering, the Lamb Himself will descend from heaven and stand in their midst while heaven celebrates their victory. The 144,000 function, moreover, as the vanguard of a countless number of redeemed Gentiles.[25] (Rev 14:1-5)

The breaking of the seventh seal brings a profound silence in heaven for an hour, a silence which portends the final coming of God. (Rev 8:1) Since the scroll symbolizes the historical future, the great silence marks the end of history and the dawning of the final judgment. Seven trumpets will soon break the silence and announce the onset of that judgment. An angel with a censor offers incense to God on the heavenly altar, an offering which symbolizes the prayers of the saints. When the angel casts the coals from the offering down upon the earth, thunder, lightning, and earthquakes usher in the first of the trumpets. (Rev 8:2-5) The prayers of the persecuted hasten the end of history and the day of their final vindication.[26]

(VI)

As we have already seen, a trumpet blast traditionally announced the gathering of Israel, the onset of the day of judgment, the triumph of the messiah, and the restoration of Israel. All of these events will soon come to pass; and the visions of the trumpets begin their realization.

The Visions of the Trumpets

As in the visions of the seals, the visions which accompany the first four trumpets have a close relationship to one another. Together they announce the destruction of one third of all physical creation and of all animals and ships upon the sea. In the ensuing darkness which consumes a third of the day, an angel warns the survivors that the next two trumpets will bring even worse disasters. (Rev 8:1-13) Moreover, the three plagues which follow afflict humanity more directly.

At the fifth trumpet, demon locusts from the Abyss of the underworld under the leadership of Abaddon, the personification of death, sting sinners with scorpion-like tails. This torment lasts for a period of five months; but the sting brings injury, not death. The demon locusts recall the plague of locusts which descended on Egypt during the Exodus (Ex 10:1-21); but their demonic character gives them more baneful power.

25. Cf. Christopher R. Smith, "The Portrayal of the Church as the New Israel in the Names and Order of the Tribes in Revelation 7. 5-8," *Journal for the Study of the New Testament*, 39(1990), pp. 111-118; Richard Bauckham, "The List of Tribes in Revelation 7 Again," *Journal for the Study of the New Testament*, 42(1991), pp. 99-115.

26. . Cf. Harrington, *op.cit.*, pp. 105-133. Ellul correctly argues that the narrative structure of Revelation takes on enhanced importance after the breaking of the seventh seal. Cf. Ellul, *op.cit.*, pp. 66-99, 144-170.

The reference to Exodus makes two implicit theological points: 1) Like the plagues in Exodus, the plague of demon locusts happens because of humanity's hardness of heart. 2) Like the Exodus plagues, this one torments the unrepentant enemies of God at the same time that it points forward to a new Exodus, a new liberation of the world from the power of evil and oppression.

At the sixth trumpet, four angels until now chained at the Euphrates lead an uncountable army of angels ("twice times ten thousand times ten thousand" [Rev 9:16]). The angels ride plague-breathing horses. The three plagues communicated by the fire, smoke and sulphur which spew from the horses' nostrils successfully slay one third of the sinful human race. Like the Pharaoh in Exodus, however, the unrepentant two thirds, respond by further hardening their own hearts: they remain steeped in idolatry, devil worship, murder, witchcraft, fornication, and theft. (Rev 9:13-21; Ex 8:15, 19, 29, 9:1, 12, 35)

In the visions of the seals, the fifth and sixth visions provided a moment of grace in the midst of catastrophe. They preceded the breaking of the seventh seal. Now, before the seventh trumpet, two visions intervene which also give hope to believers.

In the first of these two visions, an angel, modeled in part on the angel Gabriel in Dan 12:5-7 but more powerful still, proclaims the shortness of the time before God's final victory over the forces of evil. That victory will begin with the seventh trumpet, which, like the breaking of the seventh seal, marks the transition to the visions of eschatological conflict which follow. Those visions describe Jesus' first coming and initial victory over Satan.

After hearing the comforting assurance that the times of tribulation grow short and that the final struggle and victory looms, John swallows a scroll which empowers him to prophesy about events soon to ensue. (Rev 10:1-11) The swallowing of the scroll marks the visions which follow it as of special revelatory importance.

As we shall see, these visions recall the persecution of the Church under Nero and foretell the ultimate victory of those who persevere under persecution. Since John the prophet will soon portray Domitian as Nero *redivivus*, recalling the victorious martyrdoms of Peter and of Paul under Nero serves to stiffen the nerve of the churches and to prepare them to win a similar victory by suffering, if necessary, a fate similar to the martyred apostles. The deaths of Peter and Paul also foreshadow immanent persecution.

In the second consoling vision, John receives a measuring rod and with it the command to measure the temple of God, its altar, and all the people in it but not to measure the outer court of the Gentiles, which the pagans will destroy during a forty-two-month period, almost three and a half years. The prophet John derives the time span of eschatological woe from Dan 12:7. Despite the nearness of final victory, the time of suffering and persecution will continue; but since the temple precincts, altar, and those in the temple escape destruction, their measurement sets them apart for survival and assures them of divine protection and ultimate salvation.

The temple therefore symbolizes the Church and therefore those in it who will escape the perdition which awaits the enemies of the Lamb. The distinction between the inner and outer court of the temple may correspond allegorically to the heavenly sanctuary of God on which persecuted Christians should set their hearts. That sanctuary lies beyond earthly power to touch. The outer court of the Gentiles ravaged by the pagans might well symbolize the persecuted Church on earth. In any case, the second vision begins by renewing the promise of divine protection and salvation for those who persevere to the end. (Rev 11:1-2)

The Two Witnesses

The vision of the two witnesses which follows confirms this promise by recalling the victorious martyrdoms of Peter and of Paul under Nero. Moreover, the voice from heaven promises to send the same two witnesses to protect and defend the saints during the coming persecution.

John describes the two witnesses in ways which recall Zerubabel and Joshua, who presided over the restoration of the temple after the Babylonian exile. (Rev 11:3; cf. Zech 4:3, 14) The two witnesses only resemble Zerubabel and Joshua, however; for John also compares the two witnesses to other Old Testament figures. Armed like Moses and Elijah with awesome prophetic powers and the ability to call down droughts and plagues at will, the witnesses proclaim God's word fearlessly until they complete the time allotted for their ministry. Then they die in the Great City of Babylon (Rome). Their corpses lie in the Roman streets for three and a half days after which God breathes life into them again and summons them to heaven in a cloud. (Rev 11:3-12)

The prophecy of the two witnesses illustrates well the symbolic density which the language of the book of Revelation can achieve. Three interrelated levels of symbolic meaning intertwine: two past oriented, and one future oriented. The death of the two witnesses in Rome/Babylon identifies them as the apostles Peter and Paul, both martyred during the persecution of Nero. Like Zerubabel and Joshua who presided over the restoration of Israel, they presided over the building of the new Israel, the living temple of God. Their prophetic ministry to Christ makes them comparable in stature to the great prophets of the Old Testament. In fact, they enjoy even greater stature since they combine the charismatic powers of several Old Testament types, even those of Moses himself.

Assimilated to Jesus in their submission to death for three and a half days, like Jesus through the power of the Breath of God they rise again, and at a summons from heaven they ascend in a cloud to join Him in His glory. Following their ascent, a violent earthquake, symbolizing the advent of God, destroys one tenth of Rome and seven thousand of its inhabitants. John, therefore, portrays the martyrdom of the two great apostles as a prelude to their union with Christ in glory. The earthquake foreshadows Rome's ultimate destruction for persecuting the saints of God and of the Lamb.

The two witnesses also foreshadow the future which will soon dawn. John sees in the persecution under Nero which took the lives of Peter and Paul, a foreshadowing of the persecution under Domitian which will soon ensue. The courageous prophetic witness of the great apostles against the Roman beast, in the very bowels of its capitol, provides Christians facing persecution under Domitian with both an example and a hope. The churches too must now bear witness against Babylon as the apostles did. They do so, moreover, in the knowledge that they share in the sure hope for a glory which the apostles now possess.

One discerns, then, three levels of meaning in the passage: the historical level provided by the lives and witness of Peter and Paul, a typological Biblical level in which John uses symbolic images from the Old Testament in order to evoke the ministry of the great apostles, and a third prophetic and exhortatory level of meaning. The promise from heaven of two witnesses to guide the churches in the present extremity also instructs the persecuted Christians to expect God to raise up prophetic leaders who, in the tradition of the apostles, will bear witness, if necessary even with their lives.[27]

As we have seen, the scroll which the prophet John ate prepared him to utter two visions: the measuring of the temple and the two witnesses. The fact that the scroll tastes sweet in the prophet's mouth but sour in his stomach symbolizes the bittersweet character of the message he utters. Bitter persecution looms; but the consolation of assured divine protection in the midst of suffering sweetens the prophet's warning.[28] (Rev 10:8-10)

The breaking of the seventh seal had ended the seal cycle of visions on a positive note: a period of silence in heaven followed which portended the coming of God. The seventh trumpet also terminates the trumpet

---

27. Schillebeeckx's cursory handling of the book of Revelation in his analysis of a New Testament theology of grace strikes me as largely opaque to the imaginative density of the language of this most symbolic book. That opaqueness, however, accords with the rationalistic tone of Schillebeeckx's entire approach to Christology. Cf. Edward Schillebeeckx, *Christ: The Experience of Jesus as Lord*, translated by John Bowden (New York, NY: Seabury, 1980), pp. 425-462.

28. Cf. Stanley E. Porter, "The Language of the Apocalypse in Recent Discussion," *New Testament Studies*, 35(1989), p. 582-603.

cycle of visions on a positive note, even though John reminds the reader that more eschatological woes have yet to occur. (Rev 11:14) At the sounding of the seventh angelic trumpet, voices from heaven proclaim the victory of God and of His Christ and proclaim God's everlasting reign. (Rev 11:14-5) At this joyful declaration of God and Christ's final triumph, the elders surrounding the throne of God prostrate themselves before Him and praise Him for beginning His reign.

In asserting His divine authority, God also reveals His just anger against the nations who persecute His saints. At the same time, God vindicates all those who worship Him, whether small or great. The elders announce: "The time has come to destroy those who are destroying the earth." (Rev 11:16-8)

Here several points deserve mentioning. The announcement that the time of final, general judgment has arrived portends the resurrection of the dead and the vindication of the just. Moreover, the elders clearly assert that the sinfulness and perversity of God's enemies has led to the devastation of the earth, either directly or through the eschatological punishments which intransigent sinfulness has caused. Both the sinful perversity of God's enemies and the destruction of creation for which they stand responsible transform them into objects of divine wrath.

After this joyful proclamation of God's final victory, a startling revelation occurs which begins to fulfill the sign given after the seventh seal. The silence after the seventh seal promised God's coming. Now, suddenly after the seventh trumpet, the innermost sanctuary of heaven where God dwells opens wide, revealing the celestial arc of the covenant, the heavenly prototype of God's temple on earth. The traditional Old Testament signs of a theophany accompany the sudden disclosure of the very place where God dwells in heaven: thunder, lightning, an earthquake, and violent hail. (Rev 11:19)

In contrast to later Jewish apocalyptic, therefore, John the Christian prophet espouses a realized eschatology. In the coming of Jesus and through the paschal mystery God has scored a decisive victory over the forces of evil. The delay of the second coming may create the illusion that evil holds the upper hand. In fact, however, it stands already defeated. The seven historical and eschatological visions which follow spell out in greater detail these traditional Christian beliefs.[29]

(VII)

The first cycle of historical and eschatological visions follows. This cycle of visions portrays symbolically Jesus' first coming: His birth, death, and resurrection. It also depicts symbolically the historical forces of evil which opposed Jesus and which are conspiring to make the persecution of Chris-

29. Cf. Harrington, *op.cit.*, pp. 133-163.

tians under Domitian inevitable. This same cycle of visions also announces Jesus' initial victory over Satan. The vision makes it clear that the same demonic forces which sought unsuccessfully to destroy Jesus have taken historical shape in the Roman Empire. They will soon under the wicked Domitian subject the followers of Jesus to bitter persecution.

The second cycle of historical and eschatological visions parallels the first cycle. It will depict Jesus' second coming and final victory over the forces of evil and the final judgment. In between the first and second cycle, the third and final set of plagues promised in Rev 11:14 begins God's reckoning with the evil Roman empire, as angels empty the final bowls of divine wrath upon Rome and upon all those who serve it.

The visions of the bowls thus link the two cycles of historical and eschatological visions dramatically to the visions of the trumpets which began the world's final judgment. Taken together, the last three cycles of visions in the book of Revelation—namely, the first cycle of historical and eschatological visions, the visions of the bowls, and the second cycle of historical and eschatological visions—focus the generic divine wrath against sin expressed in the visions of the trumpets upon the Roman empire as its chief institutional incarnation. In the course of these final visions, John makes it clear that God's wrath has Rome and everything which it symbolizes as its special object.

These three cycles of judgmental visions—the seals, the trumpets, and the bowls—all have Christological significance. The Lamb, who is Christ, inaugurates them by breaking the seals which disclose the eschatological future over which He alone presides. Moreover, the historical visions which John weaves into these visions of divine judgment underscore the Christological import of the seals, the trumpets, and the bowls. Like the seals, bowls, and trumpets, both sets of historical visions number seven in all. The change in characters or subject matter marks one vision off literarily from the others.

The first cycle of historical visions includes the following major visions: 1) the woman and the dragon. (Rev 12:1-17); 2) the beast from the sea (Rev 12:18-13:10); 3) the beast from the land (Rev 13:11-8); 4) the Lamb and 144,000 virgins (14:1-5); 5) the three herald angels (Rev 14:6-13); 6) the harvest of the pagans (Rev 14:14-20); and 7) the triumphant celebration of those who win the victory with Christ. (Rev 15:1-4) The last vision also marks the transition to the vision of the bowls of wrath by introducing the seven angels carrying the bowls who will execute final vengeance against the Roman anti-Christ.

Visions of the End Time

In the first complex of visions, John sees a woman of goddess-like appearance: adorned with the sun, standing on the moon, and crowned with twelve stars. (Rev 12:1) Scholars have debated her identity. Her sojourn in the desert, however, identifies her as a symbol of Israel. The forty-two months which she passes in the desert equal three and a half years, which in both Revelation and Daniel designate a time of suffering and tribulation. (Rev 12:6)

Her crown of twelve stars symbolizes the twelve tribes of Israel. It seems unlikely, then, that John the prophet thought of the woman as Mary, the mother of Jesus. More likely he saw her as a symbol of Israel, whom God chose in order that it might produce the messiah. The woman also functions as a type of the heavenly Israel, the spouse of God and of Christ.

In advanced pregnancy, the woman cries out in the pangs of childbirth as she brings forth the messiah. The painful birthing of the messiah alludes, of course, to "the birth pangs of the messiah," the period of suffering and of conflict which His arrival inaugurates and which the forty-two weeks symbolize. The labor pains also allude to God's curse of Eve: that, because of her sin, she would give birth in pain. The woman's labor therefore recalls as well God's simultaneous promise to Eve of abiding enmity between her offspring and the serpent.

By the time John wrote Revelation, the figure of the serpent in Genesis had fused with the figure of Satan, the angelic enemy of God and of Christ. (Cf. Gen 3:14-6) No sooner, then, does the woman give birth to the messiah than a dragon with seven crowned heads and ten horns appears. (Rev 12:1-3) The fact that the dragon, a kind of serpent, swept a third of the stars from heaven with his tail—an allusion to the rebellion of the evil angels under Satan's leadership—identifies him as Satan, the anti-Christ and arch-demon. (Rev 12:4) The second vision will make the identification explicit.[30] (Rev 12:9)

John asserts the messianic character of the woman's male child by alluding to the messianic psalm 2, which promises that the messiah will rule the nations with a divine scepter and thus function as eschatological judge of the world. (Rev 12:5; cf. Ps 2:27) The dragon seeks to devour the child; but God takes him immediately up to heaven and allows the woman to escape to the safety of the desert. The woman's desert sojourn thus symbolizes the new Israel's time of testing before her final eschatological marriage with the Lamb. (Rev 21:2)

The dragon's assault upon the child alludes to Jesus' temptations, which culminated in the cross. His rapture into heaven alludes to His victorious glorification by the Father. These symbolic events, therefore, link Jesus' initial conflict with the powers of evil during His mortal ministry to His final conflict with those same powers when he returns from heaven as eschatological judge. They also portray the eschatological suffering of the

---

30. Cf. Paul S. Minear, "Far as the Curse Is Found: The Point of Revelation 12:15-16," *Novum Testamentum*, 33(1991), pp. 71-77.

churches as an aspect of their desert sojourn. In the desert, the new Israel, the predestined eschatological bride of Christ, experiences purifying testing.

As the first set of visions continues, the messiah's rapture into heaven begins the final struggle between Michael, the archangel of Israel, who leads the angelic hosts, and Satan who commands the demonic forces of anti-Christ. Michael wins the battle by driving Satan and his minions out of heaven.

This victory occurs after the messiah's glorification because His eschatological victory over the powers of evil through rising from the dead brings about Satan's expulsion from the heavenly court. John makes this idea explicit by having a voice proclaim that Satan's fall results from the victorious power and authority of God and of Christ. In other words, the kingdom of God which Jesus brings has no place in it for a sinister, demonic prosecuting attorney who accuses the saints night and day, as he once persecuted Job. (Job 1:1-2:7) Indeed, those Christians whom Satan has persecuted share in Christ' victory; for they triumph over Satan by the blood of the Lamb and through the witness of their own martyrdoms. (Rev 12:10-1)

Satan's expulsion from heaven, however, does not end his mischief; for he and his minions fall from heaven to earth, where they put the saints to the test through temptations and persecutions. While the heavens can rejoice that Christ's victory casts the tempter forever from heaven, the earth and sea have reason to fear the evil which Satan and his minions will inflict upon them. (Rev 12:9, 12) Only the second coming will break the power of Satan over creation.

Indeed, no sooner has Satan fallen to earth than he assaults the woman, the new Israel and future bride of Christ. God protects her by giving her eagle's wings to fly to the desert. (Rev 12:13-4) Frustrated, Satan vomits out a huge river of water to sweep the woman away; but the earth protects her by swallowing it up. (Rev 12:15-6) The vomited waters recall the waters of chaos. (Gen 1:1-2) Enraged that he cannot destroy the woman, Satan takes to persecuting the children of the new Israel, namely, "those who keep the commandments of God and bear testimony to Jesus." (Rev 12:17)

For John, then, no amount of persecution will ever destroy the Church. Despite Satan's attempt to annihilate the new Israel, God and the forces of creation which obey God's command will collaborate to frustrate him. That does not, however, make the children of the new Israel invulnerable to his assaults. On the contrary, it transforms them into the special object of demonic wrath and persecution.

A sudden change of scene marks the beginning of the second set of visions: those concerning a vision of the beast from the sea. John suddenly finds himself standing on the seashore. From the sea, the biblical symbol of chaos and rebellion (Cf. Gen 1:1-2; Ps 74:13), a leopard-like beast with the paws of a bear and head of a lion emerges. The beast has seven heads and ten horns with a coronet on each of the horns. Each head has a blasphemous title written upon it. One head has a fatal wound, but it has healed. (Rev 12:18-13:3)

The beast from the sea symbolizes the Roman empire. The seven heads represent the seven hills of Rome as well as a succession of seven emperors; the ten horns, ten client kings. (Rev 17:10-14) The blasphemous titles on the heads represent the emperor's claim to divinity and to worship by his subjects. The fatally wounded head probably symbolizes the suicide of Nero, who according to legend was supposed to return. As we shall see, John the prophet regards Domitian as Nero *redivivus*.

The beast has traits derived from the four beasts in the book of Daniel (Dan 7:4-8), which in that Old Testament book symbolized four successive, oppressive kingdoms or empires. By placing traits of all four beasts in the Roman empire, John portrays it as the heir and compendium of their wickedness and oppression.

The beast's ability to survive a mortal wound transforms it into a hideous antitype to the risen Christ. That the Roman empire embodies the Anti-Christ appears even more clearly when the dragon, Satan, hands over to it his power, throne, and worldwide authority, with the result that throughout the world, those whose names do not appear in the Lamb's book of life, worship the beast with idolatrous blasphemy. For forty-two months, the allotted time of tribulation, the beast blasphemes against God and the heavenly sanctuary; and the beast makes war against the saints of God on earth. (Rev 12:18-13:10)

In the first set of visions, Satan, enraged at his inability to destroy the new Israel, determined to make war against her children. The second set of visions portrays the Roman empire as the blasphemous instrument which Satan has devised to accomplish his evil ends. In imperial Rome, the Anti-Christ finds institutional embodiment.

The second set of visions ends with an ominous warning which recalls the seven letters which opened the book of Revelation: "If anyone is to be taken captive, to captivity he goes; if anyone slays with a sword, with the sword must he be slain. Here is a call for the endurance and faith of the saints."[31] (Rev 13:9-10) In a sense, the warning sums up the central moral message of Revelation: trial, persecution, testing are coming; prepare, then, to meet it non-violently. Retribution, however, awaits the persecutors.

The third set of visions contains only one note of comfort: the time of the beast will end. It will blaspheme and have its way for only "forty-two months." (Rev 13:5) The forty-two months could conceivably allude to

---

31. Cf. Aune, *op. cit.*, pp. 281-282.

Israel's forty years of desert testing. If so, the allusion would mark the persecution as a time of testing and purification for the saints.

In the third set of visions, another beast with horns like a lamb and a voice like a dragon arises from earth to serve the beast from the sea. The two beasts allude to the myth of Leviathan (the sea monster) and Behemoth (the land monster).

By combining traits of Christ and Satan the second beast also stands revealed as anti-Christ. The second beast serves the beast from the sea (the Roman empire) and works prodigies which persuade the people of the world to worship the statue of the beast who had been wounded by the sword and yet lived. In the vision of the first beast, the emperor wounded by the sword who lived was Nero. (Rev 13:3)

The second beast's power to work lying prodigies also identifies it with the anti-Christ. So do its other actions. In a demonic parody of the first creation (Gen 2:7), the second beast breathes life into the statue of Nero and empowers it to command the death of anyone who refuses to worship it. The prophet alludes, of course, to emperor worship and to the death penalty for refusing to engage in such idolatry.[32]

The second beast inflicts other woes on God's saints. Only those branded with the name of the beast or with the number of its statue's name can buy or sell anything. In other words, those who refuse to serve the beast must live in abject poverty and want.

Invoking ancient numerology, John equates the speaking statue's name with the number 666. John then gives the reader a further clue concerning the speaking statue's identity: the name belongs to a man. (Rev 13:11-18) In numerology, each letter has a numerical value. The sum of the letters in Nero's name apparently adds up to 666.

The beast from the land symbolizes the agents of the Roman empire who enforce emperor worship. If the deceptive prodigies and false prophecies of the second beast mark it as the Anti-Christ, so does the figure of Nero who undergoes a pseudo-resurrection. Dealt a mortal wound, he nevertheless lives. (Rev 13:3, 12)

The prophet John is alluding to a legend which arose after the death of Nero. The legend claimed that Nero had survived the attempt on his life, that he had fled to the east to rally supporters, and that he would one day return to destroy the city of Rome and punish his adversaries. The prophet John incorporates this legend into his apocalyptic scenario and transforms the "second coming" of Nero into an apocalyptic symbol of the

---

32. In Lucian's debunking work, *Alexander the False Prophet*, the author describes a talking statue not unlike the statue in Revelation. The statue's remarkable volubility results from the false prophet's chicanery and trickery. (Lucian, *Alexander the False Prophet*, 17) Cf. Stephen Sherrer, "Signs and Wonders in the Imperial Cult: A New Look at Roman Religion in the Light of Rev 13:13-15," *Journal of Biblical Literature*, 103(1984), pp. 599-610.

Anti-Christ. Later the prophet will transform the returned Nero into the instrument chosen by God to destroy Rome for all its crimes.[33]

In the present context. the talking statue of Nero which commands its own idolatrous adoration probably refers cryptically to Domitian, who is about to launch a persecution of all those who will not engage in emperor worship. The persecution under Domitian recalls the first persecution of Christians under Nero. In promoting his own idolatrous worship, Domitian acts like a second Nero and an agent of the Anti-Christ. The vision which follows supports the assimilation of Domitian to Nero, because in the vision the Lamb descends to earth to gather to Himself the martyred victims of Domitian's persecution.

In the fourth set of visions, the Lamb descends from heaven to Mount Zion and stands in the midst of the 144,000 whom an angel had sealed with His and the Father's name in Rev 7:1-8. (Rev 14:1) The angel had sealed them in order to keep them safe in the midst of persecution and suffering. Now the Lamb descends to claim them as His martyrs. Mount Zion, the mountain on which God chose to dwell, offers a counter-image to the sea of chaos and rebellion from which the first beast emerged.

John describes the 144,000 as virgins. In the Old Testament whoring symbolized idolatry. Those sealed with the name of the Lamb will not submit to idolatrous emperor worship, no matter how threatened or persecuted. Their virginity, therefore, symbolizes their repudiation of idolatry. John also describes the 144,000 as people who never allowed a lie to pass their lips; he refers, of course, to the blasphemous lie of emperor worship. (Rev 14:1, 4-5)

The Lamb descends into the midst of His victorious followers on earth with a peal of thunder which marks His appearance as a theophany. The peal of thunder, however, sounds like harps. In fact, the thunder results from the harp-playing of the elders who surround the throne of God. They and the four angelic animals are singing a new song. Like Moses after Israel's deliverance from Egypt (Ex 15:1-21), they are celebrating the final deliverance of the new Israel from the power of anti-Christ. Only the 144,000 learn the meaning of the song, however, because only they among those who dwell on earth experience the new exodus.[34]

The Romans will kill them for their refusal to pronounce the lying blasphemy of emperor worship ; but John prophesies that they will have the privilege of rising first from the dead. (Rev 14:2-3, 5) This prophecy will find fulfillment when the 144,000 rise and reign with Christ during the millennium which will precede the final judgment. (Rev 20:4) The

---

33. Cf. Adela Yarbro Collins, *The Combat Myth in the Book of Revelation* (Missoula, MT: Scholars Press, 1976).

34. . Cf. Roland Meynet, S.J., "Le cantique de Moise et le cantique de l'Agneau (Ap 15 et Ex 15)," *Gregorianum*, 73(1992), pp. 19-55.

third vision therefore celebrates the victory through martyrdom of those killed by Domitian.

A fifth vision of three prophetic angels follows. The first angel announces that the time of judgment has arrived. The second proclaims the immanent fall of Babylon, or Rome. The third foretells vengeance and torture for those who wear the sign of the beast. Finally a voice from heaven pronounces blest all those who have died in the Lord. The voice refers apparently to the 144,000 and to all Christian martyrs. The angels, therefore, announce the swift retribution which God will exact from imperial Rome for murdering His saints.[35] (Rev 14:6-13)

In the sixth set of visions, an angel resembling a son of man appears on a cloud carrying a sickle. (Rev 14:15) The image suggests the vision of the Son of Man in Daniel 7:13. This sickle bearing son of man seems to enjoy angelic status, since Rev 14:15 describes the appearance of "another angel" who commands the sickle bearer to begin the judgment by reaping the pagans. The sickle bearer's resemblance to the Son of Man in Dan 7:13 suggests that he acts in name of the Son of Man who appeared to John in Rev 1:13.

A second angel begins cutting down the pagans like vines and heaps them into a giant winepress of divine wrath outside the city of Jerusalem, the traditional place for the final destruction of the pagans. (Cf. Zech 14:2-21; Ezek 38-9) The Lamb and the 144,000 martyrs witness the destruction of their enemies. As the pagans are trodden underfoot in the winepress of God's wrath, the blood which flows from the press rises to the height of a horse's bridle. The flood of blood dramatizes the extent of the slaughter. (Rev 14:14-20)

God's vengeance against the pagans sets the stage for the annihilation of Rome itself. Seven bowl-bearing angels appear who will inflict the plagues which will destroy Rome once and for all. (Rev 15:1)

Before, however, the angels begin their work, John sees in a seventh vision all those who have fought victoriously against the beast from the sea standing by a glassy lake suffused with fire. The lake, as we have seen, lies before the throne of God. Into this flaming lake the enemies of the Lamb will soon find themselves hurled headlong. The 144,000 have harps and join in the song of the four angelic animals and the elders. They too celebrate the world's final exodus, its liberation from persecution, oppression, and idolatry. (Rev 15:2) They sing:

> Great and Wonderful are your deeds, O Lord God almighty! O King of the ages! Who shall not fear and glorify your name, O Lord? For you alone are holy. All nations shall come and worship you, for your judgments have been revealed. (Rev 15:3-4)

35. Cf. Aune, op. cit., pp. 282-283.

God will cast all the wicked into the fiery lake when, after destroying
Rome through the agency of the bowl-bearing angels, He executes judgment on the rest of the nations.[36] (Rev 20:14-5)

(VIII)

The visions of the seven bowls describe the destruction of Rome with
seven divinely inflicted plagues. The destruction of Rome by plagues ex-
plicates the exodus imagery implicit in the image of the seven plague
bearing angels. The prophet John, however, describes a cosmic exodus, as
each of the elements—earth, air, fire, and water—conspire to visit judgment and devastation on the enemies of God. The second coming which
will follow upon the visions of the bowls ushers in cosmic liberation.[37]

The Visions of the Bowls

John describes the first five visions of the bowls with a brevity which
gives the impression of a rapid crescendo of catastrophes visited upon
Rome and its minions. Only the servants of the beast suffer during the
plagues; but they remain blasphemously unrepentant to the end. (Rev
16:9, 11)

As the first angel empties its bowl all the servants of the beast break out
into disgusting an virulent sores. The emptying of the second bowl turns
the sea into blood. The emptying of the third bowl does the same for the
rivers and streams. Both plagues echo plagues in the first exodus. (Ex
7:14-24, 9:8-12) John, however, sees new symbolic meaning in the water
become blood. A voice from heaven announces that the plague of blood
justly repays Rome and its minions for the blood of the saints which they
have spilled.[38] (Rev 16:4-7) As the fourth angel empties its bowl, the sun
scorches the blaspheming servants of the beast. (Rev 16:8-9) The emptying of the fifth bowl plunges the world into darkness like the three day
darkness which preceded the plague of the firstborn in Exodus. (Rev
16:10-11; Ex 10:21-29) The darkness presages final retribution for Rome
just as it presaged final retribution for Egypt in the time of Moses.

As the sixth angel empties the sixth plague-filled bowl, the river
Euphrates dries up. In desperation the dragon Satan, the beast from the
sea (the Roman empire), and the beast from the land (the empire's human and institutional servants) all open their mouths and belch up frog
demons who rally the ten kingdoms allied to Rome. The armies gather at

36. Cf. Harrington, *op.cit.*, 164-198.
37. Cf. Adela Yarbro Collins, "The History of Religions Approach to Apocalypticism
    and the 'Angel of the Waters' (Rev. 16:4-7)," *Catholic Biblical Quarterly*, 39(1977),
    pp. 367-381.
38. Cf. Peter Staples, "Rev. XVI, 4-6 and Its Vindication Formula," *Novum Testamen-
    tum*, 14(1972), pp. 280-293.

Armageddon, the mountains of Megiddo, where the righteous king Josiah met overwhelming defeat. (2 Kings 23:29-30) Here as in Zech 12:11, Armageddon symbolizes disastrous defeat of the armies who gather there. The very gathering of the powers of evil therefore dooms them to final destruction. Before they meet utter destruction (Rev 19:17-21), however, the kings will join with Nero in his second coming in order to visit divine retribution on the city of Rome. That the prophesied "second coming" of Nero, the imperial anti-Christ, would finally destroy Rome once and for all seems to have suited the prophet John's ironic sense of justice.[39] (Rev 17:15-18)

As the seventh angel empties its bowl, a voice from heaven decrees the destruction of Rome itself. Lightning, thunder, and the most violent earthquake ever known split the city of Rome (Babylon) into three pieces. As it and all the other cities of the world collapse, giant hailstones bombard its blaspheming inhabitants. (Rev 16:17-21)

Three visions follow the emptying of the seventh bowl and describe in greater detail how Rome meets its final destruction. In the first, one of the angels carrying a bowl shows John a prostitute riding on the back of the beast from the sea carrying a gold cup filled with the filth of her fornication. On her forehead she bears the symbolic name: Babylon the Great. Drunk with the blood of Christian martyrs, she symbolizes the idolatrous city of Rome. The personification of Rome as a woman may in fact allude to the worship of the goddess Roma, which Augustus authorized in the cities of Pergamum, Nicomedia, and Nicea in the year 29 b.c.[40] (Rev 17:1-7, 18) After explaining the symbolism of the beast's seven heads and ten horns, the angel prophesies that the day will come when the nations will overcome the Roman empire and destroy the city of Rome. (Rev 17:8-18)

The next vision describes the fall of Rome. An angel descends from heaven and announces the city's immanent doom. The angel predicts that Nero, the beast who was, who is not, and who is to come, is about to destroy the city of Rome. An eighth emperor in virtue of his second coming, Nero yet belongs to the original seven emperors symbolized by the seven heads of the first beast. (Rev 17:8-11) Nero is about to assemble his allies, the ten kings symbolized by the ten horns of the first beast. (Rev 13:1) God will allow Nero the anti-Christ to rampage only for a short time, only until he destroys Rome and punishes it for all its crimes:

39. Michael Oberweis sees in Armageddon a cryptic reference to Nod and Gomorrah. In his reading, the assembled kings number among the descendants of Cain, the proto-fratricide. See: Michael Oberweis, "Erwägungen zu apokalyptischen Ortsbezeichnung," *Biblica*, 76(1995), pp. 305-324.

40. Cf. Ronald Mellor, *Thea Roma: The Worship of the Goddess Roma in the Greek World* (Göttingen: Vanderhoeck & Ruprecht, 1975), p. 140; Domingo Muños-León, "El Culto Imperial en el Apocalypsis," *Revista Biblica*, 56(1994), pp. 129-148.

And the ten horns which you saw [the ten kings], they and the beast [Nero] will hate the whore; they will make her desolate and naked; they will devour her flesh and burn her up with fire. For God has put it into their hearts to carry out his purpose by agreeing to give their kingdom to the beast until the words of God will be fulfilled. The woman you saw is the great city which rules over the kings of the earth. (Rev 17:16-18)

Another angel suddenly proclaims the fall of Rome (Babylon the great), who has corrupted the nations of the earth, fornicated idolatrously with kings, and through her merchants has grown rich at the expense of others. God calls His people out from the city before destroying it, as He once called Lot from Sodom. (Gen 19:12-26)

The prophet John has already identified Domitian as Nero *redivivus*. (Rev 13:11-18) Might one, then, see in his account of the fall of Rome an ironic use of the myth of Nero's return? By its persecution of the saints of Christ, the beast from the land, embodied in Domitian and his minions, have in fact sealed the destruction of the Roman whore (Rev 17: 1-7) in divine retribution for her and their sins. I find the suggestion somewhat speculative, but plausible.

Then all the nations and kingdoms of the earth mourn Rome's fall. (Rev 18:1-23) The merchants and seamen who, along with Rome, grew rich on Roman exploitation express special grief.[41] (Rev 18:15-20)

While the powers on earth mourn the passing of Rome, the heavens rejoice. In a third vision describing the fall of Rome, John witnesses the jubilation, which results not only from Rome's perpetual annihilation but also from the anticipation of Christ's second coming. Now that the Roman whore has died and her flesh turned into carrion the final judgment of the world can begin. (Rev 17:16; 19:1-10)

The heavenly rejoicing focuses especially on the coming marriage of the Lamb to His Bride, the new Jerusalem, (Cf. Rev 21:1-2) whose linen bridal gown will be made up of the good deeds of the saints. Though the bride of Christ receives this gown as a gift from God, nevertheless, the gift demands human collaboration: the saints' good deeds. (Rev 19: 7-9) The new Jerusalem will soon replace Rome, the idolatrous harlot.[42]

This joyous anticipation of the second coming marks the transition to the final series of visions, which describe how the second coming will transpire.[43]

---

41. Cf. Aune, *op. cit.*, pp. 284-285.
42. For an account of civil and political unrest in the Roman empire, see: Ramsay MacMullen, *Enemies of the Roman Order: Treason, Unrest, and Alienation in the Roman Empire* (Cambridge, MA: Harvard University Press, 1966).
43. Cf. Harrington, *op.cit.*, pp. 198-226.

(IX)

The first vision of the final series describes the second coming itself. Through an apocalyptic rent in the heavens symbolizing the end time, the Word of God appears riding on a white horse. John calls Him "Faithful" and "True," "a judge with integrity" and "a warrior for justice." He has the same flaming eyes of omniscience as in John's inaugural vision, eyes which penetrate to the depths of the heart and from which nothing can hide. The Word's omniscience insures the justice of the judgments which God pronounces through Him.

Visions of Final Judgment

As in the inaugural vision, moreover, a sharp sword also comes from the rider's mouth, the sword of the word of God with which He will now smite the pagans. His blood soaked cloak shows that he comes to fulfill the prophecy in Is 63:1-6 by taking vengeance on the nations. He wears on His coat and thigh the messianic titles: the King of Kings and the Lord of Lords. (Rev 19:11-16)

In the second vision of the final judgment, an angel summons carrion-eating birds to feast on the flesh of kings and of their armies, citizens, and slaves. (Rev 19:17-8) The summons foreshadows the immanent defeat of the armies of Anti-Christ which have just devastated Rome.

In the third vision, the two beasts, the Roman empire and its minions, together with their armies and allies suffer final defeat and annihilation. An angel hurls the captured beasts into the fiery lake of burning sulphur and slays all the survivors. The birds summoned in the preceding vision feast on the corpses. (Rev 19:19-21)

In the fourth vision, an angel confines Satan in the abyss for a thousand years. The 144,000 rise from their graves and during the thousand years of Satan's confinement reign with Christ. In Jewish apocalyptic the period of the end time functions as the period in which God finally fulfills the promises He made to righteous Jews through His Law and prophets. John, the Christian prophet, transforms this period of idyllic peace into a special reward for the victims of Domitian's persecution. In the book of Revelation, therefore, the millennium symbolizes the fact that those who suffer martyrdom will enjoy a special reward from God. John the prophet postpones the final destruction of Satan so that he can make this important point dramatically and narratively.

At the end of the saints' thousand-year reign, Satan emerges once again and marshals the armies of Gog and Magog to beseige God's faithful ones. Ezekiel prophesied that Gog, the king of Magog, would one day lead his armies against Israel only to suffer annihilation. (Ez 38:1-39:29) Accordingly, Satan suffers final and total defeat. Fire from heaven destroys his armies, while Satan finds himself hurled into the fiery lake to suffer the same annihilation as the two beasts. The trials of the saints have finally ended. (Rev 20:7-10)

In the fifth vision, God the Father appears seated on His throne. At His appearance the earth and sky vanish without a trace. The dead rise. The book of life is opened together with the other books in heaven which record the deeds by which God will judge the dead. (Rev 20:11-2) In the sixth vision, the dead rise from the sea of chaos and from Death and Hades. After the judgment, Death and Hades suffer the same fate as Satan, destruction in the fiery lake.[44]

In the seventh and culminating vision, the new Jerusalem descends from heaven as the bride of the Lamb. The voice from the divine throne itself, the Father's voice, proclaims the heavenly Jerusalem the city where God dwells with humans and consoles them for their former suffering.[45] (Rev 21:1-9) The heavenly city replaces imperial Rome.

One of the angels who had emptied a bowl of divine wrath upon Rome gives John a tour of the new Jerusalem. The golden city, filled with the glory of God, glitters like a jewel. It has twelve gates, three in each of its four walls. Each gate consists of a single giant pearl and bears a name of one of the tribes of Israel. At each gate stands an angel guardian like the angel who guarded the gate to Eden. (Gen 4: 24) Only the just shall enter the heavenly city. (Rev 21:8) The city's walls rise on twelve precious foundation stones which each bears the name of one of the apostles. (Rev 21:9-21) The gates and their foundation stones symbolize that the new Jerusalem embodies the glorified new Israel. The city rests upon the apostolic witness which the Old Testament prepared. In other words, the new Jerusalem sums up and fulfills both testaments, the whole of salvation history.

The city has no temple because God and the Lamb are its temple. Their radiant glory replaces the sun and moon. Darkness had ended. Nothing unclean can enter the city. The uncleanness implies more than ritual impurity. The divine presence excludes all sin from the heavenly Jerusalem.

From the throne of God and of the Lamb a crystalline river of life flows down the center of the street on whose banks grow trees of life which bear twelve times a year and whose leaves heal the nations, whose kings come streaming with gifts and treasures to its pearly gates. (Rev 21:22-22:2) The new Jerusalem exceeds Eden which had only one tree of life. (Gen 3:24) The abundance and extraordinary fruitfulness of the trees guarantees perpetual life and healing to the city's citizens.

As in Zech 14:11, the curse is lifted from the heavenly city as a sign that nothing threatens its security. The inhabitants of the city see God

---

44. Cf. Ellul, *op.cit.*, pp. 171-213.
45. Cf. Aune, *op. cit.*, pp. 286-288.

and the Lamb face to face. They bear the names of God and of the Lamb on their foreheads; and they worship God and the Lamb seated in victorious triumph on their thrones. God has become the light of the glorified saints; and with God they reign happily forever.[46] (Rev 22:3-5)

The Epilogue

The book of Revelation closes with a series of loosely related pronouncements and admonitions. Three of them have Christological significance.

In an oracle delivered by an angel, Christ identifies Himself as the Alpha and Omega, the creator and end of all things. He promises that He will come soon to reward each person according to his or her deeds. The promise suggests that the prophet John hoped that final judgment would follow upon Rome's destruction. Those who have washed their robes clean (i.e., those who have passed through the time of tribulation and been washed clean of sin by the blood of the Lamb) will enter the heavenly Jerusalem and feed forever on the trees of life, while outside its walls languish the fortune-tellers, fornicators, murderers, idolaters, and liars. (Rev 22:12-5) They suffer the second death in the fiery lake. (Rev 21:8)

In the second oracle, Jesus speaking in His own name identifies Himself as the source of John's revelation. He speaks as the messianic root of David, and as the morning star, a symbol of divinity in the near east.[47] (Rev 22:16)

The book ends with a third oracle. Jesus' promise that He will come soon. John responds to that promise: "Amen, Come, Lord Jesus." Finally, the prophet wishes "the grace of the Lord Jesus" to all the churches to which he is writing. (Rev 22:20-1)[48]

I have considered the origins and shape of Jewish apocalyptic writing and the place of the book of Revelation within the apocalyptic tradition. I have also examined the book's literary structure in an attempt to understand its message. The chapter which follows distills from Revelation a Christology of hope which speaks to the needs of contemporary Christians.

---

46. Cf. Ellul, *op.cit.*, pp. 215-255. For a discussion of the symbolism surrounding the structure of the heavenly Jerusalem, see: Farrer, *op.cit.*, pp. 185-244. See also: Gale Z. Heide, "What is New about the New Heaven and the New Earth? A Theology of Creation from Revelation 21 and 2 Peter 3," *Journal of the Evangelical Society*, 40(1997), pp. 37-56.

47. Cf. David E. Aune, "The Prophetic Circle of John of Patmos and the Exegesis of Revelation 22.16," *Journal for the Study of the New Testament*, 37(1989), pp. 103-116.

48. Cf. Harrington, *op.cit.*, pp. 226-275.

Chapter 20
Revelation as Christian Myth

This chapter reflects on the relevance of the apocalyptic Christology of the book of Revelation to contemporary Christian hope. It divides into three parts. Part one reflects on Revelation as a Christian prophecy, as a Christian myth, and as a Christian classic. Part two compares and contrasts the apocalyptic Christology of Paul and of Revelation. Part three examines the contribution which apocalyptic Christology makes to an understanding of contemporary Christian conversion.

(I)
The book of Revelation develops a special kind of narrative Christology. As we shall see in greater detail in the second volume of this study, narrative Christology makes a statement about Jesus as Christ by telling a story. The Christological statement emerges as the plot, or quasi-plot, and imagery unfold. One understands who Jesus Christ is by the way the story teller describes Him and by the way He relates to the other characters and (often personified) forces in the story.

As in the case of Jewish Apocalyptic the subversive, anti-imperial message of the book of Revelation helps explain its obscurantism; but other doctrinal concerns help shape this book's often dense and puzzling imagery. As we have seen, sometimes layers of images thicken the symbolic meaning. In point of fact, the obscurity of the imagery accords well with the mystery which surrounds the end time, the second coming, and the final judgment.

The book of Revelation made a prophecy. It foretold the destruction of the Roman empire prior to the second coming of Christ. That prophecy came true. The symbolic events which John describes did not happen exactly as he narrates them; but the prophet John never intended to write a literal account of future events. In fact, Rome and its empire did suffer the annihilation which he predicted symbolically and metaphorically.

Revelation, however, does more than predict the fall of Rome. It constructs a myth about the end time. Myths differ from fairy tales. By a fairy tale I mean a story which one can give as a gift to a small child. Myths do not address children; they address adults.

Viewed as narrative, myths and parables have diametrically opposed purposes. A parable tells a story which subverts a familiar world in order to open the hearer to new ways of perceiving reality. A myth, by contrast, creates an adult world of reality, value, and meaning in which to live.

Not all myths count as religious. Literary myths, for example, create fictional worlds. The myth of Yoknapatapha county, for example, creates the world in which William Faulkner's characters live, love, hate, and die. *The Silmarillion* creates Middle Earth.

Religious myths create religious worlds of reality, value, and meaning. Moreover, religious myths about either the creation or end of all things make a statement which aspires to universality because it describes the origin or destiny of all created reality. Myths of origins and of ends, therefore, function in intuitive thinking in the same way in which metaphysical hypotheses function in inferential thinking. Both give an account of reality in general.

A classic piece of literature speaks not only to the people in the generation which gave rise to it but also to subsequent generations. When we view the book of Revelation as a Christian myth of the end time, it takes on the characteristics of a Christian classic; for, when read as myth, Revelation acquires the power to speak to the needs of every generation of Christians. In order to analyze the book of Revelation as a Christian myth and understand it as a Christian classic, one needs then to answer the question: What kind of religious world does this story create?

Myths create worlds of reality, value, and meaning. What kinds of religious realities, then, does Revelation describe? Revelation proclaims Jesus as God incarnate. Jesus possesses the divine name. In describing Jesus as eschatological judge, John combines in Him traits derived both from the Son of Man and from the Ancient of Days in the book of Daniel. Jesus' possession of the same traits as Yahweh, the Ancient of Days, symbolizes His union with the Father. At the same time, the risen Christ's simultaneous identification with Daniel's Son of Man also makes Him human and distinct from the Father. In virtue of His incarnation, atoning death, and resurrection, the risen Christ confronts the world as its divine, glorified, eschatological judge.

Besides identifying Jesus with the Ancient of Days, John uses other descriptive imagery in order to assert His divinity. He holds the angels in His hand and commands their obedience, something only God can do. His seven eyes symbolize the omniscient perfection of His knowledge, as does His fiery, all-penetrating gaze. With the Father, the Son creates the world. With the Father, He embodies the reason why everything exists.

Jesus' incarnation, death, and resurrection constitute Him final judge of the world. His atoning death washes away the sins of all who believe in Him. It reveals Him as the paschal lamb whose sacrificial blood seals a new covenant. His death also identifies Him as the suffering servant whose innocent passion reconciles the repentant to God. Jesus' resurrection reveals Him as the victorious Lamb of Jewish apocalyptic.

Since only God forgives sin, the fact that Jesus' death and resurrection effect the forgiveness of sin reveals that He possesses divine judicial authority. God has appointed Him to judge the world. Jesus' unique possession of divine judicial authority empowers Him and Him alone to break the seals which reveal the course of history and ultimately the final judgment. As apocalyptic judge the risen Christ presides over the entire course of salvation history.

The divine authority revealed in the death and glorification of Jesus imply His creative power; for, if the Son stands historically revealed through His death and glorification as the one through whom God acts upon the world to save and judge it, then the Son also stands historically revealed as the spoken Word of God, as the one through whom God does whatever He chooses to do to creation, including its origination.

The resurrection reveals the divinity of Christ. John does not speak in Revelation of Jesus' sending of the Holy Breath; but he does describe Jesus as present and actively addressing the Church through the power of the Breath, especially through the Breath of prophecy.

The words inspired by the prophetic Breath, count as Jesus' own words to His churches. Moreover, Christ, the victorious Lamb, remains actively present to and within the churches despite suffering, persecution, or even martyrdom. He protects them from sin but not from suffering; for they, like He, enter into glory through sharing in the suffering of His passion, in which they participate as His priestly people.

John the prophet portrays human suffering, misery, and oppression as the direct consequence of sin. Like sin, suffering results from the intransigent refusal of the human heart to repent and accept the forgiveness of Christ. Sin destroys both people and nature. In Revelation sin alone motivates God's cataclysmic acts of judgment. Moreover, the violence with which God punishes sin dramatizes its heinousness. The more sinners heap up crimes, the more they transform themselves into His enemies.

In virtue of His incarnation, death, and glorification, Jesus also confronts the reader as priest and messiah, as the unique mediator between heaven and earth. His atoning death washes away sin. His death and glorification establish a new covenant with God, a marriage covenant of love which transforms the redeemed into the bride of Christ.

In Revelation, moreover, Jesus's judicial, messianic, and priestly authority all coincide. As messianic king and judge, the glorified Christ casts Satan out of heaven, because the court of the Father has no need for an accusing, angelic prosecuting attorney. The decisive victory He wins by dying and rising insures that the powers of evil will never overcome the new Israel He has established no matter how cruelly those powers persecute her members. Moreover, Jesus shares both His priestly mediatorial authority and his messianic, judicial authority with those who confess Him faithfully even to death. The new priestly Israel mediates God to the world and in virtue of its faithful witness will sit with the messiah on thrones of judgment. In other words, their witness to Christ prepares God's final judgment of their enemies.

Like Jesus Himself, Revelation inculcates non-violent prophetic opposition to the forces of anti-Christ. That opposition draws the saints into Jesus' atoning passion and victory over sin, suffering, and death. The sufferings of the Church prolong the passion of Jesus. The same forces which conspired to kill Him now slaughter His holy ones.

In a sense, moreover, the historical disclosure of God's judgment upon human sin prolongs in space and time the revelation of Jesus' resurrection. It does so by disclosing the full scope of His victory of over sin, suffering, oppression, and finally over death itself. The resurrection empowers saints of every generation to bear faithful witness to Christ even through martyrdom.[1]

Myths endow realities with meaning. Religious myths make a statement about both created and transcendent realities. Myths, however, also inculcate values. They do so by describing the conflict between good and evil. They require, therefore, that those who live within the myth identify with the forces of good and repudiate the forces of evil. Viewed as myth, the book of Revelation describes the battle between the risen Christ and the forces of anti-Christ.

In the final conflict between God and the Lamb, on the one hand, and Satan and the forces of evil, on the other, politically oppressive, economically exploitative, and religiously blasphemous institutions like the Roman empire embody the anti-Christ. They incarnate everything which contradicts the revelation of divine forgiveness in Christ. The violence of the forces of anti-Christ causes their own violent destruction at the hands of the divine judge. Those who choose to live by the sword also perish by it. (Rev 13:14) Although John focuses, for obvious historical reasons, on the oppressive Roman empire, what he says applies to any analogous systematic human institutionalization of sin, injustice, oppression, and unbelief.

Resurrection with Christ incorporates one into the heavenly Jerusalem. It transforms one into the bride of Christ by bringing to consummation the love which here on earth binds believers to the risen Lord. Those who experience that consummation see God face-to-face and respond to that revelation with joyous love and praise. This everlasting consummation of love between a creating, redeeming God and those who confess Him reveals the full scope of the divine love incarnate in the

---

1. Cf. Adela Yarbro Collins, "The Political Perspective of the Revelation of John," *Journal of Biblical Literature*, 96(1977), pp. 241-256.

death and resurrection of Jesus. John the prophet hoped, probably expected, that the second coming of Christ would happen soon. In that he echoed the longing of the early Church for the final consummation of the love it bore to the Lamb and to the Father He discloses.

I have reflected on Revelation as a Christian myth of the end time and distilled from it an apocalyptic Christology of hope. In the following section, I shall compare and contrast the apocalyptic Christologies of Paul the apostle and of John the prophet.

(II)

One finds some remarkable points of convergence and of agreement between Paul's understanding of Christ and the Christ portrayed in the book of Revelation. In both Christologies, the resurrection reveals the divinity of Jesus. In both, the Father judges the world through the Son, the Lamb. In both Paul and Revelation, the disclosure of Jesus' divinity in His resurrection simultaneously manifests His messianic authority to rule and judge the nations.

Both Paul and Revelation see in the death of Jesus a sacrificial act of atonement which reconciles believers to God. Both regard His death as a covenant sacrifice.

In both Paul and Revelation, the sufferings of the Church prolong historically the passion of Jesus. Both therefore look upon salvation history with sober realism. The redemption which Jesus brings keeps one safe (i.e., saved, united to God) in the midst of natural disasters, suffering, and persecution; but it does not necessarily exempt one from these evils. Rather through union with Jesus in His redemptive death one triumphs over the dark powers.

In both Paul and Revelation, incorporation into the new Israel commits one to do active battle with the principalities and power of this world. In both Christologies, the salvation and the judgment which Jesus brings have both social and cosmic consequences.

In both Paul and Revelation, final resurrection culminates in personal and communal union with God and Christ. The apocalyptic Paul speaks of that union in terms of rapture into heaven with Christ. Elsewhere he describes it as the culmination of the pneumatic life which baptism communicates to believers, or as face-to-face vision, or as the perfection of love. Revelation imagines perfect union with God as the heavenly Jerusalem. John portrays the heavenly city as the bride of Christ and union with God as the consummation of one's marital covenant with God. Both Paul and the prophet John believe that in the next life the saints enjoy the immediate, face-to-face vision of God, who imparts to them a share in the risen life of Christ.

One also finds significant contrasts between Pauline Christology and the apocalyptic Christology of the book of Revelation. The book of Revelation stresses more than Paul does Christ's priesthood and the Church's participation through prayer and suffering in His priestly mediation between God and the world. The apocalyptic Christology of the book of Revelation also insists much more explicitly than Paul does that the risen Christ, the victorious Lamb who was slain, presides over the whole of salvation history as well as over the final judgment.

Needless to say, the book of Revelation provides a much richer font of apocalyptic images than does the surviving apocalyptic Christology of Paul. One thinks of cosmic woes, plague breathing horses, demon locusts, the beasts from the sea and land, angelic battles, the heavenly sanctuary, the fiery lake, the heavenly Jerusalem. I shall reflect below on the emotional impact of these images.

The book of Revelation also renders with much greater concreteness than Paul the nature of human opposition to God. Paul, in second Thessalonians, refers, as we have seen, to "the man of lawlessness" and to a final rebellion against God. Paul also speaks of doing battle against the principalities and powers of this world. In the book of Revelation, human opposition to God takes concrete, historical shape in the Roman Empire, in its minions, and in its allies. They become symbolically incarnated in the beasts from the sea and land, in the blasphemous talking statue, and in the whore of Babylon.

John the Prophet clearly hoped, vainly as it turned out, that with the collapse of Rome the reign of Satan would end. The apocalyptic Christology of Paul and of Revelation would, however, seem to agree in expecting human opposition to God to intensify before the final judgment; but they use different images to symbolize that opposition.

Perhaps Pauline Christology and the Christology of Revelation differ most dramatically in the way in which they depict the relationship of Christ to the Breath. As we have seen, at the heart of the Pauline witness to the risen Christ lies the apostle's testimony that in His resurrection Jesus "became a life-giving Breath." For Paul the emanation of the Breath from the risen Christ reveals their vital and functional identity. In Paul the Breath of the risen Christ comes to those who believe in order to conform them to Him through justification, sanctification, and charismatic empowerment. Her procession from the risen Jesus reveals Him as fully divine. The notion of God's Breath, however, remains undeveloped in Revelation. The book of Revelation refers only to a Breath of prophecy, whose relationship to "the Holy Breath" remains symbolically vague, even though the two may very well coincide.

Pauline Christology also insists more than does the Christology of Revelation on the universality of the salvation accomplished in Christ. The image of Christ as the last Adam symbolizes for Paul the graced recreation of the whole human race through its share in the paschal mystery. Paul's insistence on universal salvation in Christ reflects, of course, his struggle to include baptized Gentiles in the new Israel on the same footing as baptized Jews.

The book of Revelation apparently emerges from an embattled Church on the eve of persecution. It therefore tends to view the Gentile world with uniform hostility. Paganism finds its ultimate sinful embodiment in the Roman empire and in every evil which it symbolizes. The beast of Rome precisely because it incarnates everything opposed to Christ must in the end suffer the same fate as Satan: the second death by drowning in the fiery lake of divine judgment, just as Pharaoh and his armies perished in the Red Sea.

The adversarial stance which the book of Revelation takes toward a hostile pagan world of sinfulness and unbelief politicizes its rhetoric. More than Pauline Christology, the apocalyptic Christology of the book of Revelation insists on social, political, and economic implications of hope in Jesus the savior. In the eyes of John the prophet, the social, political, and economical oppression wrought by the Roman empire marks it as the anti-Christ. As Satan's instrument, the empire persecutes Christians and others who refuse to perform the blasphemous act of emperor worship. Rome incarnates everything which contradicts the redemption which Christ came to bring: greed, economic exploitation of the poor and helpless, coercive violence, and political oppression.

Both Paul and Revelation agree that faith and hope in Jesus Christ pits one against the forces of anti-Christ. The book of Revelation, however, addresses a Church threatened with immanent persecution at the hands of imperial Rome. The violence and injustice of that confrontation leaves no doubt in the prophet John's mind that the kingdom of Satan takes institutional shape in imperial Rome. As a consequence, the apocalyptic Christology in Revelation makes it even clearer than does Pauline Christology, that Christian hope pits one in implacable opposition to all such corrupt and corrupting institutional forces.

The book of Revelation also insists even more explicitly than Paul does on the non-violent character of that opposition. Christians in Revelation oppose the beasts from the land and from the sea with no other weapons than the prophetic word of Christ. Armed with the word, the victims of persecution must trust in Jesus' ability to save them through their participation in His passion.

The author of Revelation denounces prophetically the violence of oppressive political structures like the Roman empire. He does so in full expectation that such opposition will lead to martyrdom. That danger, however, does not allow the Christian prophet either to mince words or to hide his identity behind a pseudonym. He names without flinching the evil embodied in the beasts from the sea and from the land at the same time that he longs for their ultimate destruction and replacement by the heavenly Jerusalem.

The book of Revelation narrates, then, a non-violent Christology of liberation. Revelation also asserts more clearly than Paul does that non-violent confrontation with the institutional forces of sin, unbelief, oppression, and violence lies at the heart of Christian hope. In longing for the second coming, Christians of necessity simultaneously yearn for the destruction of Satan's empire. That empire takes concrete, blasphemous, and incarnate form in all human institutions of enslavement and oppression.

(III)

The preceding sections of this chapter have virtually completed the implementation of the strategy I suggested for solving the problem of contemporary access to the book of Revelation. Only one task remains: namely, to reflect on the contribution which the book of Revelation makes to a contemporary theology of conversion.

This chapter and the preceding one have studied the book of Revelation for the light its Christology throws upon the experience of Christian conversion. Apocalyptic Christology speaks in a special way to Christian hope. It informs Christian longing for the future with a vision of salvation history and of the end time. What, then, does this book of the New Testament have to tell us about the way in which faith in Jesus Christ transforms and transvalues natural and sinful human hopes?

Imagination and Hope

First of all, the book of Revelation forces contemporary Christians to face in a dramatic way the intimate relation between imagination and Christian hope. Christian hope seeks to transform human affective longing for the future. One cannot, however, long for a Christian future until one begins to imagine reality in a Christian way.

Like Pauline Christology, the book of Revelation makes it clear that a Christian imaginative vision of the world has to root itself in the paschal mystery and in the incarnational realities which it reveals. In order to hope as a Christian one needs to be able to imagine God incarnate, the very reality of deity embodied in the crucified and glorified Jesus.

Not every human imagination can do that. The Christian imagination finds ultimate meaning, ultimate reality, ultimate purpose embodied in reality when created reality undergoes saving transformation in the reality of God.

Some natural human imaginations, by contrast, recoil in suspicion or even disgust from the concrete, the sensible, the physical. They seek instead to find ultimate meaning, purpose, and reality exclusively within human subjectivity. Such an imagination often characterizes the inflated, introverted ego. Other human imaginations can only see in physical reality something to exploit, often for selfish or myopic human ends. They find in the concrete, the sensible, the physical only an instrument for achieving self-reliantly one's own self-fulfillment or self-advancement. Such an imagination often typifies an inflated, extraverted ego. Some people have imaginations of despair. They find no meaning in the concrete sensible world; and, when they seek for meaning in their own subjective consciousness, they find there only chaos, confusion, disorder. Such tormented souls run the risk of sinking helplessly into madness and self-destruction. Such an imagination often flows from a deflated, introverted ego. Some people have cynical imaginations. They can imagine nothing beyond concrete sensible facts, nothing beyond the physical universe. They face death as meaningless annihilation. Such an imagination often expresses a deflated, extraverted ego.[2]

The imaginative visions of the book of Revelation call the unconverted human imagination beyond the emotional inflation and deflation exemplified in each of the preceding natural and sinful human imaginations. The book of Revelation portrays a world in process of transformation in the paschal mystery: in the death and glorification of the incarnate Son of God. Here Pauline Christology can supplement the book of Revelation by calling more explicit attention than it does to the role which the saving Breath of God plays within the paschal mystery.

Revelation itself, however, envisions the world as a cosmic reality into which the paschal mystery has suddenly and unpredictably erupted. It depicts the victorious Lamb as the Lord of history. He alone has the authority to break the seal and unroll the scroll of the future. The book of Revelation discovers in Jesus, the failed and crucified prophet of Nazareth, the Son of God made flesh, co-creator with the Father, and apocalyptic judge of the universe.

Besides challenging the Christian convert to imagine reality in thoroughly incarnational terms, the book of Revelation also challenges Christians, both personally and collectively to constant self-scrutiny and ongoing conversion. Revelation paints no idyllic vision of the world in which

2. For further discussion of the modalities of the imagination, see: William Lynch, *Christ and Apollo* (New York, NY: Mentor, 1960); Donald L. Gelpi, S.J. *Experiencing God: A Theology of Human Emergence* (Lanham, MD: University Press of America, 1987), pp. 135-152; Gerald J. Bednar, *Faith as Imagination: The Contribution of William F. Lynch, S.J.* (Kansas City, KA: Sheed & Ward, 1996).

we live. It tells us to expect a future marked by suffering and natural disasters. It warns that until the second coming the followers of Jesus must do battle with Satan, with his beasts, and with the institutionalized unbelief and oppression which they symbolize.

In our day, the Satanic beasts take different institutional form: economic colonialism, capitalistic greed, militarism, arms proliferation, homelessness, racism, sexism, homophobia, anti-Semitism, chauvinism, classism, ruthless political regimes, secular unbelief. Contemporary Christians need to name with the same unflinching honesty as John the prophet the shape which the beast from the land takes in our own day.

Given the fragility, tragedy, and suffering of the human condition and given the implacable enmity of both the Satanic beasts, Christians have no choice, the book of Revelation warns, but to face squarely the challenge of ongoing conversion. Moreover, that conversion must unfold in non-violent confrontation with institutionalized evil (the beast from the sea) and with those whom it corrupts (the beast from the land).

Revelation also teaches contemporary Christians to recognize that conversion has both a personal and an ecclesial aspect. Revelation does not require only individual Christians to convert. The angels of the churches must convert as well. Those "angels" personify the way in which any give Christian community, whether local or world-wide, has incarnated either repentant faith or religious hypocrisy.

As ongoing converts, therefore, Christians must deal simultaneously with two different but interrelated institutionalizations of evil: one secular, the other ecclesiastical. Besides facing the impact of secular sin upon their lives, they must also confront the ways in which the churches themselves encourage complacency, religious hypocrisy, and the lack of converted commitment to Christ. The danger to Christian commitment posed by secular institutionalizations of evil poses challenge enough. When one adds to it the danger which stems from institutionalized hypocrisy and oppression within the Church itself, one can only respond adequately to both challenges by constant vigilance, as the book of Revelation eloquently warns.

The book of Revelation preaches a Christian ethic of non-violent, prophetic opposition to evil; yet the book teems with images of violence. Adela Yarbro Collins has argued persuasively that the violent cataclysmic images of Revelation originally served a cathartic purpose. They allowed a powerless Church threatened with persecution and martyrdom to express and to face its fear and resentment of Roman violence without imitating that violence.[3]

---

3. Cf Adela Yarbro Collins, *Crisis and Catharsis: The Power of Apocalypse* (Philadelphia, PA: Westminster, 1984).

The violence of the apocalyptic Christian imagery also conveys through narrative the heinousness of institutionalized evil. The violent images dramatize both the destructive power and the self-destructive potential of institutionalized sin.

The violent images of Revelation do not sanction Christian violence. Instead, they warn Christians of the disastrous consequences of being co-opted by institutional violence and oppression. Intransigent sinfulness and the refusal to hear the gospel will inexorably result in human tragedy and in cosmic disaster. Today in a world which still confronts the possibility of nuclear holocaust and which is only beginning to face the consequences of planetary environmental degradation, the images of cosmic woe in the book of Revelation contain an ominous warning.

The prophetic tone of Revelation invites its readers to repentance, conversion, and healing. The cataclysmic violence of the book warns of the tragic consequences of the sinful abuse of human freedom. Humans must choose finally between salvation and damnation, between human life or human destruction, between cosmic healing or cosmic devastation.

The book of Revelation makes no bones about the fact that following Jesus draws one inexorably into His passion. Non-violent resistance to both the Satanic beasts does not, however, mean supine suffering at their violent hands. On the contrary, it demands prophetic confrontation with those same forces, even though the confrontation cost one one's life. The book of Revelation also proclaims that non-violent confrontation with the Satanic beasts springs from confident assurance that the Lamb who was slain has already won the victory.

Finally, the book of Revelation challenges contemporary Christian converts to revive their longing for the second coming of Christ. Christians have long since ceased to expect the second coming to happen tomorrow. Longing for the second coming, however, roots itself in more than in the expectation of its immanence. Christian apocalyptic yearns for an end to the "birth pangs of the messiah." Those sufferings will end only when the evil forces of Anti-Christ have yielded to the full and final realization of God's reign.

Ordinarily, one can measure the intensity of Christian longing for the heavenly Jerusalem by the intensity of Christian opposition to institutional violence and to those who inflict it. Too many contemporary Christians have lost interest in the heavenly Jerusalem because they live insulated by comfort and affluence from the suffering, oppression, and injustice which the poor confront on a day-to-day basis.

Christian conversion challenges sheltered and affluent Christians to shed their complacency. In order to do that, they need to enter personally and collectively into the struggle with corporate sin and injustice. They need to see with their own eyes the consequences of corporate injustice in the pain-filled faces of the hungry, the broken, and the tortured. They need to begin to learn to confront the forces of anti-Christ with the same courage as the prophet John. When contemporary Christians enter into militant, non-violent opposition to the kingdom of Satan in all of its intransigent institutional incarnations, they will, I predict, find new meaning in the prayer which closes the book of Revelation: "*Maranatha.* Come, Lord Jesus."

The apocalyptic Christology in the book of Revelation provides an important complement to a Pauline Christology of hope. Pauline Christology articulates in many ways a more adequate doctrinal foundation for Christological hope. The apostle's insight into the way in which the paschal mystery transforms the future gives eloquent expression to shared Christian longing. The apocalyptic Christology of the book of Revelation, however, emerges from a Church in direct and violent confrontation with institutional injustice at its intransigent worst. Its Christological vision succeeds better than Paul's does in making it clear to converts that Christian hope remains immature and partial until it draws one actively into direct, non-violent, prophetic confrontation with the institutional forces of anti-Christ. Unless confronted and transformed in the redeeming love of Christ, those same forces have the power to co-opt and to corrupt both Church and secular society. Corrupt institutions warp human consciences to violent and Satanic ends.

I am not suggesting that every converting Christian needs to master the book of Revelation's arcane imagery. Every converting Christian does, however, need to respond to the challenges which its apocalyptic Christology poses. Those challenges include the following: 1) the development of a thoroughly incarnational imagination; 2) the necessity for a socio-political conversion which deals actively and prophetically with institutional injustice; 3) responsible criticism of ecclesial institutionalizations of religious hypocrisy and mediocrity; and 4) an eschatological yearning for the second coming rooted in compassion for perennial human suffering and tragedy. Any RCIA program which fails to inculcate all these attitudes sells its adult catechumens seriously short. Any Christian who fails to appropriate all these attitudes still has much to learn about the demands of integral conversion.

Glossary

ABDUCTION: in pragmatic logic, an inference which concludes to a case from a rule and a result; in other words, an inference which gives an initial classification to data in need of explanation on the basis of a law assumed to function in reality; the formulation of an hypothesis

ABSOLUTE: unconditioned; as an ethical category, commitment to particular ideals and principles no matter what the circumstance

ABSTRACT: lacking concreteness

ACCOMMODATION: adjustment; in developmental psychology, adaptive growth

ACT: as a technical philosophical term, the determination of a potency

ACTUAL: in a metaphysics of experience, factual, or pertaining to the realm of decision

ADAPTATION: change with regard to a situation; in developmental psychology, adjustment to an environment through accommodation or assimilation

ADOPTIONISM: the heterodox doctrine that Jesus first existed as a human person and only subsequently became the Son of God by an act of divine grace

AESTHETICS: in pragmatic logic, the normative study of ideals and of the habitual forms of behavior which appreciate and respond to them

AFFECT ATTUNEMENT: in social psychology, the capacity of an adult to share empathetically and symbolically in the emotional experiences of an infant and vice versa

AFFECTION: in a metaphysics of experience, the emotive perception or judgment of reality

AFFECTIVE CONVERSION: the decision to take adult responsibility for one's own subsequent emotional development

ANALOGY: similarity in difference

ANALYTIC: dividing into elemental parts or basic principles

ANONYMOUS CHRISTIAN: the questionable theological doctrine that all persons experience an *a priori*, graced orientation to Jesus Christ prior to the act of faith in Him

ANTHROPOLOGY: a more or less organized account of the human

APOCALYPTIC: revelatory

APOCALYPTIC THEOLOGY: a visionary account of the end time: i.e., of the final stage or salvation and of final judgment

APOLLONARIANISM: the heterodox doctrine that in the incarnation Jesus' divinity and humanity blend into a third theandric reality

APOPHATIC THEOLOGY: a doctrine of God which holds that created reality can only reveal what God is not

A PRIORI: before the fact; the character of an argument which fallaciously claims validity without evidence to support it

ARIANISM: the heterodox theological denial of the divinity of Jesus and of his divine Breath

ASSIMILATION: in developmental psychology, biological adaptation through ingestion

ATHEISM: the denial of the reality of God
  PRACTICAL: the failure to accept the practical consequences of one's alleged belief in God
ATONEMENT: reconciliation; the restoration of a ruptured relationship by accepting the suffering which reconciliation requires
AUTONOMY: in a metaphysics of experience, the bare capacity to initiate activity
BEATIFIC VISION: the face-to-face vision of God in the next life
BEAUTY: the intuitive perception of excellence; the simultaneous intuitive grasp of goodness and of truth in some reality
BEING: really existing
BELIEF: in pragmatic logic, a proposition for whose consequences one stands willing to assume responsibility
BIBLICAL CHRISTOLOGY: an account of what the New Testament says about Jesus Christ
BIGOTRY: rigid stereotyping of the members of an out-group combined with overt hostility toward them
BLASPHEMY: insulting God
BODY: in a metaphysics of experience, the immediate environment from which a finite self emerges
CAPITALISM: an economic system which buys human labor for producing, handling and marketing goods, which promotes a so-called[1] free market system as well as the private and corporate ownership of the means of production, and which seeks to maximize the profits of businesses and corporate investors
CASE: in pragmatic logic, the classification of data in inferential thinking
CATECHUMENATE: an organized period of preparation for receiving the sacraments of Christian initiation
CATEGORY: a predicate; an concept used in interpreting reality
CELIBACY: the deliberate renunciation of genital sex
CERTAIN: beyond the shadow of a doubt
CHALCEDONIAN CHRISTOLOGY: the doctrine that the person of Jesus unites His divinity and His humanity without blending them into a third reality
CHRISTIAN CONVERSION: the decision to respond to the revelation of God in Jesus Christ and in the mission of His Breath on the terms which that revelation demands
CHRISTIAN ORIGINS, CRITERION OF: a norm for authenticating historically words or actions of Jesus which asserts that any historical portrait of Jesus must offer a plausible account of how the movement He headed could have evolved into the Christian Church
CHRISTOLOGICAL QUESTION, THE: asking how divinity and humanity relate in the person of Jesus

---

1. The freedom of the capitalistic market varies with one's economic assets. Wealthy corporations, the rich, and the affluent experience considerable freedom in a capitalistic market. The starving poor tend to find it oppressive rather than liberating.

CHRISTOLOGY: a more or less organized account of the person and ministry of Jesus Christ

OF HOPE: a foundational theological account of how commitment to Jesus Christ in justifying faith heals, perfects, and elevates natural and sinful human hopes

NARRATIVE: a foundational theological account of how commitment to Jesus Christ in justifying faith transforms intuitive perceptions of His person and mission communicated in story form

DOCTRINAL: a foundational theological account of how commitment to Jesus Christ in justifying faith transforms inferential perceptions in faith of His person and mission

PRACTICAL: a foundational theological account of how commitment to Jesus Christ in justifying faith transforms both personal moral conversion and socio-political conversion

CHRISTOPRAXIS: living out the practical consequences of commitment to Jesus Christ in justifying faith

CLASSIC: a work of art or literature which from generation to generation makes human life and experience meaningful

CLASSISM: the fallacious ideological justification of giving to one or more social groups privileged access to the benefits of a society to the detriment and even oppression of other social groups

CO-EXISTENCE: the simultaneous enjoyment of reality

COHERENCE, CRITERION OF: a norm for authenticating as historical words and actions of Jesus on the basis of their compatibility with other words and actions already authenticated by other norms

COLONIALISM: a policy which extends and maintains the control of one nation over foreign dependencies

COMMON GOOD: a social arrangement which ensures that every member of society has the opportunity to share with reasonable adequacy in that society's benefits and to contribute to those same benefits

COMMON SENSE: colloquially, the ability to deal realistically with one's world; as a technical philosophical term, the power to correlate sense perceptions

COMMUNICATIO IDIOMATUM: literally, Latin for "the communication of traits"; in theology, a doctrinal account of the way human and divine traits relate in Jesus Christ

COMMUNICATION: in a metaphysics of experience, symbolic activity which expresses to one mind the evaluative perceptions of another about some entity

COMMUNICATIONS: a functional theological specialty which uses the results of theological reflection in order to re-establish dialogue among the members of a religious community when lack of conversion causes dialogue to break down

CONCEPT: in a metaphysics of experience, a particular way of responding evaluatively to one's world

CONCUPISCENCE: those corrupting forces in the environment of a baptized person immanent to experience which differ from that person's own sins but which nevertheless come from sin and lead to sin

CONSCIENCE: personal judgment of moral right and wrong

CONSCIOUSNESS: awareness

PERSONAL: awareness which begins with distinguishing one's own body from its surrounding environment and which develops by making distinctions and asserting relationships

COMMUNAL: the consciousness of a community which results from its shared memories, shared hopes, shared lives, practice of atoning love and degree of conversion

CONVERSION: the decision to pass from irresponsible to responsible behavior in some realm of human experience

INITIAL: one's first assumption of adult responsibility in some realm of experience

ONGOING: living out the consequences of initial conversion

COORDINATION OF CATEGORIES, THE: reflection on the relationship of categories which derive from different disciplines which study the same or related realities

CONSUMERISM: an economic system which seeks to persuade buyers to regard luxuries, i.e., possessions which enhance class status, as necessities

CORRELATION, METHOD OF: a mode of thinking which interrelates different realities under investigation

COUNCIL OF THE CHURCH: a plenary meeting of leaders and teachers of the Christian community in order to decide doctrinal and pastoral questions

COUNTERDYNAMIC OF CONVERSION: the tendency of the lack of conversion in one realm of experience to undermine the presence of conversion in another realm of experience

COVENANT: a mutually binding agreement among persons

CREATION: as a divine act, God's ongoing constitution of the developing universe as a reality; as an object, the developing spatio-temporal universe viewed as a product of divine activity

CRITICAL COMMON SENSISM: a doctrine of pragmatic logic which maintains that if one attempts to doubt seriously one's spontaneous beliefs, one will find some beliefs which one cannot doubt

CULTURE: reality mediated and conditioned by human symbolic behavior

DECISION: in a metaphysics of experience, an action which makes reality concretely this rather than that; a fact

DEDUCTION: in pragmatic logic, an inference which concludes from a case and a rule to a result; in other words, the prediction of facts not yet in evidence but implied by a particular abduction

DEISM: a philosophical system which posits the existence of God, the immortality of the soul, and universal moral principles but which denies divine intervention in human history

DELIBERATION: in a metaphysics of experience, disjunctive thinking; the weighing of mutually exclusive alternatives for choice

AESTHETIC: disjunctive thinking about how best to communicate an intuitive grasp of excellence

PRUDENTIAL: disjunctive thinking about ethical choices

PRACTICAL: disjunctive thinking about how best to get a job done

DEMIURGE: in Platonic philosophy, a quasi-deity who fashions the material universe

DEMYTHOLOGIZATION: the substitution of rational explanation for a mythic grasp of reality

DE-OBJECTIFICATION: the process of replacing inferential thinking which claims to grasp things as they are in themselves with a mode of thought which recognizes the relational character of all reality and of all knowing

DEPRAVITY: moral corruption; as a theological term, the doctrine that sin has so corrupted human nature that it can of itself perform no morally good acts

DIALECTICS: a functional theological specialty which compares and contrasts different doctrinal frames of reference in order to assess if and why they agree or disagree

DIOHYPOSTATIC THEOLOGY: an early form of heterodox trinitarian theology which focused on the existence of two subsistent realities in the Christian Godhead, the Father and the Son, but which left the Son's eternal existence and co-equality with the Father vague

DI-POLAR NOMINALISM: a philosophical doctrine which reduces human knowing to the subjective interrelation of concrete percepts and abstract concepts

DISCERNMENT: a charism of the Holy Breath which renders human deliberation receptive to Her inspirations

DISCONTINUITY, CRITERION OF: a principle for authenticating historically words and actions attributed to Jesus which argues that if one cannot trace them either to the milieu in which Jesus lived or to the apostolic Church they probably originated in Jesus Himself

DISPENSATIONAL THEOLOGY: a descriptive account of God's saving action in human history

DIVINITY: divine reality; the nature of deity

DOCTRINES: a functional theological specialty which distinguishes sound from unsound doctrine by the former's ability to advance an integral five-fold conversion and by the latter's tendency to undermine integral five-fold conversion

DUALISM: the fallacious conception of two interrelated realities in such a way that their real relationship to one another becomes subsequently unintelligible

COSMIC: conceiving time and eternity in such a way that their real relationship to one another becomes subsequently unintelligible

MATTER-SPIRIT: the characterization of reality as divided into essentially different realms, one embodied and the other disembodied, with the result that their interrelationship becomes subsequently unintelligible

OPERATIONAL: the conception of human powers of activity in such a way that their interaction becomes subsequently unintelligible

SUBSTANTIAL: the division of the human person into two essentially different substances whose essential difference makes the unity of the person unthinkable

SUBJECT-OBJECT: an interpretation of a cognitive relationship in such a way that the act of knowing becomes subsequently unintelligible

DUTY: a moral obligation to respond to the need of some person or persons

DYNAMIC OF CONVERSION: the tendency of one kind of conversion to re-enforce another

ECCLESIOLOGY: a more or less organized account of the Church

ECLECTICISM: the endorsement of beliefs on the basis of taste and without much concern for their mutual compatibility

EGO: in psychology, the conscious person

EGO DEFLATION: the painful, conflicted psychological state of one whose ego-inflation has led to positing an act with destructive consequences to one-self and/or others

EGO INERTIA: in clinical psychology, the human tendency to resist challenges to personal attitudes, beliefs, or commitments

EGO INFLATION: a psychological state of exaggerated self-confidence resulting from lack of realistic contact with potentially destructive, unconscious impulses and with one's own limitations

EMBARRASSMENT, CRITERION OF: a norm for authenticating historically words or actions of Jesus which argues that, if a New Testament author records something about Jesus disconcerting either to the one who records it or to the Christian community, then the event in question probably took place

EMOTION: in a metaphysics of experience, the affective perception or judgment of reality

SYMPATHETIC: a benevolent attitudinal response like affection, sympathy, friendship, love which functions as the affective equivalent of a logical "yes"

NEGATIVE: an attitudinal response which function as the affective equivalent of a logical "not," like fear, anger, shame, guilt

EMPIRICAL THEOLOGY: a theology which requires that all theological propositions find verification in the historical events which reveal God in space and time

ENLIGHTENMENT, THE: an intellectual movement in the eighteenth century which defended the superiority of scientific knowing nominalistically conceived, moral individualism, the purely subjective character of moral and religious judgments, and social contract theory

ENLIGHTENMENT FUNDAMENTALISM: the spontaneous and dogmatic endorsement of the untenable aspects of Enlightenment philosophy

ENVIRONMENT: in a metaphysics of experience, the physical universe from which the self emerges, most immediately its own body but also the surrounding world from which it derives its physical life

EPISTEMOLOGY: a philosophical account of human knowing

ESSENCE: what something is; in a metaphysics of experience, a mode of evaluative perception abstracted from the one perceiving and the reality perceived

ESSENCE FALLACY: the indefensible reification of essences as existing in experienced reality instead of regarding them as fallible modes of perception

ESSENTIALISM: a philosophy which endorses the essence fallacy

ETERNAL OBJECT: in Whiteheadean philosophy, a concept in the conceptual pole of the divine experience

ETHICS: a moral code which measures human conduct by norms, principles, and ideals which make absolute and ultimate claims

EVALUATION: in a metaphysics of experience, a quality of experience viewed as an intentional, cognitive relationship

EVALUATIVE CONTINUUM: in a metaphysics of experience, the entire network of intentional, evaluative relationships in human experience which includes, sensation, emotion, memory, intuition, inference, and deliberation

EXCELLENCE: a reality's capacity to evoke in another the simultaneous intuitive perception of goodness and of truth

EXEGESIS: the interpretation of texts

EXISTENTIALISM: a phenomenological account of the human subject's relationship to Being understood as the total pattern of meaning

EXPERIENCE: in a metaphysics of experience, a process composed to relational elements called feelings; the higher forms of experience contain three kinds of relational elements: evaluations, decisions, and tendencies

    REALM OF: an distinctive habitual way of responding evaluatively or decisively

FACT: in a metaphysics of experience, a decision, an action which makes reality concretely this rather than that

FACULTY PSYCHOLOGY: an account of the human person which explains human activity by grounding it in really and essentially distinct powers with fixed formal objects

FAITH: commitment to a self-revealing God on the terms which that self-revelation demands

    JUSTIFYING: an initial religious conversion which conforms the convert to the divine will and therefore commits one to ongoing religious conversion

    THEOLOGICAL: the graced transformation of intellectual conversion

    CHARISM OF: a gift of the Holy Breath which enhances the social visibility of one's commitment to God by rendering it more prayerful, more docile to the movements of grace, and more willing to take personal risks for the sake of God

FALLACY OF UNIVERSAL TEXTUALITY, THE: the false belief that one can characterize every entity as a text

FALLIBILISM: in pragmatic logic, the philosophical doctrine that if one admits that one can err in interpreting reality one has a better chance of reaching the truth than if one denies one's capacity for error

FALSE: the characteristic of a belief which contradicts the evidence

FEELING: in a metaphysics of experience, a relational element within experience, which in its higher forms manifests three kinds of such relational elements: evaluations, decisions, and tendencies

FEMINISM: a movement of social reform with scholarly and theological underpinnings which seeks to vindicate the rights of women to freedom from personal and institutional oppression on the basis of sex

FINITUDE: limitation

FORMAL OBJECT: the object of a power of operation which defines the essence of that power by specifying the aspect under which it operates on its object

FOUNDATIONS: a functional theological specialty which proposes a strictly normative account of the forms, dynamics, and counterdynamics of conversion

FREEDOM, ELEMENTARY: the power to act or not or to choose to do this rather than that

FUNCTIONAL SPECIALTY: a realm of theological investigation which raises a particular kind of theological question requiring a distinctive method to answer it

GOODNESS: desirability, the exemplification of excellence

GRACE: as a theological term, God's utterly gratuitous intervention in human history in order to undo the consequences of human sinfulness and in order to unite humans to God and to one another

HERESY: the tenacious defence and propagation of a heterodox belief

HERESIARCH: the principal intransigent propounder of a heresy

HERMENEUTICAL CIRCLE, CLOSING THE: a theological method characteristic of liberation theology which beings by investigating a situation of institutional injustice, searches divine revelation for norms which promise to rectify the injustice, and then devises specific strategies for effecting the desired rectification

HERMENEUTICS: a theory of interpretation

HETERODOX: in theology, the characteristic of a belief which interprets divine revelation incorrectly

HIGH CHRISTOLOGY: an account of the person and mission of Jesus which beings with reflection on His divinity and which sometimes sacrifices His humanity to His divinity

HISTORICAL-CRITICAL METHOD: the scholarly interpretation of a text in the light of the circumstances which originally inspired its composition

HISTORY: developments in space and time; in the metaphysics of experience, the unfolding of spatio-temporal experience; as a functional theological specialty, a scholarly account of a religious community's development

HOLY BREATH: the third person of the trinity conceived as a sanctifying source of divine life

HOMOIOUSIOS: similar in being; a technical Greek theological term for asserting that the Son and Holy Breath have a divine reality similar to the Father's

HOMOOUSIOS: one in being; a technical Greek theological term for asserting that the Son and the Holy Breath have identically the same divine reality as the Father

HOPE: in a metaphysics of experience, the intuitive perception of a desirable future

HUMANITY: the nature possessed by finite embodied persons

HYLEMORPHISM: a philosophical doctrine which asserts that finite substances consist of a potential principle called matter (in Greek, *hylê*) and an actual principle called form (in Greek *morphê*)

HYPOSTATIC UNION: the uniting of divinity and humanity in the second person of the trinity without their blending into some third reality neither fully divine nor fully human

HYPOSTASIS: in theology, the Greek term for a particular, subsistent reality

HYPOTHESIS: an abduction

IDEAL: a desirable possibility which makes normative claims

IDEOLOGY: the false and deceptive rationalization of a situation of injustice

IMAGINATION: the capacity to interpret reality through the use of images

IMMATERIAL: purely spiritual, devoid of matter

IMMORALITY: the decisive violation of ethical ideals and principles

IMMUTABILITY: the inability to change

IMPASSIBILITY: the inability to suffer

IMPOSSIBLE: what cannot or could not have happened; the character of a belief which defies verification under any circumstances

IMPLAUSIBLE: the character of a belief which the preponderance of the evidence calls into question without, however, ruling it out altogether as false or impossible

IMPROBABLE: the characteristic of a belief which the evidence calls seriously into question but without establishing the likelihood of another interpretation

INCARNATION: embodiment; as a theological term, the embodiment of the second person of the trinity

INCULTURATION: evangelization or theological thinking which uses the symbols of a particular culture, which invokes the gospel to challenge that culture's sinfulness, and which establishes a dialogue between a particular culture and the Church universal

INDIVIDUALISM: the ideological belief that society consists of atomic individuals with only accidental and artificial relations to one another

EXPRESSIVE: the self-isolating ideological belief that one must defend one's "core self" from the incursions of others

UTILITARIAN: the ideological belief that one can justifiably do anything necessary to advance one's own interests and to succeed

THERAPEUTIC: psychological theories and healing practices which inculcate the ideological belief in oneself as an atomic individual with only accidental and artificial relationships with others, relations which one can sacrifice as needed in order to ensure personal self-fulfillment

INDIVIDUALITY: the results of individuation; the traits which make one individual differ qualitatively from another

INDIVIDUATION: the process of becoming an individual qualitatively distinct from other individuals

INDUCTION: in pragmatic logic, an inference which concludes from a result and a case to a rule; the verification of a deductively clarified abduction which establishes the reality of the rule which a prior abduction presumed to obtain in reality

INFERENCE: in pragmatic logic, an argument which interrelates a rule, a case, and a result

INFINITE: that which encompasses every other thing and is encompassed by nothing

INFUSED KNOWLEDGE: preternaturally communicated perceptions of reality

INSTITUTION: groups of persons acting in socially sanctioned ways

INTELLECT: in philosophy, the spiritual power which grasps Being cognitively as true

AGENT: in scholastic philosophy, the spiritual power of the human soul which uses an image in the imagination as an instrument for imprinting an idea on the passive intellect

PASSIVE: in scholastic philosophy, the spiritual power of the soul which the active intellect enables to grasp sensible being as true

INTELLECTUAL CONVERSION: the decision to take adult responsibility for the truth or falsity of one's beliefs and for the adequacy or inadequacy of the frames of reference in which one fixes one's beliefs

INTELLIGIBILITY: something possessing significance or meaning

INTERPLAY OF CATEGORIES: the interpretation of categories derived from one intellectual discipline by categories derived from another intellectual discipline

INTERPRETATION: a meaningful account of symbolic significance; as a functional theological specialty, exegesis, or a scholarly account of the significance of religious texts and artifacts

INTUITION: in a metaphysics of experience, knowledge mediated by images and affections

JESUSOLOGY: a rational account of Jesus' humanity and mortal ministry

JUDGMENT: in pragmatic logic, the fixation of a belief

JUSTIFICATION: in theology, passage from a state of sin to the obedience of faith

KENOSIS: the Son of God's free self-emptying in becoming human and suffering crucifixion

KENOTIC CHRISTOLOGY: a Christology which interprets the meaning of the divine self-emptying which occurred in the incarnation

KINGDOM OF GOD: Jesus' central message; Jesus' egalitarian vision of a new Israel founded 1) on unconditioned trust in God; 2) on the free sharing of the physical supports of life, especially with the poor, the marginal, and the expendable; 4) on prayer; 5) on mutual forgiveness even of one's enemies; and 6) on non-violence

LAW: in the metaphysics of experience, a general tendency

LIBERATION THEOLOGY: a theology which takes as its starting point social, economic, and political injustice and which invokes gospel values to overcome such injustice

LIBERTY: in a metaphysics of experience, responsible human freedom; freedom to live for the beautiful, the good, and the true

LOGIC: a normative account of the way the human mind ought to think

KANTIAN: transcendental logic, which recognizes only deductive inference and which offers an *a priori* account of the structure of human subjectivity

LOGICAL: inferentially self-consistent; lacking internal contradictions in meaning

LOGICAL ADEQUACY: in pragmatic logic, the ability of a theory to interpret all relevant data

LOGICAL APPLICABILITY: in pragmatic logic, the ability of a theory to interpret some relevant data

LOGICAL COHERENCE: the characteristic of a theory whose key terms remain unintelligible apart from one another

LOGOS: the Greek term for word; as a Christological term, a title of the incarnate second person of the trinity which portrays Him as a divine communication

LOGOS-ANTHROPOS CHRISTOLOGY: a Christology which claims that the incarnate Son of God possesses a complete humanity which consists of both a body and a soul

LOGOS-SARX CHRISTOLOGY: a heterodox Christology which claims that in the incarnation the divine *Logos* replaces the human soul in Jesus' humanity with the result that the second person of the trinity in becoming incarnate possesses a human body but not a human soul

LOW CHRISTOLOGY: a Christology which begins by reflecting on Jesus' humanity but which sometimes fails to offer an adequate account of His divinity

MATTER: physical reality; in Aristotelian philosophy, the pure potency for substantial change

MEANING: in a metaphysics of experience, evaluation viewed as the intentional grasp of significance

MEDIATION: the establishment of a relationship between or among distinct realities

MEMORY: the ability of recall past experiences

MESSIAH: the anointed one; in Jewish apocalyptic theology one anointed by God to effect the deliverance and salvation of Israel

METAPHOR: the intuitive grasp of analogy through the verbal identification of two partially similar realities

METAPHYSICS: an organized account of reality in general; a theory of the whole of reality which develops systematically a root metaphor for Being

METAPHYSICS OF EXPERIENCE: a theory of the whole which takes experience as a root metaphor for the whole of reality

METHOD: a set of recurrent and related operations yielding cumulative and progressive results

MIAHYPOSTATIC THEOLOGY: an early heterodox form of theology which discovers only one subsistent reality in the Christian deity

MIA PHYSIS: the Greek phrase meaning "one nature"; as a Christological term, Cyril of Alexandria's unusual term for the person of the incarnate Word

MODEL: a representation of some reality

MONOPHYSITISM: Apollonarianism; the heterodox Christological doctrine which taught that the divinity and humanity of the incarnate Word blend into a third nature neither fully divine nor fully human

MORALITY: a code of conduct which measures choices by ideals, principles, and realities which make ultimate and absolute claims on the human conscience

PERSONAL: a code of conduct which invokes rights and duties in resolving interpersonal conflicts

PUBLIC: a code of conduct which measures institutional justice by the common good

MULTIPLE ATTESTATION, CRITERION OF: a principle for validating historically words and actions of Jesus which claims that, when different New Testament authors bear witness to the fact that Jesus said or did something, He probably did, especially if the authors in question represent independent historical traditions about Jesus

MYSTAGOGY: the last phase of the catechumenate which instructs newly baptized Christians in the demands of Christian living

MYTH: a story which creates an adult world of value

NARCISSISM: morbid self-preoccupation

NARRATIVE: a tale told by a story-teller to an audience about a world

NATURAL: in a metaphysics of experience, the character of an experience which responds legitimately to created value only and which ignores the historical self-revelation of God

NATURE: in philosophy, a reality's essence viewed as the source of its activity; in theology, created reality untransformed by saving, supernatural grace

NATIONAL SECURITY: an ideology which claims that a government has the right to do anything at all which secures its own interests

NEO-ARIANISM: the heterodox tendency in contemporary Christology to portray Jesus as a graced human person

NEO-ORTHODOXY: a movement in Protestant theology which rejects metaphysical thinking and which recognizes only the analogy of faith as a legitimate theological method

NEO-PLATONISM: a school of Platonism which fused middle Platonic philosophy and contemplative religious impulses

NESTORIANISM: the heterodox denial that Mary is the mother of God

NOMINALISM: the philosophical denial of real generality

 CLASSICAL: the reduction of universal concepts to mere spoken words and of reality to concrete sensibles

 CONCEPTUAL: the restriction of real generality to conceptual universals which exist only in human subjectivity

NORM: that which measures something else

NORMATIVE SCIENCES: philosophical disciplines which reflect on the way in which one ought to respond to reality aesthetically, ethically, and logically

NOTE: in theology, a category which assigns to a particular belief a degree of verifiability

OBJECTIFICATION: the attempt to portray reality as it exists in itself instead of portraying it as inherently relational

ONTOLOGICAL: metaphysical; pertaining to a theory of the whole

ONTOLOGISM: the philosophical doctrine which claims that created minds have immediate access to the ideas in the mind of God

OPERATIONAL: pertaining to activity

OPTIMISM: the tendency to focus on good and pleasant realities rather than on evil and unpleasant realities

ORALITY: the characteristic of a culture which communicates through the spoken rather than through the written word

 PRIMARY: the way language functions in purely oral cultures

 SECONDARY: the way orality functions in literate cultures

ORTHOPRAXIS: decisive behavior which conforms to appropriate norms

ORTHODOXY: shared religious beliefs which conform to the norms of truth and adequacy in interpreting the historical self-revelation of God

ORIGINAL SIN: the totality of human sinfulness minus one's own personal sins

OUSIA: a Greek term for being; as a technical trinitarian term, the reality common to the three members of the trinity

PARABLE: a comparison, which, when expressed in narrative form, seeks to subvert a familiar world in order to open its audience to an alternative way of viewing reality

PARADIGM: in grammar, a list of inflectional forms; in the philosophy of science, an organized way of asking and answering questions which invokes an appropriate method, appropriate instrumentation, appropriate models, and appropriate concepts for dealing with a problem

PARADIGM SHIFT: the abandonment of one organized rational way of asking and answering questions for another

PASSION: the affective perception of interpersonal relationships

PERCEPT: a concrete, sensible reality viewed as an object of knowledge

PERSON: an autonomous, subsistent, self-conscious reality enjoying continuity of life and capable of entering into responsible social relationships with other realities like itself

PERSONAL MORAL CONVERSION: the decision to take adult responsibility for respecting the rights and duties of others

PESSIMISM: the tendency to focus on evil and suffering rather than on good, pleasant, beneficial realities

PHANTASM: in scholastic philosophy, a term for an image in the imagination

PHARISEE: the member of a Jewish sect which resisted the Hellenization of Jewish religious faith by requiring that Jews observe not only the Torah but pious oral traditions as well

PHENOMENOLOGY: the organized description of what appears in experience without attempting to distinguish between reality and illusion

PHILOSOPHY: critical reflection on lived human experience

PHYSIS: the Greek term for nature

PLATONISM: the school of philosophy founded by Plato in the fourth century b.c. which divides reality into an unchanging, spiritual realm of ideas and ideals and a material realm of constant change and illusion

    MIDDLE: a school of Platonism which located ideas and ideals in a quasi-divine intellect

PLAUSIBLE: the character of a belief supported by some evidence without that evidence ruling out other possible or even probable interpretations

PLURALISM: the characteristic or a situation which permits of a variety of interpretative approaches and evaluations

PNEUMATOLOGY: a more or less organized account of the Holy Breath, the third person of the trinity

POLICY: an institutionally sanctioned practice

POSSIBLE: the character of a belief which could conceivably enjoy verifiability despite the fact that little evidence supports it

POSSIBILITY: that which could occur; an idea or ideal capable of real or actual exemplification

POST-MODERNISM: a vaguely organized movement in contemporary western thought which seeks to advance beyond the presuppositions of modern culture, sometimes characterized by the denial of any subject of discourse and by extreme skepticism concerning linguistic meaning

POTENCY: as a technical philosophical term, the capacity for actualization

PRAGMATIC LOGIC: a theory of inference which holds that the deductive operational consequences of any abduction define the whole of its meaning

PRAXIS: decisive activity which seeks to transform reality, especially oppressive social institutions

PRE-CATECHUMENATE: the first phase in the instruction of candidates for Christian baptism which seeks to introduce them to the Christian community and to evoke from them an initial Christian conversion

PRECONSCIOUS: capable of recall

PRE-EXISTENCE: a technical Christological term for the mode of being enjoyed by the second person of the trinity prior to the incarnation

PREFERENTIAL OPTION FOR THE POOR: a principle of Christian ethics which insists that in the resolution of disputed questions of public morality the needs of the socially, economically, and politically disadvantaged take precedence over those of the advantaged and affluent

PREHENSION: in Whiteheadean philosophy, a concrete fact of relatedness which includes a subject, its initial datum (or what it prehends at the beginning of its processing), the subject's objective datum (or perspective on the universe), its negative prehensions (which distinguish it from other prehensions), and its subjective form (or way of prehending the universe)

PREJUDICE: an opinion formed without sufficient attention to the facts

PRE-OPERATIONAL: in developmental psychology, a characteristic of the cognitive behavior of children who have yet to develop the capacity for abstract rational thought

PRESENTATIONAL IMMEDIACY: in a metaphysics of experience, the way in which an evaluative response makes the mind present to its world and the world to it

PRETERNATURAL: beyond the powers of created nature

PRIEST: one who mediates between God and humanity

PRINCIPLE: a rule of conduct derived from an ideal

PRINCIPLE OF ALTERNATION: in logic, a rule which asserts that the mind should focus by turns on the investigation of particular problems and the readjustment of its metaphysical theory of the whole in the light of the results of a focused investigation

PROBABLE: the character of a belief which the preponderance of the evidence favors without, however, establishing its certitude

PROCESS THEOLOGY: an account of God which equates all reality with change and development

PROPHET: one who speaks for God in summoning a community to repentance and to hope

PROSÔPON: a Greek term for the mask worn by an actor in classical Greek theater; as a theological term, *prosôpon* has many different meanings, some orthodox, some heterodox

PRUDENCE: deliberation ruled by sound moral principles

PSYCHIC CONVERSION: Robert Doran's term for the kind of conversion which transforms human affectivity; ordering disordered affectivity in the light of sound insights generated by intellectual conversion

PSYCHOLOGY: the scientific study of human behavior

EMPIRICAL: the scientific study of human behavior which measures its hypotheses against the behavior of control groups

DEVELOPMENTAL: a branch of empirical psychology which argues that human behavior develops in predictable stages

SOCIAL: the scientific study of how individual persons and institutions interact

QUALITY: in a metaphysics of experience, an instance of particular suchness

QUESTS FOR THE HISTORICAL JESUS: the rational attempt to validate words and actions of Jesus (the new quest) and to situate them in the historical context in which He lived (the third quest)

RACISM: prejudice and bigotry directed toward the members of a particular race

RCIA: The Rite of Christian Initiation of Adults; the restored catechumenate

REACTION: a way of dealing with an impinging reality

CIRCULAR: in developmental psychology, an activity whose pleasurable character tends to motivate its repetition

PRIMARY: in developmental psychology, an infantile circular reaction which focuses on the infant's own body

SECONDARY: in developmental psychology, an infantile circular reaction which focuses on object other than the infant's own body

TERTIARY: in developmental psychology, an infantile circular reaction which explores the child's environment

REAL: in a metaphysics of experience, pertaining to the mode of existence of a tendency

REALISM: in philosophy, a defense of the mind's ability to grasp reality in opposition to subjectivism, or a defence of the existence of real generality in opposition to nominalism, or the simultaneous defence of both positions

REDACTION CRITICISM: the interpretation of a text in the light of its editing

REDEMPTION: reacquisition; as a theological term, salvation viewed as the divine reacquisition of a religious backslider

REFORMED SUBJECTIVIST PRINCIPLE: an axiom of Whiteheadean philosophy which asserts that apart from the experiencing of subjects there is nothing, nothing, nothing, bare nothingness

REJECTION AND EXECUTION, CRITERION OF: a norm for authenticating historically words and actions of Jesus which asserts that any historical portrait of Jesus must offer a plausible account of why He suffered condemnation and crucifixion

RELATIVISM: the philosophical denial of binding, universal norms for human behavior and cognition

RELIGION: an organized way of relating to God

REPENTANCE: the conscious repudiation of one's former sinfulness

RESEARCH: in theology, a functional specialty which provides other theologians with the tools which they need in order to think theologically

RESPONSIBILITY: accountability to oneself, to others, and ultimately to God

RESPONSIBLE, PERSONAL FREEDOM: the liberty to choose the beautiful, the true and the good which results from an integral five-fold conversion

RESULT: in pragmatic logic, the descriptive identification of data in need of explanation

RESURRECTION: total transformation in God after death

REVELATION: in theology, God's historical self-disclosure

REVERSION: a technical term in Whiteheadean philosophy for the experience of novel possibility by prehending an eternal object in the mind of God

RHETORIC: the study and practice of the art of persuasion

RIGHT: a personal need which makes legitimate claims on another person or persons

ROOT METAPHOR: in philosophy, an intuitive grasp of analogy which serves as a conceptual model for Being in general

RUAH: the Hebrew word for breath or wind in motion; in Christian theology a Hebrew term for the third person of the trinity

RULE: in pragmatic logic, the conceptual formulation of a real law or tendency

SACRAMENT: most broadly, an event which simultaneously reveals and conceals the reality of God; in sacramental theology, an official act of new covenant worship whichexpresses the shared faith of the Christian community, which therefore requires a minister sanctioned by that same community, and which challenges Christians assembled in worship to committed faith in the paschal mystery and in the triune God which the paschal mystery reveals

SADDUCEES: a religious sect in Judaism which fostered obedience to the Torah but which, in contrast to the Pharisees, denied bodily resurrection, the existence of angels, and did not regard unwritten Jewish religious practices as binding

SALVATION: in theology, the state of standing in a life-giving relationship with the triune God

SATAN: the Biblical personification of all those forces which oppose God and put those who believe in God to the test; in the New Testament, the personification of anti-Christ

SAVIOR: one who puts another in a life-giving relationship with the triune God

SCHEMA: in developmental psychology, a technical psychological term for an acquired cognitive habit

SCIENTIA BEATA: in theology, a Latin term for the special transformation of Jesus human self-awareness effected by the incarnation

SECULARISM: an ethos which either subordinates religious values and realities to values and realities which have nothing to do with religion or which replaces religious realities and values with non religious ones

SELF: in the metaphysics of experience, an autonomously functioning tendency

SENSATION: initial perception of environmental impact on a conscious animal

SEXISM: discrimination and oppression for reasons of gender

SIGNIFICANCE: in the metaphysics of experience, the intelligibility of events and of symbolic communications

SIN: a deliberate violation of the will of God

SINLESSNESS: perfect obedience to the divine will

SOCIO-POLITICAL CONVERSION: the decision to take responsibility for seeking to end institutional oppression through commitment to some just cause of universal human significance

SOUL: an animating principle

SOTERIOLOGY: a more or less organized account of God's saving activity in human history

SPIRIT: in philosophy, immaterial reality

SPIRIT CHRISTOLOGY: an explanation of the person and ministry of Jesus which highlights His relationship to the divine Breath

STRATEGY: a concrete plan for implementing a policy or principle

STRICTLY NORMATIVE THINKING: critical reflection of one's own behavior in the light of ideals and principles which one has appropriated and interiorized

SUBJECT: in a metaphysics of experience, an emerging, experiencing self; in substance philosophy, an underlying reality

SUBJECTIVISM: the philosophical belief that one can experience only one's own subjectivity

SUBJECTIVITY: the evaluative responses of an experiencing self contrasted with the realities that self experiences

SUBSISTENCE: in a metaphysics of experience, autonomous functioning

SUBSTANCE: in philosophy, that which exists in itself and not in anything else as a subject of inhesion

SUPERNATURAL: that which exceeds the power of created nature; in theology, pertaining to the realm of saving grace

SUPERNATURAL EXISTENTIAL: an alleged *a priori*, graced expansion of the formal object of the agent intellect which endows it with a spontaneous longing for the beatific vision and for the God revealed in Jesus Christ

SYMBOL: in the metaphysics of experience, whatever mediates the symbolic grasp of significance

COMMUNICATION: an evaluative response expressed by one mind to another through decisive activity

EXPRESSIVE: a significant event

INTERPRETATIVE: an unexpressed evaluative response

SYNECHISM: the philosophical assertion of continuity in development

SYNTHETIC: pertaining to the perception of relationship and of unified wholes

SYSTEMATICS: in theology, a functional specialty which examines relationships among sound theological doctrines

TENDENCY: in a metaphysics of experience, a general law in reality; a habitual orientation to decide or evaluate in a particular way

THEANDRIC: combining divine and human traits

THEISM: belief in the reality of God

THEOLOGY: a more or less organized account of God

MEDIATING: the theological retrieval of a religious tradition; the functional specialties of research, interpretation, history, and dialectics

MEDIATED: the theological reformulation of a religious tradition; the functional specialties of foundations, doctrines, systematics, and communications

THEOTOKOS: a Greek term meaning "mother of God"; in theology, the doctrine that Mary is the mother of the second person of the trinity

THERAPEUTIC CHRISTOLOGY: an interpretation of the person and mission of Jesus in the light of the psychological study of human behavior

THOMISM: philosophical and theological ways of thinking inspired by the thought Thomas Aquinas

TIME: the present transformation of a past into a future

CLOCK: measured motion

REAL: in a metaphysics of experience, the present movement of experience from a past toward a future

TRANSACTION: decisions which put autonomous selves into social relationship

TRANSCENDENTAL THOMISM: the reformulation of the thought of Thomas Aquinas in the light of Kantian logic and the turn to the subject

TRANSDUCTIVE: in developmental psychology, pre-rational, intuitive thinking

TRANSMUTATION: change relationally, aesthetically, and organically conceived

TRANSVALUATION: the re-evaluation of a reality, actuality, or possibility by transposing it from one frame of reference to another

TRINITY: three persons in one God; the Christian deity

TRIUMPHALISM: a view of the Catholic Church which presents it alone as the one, true Church and which de-emphasizes or denies its flaws and sinfulness

TRUTH: the correct interpretation of reality

TURN TO COMMUNITY, THE: a methodological shift from preoccupation with the individual subject to concern with the way in which persons interrelate socially and institutionally

TURN TO EXPERIENCE, THE: the systematic use of "experience" as central category in one's account of reality

TURN TO THE SUBJECT, THE: critical reflection on human intentionality which typically invokes Kantian logic

ULTIMATE: final; in ethics, the characteristic of some reality or value worth not only living for but, if necessary, worth dying for; in Whiteheadean philosophy, universally predicable

UNCERTAIN: in logic, unsupported by evidence which would force a judgment one way or the other

UNCONSCIOUS: lacking awareness

VAGUE: the character of a belief which one can neither verify or falsify until one first clarifies its meaning

VALIDITY: in logic, the characteristic of thinking which follows sound methodological principles

VALUE: desirability; in a metaphysics of experience, a particular mode of perception

VIRTUAL INFINITY: the alleged ability of a finite power of operation to aspire to infinite satisfaction

WILL: in philosophy, a spiritual power to make decisions

WOMANIST THEOLOGY: a strain in feminism usually promoted by women of color which criticizes the ethnic and class bias of white feminists

WORLD RELIGION: an organized way of relating to God professed by a large number of people of different racial, national, and cultural backgrounds

WORLD SOUL: in philosophy, the animating principle of the universe

Marquette Studies in Philosophy
Andrew Tallon, Editor
Standing orders accepted
All books available as eBook

Harry Klocker, S.J. *William of Ockham and the Divine Freedom.* ISBN 0-87462-001-5. 141 pages, pp., index. $15. Second edition, reviewed, corrected and with a new Introduction.

Margaret Monahan Hogan. *Finality and Marriage.* ISBN 0-87462-600-5. 122 pp. Paper. $15.

Gerald A. McCool, S.J. *The Neo-Thomists.* ISBN 0-87462-601-1. 175 pp. Paper. $20.

Max Scheler. *Ressentiment.* ISBN 0-87462-602-1. 172 pp. Paper. $20. New Introduction by Manfred S. Frings.

Knud Løgstrup. *Metaphysics.* Translated by Dr. Russell Dees ISBN 0-87462-603-X. Volume I, 342 pp. Paper. $35. ISBN 0-67462-607-2. Volume II, 402 pp. Paper. $40. Two volume set priced at $70.

Howard P. Kainz. *Democracy and the "Kingdom of God".* ISBN 0-87462-610-2. 250 pp. Paper. $25.

Manfred Frings. *Max Scheler. A Concise Introduction into the World of a Great Thinker* ISBN 0-87462-605-6. 200 pp. Paper. $20. Second ed., rev. New Foreword by the author.

G. Heath King. *Existence Thought Style: Perspectives of a Primary Relation, portrayed through the work of Søren Kierkegaard.* English edition by Timothy Kircher. ISBN 0-87462-606-4. 187 pp., index. Paper. $20.

Augustine Shutte. *Philosophy for Africa.* ISBN 0-87462-608-0. 184 pp. Paper. $20.

Paul Ricoeur. *Key to Husserl's Ideas I.* Translated by Bond Harris and Jacqueline Bouchard Spurlock.With a Foreword by Pol Vandevelde. ISBN 0-87462-609-9. 176 pp., index. Paper. $20.

Karl Jaspers. *Reason and Existenz.* Afterword by Pol Vandevelde. ISBN 0-87462-611-0. 180 pp. Paper. $20.

Gregory R. Beabout. *Freedom and Its Misuses: Kierkegaard on Anxiety and Despair* ISBN 0-87462-612-9. 192 pp., index. Paper. $20.

Manfred S. Frings. *The Mind of Max Scheler. The First Comprehensive Guide Based on the Complete Works* ISBN 0-87462-613-7. 328 pp. Paper. $35.

Claude Pavur. *Nietzsche Humanist.* ISBN 0-87462-614-5. 214 pp., index. Paper. $25.

Pierre Rousselot. *Intelligence: Sense of Being, Faculty of God.* Translation of *L'Intellectualismse de saint Thomas* with a Foreword and Notes by Andrew Tallon. ISBN 0-87462-615-3. 236 pp., index. Paper. $25.

Immanuel Kant. *Critique of Practical Reason.* Translation by H.W. Cassirer. Edited by G. Heath King and Ronald Weitzman and with an Introduction by D.M. MacKinnon. ISBN 0-87462-616-1. Paper. 218 pp. $20.

Gabriel Marcel's Perspectives on The Broken World. Translated by Katharine Rose Hanley. *The Broken World,* A Four-Act Play followed by "Concrete Approaches to Investigating the Ontological Mystery." Six orignal illustrations by Stephen Healy. Commentaries by Henri Gouhier and Marcel Belay. Eight Appendices. Introduction by Ralph McInerny. Bibliographies. ISBN 0-87462-617-X. paperbound. 242 pp. $25.

Karl-Otto Apel. *Towards a Transformation of Philosophy.* New Fore-word by Pol Vandevelde.ISBN 0-87462-619-6. Paper. 308 pp. $35.

Gene Fendt. *Is Hamlet a Religious Drama? As Essay on a Question in Kierkegaard.* ISBN 0-87462-620-X. Paper. 264 pp. $30.

Marquette Studies in Theology
Andrew Tallon, Editor
Standing orders accepted
All books available as eBook

Frederick M. Bliss. *Understanding Reception.* ISBN 0-87462-625-0. 180 pp., index, bibliography. Paper. $20.

Martin Albl, Paul Eddy, Renée Mirkes, OSF, Editors. *Directions in NewTestament Methods* ISBN 0-87462-626-9. 129 pp. Annotated bibliography. Paper. $15. Foreword by William S. Kurz.

Robert M. Doran. *Subject and Psyche.* ISBN 0-87462-627-7. 285 pp. Paper. $25. Second ed., rev. With a new Foreword by the author.

Kenneth Hagen, editor. *The Bible in the Churches. How Various Christians Interpret the Scriptures* ISBN 0-87462-628-5. 218 pp. Paper. $25. Third, revised editon. New chapter on Reformed tradition. Index.

Jamie T. Phelps, O.P., Editor. *Black and Catholic: The Challenge and Gift of Black Folk. Contributions of African American Experience and Thought to Catholic Theology.* ISBN 0-87462-629-3. 182 pp. Index. Paper. $20. Foreword by Patrick Carey.

Karl Rahner. *Spirit in the World.* New, Corrected Translation by William Dych. Foreword by Francis Fiorenza. ISBN 0-87462-630-7. COMPUTER DISK VERSION. $10. Available on 3.5 inch disk; specify Macintosh or Windows. By a special arrangement with Continuum Publishing Co.

Karl Rahner. *Hearer of the Word.* New Translation of the First Edition by Joseph Donceel. Edited and with anIntroduction by Andrew Tallon. By a special arrangement with Continuum Publishing Co. ISBN 0-87462-631-5. COMPUTER DISK VERSION. $10. Available on 3.5 inch disk; specify Macintosh or Windows.

Robert M. Doran. *Theological Foundations. Vol. 1 Intentionality and Psyche.* ISBN 0-87462-632-3. 484 pp. Paper. $50.

Robert M. Doran. *Theological Foundations. Vol. 2 Theology and Culture.* ISBN 0-87462-633-1. 533 pp. Paper. $55.

Patrick W. Carey. *Orestes A. Brownson: A Bibliography, 1826-1876.* ISBN 0-87462-634-X. 212 pp. Index. Paper. $25.

John Martinetti, S.J. *Reason to Believe Today.* ISBN 0-87462-635-8. 216 pp. Paper. $25.

George H. Tavard. *Trina Deitas: The Controversy between Hincmar and Gottschalk* ISBN 0-87462-636-6. 160 pp. Paper. $20.

Jeanne Cover, IBVM. *Love–The Driving Force. Mary Ward's Spirituality. Its Significance for Moral Theology* ISBN 0-87462-637-4. 217 pp. Paper. $25.

David A. Boileau, Editor. *Principles of Catholic Social Teaching.* ISBN 0-87462-638-2. 204 pp. Paper. $25.

Michael Purcell. *Mystery and Method: The Other in Rahner and Levinas.* With a Foreword by Andrew Tallon. ISBN 0-87462-639-0. Paper. 394 pp. $40.

W.W. Meissner, S.J., M.D. *To the Greater Glory: A Psychological Study of Ignatian Spirituality.* ISBN 0-87462-640-4. Paper. 657 pp. $50.

Catholic Theology in the University: Source of Wholeness. Virginia M. Shaddy, editor. ISBN 0-87462-641-2. Paper. 120 pp. $15.

Subscibe to *eNews from Marquette University Press*
Email universitypress@marquette.edu with the word "subscribe" as the subject.
Visit Marquette University Press online: **www.marquette.edu/mupress/**

About
The Firstborn of Many
A Christology for Converting Christians

"Donald Gelpi's Christological trilogy is an important contribution to the discipline combining as it does both foundational and constructive Christology. Gelpi carefully establishes his methodological choices and situates them amid other theological options on the present scene. He then builds his case by moving through the foundational issues and explicating them in regard to their import for a systematic Christology. Connections are made with his earlier work and here Gelpi continues his theological project of establishing a new foundationalism (with its Peircean pragmatic logic of consequences, the turn to community, and a fallibilistic metaphysics of experience) and exploits it for doctrinal theology. Gelpi's proposals will certainly not be without its critics but his attempt to inculturate the philosophical issues in a North American idiom should be on the table.

"The strength of Gelpi's volumes is the care with which he examines the issues on the agenda of any contemporary Christology. These include in addition to methodological issues (not always consciously attended to and seldom with the philosophical attention which Gelpi gives them), the quest for the historical Jesus, and the diversity of New Testament Christologies. Gelpi's contribution is to take these issues seriously and weave them into a constructive narrative of contemporary Christological development, at each point highlighting how they address the pertinent issues in theological foundations. Hence the bulk of his efforts is working through New Testament material in order to establish the constructive sequence: Jesus of history, kerygmatic Christology (Pauline corpus), apocalyptic Christology (book of Revelation), narrative Christology (synoptic gospels), doctrinal Christology (picking up from the particular narrative Christology of the Gospel of John, Chalcedon and post-Chalcedonian developments), and practical Christology (working with liberationist themes but consistent with his foundational pragmatism). All are related to a foundational theology of conversion and are rendered pastoral by addressing their implications for Roman Catholic RCIA practice."

Ralph Del Colle
Marquette University

ISBN 0-87462-644-7

54000

9 780874 626445